DATE			

Studies in Church History

9

SCHISM, HERESY AND RELIGIOUS PROTEST

SCHISM, HERESY AND RELIGIOUS PROTEST

PAPERS READ AT
THE TENTH SUMMER MEETING AND
THE ELEVENTH WINTER MEETING
OF THE
ECCLESIASTICAL HISTORY SOCIETY

EDITED BY
DEREK BAKER

CAMBRIDGE
AT THE UNIVERSITY PRESS
1972

Published by the Syndics of the Cambridge University Press
Bentley House, 200 Euston Road, London NW1 2DB
American Branch: 32 East 57th Street, New York, N.Y.10022

Library of Congress Catalogue Card Number: 75–184899

ISBN: 0 521 08486 5

Printed in Great Britain
at the University Printing House, Cambridge
(Brooke Crutchley, University Printer)

PREFACE

The present volume of *Studies in Church History* is the ninth to be produced by the Ecclesiastical History Society, and the fourth to be published by the Cambridge University Press. 'Heresy, Schism and Religious Protest' was the theme of the tenth summer meeting (held at University College, Durham) and the eleventh winter meeting of the Society. All the thirty papers included in this volume were read at one or other of these meetings, and are arranged in chronological order of subject matter.

DEREK BAKER

CONTENTS

CONTENTS

CONTENTS

CONTRIBUTORS

DEREK BAKER, lecturer in history, university of Edinburgh

J. M. BARKLEY, professor of church history, Presbyterian College, Belfast

BRENDA BOLTON, senior lecturer in history, polytechnic of North London

MARGARET BOWKER, lecturer in history, university of Cambridge

CLAIRE CROSS, senior lecturer in history, university of York

WAYNE DETZLER, tutor in ecclesiastical history, Moorlands Bible College

GORDON DONALDSON, professor of Scottish history, university of Edinburgh

EVERETT FERGUSON, professor, Abilene Christian College, Texas

W. H. C. FREND, professor of ecclesiastical history, university of Glasgow

JOAN G. GREATREX, assistant professor of history, Carleton university, Ottawa

S. L. GREENSLADE, regius professor of ecclesiastical history, university of Oxford

KEITH HAMPSON, lecturer in history, university of Edinburgh

MARGARET HARVEY, lecturer in history, university of Durham

FELICITY HEAL, fellow of Newnham College, Cambridge

PETER HINCHLIFF, secretary, Missionary Ecumenical Council of the Church of England

ANNE HUDSON, fellow of Lady Margaret Hall, Oxford

D. M. LUNN, Downside Abbey

A. K. MCHARDY, Somerville College, Oxford

CONTRIBUTORS

R. A. MARKUS, reader in medieval history, university of Liverpool

STUART MEWS, lecturer in the sociology of religion, university of Lancaster

JANET L. NELSON, lecturer in history, King's College, university of London

W. B. PATTERSON, associate professor of history, Davidson College, North Carolina

P. G. SCOTT, lecturer in English literature, university of Edinburgh

PAUL SLACK, lecturer in history, university of York

MARGARET SPUFFORD, Calouste Gulbenkian research fellow, Lucy Cavendish College, Cambridge

WALTER ULLMANN, professor of medieval ecclesiastical history, university of Cambridge

W. R. WARD, professor of modern history, university of Durham

K. T. WARE, Spalding lecturer in Eastern Orthodox Studies, university of Oxford

A. R. WINNETT, rector of Ockham, Surrey

MICHAEL WILKS, reader in the history of political thought, Birkbeck College, university of London

ABBREVIATIONS

ACO	*Acta Conciliorum Oecumenicorum*, ed E. Schwartz (Berlin/Leipzig 1914–40)
ACW	*Ancient Christian Writers*, ed J. Quasten and J. C. Plumpe (Westminster, Maryland/London 1946–)
An Bol	*Analecta Bollandiana* (Brussels 1882–)
ASOC	*Analecta Sacri Ordinis Cisterciensis* (*Analecta Cisterciensia* since 1965) Rome 1945–
BIHR	*Bulletin of the Institute of Historical Research* (London 1923–)
BJRL	*Bulletin of the John Rylands Library* (Manchester 1903–)
BM	British Museum, London
BZ	*Byzantion* (Brussels, Boston, 1924–)
Cam S	*Camden Series* (London 1838–)
CHJ	*Cambridge Historical Journal* (Cambridge 1923–57)
CSCO	*Corpus Scriptorum Christianorum Orientalium* (Paris 1903–)
CSEL	*Corpus Scriptorum Ecclesiasticorum Latinorum* (Vienna 1866–)
CSHByz	*Corpus Scriptorum Historiae Byzantinae* (Bonn 1828–78)
DACL	*Dictionnaire d'Archéologie chrétienne et de Liturgie*, ed F. Cabrol and H. Leclercq (Paris 1924–)
DDC	*Dictionnaire de Droit Canonique*, ed R. Naz (Paris 1935–)
DHGE	*Dictionnaire d'Histoire et de Géographie ecclésiastiques*, ed A. Baudrillart etc (Paris 1912–)
DNB	*Dictionary of National Biography* (London 1885–)
DSAM	*Dictionnaire de Spiritualité, Ascétique et Mystique*, ed M. Viller (Paris 1932–)
Ec.HR	*Economic History Review* (London 1927–)
EHR	*English Historical Review* (London 1886–)
GCS	*Die griechischen christlichen Schriftsteller der erste drei Jahrhunderte* (Leipzig 1897–)
HE	*Historia Ecclesiastica*
HJ	*Historical Journal* (Cambridge 1958–)
HMC	Historical Manuscripts Commission

HMSO	Her Majesty's Stationery Office, London
Jaffé	*Regesta Pontificum Romanorum ab condita ecclesia ad a. 1198,* 2 ed S. Loewenfeld, F. Kaltenbrunner, P. Ewald, 2 vols (Berlin 1885–8, repr Graz 1958)
JEH	*Journal of Ecclesiastical History* (London 1950–)
JMH	*Journal of Modern History* (Chicago 1929–)
JRS	*Journal of Roman Studies* (London 1910–)
JTS	*Journal of Theological Studies* (London/Oxford 1899–)
LRS	*Lincoln Record Society*
MA	*Monasticon Anglicanum,* ed R. Dodsworth and W. Dugdale, 3 vols (London 1655–73); new ed J. Caley, H. Ellis, B. Bandinel, 6 vols in 8 (London 1817–30)
Mansi	J. D. Mansi, *Sacrorum conciliorum nova et amplissima collectio,* 31 vols (Florence/Venice 1757–98); new impression and continuation, ed L. Petit and J. B. Martin, 60 vols (Paris 1899–1927)
MGH	*Monumenta Germaniae Historica inde ab a. c. 500 usque ad a. 1500,* ed G. H. Pertz etc. (Berlin, Hanover, 1826–)
AA	*Auctores Antiquissimi*
Dip.	*Diplomata*
Epp.	*Epistolae*
Leg.	*Leges*
SS	*Scriptores*
SRL	*Scriptores rerum langobardicarum et italicarum*
SRM	*Scriptores rerum merovingicarum*
NH	*Northern History* (Leeds 1966–)
ODCC	*Oxford Dictionary of the Christian Church,* ed F. L. Cross (Oxford 1957)
PG	*Patrologia Graeca,* ed J. P. Migne, 161 vols (Paris 1857–66)
PL	*Patrologia Latina,* ed J. P. Migne, 217+4 index vols (Paris 1841–64)
PO	*Patrologia Orientalis,* ed J. Graffin and F. Nau (Paris 1903–)
Potthast	*Regesta Pontificum Romanorum inde ab a. post Christum natum MCXCVIII ad a. MCCCIV,* ed A. Potthast 2 vols (repr Graz 1957)
PP	*Past and Present* (London 1952–)

ABBREVIATIONS

PRO	Public Record Office, London
PW	*Paulys Realencyklopëdie der klassischen Altertumswissenschaft*, new ed G. Wissowa and W. Kroll (Stuttgart 1893–)
RB	*Revue Bénédictine* (Maredsous 1884–)
RHE	*Revue d'Histoire Ecclésiastique* (Louvain 1900–)
RHEF	*Revue d'Histoire de l'Eglise de France* (Paris 1910–)
RR	*Regesta Regum Anglo-Normannorum*, ed H. W. C. Davis, H. A. Cronne, R. H. C. Davis, 4 vols (Oxford 1913–1969)
RS	*Rerum Brittanicarum Medii Aevi Scriptores*, 99 vols (London 1858–1911). *Rolls Series*
SA	*Studia Anselmiana* (Rome 1933–)
SCH	*Studies in Church History* (London 1964–)
Speculum	*Speculum, A Journal of Medieval Studies* (Cambridge, Mass 1926–)
SS	*Surtees Society* (Newcastle 1835–)
TRHS	*Transactions of the Royal Historical Society* (London 1871–)
VCH	*Victoria County History* (London 1900–)
WA	*D. Martin Luthers Werke*, ed J. C. F. Knaake, Weimare Ausgabe (Weimar 1883–)
YAJ	*Yorkshire Archaeological Journal* (London, Leeds 1870–)
RecS	*Record Series* (1885–)

HERESY AND SCHISM IN THE
LATER ROMAN EMPIRE

by S. L. GREENSLADE

FEW Paris theologians like Beda's bitterness. How can you win if you drive those who disagree with Luther into his camp? Hatred like this made Arius a heresiarch, drove Tertullian out of the Church. This is the way to make heretics.'[1] So Erasmus, and elsewhere he reflects how he exposed himself to the charge of heresy by trying to be just to heretics. He was kinder than Tertullian who had no mercy for them. Heresy is the devil's work, one of the manifold ways he attacks truth. It is evil, it is sin; it is worse than schism, it is blasphemy, a kind of adultery, close to idolatry. Heresy brings eternal death, while persecution at least gives birth to martyrs. Heretics are the ravening wolves who attack Christ's flock. Humanly considered, heresy is a sin of the flesh for, as an act of choice, it is self-assertion against God, and so the heretic is self-condemned. More properly it is demonic, the spiritual wickednesses from which it comes were sent by the devil.[2]

Not only the fiery Tertullian so speaks. To Irenaeus the peace-lover heretics are self-condemned since they oppose their own salvation, they are blasphemous, they are slippery snakes, they will go to eternal fire. Since they bring strange fire to the altar, they will be burned up by fire from heaven, like Nadab and Abihu. To Origen the truth-seeker they are traitors: all heretics, like Judas, call Jesus 'Rabbi' – and kiss him.[3]

Here is already an entrenched notion of heresy. How did it come about? This study will be more theological than sociological, for, although the Church lives in history and its members are exposed to all manner of social and cultural influences, it is still the Church, charged to be itself and to fulfil its mission.

The New Testament occasionally calls a group *haeresis* without pejorative implication. But when Paul blamed the Corinthians for their divisions (*schismata*), he continued with a fateful proof-text:

---

[1] Erasmus, *Opus Epistolarum*, ed P. S. Allen, VI: 1721, VIII: 2136 (Oxford 1926, 1934).
[2] Tertullian, *Adversus Praxean* 1, *De Praescriptionibus* 1–6 and *passim*.
[3] Irenaeus, [*Adversus Haereses*], ed W. W. Harvey (Cambridge 1857), I ix, II viii, IV xl. Origen, *Commentariorum Series*, 100.

There must be *haereseis* so that the *dokimoi*, the sound, among you may be manifest (1 Cor., 11:19). The blame is moral, for faction, and in the context the soundness is not explicitly doctrinal, though a comprehensive loyalty may be intended. In the *Pastorals*, which Irenaeus and the rest took to be Pauline, the concept is doctrinal. There is sound religious teaching and false, *heterodidaskalia*; the false teacher is ignorant and diseased. The heretic is obstinate, self-condemned, and if he will not respond to warnings twice given, he is to be shunned – more fateful proof-texts (1 Tim., 6:3–5; Titus, 3:10).

It sounds harsh: no sympathy with the genuinely puzzled, no concern for intellectual liberty. But it has point. As Israel was delivered from exile to be a holy, separate people, so Christians, delivered from the world, must be a holy people unto the Lord, his own possession, though with a mission to the world. To discharge that mission the Church must make clear to itself and others what it stands for in thought and action, must develop the institutions proper to its nature and mission, must be different from the world till it conquers the world. It must also be manifestly a single entity, one Church. In a pagan environment one proof-text, however balanced with others, will be, 'Come ye out from among them, and be ye separate, and touch not the unclean thing' (2 Cor., 6:17, citing Isa., 52:11). No moral compromise, no doctrinal syncretism. This was not sociological aspiration but theological demand. Brought into being by divine action first in Israel, finally in Christ, the Church was anchored in history to an event in Christ, mediated by a historical group of apostles and maintained by God through the Spirit of Christ active in historical processes. It was charged with a historical mission now seen as universal: 'Go ye, and make disciples of all nations.'

On the one hand, then, the Church must look backwards to Christ, to the apostles, their teachings and institutions, thus preserving its God-given identity. On the other hand it must discover the fulness of its resources by responding in the course of its mission to the Spirit's activity. Here it must look forwards, sensitive to changing needs of the world, intellectual and moral. Problems were inevitable, through ignorance, sin and circumstance: there must needs be choices, and some will be wrong. Tensions between – in modern terms – individual rights and the establishment will often be acute. Behind both heresy and schism lie basic questions: for the Church, Am I remaining my true self?; for the individual, On what terms can I join?, or, Do I really belong?. Historians ask why individuals were not at ease in

Zion, why groups broke away, how they were treated, whether the Church chose the right means to keep its identity and unity, how it responded to suffering and to success and power. All this has its sociological side to which I try, if but briefly, to do justice. But the theological issues and criteria are paramount. How could the Church be loyal both to what was given in Christ in a few years of the first century and to the forward-leading Spirit, responding to the needs of mankind?

2

Return for a moment to Paul. He stood for Christ as Lord, as authority. He stood also for liberty against law, the freedom with which Christ set us free. You can extract a creed from Paul, who was passionately anxious that no one should preach another gospel, but he wants allegiance to this Lord to spring from *pistis*, personal commitment, and to bring life in Christ and thereby in the christian community, which is not an amorphous group of individuals but is delimited by some clear beliefs, like the Resurrection of Christ, and by some institutions, like baptism and eucharist, and by a real, if undefined, acceptance of an apostolic authority derived from Christ. Liberty cannot be unrestrained – we see this in his dealings with Corinth – yet Christ's gift of freedom must be cherished. The ideal is not, as the *Pastorals* almost suggest, a collection of children believing and doing what instructors of unquestionable authority tell them, but growth into the full stature of Christ through, and into, freedom. Hence another inescapable tension, between accepting the given and freely giving oneself. How did choices demonstrate the sound members?

The gnostic challenge, though crucial, need not be described in detail. In a sense Gnostics stood for freedom of thought and organisation, claiming both to be progressive Christians on some speculative or eclectic or syncretistic basis, and to be true to scripture properly understood or to tradition, perhaps their own secret traditions. Some teachers were attracted by this outlook, and they must have been difficult for early bishops to size up and handle, while most ordinary Christians probably sensed that something was wrong. So came a crisis of authority, resolved fairly quickly by standing upon the backward-looking note of apostolicity. Faced by faction at Corinth, Clement of Rome had stressed order, obedience and the rights of a ministry sent by God through Jesus and the apostles. Ignatius, fearing not only faction but evaporation of the historicity of Christ through

3   I-2

gnostic speculation, had found a simple solution in the maxim, Hold to your bishop, whatever he approves pleases God.[1] Before long the meaning of apostolicity as the hall-mark of authentic Christianity had been developed and formalised, especially by Irenaeus and Tertullian. Saving truth has been revealed in Christ and given by him to the apostles and by them to the Church. Trust them. Their teaching is known primarily in the apostolic scriptures, the Old Testament accepted by them and their own writings or those of close companions (the essentials of the New Testament canon were almost settled by Irenaeus's time) and it is by scripture that heresy should be refuted. The obvious problem of interpretation was eased as to fundamental beliefs by confidence in a rule of faith (*regula fidei* or *veritatis*) apostolic in origin, which sets bounds to liberty of exegesis. Then there was the tradition of important churches, also authoritative where trust in its continuity from the apostles seemed warranted by apostolic foundation and an unbroken succession of bishops with a duty to preserve the apostolic faith and institutions. When such churches plainly agreed, confidence reached its maximum. 'Is it likely that so many churches would have erred into one faith?' asked Tertullian. 'Where uniformity is found among many, it is not error but tradition.' Christianity is salvation, not philosophy, *divinum negotium*, something already done once for all and given to us by God. A time comes when you have to accept or reject it, you cannot endlessly seek without finding. Heresy is persistent contradiction of scripture as epitomised in the rule of faith agreed among apostolic churches.[2]

We see dangers in this backward-looking position. Is scripture clear and uniform, how is it related to tradition, did the apostles know and understand so much, cannot bishops or the bulk of the Church go astray, will not ecclesiastical authority eventually triumph over scripture? What room for liberty, for charity? Yet in principle Christians cannot evade the implications of their faith's givenness and particularity, while in practice the early Church could probably not have preserved its identity and saved itself from dissolution through syncretism without such confidence in apostolicity. Besides, the scope of heresy was at this time limited to 'things necessary to salvation', and though the notion of essential beliefs contains its own problems, it allows and even safeguards some freedom. It was the basis of Origen's exegesis. It allows

---

[1] I Clement 40–4; Ignatius, for example *Ephesians* 3–6, *Smyrnaeans* 8.
[2] Irenaeus, I *praefatio*, ii; III i–iv; v xx. Tertullian, *De Praescriptionibus* 14, 28 and *passim*. See Origen, *De Principiis* I *praefatio*.

also for charity in that there can be differences of opinion within the unity of a comprehensive Church. What had happened so far was not that the whole content of orthodoxy had been investigated and formulated, but rather that its norms had been generally accepted. Discipline had not yet been codified. Room was left for response to the Spirit in the inner life of the Church and its mission. But the theology of authority had not been finally settled, and its exercise was already open to abuse by those who possessed or sought power.

The initial popularity of Montanism points to anxiety and discontent. It stood for, though it distorted, some things which had been prominent in primitive Christianity: confidence in immediate action of the Holy Spirit, prophecy as its normal medium, expectation of a speedy *Parousia*, stern preparation for it. Montanism did not precipitate a doctrinal crisis, since it did not deny the finality of scripture for the faith nor dissent from the rule of truth. The Paraclete would expound scripture, not contradict it, nor invent new saving doctrines. In morals and discipline, however, the Spirit would teach the Church how to live. Here, though it may not have been originally a reaction from institutionalism, Montanism threatened to disrupt the rather authoritarian pattern which was being designed to meet Gnosticism, and to replace it, not by freedom, but by a different authority. In Tertullian moral and disciplinary decisions, involving excommunication and so one's chance of salvation, belong to *spiritales homines* in the Church which is *spiritus*, not *numerus episcoporum*.[1] This implies a different ecclesiology. Had Montanism prevailed, its emphasis upon prophets rather than episcopal guardians of apostolic tradition must, for all Tertullian's denials, have unwound the triple cord of apostolic scripture, rule and ministry. Perhaps the shake-up would have been salutary. The Church, however, set itself to strengthen precisely these defences: the Canon was not quite closed, but later candidates needed strong backing from apostolic churches, prophets were discounted, bishops seen as succeeding to apostolic authority and their control of discipline taken for granted. This apostolic Church was the mediator of salvation, the home of the saved, including sinners. Certainly it must keep the faith, but heresy was not the chief issue in the third century, since the central problems set by the Modalists and Origen and Paul of Samosata did not come to a head until the fourth. More concentrated attention was given to problems of discipline and, with them, of schism. So we come to Cyprian.

[1] Tertullian, *De Pudicitia* 21.

5

3

For him the Church is by nature one and cannot be divided. Its inner unity and uniqueness are supported and defined by its apostolic structure in which bishops are heirs to the apostles *vicaria ordinatione* – apostles, as Clarus put it concisely in 256, 'quibus nos successimus eadem potestate ecclesiam Domini gubernantes'.[1] Locally and universally bishops are the glue of the Church, their responsibility to God carrying with it a right to obedience from the faithful. Succession is to one's predecessor in a see, not one's consecrator, though lawful choice and consecration are necessary. If a splinter-group pretends to appoint a bishop, he can only be *pseudepiscopus, nemini succedens*, however many bishops consecrated him. In Rome Novatian could find no empty *cathedra* to sit on. Any such group is non-church, has no ministry, no sacraments, no Holy Spirit. There is no salvation in it. Without the Spirit, it must soon wither away, a vulnerable spot in Cyprian's doctrine. Right or wrong, it is a clear and coherent theory, binding Church, ministry and sacraments together. It has no hesitation about episcopal authority in doctrine and discipline. Only about their independence in relation to one another or to a council does Cyprian lack clarity.

This apostolic Church confidently declared itself alone the divinely guaranteed instrument of salvation, quite unconscious of the derogatory sense Harnack would one day attach to *Heilsanstalt*. No plurality of churches was acknowledged. Subsequent history brings out the threat of a conforming, mechanical Christianity lurking in this institutional confidence. Already, indeed, Clement and Origen were more interested in teachers than in bishops, in Christians of advanced spiritual understanding than in those who worked their passage obediently through the practical life to salvation – an attitude which might set ecclesiological problems. Others took up the ecclesiological issue directly. If the Church is by nature one, it is also by nature holy and can lose its *esse* through the unholiness of its members. The point was made in disputes between Callistus and Hippolytus and between Tertullian and Callistus or the bishop of Carthage over adultery, and in Cyprian's anxieties over the discipline of Christians who compromised or lapsed into idolatry under persecution. Whatever personal factors –

---

[1] Cyprian, *Ep* 66: 4; *Sententiae* 79. For Cyprian's ecclesiology see G. S. M. Walker, *The Churchmanship of St Cyprian* (London 1968) and my *Schism [in the Early Church]* (2nd ed London 1964).

and they were many – affected the lax Novatus and the rigorist Novatian, it was the resulting theology of the Church that mattered in the long run. Is it a society of saints kept exclusive by stern discipline or a school and home for forgiven sinners?

Groups which took the former line were not being liberal or uninstitutional. Novatianists, and Donatists after them, claimed to be exclusively the Church. And at this date grave problems could neither be resolved by a tolerant denominationalism within a wider catholicity nor ended by papal fiat, as is plain from the storm raised by Victor's action in the Quartodeciman controversy and by the joint resistance of Cyprian of Carthage and Firmilian of Caesarea to Stephen. Councils were emerging as organs of catholicity: they were used in the Easter debates, against Montanism and Novatianism, and later against Paul of Samosata. But the theory of councils was not yet developed, and their authority and power *vis-à-vis* such great sees as Alexandria, Antioch, Ephesus, Carthage, and above all Rome, was quite unclear.

Before Constantine, the Church was fighting for its life: not always for the mere right to exist, but for freedom to be itself and discharge a mission seen mainly as rescuing souls from paganism for eternity, though since good conduct was a means to that end, the hope of changing society dawned. Institutions proper to the mission had to be developed, and risks intrinsic to institutional life were taken: the danger of codification in thought and practice, of undue submission to authority, of complacency, of getting by on minimum standards for salvation. One can fairly ask how far devotion to the person Christ had been exchanged, before the third century ended, for devotion to a christian system, though we know too little about ordinary Christians of the time to answer the question. Even if the Church rejected élitism, the social consequences of professing Christianity and, at times, the selective process of actual persecution kept standards up. There is something grand in the sense of unity and catholicity which inspired the institution to offer all men new life within a visible fellowship of the Spirit. How would the Spirit fare against human frailty when the Church was offered a privileged status in the world?

4

Two movements cover most of the fourth century problems: the Donatist schism and the Arian heresy. Not that schism and heresy can always be distinguished. Asked what heresy Novatian introduced,

7

Cyprian replied that we should not be curious about what he taught since he taught outside. Elsewhere he argued that Novatianists do not observe the catholic *lex* and *symbolum* since, when they profess belief in holy Church, they lie, not possessing the Church. Thus they are both schismatics and heretics. When Cresconius denied that Donatists were heretics, Augustine answered that inveterate schism amounts to heresy.[1]

Non-theological factors entered largely into Donatism: pique of a woman *pecuniosissima et factiosissima* reproved by an archdeacon, Numidian jealousy of Carthage, regional if not strictly national feeling against Rome, economic grievances of poor against rich, country against city – all probably played some part in the course of the long schism, and without them the theological debate might have proved less intractable. Full weight must be given to these elements, discussed in detail by Dr Frend and others, including some Marxists.[2] The theological issues, however, were real, important, and of lasting consequence – and more exciting than the dry words of Article 26, 'Of the Unworthiness of the Ministers, which hinders not the effect of the Sacrament'.

The main ecclesiological tradition in Africa was Cyprian's unique apostolic Church outside which are no ministry or sacraments. But rigorism was also powerful. One breach in Cyprian's stronghold was made by pope Stephen who, though he fully shared Cyprian's concept of apostolicity and held with him that there is no salvation outside the apostolic body, did allow a certain validity to baptism performed by heretics or schismatics. If the recipient came over to the true Church, the baptism need not be repeated; it began to work.[3] This view had been widely accepted before Donatism began. Another breach was due to Cyprian himself when, perhaps illogically, he told some Spanish churches that a Godfearing *plebs* ought to separate itself from a sinful (read, lapsed) bishop, since it could not be immune from the contagion of his communion and would be contaminated by sharing in his sacrifices (read, eucharists) which God could not accept.[4] Fateful generalisation from a single case! The second breach was fundamental to the Donatist position, the first to the catholic rejoinder.

In 304 the imprisoned confessors of Abitinae ventured to excommunicate *traditores* and their *consortes*, and, if we trust a second account, delivered this verdict: 'Si quis traditoribus communicaverit, nobiscum

---

[1] Cyprian, *Ep* 55:24; Augustine, *Contra Cresconium* II 4.
[2] W. H. C. Frend, *The Donatist Church* (2nd ed Oxford 1971) with the bibliography and introductory note.
[3] Cyprian, *Epp* 69–75, especially 75:8–15.   [4] Cyprian, *Ep* 67.

partem in regnis caelestibus non habebit.'[1] This infection-principle
was formalised in Donatist theology. They did not repudiate Cyprian's
apostolic Church; they claimed to be that Church, since, by Cyprian's
own statement, apostate bishops are *ipso facto* excommunicate before
official deposition, and their sacramental acts – baptisms, eucharists,
ordinations – are automatically null and void. In particular Caecilian
had been consecrated by a *traditor*, that is, not consecrated, so that their
man Majorinus duly succeeded to the vacant see of Carthage. To accept
a traitor's sacraments, to adhere to Caecilian, must infect the Church.
The Donatists, alone both holy and apostolic, were the catholic Church.
And by another Cyprianic principle, only within that Church were
baptisms valid. Therefore they rebaptized. So this schism had its own
theology, even if not one formally heretical by contradicting the creeds
verbatim.

Though Donatism owed much of its strength to other factors, this
holiness theology, as later events have often shown, required an answer,
which, when it came, was constructed from accepted principles but was
potentially revolutionary. Take first the non-Donatists, to most eyes
the catholic Church. Augustine accepted Cyprian's teaching on its
apostolic structure and then, emphasising the action of Christ as
minister of all sacraments, argued that where they are duly celebrated
by a minister of the Church, his moral condition will not prevent
Christ from fulfilling his promises. Baptism and ordination happen.
On this argument Donatists were non-suited for lack of apostolic
succession. They had left the Church.

But Augustine genuinely wanted to get them back, and was willing
to investigate the bearings of his own argument upon their present
status in schism; for they were not pagans nor credally heretics. So the
old concession about baptism *extra ecclesiam* was extended to ordination
and theologically deepened. In both Christ, as minister, confers a
consecratio: the recipient is a baptized or ordained person. Though
outside the catholic Church they are not effective to salvation, these
actions need not be repeated if he enters it. Already valid, they become
efficacious. On these terms men might more readily come in, and
bishops could be received as bishops, *cum honoribus*, especially if
accompanied by their flock. Augustine made other points: that
Donatists in Africa, unrecognised abroad, lacked the catholicity
inherent in God's promise to establish the Church in all nations, that
their uncharitable temper proved their want of the Holy Spirit, the

---

[1] *Acta Saturnini*, PL 8 (1844) cols 690–703. See *Schism*, pp 117–20.

mark of the true Church. His ecclesiology created a new situation, though it was not at once accepted, by popes Innocent and Leo for example.[1]

After some conciliatory overtures and much bitter conflict Donatism was defeated less by argument than by coercion. Comment on this must wait till something has been said of Arianism, since state intervention in church affairs is one story. Meanwhile, observe one theological consequence of Augustine's thinking. It can unsettle confidence in discerning the true Church by its structure. Men go on asking if they should not separate from a body which authoritatively rejects adequate discipline, or if charity is a safe test of the Spirit's indwelling. To find catholicity should we look first for apostolic structure or apostolic faith? Can they never clash, and if they seem to, what authority decides the case? Some answers to problems intensified by his ecclesiology are now freshening ecumenical dialogue, while others long ago convinced the Reformers that they had true churches by virtue of loyalty to the apostolic Gospel. Is it orthodoxy, then, that determines catholicity, and if so, what is heresy?

Despite high counts by hereseologues from Hippolytus on, it had no wide range of content in the ante-Nicene church. To be taken with the seriousness found in Irenaeus or Tertullian, it must usually concern the nature of God or the person of Christ. Paul of Samosata was banned because his teaching seemed utterly contrary to the christian faith. But, though some Modalists were condemned, modalist thinking continued as one tradition within the Church, as did some Logos-doctrine which was later denounced. Origen was attacked, but not excommunicated, Dionysius of Alexandria easily made his peace with Rome. For even within this narrow range implications were rarely worked out in detail, while many fundamental doctrines – atonement, eucharist, Holy Spirit – were left undefined. Orthodoxy meant broad acceptance of living tradition, not of a precise theological scheme. With Arianism every implication was wrung out, controversy was more public, far more participated in it, far more power-politics affected it.

Our concern is rather with methods of controversy than the doctrine itself. First, philosophy. Tertullian (in some moods) and Hippolytus

---

[1] I have tried to work out the implications of Donatism and Augustine's reply in *Schism*. On the subsequent history of reordination consult L. Saltet, *Les Réordinations* (Paris 1907) and H. E. J. Cowdrey, 'The Dissemination of St Augustine's Doctrine of Holy Orders during the later Patristic Age', *JTS*, new series, XX (1969) pp 448–81.

had cast it for the role of the devil; now, if christian theology was to be taken seriously by the world, it must take philosophy seriously. Aristotelian logic entered into the late Arianism of Eunomius, Middle Platonism in the tradition of Origen affected Arians and their opponents, Athanasius as well as the Cappadocians. Neoplatonism made its mark. Philosophical argument was inescapable, despite its danger to the biblical ideas of God which Athanasius affirmed when he argued from Christ as Saviour to Christ as God.

But Arians appealed also to scripture, finding proof-texts in plenty like Proverbs, 8:22, 'The Lord created me', and Colossians, 1:15, 'first-born of all creation'; and they appealed to tradition, to Origen calling the Logos *ktisma*, to other subordinationist statements, the material later collected by Petavius and triumphantly, as he thought, explained away by Bull.[1] In addition they objected to forcing a non-scriptural term into a creed as the test of orthodoxy, reversing the old view that orthodoxy is prior to heresy, which is recognisable by its novelty. So controversy must now turn not only on exegesis but on the respective authority of scripture, tradition and reason. Would truth best emerge from prolonged thought? Could discussion be open-minded enough for truth to be a likely result?

In retrospect we know how much worked against that. There was the difference between eastern and western Christianity in language, temperament and background. Within this area of controversy were already traditional loyalties, to Origenism in the East, in the West to that near-modalism (despite Tertullian and Novatian) which alarmed the East. The Greek lands had nearly all the apostolic foundations, the majority of Christians, more bishops, more learning. They resented Roman claims – see Firmilian's letter to Cyprian and Eusebius's account of Victor, gleefully citing Polycrates of Ephesus's reply. And the doctrinal debate is shot through with rivalry between sees after the rise of Constantinople had thrown Alexandria into the Roman alliance, as comes out so clearly when Julius was defending Athanasius against the Eusebians.[2]

Despite all this, the theological debate was earnest and intelligent. It probed the soteriological principle, it asked on what grounds Christ and the Spirit could be worshipped and what that would imply

---

[1] D. Petavius, *De Theologicis Dogmatibus*, 1644–50; G. Bull, *Defensio Fidei Nicaenae*, 1685. See also O. Chadwick, *From Bossuet to Newman* (Cambridge 1957).

[2] Cyprian, *Ep* 75; Eusebius, *HE* v 24; Julius in Athanasius, *Apologia contra Arianos*, 21–35.

for the essential being of God. Plenty of scope for research. But since the Church is not a theology faculty but a worshipping community, some settlement was imperative, and much church history in this period concerns how you can get one. If it should not be left to academics, authority, it seemed, must step in. But the rule of faith and baptismal creeds were too vague, while appeal to scripture and tradition still involved scholars. Of the accepted norms there remained the apostolic ministry, bishops meeting together. This was not a simple solution. Bishops could execute the decisions of provincial councils locally, but for something to bind the whole Church there was as yet neither legal provision under a constitution nor a theology of conciliar authority. If agreement was reached, you could attribute it to common sense or the Holy Spirit. If not, you must raise constitutional and theological problems. Had a council at Tyre any right to try the bishop of Alexandria? Had a Roman council any right to restore Athanasius when he had been condemned by Tyre? At Sardica was he properly defendant or sitting member? How does a bishops' meeting become a council? Is there an appeal, and if so, to what? To any larger council? More theologically, was Nicaea binding because it reached the right conclusion from scripture and tradition, as Athanasius says in his earlier writings, or did it have an intrinsic right to decide, *qua magisterium* or through the promised guidance of the Spirit? Or were bishops there to represent their flocks who had, *qua* Church, the right to take the final decision by receiving the council? Until there was substantial agreement on such points, councils alone could not deal finally with heresy or schism.[1]

In the event decision was not left to ecclesiastical authority alone. The state came on the scene, eager for unity. But on what principles, by whose advice, should the emperor act? With Donatism Constantine began naturally enough by recognising at Carthage the bishop in possession, Caecilian, duly appointed, it seemed, and acknowledged by the churches overseas. The Donatists responded with charges against him which Constantine agreed to have sifted by an episcopal tribunal that Miltiades of Rome turned into a small council. When its proceedings were disputed, the emperor summoned the council of Arles, and waxed indignant when Donatists repudiated even this authority.

[1] On the nature and authority of early councils see G. Kretschmar's chapter in *The Councils of the Church*, ed H. J. Margull (Philadelphia 1966) and P. Camelot's in B. Botte etc, *Le Concile et les Conciles* (Paris 1960); also *Councils and the Ecumenical Movement*, ed L. Vischer (World Council of Churches, Geneva 1968).

Were they ignorant that the episcopal judgement is equivalent to God's? In these few years precedents were set for the imperial summons and confirmation of councils, for the state to banish bishops deposed by them, but also for some distinction between the duties of emperor and bishops.

Arianism followed quickly upon Donatism, again Constantine thought a council could settle it, again he managed the council, and again distinguished his functions from the doctrinal decisions of the bishops, which, he said, must be accepted as God's own mind and will communicated to them by the Holy Spirit. However that might be, imperial control of councils had set in, and their story was very human. Councils could be packed, like Tyre and Constantinople, or split, like Sardica and the crafty division of a proposed Nicaea II into Seleucia and Ariminum. There might be good councils like Alexandria, but none unreservedly open to the Holy Spirit. Parties strove for the ear of emperors who found neutrality impracticable, though Valentinian I is supposed to have tried it. Even when sole emperor, Constantine was hard put to it to secure the imperial interest in unity by insisting on Nicaea, his council, and for Constantius it was much harder. There was a good case for counting the bishops of the East (his first responsibility) better theological authority than those of the West. But many of them were Origenists, they plainly disliked *homoousios*, or the modalist sense given to it in the West, as they believed. Besides, they favoured comprehension under vague homoean formulas, and it might seem right in principle to preserve unity as the best means of discovering truth. Understandably he supported the homoeans and against wavering opposition carried their policy into the West when he became sole emperor. One wonders what would have happened had the anti-Nicenes remained vaguely homoean. But when undisguised anomoeanism grew out of it, traditional Christianity everywhere felt that to be wrong, and from longing after peace and constructive Cappadocian theology a solution was found at Constantinople, though only with the help of Theodosius and at the cost of erecting secular coercion of dissidents into an ecclesiastical principle. An orthodox Church was established by imperial legislation, and heretics, condemned by the Church, were deprived of their churches by the state. Ten years later came legislation against pagan cults, and soon Donatists were struggling to prove that they were not heretics liable to the penalties prescribed against such. In this they failed, the Church in Africa now, against its earlier policy, pressing Honorius to proceed against Donatists by name. Augustine's conversion to coercion is too familiar to need comment.[1]

Thus one consequence of heresy and schism was coercion in religion, against which Christians had once so vehemently protested. Protests were not lacking now. When Constans sent his commissioners, *operarios unitatis*, into Africa, Donatus asked, 'Quid imperatori cum ecclesia?' When Constantius threatened Nicaea and Athanasius, Hosius boldly told him not to intrude into ecclesiastical matters which God had committed to us (the bishops) alone. Hilary, Basil, Chrysostom protested, no less than the hot-head Lucifer. Ambrose defended *causa Dei* against emperors, though unhappily he believed that coercion of pagans was a *causa Dei* to be carried out by the state. But with the principle of coercion added to general belief that the state cannot hold aloof from religious affairs, since Church and state are one community, it was long odds against any theological controversy being settled by friendly dialogue. On the other hand the Church was unlikely to submit to sheer dictation, since recent controversy had issued in an established orthodoxy on which the Church could now stand as its agreed tradition, not needing re-examination by renewed study of scripture or philosophy. This becomes clearer in the fifth century.

5

Constantinople anathematised all heresies, in particular (*idikōs*) Eunomians, Arians, Semiarians, Sabellians, Marcellians, Photinians and Apollinarians – all trinitarian or christological heresies. Manichees had already been proscribed by the state. Theodosius's immediate concern was trinitarian heresy, as the law *Episcopis tradi* of 381 shows. It uses the positive test of communion with named orthodox bishops, it aims to make heretics manifest (see 1 Cor., 11:19) and establish the Nicene faith. Would the range of punishable heresy be extended? Filaster and Epiphanius had been busy cataloguing. Augustine, persuaded to write a *De Haeresibus*, used common sense – not every error is heresy – but failed to write the second book in which he had intended to discuss what constituted heresy. While grasping what it really is, theology which keeps men from salvation in Christ, he could not clarify the formal standard by which it is to be judged and

---

[1] Most of the legislation is in *Codex Theodosianus* XVI, chs 1, 2, 5. On Theodosius I, N. Q. King, *The Emperor Theodosius and the Establishment of Christianity* (London 1961).

was pushed more and more towards the present authority of the Church, especially in council. Vincent of Lerins, in 434, formulated a criterion, *Quod ubique, quod semper, quod ab omnibus*, with the emphasis on antiquity, the consent of the Fathers seen in the rule of faith, but he treats Novatian, Donatus, Priscillian, Jovinian and Pelagius as heretics. He had not resolved a confusion between heresy determined by the simple rule which Tertullian knew and heresy measured by what the Church now teaches. Against his intention he opens the way to a position in which the criterion of antiquity is soft-pedalled and the criterion of consent used to mean the present belief of the *ecclesia docens*. Then the central problem becomes the relation of divine and human in the *magisterium*.

A few new names crept into Theodosius's edicts, but they were kinds of Arians or Manichees. Then, in March 395, Arcadius and Honorius forbade all heretics contained in the innumerable laws of their father to assemble or perform ordinations. If that was not clear enough, they decreed in September that all who deviate *vel levi argumento* from the catholic religion are included in the word heretic and liable to the legal penalties. By 405, and after a struggle again in 408, the Donatists are expressly called heretics and penalised as such. What is *catholica religio*?

Origenism might have provided a test case, had not that quarrel been so complicated by ecclesiastical politics and by the family ties and personal allegiances which Peter Brown so fascinatingly describes that the principles and mechanics of condemnation get lost in the smoke.[1] Though Pelagianism had similar complications, it puts one central problem more plainly. Pelagius claimed that, even if erroneous, his teaching on grace and freedom was not heretical since these topics had not been defined by authority. At Diospolis the bishops agreed that many of his disputed statements were not *aliena ab ecclesiastica doctrina*, while he anathematised the authors of some statements attributed to himself 'quasi stultos, non quasi haereticos; siquidem non est dogma'. Caelestius argued that original sin was *res quaestionis, non haeresis*; he was no heretic since he did not pretend to define dogma. Pope Zosimus warned Caelestius and the bishops against hairsplitting, unedifying debates, contagious curiosity and conceit. All this put Augustine in a quandary, for he acknowledged the problem *Quomodo*

[1] Peter Brown, 'The Patrons of Pelagius', *JTS*, new series, XXI (1970) pp 56–72; see R. F. Evans, *Pelagius: Inquiries and Reappraisals* (London 1968), ch 2: 'Pelagius and the Revival of the Origenist Controversy'.

sit definiendus haereticus. He appealed to creeds and the rule of faith, but these were not decisive, though he hoped to catch Caelestius out credally under the clause 'one baptism for the remission of sins', which must, he said, apply to infants. Unaware how much Greek theology favoured the Pelagians, utterly convinced that the faith was at stake, he went on debating the *quaestiones* on the basis of scripture, the western tradition and the immense resources of his own genius, but simultaneously worked to get Pelagianism condemned as heresy. Diospolis, in acquitting Pelagius, had condemned the heresy of which it acquitted him. Africa had condemned it, Rome had condemned it; so must the state. This he obtained, aided by the usual non-theological factors, though why the state came down against the Pelagians and exerted pressure on Rome is not clear from the extant evidence. Later events proved this sort of condemnation inadequate, for Julian of Eclanum knew as well as Augustine that fundamental issues had been raised and boldly insisted on more theology. His condemnation at Ephesus in 431, veiled under the name of Caelestius and surprisingly secured from an eastern council because Cyril of Alexandria hoped it would strengthen his alliance with Rome, was not theologically conclusive, nor were the *capitula* of Orange (529) though they stopped actual controversy for a time.

We must take stock. What is heresy? Arianism might have shown the inadequacy of appeal to baptismal creeds in theological debate, words like Son, *Logos*, incarnate, salvation, rather pointing to than settling problems, but, with tradition and theology, council and state cooperating, that controversy brought forth not a dogmatic constitution *De Trinitate* but a new creed. Pelagianism again proved that creeds cannot sufficiently define orthodoxy without much agreement to differ within the Church. Possible with laymen, that is awkward with accredited teachers. As controversy spread, liberty was confined in several ways. One was by coercion, another by tradition as a general notion, meaning in practice: Trust the mind of the Church in official preaching and worship (*lex orandi, lex credendi*). A third was to translate tradition into dogma and, on conciliar authority, to demand assent to a string of propositions like those put to Caelestius at Carthage or to a document like the Chalcedonian definition and its appendages. Another, to open problems up by re-examining scripture or tradition, was unpopular: it risked speedy condemnation for novelty. The trend to authoritarianism is obvious. Even so we observe a different outcome in East and West: the East holding indeed to the authority of councils but content with those few early ones which safeguard the doctrine of the Incarnation, and requiring reception by the *consensus fidelium*, with great confidence in a loosely defined tradition preserved in liturgy; the West increasingly stressing the contemporary *magisterium*, multiplying councils but accepting reception by the pope as necessary and sufficient, moving towards a codification of orthodoxy over a wider range of doctrines.

The movements in both directions were not purely theological, and historians properly investigate secular influences. I could tell lurid stories of Ephesus and Chalcedon. It became ever harder to hold East and West together in one institution. Rome and Constantinople were rivals, Alexandria resented subordination to Constantinople, Jerusalem wanted a patriarchate at the expense of Antioch. In a multi-racial empire social discontent brought grievances against the central administration, and centrifugal, if not nationalistic, tendencies involved the Church more completely now that most people were Christians. Large-scale faction must both alarm the emperor and give opportunity to curry his favour. State coercion bred church pressure groups. In short, problems apparent under Constantius were now more intense, with fresh ones added by the increased proportion of non-Greeks in the eastern Church and by barbarian invasions in the West. How fascinating to study the human element! Suppose Cyril or Nestorius or Dioscorus had been born with different genes or Theodosius had not died in 450? But I must pursue my theological course. Granted that under familiar human pressures the Church fell below true christian standards, what, by the mid-fifth century, had it made of its battle with heresy and schism? what had they made of it?

Schism, division as such, normally weakens the Church as Donatism and christological divisions weakened it against Islam. But personal and social factors which account for the extent and intensity of so many schisms should not be seen only as causes of this or that split, but also as recurrent symptoms of weakness and consequences of failure in the christian mission to the world. So longing for holiness shows itself ecclesiologically in perfectionist sects throughout history. It has a different parallel in current readiness, even within ecumenism, to see the *esse* of the Church in its service to society, over-riding structural considerations. My period ends with the old ecclesiology still dominant. The Church is one institution, holy in virtue of Holy Spirit, holy scripture, holy sacraments, rather than individual sanctity, catholic and apostolic by doctrinal and structural continuity. Monasticism sometimes approached schism through its different outlook. Schismatic bodies claimed to be this Church, not churches. Some modifications were possible. Mutual excommunication might be hopefully delayed, and temporary compromise helped by mediate communion as in the Antiochene schism when Antioch was in communion with Alexandria but not with Rome while Rome was in communion with Alexandria, when Basil communicated with Athanasius and Meletius, Athanasius with Paulinus, Nectarius with Damasus and Flavian, Damasus with Nectarius and Paulinus.[1] Potentially more important was Augustinian ecclesiology, since valid ordinations *extra ecclesiam* may be a step to plurality of churches. Rome's attitude to the Orthodox Church has often been obscure, and the concessions made to it now in *De Ecumenismo* are spreading to other ecclesial bodies, outrunning Cyprian and Augustine by allowing saving baptism by incorporation into Christ within them and moving cautiously towards the acknowledgement of schism within the Church. In the fifth century, however, apostolic structure was deemed of the *esse* of the Church and that apostolic body claimed to determine orthodoxy along the lines of Tertullian's prescriptions: apostolic scripture, tradition and authority belong to us. Hence Chalcedon.

To assess the effects of heresy is more difficult, for it can weaken or strengthen the Church. Coercion was a wrong turning, damaging it spiritually. In the realm of thought, however, by sifting beliefs heresy can (often did) lead to clearer or deeper theology. That strengthens. Unfortunately the chosen instrument of decision, the council, noble in idea, was in practice dangerous. Even if, *per impossibile*, we set aside the manipulations and quarrels and the imperial control (which was sometimes beneficial), they were theologically dangerous. Take Ephesus (431). Overlook the rivalry of Alexandria and Constantinople and consider its theological method. The creed of Nicaea was read, then letters of Cyril and Nestorius. Rapidly, with scant discussion, Cyril was declared consistent with Nicaea, Nestorius inconsistent and so condemned. Then a long patristic catena was read, not wholly one-sided but lacking any Antiochene component. Again Nestorius was quickly found guilty of opposing tradition, as if the creed of 325 decided christological problems then unforeseen and as if orthodox tradition were already formulated by fourth century Fathers of the Church. In

[1] On the Antiochene schism: F. Cavallera, *Le schisme d'Antioche* (Paris 1905); E. Schwartz, *Gesammelte Schriften*, IV (Berlin 1960) pp 39–110; A. M. Ritter, *Das Konzil von Konstantinopel* (Göttingen 1965) pp 57–68.

such an intellectual climate how many theologians would be brave enough to rethink the implications of scripture rather than interpret it by tradition?

Paradoxically, councils were now more self-consciously theological about their own authority. Ephesus judged by tradition, but claimed too, on poor grounds, to be ecumenical by representation. It also heard letters from Celestine of Rome and Capreolus of Carthage magnifying the Holy Spirit's operation in councils, though neither inferred automatic infallibility. Chalcedon, of course without denying the authority of scripture and tradition and never regarding its deliberations as a search for truth yet unknown, emphasised both its authority as ecumenical by representation and the assistance of the Spirit, attested by the loud acclamations of a Spirit-given unanimity.

Representation, unless allied to reception, rests on the teaching authority of bishops as such, and confidence in the Spirit points to the intrinsic authority of councils. In 451 Chalcedon claimed to formulate tradition authoritatively in its *Definition*. Now the *Definition* was orthodoxy, to reject it heresy. Yet it was rejected by large parts of what had been the Church in 450. The criterion of reception failed, except on a circular argument that non-receivers were not part of the Church. The state had to step in. Should councils, then, be content with constitutional authority to produce practical solutions, a *modus vivendi*, or should they claim an intrinsic and absolute authority, perhaps infallibility? Where their intrinsic authority is accepted, they are tempted to define more dogmas more precisely, hindering the Church from rectifying past errors. But – here is the paradox – such councils can be organs of development rather than traditionalism. Rome has sometimes welcomed this, and a critic of Jewel said that to recall the Church to the state of the apostles' time was to enforce a tall man to cry alarm again in his cradle.[1] But traditional Anglicans suspected development, believing the first centuries truer to scripture. The problem of revelation remains. What should be defined, what may be left open? Is loyalty to the person of Christ sufficient for authentic Christianity? To criticise the early councils is not to refuse them sympathy in their anxieties. Empirically, at the price of losing thousands who should have been kept, they gave solidity to the Church and helped it to speak with authority to new and uneducated peoples.

[1] Anon, *An Apology of Private Mass*, p 10, in the Parker Society edition of T. Cooper's *Answer* (Cambridge 1850).

Theologically, in so far as they tried both to respect revelation in past history and to be open to the guiding Spirit, they were on the right lines. In so far as they limited his guidance to the clergy they were wrong. Prophets, saints, scholars, sensible laymen were all needed. When the mission of the Church is to be decided, the Spirit must be allowed to blow where he listeth.

CHRISTIANITY AND
DISSENT IN ROMAN NORTH AFRICA:
CHANGING PERSPECTIVES IN
RECENT WORK

by R. A. MARKUS

THE history of North African Christianity in antiquity is a
peculiar blend of the local and the universal. Whether we
consider the 'catholic' or the 'dissenting' traditions represented
in it, we find ourselves at the intersection of two worlds. It was not
only the 'Catholicism' of Optatus, Augustine and Aurelius and their
friends and successors that linked the African Church with the Great
Church across the seas. Professor Frend long ago drew attention to the
similarities between the ecclesiologies of the Donatist and of other
western schismatic churches.[1] More recently we have been given a
portrait of another such 'dissident' Church by M. Meslin in his
impressive study of the Arian communities of the Danubian lands.[2]
As these developed in the course of the later fourth century, after
earlier flirtation with the idea of an imperial Church cast in some
'Arian' mould, they came to bear many of the same features of
'dissent' which distinguished the Donatists. Donatism was no mere
aberration; it was the local expression of a permanent religious option.
But unlike the other 'dissenting' churches of the Roman world,
Donatists did not adopt their dissenting posture as a mere response of
defeated men driven into a corner by a hostile imperial and ecclesiastical
establishment. It had a long pre-history in the African tradition of
Christianity.

Like the province itself, throughout most of its history part of a
large empire, African Christianity also lay at the intersection of two
worlds. It provides a classic illustration of the co-existence and tension
of particular and universal. By the fourth century Africa had become
a stronghold of Christianity. Until the submergence of African Christianity in the seventh century, the North African Church remained

---

[1] 'The Roman Empire [in the eyes of Western schismatics during the fourth century
A.D.', *Miscellanea historiae ecclesiasticae Stockholm 1960*] (Louvain 1961) pp 9–22.
[2] *Les Ariens d'Occident 335–430, Patristica Sorbonensia* 8 (Paris 1967).

one of the chief centres of religious and intellectual vitality in the Latin Church. Thereafter Christianity survived only in isolated communities in North Africa. Its near-disappearance under the Arab conquest inevitably overshadows the historiography of the period of its greatness in the late Roman period. It is no accident that the interplay between the local and the universal should have fascinated its historians.

The landmark which dominates all modern discussion of Christianity in Roman Africa is W. H. C. Frend's book, *The Donatist Church* (Oxford 1952, reprinted 1971). It is a work whose seminal power has been revealed in the extent to which it has set the terms of every discussion of the subject since its appearance. Frend's aim was to relate the schism which divided African Christianity throughout the fourth century and, apparently, until the very end of Roman rule in Africa, to its local roots. The schism between Catholics and Donatists was far more tenacious than similar divisions elsewhere. Why, Frend asked, did the contested episcopal election to the see of Carthage in 312 play the part in the subsequent history of the province which it did? Why did the Donatist schism, as it came to be called, assume an importance which, for example, the Melitian schism in Egypt never assumed, although it had arisen, like its Donatist counterpart, from differences of opinion in the Church over churchmen who had been compromised or suspected of defection during the 'great persecution' of 303–5? Frend's answer emerged from his study of the geographical prevalence of the schism, the distribution of Donatist centres and his success in relating the areas where its appeal was apparently strongest to the ethnic, social, economic, climatic and cultural divisions in the province. 'The main divisions between the two churches is shown to be that between the Donatism of the inland plains and the Catholicism of the cities and towns on the Tell' (p 52). A considerable degree of coincidence came to light between the distribution of Donatism and the areas of 'Berber' speech.[1] The distribution maps pointed towards the conclusion that in the religious movement of Donatism the aspirations of the African under-privileged, the relatively un-Romanised, the native poor, made itself felt against the respectable religion of the wealthy, Romanised urban bourgeoisie and the land-owning aristocracy, and those within their sphere of influence. This conclusion provided a framework in which the known relations between the two churches

---

[1] On this very problematic concept, see most recently F. Millar, 'Local cultures in the Roman Empire: Lybian, Punic and Latin in Roman Africa', *JRS*, LVIII (1968) pp 126–34, and [Peter Brown], 'Christianity and local culture [in late Roman Africa]', *ibid* pp 85–95.

made good sense. The schismatic Church rallied the support of those who had little or no stake in Roman society. The itinerant *circumcelliones* acted as its shock-troops (and have given rise to a fair body of literature which I leave on one side here), combining the fanaticism of religion with that of the social revolutionary. The state called in its forces to repress the dispossessed and to maintain the *status quo*. The Catholic Church, leaning on the support of the imperial power, became the object of an opposition in which cultural, social and economic forces all played a part.

This is too bald a summary to do justice to a powerful historical synthesis. Not only did it offer an interpretation of the known facts, but it offered, at the same time, an explanation of the ultimate fate of Christianity in North Africa in terms of the interplay of the 'particular' and the 'universal'. 'One can see', Frend wrote, 'in Donatism one of the movements which led to the extinction of classical culture over a large part of the Mediterranean.' 'If the Moslems were able to absorb the populations which they conquered into a mould so different from the classical, it was because by the seventh century AD the masses had already renounced Greco-Roman culture, or had remained untouched by it.' 'The survival of the Catholic Church...depended in Africa as in other parts of the Mediterranean on the survival of the material institutions of the Empire. When these failed, as they did in the fifth and sixth centuries, Catholicism had no appeal for the masses of the native population. It had no message of effective social reform. The Catholic Church in Africa ultimately suffered the fate of its counterpart, the Melkite Church in Egypt.'[1]

Frend was not, of course, the first to suggest that more than merely religious differences were involved in the schism. Gottfrid Arnold, the German pietist historian, had already in 1699 seen orthodoxy more in terms of an 'ecclesiastical vested interest'[2] than in terms of doctrine, and as Frend himself notes (p 331), F. Martroye had in 1904 pointed out 'that one of the causes of Donatism was probably the suspicion that the Caecilianists had surrendered not only sacred objects but equally the sense of social justice which had inspired the primitive christian community'. More than half a century ago Sir Llewellyn Woodward, in his *Christianity and nationalism in the later Roman Empire* (London 1916) generalised the view that the great mass heresies

---

[1] Quotations from *The Donatist Church* (Oxford 1952) pp 333–5.

[2] I owe the reference to his *Unparteyische Kirchen- und Ketzer-Historie...*(Frankfurt-a.-M. 1699) to [P. R. L. Brown,] 'Religious dissent [in the later Roman Empire'], *History*, XLVI (1961) pp 83–101, n 9.

could not be explained in exclusively religious terms; and Paul
Monceaux, in his great work – unfortunately never completed –
Histoire littéraire [*de l'Afrique chrétienne*] (7 vols, Paris 1901–23), though
ejecting the conclusion that Donatism was a 'national movement or a
party of political opposition' (IV, p 190) as too simple, took such
considerations very seriously into account in his summary of the
'apparent and the profound causes' of the schism, and of its 'character
and its social role' (IV, pp 163–92). Frend's approach was not, then,
unprecedented, nor were his conclusions revolutionary.

That his book has nevertheless come to mark a turning-point in the
study of African Christianity is due to two facts. In the first place, his
study was – and still remains – the first full-scale account of its theme
which drew on the discovery of the largely unknown Africa of the
High Plains, made possible by the work of French archaeologists from
Gsell to Berthier. It is not without significance that ten years before
the publication of his book, Frend had already blazed the trail for it
with a paper on 'The revival of Berber art'.[1] The soil of Numidia
provides evidence which does not only supplement the literary evidence,
but discloses a world which the literary evidence scarcely allows us to
glimpse. In the second place, Frend's study drew together all these
threads at a time when Michael Rostovtzeff's great work, *Social and
economic history of the Roman Empire* (Oxford 1926; 2nd ed 1957) had
already introduced historians to a vision of the crisis of the Roman
world in terms of the destruction of its urban culture by the under-
privileged and unassimilated countryside which had sustained it.
Frend's work has to be seen against a wider horizon: it was the working
out for one region of an ambitious attempt at historical interpretation
on the grand scale. Moreover, it slipped neatly into a still longer
perspective on African history. 'Is Donatism part of a continuous
native religious tradition', Frend asked himself, 'as fundamentally
unchanging as the Berbers themselves in the routine of their daily
lives?'[2] and his answer can take its place alongside works such as
C. Courtois's *Les Vandales et l'Afrique* (Paris 1955) and E. F. Gautier's
Le passé de l'Afrique du Nord: les siècles obscurs (Paris 1937), not to
mention more recent studies on the sociology of the Maghreb, as
concerned with the permanent 'rhythm' underlying North African
history.

It is no wonder that *The Donatist Church* should have come to

[1] *Antiquity* (London 1942) pp 342–52.
[2] *The Donatist Church*, p xvi.

dominate the landscape of scholarship in this field.[1] Work carried out very largely within the perspectives set by Frend, though sometimes useful and interesting, is of little importance for this study of *changing* perspectives. Among these, however, the studies of the East-German scholar, H. J. Diesner, especially those concerned with the *circumcelliones*, deserve mention.[2] J. P. Brisson, the blind scholar whose work *Autonomisme et christianisme dans l'Afrique romaine* (Paris 1958), though published some years after *The Donatist Church* was apparently written independently of Frend's book, has made an important contribution which we shall need to consider below; but in so far as his views on the social roots of Donatism are concerned, they fit well into the same perspective. The second part of his book (pp 325–410) explores the Donatist Church as the Church of the poor and dispossessed.

The account of Donatism as a movement of protest has gained momentum; but it has also been exposed to severe attack. The late A. H. M. Jones, in a soberly astringent paper,[3] has posed the question in terms which will scarcely admit of an affirmative answer:

What the sectaries actually said in public, so far as our record goes, was...'The Donatist Church is the true Catholic Church, and we will never communicate with *traditores*', but what they thought, we are asked to believe, was: 'We are Africans and hate the Rome government; we will have nothing to do with the Romans and will maintain our African Church and if possible our African state.' This is a thesis which it is obviously difficult to prove or to disprove, for one cannot easily read the secret thoughts of men who lived 1500 years ago.

[1] It has not, of course, been universally accepted. The range of 'moderate' assessments may be represented by the following: S. L. Greenslade, *Schism in the early Church* (London 1953; 2nd ed 1964) pp 58–61 (general agreement); B. H. Warmington, *The North African provinces from Diocletian to the Vandal conquest* (Cambridge 1954, though completed before *The Donatist Church*, 1952) pp 76–102 (qualified assent); H. Chadwick, *The early Church* (London 1967) pp 219–25 ('the tension between the two communities was all the sharper because class and economic factors had not been the prime cause of the division' – p 220); R. MacMullen, *Enemies of the Roman order* (Cambridge, Mass. 1967) pp 201–7 (sceptical; a somewhat different direction emerges from the same writer's 'Provincial languages in the Roman Empire', *American Journal of Philology*, LXXXVII (Baltimore 1966) pp 1–14.

[2] The most important of these are collected in his *Kirche und Staat im spätrömischen Reich* (Berlin 1963); see also his survey *Der Untergang der römischen Herrschaft in Nordafrika* (Weimar 1964). The principal contribution of Soviet scholarship in this field also appears to have been concentrated on this point. See P. Gacic, 'En Afrique romaine: classes et luttes sociales, d'après les historiens soviétiques', *Annales*, XII (Paris 1957) pp 650–61, at 659–60. I am unable to assess their work at first hand.

[3] 'Were the ancient heresies national or social movements in disguise?', *JTS*, n.s. x (1959) pp 280–95. Quotation from p 281.

Jones's attack is concentrated on the 'nationalist' form of the thesis. He discounts the alliance between (some) Donatist bishops and the African rebels Firmus and Gildo as insufficient to bear the weight of serving as evidence for any African nationalism. He further questions the identification of the Catholic Church with Latin and the Donatist with native culture; but despite his scepticism, he allows that 'there is some solid evidence' behind the view of Donatism as a social movement of the poor (pp 294–5). Doctrine, he reminds us finally, could be far more divisive in the Roman world than nationalism or socialism.

Some of Frend's arguments, and indeed the evidence on which they were based, have been called into question by Emin Tengström, in his meticulous study *Donatisten und Katholiken: soziale, wirtschaftliche und politische Aspekte einer nordafrikanischen Kirchenspaltung (Studia graeca et latina Gothoburgensia, xviii, 1964)*. This book, confined to carefully limited analysis of some key texts and their implications, subjects some of the evidence on which Frend's thesis was based to relentless scrutiny. Tengström criticised the inference from the sporadic alliance between some of the Donatist leaders and circumcellion terrorists to the conclusion that social protest and reform were the chief moving forces behind the schism; he discounted the links between some of the Donatist bishops and the rebels Firmus and Gildo as evidence for any general alliance between Donatism and African nationalism, and cast doubt upon some of the evidence for the overwhelming concentration of Donatism in Numidia. We cannot consider his arguments on these points here. More fundamentally, however, he pointed to the decisive role of force. What determined the distribution and the prevalence of the two churches were not so much factors such as culture, race or wealth, as pressure: on the Donatist side, the pressure of circumcellion terrorism, which, on Tengström's hypothesis, restricted the evangelisation of the countryside (where, according to his theory, they were active as wandering labourers employed on the seasonal work of olive-harvesting) by catholic clergy; on the catholic side, the attitude of the government was decisive, and that on two counts. First, much depended – especially in the towns, the centres of government – on the energy with which the African administrative personnel were prepared to give effect to repressive measures of the emperors. In the second place, much depended on the extent to which landowners were inclined to shelter schismatics on their estates. Unlike Frend, Tengström saw the great landowners as the protectors of their Donatist dependants, so long as economic interests demanded that they should protect schismatic *coloni*. The landowners' attitude changed only – according to an ingenious, possibly a too ingenious, analysis of the legislation offered by Tengström – when the government made it possible for landowners to risk losing a persecuted peasantry without fear of financial loss.

Tengström's critique, though far from uniformly compelling, prompts some reserve towards the Frend-thesis. But it must be acknowledged that, apart from the important reminder it contains of the decisive role played by force, it does nothing to explain the roots of the schism and little to account for its tenacity. Above all, it restricts itself to a range of evidence too narrow to allow a satisfying account of Donatism to emerge as an alternative to the thesis it criticises. In his penetrating review of Tengström's book P. R. L. Brown has summed up its shortcoming in this fundamental respect thus: 'The historian of Donatism must start, not with the social history of North Africa, but with the implication of two distinct views of the role of a religious group in society.'[1]

Brown characterised the two views in the following terms: 'the one, that the group exists above all to defend its identity – to preserve a divinely-given law, *Machabaeico more*; the other, that it may dominate, "baptize" and absorb, by constraint if need be, the society in which it is placed'.[2] While this dichotomy appears to me too simple to do justice to the possible variety of ways in which a religious group might conceive its place in society, we are brought at this point to the theological issues at stake in the schism. The reminder has become necessary, though, interestingly, Frend himself perceived that the conception of the Church in its relation to the secular world was at the core of the conflict. The characteristic way in which Donatists conceived this relation was part of an older and a wider theological tradition.[3] Outside the *milieu* of Alexandrian Christianity it was common in the pre-Constantinian period to think of the Church as 'set over against' a secular world and caught up in a permanent conflict with all its

---

[1] *JRS*, LV (1965) pp 281–3. Quotation from pp. 282–3.

[2] *Ibid*, p 283. For a masterly evocation of the contrast see his *Augustine of Hippo* [*: a biography*] (London 1967) pp 212–43.

[3] See W. H. C. Frend, 'The Roman Empire', referred to above, p 21 and also his 'The Roman Empire in eastern and Western historiography', *Proceedings of the Cambridge Philological Society*, CXCIV (Cambridge 1968) pp 19–32. A further dimension of the problem is the relation between Judaism and Christianity in North Africa. On this see M. Simon, 'Le judaisme berbère dans l'Afrique ancienne', *Revue d'histoire et de philosophie religieuses*, XXVI (Strasbourg 1946) pp 1–31, 105–45; reprinted in his *Recherches d'histoire Judéo-chrétienne* (Paris 1962) pp 30–87; and W. H. C. Frend, 'The Gnostic-Manichaean tradition in Roman North Africa', *JEH*, IV (1953) pp 13–26.

works and its powers. The community of the elect was gathered out of the world, would always be at odds with it and persecuted by it. Tertullian – an African! – had provided the classic statement of this mode of understanding the christian presence in the world. The sharp antithesis between light and darkness, holiness and sin, truth and error in terms of which he was apt to see the division between the christian Church and secular society around 200 survived into the fourth century. Donatist fervour in seeking martyrdom was far more than the zeal released by persecution, of a rigorist and fanatical religious minority; it was the expression of their inward posture in the world, their sense of identity as the 'holy' and 'unspotted' Church face to face with a sinful world and its agencies and with a pseudo-Church that had become identified with it, and had thereby ceased to be the true Church of the saints. A conception on such lines had not only dominated the larger part of pre-Constantinian Christianity, but, as Frend noted in these papers, remained alive in the fourth century among various groups on the edges of orthodoxy. It was no monopoly of Donatism.

The outstanding merit of J. P. Brisson's book *Autonomisme et Christianisme dans l'Afrique romaine* (Paris 1958) is that it approached the problem of Donatism, in the first place, in its own, that is in religious terms. The first part of the book (on the second part see above, p 25) is a thorough examination of Saint Cyprian's theology of the Church, of the ministry and of baptism, and this is followed by a discussion of the treatment given to these themes in Donatist theology. This impressive study,[1] though occasionally marred by some impetuous inference or some unguarded expression, has to my mind established the considerable extent of the continuity between the old, Cyprianic (and we need no reminder of Cyprian's debt to Tertullian) tradition of African theology and Donatism. In its understanding of what kind of community the Church was, of what was decisive for its identity in the world, Donatism was no new creation. It was the representative in the fourth century of an older African theological tradition with deep roots in its characteristic religious mentality.

Brisson came close to the fundamental insight that, from the point of view of African Christianity, it would be less misleading to speak of a 'catholic' than of a 'Donatist' schism. Augustine had to face the

[1] It has been subjected to severe criticism by A. Mandouze, 'Encore le Donatisme: problèmes de méthode posés par la thèse de J. P. Brisson', *L'antiquité classique*, XXIX (Paris 1960) pp 61–107. For a less ungenerous estimate see the sane and balanced survey by Y. M. J. Congar in his introduction to *Oeuvres de saint Augustin*, XXVIII: *Traités anti-Donatistes*, I (Paris 1963) pp 7–133, at p 31.

fact, when writing his *De baptismo contra Donatistas* in 400–1, that when it came to tracing a theological pedigree, the Donatists could claim the heritage of Cyprian at least as readily as the Catholics: the Donatists had Cyprian's theology: the Catholics, Augustine thought, his charity. It was only Augustine's own labour of theological re-interpretation that gave African Catholics some share in that heritage. Up to this time, the central thread of African ecclesiological tradition had been discernible in Donatist rather than in catholic theology. Looked at from the point of view of theological continuity, or of continuity of consciousness of what constituted being the Church in the world, Donatism was, quite simply, the continuation of the old African Christian tradition in the post-Constantinian world. It was the world that had changed, not African Christianity.

From the scanty evidence we have,[1] the last forty years of the third century appear to have been the great age of the christianisation of North Africa. The African Church, in other words, grew into its definitive shape under the sign of Cyprianic Christianity. It bore the impress of the Cyprianic theology of Church and baptism to which the African episcopate had committed itself, in the teeth of Roman opposition, on the eve of the Valerianic persecution. Cyprian himself perished in that persecution, and his martyrdom undoubtedly helped to establish his legacy as part of the African Church's sacred endowment. It was a 'Cyprianic Church' that entered the 'great persecution' of Diocletian in 303, and the same Cyprianic Church that emerged when it ended, in 305 in Africa. Now, however, it was rent by conflicting passions released by the aftermath of persecution. Failure of nerve under the stress of persecution inevitably aroused suspicion, rancour and bitter hostilities. A contested election to the see of Carthage on the death of Mensurius in 311 or 312 provided an outlet for these passions.

What transformed this contested election into the great African schism was the dramatic change in the situation from 312: the emperor was now Constantine, and it was to him that appeals went from the African Church to settle the dispute. It was the emperor, and the 'Church across the seas' who now defined the terms of orthodoxy. The party of Caecilian in the Carthaginian schism was prepared to fall into line – it is not possible to determine precisely when – with Italian and Gallic baptismal practice, and along with the practice, to adopt

---

[1] On the literary evidence, see Monceaux, *Histoire littéraire* (referred to above, p 24) III, pp 3–20; on the archaeological and epigraphic evidence see Frend, *The Donatist Church*, pp 76–93.

an ecclesiology very different from the Cyprianic. The party of Majorinus, faithful to the Cyprianic theology of the African Church and not prepared to surrender the traditional practice of rebaptism, found itself labelled the 'heresy of Donatus'. Almost overnight, the traditional orthodoxy of the African Church had become heresy. The Constantinian settlement imposed on Africa the orthodoxy of the 'transmarine churches'. Seen from Africa, however, Catholicism was the new importation, and the emperor and his government the agents of a schism in upholding the claims of a *figmentum*: a human work masquerading as the Church. The Catholic Church in Africa owed its sense of identity to its being in communion with the churches over the seas, and its standing in African society to this association with a wider world and with a Church which, progressively in the course of the fourth century, came to conquer and to dominate that world. The two churches in Africa were divided precisely on the question of what it meant to be the Church in the world.

In terms such as these Peter Brown has interpreted the African schism as part of the 'Constantinian problem' in a paper which is so far the most fundamental contribution to the discussion: 'The issue at stake is not the protest of a particularist group, but the autonomy of a provincial tradition of Christianity in a universal and parasitic Empire. It was Constantine who provoked this struggle by allying the Empire with the universal Catholic Church.'[1] In a perspective such as this doubts of the kind raised by Jones about social or national protest movements disguised as heresies simply do not arise, for Donatism is no longer seen as a movement. If there was a religious 'movement' in late Roman Africa, it is that of Catholicism. The problem is not to trace the roots of Donatism, but rather to assess the factors which assisted the advance of Catholicism in the face of the indigenous Christianity of Africa. It is only in this perspective that one can fully appreciate the importance of Tengström's valuable contribution (see above, p 26) in spotlighting the part played by the force either of terrorism or of official pressure. Moreover, evidence of the kind adduced by Frend, concerning the relative distribution of Catholicism and Donatism (and on any reckoning much of it survives even Tengström's critique) falls into place. There is no cause for surprise in the fact that Catholicism should have established itself most firmly in the most Romanised areas, especially in the towns and the coastal plains most exposed to 'overseas' influence and pressure. There is no need to

[1] 'Religious dissent', p 97.

explain Donatism as the religious expression of pre-existing tensions in order to appreciate why it should have survived longest and in greatest concentration in areas less susceptible to such influences. Nor does the indisputably 'Latin', urban and cultured side of Donatist religion constitute any difficulty on such an interpretation. The notion – odd in any case – of a rural Christianity hostile to the towns becomes superfluous; and the existence among the Donatist clergy of a Latin oratorical and theological culture not a whit less 'Roman' than that of their catholic colleagues, or their pride in magnificent cathedrals in great urban centres as at Timgad, will not appear anomalous. In a recent paper[1] Peter Brown has dealt a severe blow to any interpretation of Donatism as a vehicle for a local culture: for in the Latin language which Donatists shared with Catholics both were being drawn into the orbit of the same late Roman, Latin, ecclesiastical culture. To seek an interpretation of Donatism as a distinctively rural form of Christianity is to do scant justice to the religious language, the theology, the architecture and generally, the Latin culture it shared with Catholicism, and to the importance of its great urban centres. Moreover, it may be that we are too easily bewitched by Rostovtzeff's opposition of town and country. P. A. Février has recently subjected the customary antithesis of town and countryside in fourth century North Africa to some radical questioning in a paper on Tengström's thesis.[2]

It seems as if Frend's thesis has been, not so much eroded, but left – more or less – intact, only turned upside down. One of its facets, however, has survived this revolution in almost its original position: the assessment of the opposition to Donatism, and notably of the figure of Augustine of Hippo. In making himself the champion, from 393 onwards, of the 'universal' Church, *toto orbe diffusa*, Augustine did, of course, align himself against the claim of the Donatists to being the true Church in Africa. From his cosmopolitan point of view they were frogs croaking parochially from their pond 'Only we are true Christians'. It is true that the catholic episcopate in Africa, and Augustine as one of its acknowledged leaders in the decisive period between 393 and 411 (the conference of Carthage), helped to cement the alliance between the Catholic Church and the empire, endorsed the recourse to force against the schismatics, and brought the African Church more into the orbit of the Roman see, and that precisely at a time when the

---

[1] 'Christianity and local culture.'

[2] 'Toujours le Donatisme. À quand l'Afrique?', *Rivista di storia e lettere religiose*, II (Florence 1966) pp 228–40.

Roman bishops, notably Innocent I, were seeking to transform the authority of their see in the Church and to establish it *vis à vis* the autonomy of provinces such as the African. Frend's estimate of Augustine is entirely within this perspective: Augustine as the great architect of the alliance between Church and state, as the champion of the religious establishment of the Theodosian empire. The same is true of the more hostile estimates by Brisson (see above, p 25) and H. J. Diesner in his book *Studien zur Gesellschaftslehre und sozialen Haltung Augustins* (Halle 1954), a book hagridden by the need to represent Augustine as a copy-book example of the defender of wealth, privilege and establishment in every detail. The portrait – though infinitely richer in its depth and more varied in its nuances – in Peter Brown's superb biography *Augustine of Hippo*, is not fundamentally different. Though Brown finds evidence that from *c* 413 Augustine became disillusioned about the alliance of Church and state, he nevertheless emerges as the theorist of the Constantinian revolution.

That there is much justice in this picture of Augustine cannot be denied; but it is open to doubt whether it does justice to him precisely as a thinker. Augustine's debt to the dissident Donatist theologian Tyconius has long been appreciated. More recently we have had further reminders of the large extent of common territory between Augustine and his Donatist opponents, and especially, of the extent to which both sides were drawing on a common fund of African theology. In the field of ecclesiology, in particular, J. Ratzinger in his *Volk und Haus Gottes in Augustins Lehre von der Kirche* (*Münchener theol. Studien*, II, 7, 1954) has presented Augustine's thought as sharing with Donatist ecclesiology a central position within the mainstream of the African theological tradition. We have allowed Augustine's political position, his social standing as a catholic bishop, and his polemical writings as an anti-Donatist controversialist to obscure some important affinities between his theology and Donatist thought. I have tried to explore his thought from this point of view in various papers and in my book *Saeculum: history and society in the theology of Saint Augustine* (Cambridge 1970), and concluded that when studied in its full range and its developing complexity, it is very far from being a theology of the Constantinian establishment.

The observation that in some important respects even Augustine belongs, with Donatism, to the central strand in the tradition of African Christianity from Tertullian and Cyprian prompts the question, not unlike Frend's (see above, p 24) question concerning an abiding

Christianity and dissent in Roman North Africa

Berber presence behind the religious history of North Africa – whether and how far the permanent tradition of African Christianity is one of 'dissent', to what an extent the conforming religion of the Catholics was only a 'façade' which came to efface, temporarily and not entirely, the more fundamental and more permanent features of the indigenous 'reality'? We are, of course, very much less fully informed about the life and thought of the African Church after the Vandal conquest (430) and under the Byzantine rule re-established a century later and destined to last until the Arab conquest in the eighth century than we are for the fourth and the early fifth centuries. During the Vandal period the relation of the two churches is very obscure[1] and the whole evidence for the survival of Donatism needs careful re-examination. That it survived beyond the conference of 411 and at any rate into the earlier part of the Vandal period need not be doubted; but it seems probable that the divisions between the two churches became blurred in the course of their common opposition to the Arian Church of the Vandal kingdom.

Under Byzantine rule, at any rate until the end of the sixth century, we hear no more about Donatism. But the dissenting tradition in African Christianity was not spent: it merely found another outlet. Justinian's edict 'On the three chapters', and the whole course of his *Kirchenpolitik* leading up to it, were seen by most of the African bishops as tyrannous imperial meddling with Chalcedonian orthodoxy. The African Church led the opposition. Its leaders, like bishop Facundus of Hermiane, drew on its old traditions of 'dissent': in the accents of Tertullian and of the Donatists they denounced the 'manufactured' churches, upheld by the imperial edicts not by the Gospel. With time-servers among the clergy more ready to bow to the imperial will such protests against the *Reichskirche* earned Facundus and like-minded churchmen the reputation of being Donatists in disguise.[2]

At the end of the century we again hear of a resurgence of Donatism in the voluminous surviving correspondence of pope Gregory the Great. This has universally, so far as I know, been taken as the main body of evidence for the survival of the schism at least down to

---

[1] See Monceaux, *Histoire littéraire*, IV, pp 97 et seq, to which on this point C. Courtois, (*Les Vandales*) adds little, and H. J. Diesner, *Das Vandalenreich: Aufstieg und Untergang* (Stuttgart 1966) less.

[2] On this episode, considered in relation to the 'dissenting' tradition in African Christianity, see my paper 'Reflections [on religious dissent in North Africa in the Byzantine period]', *SCH*, III (1966) pp 140–9, where references to other accounts are given.

Gregory's time in the 590s. I have examined this evidence[1] and suggested that its real bearing is quite different. A careful scrutiny shows that if there were still two ecclesiastical communities in Africa – a matter itself in doubt – they could live together in remarkable amity. If there was a division within the African Church, it was one projected by the pope on to the tension between a few unpopular churchmen on the one hand who were prepared to act as his agents and a majority who were not inclined to welcome such intervention. There is no evidence of anything that would have been recognised as the old schism in Africa, and it looks as if pope Gregory's 'Donatists' were merely Numidian bishops who valued their autonomy. The schism seems to be a creation of Italian minds seeking to understand the unfamiliar phenomenon of a tradition of dissent and autonomy in terms of a fiction which had once corresponded to the facts, but now bore little relation to them. The survival of Donatism much beyond 430, in the strict sense implying a schism between two identifiable ecclesiastical groupings, must be considered an open question, which only the spade may help us to answer. The whole of the literary evidence, and especially such hints as are provided by European material, for instance papal formularies,[2] is ripe for careful reassessment.

If there is no unambiguous evidence of the continued survival of Donatism, there is clear evidence of a continuous tradition of African autonomy, not only in relation to the see of Rome, but also in relation to the government. In the seventh century, under Heraclius and Constans II it was once again the African Church that took the lead in the fight against the monothelitism of the emperor and the attempt to impose it on the Church. From its beginnings until almost the moment of its submergence African Christianity is marked by the same quality of intransigence, a jealous sense of its independence and a peculiar identity over against the 'churches across the sea', against the empire and the secular world as a whole, and against the pseudo-Church which is their creature. The Church of Tertullian and Cyprian, the Church of Donatus and Parmenian, the Church of Facundus and of

---

[1] 'Donatism: [the last phase'], *SCH*, I (1964) pp 118–26, and 'The imperial administration and the Church in Byzantine Africa', *Church History*, xxxvi (Chicago 1967) pp 3–8.

[2] I single this out because references to *rebaptizati* in papal formularies as late as the seventh century are still held to provide formal proof of the existence of Donatists in Africa at that time. I think I have demonstrated that no such inference can be made from either papal formularies or papal letters based upon them; and that in any case the *rebaptizati* referred to are not Donatists, even at the time when the formula originated. See my 'Reflections', p 145 n 1, together with 'Donatism', p 124.

Maximus the Confessor are cast in the one mould. 'Dissent', we may say, was its instinctive posture in society. In this perspective the Donatist schism is one of the manifestations of this basic orientation, one relatively transitory, which lasted while African Christianity was brought into contact with the Church of the imperial 'establishment'; when the pressure exerted by the 'establishment' was relaxed, the ranks once again closed. It is the Catholic Church of Optatus and Augustine, between Constantine and the disappearance of Roman rule in 430, that constitutes the anomaly in African Christianity; and if I understand him aright, even Augustine is no outsider, in the fundamental cast of his mind, to the main stream of the African tradition. It may be that his theology played some part in assimilating the old tradition of African ecclesiology to the permanent capital of African, indeed of European Christianity. Facundus, at any rate, more than a hundred years after Augustine's death, certainly saw him as an illustrious link in the chain of the tradition in which he was taking his stand. The late Christian Courtois's remark on the Africans of the fifth century is true of African Christianity as a whole: 'in some obscure corner of men's minds there was something that said "no" to the Empire' (*Les Vandales*, p 148); and, we may add, 'no' not only to the Empire, but also to the Roman Church.

In *The Donatist Church* Frend opened a chapter in the study of African Christianity which is far from closed. For an understanding of its character and its place in North African society, scholarship of several kinds still has much to contribute. M. Février has remarked (in his article referred to above, p 31) on the need for inter-disciplinary studies in this field. It is amply clear that a satisfying and adequately grounded account of Christianity in Roman Africa will only come from a fruitful marriage of labours such as M. Février's own and M. Lancel's on the North African setting, and the work of historians of theology. The interest of the subject to students of North Africa, particularly of the Berber 'presence' throughout its history, needs no comment. It is also of central relevance to the historian of the late Roman world, to any attempt to discern in its collapse the interplay of opposing forces of cultural fragmentation and imperial centralisation. To the historian of religion it offers a rewarding quarry of material for the study of the ways in which a religious group may conceive its place in society. For the theologian, finally, it offers more than a tradition of thought about the Church, the ministry and the sacraments (well-trodden ground, this) which is still capable of furnishing some insight into the problems of twentieth-century theology. Beyond such insights, the history of African Christianity is one of the crucial cases for the current discussions of 'the problem of the confessions'.[1] The whole history of North African Christianity could lend substance to the view, increasingly widely canvassed in ecumenical discussions, that the problem of the christian denominations is as old as Christianity itself; that it was the Constantinian revolution that transformed the meaning and the limits of 'orthodoxy' and thus transformed the coexistence of different christian traditions in the 'great Church' into a problem of 'confessions'. The theologian is at this point, as so often, the beneficiary of historical scholarship.

For theologians, for historians of the late Roman world and for Africanists, the study of North African Christianity offers a field of crucial importance for very much wider concerns.

[1] This is the title of an essay, itself one of the most distinguished contributions to this discussion, by Gerhard Ebeling, reprinted in his *The Word of God and tradition* (Engl trans London 1968).

HERESY AND SCHISM AS SOCIAL AND NATIONAL MOVEMENTS

by W. H. C. FREND

(*Presidential address*)

ON 6 July 1439 the delegates of the Greek and Latin Churches signed at Florence a decree of union that ostensibly ended the schism that had lasted for nearly four centuries. The Greeks had accepted the Latin views of purgatory, the eucharist, the Holy Spirit and the Roman primacy. The emperor John VIII received communion at the hands of pope Eugenius IV, and in a solemn mass the Greek and Latin bishops clad in resplendent robes exchanged the kiss of peace. There was dancing in the streets of Florence, and in the western European capitals, especially in the London of Henry VI, processions, festivals and Te Deums. In the next few years, Armenians, Jacobites and Copts trod the same path to Italy and signed similar formulae of union. By the end of 1445 the unity of Christendom appeared to have been restored for the first time since the crisis of the christological controversy almost precisely a thousand years before.[1]

The agreement, however, had been worked out by the leaders of the two communions under the dire pressure of the threat of a Turkish conquest of eastern Europe. The Greeks had submitted ultimately because they realised that the survival of the independence of a few square miles round the city of Constantinople and outposts in Greece and Asia Minor depended almost exclusively on Latin military aid. When that failed at the battle of Varna in November 1444 the flimsy façade of unity was torn down. Popular suspicions re-asserted themselves. The 'Greco-Latins' as those who accepted union were called, were hounded from public life. 'We have sold our faith', some were said to have admitted.[2] In Sancta Sophia the pope was not commemorated at the eucharist as an orthodox prelate. In the few years remaining before the final crisis of the siege of Constantinople Greek opinion

---

[1] The best account of the negotiations between the Greeks and the Latins at Florence is that by [Joseph] Gill, [*The Council of Florence*] (Cambridge 1959). For the celebrations in London see p 299.

[2] Ducas, *Historia byzantina*, ed I. Bekker (Bonn 1834) xxxii, p 216. See Gill, p 349.

rallied behind those who declared that they 'would rather see the sultan's turban than the Pope's mitre' in Constantinople.[1] They had their way. All that remained from the years of effort towards the restoration of a united Christendom were a few illustrious converts to the Latin view of which cardinal Bessarion was the most famous. In this instance, instinctive popular pressure had triumphed over theological formulae worked out by the leaders of the two communions with great conscientiousness. The forces of culture and civilisation which had found expression in the schism between the churches centuries before were not to be denied. In this paper we look more closely at the nature of some of these forces and their influence in fomenting and perpetuating divisions in the early centuries of the Church.

Divisions have contributed much to the history of the Church. One does not have to be an expert in New Testament criticism to realise that in the generation after the Crucifixion there were serious divisions between Jesus's adherents. Paul and James represented differing outlooks towards the status of Gentiles within the Church: at Antioch there was a breach between Peter and Paul on the same issue (Gal., 2:11), and in Corinth we hear of baptisms in the name of Apollos, Cephas and Christ and resulting divisions within the community (1 Cor., 1:12). Associated within these divergencies was the creation of differing types of church organisation. In Jerusalem the position of James delivering formal judgement at the apostolic council and directing the mission of the Church resembled that of the high priest to whom later generations compared him. His was the monarchical tradition of episcopacy with a focus of worship provided by the existence of the Temple.[2] Beyond the immediate influence of Jerusalem we find, however, prophets and teachers as the bearers of ministerial office, and the Pauline mission churches were ruled by individuals whom Paul addressed sometimes as 'presbyters' and sometimes as 'bishops'. What would have happened if James had had successors of comparable ability to himself or if Jerusalem had not fallen in 70, thus bringing the Palestinian Church to a virtual close, cannot be guessed at. It is evident, however, that even then the christian community was tending to divide along cultural lines, the Churches with the background of the Jewish dispersion adopting different forms of organisation with a less positive emphasis towards the Temple, its

[1] Ibid xxxvii, p 264, A statement attributed to Gennadius.
[2] On the cultural and geographical factors behind the various types of church government in the time of the apostles and their successors see A. A. T. Ehrhardt, *The Apostolic Succession* (London 1953) ch III.

cult and its hierarchical tradition from those favoured by the Jerusalem Christians. The difficulty of adapting a message of repentance and salvation preached to an Aramaic-speaking Palestinian countryside to the provincials of the remainder of the Greco-Roman world whose personal religion was often that of the mystery-cult was becoming evident even at this early stage.

So much may be judged from the events recorded in Acts and by St Paul in his letters, but one would be surprised if either Paul or his opponents had recognised these as among the underlying reasons for their quarrels. The tendencies which each represented only become plain gradually in the light of later events. This is a truism, but it is worth restating, since silence on the part of the participants concerning their non-theological motives has encouraged scholars sometimes to suppose that these did not exist. We must not ask too much of our evidence. We should be surprised to find a Montanist or a Donatist leader describing his opposition to the religion of the catholic clergy in terms of nineteenth-century nationalism. Yet when confronted by the emphasis on prophecy and martyrdom, and on the literal interpretation of the New Testament, especially its apocalyptic passages that characterised both these movements, the historian may be pardoned if he asks himself whether a pattern emerges that links the various rural Christianities in the early Church with each other; and distinguishes their outlook from that of the more conventional established communities in the cities.

This is as far as anyone would like to go, and for the purposes of demonstration I intend to move once again down the beaten trackways of Donatism and Monophysitism. Despite all that has been written in the last twenty years,[1] these seem to provide the best starting points for enquiring into the importance of the non-theological aspects of divisions in the Church in the patristic era in west and east respectively.

It must be sufficiently obvious that the storm that blew up in 311–12 over the election of the archdeacon, Caecilian, as bishop of Carthage, had a long history behind it. From the vantage points of time and distance one can see how the seeds of the controversy are to be found in developments that were present almost from the moment of the foundation of the Church in North Africa more than a century before. The christian mission there, whatever its source, had been confronted

---

[1] For a bibliography and discussion see my *The Donatist Church* (2nd ed, Oxford 1971) pp v–vi.

with problems different from those encountered in the Greek-speaking world. Roman Africa was ostensibly Latin, but beneath the outward form of latinisation, the population retained much of the religious and cultural heritage of Carthage. In addition, the Jews whose communities extended all the way from Carthage to Volubilis in Morocco [1] and formed a strong element in the background of the development of Christianity there, as elsewhere in the Mediterranean, seem to have been of a strict and legalistic type.[2] They differed considerably in outlook from the Jewish philosophers of Alexandria. For some years, too, the Christians were regarded by the Carthaginian Jews as 'Nazarenes', that is, schismatics from their own body.[3]

Theirs was an exclusive outlook and a harsh one also. Tertullian tells us as a matter of course how the Carthaginian Christians readily regarded themselves as a sect or school 'bound together by common religious purpose and unity of discipline',[4] whose sense of righteousness involved defiance against every manifestation of the existing order and a readiness to die for their convictions. The antitheses Athens versus Jerusalem, the Bible versus philosophy, Christ versus Belial, came readily to them.[5] Intense in their expectations of the approaching end of the world they believed in a judgement in which they would be revenged and would see their idolatrous foes committed to everlasting flames.[6] Believing in the continuous work of the Spirit among baptised Christians, their object was to keep the Church free from every form of defilement, particularly from contact with the pagan world, and they were merciless towards those of their number who appeared to make the slightest concession to the idolater. Their ideas, indeed, had much in common with those of Palestinian Jews in the Maccabaean period. There was the same sense of election, entailing the same rigorous attitude towards the outside world, the same emphasis on an uncompromising adherence to the prescriptions of their covenant and the same hope for the reversal of roles in one final day of reckoning. Indeed, consciousness of the legacy of the Maccabees was to be a factor in the immediate outbreak of the Donatist

---

[1] For Volubilis see P. Berger, *Bulletin Archéologique du Comité des Travaux Historiques* (Paris 1892) p 64, and R. Thouvenot, *Révue des Etudes Africaines* (Paris 1969) pp 352–9.

[2] See the comments of P. Monceaux in *Histoire littéraire de l'Afrique du Nord* (Paris 1901) ch I.

[3] Tertullian, *Adversus Marcionem*, III, 8.

[4] Tertullian, *Apologia*, XXXIX, 1 and *De Spectaculis*. II.

[5] For instance Tertullian, *De Praescriptione*, VII and *De Idololatria*, XIX.

[6] Tertullian, *De Spectaculis*, XXX.

crisis, and among the leaders of the Donatist Church during the fourth and early fifth centuries.[1]

The relatively full information about the African Church provided by Cyprian's correspondence half a century later and other writings of this time shows the same factors at work. Though the place of the confessor and prophet as the direct agents of the Spirit and guiding influences in the Church had now been taken by the bishop, the same ideals of apostolic purity and freedom from contagion with the secular world still predominated. 'No salvation outside the Church' rendered definition of the Church and its authority the most important doctrinal issues among the African Christians. The distinction between schism and misbelief tended to become blurred in a general condemnation of anything deemed to be 'outside the Church'. Breach of unity was regarded as the worst of sins, calling down on the heads of the culprits the penalty of Abiram, Dathan and Korah.[2] At the same time, the Church was the 'closed garden' and 'lily among thorns', its purity to be safeguarded at all costs. Even though backsliders among the laity might be tolerated as they had been in Israel there was no place for a cleric who had committed one of the traditional Jewish deadly sins, apostasy (including idolatry), bloodshed and adultery.[3] Not only that, but sacraments offered by such could turn to the detriment of those who partook of them. A congregation had the right and duty to separate itself from a cleric who had lapsed into deadly sin.[4] Final sanction of divine authority for these attitudes was seen in the death of Cyprian as a martyr on 14 September 258.

During Cyprian's episcopate African Christianity was still mainly an urban religion. Its adherents were usually small artisans some of whom, like Soliassus the mule-keeper and Paula a maker of mats, could win reputations for themselves by their wholehearted support of Cyprian's rivals.[5] The leadership, however, lay with a few strong-willed individuals who, like Cyprian himself, had accepted conversion as a radical alternative to the classical heritage and pagan society in which they had been reared. The scale of these conversions should not, however, be overestimated, for a generation later Lactantius a fellow

[1] As shown by the Numidian leader Secundus of Tigisis claiming how in contrast to the primate of Africa, Mensurius of Carthage, his stand during the persecution might be compared with that of Eleazer, the martyr priest in the saga of the Maccabees (2 *Macc.* 6:21). Augustine, *Brev[iculus] Coll[ationis cum Donatistis]*, III, 13, 25.

[2] Cyprian, *Epistolae*, ed W. Hartel, 3 vols, *CSEL*, III (1868–71), LXVII, 3, LXIX, 8.

[3] *Ibid ep* LXIX; *De Unitate Ecclesiae*, VI.

[4] Cyprian, *ep* LXVII, 3–6 (the case of the Spanish bishops).

[5] *Ibid ep* XLII, 1.

41

African tells us that he had few followers among the lettered classes and many thought him a crank.[1] Even in the beleaguered garrison that was the African Christian Church in the time of Decius and Valerian one can detect the emergence of incipient rifts along social lines. In time of crisis, the mass of the poorer Christians though open-handed when it came to rendering favours to relatives who had sacrificed to the gods tended to accept a rigorous doctrine of the Church with its hopes of recompense hereafter, whereas the wealthier members were often prepared to insure themselves with the authorities at least to the extent of accepting certificates of sacrifice.[2] Their breach with Roman civilisation was not total.

Fifty years later, the picture was essentially the same, though the relative strength and distribution of the different interests within the Church had modified considerably. Many of the urban communities were now, so far as the evidence goes, firmly in the hands of the moderates. These were people who accepted the state, and, unless told to do otherwise, the authorities accepted them. In return, some elements in Cyprianic rigorism including the emphasis placed on the requirement for baptism to be performed by a priest in every way in a state of grace was falling into desuetude.[3] In contrast to this, the artisan element had been reinforced powerfully by a fairly rapid spread of Christianity in the countryside and in particular in Numidia. There had also developed a growing sense of self-identification among the Numidian Christians, whose primate in the years between 260 and 300 acquired the right of consecrating the bishop of Carthage.

These new Christians brought to the Church much of the idealistic sectarianism that had characterised the African Church a century before. Denial of duties to the state, including military service, sense of brotherhood, acceptance of martyrdom, including voluntary martyrdom, a readiness to model conduct on the example of the Maccabees, and a fanaticism that could vent itself on more moderate attitudes were all apparent in Numidia and in the rural areas generally before the outbreak of the schism in 312.[4] So, at the very moment when Christianity among the citizens and wealthier people was becoming more conformist and more part of the general provincial scene, the masses

---

[1] Lactantius, *Divinae Institutiones*, ed S. Brandt, *CSEL*, XIX (1890) V, I, 24.

[2] Thus Cyprian's comment in *De Lapsis* XI concerning wealthy *libellatici* 'Decepit multos patrimonii sui amor caecas', ed W. Hartel, *CSEL*, III, I, p 244.

[3] This requirement was dropped with the agreement of the Caecilianists at the council of Arles in 314 (canon 9).

[4] See *The Donatist Church*, ch I and pp 141–4.

showed no tendencies towards abandoning the rigorist traditions of the African Church. The mention, too, of avoidance of the consequences of fiscal debt as one of the motives for voluntary martyrdom during the great persecution provides just a hint that some of the anti-pagan fanaticism of the countryside was shared by the poorer element among the Christians in Carthage.[1] Perhaps as Lactantius suggests, the economic reforms of the Tetrarchy, particularly the attempt to resuscitate the African cities after a generation of decay, and the multiplication of the bureaucracy following the provincial reforms had caused hardship and anger.[2] This found its outlet in violent protest against the edicts of persecution in 303 and 304.

Donatism was the heir to all this latent discontent. If one looks carefully at the events which led up to the schism one finds both in Numidia and in Carthage the Donatists being swept into office by popular acclaim regardless of their personal worthiness. At Cirta in 305 for instance, the capital of Numidia, the mob incarcerated the christian citizens in the cemetery of the martyrs, while a tumultuary election of the sub-deacon Silvanus as bishop was carried through by what was described as a crowd of peasants, quarry workers and women of the town.[3] Though their protest was supposed to be against the clergy, like the deceased bishop Paul who had handed over the scriptures to the authorities and thus become a *traditor*, the man they chose in his place had been almost equally guilty; he had handed over the church plate.[4] At Carthage in 312, the archdeacon Caecilian had the support of the citizens when he was elected as bishop but was unpopular with the people, and they accepted the leadership of the Numidians who saw their own interests threatened by Caecilian's election.[5] In addition to this, the Donatists represented the rigorist tradition of African theology true in every particular to the outlook and doctrine of the Church in the time of Cyprian. They were harsh towards backsliders, especially the *traditores* who were regarded as guilty of committing the word of God to the flames. They proclaimed the purity of the Church purged through the suffering of its martyrs. They

---

[1] Augustine, *Brev Coll*, iii, 13, 25 'et fisci debitores, qui occasione persecutionis vel carere vellent onerosa multis debita vita...vel certe acquirere pecuniam'.

[2] Lactantius, *De Mortibus Persecutorum*, ed J. Moreau, 2 vols, S[ources] Ch[rétiens] xxxix (Paris 1954) vii, xxiii.

[3] *Gesta apud Zenophilum*, ed C. Ziwsa, CSEL, xxvi (1893) p 196, 'Campenses et harenarii fecerunt illum [Silvanum] episcopum...Prostibulae illic fuerunt'.

[4] *Ibid* pp 188–9.

[5] Optatus, [*De Schismate Donatistorum*], ed C. Ziwsa, CSEL, xxvi (1893) i, 18.

had a vivid concept of divine wrath and judgement, and they rejected with horror the possibility of an alliance with the Constantinian state. The emperor to be sure, might be 'of God', and worthy to act as umpire in a dispute with the Catholics, but his sphere of action was a limited one. His duty was to secure earthly peace and liberty for the Church, but not otherwise to intervene in its affairs, let alone coerce its members. In all this the Donatists were by no means isolated from the main stream of western thought as the writings of Victor of Pettau or the schism of the Luciferians later in the century shows,[1] but in Africa the strength of Christianity as the religion of town and countryside alike had allowed parties to form representing irreconcilable interests reinforced by provincial divisions. Under the pressure of the great persecution schism was the inevitable result.

The Donatist outlook remained consistent throughout the whole period of the schism. Though in social terms they were strongest among the populace of Carthage and in rural Numidia the background to their movement was always religious.[2] They claimed strict adherence to the teaching of Cyprian regarding the nature of the Church and the inviolability of its sacraments, the purity of its membership, and its complete separation from the world. A Donatist on being baptised would be expected to renounce all connection with the secular world and cleave to the Bible and its teaching only.[3] 'The servants of God are those who are hated by the world', so ran the title of a Donatist work which at the end of the fifth century Gennadius, the presbyter of Marseilles, was to pronounce as irreproachable in its orthodoxy.[4] This combat was always against the Devil and his allies; the goal of christian life was the imitation of Christ through penance and suffering leading to the martyr's death.

These objectives had, however, the effect of widening the scope of the Donatist protest. It was not merely that the value to the Church of the Constantinian revolution was denied. The Donatist saw the rulers of the present age as permanently on the side of the Devil against the servants of God. In a catena of denunciation which recalls 4 Maccabees in its vituperative power, Petilian, bishop of Constantine (Cirta)

---

[1] On this theme, see my note on 'The Roman Empire in the Eyes of the Western Schismatics', *Miscellanea Historiae Ecclesiasticae*, II (Louvain 1961) pp 5–22.

[2] This aspect is brilliantly treated by [J. P.] Brisson, [*Autonomisme et Christianisme dans l'Afrique romaine de Septime Sévère à l'invasion vandale*] (Paris 1958) ch I.

[3] As made clear in the case of bishop Marculus, *Passio Marculi*, PL 8 (1844) I, col 760.

[4] Gennadius, *De Scriptoribus Ecclesiasticis*, PL 59 (1862) IV, col 1059, concerning Vitellius Afer, 'Si tacuisset de nostro velut persecutorum nomine egregiam doctrinam ediderat'.

writing *c* 400, recalled to his clergy how from creation to his own day, from the time of Abel's murder onwards, the righteous had received nothing but oppression from the world's rulers. 'But what have you to do with the kings of this world, in whom Christianity has never found anything save envy towards her? And to teach you shortly the truth of what I say: a king persecuted the brethren of the Maccabees. A king also condemned the three children to the sanctifying flames, being ignorant what he did, seeing that he himself was fighting against God. A king sought the life of the infant Saviour. A king exposed Daniel, as he thought, to be eaten by wild beasts. And the Lord Christ Himself was slain by a king's most wicked judge.'[1] Similarly, during the period of catholic ascendancy after the exile of Donatus in 347, the emperor Constans, good Nicene Christian though he was, found himself denounced as 'Anti-Christ' and his government as that of the Devil by Donatist pamphleteers in Carthage.[2]

These attitudes can be traced back to the period of the Maccabees when they reflected the religious attitudes of Jews striving for religious liberty against the Seleucids. The same outlook is reproduced almost exactly among the African Christians of the third century and continued by the Donatists. Indeed it is far from true to claim as some ancient historians have been tempted to do that 'it was only when the verdict of Constantine went against them that the Donatists evolved the doctrine that the Church should be independent of the state'.[3] Theirs was an attitude that belonged to the western tradition from its beginning, and behind that it looked back to some of the attitudes of Palestinian Judaism. The Donatist, like Tertullian two centuries before, was against 'the world'. His identification of the world with secular rule was not confined to the Roman empire and not to any individual emperor. After the empire's disappearance and replacement by the Vandals, Gaiseric was to be denounced with equal force by Donatist writers.[4] Nor does Donatist support for the African rebel leaders, Firmus and Gildo, necessarily suggest that they aimed at political separation from the Roman empire. The ultimate aim of both

---

[1] Augustine, *Contra Litteras Petiliani*, II, 92, 202.
[2] Especially in the *Passio Marculi* and *Passio Maximiani et Isaaci*, PL 8 (1844), cols 760–72.
[3] Thus A. H. M. Jones, 'Were ancient heresies national or social movements in disguise?', *JTS*, new series X, 2 (1959) pp 280–98 at p 282. Compare G. E. M. de Ste Croix, 'Christianity's encounter with the Roman government', *Crucible of Christianity* (London 1969) p 351.
[4] *Liber Genealogus*, ed T. Mommsen, *MGH, AA*, IX (Berlin 1892) p 195.

rebels is uncertain, but it is doubtful whether either saw themselves as independent rulers. Perhaps a 'kingdom of Africa' on the lines of Matsumas's 'kingdom of Moors and Romans' in the next century was the limit of their horizons.[1] To that extent, however, the Donatists may have been prepared to accept a change of political masters. Augustine's suggestion, albeit from the catholic standpoint, that small kingdoms living in harmony with each other were preferable to great empires,[2] may reflect a fragment of floating political tradition common to both parties in Africa at the end of the fourth century.

Mere change of secular masters was, however, not high on the Donatist list of priorities. Firmus's revolt in 372, however, seems to have been precipitated as a protest against overtaxation, in particular the tax which struck the rural population hardest, the *annona*.[3] It is on this level that the point of junction between the religious and non-religious factors in the Donatist schism may be found. A 'realised apocalyptic' designed to end all oppression provided a focus for the dual element in Donatist teaching. The idea of the end of the existing age presaging judgement associated with a massive reversal of fortunes struck the imagination of the people. It found a particularly ready acceptance in rural Numidia and Mauretania where extortionate taxation and perhaps over-population led to chronic indebtedness, and as a result, produced a restless rural proletariat fanatically christian, and ready to listen to preachers who promised the overthrow of the landowners and their bailiffs in the name of God. There is no evidence to show why the circumcellion movement should have come to notice in 340, except that 'extortionate exactions' seem to have been levied from imperial estates in Africa for a generation past, but in the three quarters of a century of its recorded existence it impressed its characteristics on contemporaries whether violently hostile or mildly admonishing, like Tyconius, in precisely the same way. Its leaders proclaimed themselves 'leaders of the saints' and combined the religious drive of men and women on perpetual pilgrimage among the shrines of the local martyrs with a revolutionary zeal aimed ultimately at winning the crown of martyrdom for themselves.[4]

The programme of social reform is unmistakable. Optatus of Milevis writing *c* 365 states that thanks to Fasir and Axeido, the

---

[1] See J. Carcofino, 'Un empereur maure inconnu', *Révue des Etudes anciennes*, XLVI (Paris 1944) pp 94–120. [2] *De Civitate Dei*, IV, 3.
[3] Zosimus, *Historia Nova* ed L. Mendelssohn (Leipzig 1887) IV, 16.
[4] Optatus, III, 4. See *The Donatist Church*, pp 172–6; Brisson, chapter on 'L'Impatience populaire'; H. J. Diesner, *Kirche und Staat in spätromischen Reich* (Berlin 1963) pp 110 ff.

circumcellion leaders, 'no one could feel secure in his estates' and that the debtor's bond lost its force. No creditor possessed the liberty of exacting payment of a debt.[1] More than merely defending the unfortunate, the Circumcellions reversed earthly fortunes whenever chance arose. Rich men driving comfortable vehicles would be pitched out of them and made to run behind their carriages which were now occupied by their slaves.[2] This was not an isolated account. Seventy years later Augustine reports with lurid detail similar events.[3] His rival bishop of Hippo found himself in the position of leader of one of these bands operating against villas in the neighbourhood of the town.[4] There is the same catalogue of outrages, destruction of creditors' bonds, enforcement of slave labour on the possessing classes, compulsory freeing of slaves and threat of reprisal in case of disobedience. There is no reason to believe either, that the Circumcellions were other than religious fanatics. Augustine has much to say about their war cry 'Deo Laudes', their false pilgrimages and suicides under the pretext of seeking martyrdom, but makes no reference to any activities as day labourers using their clubs to knock down the olives ready for harvest.[5] It might be added too, that such evidence as exists, suggests that in the towns also the Donatists tended to represent the outlook of the serving and working rather than the privileged community.[6]

So far as Donatism is concerned the links between religious belief and popular discontent seem to be established. The clue however lies in the eschatology of the movement. Over all loomed the spectre of divine judgement. The battle against the Devil was unending. From resistance against Antichrist reflected in the persecuting authorities of the secular world in the third century,[7] the Christian moved towards overthrowing the Devil in the form of oppressive magistrates and extortionate landowners after the conversion of Constantine. In both the goal was victory not over 'flesh and blood' but over spiritual powers of wickedness, and if the weapon was usually the circumcellion's club, the ideal was self-immolation in the glory of martyrdom and assurance of vengeance at the Last Day.[8]

[1] Optatus, III, 4.
[2] *Ibid.* [3] Augustine, *Epistolae*, CLXXXV, 4, 15 (written in 417). [4] *Ibid* CVIII, 5, 14.
[5] As E. Tengström, *Donatisten und Katholiken* (Göteberg 1964) pp 51–2.
[6] Augustine, *Contra Litteras Petiliani*, II, 83, 184 (Donatist *inquilini* in Hippo).
[7] For the emperor Decius being regarded as the 'forerunner of Antichrist' in the popular view among African Christians see Cyprian, *Ep* LV, 9. Decius was 'ipsum anguem maiorem metatorem antichristi'.
[8] As defined by Petilian of Constantine, cited by Augustine, *Contra Litteras Petiliani*, II, 89, 196.

The equation of social revolutionary zeal coupled with eschatological hopes and the rejection of the established forms and organisation of religion was not a phenomenon confined to fourth-century North Africa. If one looks back to the past, one also finds it a recurring theme of late Jewish history; it is present as one of the themes in the second part of the Book of Daniel; in the great revolt against Rome in 66 we find the Zealots as hostile to the men of wealth among the Jews and the priestly caste, as they were bitter enemies of Rome.[1] Debtors' bonds were destroyed with their owners in best circumcellion style. Then as one looks ahead into the history of popular religious movements in medieval and reformation Europe the same phenomena are discernible. We have only to think of the Peasants' Revolt of 1381 and the jingle 'When Adam delved and Eve span, Who was then a gentleman', used as a text by John Ball, monk of St Albans, at the period of the rising, to see how biblical literalism could form a focus for political and social discontent. A generation later, in the 1420s, the Czech Adamites preached the approaching judgement and the duty of imitating Adam and Eve and wearing no clothes, but also not to pay any interest to anyone and to defy the authorities, including that of the Czech patriot Ziska.[2]

Ziska's Taborites were Millenarists, believing that all lords, nobles and knights would be cut down and exterminated in the forests like outlaws and the millennium established.[3] Their armed bands included a heterogeneous company of artisans, indentured servants, beggars and prostitutes, which could easily have been exchanged for the mobs that produced and sustained the Donatist leadership in fourth-century North Africa. In another part of central Europe, Thuringia, apocalyptic movements reflected peasant discontent for a century before the outbreak of the Peasants' Revolt in 1525. The militant Anabaptist, Thomas Müntzer (1485–1525) believed the uprising would herald the descent of New Jerusalem, and he believed too, like the circumcellion leaders, in an egalitarianism based on the Gospel, in which princes and lords would lose their traditional roles. In struggles against baronial and ecclesiastical oppression in Europe extending over a thousand years

---

1 Josephus, *Wars*, IV, 3.2; IV, 6, 1. Zealots 'thirsting after the blood of valiant men and men of good families'. For zealot attitudes see M. Hengel, *Die Zeloten* (Leiden/Köln 1961) pp 266 ff.

2 See T. Büttner and E. Werner, *Circumcellionen und Adamiten zwei Formen mittelalter-licher Haeresie* (Berlin 1959) pp 79–83

3 See N. Cohn, *The Pursuit of the Millennium* (2nd ed, London 1970) pp 238 ff; G. Rupp, *Patterns of Reformation* (London 1969) pp 298–302.

we can point to the same features activating popular revolt. Prophecy and hope of martyrdom in expectation of future vindication motivated by the Book of Daniel and Revelation provided much of the inspiration for the peasant armies. In these movements the African Donatists paved the way for western Europe as a whole.

One turns now to the more complicated situation presented by the monophysite movement in the East. At first sight the Monophysites resembled the Donatists. They were schismatics, they drew their support from the masses of the people in Egypt and Syria, and even more than the Donatists their churches developed along national or territorial lines. By 600 they were dominant in a great band of territory extending from the Black Sea to the sources of the Nile embracing Armenia, much of Syria, many of the Arab tribes, Egypt, Nubia and Ethiopia. Theirs was a third religious force, territorially more extensive than Byzantine and Latin Christianity combined. The end product of an independent hierarchy based on national or territorial allegiances has tempted historians to see Monophysitism at its outset as an expression of popular will directed against the Byzantine emperor and the Chalcedonian faith that he represented. It is for the east, however, that the challenge contained in the article by my late mentor and friend A. H. M. Jones, 'Were the ancient heresies national and social movements in disguise?', has most validity.[1] At the same time, it has yet to be stated how and why the story of Monophysitism differs from that of the Donatists.

The first mistake that historians usually make is to place the emergence of a schismatic monophysite Church immediately after the council of Chalcedon in 451. It is then asserted that this Church reflected the hatred of the Coptic and Syrian peasantry for their Byzantine overlords, and that this hostility made what to all intents and purposes was simply a difference over words impossible to settle.[2] A study of the available evidence suggests that this interpretation of events, even if it were related to the period immediately before the Arab invasions in the 630s is an over-simplification, and that the monophysite movement cannot be interpreted by the same categories that are valid for Donatism and its successors in the west.

The acceptance in the Chalcedonian definition of the Two-Nature formula (Christ was to be acknowledged 'in two natures inseparably

---

[1] *JTS*, new series x, 2 (1959) pp 280–98.
[2] For the 'nationalist' thesis as applied to Monophysitism see E. L. Woodward, *Christianity and Nationalism in the Later Roman Empire* (London 1916) ch II.

united') indeed caused a spontaneous outbreak of popular anger unparalleled in the history of the east Roman provinces.[1] Most Christians had come to accept the arguments of Cyril of Alexandria (died 444) and his turbulent successor Dioscorus (died 454) that in order to safeguard the full deity of Christ and his saving work for humanity, He must be confessed as being formed 'out of the two natures of God and Man, one incarnate nature', that of the Divine Logos assuming flesh from the Virgin. Chalcedon was regarded as a betrayal and violent hostility awaited many of the bishops who signed the definition on their return to their sees. In Egypt the presbyter Proterius who accepted consecration as patriarch in Dioscorus's stead was shunned and on Maundy Thursday 457 lynched by the Alexandrian mob, while in Palestine the powerful and ambitious Juvenal of Jerusalem had to flee for his life.[2] Despite the depth of hostility, however, no formal schism developed. No 'altar was set up against altar' in western style. Even in Egypt, the constant objective of the anti-Chalcedonian line of patriarchs was to get the emperor to renounce the Two-Nature christology and Chalcedon and make Cyril's theology in its entirety the theology of the empire as a whole. On the first point they had some success, for the letter which the emperor Zeno sent to the Egyptian clergy, monks and laity in July 482, known to history as the *Henotikon*, expressly declared that Christ must be acknowledged as 'one and not two', and that any other opinion expressed whether at Chalcedon or elsewhere was anathema.[3] On the other hand, no emperor could renounce Chalcedon as a whole, because the title deeds of the see of Constantinople accepting its ecclesiastical preeminence next to that of Old Rome rested on the 28th canon of the council. Leo's *Tome* might be expendable but not the council itself.

Hence the stalemate that developed between Alexandria and the other important sees of the east. For many years, however, there was no thought in Alexandria of establishing a separate Church in Egypt whose orthodoxy alone could be guaranteed, and even the idea that at any time during the fifth century the Monophysites represented the

[1] See, for instance, the catalogue of incidents recorded in John Rufus, *Plerophoria*, PO 8, 1 (1911) and in Michael the Syrian, [*Chronicle*], ed J. B. Chabot (Paris 1901) VIII, 11–12.

[2] Zacharius Rhetor, *HE*, ed E. W. Brooks, *CSCO*, Series III, *Syriaci Scriptores*, V–VI (1919–24) bk III, 3, p 107.

[3] For the text see E. Schwartz, 'Eine antichalkedonische Sammlung aus der Zeit Kaiser Zenos', *Abhandlung en der bayerischen Akademie der Wissenschaften*, Philologische-Historische Klasse, VI (Munich 1927) p 52. For an English translation and notes see R. M. Coleman Norton, *Roman Empire and Church* (London 1966) pp 924–33.

Copts while the Chalcedonians represented the Greeks in Egypt is fallacious. As far back as 346 when Athanasius had been welcomed home from exile by the Greek-speaking magistrates of Alexandria who went out 100 miles from the city to meet him (ten miles was a more normal mark of respect for a visiting dignitary) and joined hands with the Coptic monks from the deserts, the patriarch of Alexandria had been the leader of the Egyptian people as a whole. Athanasius and Donatus represented analogous situations in Egypt and North Africa. At the heart of the monophysite position as with the Donatist, lay loyalty to a theological tradition personified in a single great leader, Cyril on the one hand, Cyprian on the other.

Cyril had united Egypt around his doctrine and his personality. His successor Dioscorus, however, had endangered this unity through his abominable conduct against, among others, Cyril's relatives.[1] The Chalcedonian party that formed in Egypt after 451, while including imperial officials also numbered a considerable force of Pachomian monks and laity who considered that Dioscorus had deserved the condemnation passed on him at Chalcedon. Similarly, Alexandrians of all classes and monks accepted his monophysite successor, Timothy the Cat. Contemporary sources indicate that the rift between the parties divided families and not racial communities.[2] In 455 the emperor Marcian wrote to the prefect of Egypt, Palladius, to the effect that both Alexandria and the rest of Egypt was a prey to Apollinarian heresy.[3] This pattern was to persist until the sixth century at least. Indeed, only in the time of Heraclius do we find Coptic monks equating the fact of their being Egyptian with their opposition to the emperor's Chalcedonian creed.[4] Even in the Arab invasion one looks in vain for evidence of a Coptic rising against Byzantine landlords.

Another point. We have seen how separation of church from state was a cardinal point in Donatist and indeed all western schismatic thinking. Among the Monophysites, however, the opposite was true. For many, the One Nature of Christ implied also the unity of the Roman empire under one ruler who was God's vice-regent on earth. In a letter to the emperor Justin I, James of Saroug, one of the monophysite leaders, asked why the emperor wore a cross on his crown if he

---

[1] Outlined in the letter of the presbyter Athanasius to the council of Chalcedon, Mansi VI, col 1029.

[2] *Plerophoria*, LXI, no greetings exchanged in the streets between the families of rival allegiances.

[3] Text in *ACO*, II, ii, 2, pp 24–6.

[4] *History of the Patriarchs*, ed B. Evetts, PO I (1907) I, ch XIV, p 498.

did not believe in the unity of Christ and the unity of the empire.[1] Among the torrent of abuse which the Monophysites heaped upon the emperor Marcian for his furtherance of Chalcedon was that he had divided the empire just as the definition accepted by the council divided Christ and divided the Church.[2] Far from uttering defiance at the emperor and his representatives as Donatus of Carthage had done, the monophysite leaders lost no opportunity of asserting their loyalty to the emperor, while their chroniclers such as John of Ephesus seem to go out of the way to record the 'God-loving' character of the rulers. The Egyptian monks too, arrogant and rumbustuous though their spokesmen were, reserved any miraculous powers of destruction for the benefit of pagan landowners. They felt a sense of identity against the stranger, but until the seventh century this did not imply a national hostility towards the creed of the capital. Indeed, down to the time of Heraclius their relationship with the emperor and his officials was almost always one of mutual respect. Like their leaders in Alexandria their prime object was to secure the renunciation of Chalcedon by the emperor as the only means of preserving for humanity divine favour and ultimate salvation.

Against this background it is not easy to speak in terms of nationalism or social revolution when one considers the formation of the monophysite kingdoms. The Byzantine Church always tended to the development of autocephalous patriarchates and metropolitans, and in Armenia, Nubia and Abyssinia these came early in course of time to be identified with a national religion which was Monophysitism. It took eighty years from the time of the council of Chalcedon before any move was made to establish an anti-Chalcedonian hierarchy in the empire, and then Severus of Antioch and his associates in exile at Alexandria acted with great reluctance. In 530 after ten years of persecution by Justin and Justinian the numbers of clergy loyal to them was waning. Their concern became the maintenance of an 'orthodox' hierarchy who could dispense the sacraments to the faithful. Any idea that they were serving the cause of permanent religious separation would have been laughed to scorn. At the same time, the great volume of public support, not only in Egypt and Syria but also in Asia Minor, to the monophysite ideal made itself clear. 'Thousands', we are told, 'offered themselves for ordination'.[3] A new Church came into being despite itself.

---

[1] Cited from A. Vasiliev, *Justin the First* (Harvard 1950) p 234.

[2] Michael the Syrian, VIII, 14, p 122.

[3] See John of Ephesus, *Lives of the Eastern Saints; John of Tella*, ed E. W. Brooks, PO XVIII, 4 (1924) pp 518–19.

Heresy and schism as social and national movements

At this point, however, other factors contributing to the establishment of Monophysitism on a territorial basis began to assert themselves. From sources as disparate as Schenute of Atripe and Theodoret of Cyrrhus one gathers that in parts of Egypt and Syria social and economic conditions were as bad as they were in North Africa.[1] Taxation bore heavily on the cultivator, there were merciless landowners and degrading conditions were imposed on the debtor. These territories had, however, produced monks and not circumcellions, and by the latter half of the fifth century, fed by bequests and donations, as well as the fruits of their own husbandry, the monks were beginning to become a power economically as well as spiritually. In northern Syria it seems that the regime of the secular landowner often gave way to that of the monastery, and the same appears to have been happening in parts of Egypt.[2] The influence which the monks exerted on the villagers among whom they settled was thus consolidated. As the monks were in the vast majority anti-Chalcedonian, Monophysitism gradually began to take on a territorial aspect, which except in Egypt it had previously lacked. Even so, to speak of this development as one representing a native Syrian movement hostile to the continuance of imperial authority can hardly be sustained.

As one searches for the reasons for the differing attitudes of the eastern and western schismatics towards the Roman empire two factors suggest themselves. The first concerns public relations and the second theology. Anyone looking at the history of the Roman empire in the fourth and fifth centuries must be impressed by the enormous difference in approach which marked the relations between the emperor and his subjects, especially his christian subjects in the two halves of the empire. Constantine's embrace at the council of Nicaea of the confessor, Paphnutius, cruelly maimed in the great persecution, was a masterpiece of tact, and ensured that hatred of the slayers of the martyrs among the Copts was confined strictly to his pagan predecessors.[3] Sixty years later, in 387, Theodosius I was prepared to lend a kindly ear to the solicitations of Macedonius, the Barley-eater, and spare the city of Antioch whose punishment he had intended.[4] No such mercy was granted to Thessalonica four years later. Ambrose could only excommunicate the emperor when the deed was done. Indeed the

---

[1] Besa, *Life of Schenute*, ed J. Leipoldt, *CSCO*, Series II, *Scriptores Coptici*, II; IV, 3; V, 4 (1906–13) latin translation H. Wiesmann (1931–6) LXXXI. Theodoret, *Letters*, ed Y. Azéma, *SC* XI, XCVIII, CXI (1955–65) no 42.

[2] G. Tchalenko, *Villages, antiques de la Syrie du Nord* (Paris/Beyrouth 1953) I, p 178.

[3] Socrates, *HE*, I, 11   [4] Theodoret, *HE*, v, 20

monks formed an essential link in a chain of relationships which brought the emperor into direct touch with his eastern subjects, and the reward was their loyalty against Hun and Persian alike.

The mutual respect of emperor and monks might not have been so deep-seated if the east had shared the theological assumptions of the west. Ever since Justin Martyr and Melito of Sardes had stressed the harmony of church and empire theologians had striven to provide this concept with divine sanction. As in so much else in Greek theology, Platonism contributed largely to the answer. All the world was ultimately God's world, the Church and its liturgy was a reflection of the celestial hierarchy and its service to God. Through the right training of body and mind individuals moved along the road towards communion with God. The monks were the true philosophers challenging the demons, confronting the forces of unreason and obstruction to human progress towards God with their feats of asceticism and prayer. To the emperor was due the obedience of all humanity, not merely because this was commanded in scripture but because the emperor reflected the image of Christ and controlled all the affairs, civil and ecclesiastical of the civilised world.[1] Judgement and divine anger that played so great a part in western theology received less consideration. Original sin was conceived as loss of the image of God to be made good by human effort, not as a fatal disease passed down from Adam to his descendants. There was no opposition of interest between emperor and his subjects, and no 'two swords' relationship with the Church. However bitter the christological debate, none would deny that the emperor as well as his theological opponents belonged to the same christian *oikoumene*. 'Long live the emperor', 'Long live the Roman empire', echoing in the streets of monophysite Edessa in 449,[2] was not a cry often heard in the west.

The contrast with the Latins remained in this and other respects. The Greek Christians could never understand why the Latins insisted that the definition of Chalcedon and the council's canons (except the 28th, which they refused to accept) were not subject to the slightest modification or negotiation, whereas they took their own stand on Nicaea alone. The definition of Chalcedon was a valuable bulwark against Nestorian or Eutychian heresy, but the only symbol of faith which they recognised was that of Nicaea supplemented by Constan-

---

[1] Thus Eusebius, Tricennial Oration I, 6; see N. H. Baynes, 'The Byzantine State', in *Byzantine Studies and Other Essays* (London 1955) pp 53–8.
[2] Ed J. Flemming, *Nachrichten der Gesellschaft der Wissenschaften zu Göttingen*, new series XV (1917) p 33.

tinople in 381 and confirmed at the first council of Ephesus. What to Rome was simply the assertion of the paternal care of all churches entrusted by Christ to Peter and his heirs was to the Greek churches innovation and arrogance: for them the Church was governed by autocephalous patriarchs, with the emperor as descendant of Constantine, the 'friend of God' and 'thirteenth apostle' speaking for them all. Between these views nothing that happened in the next thousand years succeeded in providing a compromise. When at Florence in 1439 the theological arguments between the two sides appeared to be settled, the people of Constantinople remembered as they had after the council of Lyons in 1274 the successive humiliations they had received at the hands of the Latins, and even with the Turk at their gates preferred the turban to the mitre as ruler of New Rome.

The question therefore how far schisms in the early Church may be regarded as reflections of social and political dissent may be answered more positively than sometimes has been the case. The religious issue indeed is always primary. The Donatists would not have existed without Cyprian any more than the Monophysites would without Cyril, but in both cases the teaching represented by these leaders struck a responsive chord among the humbler Christians who had no training or interest in the subtleties of ecclesiastical debate. In the West, however, the links between the Donatists and the aspirations of the poor and downtrodden are clearer cut and easier to understand than in the case of the Monophysites. They put into a practical form the hopes that Christianity involved some sort of great revolution and reversal of roles that one finds in the verses of the poet Commodian. Moreover, as one follows their legacy through the Middle Ages to better documented periods nearer our own day, the association of biblical-inspired religion and political nonconformity becomes more evident. In western Europe anabaptist-inspired peasants in Germany, Covenanters in Highland crofts, and first-generation Methodists in northern industrial towns continue to represent similar patterns of thought and action. In the East, however, such equations are less easy to establish. There, the ideal was of the christian *oikoumene* guided by the emperor, and of the individual's communion with God. Both aspirations led to a more optimistic and universalist view of human salvation which blurred the edges of religious controversy and delayed the formation of separatist religious communities along hard and fast lines. At no time before the Arab invasions did the monophysite leaders abandon hope of ultimate reunion with the emperor's Church. Only as decade succeeded decade and no formula could be found which would vindicate both Cyril and the Chalcedonian definition did the monophysite churches consolidate into national and regional areas. In addition, in Armenia, Syria, Nubia and Abyssinia, Monophysitism came to reflect national consciousness through a vernacular liturgy and script that no other force has since been able to achieve. Like the Byzantines themselves they conceived national independence in terms of religious allegiance. Such are some of the factors that have moved humanity through the ages down almost to our own day. It has been said not untruly that the real history of man is the history of religion. Throughout the period we have been dealing with, religion was what made men 'tick'. Those who would seek to unify the Churches will have little success if they fail to realise the strength of this legacy from a time when religion included man's experience in its entirety.

ATTITUDES TO SCHISM AT THE COUNCIL OF NICAEA

by EVERETT FERGUSON

THE council of Nicaea in AD 325 had to deal with disciplinary matters related to three schisms or heresies in addition to Arianism. The persons involved were the clergy among the followers of Meletius, Novatian, and Paul of Samosata.

The interpretation given in the standard history of the councils by Hefele and Leclercq[1] is that the fathers at Nicaea did not require a new ordination of Novatian and Meletian clergymen who returned to the catholic Church. Their previous ordinations were valid but irregular. When this irregularity was corrected, the persons involved could then function in the clergy of the great Church. Later theory about the indelibility of ordination appears to have influenced unduly this interpretation.[2]

Let us look at the three main texts from the council. The fullest and least ambiguous is the synodal letter sent to the Egyptian and neighbouring churches concerning the adherents of Meletius.

Since the synod was disposed to act kindly (for in strict justice he was worthy of no leniency), it was decreed that Meletius should remain in his own city and have no authority to make appointments [*procheirizesthai*][3] or to lay on hands [*cheirothetein*] or to appear in any city or village for this purpose, but should possess only the bare title of his rank [bishop]. Those who have been appointed [*katastathentas*] by him, after they have been confirmed by a more sacred ordination [*mystikōtera cheirotonia*], may on these conditions be fellowshipped and have their rank and officiate, but they shall be the inferiors of those enrolled [*exetazomenōn*] in each parish and church who have been appointed [*prokecheirismenōn*] by our most honourable colleague Alexander. These have no authority to make appointments [*procheirizesthai*] of persons pleasing to

---

[1] [C. J.] Hefele and [H.] Leclercq, [*Histoire des conciles*] (Paris 1907) I, pp 576–87, 615–18. Translations of the canons are made from their text.

[2] E. Amann, 'Réordinations', *DTC*, XIII (1936), cols 2390–2, sees some uncertainty in the thought of the fathers at Nicaea about the validity of the Novatian and Meletian ordinations, but rather than speak of a new ordination he says their clergy received a rite giving a guarantee of validity to their ordination. The later doctrine of the indelibility of ordination still influences an otherwise fine treatment of the sources.

[3] Gelasius reads *Cheirotonein mēte cheirizein*.

them or to propose names or to do anything without the permission of the bishop of the catholic and apostolic church serving under Alexander...If it should happen that any at that time in the church die, then those who have been recently received are to succeed to the office of the deceased, only if they appear worthy, and the people choose them, with the catholic bishop of Alexandria concurring in the election and ratifying it.[1]

The most frequently used word in the passage is *procheirizomai*. Instead of the older translation 'nominate', I have rendered it 'make appointments'.[2] The idea of proposing names seems excluded by the word's usage alongside phrases literally meaning this.[3] The term might include designations of lower clergy whom a bishop selected directly, or it might mean the participation in or concurrence with an ordination by bishops or presbyters who did not directly engage in the laying on of hands.[4] Primary attention attaches to the use of the word *cheirothetein* ('to lay on hands'). There can be no doubt that the word means in this context 'to lay on hands in ordination'.[5]

The key word for the thesis of this paper is *cheirotonia* ('ordination'). In requiring a more mystical (*mystikōtera* – shall we say 'more sacramental'?) ordination, the council seems to speak clearly of its concept of ordination. Hefele takes *cheirotonia* here of benediction, which indeed he must in order to maintain his position. Such a singular use is wholly unparalleled in the early centuries and the interpretation is quite arbitrary. *Cheirotonia* here must mean 'ordination', and the passage must mean that the Meletian clergy are to receive a new ordination. Note that before the former Meletian clergyman succeeded to a new charge in the catholic Church he must be elected by the people and have the approval of the patriarch of Alexandria, as would anyone else.

It is generally recognised that Nicaea accorded the same treatment to restored Novatians and to restored Meletians.[6] Since both groups were doctrinally orthodox and separated from the main Church on the grounds of moral rigorism, especially as regarded the reconciliation to the Church of apostates during persecution, a common policy was consistent. The decision on the Novatians is contained in canon 8.

---

[1] The text with minor variants in wording is preserved in Socrates, *HE* I.9; Theodoret, *HE* I.ix.7ff; and Gelasius, *HE* II.33. My translation is made from Theodoret, ed L. Parmentier and F. Schneidweiler in *GCS* (second edition; Berlin 1954) pp 39–41.
[2] [G. W. H.] Lampe, [*A Patristic Greek Lexicon*] (Oxford 1968) gives the meanings 'put forward for office, appoint'. [3] *hypoballein onomata* and *epilegesthai onomata*.
[4] See my 'Eusebius and Ordination', *JEH*, XIII, 2 (1962), pp 141ff.
[5] Lampe cites more instances of this meaning than any other.
[6] Hefele and Leclercq, p 582; [William] Bright, [*Notes on the Canons of the First Four General Councils*] (Oxford 1882) p 26.

Concerning those who call themselves Cathari, if they [who are clerics] come over to the catholic and apostolic church, it is decreed by the holy and great synod that upon receiving a laying on of hands [*cheirothetoumenous*] they are to continue in the clergy...If, then, whether in villages or cities, all of the ordained (*cheirotonēthentes*] are found to be Cathari only, let them remain in the clergy and in the same rank in which they are found. But if some come over where there is a bishop or presbyter of the catholic church, it is evident that the bishop of the church has the rank of the episcopate; and the one named a bishop by those called Cathari has the honour of the presbytery, unless it seem fitting to the bishop to share with him the honour of his title. If this is not satisfactory, he shall provide for him a place as chorepiscopus or presbyter, in order that he may be seen to be of the clergy, and that there may not be two bishops in the city.

Commentators have differed over the significance of the 'laying on of hands' in this text. Does the word mean 'those who have previously received a laying on of hands in the Novatian sect'[1] or 'those receiving a laying on of hands on their return to the catholic Church'? The use of the present tense would favour the latter.[2] In either case the reference would be to a laying of hands on ecclesiastics, for it is only they who are in view. If the reference were to a Novatian imposition of hands, the ordination laying on of hands would be the obvious meaning. The council does use *cheirotonia*, ordination, for what Novatian clerics had received. If, however, we follow the Latin translators, then there is a question whether the laying on of hands pertained to the absolution of penitents, signifying their reconciliation to the fellowship of the Church,[3] or to a laying on of hands in ordination. Hefele and Leclercq rejected Gratian's interpretation requiring a reordination and chose the former interpretation, namely that Nicaea required 'a simple imposition of hands with the value of a benediction which restores the irregularity'.[4]

William Bright's *Notes on the Canons of the First Four General Councils* nearly a century ago, although appearing to favour Hefele's view, gave the arguments in support of understanding the text as requiring a fresh ordination.[5] The *cheirothesia* family of words is not generally used of any laying on of hands other than that in ordination

---

[1] This was the view of Rufinus, the Greek commentators, and others – Hefele and Leclercq, pp 583ff. I would suspect that Zonaras and Balsamon knew that the word meant ordination, but since reordination was no longer the practice in their time, they referred it to Novatian ordination.

[2] *Ibid.* Hefele adds the point that the absence of the article and use of the pronoun with the participle favor this interpretation.

[3] J. Coppens, *L'Imposition des mains et les rites connexes* (Paris 1925) chapter 5 for instances.

[4] Hefele and Leclercq, pp 583ff.   [5] Bright, pp 25ff.

before the *Apostolic Constitutions*.[1] The earliest Greek writer to cite the canon, Theophilus of Alexandria at the end of the fourth century, understood the canon as enjoining a fresh ordination and substituted *cheirotonia* for *cheirothesia*.[2] This usage accords with that of the synodal letter about the Meletians.

Canon 19 about the followers of Paul of Samosata is conclusive that the Nicene bishops used *cheirothesia* for ordination.

Concerning the Paulianists who have fled for refuge to the catholic church, it has been decreed that they must by all means be rebaptized. If any of them who in time past were found in the clergy and if they appear to be blameless and without reproach, when they have been rebaptized, they are to be ordained [*cheirotoneisthōsan*] by the bishop of the catholic church. But if the examination finds them unfit, they are to be rejected. Likewise in the case of their deaconesses and generally concerning those enrolled on the canon, the same policy shall be observed. We make mention of deaconesses enrolled on the list, since they do not have any laying on of hands [*cheirothesian*], that they are numbered only among the laity.

Supposed difficulties have led to drastic solutions, such as removing the last sentence as an interpolation made by someone embarrassed at the possibility of deaconesses seemingly being counted in the clergy. This is unnecessary, as is Hefele's suggestion, for which there is evidence, to read 'deacon' for the first occurrence of 'deaconess'. There is a 'formal contradiction' with the end of the decree only if one understands *kanōn* as meaning 'clergy'. The canon or 'roll' of the Church would have included any special classes in the Church and benevolent cases as well as the clergy.[3] The council is saying that the same procedure is to be followed in regard to all the enrolled persons as is followed for the ordained. All may take up the same position, if worthy, they had among the Paulianists, but they have to go through the same process

[1] C. H. Turner, '*Cheirotonia, Cheirothesia, Epithesis Cheirōn*', *JTS*, XXIV (1923) p 502. Eusebius, a participant at Nicaea, does not use the verb, but the one occurrence of the noun in his *Ecclesiastical History* refers to ordination (VI.xxiii.4).

[2] 'Since the great synod held at Nicaea decreed that the Novatians coming over to the church be ordained, do you ordain those who wish to come over to the church, if their life is upright and there is no objection', Theophilus, *Narratio de iis qui dicuntur Cathari*, PG 65 (1868) col 446.

[3] Canon 16 of Nicaea has only clergy in view, but Chalcedon, canon 2, illustrates the broader meaning of *kanōn*. Cornelius's list of presbyters, deacons, subdeacons, acolytes, exorcists, readers, doorkeepers, and widows (Eusebius, *HE* VI.xliii.11) would constitute the 'canon' of the church at Rome. Hippolytus, *Apostolic Tradition* I.x–xiv takes up confessors, widows, readers, virgins, subdeacons, and those with the gift of healing after the bishops, presbyters, and deacons. A similar explanation is given by H. J. Schroeder, *Disciplinary Decrees of the General Councils* (London 1937) pp 55–7.

used in appointing the faithful to the respective positions. *Cheirotonia* means ordination, as it does generally. *Cheirothesia* is the laying on of hands in ordination. This act deaconesses do not receive,[1] hence they are technically 'laity' although among the enrolled persons of the Church. The council is at pains to specify the status of deaconesses perhaps because of some special prominence among the Paulianists.[2]

Since Paulianists were considered heretical in their view of the divine Trinity, their baptism in the triune name was not considered valid.[3] Since their baptism was not recognised, obviously their ordination was not. Silence about baptism in canon 8 implies that Novatians were not rebaptised.[4] If ordination was required of heretical Paulianist clergy, the same terminology must mean the same thing in the decisions relative to the schismatic Meletians and Novatians.

A look at the meaning of ordination in the fourth-century Church provides a further confirmation of the interpretation which has been given to these Nicene decisions. Ordination consisted of prayer and the laying on of hands. The act was understood as a blessing. The imposition of hands designated or marked out the person being ordained for divine favour which was invoked in the prayer. Laying on of hands in early Christian thought signified a blessing, and in ordination the prayer specified the blessing intended.[5] It was indeed the central feature and the imposition of hands was an accompaniment to the prayer.

A few passages will show the theological interpretation. 'Blessed was he in being counted worthy to cover such a head with his hand and to bless so noble a soul with his voice' (*Life of Polycarp*, xi). Chrysostom defines the ordination as the prayer for God to bless: '[Luke] says not how, but simply that they were ordained by prayer; for this is the ordination. The hand of man is laid on, but God performs everything, and it is God's hand which touches the head of the

---

[1] *Apostolic Constitutions* VIII.xix–xx provides for a laying on of hands at the appointment of deaconesses. J. Cotsonis, 'A Contribution to the Interpretation of the 19th Canon of the First Ecumenical Council', *Revue des études Byzantines*, XIX (Paris 1961) pp 184–97, takes the *cheirothesia* of benediction and not the conferral of holy orders, but he does see the canon as implying that deaconesses were canonically ordained like other members of the clergy. He explains the canon as referring to some who took the habit at an early age and then were ordained later.

[2] Eusebius, *HE* VII.xxx.10, 12ff indicates something of the importance of women in Paul's following.

[3] Athanasius, *Orationes contra Arianos* II.xviii.41, 43.

[4] Compare Arles, canon 8.

[5] For a preliminary statement of the case see my 'Jewish and Christian Ordination', *Harvard Theological Review* LVI, 1 (Cambridge, Mass., 1963) p 15.

one being ordained, if he is truly ordained.'[1] Gregory of Nyssa in his sermon *On the Baptism of Christ* defines ordination as a change effected by benediction.[2] Jerome implies primacy for the prayer in his definition of the Greek word *cheirotonia*: 'the ordination of the clergy which is accomplished not only at the verbal prayer but at the imposition of the hand (lest indeed in mockery someone be ordained ignorantly to the clergy by a secret prayer)'.[3]

Ordination thus was a particular kind of blessing. A new prayer for each ministry (deacon, presbyter, bishop) shows the specific nature of the ordination blessing. And the ordination was for service in a particular church.[4] The early Church expected a person to remain for life in the church where he was ordained. The frequent translations in the imperial Church called forth repeated protests in the canonical legislation against the practice, as already in Nicaea, canon 16.

It is not always clear whether a new ordination was involved in such translations. Since they often involved a promotion, such would be expected. But reordinations were performed where no promotion was involved. Apostolic Canons 68 decrees as follows:

> If any bishop, presbyter, or deacon receives a second ordination from any one, let him be deprived, and the person who ordained him, unless he can show that his former ordination was from the heretics; for those that are either baptized or ordained by such as these, can be neither Christians nor clergymen.

We may apply the rule, If somebody forbids it somebody is doing it. If there was a reordination in transferring a clergyman from one diocese to another, certainly there would have been in bringing him from a schismatic body to the catholic Church.

Hefele and Leclercq understood the Nicene fathers to use *cheirotonia* as equivalent to *cheirothesia*, meaning a benediction.[5] The situation is rather the reverse – *cheirothesia* supplied the meaning and content for ordination. The meaning of benediction is correct, but not in the weak or accommodative sense implied. There was not a 'real' ordination earlier which now had to be regularised. *Cheirothesia* was used at Nicaea for the laying on of hands at ordination, because the meaning of ordination itself was a benediction for ministry. In view of this significance for the act, clearly a new act of ordination was required

---

[1] *Homilies xiv in Acts* 6, PG 60 (1862) col 116. We have translated according to the punctuation which the Greek text seems to require.
[2] *De baptismo Christi*, PG 46 (1863) col 581d.
[3] *In Isaiam* XVI.58, PL 24 (1865) col 591.
[4] Chalcedon, canon 6.   [5] Hefele and Leclercq, pp 584, 617ff.

for reconciled schismatics before they could take up a ministry in the Church. This had nothing to do with any question of the 'validity' of the former ordination. Such is a later and foreign concept to the terminology of Nicaea. Sacramental theology had not advanced as far about ordination as it had about baptism.

The readiness to accept schismatic clergymen into the clergy of the catholic Church was a realisation that qualified leaders in the sect could be qualified leaders in the Church and that it was prudent in bringing such men back into the fellowship of the parent body to permit them to continue in the honours to which they were accustomed. The council protected the rights of catholic clergy and the needs of good order. The council could not give schismatics a charge in the catholic Church without a new act of appointment to service. A simple reconciliation to the Church did not automatically guarantee one's ministry in the Church. There is no question of validity or non-validity of the previous appointment. Such questions were irrelevant, given the understanding of ordination which we have found in the fourth century, pre-Augustinian sources.

SOCIETY, THEODICY AND
THE ORIGINS OF HERESY:
TOWARDS A REASSESSMENT
OF THE MEDIEVAL EVIDENCE

by JANET L. NELSON

I shall not be presenting in this communication the fruits of any original research: my aim will be simply to put together some of the results of recent work by others, and on that basis to offer a little contribution to 'the great seven-storey library' which professor Le Bras hopes will one day 'be devoted to studies of the structure and whole life of every religion at every moment of its history'.[1]

It is best to begin with some explanation of my title: much of the debate on the origins of heresy has centred on the question of whether or not it represented a 'social problem'. Thus when Grundmann asks if social questions were at the root of heresy, he means, was heresy the expression of material deprivation on the part of the unprivileged?[2] This sort of connection has of course been made by historians usually stigmatised as Marxist (though Marx himself would, I think, have disowned some of their crude anachronisms); Werner, for example, explains heresy as a protest movement against the economic and social exploitation of the feudal system.[3] Grundmann and others have ably exposed the weaknesses of that thesis: indeed to continue the debate in such terms has become a sterile exercise. And I am not proposing now to discuss the origins of heresy as a social problem in that narrow sense. My concern is with society as an inclusive system of human relationships and organisation within which religion constitutes a major component. Now Christianity even in early medieval society had achieved a considerable degree of differentiation,

---

[1] 'Sociologie de l'Église dans le Haut Moyen Âge', in Settimane [di studio del centro Italiano di studi sull'Alto Medioevo], VII (Spoleto 1960) II, p 611.
[2] Religiöse Bewegungen im Mittelalter (2 ed Darmstadt 1961) pp 519ff.
[3] Die gesellschaftlichen Grundlagen der Klosterreform im 11. Jahrhundert (Berlin 1953), and Pauperes Christi. [Studien zu sozialreligiösen Bewegungen im Zeitalter des Reformpapsttums] (Leipzig 1956). But see also [G.] Koch, Frauenfrage [und Ketzertum im Mittelalter] (Berlin 1962) – a work of insight and fine judgement.

with its own well-established traditions and institutions. But religious change needs to be studied along with economic, political and social change, varying both with, and independently of, these other processes. Religion, as an aspect of human activity, can only be fully understood in this total context.

By theodicy I mean the problem which arises within a belief-system when the individual's experience involves suffering which the system fails to accommodate or explain. Any religion of benevolent monotheism faces a problem in accounting for God's permission of suffering: it requires a constant vindication of divine providence – what C. S. Lewis referred to as 'explaining or explaining away the miseries of life'.[1] A theology of good fortune for the fortunate is unlikely to satisfy this demand. It is important to stress the cognitive basis of the theodicy problem: that is to say, it arises, not directly or automatically from experience, but from dissonance between that experience and received knowledge or belief. So, to the extent that a given cosmology is adapted to certain types of social experience, it is likely to be felt inapposite or outmoded in situations of social change. The extent of disaffection will vary both with the scale and intensity of individuals' perception of such change, as well as with psychological factors with which I do not propose to deal.[2]

So there is no necessary connection between theodicy and material suffering. Disorientation arising from a failure of actual experience to tally with learned perception and classification, can obviously arise as readily for the *nouveau riche* as for the dispossessed. Mobility in any dimension – horizontally in space as well as vertically in a social hierarchy – will tend to raise new problems of adaptation for the 'displaced person'. Therefore any significant increase in such mobility will increase the likelihood of a crisis of theodicy within the framework of a given religious organisation, belief and practice. Ultimately the religious authorities may face stark alternatives: adaptive change or obsolescence. If they opt for the former, they must still preserve tradition: the successful containment of novelty requires a definition

[1] *The Problem of Pain* (London 1941) p 4. I have learned much from G. Obeyesekere, 'Theodicy, Sin and Salvation in a Sociology of Buddhism', in *Dialectic in Practical Religion*, ed E. R. Leach (Cambridge 1968) pp 7–40. On dissonance and personal commitment, see L. Festinger, H. W. Riecken and S. Schachter, *When Prophecy Fails* (Minneapolis 1956) esp pp 25ff, and B. R. Wilson, 'A typology of sects in dynamic and comparative perspective', *Archives de Sociologie des Religions*, XVI (Paris 1963) pp 49–63.
[2] But see H. Toch, *The Social Psychology of Social Movements* (London 1966), and W. Sargant, 'The Physiology of Faith', *British Journal of Psychiatry*, CXV (London 1969) pp 505–18.

of new boundaries. But that very definition will mean the exclusion of further change. The new orthodoxy thus creates heresy as its antitype.

I should perhaps make clear at this point that I shall not be concerned with the much-disputed question of Bogomil influence on the origins of heresy in the medieval West.[1] I am inclined in any case to leave this possibility open, while focusing on the indigenous factors within western society which from *c* 1000 onwards were tending to produce a crisis of theodicy. Historians have long since drawn attention to certain qualitative changes in medieval Catholicism at this period, and many of them have suggested a vague relationship with contemporary developments in the wider society. The origins of heresy, we are told, are to be found in 'un réveil collectif d'une conscience neuve et d'une sensibilité nouvelle',[2] in 'nascent religious sentiments...ascetic and spiritual impulses',[3] in a 'deep religious dynamic',[4] in 'a widely and strongly felt popular need...the product of a transition from a comparatively simple to a more sophisticated world of opinion'.[5] To term such remarks no more than suggestive, is, I hope, by no means to ignore the profound and sensitive scholarship that lies behind them. To the impressionist school we owe pictures of intense colour and marvellous subtlety. As historians, however, we need to face squarely the problem of historical causation: *why* the new consciousness? *why* the new spiritual needs? Recent American historiography presents us with a 'Janus-complex' in christian history, a 'counterpoint' of tradition and reform, orthodoxy and dissent:[6] but is this sort of scheme anything more than a re-description and re-classification of familiar materials? The assumption appears to be that the christian religion pre-programmes its adherents to a kind of behavioural oscillation. But human beings aren't computers: they are themselves the programmers,

[1] For a guide to the huge bibliography on this subject, see J. B. Russell, 'Some Interpretations of the Origins of Medieval Heresy', *Medieval Studies*, XXV (Toronto 1963) pp 26–53. See now also R. I. Moore, 'The Origins of Medieval Heresy', *History*, CLXXXIII (London 1970) pp 21–36; and the judicious remarks of C. N. L. Brooke in *JTS*, XVIII (1967) pp 256–8, reviewing J. B. Russell's book, *Dissent [and Reform in the Early Middle Ages]* (Berkeley 1965). T. Manteuffel, *Die Geburt der Ketzerei* (Vienna 1965) has unfortunately been inaccessible.

[2] R. Morghen, 'Problèmes sur l'origine de l'hérésie au Moyen Âge', *Revue Historique*, CCXXXVI (1966) pp 1–16, at p 10.

[3] W. L. Wakefield and A. P. Evans, *Heresies of the High Middle Ages* (New York 1969) Introduction, pp 21–2.

[4] A. Franzen, *A Concise History of the Church*, ed J. P. Dolan (rev ed London 1969) pp 187ff.

[5] [C. N. L.] Brooke, 'Heresy [and Religious Sentiment: 1000–1250'], *BIHR*, XLI (1968) pp 115ff.

[6] See Russell, *Dissent*, and K. F. Morrison, *Tradition and Authority in the Western Church, 300–1140* (Princeton 1969).

3-2

the subjects not the objects of history. At a given moment, the religious tradition exists as a repertoire of symbols: why choose to employ some rather than others? And what determines the timing of the choice? It is, I think, the responsibility of the ecclesiastical historian to undertake the same kind of enquiry that his colleagues in social and comparative history have been pursuing in the field of non-European cultures. If, for instance, the Arabist seeks to explain the striking differences between urban and rural forms of Islam, he will not be content to say that both are validated by the same religious tradition, but asks why certain elements are stressed in one social environment rather than another, and when and how these transformations came about.[1] I suggest that we might usefully pose these same questions in regard to medieval Europe.

Turning now to the problem of the origins of medieval heresy, I want to outline the way in which religious and social structures interlocked in the relatively stable society of the early middle ages, which, though subject to external attack and natural catastrophe, possessed a resilient and perduring internal structure. First then, a necessarily brief and generalised sketch of a western European kingdom of the ninth or tenth century.[2] Its material base is a patrimonial peasant economy almost wholly agricultural, and poorly equipped technologically; the population remains stable, at near-subsistence level. Ties of cognatic kinship and village community provide social cement. The role of the patrimonial lord whom the peasantry supports is protective and in some measure redistributive: status distinctions are based on rank, not caste, and status is gained by giving. Ecclesiastical and political structures are closely aligned, often staffed by the same personnel; status is to a considerable extent concomitant in both, and the same forms of display expenditure characterise both rank-systems. It is regarded as perfectly appropriate that a great monastery should excel both in *divitiis et sanctitate*.[3] Literacy is the preserve of a small and culturally conservative élite. At all social levels,

---

[1] E. Gellner, 'A pendulum swing theory of Islam', *Annales Sociologiques* (Paris 1968) pp 5–14, and *Saints of the Atlas* (London 1969).

[2] Among historians, the following survey owes most to M. Bloch, *Feudal Society* (London 1961), G. Duby, *Rural Economy and Country Life in the Medieval West* (London 1968), and [R. W.] Southern, *Western Society [and the Church in the Middle Ages]* (Harmondsworth 1970); among social scientists, to E. R. Wolf, *Peasants* (Englewood Cliffs 1966) and M. Fried, *The Evolution of Political Society* (New York 1967).

[3] So Ralph Glaber, praising the achievement of a cluniac abbot, stressing at the same time his noble birth, and that 'summum in palaciis regum ac ceterorum principum obtinebat locum'. *Historiarum Libri Quinque*, III, v, c. 16, ed M. Prou (Paris 1886) p 66.

sex, age, and hierarchical position indicate prescribed roles. The norm is cooperation, in settled agrarian communities. Above all, at the centre of the system and himself symbolising its unity, stands the king. His job, as Alcuin tells Charlemagne, is 'to purify and protect the churches of Christendom internally from the doctrines of false brethren, externally from destruction by pagans'.[1] It is the king's job too to hold the system together as a functioning whole by controlling mobility within it, and so preserving prescribed balanced relations between all its parts. The Church elaborates a royal ideology, and calls on the king in an outburst of alliterative rhymed prose to be: 'amicis adiutorium, inimicis obstaculum, humilibus solatium, elevatis correptio, divitibus doctrina, pauperibus pietas, peregrinis pacificatio, propriis in patria pax et securitas'.[2]

Early medieval religion fitted into this society, both ideologically and institutionally, by pronouncing and affirming the values of stability and tradition, by sanctioning the established structures of political and economic control especially in its support of kingship and development of theocratic doctrine, by enjoining on individuals the fulfilment of ascribed roles, by asserting the efficacy of ritual practice in coping with nature and supernature. It is a religion of emphasis on shame rather than sin, atonement rather than repentance, orthopraxy rather than orthodoxy, of locally-based cults, each rural community equipped with the relics of its patron saint, each individual striking his own bargain with invisible protectors. The life hereafter is believed to be continuous with arrangements on earth: dead kings reign in heaven, where they, together with the clergy, continue to be answerable for the shortcomings of their earthly flock.[3] Suffering in this world is regarded as an effect of divine displeasure or revenge, punishing human interference with *ordo* rather than any moral offence. Thus tyranny is identified as kingship acquired against the rules, not royal misgovernment or wrong-doing.[4] The confident manipulation of

---

[1] Ep. 171, *MGH Epp.* III, *Epistolae Karolini Aevi*, II, ed E. Dümmler etc (Berlin 1895) p 282.

[2] From the prayer 'In diebus' in the royal consecration *Ordo* edited by P. E. Schramm, 'Die Krönung bei den Westfranken und Angelsachsen von 878 bis zum 1000', *Zeitschrift der Savigny Stiftung für Rechtsgeschichte, Kan. Abt*, XXIV (Weimar 1934) pp 211ff. Schramm's opinions on the origin and date of this *Ordo* stand in need of revision.

[3] See Schramm, 'Mittherrschaft im Himmel: Ein Topos des Herrscherkults in christlicher Einkleidung', in his collected papers, *Kaiser, Könige und Päpste* (Stuttgart 1968) I, pp 79–85.

[4] See M. Reydellet, 'La Conception du Souverain chez Isidore de Séville', in *Isidoriana*, ed M. Diaz y Diaz (Leon 1961) pp 457–66; W. Schlesinger, *Beiträge zur deutschen*

recognised symbols by ritual specialists is believed to restore equilibrium between natural and supernatural worlds: the divinity is appeased or swayed by correctly performed sacrifice or the penance by proxy of monks. Humbler folk use christian or pagan magic for self-protection.

Occasionally, individuals fall foul of the ecclesiastical authorities because of some idiosyncratic belief or practice, or as charismatic leaders of ephemeral peasant followings, often in conditions of political upheaval.[1] Within the monastic culture an individual scholar might produce novel interpretations of doctrine, but in these narrow confines, as the case of Gottschalk shows, the authorities had little difficulty in suppressing heterodoxy.[2] Spanish Adoptionism perhaps constitutes a special case, reminiscent of certain forms of religious provincialism in late antiquity, though even here the issue seems to have concerned only a small group of dissident higher clergy.[3] But heresy, as a recurrent problem of ongoing doctrinal and institutional deviance on the scale of a popular movement: this I take to be unknown in the early Middle Ages. If I regard the heresy of the high Middle Ages as an indigenous growth, this is not because of the prior existence of a continuous tradition of dissent.

What confronts the historian from c 1000 onwards is a series of far-reaching changes in economic and political organisation.[4] The under-

---

Verfassungsgeschichte des Mittelalters (Göttingen 1963) pp 109, 111, notes the appearance of the distinction between *rex* and *tyrannus* in ninth-century Frankish chronicles, with similar implications.

[1] For details, see Russell, *Dissent*. But some of the categories imposed here ('eccentrics', 'reformists') are unhelpful, while in general, the social environment of religious phenomena receives too little attention: for example, Russell chronicles the brief career of the prophetess Theuda, reprimanded by the synodists at Mainz in 848, without any reference to the troubled political situation at that period in her homeland, Alemannia.

[2] K. Vielhaber, *Gottschalk der Sachse* (Bonn 1956) gives a sympathetic account. S. Epperlein, 'Sachsen im frühen Mittelalter', *Jahrbuch für Wirtschaftsgeschichte* (Berlin 1966) pp 206ff, argues that Gottschalk's doctrine reflected Saxon opposition to the 'Feudalisierungspolitik' of the Frankish church. But the only evidence he can cite for the view that Gottschalk's teaching was taken up by the population at large – *MGH, Epp.* v, *Epistolae Karolini Aevi*, III, ed E. Dümmler and K. Hampe (Berlin 1899) p 481 – turns out to relate to the monk's activities, not in Saxony, but in Italy! Mr J. B. Gillingham kindly drew my attention to Epperlein's article.

[3] W. Heil, 'Der Adoptionismus, Alkuin und Spanien', in *Karl der Grosse. Lebenswerk und Nachleben*, ed B. Bischoff (Düsseldorf 1965) II, pp 95–155.

[4] Some aspects of these changes are brilliantly analysed by J. F. Lemarignier, 'Political and monastic structures in France at the end of the tenth and the beginning of the eleventh century', reprinted and translated by [F. L.] Cheyette, *Lordship and Community [in Medieval Europe]* (New York 1968) pp 100–27; J. Dhondt, 'Les solidarités médi-

lying dynamic seems to have been demographic growth, probably attributable to technological improvements, in turn setting up new pressures at every social level, stimulating both intra-rural migration and even more significant, rural–urban migration and the growth of towns. Though the migrants form new solidarities consonant with their new environment, these are less all-embracing than the groupings of village and kindred: in the town, the individual's roles as kinsman, citizen, worker, are increasingly differentiated. For displaced persons in the countryside – the guest-people on the village-fringe, the colonists of the waste, travelling artisans in cloth and metal – the old kindred supports become more difficult to activate and take time to re-establish.

Old patternings suffer dislocation too, through a general (though differential) trend towards undivided inheritance of patrimonies. The prestige and independent status of women, at least in landowning families, declines markedly with the consolidation of agnatic lines of descent and with husbands exercising control of their wives' dowries.

The *juvenes* jostle to assert their individual claims to status, whether in clerical or knightly life-styles. For some of them, education will provide the key to advancement in the service of prince or prelate: new lines of learned inquiry are pursued in the schools by a veritable throng of students.[1]

Lords have to struggle to maintain their families' wealth and prestige: the seigneurial aristocracy becomes a caste with less to spare for dowries, for monastic foundations, for feeding the poor. Peasants feel the burden of seigneurial power, now more often perceived as oppressive rather

évales. Une société en transition: la Flandre en 1127–1128', *Annales. É[conomies]. S[ociétés]. C[ivilisations]*, XII (Paris 1957) pp 529–60; G. Duby, 'Les "jeunes" dans la société aristocratique', *Annales. E.S.C.*, XIX (1964) pp 835–46, and 'Les sociétés médiévales: une approche d'ensemble', *Annales. E.S.C.*, XXVI (1971) pp 1–13; G. Luzzatto, 'Mutamenti nell'economia agraria italiana dalla caduta dei Carolingi al principio del sec. XI', in *Settimane*, II (1955) pp 601–22; K. Leyser, 'The German Aristocracy from the ninth to the early twelfth century: a historical and cultural sketch', *PP*, XLI (1968) pp 25–53. Two valuable area-studies are G. Duby, *La Société aux XIe et XIIe siècles dans la région mâconnaise* (Paris 1953), and [R.] Fossier, *La Terre et les Hommes en Picardie [jusqu'à la Fin du XIIIe siècle]* (Paris 1968). J. Le Goff, 'Note sur société tripartite, idéologie monarchique et renouveau économique dans la chrétienté du IXe au XIIe siècle', in *L'Europe au IXe au XIe Siècle*, ed T. Manteuffel and A. Gieysztor (Warsaw 1968) pp 63–71, suggests some interesting correlations between social and ideological change.

[1] Abbot Philip of Harvengt wrote of Paris in the mid-twelfth century (*PL* 203 (1855) col 31): 'Hic ad pulsandum tantus concursus, tanta frequentia clericorum, ut contendat supergredi numerosam multitudinem laicorum!' I am grateful to professor W. Ullmann for pointing out to me the significance of developments in education.

than partly protective: and it is not until the later twelfth century that there is much evidence of the village community successfully closing its ranks to resist the lord's new demands. The keynote – in limited but crucial areas of this society – is competition: an increasing number of individuals, possibly deprived of former kin or communal supports, face the need to prove themselves – to achieve status rather than to play out ascribed roles.

But the social impact of this increased mobility and competition depends upon a further key variable in the social system: namely, the extent to which an overarching political authority survives to co-ordinate and control some of the effects of these developments. I believe that the relative strength or weakness of monarchy is of crucial importance in determining the form and extent of religious change: it seems no coincidence that the main impulse to reform and heresy alike comes not initially from England or Germany or Spain (though they might of course be taken up in those areas later) but from Lorraine, southern and eastern France and northern Italy. Again, continental heresy meets with a very cool reception in twelfth-century England, where not only does the royal government concern itself actively with, for example, the protection of urban liberties and the status of freemen, making itself felt also at the level of rural communities, but to a considerable extent the early medieval type of royal ideology retains its force.

But, all the more where strong political authority is absent, certain individuals are exposed to new types of social experience for which their religion offers no meaningful patterning. What relevance has a religion of stability to a life of mobility, competition and uncertainty? Will a God who reinforces social order and conformity, integrating political with religious structures, have regard for the 'marginal man' in the chinks of the social structure or in physical or social transition? Here is the genesis of a new problem of theodicy: and just as the occurrence of social change is highly differential, so are religious crisis and its resolution. But where that crisis *is* experienced, the response is broadly two-fold, in two distinct phases.

The first is a resolution of the theodicy in terms of a heavy reinvestment of religious capital in received religious belief and practice:[1]

[1] See Southern, *Western Society*; M. Chenu, *Nature, Man and Society* [*in the Twelfth Century*] (Chicago 1968); among recent detailed studies in English, H. E. J. Cowdrey, 'The peace and the truce of God in the eleventh century', *PP*, XLVI (1970) pp 42–67, and Brooke, 'Heresy'. [R. W.] Southern, *St Anselm* [*and his Biographer*] (Cambridge 1963) shows the varieties of religious change in the mirror of monastic life and thought.

there is a blossoming of devotional piety, manifested in pilgrimages, in the Peace Movement, in the Crusades, in church-building, in the heyday of patronage for the Cluniacs. At the belief level, there is adaptation through redefinition of doctrines, a reaffirmation of the efficacy of eucharistic ritual expressed in the doctrine of the Real Presence (there Berengar was the conservative !) and a holding-out of hope to sinners through indulgences and the doctrine of Purgatory. Renewed emphasis on ritual efficacy presupposes the ritual cleanliness of the practitioners: there is a demand for clerical conformity to the norms of purity already exemplified in the monastic life, with a primary insistence on chastity, and a secondary onslaught on simony. At the same time, the laity set for themselves new standards of purity: moral values are increasingly internalised, sin and guilt replacing shame, repentance replacing ritual atonement. Perhaps most significant of all, there is renewed emphasis on institutional unity, and the common religious heritage of Christendom as a whole: the trend is centripetal, towards increased conformity.

Thus the Gregorian reform, involving a new degree of religious differentiation within the wider social system, and revaluation of religious commitments for all adherents, was the answer to newly-felt demands. Anselm and Damian witness this in reaffirming the consonance of divine justice and divine mercy, and in seeking the reintegration of christian cosmology epitomised in Anselm's assertion that 'even the smallest inconsistency in God is impossible'.[1] It was not only that western society before the eleventh century had been unable to afford ecclesiastical reform. Certainly, resources and personnel now became available: the real dynamic of religious change, however, was popular demand.

But, as I suggested earlier, the commitment to adaptation on the part of ecclesiastical authorities produced its own 'freezing-effect' in the

A useful perspective on this material may be found in M. Weber, *The Sociology of Religion* (London 1965). T. Parsons, 'Christianity and modern industrial society,' in *Sociological Theory, Values and Sociocultural Change. Essays in Honour of P. A. Sorokin*, ed E. A. Tiryakian (Glencoe 1963) pp 33–70, at pp 33–49, analyses changes in medieval Christianity but disappointingly sidesteps the crucial problem of causation. Much greater finesse seems to have been applied to comparable problems by social anthropologists. In preparing this paper, I have found particularly valuable [M.] Douglas, *Natural Symbols* (London 1970); R. Horton, 'African Conversion', *Africa*, XLI (London 1971) pp 85–108; and [V. W.] Turner, *The Ritual Process[: structure and anti-structure]* (London 1969).

[1] Quoted by Southern, *St Anselm*, p 120. On Damian's asceticism, see P. McNulty's introduction to *St Peter Damian. Selected Writings on the Spiritual Life* (London 1959).

crystallisation of new structures – which in turn created new marginal men. The same social pressures that brought about the original theodicy crisis actually grew more acute, in that more people were affected by increasing mobility (especially through urbanisation) and by a continuing political disintegration which seems to have reached its maximum in certain key areas *c* 1100. In short, ecclesiastical structures became less flexible while pressure was building up within.

Twelfth-century heresy was in an important sense anti-structural: this was why the issue of obedience was crucial, and why doctrine was not necessarily involved.[1] Not surprisingly, monks, clerks and hermits, for whom the conflict between personal striving for the *visio dei* and required discipline presented itself in most acute form, were often the instigators and disseminators of heresy. They could no longer accept the Gregorian synthesis whereby religious *libertas* was integrated within hierarchical *ordo*. Educational developments from the later eleventh century onwards meant that more and more people, both clerks and eventually laymen also, in the towns were capable of doctrinal speculation. Perhaps too heresy took root most firmly in areas where political and religious structures were most closely articulated, both because ecclesiastical authority was there experienced as peculiarly oppressive (for example in some Italian towns), and because such ecclesiastical structures offered little hope of achieving either personal status (is it a coincidence that many of the Cathar adepts – the *Perfecti* – were members of the struggling lesser nobility, women, and even men of humble origin?) or any collective sense of *communitas* (again Catharism could supply this deficiency).[2] This much basis might be admitted, too, for the *Frauenfrage* postulated by East German historians, that one effect of the Gregorian reform was to diminish the possibilities of active female participation in formal religious organisations at the exalted level afforded, in some areas at least, by early medieval convents.[3]

[1] Some excellent studies, together with a guide to the bibliography, are contained in the collection, *Hérésies et sociétés [dans l'Europe préindustrielle, 11e–18e siècles]*, ed J. Le Goff (Paris 1968). The importance of the obedience issue is indicated elsewhere in the present volume by Miss B. Bolton, 'Tradition and Temerity' (below, pp 79–91).

[2] See A. Borst, *Die Katharer* (Stuttgart 1953), and, for a brief discussion, the article, 'Cathari', by Y. Dossat in the *New Catholic Encyclopedia*, III, pp 246ff. The geography of heresy is illuminated by [C.] Violante, 'Hérésies urbaines [et hérésies rurales en Italie du 11e au 13e siècle',] in *Hérésies et Sociétés*, pp 171–98, and by the short articles of R. Manselli and P. Wolff (*ibid*). Turner, *Ritual Process*, chs III and IV, explores the meaning of *communitas*.

[3] On the complexity of female motivations see Koch, *Frauenfrage*, esp pp 23ff. Werner, *Pauperes Christi*, pp 53ff compares the role of women in early medieval religious life with their disadvantageous position in feudal society.

Society, theodicy and the origins of medieval heresy

Would it be going too far to speak of a deliberate devaluation of the intercessory function of women in religion?

The most important point, however, is that heresy meant literally opting out: a deliberate rejection of the 'standard cosmology'[1] and the religious organisation with which it was identified. It seems to me, leaving aside ephemeral outbursts of chiliasm which (as professor Frend reminds us)[2] have been a recurrent feature of western Christendom, that there were broadly two types of heresy: one involving not only a new belief-system but also a new life-style, the *vita apostolica*. This meant resolution of theodicy by renewed search for communion, even identification, with the divine through personal commitment to asceticism. Poverty was primarily a means to this end, whatever connotations of economic protest it could later acquire.[3] The second type of heresy afforded a different resolution of the theodicy: Cathar dualism may be seen as a typically sectarian response, combining affirmation of the purity and internal solidarity of a new group with rejection of corrupt external institutions; the gulf between them is mirrored in the cosmic polarity. It is tempting to accept a recent suggestion that Catharism was the 'natural' religion of the twelfth-century Italian *bonne bourgeoisie*:[4] the liturgy was simple; poverty was not prescribed for ordinary adherents; usury was permitted; and bloodshed, glorified by the knightly ethos, was prohibited.

Observe, finally, the 'freezing-effect' in the attitude of the ecclesiastical authorities to heresy from the eleventh century onwards, especially after the Gregorian reform. It seems to me misleading to characterise their earlier attitude as 'relatively liberal'.[5] Without adequate central co-ordination, internal organisation or infrastructure, the early medieval Church had no alternative to accommodation with regard to what our French colleagues term *phénomènes folkloriques*. It was only with the organisation of rural parishes, in few areas effective before the tenth century, that the Church really got to grips with pagan survivals in the

---

[1] M. Chenu, 'Orthodoxie et hérésie', in *Hérésies et Sociétés*, pp 9–14.
[2] In the present volume, above, p 48. See also N. Cohn, *The Pursuit of the Millennium* (rev ed London 1970).
[3] See Chenu, *Nature, Man and Society*, ch VI: 'Monks, Canons, and Laymen in Search of the Apostolic Life', and ch VII: 'The Evangelical Awakening'. Both chastity and poverty seem to me to have been 'natural symbols', in professor Douglas's sense, of personal and social *renovatio*.
[4] Violante, 'Hérésies urbaines', p 185. On dualist cosmology and its social referent, see Douglas, *Natural Symbols*, pp 119ff.
[5] Russell, *Dissent*, p 262.

countryside.[1] One significant index of a new offensive can be seen in the Church's attitude to witchcraft and sorcery, which I suspect were very widely-used instruments of social control in the early Middle Ages. The Church now asserted a monopoly of such instruments, identified witchcraft with heresy and later mobilised the Inquisition against both.[2] How far did heresy, still more perhaps accusations of heresy, replace the function of early medieval witchcraft? This is the sort of question that ecclesiastical historians of the future may be able to answer!

By way of conclusion, I should like to stress three kinds of distinction which underpin the foregoing argument. First, the distinction between primary causes and secondary phenomena: in contrast to the current tendency to regard social conditions merely as the environment of religious change, for example assisting its diffusion, I see social change as primary, generating adaptation in religious systems. But the second distinction is between origins and developments within the process of religious change itself: here the dialectic between 'learned' and 'popular' heresy[3] is crucial, for in the course of its appropriation and elaboration by members of the literate élite, doctrine could assume very different forms and functions from those it originally possessed. It could also be manipulated by powerful adherents to play a directly political role, for instance in the aristocratic Catharism of Languedoc, and thus itself assume causal significance in relation to further political and social change. But I have been concerned with origins rather than

[1] See G. Fournier, 'Rural churches and rural communities in early medieval Auvergne', in Cheyette, *Lordship and Community*, pp 315–40; Fossier, *La Terre et les Hommes en Picardie*, I, pp 167ff (conversion only completed in Carolingian times); and, for indirect evidence, G. Constable, *Monastic Tithes from their Origins to the Twelfth Century* (Cambridge 1964). The differential nature of this development, with parish organisation existing much earlier in some dioceses, is stressed by J. F. Lemarignier, 'Quelques remarques sur l'organisation ecclésiastique de la Gaule du VIIe à la fin du IXe siècle', and the comments thereon of J. Semmler, in *Settimane*, XIII (1966) pp 451–86 and 571ff.

[2] Evidence from medieval sources is presented, though in a rather unsystematic way, by H. C. Lea, *Materials toward a History of Witchcraft*, ed A. C. Howland (New York 1939), and by J. C. Baroja, *The World of the Witches* (London 1964). It is to be hoped that a medievalist will soon study this important subject, despite the gaps in his evidence, with the sensitivity that A. Macfarlane and K. Thomas have recently brought to their researches on witchcraft beliefs in the early modern period. Meanwhile students of medieval heresy can find much food for thought in Douglas, *Natural Symbols*, ch VIII, and in many of the readings in *Witchcraft and Sorcery*, ed M. Marwick (Harmondsworth 1970): in his postscript, for example, the editor draws attention to evidence for the decline of witchcraft beliefs following on urbanisation and differentiation.

[3] See Grundmann, 'Hérésies savantes et Hérésies populaires au Moyen Âge', along with the comments of Le Goff, in *Hérésies et Sociétés*, pp 209–14 and p 216.

with such secondary developments. For I am convinced that even in the case of long-established and highly articulated universal religions like medieval Christianity, with its inbuilt dynamic and propensity to internal evolution, major change is set in motion by 'push factors' operating in the wider society.

Finally, I stress the differential nature and impact of these factors in the diverse social levels and geographical areas of eleventh- and twelfth-century Europe. To accommodate so many variables with so complex an interaction requires extreme finesse in scholarly approach. All I have been able to offer here is a crude, preliminary and highly provisional hypothesis: if it provokes others to supply more convincing answers, it will have served its purpose.

TRADITION AND TEMERITY: PAPAL ATTITUDES TO DEVIANTS, 1159–1216[1]

by BRENDA BOLTON

THE fourth Lateran council of 1215 represented a watershed in the official attitude towards heresy. It marked the end of a period of considerable flexibility and real experiment in dealing with dissident movements. For nearly sixty years, the Church had been seeking possible solutions to the problems posed by the formation of new religious groups which not only deviated in various ways from orthodox belief but which also failed to conform to accepted social patterns within the christian community. Tradition and temerity were two elements in papal policy at this time. The tentative developments of the pontificate of Alexander III were given positive direction by the energetic actions of Innocent III who examined some of these groups to find a way by which they might be contained within the Church and thus allowed to fulfil their vocation. But at the same time, the Church was becoming institutionalised and its framework more rigid. The freedom of manoeuvre of the pope was limited. The episcopate and the regular orders saw Innocent's actions as inimical to the hier-archical structure of the Church and, therefore, brought the whole weight of traditional opinion and influence to bear against the continua-tion of such policies.

Before 1215, several groups had presented themselves to the Curia. In 1162, some Flemings came to Alexander III at Tours[2] and Waldes visited him in Rome during the third Lateran council of

---

[1] The most useful secondary works on heresy and the religious movements of this period have been [H.] Grundmann, *Religiöse Bewegungen [im Mittelalter]* (2 ed Hilde-sheim 1961); [H.] Maisonneuve, *[Études sur les] origines de l'Inquisition* (2 ed Paris 1960); [C.] Thouzellier, *Catharisme et Valdéisme [en Languedoc à la fin du xiie siècle]* (2 ed Louvain 1969) and [J.] Le Goff, *Hérésies et sociétés [dans l'Europe pré-industrielle 11–18 siècles]*, École pratique des hautes études: Civilisations et Sociétés, x (Paris 1968) which contains an excellent bibliography. W. Wakefield & A. P. Evans, *Heresies of the High Middle Ages* (New York 1969), present a selection of translated sources. Mr John Gillingham, Dr F. D. Logan, Dr Janet Nelson and Dr Colin Tite have read this paper at different stages and my most sincere thanks is due to them for their critical and helpful sugges-tions.

[2] [M.] Bouquet, *Recueil [des historiens des Gaules et de la France]*, xv (Paris 1808) pp 790, 792, 799; *PL*, 200 (1855) col 187.

1179.[1] The *Humiliati* of Lombardy came to Innocent III in 1199,[2] seeking recognition of their way of life, and in the same year the evidence of the laymen and women of Metz was heard.[3] In 1208, Durand de Huesca and his followers made a profession of faith.[4] Both Bernard Prim and Francis of Assisi sought Innocent's approval in 1210[5] and details of a penitential community at Elne were investigated in 1212.[6]

A major problem for the Curia was to establish the distinction between heresy and disobedience. The sectarian movement contained two essentially dissimilar elements which demanded different treatment. The Cathars were automatically excluded from the Church, for their beliefs were clearly contrary to christian doctrine.[7] Missionaries were sent to convert them, codes of repressive legislation foreshadowing the Inquisition were enforced and, when these measures showed little or no result, appeal to temporal power was made and crusade preached against them. On the other hand, there were those communities which were formulating new ways of life by attempting to apply the evangelical precept of voluntary poverty.[8] Such groups hovered on the border between heterodoxy and orthodoxy. Could lay preaching organised from an independent centre, be tolerated within the framework of an institutional Church? This was the main point at issue. Separation from the Church was a gradual process. A refusal to submit

---

1 *Chronicon Universale Anonymi Laudunensis,* [ed A. Cartellieri et W. Stechèle] (Paris 1909) pp 28–30; Walter Map, *De Nugis Curialium,* [ed M. R. James], I, xxxi, *Anecdota Oxoniensia,* Medieval and Modern Series, xiv (Oxford 1914) pp 60–2.

2 *PL*, 214 (1855) col 921; G. Tiraboschi, *V[etera] H[umiliatorum] M[onumenta]* (Milan 1766–8) II, p 139.

3 *PL*, 214 (1855) cols 695–9; *PL*, 216 (1855) cols 1210–14.

4 *PL*, 215 (1855) cols 1510–14; Potthast I, nos 3571–3, p 308.

5 *PL*, 216 (1855) cols 289–93; Potthast I, nos 4014, 4015, p 346. On Francis's visit to Rome see Grundmann, *Religiöse Bewegungen,* p 127 note 111 and p 132 note 116.

6 *PL*, 216 (1855) col 601; Potthast I, no 4505, p 389.

7 There is a very clear account of cathar beliefs in S. Runciman, *The Medieval Manichee. A Study of the Christian Dualist Heresy* (Cambridge 1947). See also A. Borst, *Die Katharer, MGH* SS, xii (Stuttgart 1953).

8 Some of the problems which such groups experienced are dealt with by M. D. Chenu, 'Moines, clercs, laïcs au carrefour de la vie évangelique [au xiie siècle]', *RHE,* xlix (1954) pp 59–89. See [M.] Maccarrone, 'Riforma e sviluppo della vita religiosa [con Innocenzo III]', *R[ivista di storia della] C[hiesa in] I[talia],* xvi (Rome 1962) pp 29–72 for an account of Innocent III's interest in religious movements and C. Violante, 'Hérésies urbaines et rurales en Italie du 11e au 13e siècle' in Le Goff, *Hérésies et sociétés,* pp 171–97 who attempts an analysis of the movement towards the *vita apostolica.* Also valuable is the volume 'Movimenti religiosi popolari ed eresie del Medioevo', *Relazioni del X Congresso internazionale di scienze storiche Roma 4–11 sett. 1955,* III; *Storia del Medioevo* (Florence 1955) pp 305–541: see R. Morghen, 'Movimenti religiosi popolari nel periodo della riforma della chiesa', pp 333–56; H. Grundmann, 'Eresie e nuovi ordini religiosi nel secolo xii', pp 357–402. Also Grundmann, *Religiöse Bewegungen,* pp 503–13.

to the decisions of the ecclesiastical authorities brought condemnation of the minority while complete submission usually guaranteed a degree of toleration. As these movements proliferated after 1159, the papacy began to recognise that their essential aims were orthodox in principle and attempted to discriminate between such groups and others which rejected outright the priesthood and sacraments of the Church.

The Church's response to the spread of heresy was not simply one of negative repression but a positive attempt to set its own house in order and to meet the requirements of some dissident lay groups by purifying itself. Deviants of all kinds struck a note of simplicity beside the opulence of the hierarchical and elitist prelates. In Languedoc especially, few bishops could command a fraction of the respect given to the Cathar leaders, either for the purity of their lives or for the force of their preaching and the *vita apostolica* of the evangelical groups provided an equally sharp contrast. In 1179 and 1184 papal injunctions specifically warned the bishops to be much more rigorous in their own behaviour and in their attitude to visitation.[1] They were rich, idle and passive. Innocent, rebuking them for their inability to preach, called them 'dumb dogs who don't know how to bark'.[2] Some were merely incompetent but others subscribed to heretical beliefs themselves. Several bishops were in fact removed from their sees.[3]

The ignorance of the lower clergy posed an active problem at a time when there was an increasing demand from the laity for a really effective preaching programme. It was strongly felt that argument and

[1] Caps III and IV Lateran III in *Conciliorum Oecumenicorum Decreta* [ed J. Alberigo *et al*] (2 ed Freiburg 1962) pp 188–9; Mansi XXII, cols 491–2.

[2] Isa. 56: 10. Innocent might well have been referring to Pons d'Arsac, deposed in 1181 by the cardinal of Albano because he was too feeble to enforce measures against heretics, [C.] Devic and [J.] Vaissète, [*Histoire du Languedoc,*] VI (Toulouse 1879) p 5. During his own pontificate, the bishop of Fréjus was declared incapable in October 1198, *PL*, 214 (1855) col 374 and Otto of Carcassone, who was senile, was removed from his diocese in December 1198, *PL*, 214 (1855) cols 457–8.

[3] In December 1203 the bishop of Toulouse was deposed: *PL*, 217 (1855) col 159; in February 1204 the bishop of Béziers was accused of associating with heretics and was deprived: *PL*, 215 (1855) cols 272–3; in June 1204 Peter, bishop of Vence, was removed for his scandalous behaviour: 'quoniam igitur putridi dentes executiendi sunt de faucibus ecclesiae', *PL*, 215 (1855) cols 366–8; in April 1211 the archbishop of Auch was deposed: *PL*, 216 (1855) col 283; together with the bishop of Rodez: *PL*, 216 (1855) cols 408–9. But the most notorious and most difficult to deal with was Berengar, archbishop of Narbonne, illegitimate son of Raymond Berengar, count of Barcelona. In May 1207 an attempt was made to remove him: *PL*, 215 (1855) cols 1164–5; Potthast I, no 3113, p 265; but he was not finally deposed until 1211 or 1213: Devic and Vaissète, VI, p 137. On Italian heretical bishops see A. Dondaine, 'La hiérarchie cathare en Italie', A[rchivium] F[ratrum] P[raedicatorum], XIX (Rome 1949) pp 280–312.

biblical exposition would bring the stray sheep to see their error and no opportunity was lost to engage heretics in disputation. Groups of learned men were authorised to visit Toulouse to confront the Cathars as early as 1165 but they were booed, denounced as apostates or simply ignored.[1] Roland of Daventry acted as arbiter in a discussion of the position of the hierarchy and the nature of preaching in which both Catholics and heretics participated.[2] Alexander III approved the mission of Henry of Clairvaux to Toulouse in 1178 and empowered him to preach.[3] The Cistercian order was once again mobilised and was invited to transform itself into a preaching order. In 1204, the bull *Etsi nostri navicula* confirmed the legation of Renier de Ponza, Guy, Peter de Castelnau, Raoul de Fontfroide and Arnald-Amaury, abbot of Cîteaux and instructed them to convert by preaching and example *in opere et sermone* and to allow nothing in their actions to provoke 'the reprobation of a heretic'.[4] By 1206, however, the Cistercians were ready to return to the cloister. They hesitated to arrogate exclusively to themselves the function of preaching and they found it difficult to fulfil the provision of absolute poverty.

But by this time, Innocent had harnessed what he felt might be an effective new method of evangelism. Diego of Osma and Dominic had been diverted to aid the Cistercians in Languedoc.[5] The one hope of conversion, it was felt, lay in a demonstration of equal austerity and purity of life. The Mendicants were to live like the heretics but teach like the Church. By the example of their conduct and their skill in words, they were to recall the heretic from error. But in the long run, these missionary activities were only partially successful. The attempts at dialogue with the heretics were of little avail and Dominic's preaching was poorly supported by the local clergy. The conversion of Durand de Huesca and his followers was perhaps Dominic's chief success at

---

[1] Devic and Vaissète, VI, p 5; Maisonneuve, *Origines de l'Inquisition*, pp 127–9.

[2] *Ibid* pp 136–7. See also A. Dondaine, 'Les actes du concile albigeois de Saint-Félix de Caraman', *Miscellanea Giovanni Mercati* V, *Studi e Testi*, 125 (Vatican City 1946) pp 324–55.

[3] *PL*, 204 (1855) cols 223–5; Maisonneuve, *Origines de l'Inquisition*, p 132 note 224; Thouzellier, *Catharisme et Valdéisme*, pp 19–23. See also Y. M. J. Congar, 'Henry de Marcy, abbé de Clairvaux, cardinal-évêque d'Albano et légat pontifical', *SA* (1958) pp 1–38. Other letters about this mission are printed in *PL*, 204 (1855) cols 235–42 and *PL*, 199 (1855) cols 1120–4.

[4] *PL*, 215 (1855) cols 355–60; *Potthast* I, no 2229, p 192.

[5] *PL*, 215 (1855) cols 1024–5. C. Thouzellier, 'La pauvreté, arme contre l'albigéisme, en 1206', *Révue de l'histoire des religions*, CLI (Paris 1957) pp 79–92.

this time.[1] Thereby the Poor Catholics were disengaged from the laity and yet contained within the Church.

Alexander III introduced Bolognese doctrine into the Church and took from it his ideas on the treatment of heretics. They were to be pursued, not in order to burn them but to bring them back to orthodoxy. Any punishment was to be carried out in a spirit of charity rather than vengeance. Penalties of a medicinal nature, such as exile, the confiscation of goods and even excommunication, were aimed at isolating the heretic and *thus* compelling him to recognise his error and return to the fold.[2] Yet attitudes towards those who were doctrinal deviants were beginning to harden. The Councils of Montpellier 1162 and Tours 1163 enacted severe measures against the Cathars in Languedoc.[3] The secular princes were reminded of their duty, *vis coactiva*, towards the Church on pain of anathema. Clerics were urged to do their duty by enquiring into personal beliefs and by encouraging the denunciation of heretics by the laity. In 1178, an inquisitorial tribunal under Henry of Clairvaux functioned in the county of Toulouse, a mission which Alexander regarded as equal in importance to his projected crusade to the Holy Land.[4] The third Lateran council of 1179 empowered the bishops to levy troops and to issue indulgences as if for a crusade against the infidel.[5] Deviation from the basic tenets of the Church and the refusal to swear an oath were standard marks of heresy but on the questions of preaching and voluntary poverty, papal policy was still to be formulated. In 1162, a group of Flemings, accused of heresy by the archbishop of Rheims, came to seek a papal judgement on their case.[6] They may have felt that this was less well-defined and, therefore, less severe than that which they might expect to receive from Louis VII. Although there is evidence that they had access to a considerable sum of money, their way of life was undoubtedly praiseworthy and they refuted the accusation of heresy when they presented themselves to the pope. Alexander wrote that he received them *with asperity* but

---

[1] *PL*, 215 (1855) cols 1510–14.

[2] 'Ut solatio saltem humanitatis amisso ab errore viae suae respiscere compellantur', Cap XXIII, Council of Tours. Mansi XXI, col 1178; Maisonneuve, *Origines de l'Inquisition*, p 127 note 198.

[3] Mansi XXI, cols 1159–60 and cols 1177–8; Maisonneuve, *Origines de l'Inquisition*, p 126.

[4] *Ibid* p 133.

[5] Cap XXVII Lateran III in *Conciliorum Oecumenicorum Decreta*, pp 200–1.

[6] Bouquet, *Recueil*, xv, 790, 792, 799. I am indebted to Mr Robert Moore for allowing me to see his translations of these texts in proof-copy. Alexander III's position was difficult. The archbishop of Rheims was Louis VII's brother while the pope was merely an exile in France, dependent for help and recognition upon the French king.

his attitude softened when he saw how earnest was their desire to have the matter sorted out, not in Rheims, but in the Curia. He instructed the archbishop to investigate the Flemings' case carefully – with the help of *religiosi viri*—and declared that he would then give judgement. Meanwhile they themselves were not to be molested and their property was to be guaranteed. The outcome of their request is unknown but Alexander's attitude towards them is interesting. He warned the archbishop of Rheims that it was better to absolve the guilty than to condemn the innocent and advised him not to be overscrupulous in his examination of heretics.[1] Alexander was obviously dissatisfied with episcopal judgement alone, and in a letter of 1170 to the archbishops of Rheims, Bourges, Tours and Rouen suggested that 'wise and religious men' should also participate in such decisions.[2]

In 1179, Alexander was visited by Waldes whose popular preaching and translations of the gospels *in vulgari* had reached the attention of the archbishop of Lyons.[3] Waldes and his followers wanted papal recognition and felt that the episcopal ban imposed on them, contradicted the biblical admonition to preach and live an apostolic life. Alexander responded warmly to Waldes's voluntary renunciation of property and approved his way of life. The translations, which were submitted to the Curia for inspection, were tested neither for accuracy nor for orthodoxy but the right to preach was made dependent on theological examination. The Waldenses were declared deficient in their understanding of doctrine and Alexander refused to grant them the right to preach *unless asked to do so by priests*.[4] This was virtually an unconditional ban since preaching was strictly forbidden to all save those specifically ordained or commissioned.[5] Walter Map, who carried out the examination, was presumably one of those *religious men* whom the

---

[1] 'Scire autem debet tuae discretionis prudentia quia cautius et minus malum est nocentes et condemnatos absolvere quam vitam innocentiam severitate ecclesiastica condemnare', *PL*, 200 (1855) col 187.

[2] 'Quia negligentiae praelatorum Ecclesiae posset attribui, si non curarent evellere quae sunt ab universis fidelibus penitus resecanda', *PL*, 200 (1855) cols 684–5; Bouquet, *Recueil*, xv, 888; *Jaffé*, no 11809, p 237. The *religiosi viri* were by no means necessarily churchmen.

[3] Guichard, a cistercian monk and archbishop of Lyons 1165–81. Thouzellier, *Catharisme et Valdéisme*, p 17. *Chronicon Universale Anonymi Laudunensis*, p 28.

[4] 'Nisi rogantibus sacerdotibus', *ibid* p 29. The scriptural justification is to be found in Rom. 10: 15 'Quomodo praedicabunt, nisi mittantur?' and was used by St Bernard in his Toulouse campaign: *PL*, 182 (1854) col 436.

[5] For a discussion of this prohibition see Grundmann, *Religiöse Bewegungen*, p 64. See also B. Marthaler, 'Forerunners of the Franciscans: the Waldenses', *Franciscan Studies*, xviii (New York 1958) pp 133–42; A. Dondaine, 'Aux origines du Valdéisme: Une profession de foi de Valdès', *AFP*, xvi (1946) pp 231–2.

bishops called in to aid them.[1] He was scornful of these *idiotae et illiterati* who believed themselves called to preach and rejected their arrogant mendicity. They had tampered with scriptural dynamite by using written translations which would persist for use by others. This represented a tremendous threat to tradition: in the last resort, the interests of the pope were not separate from those of the secular clergy and Alexander did nothing to contain Waldes within the Church.

In 1184, with the support of the emperor, Lucius III agreed to take radical and severe measures against all forms of heresy. The decretal *ab abolendam* may be seen as the first attempt to define the official attitude to manifest dissent.[2] A whole group of heretics listed as Cathars, Patarines, *Humiliati* or those falsely named Poor of Lyons, Passagians, Josephines and Arnaldists were indiscriminately anathematised. Two distinct groups of deviants are mentioned: the first are those who have arrogated to themselves the right to preach either publicly or privately without papal authorisation; and the second, those who have taught doctrines contrary to the Catholic Church on sacramental questions. As a result of the decretal, Waldes and his followers were not strictly speaking heretics but anathematised schismatics. Judgement was made not on their doctrines but on their tenacious *contumacia*.[3] They would not observe the proscription on preaching and had lapsed into disobedience. Yet they, and other groups, remained impenitent, certain of their apostolic vocation and their right to represent the true Christian Church. Other provisions of the decretal declared that clerics were to be degraded and handed over to the secular power if they themselves were found to subscribe to heretical beliefs or to know of the existence of heretics. Bishops who did not publish these penalties were to be suspended for three years. Three respectable people in each diocese were to denounce, on oath to their bishop, those who held secret conventicles or who differed in their way of life from the faithful. For the first time, regular *inquisitiones* were to be held and the guilty punished by the secular power according to the *animaversio debita*.[4]

Innocent III's attitude to heresy was drawn from both imperial and

---

[1] Walter Map *c* 1140–*c* 1208. *De Nugis Curialium*, pp 60–2. See also Grundmann, *Religiöse Bewegungen*, pp 64–5 for a critical view of Map's beliefs.

[2] Mansi XXII, cols 476–8; *PL*, 201 (1855) cols 1297–1300. C. Thouzellier, 'La répression de l'hérésie et les débuts de l'Inquisition', in A. Fliche et V. Martin, *Histoire de l'Eglise*, X (Paris 1950) pp 291–340. Maisonneuve, *Origines de l'Inquisition*, pp 151–5.

[3] Thouzellier, *Catharisme et Valdéisme*, p 46.

[4] Maisonneuve, *Origines de l'Inquisition*, p 154.

canonical tradition. In 1199, in the decretal *vergentis in senium*, addressed to the clergy and people of Viterbo, heresy was for the first time equated with treason.[1] Thus the confiscation of lands and goods was radical and final and the heirs of the heretics, even if they themselves were orthodox, were totally and perpetually disinherited. But like Alexander III, Innocent showed that he could be merciful. 'When those isolated desire reconciliation with the Church and when temporal punishment corrects those untouched by spiritual punishment, then to these converted people will be restored civil and political rights and also their goods'.[2] Only after 1208 was the spiritual sword cast aside, 'iron was to conquer those whom persuasion would not convince' and the obdurate heretics of Languedoc were given up to the envious lords of northern France.[3] The radical departure from traditional theory stemmed not only from the revived study of Roman law but also from the unitary, theocratic conception of christian society towards which the papacy tended.

Innocent III possessed a breadth of vision which enabled him to put into perspective the problem of the rapidly increasing number of dissident groups. He attempted to contain several such movements by fairly consistent procedures, some of which develop from those used by his predecessor, Alexander. He asked these groups to present *proposita* or short statements to indicate their willingness to devote themselves to lives of christian piety. He set up commissions, usually of three men drawn from the regular and secular orders, to investigate this evidence. While the inquiries were proceeding, the bishops were warned to cease penalties against these groups and to protect their goods and property. Permission to preach was granted on definite terms and under episcopal licence and, whenever appropriate, these movements were placed in some sort of rule. Innocent seems to have regarded previous episcopal policies as too severe. He urged his bishops to act like doctors. Mere diagnosis of the symptoms was insufficient; effective treatment of each case was urged whether by the amputation of a malignant limb to save the body or by the soothing of wounds, though with oil not wine. Innocent, like Alexander, urged that the

---

[1] For elucidation on this point see W. Ullman, 'The significance of Innocent III's decretal *Vergentis*', in *Etudes d'histoire du droit canonique dediées à G. Le Bras*, I (Paris 1965) pp 729–41.

[2] Maisonneuve, *Origines de l'Inquisition*, p 157 note 37.

[3] 'Ideoque, cum ferro abscidenda sint vulnera quae fomentorum non sentiunt medicinam et qui correctionem ecclesiasticam vilipendunt brachio sint saecularis potentiae comprimendi, auxilium tuum...invocandum duximus'; *PL*, 215 (1855) cols 1246–8; *Potthast* I, no 3223, p 275; Thouzellier, *Catharisme et Valdéisme*, pp 204–12.

guilty should be acquitted rather than that the innocent should be condemned, and warned his bishops that they would turn piety into heresy by harsh and precipitate action.[1] A way back into the Church was to be opened for those unwillingly or unjustly excluded.

In 1199, Innocent wrote to the bishop of Verona ordering him to cease discrimination against the *Humiliati* and to give them absolution if they were prepared to acknowledge their error and to submit to papal authority.[2] He declared himself unable to grant their request for official recognition without considerable thought and investigation since their way of life was so different from that followed by any existing religious community. A commission composed of two cistercian abbots and one bishop was set up to examine them and reported favourably.[3] The *Humiliati* were given permission to preach as long as they avoided theological questions and dealt only with exhortations to a pious and earnest life. Innocent showed flexibility by retaining the essential form of their movement, yet disciplined and regulated them so that they could be reabsorbed into the Church.[4]

But it was more difficult to find a place for the followers of Waldes. They were wandering preachers, widely dispersed, who basically rejected Church organisation and believed that the right to preach and administer the sacraments was based on *meritum* and not on *ordo* or *officium*.[5] The best that Innocent could do was to deal with the individual groups of Waldenses which came to him and to treat each case on merit.

In 1199, a group of laymen and women in Metz was accused of reading from a French translation of the Scriptures and of disobedience to their bishop.[6] Innocent's attitude to them was similar to that of Alexander towards Waldes. He approved of their desire to understand the Scriptures and acknowledged that they were not entirely uninformed but pointed out the depth of meaning of the texts which not even learned men could understand. He emphasised that the Church possessed doctors specially charged to preach whose function the

---

[1] 'Quia vero non est nostrae intentionis innoxios cum nocentibus condemnare', *PL*, 214 (1855) col 789.

[2] *Ibid* col 789.

[3] The cistercian abbots of Lodi and Cerreto and the bishop of Vercelli: *PL*, 214 (1855) col 922; *VHM*, II, p 136.

[4] On the *Humiliati* see L. Zanoni, *Gli Umiliati nei loro rapporto con l'eresia, l'industria della lana ed i communi nei secoli xii e xiii*, Biblioteca historica italia, Serie II, 2 (Milan 1911); H. Grundmann, *Religiöse Bewegungen* especially pp 70–97 and pp 487–538 and my article 'Innocent III's treatment of the *Humiliati*' in *SCH*, VIII (1971) pp 73–82.

[5] Grundmann, *Religiöse Bewegungen*, p 95 and note 46.

[6] *PL*, 214 (1855) cols 695–9; *PL*, 216 (1855) cols 1210–14; *Potthast* I, no 781; Grundmann, *Religiöse Bewegungen*, pp 97–100.

laity had no right to usurp.[1] Although he disapproved of their conventicles and ideas on the priesthood, Innocent sensed that to act peremptorily might weaken the faith of these simple people.[2] He refused to judge them before he possessed all the facts of the case as he could not tell whether the matter centred on a slight error in faith or in notorious doctrinal differences.[3] The bishop of Metz was instructed to inquire into the authorship and intention of the biblical translations, the beliefs of those who read them and the teachings of these people. Finally he was to ask whether due respect was shown for the pope and the Church. The bishop reported the continued disobedience of the Metz sectaries but Innocent still felt that he possessed insufficient evidence and again turned to a commission for advice.[4] Three cistercian abbots declared the writings heretical and apparently the books were burned.[5] In this case, Innocent was attempting to establish the *distinctio* between believers and irrevocable heretics. He gave the Metz sectaries a fair chance but, as in the case of Waldes in 1179, written translations and the rejection of the priesthood could not be tolerated by the hierarchy.

In 1208, Durand de Huesca, a former Waldensian, and his companions received official confirmation of their *propositum conversationis*.[6] Innocent praised their work as mendicant preachers but pointed out that the Church could make no concessions on certain points. The fundamental conditions for the existence of the Poor Catholics were that their members should accept the validity of the hierarchical Church and that they should recognise the sacraments which could only be administered by an officially ordained priest, irrespective of his worth.[7] While accepting these conditions, the Poor Catholics gave up few of their former tenets and habits. They could live in voluntary poverty and could preach as a community as long as they conceded that this was linked with their specific papal commission. The Poor Catholics soon met with hostility from the hierarchy. Innocent warned the

---

[1] *PL*, 214 (1855) cols 697; Potthast I, no 780.

[2] 'Sic *enervari* non debet religiosa simplicitas', *PL*, 214 (1855) col 699.

[3] *Ibid* col 699. Innocent recognised that the Metz sectaries were erudite men and appreciated their *scientia*.

[4] This commission was composed of the abbots of Cîteaux, La Crête and Morimond; *PL*, 214 (1855) cols 793-6.

[5] 'Item in urbe Metensi pullulante secta quae dicitur Valdensium, directi sunt quidam abbates ad praedicandum, qui quosdam libros de latino in romanum versos combusserant et praedictam sectam extirpaverunt', Aubry de Trois Fontaines, *Chronicon*, *MGH* SS xxiii (Hanover 1874) p 878.

[6] *PL*, 215 (1855) cols 1510-14; Potthast I, nos 3571-3, p 308.

[7] Grundmann, *Religiöse Bewegungen*, pp 107-8.

archbishops of Narbonne and Tarragona to act charitably towards them[1] and informed Durand de Huesca of the complaints against him.[2] In spite of Innocent's support, the Poor Catholics did not survive long in the face of this essentially parochial prejudice. In 1210, Innocent accused his bishops of driving people away from the Church by their severity, a warning reminiscent of that made by Alexander III.[3]

In 1210, Bernard Prim undertook to obey papal and episcopal authority and assured Innocent that he and his group of lay penitents would behave respectfully towards the Church.[4] He promised to defend the Church vigorously *usque ad animam et sanguinem* against all heretical sects and to try to prevent simple believers from becoming hardened heretics. His *propositum* was confirmed in 1212.[5] In the same year, a penitential community at Elne was to be approved if the bishop of Elne could guarantee purity of belief among its members.[6]

When Francis came to the Curia in 1210, Innocent had to formulate his attitude to a movement which, like others, was developing in response to the spiritual needs of the time but which, unlike the Waldenses and the *Humiliati*, had not been accused of disobedience.[7] Whereas in the case of the more developed movements, he had asked for evidence and had called upon outside advice, Innocent decided to wait and see what form the new community might take. Francis had already indicated his unwillingness to accept an existing rule but he was allowed to continue on the condition that he and his companions, tonsured like clerks, promised to be 'in all things obedient to the Holy See'. Innocent granted him oral permission to preach and allowed him to transmit this right individually to each brother.[8]

In 1215, the Lateran council stated its attitude towards heresy quite

---

[1] *PL*, 216 (1855) cols 73–4.

[2] *Ibid* cols 75–7.

[3] 'nolentes, sicut etiam nec velle debemus, ut qui trahi gratia divina creduntur, per duritiam vestram ab infinita Dei misericordia repellantur', *ibid* cols 274–5.

[4] *PL*, 216 (1855) cols 289–93; Potthast I, nos 4014, 4015, p 346.

[5] *PL*, 216 (1855) cols 648–50; Potthast I, no 4567, p 394.

[6] 'sub disciplina et visitatione catholicorum pauperum permansuri', *PL*, 216 (1855) cols 601–2; *Potthast* I. no 4505, p 389.

[7] Grundmann, *Religiöse Bewegungen*, pp 127–35. The question of Francis's acceptance by the Holy See is dealt with by T. Manteuffel, 'Naissance d'une hérésie', in Le Goff, *Hérésies et sociétés*, pp 97–103 especially p 99. He attributes to Innocent III the credit for the farsighted and flexible policy adopted towards Francis and his followers. The crucial issue was that of obedience to the Holy See. Francis not only had episcopal support but had also submitted to the decisions of the ecclesiastical authorities.

[8] Grundmann, *Religiöse Bewegungen*, p 133 notes 117 and 118.

unequivocally.[1] Catholic doctrine had become increasingly well-defined as it was defended against the challenge of dissident groups. Henceforth dogma was to be the criterion for distinguishing between orthodox belief and heresy. All heretics were to be condemned '...no matter by what names they are known: they may have different faces but they are all tied together by their tails since they are united by their emptiness'.[2] The creation of new religious orders was banned and founders of new religious houses were to accept the rule of an approved order.[3] This proscription was justified on the grounds that too great a differentiation of orders would cause confusion in the Church. The council, therefore, presented little in the way of choice to those who deviated. They could either return to the fold or suffer persecution. These decisions were totally at variance with the earlier policies of Innocent. Two forces militated against him. On the one hand were the bishops and prelates who saw not only their pastoral rights but their purses threatened and on the other were the Cistercians and representatives of the traditional, regular orders who thought their rules sufficient for anyone truly seeking sanctity.

Since 1159 then, the Church had been continuously assessing the various measures by which it could deal with deviants. It had attempted definite reform rather than purely negative repression and had ordered its clergy to live and preach on the same terms as the heretics. It had contained some groups like the *Humiliati* and the Poor Catholics by setting up commissions to investigate belief and practice and had reversed the anathema of 1184 which had forced them into heresy. Finally it had taken measures against those like Waldes and the Metz sectaries who were not prepared to enter on official terms. In the process, it had emerged, almost incidentally, with its doctrines defined and

[1] There is no evidence of the names of individual bishops at the council or of their attitudes towards heresy but 'A new eye-witness account of the Fourth Lateran Council', Stephan Kuttner and Antonio García y García, *Traditio*, xx (New York 1964) pp 115–78 especially lines 168–78 p 128 shows Innocent III in a very human light, making sarcastic remarks and ordering Siegfried, archbishop of Mainz, to sit down three times in the course of one session.

[2] Caps I and III, Lateran IV in *Conciliorum Oecumenicorum Decreta*, pp 206–7, 209–11. Translated by B. Pullan, *Sources for the History of Medieval Europe* (Oxford 1966) p 91.

[3] Cap XIII, Lateran IV in *Conciliorum Oecumenicorum Decreta*, p 218. See also Maccarrone, 'Riforma e sviluppo della vita religiosa', *RCI*, xvi (1962) pp 60–9. Grundmann, *Religiöse Bewegungen*, pp 135–56 discusses Innocent III's reaction to the Council's decision and attempts to trace the means whereby the Franciscans became an approved order without adopting a recognised rule as required. Innocent seems to have taken steps to ensure their survival and papal protection was willingly granted to them in return for their obedience to the Holy See.

redefined. In 1215, after almost sixty years' experience in the formulation of different approaches to heretics, the Church had to decide on one particular policy and one particular path. Which direction would it take? It took the most traditional way and reversed those policies which seemed to create a dangerous precedent. Innocent III's temerity was not tolerated by the hierarchy which had continually expressed resentment against repentant heretics. The bishops saw their teaching and preaching authority under attack and knew that it was only possible for the Church to survive by keeping to the rules. Tradition triumphed. After 1215, the structure of the Church became too rigid to contain the contemporary phenomena of new religious groups and such spontaneous movements were, like the non-christian heresies, placed almost inevitably outside the communion of the Church.

HERESY AND LEARNING IN EARLY CISTERCIANISM

by DEREK BAKER

IN 1245 the General Chapter of the Cistercian Order gave reluctant approval to the establishment of a house of studies at Paris,[1] and in so doing sanctioned a major breach with the traditions and practice of the Order. The new house grew rapidly. Accorded papal protection in 1246, it was already necessary to move to a more extensive site a year later. By 1250 student monks had been admitted to the new buildings of the Chardonnet, and, though its constitution continued to be the subject of capitular legislation, the new house was fully established, under the jurisdiction of the abbot of Clairvaux, but as a centre of studies for the whole Order. In January 1256, ten years after the decision of the General Chapter, Guy, abbot of l'Aumône, became the first cistercian to incept in theology and to receive the licence to teach.[2]

The background to this remarkable volte-face was, of course, the organisation and development of higher studies in university centres in the thirteenth century, and the rapid establishment of the mendicants at these centres. In this process monks played no part. Their schools, increasingly isolated with the rise of the secular cathedral schools in

---

[1] [J. M.] Canivez, [*Statuta Capitulorum Generalium Ordinis Cisterciensis, ab anno 1116 ad annum 1786,*] 8 vols (Louvain 1933–41) II, p 290. The same Chapter had approved the establishment of local and provincial *studia* – 'Ut in singulis abbatiis Ordinis nostri, in quibus abbates habere potuerint vel voluerint, habeatur studium, ita quod ad minus in singulis provinciis provideatur abbatia una in qua habeatur studium theologiae...Ad dictas abbatias mittere poterunt de monachis suis quos ad hoc magis idoneos viderint, ita tamen quod ad id compelli non poterunt quibus facultas deerit vel voluntas...' *Ibid* pp 289–90.

[2] For the development of cistercian studies, and the part played in it by Stephen of Lexington, see [C. H.] Lawrence, ['Stephen of Lexington and Cistercian University Studies in the thirteenth Century'], *JEH*, XI, 2 (1960) pp 164–78; [B.] Griesser, ['Registrum Epistolarum Stephani de Lexinton'], *ASOC*, II (1946) pp 1–118, VIII (1952) pp 181–378; [J. A.] Watt, [*The Church and the two Nations in medieval Ireland*] (Cambridge 1970) pp 85–107; [Derek] Baker, 'Sancta rusticitas [and docta iustitia'], *Ampleforth Journal*, LXXVII, 2 (1972); J.-B. Mahn, *Le Pape Benoit XII et les Cisterciens* (Paris 1944); [C. H.] Talbot, [*Letters from the English Abbots to the Chapter at Cîteaux, 1442–1521,*] *Cam. S*, 4th series, IV (1967). On Guy of l'Aumône see P. Michaud-Quantin, 'Guy de l'Aumône, premier maître cistercien de l'université de Paris', *ASOC*, XV (1959) pp 194–219.

the twelfth century, had become irrelevant to the pursuit of higher education, and the recruits of ability whom they had continued to attract into the early thirteenth century were now turning to the mendicants. Monastic reaction and concern is well-expressed by the abbots of the English black monk houses meeting in Chapter.[1] They make it explicitly plain that they are desperately concerned to rival the mendicants, and to stay in touch with academic developments, and in their anxiety are prepared to consider a radical revision of their observance in order to encourage study and the studious.[2] This is a theme which runs through the great controversies of the fourteenth century, and persists until the end of the Middle Ages. In the later fifteenth century Marmaduke Huby,[3] the greatest of the later English cistercians, can be found pressing forward the completion of the cistercian college at Oxford against constant reference to the scandal caused by its incompleteness, and to the invidious comparison of cistercian incompetence and mendicant success – 'Behold,' they say, 'these men began to build sixty years ago, and they are not able to finish, or else, led astray by false desire, they do not wish to.'[4]

For all their great traditions of scholarship, however, and in spite of their concern at their increasing intellectual isolation, it was not the black monks who first associated themselves directly with the new developments in the thirteenth century, but the cistercians. This surprising initiative has generally, and rightly, been associated with the career of Stephen of Lexington,[5] and without his energy it is doubtful if the Chardonnet would have been established at all.

The main outline of his career is well-known. Born in Northampton-shire, and taking his name from the modern Laxton, Stephen of Lexington was early destined for a career as one of those 'sublime and lettered persons' to whom the twenty-ninth decree of the fourth Lateran council referred.[6] He studied Arts at Paris; was a prebendary of Southwell in 1215, and not long afterwards returned to the schools to study theology under Edmund of Abingdon at Oxford.[7] There, as

---

[1] For discussion of the institution and development of these Chapters see [David Knowles, The] R[eligious] O[rders in England], I (Cambridge 1948) pp 9–27; [W. A.] Pantin, [Chapters of the English Black Monks 1215–1540, Cam. S, 3rd Series, XLV, XLVIII, LIV (1931–7).

[2] See the constitutions of 1277, Pantin I, particularly pp 64–5, 75.

[3] For Huby see the references in Talbot; RO, III (1959) pp 28–38; Memorials [of the Abbey of St Mary of Fountains], I, ed J. R. Walbran, SS, XLII (1863) pp 151, 155, 221, 230, 231, 235, 239, 240, 242, 277, 281, 325, 349, 422.

[4] Talbot, no 34 (1482), see also Baker, 'Sancta rusticitas'.

[5] See above, p 93, n 2.   [6] Mansi XXII, col 1017.   [7] See Lawrence p 167.

the dominican Robert Bacon relates,[1] his career took a dramatic turn: he was one of the seven brands plucked from the burning by the abbot of Quarr and, probably in 1221, he entered the Cistercian Order. As so often, however, conversion seems to have furthered rather than stunted his career. Abbot of Stanley as early as 1223, he was entrusted with visitation of the Irish monasteries of the Order four years later.[2] His success in coping with the *conspiratio Mellifontis*, and his reorganisation of the Irish houses, paved the way to his election to Savigny in 1229. Thirteen years later, in 1242, he was elected abbot of Clairvaux, a post he held until his controversial deposition in 1256.[3] He died two years later, frustrating, it seems, a papal proposal to appoint him to the archdiocese of York, vacant on the death of Sewall de Bovill.[4]

Stephen of Lexington's thirty-five years as a cistercian were full of activity and controversy, but his most signal achievement was the establishment of cistercian university studies. A product of the schools himself he was convinced of the value of higher studies. In 1228 he had ordered the Irish abbots to send their postulants to Paris or Oxford[5] to receive a rudimentary education, remarking in a letter to the abbot of Clairvaux 'how can a man be a lover of the cloister or of books if he knows nothing but Irish'.[6] About eight years later (*c* 1236) he wrote to abbot John of Pontigny[7] in his campaign to establish a cistercian house of studies at Paris. John is to write to his friends at the papal curia, and through them to bring papal pressure to bear upon the reluctant senior abbots of the Order. The letter is a veritable jeremiad on the state of cistercian learning and instruction. 'Zealous and learned men' are vital to the health, well-being and reputation of the Order; there is great danger in lack of letters, and never more so than now – 'for the past thirteen years no scholar of renown, no master of the sacred page, has entered the Order, and those already of the habit grow old, and go the way of all flesh'.[8] That there were others within the Order who felt like Stephen of Lexington is clear. The idea for a house of studies at

---

[1] *Ibid* p 167, n 3.   [2] See Watt pp 85–107; Lawrence pp 167–8, 173.
[3] See Lawrence pp 170–7.   [4] *Ibid* p 177, n 2.
[5] Griesser, *ASOC*, II, p 47. 'Quapropter Hiberniensibus iniunximus, quod si quem de suis in ordine de cetero recipi desiderent, Parisius vel Oxonium vel ad alias civitates famosas mittere studeant, ubi litteras et loquele peritiam addiscant morumque compositionem, manifestiusque ipsis ostendimus, quod nullam intendit ordo excludere nationem, sed solummodo ineptos et inutiles et moribus humanis dissidentes...'
[6] *Ibid*. 'Quomodo autem diliget claustrum aut librum, qui nichil novit nisi Hibernicum?'
[7] *Ibid* pp 116–18.
[8] 'a retroactis iam annis XIII^{cim} nullus famose litteratus precipue in sacra pagina ad nos se transtulerit et qui iam sunt in ordine senescunt et tendunt ad viam universe carnis'.

Paris seems to have originated with one of Stephen of Lexington's predecessors at Clairvaux – abbot Evrard[1] (died 1238) – and the letter to John of Pontigny indicates that the matter was already the subject of lively debate and tortuous diplomacy. Debate and opposition continued, however, even after the house was established. The abbot of Villers, Arnulf of Louvain,[2] may be taken to speak for many of his contemporaries when he refused a subsidy for the new house, and declared 'it hath not been the custom hitherto for monks to leave their claustral exercises, which most befit their profession, in order to give themselves over to the study of letters'.[3] It was this opposition, in all probability, resentful of the curial support which Stephen of Lexington had been able to enlist, which engineered his deposition from Clairvaux in 1256, the year of Guy of l'Aumône's inception in theology.[4]

Whatever success the opponents of Stephen of Lexington achieved in 1256, however, they were not able to check the development of cistercian studies. Montpellier (1262), Toulouse (1281–3) and Oxford (1282) were all established as *studia generalia* modelled on the Chardonnet. In 1287 the General Chapter ordained that every house should support one in twenty of its monks at university,[5] while the decrees of the cistercian pope Benedict XII in 1335[6] put the seal on an already flourishing situation.

Stephen of Lexington's work had borne ample fruit, but it is questionable if this would have been entirely to his taste. In the fifteenth century the refusal of John Greenwell, one of the ablest of English cistercians, to accept the abbacy of Vaudey or Waverley 'preferring rather to stay at Oxford in order to study'[7] stands in sharp contrast to Stephen of Lexington's vision of study supplying those 'zealous and learned men' whom the Order required. It is all too easy, in the light of his career and training, to class Stephen of Lexington with contemporary English black monk abbots, or with Huby, and to see his concern for the establishment of cistercian studies as arising from academic rivalry, a fear of intellectual isolation and the personal inclination of the scholar. But this is to do him an injustice. In 1448

---

[1] See Lawrence p 169. It would appear from the letters of John of Limoges that a number of monks from Clairvaux were already attending the theological schools at Paris in the 1230s, see Lawrence p 173.   [2] Abbot 1240–8.
[3] Quoted Lawrence p 176.   [4] *Ibid*.
[5] Canivez III, p 238.
[6] *Fulgens sicut terra* (12/7/1335) is printed in Canivez III, pp 410–36. Eleven out of the forty clauses are concerned with the organisation of cistercian studies.
[7] *Memorials* I, pp 149–50.

the abbot of Cîteaux delegated extensive powers to John Greenwell, by then abbot of Fountains, and described him as a man 'whose mature wisdom had been commended to me by so many people and on so many occasions'.[1] This was precisely the sort of man, educated, capable of high office, active in the government of the Order, that Stephen of Lexington hoped to produce through the process of cistercian studies: not ivory-tower scholars, but men like Stephen himself, trained and able to cope with all the problems of the Order.

In his letters and career Stephen of Lexington emerges as a practical man of affairs rather than as an academic. To him, education and learning were useful, and at times essential. His early experience in Ireland had emphasised to him the dangers that threaten when even the most elementary educational standards were lacking. Ireland, of course, with its two nations and its two cultures, was a special case,[2] but the same general problems of assimilation to a common continental observance, tradition and standards were repeated in all the fringe areas of the western European world. When the cistercian statutes expatiate on the drunkenness of English monks;[3] deplore the insubordination of Welsh conversi,[4] and investigate trouble in Norwegian houses[5] they are talking in legalistic and disciplinary terms of problems which have their roots as much in cultural and linguistic immaturity and discontinuity as in simple failure of control.

These were problems to which cistercianism was, by its very nature, particularly susceptible. The deliberate isolation of the communities and their establishment in remote wastelands, located them, in many cases, on the fringes of civilisation. The emphasis on manual labour; the prohibition of intellectual activity[6] and the recruitment of large numbers of conversi placed a premium on leadership, and presupposed considerable ability and dedication on the part of the cistercian abbots and their officers.[7] Such circumstances and demands were far removed

---

[1] Talbot, no 1, p 18.

[2] For the most recent discussion of the problems arising from the duality see Watt.

[3] Canivez I, pp 123, 149, 193, 202. See Knowles, *MO* pp 654–61.

[4] *Ibid* I, pp 123, 138, 191, 193, 262, 281, 324, 343–5.

[5] *Ibid* I, pp 375–6, 387, 396, 406, 422.

[6] Nulli liceat abbati, nec monacho, nec novitio, libros facere, nisi forte cuiquam in generali capitulo concessum fuerit, Canivez I, p 26.

[7] The burdens placed upon the cistercian abbots by the phenomenal growth both of individual houses and of the Order, can be clearly seen in Walter Daniel's account of Ailred, and in the Foundation History of Fountains Abbey (*Memorials* I, pp 1–129). Where abbots became involved in wider issues as well the pressures could become almost intolerable – see St Bernard's letters during the papal schism of 1130–9.

from the simple asceticism of the cistercian fathers, and early cistercian history is littered with the sad careers of men of great sanctity and asceticism who were overtaken by the phenomenal success of the way of life which they had chosen, and saddled with responsibilities for which they had no mind and, often, little ability: men like Adam of Meaux, a veteran of the refoundation of Whitby, whose abbacy ended in the temporary dissolution of his house;[1] Gervase of Louth Park, who finally resigned his office 'because of my insufficiency and weakness',[2] or Richard, second abbot of Fountains, who 'longed with his whole being for the desert'.[3] Fortunately for the Order it had, throughout the twelfth century, recruited men like St Bernard himself, William of Rievaulx,[4] Richard I of Fountains,[5] Ailred,[6] Henry Murdac:[7] men who combined sanctity of life with administrative ability and considerable education. For all its initial renunciation of the world and learning the Cistercian Order had quickly come to depend upon the recruitment of men of this type and calibre for the maintenance of its observance and standards, and the size of its communities, the complexity of its organisation and the nature of its life made it more dependent on them than most other forms of western monasticism. By the second quarter of the thirteenth century such recruits were not forthcoming, and, as Stephen of Lexington pointed out, there were great dangers in this situation. Nor was it simple accident or personal whim which led him to emphasise the lack of 'scholars of renown and masters of the sacred page': as his letter to John of Pontigny makes clear one threat in particular was most urgent.

The letter opens with conventional pious exhortation to John of Pontigny to deal with the lax observance of the brethren of Cadouin and its daughter-houses,[8] but it proceeds quickly to 'unheard of things' of greater importance. In the abbey of Gondon, a daughter-house of Cadouin, there are said to be seven heretical monks, and this at a time when the pope had appointed special *predicatores litteratos* to search out heresy throughout the Church.[9] Further, a papal inquisitor preaching at Orleans had recently indicted cistercians amongst the supporters

[1] See Derek Baker, 'The Desert in the North', *NH*, v (1970) pp 1-11.
[2] *Ibid*, and the references there given.   [3] *Ibid*; *Memorials* I, pp 73-8.
[4] See [Walter] Daniel, [*Life of Ailred*,] ed F. M. Powicke (London 1950) p 32; [Ailred], *De Anima*, ed C. H. Talbot, *Medieval and Renaissance Studies*, Supplement I (London 1952) p 5, n 4.   [5] See *Memorials* I, pp 6-72.   [6] See Daniel.
[7] See *Memorials* I, pp 84-108; *The Letters of St Bernard*, trans B. S. James (London 1953) no 107, pp 155-6.   [8] Griesser, II, p 116.
[9] 'Cum igitur iam papa speciales fere ubique predicatores litteratos et in hac parte industrios deputaverit ad indagandos hereticos...', Griesser, II, p 116.

of 'a certain German count', the protector of heretics, and a heretic himself. There was real danger of inquisition into the Order, and John of Pontigny is urged to draw his sword, and by cutting out the offence at Gondon to spare the Order the shame and scandal of such inquiry.

For all Stephen of Lexington's concern, however, and the evident seriousness of the matter, there is scant reference to it in the deliberations of the cistercian General Chapter. In 1234[1] the abbot of Pontigny was ordered to report to the next General Chapter on the many unspecified evils alleged against the houses of Cadouin and Gondon, but there is in fact no reference to this commission in the capitular proceedings of 1235 or 1236: when the abbots of the two houses next appear, in 1277,[2] it is in the course of ordinary capitular business. From the records it would appear that there had been no such process of inspection and correction with Cadouin and Gondon as had occurred with a number of other houses at this time. It may be that John of Pontigny had acted with such speed and decision that there was no need to refer to the matter again, but Stephen of Lexington's letter, which may be placed soon after the arrival in France in 1235 of the dominican inquisitor Robert le Bougre,[3] would lead us to think otherwise. It is more likely that both John of Pontigny and the General Chapter allowed the matter to go by default. This, coupled with the absence from the capitular records of any reference to the heretical involvement of German cistercians, might lead us to think that Stephen of Lexington was being unduly alarmist, but there is other evidence to show that he had good cause for concern. In 1236[4] the General Chapter decreed a general inquisition for heresy in the cistercian houses of the province of Tarragona, and twenty years later two Italian abbots, of Locedio and Aqualunga, were deposed for continuing to consort with proven heretics.[5] These few references might be taken to suggest that the heretical tendencies and sympathies of southern cistercian houses were more pronounced than of those in the north, and when the activity of contemporary cathars and Albigenses is considered such a conclusion would not be improbable.

This view would accord with Stephen of Lexington's comments on heresy at Gondon, itself in Languedoc. It does not, however, account for what appears from him to be a more general heretical involvement in

---

[1] Canivez II, p 138.   [2] *Ibid* pp 175-6.

[3] See C. H. Haskins, 'Robert le Bougre and the beginnings of the Inquisition in Northern France', *American Historical Review*, VII (New York 1902) pp 437-57, 631-52; Lawrence p 173; Griesser, II, p 116, n 2.

[4] Canivez II, p 159.   [5] *Ibid* pp 451, 452.

at least one part of Germany, and there are other indications that heresy was not simply confined to the southern houses of the Order. Indeed, it might be argued that heresy first became a problem amongst the cistercians in northern Europe. The earliest reference to heresy in the cistercian statutes occurs in those for 1219,[1] when the cistercian abbots concerned in the legatine visitation of that year were given a direct instruction to seek out the supporters of heretics amongst their monks and lay-brethren and to exile them to the most remote houses of the Order. If they refused exile they were to be stripped of the cistercian habit. Heresy is next mentioned in 1235,[2] and again it occurs in the north. In that year the abbot of Le Loroux, in Anjou, was accused of heresy in General Chapter, and the resultant inquiry was delegated to the abbot of Cîteaux himself.

These references are, of course, too few to allow any full description of the anatomy of cistercian heresy, but taken together they do suggest certain general conclusions. All the references to heresy in the decrees of the General Chapter except one – an isolated entry in 1411[3] – occur in the forty years from 1219 to 1259. It would seem, therefore, either that heresy infiltrated the Order in that period, or that existing practices and views became suspect in the context of the prevailing anxiety about heresy within the Church as a whole, and of the policies of inquisition and repression which sprang from that concern. That the cancer was of recent growth amongst the cistercians is suggested by the references to it – it is unheard of, infamous, a great scandal – and if the capitular decrees are any reliable indication it seems to have ceased to be a threat to the health of the Order soon after the middle of the century. It was at its most virulent at precisely the time that Stephen of Lexington was writing to John of Pontigny, and his letter is valuable evidence that the problem was of wider significance than the cistercian statutes, taken by themselves, suggest.

This handful of references demonstrates the existence of heresy within the Cistercian Order, but it does little more than that, and, in particular, does nothing to make possible the identification of any specific heretical creed or practice. In the statutes heresy occurs simply as the reason for the disciplinary action decreed, and only Stephen of Lexington's letter gives the subject more extensive treatment. Even here, however, there is no precision on matters of belief or observance – heresy is rife; there are papal inquisitors abroad charged with its eradication, and all cistercians, orthodox as well as heretical, will

---

[1] *Ibid* I, p 510.   [2] *Ibid* II, p 143.   [3] *Ibid* IV, p 150.

suffer inquisition unless they put their house in order. There seems no chance here of identifying the errors which had subverted cistercian purity, and yet if the letter is taken as a whole the nature of the problem which preoccupied Stephen of Lexington does become more apparent.

The letter culminates, as has been said, in the plea to John of Pontigny to use all his influence to ensure the provision of zealous and literate men for the direction of the Order. By them the ignorance of sacred texts, the deficiency in letters, which Stephen of Lexington deplored would be redressed. Without them the glories of the past could not be recalled: with them all could be renewed in its pristine virtue.[1] The immediate object of the letter is plain, but it should not be interpreted in too narrowly an educational or doctrinal sense. The purpose of the educational provision Stephen of Lexington sought was the renewal of spiritual fervour within the Order:[2] its context was the need to restore the purity of cistercian observance, and through the reaffirmation of essential principles – silence and solitude – to regain the strength of purpose and sense of direction that sprang from them. The great problem – *rem...satis detestabilem et ordini valde periculosam*[3] – with which Stephen of Lexington was concerned was the failure of leadership and the decay of discipline, and from this all else stemmed. In beginning his letter by referring to the entirely unremarkable shortcomings of Cadouin and its dependencies[4] he emphasised this point. At Gondon[5] discipline was lax and leadership lacking, and in its absence free rein was given to eccentricity of life and of doctrine –

---

[1] 'Unde, si placet, bonum nobis videretur, ut efficaciter scriberetis amicis vestris in curia, quatinus suggereretis domino pape, non de prescribenda certa forma studendi, sed ut dominus papa efficaciter det in mandatis abbati Cisterciensi et IIII^or primis, ut convocatis de maioribus et sanioris ordinis nostri abbatibus [lacuna] conveniant in aliquo loco competenti prope Parisius et deliberent apud se, dum vigent in ordine ipsius ordinis zelatores et viri litterati, qualiter huic periculo de defectu litterature, in quo timetur ipsi ordini futuris temporibus, possint provideri; nam procul dubio, si in hoc solo articulo bene cautum esset ordini nostro, non credimus, quod unquam ordo in aliquibus preteritis temporibus ita floruisset, ut non refloreret nec esset sibi unquam de cetero de lapsu formidandum. Ceterum ipse ordo, qui iam vilescit, resurgeret indubitanter in gloriam et honorem apud Deum et homines in confusionem detrahencium et obloquencium sibi.' Griesser, II, pp 117–18.

[2] 'Pater in Christe karissime, ipsa tempora periculosa, que iam instant, nos ammonent de vigilancia et sollicitudine pro statu ordinis maxime in spiritualibus.' *Ibid* p 117.

[3] *Ibid* p 116.

[4] 'Ipsa namque nulli monachorum suorum annuatim vestimenta ministrat, sed generaliter unusquisque suas vacas aut boves aut aliquid huiusmodi proprietatis genus habere dicitur sub pretextu huiuscemodi. Quot vero exinde sequantur inconvenientia et animarum pericula ac ordinis scandala, leve est perpendere.' *Ibid*.

[5] See Griesser, II, p 116, n 2 for the appearance of Cadouin and Gondon in the statutes of the General Chapter under a number of disciplinary headings.

'from all this', he declared, 'it can be most clearly seen what great sin and peril spring from the failure of discipline'.[1] It is, of course, commonplace to suggest that the morale of an institution depends upon the quality of its leadership, and there can be little doubt that thirteenth-century cistercian heterodoxy owed much to contemporary debate and experiment both within the established Church and outside it. Yet Stephen of Lexington's views do not constitute a superficial, oversimplified diagnosis of a complex condition. His earlier career in Ireland had demonstrated a ready and practical appreciation of problems which is still evident here. There was, as has been said, a particular need for able and informed leaders in an Order which combined complex organisation with simplicity of life, and this necessity was emphasised at a time when the best men and best minds were being recruited into the ranks of the mendicants. But the matter does not rest there. In the absence of those learned and spiritual leaders whom Stephen of Lexington sought to provide heterodoxy was likely to flourish amongst cistercians, for this was an Order whose spiritual strength and inspiration was based upon the individual experience of the monk-ascetic in personal communion with his God.

Amongst twelfth-century cistercians men with this dynamic, deeply felt spirituality abound. If St Bernard himself is the supreme example, men like William of Rievaulx, Richard II of Fountains, Ailred, come readily to mind in an English context. Not only were they admirable in themselves, but they were decisive for the spirit and standard of the cistercian life in their century. Their example was, of course, salutary, but it was not simply by example that they taught. Ailred's instruction of the novices at Rievaulx, and the ready access of his monks to him when he was abbot, are well known. William of Rievaulx's influence,[2] though less well-chronicled, was equally decisive, while Richard II of Fountains made a lasting impression on his monks with his spiritual discourses and counsels.[3] Intensely personal though their influence and instruction was, however, there was no hint of eccentricity about it, no departure from established truth, whether of doctrine or observance, for these were all educated men,

---

[1] 'ex quo liquido patere potest, quanta et quam enormia pariat peccata atque pericula defectus discipline'. *Ibid.*

[2] See above, p 98, n 4.

[3] 'Virtus animi in vultu radiabat, et ipse homo exterior interioris ymaginem praeferebat ...Deum testor, nunquam apud hominem tantam inveni gratiam, ad moestum consolandum, ad lapsum relevandum et ad lesae conscientiae latentes causas dinoscendum.' *Memorials* I, p 74.

trained in a secure theological tradition.[1] William of Rievaulx had been St Bernard's secretary. Richard II of Fountains had been sacristan of St Mary's, York, and the spiritual leader of the reformers there.[2] Ailred, though he might admit to 'little grammar and less learning'[3] when he entered the cloister, and even at the end of his life declare 'I am not wise or learned, but just a simple, uneducated man, more like a fisherman than a preacher',[4] was one of the foremost scholars of his age. Like St Bernard himself Ailred acquired his learning in the cloister, and he owed much to the abbot of Clairvaux both in direct encouragement and advice, and in the indirect transmission of the saint's teaching through disciples like William of Rievaulx.[5] Though Ailred might never, like St Bernard, have been consulted on knotty points of theology by Hugh of St Victor,[6] his *De Anima* showed that he could handle complex theological questions and was quite clear where orthodoxy lay.[7] Ailred, of course, like St Bernard, was exceptional, but the education which both men were able to acquire as cistercian monks demonstrates the ability of the Order to inculcate sound theology and to foster spiritual qualities in its recruits: even, as the career of another English cistercian shows, in recruits of much less ability and potential than an Ailred.

In 1190 Ralph Haget,[8] a member of a locally important Yorkshire family succeeded William of Newminster as abbot of Fountains. He had entered the Order late, receiving the habit when he was about thirty from Robert of Pipewell sometime between 1170–9. Until then he had pursued a normal knightly career, and, unlike Ailred, does not seem to have received any instruction at all prior to entering the cloister.[9] All his education was gained at Fountains, and it says a great deal for it that as early as 1181 he should have become abbot of

---

[1] See Talbot's comments on the course and tradition of cistercian studies in the twelfth century, *De Anima*, pp 9–23.

[2] *Memorials* I, p 73.

[3] *Speculum Caritatis, PL,* 195 (1855) col 503.

[4] Quoted *De Anima,* p 10.

[5] See *De Anima,* pp 9–13, 22, in particular the extract from Ailred's *De spirituali amicitia* given at p 12, n 4: 'In turba fratrum me residente, cum omnes undique circumstreperent, et alius quaereret, alius disputaret, et iste de Scripturis, ille de moribus, alter de vitiis, de virtutibus alter quaestiones ingererent, tu solus tacebas.'

[6] *Ibid* pp 10–11.

[7] See his discussion, in some detail, of the heretics who appeared in England in 1166, *De Anima,* bk I, pp 90–1.

[8] For Haget see *Memorials* I, pp 117–25, 133.

[9] 'Intermiserat litterarum studia, tempore quo in armis agebat, sed lectionis assiduitate intermissi temporis dampna redimebat; legens magis in libro experientiae, quod alii in codice actitabant.' *Ibid* p 118.

Kirkstall, a daughter-house of Fountains, returning as abbot to the mother-house nine years later. Haget was no scholar or theologian, and he made no mark in the wider affairs of his Order or his country. As the father of his monks, however, he is clearly in the tradition of Ailred. To Hugh of Kirkstall he was 'the mirror of religion, the flower of the Order, the model of discipline',[1] solicitous for the purity of cistercian observance, setting an example of personal holiness, and recounting to his monks with tears in his eyes[2] his experience of the unutterable sweetness of God,[3] and his visions of the fear of the Lord[4] and of the Trinity.[5] For the insight it gives into the quality of life of a cistercian community under what might be termed an ordinary abbot the account is invaluable, but this apart Hugh of Kirkstall gives a unique insight into the spirituality of the first century of English cistercianism when he relates the circumstances of Ralph Haget's conversion to the regular life.[6]

While still in the world Haget had begun to be exercised about his secular way of life. The matter increasingly preyed on his mind until finally, after having consulted a member of the community at Fountains, he experienced a direct summons while in prayer before a crucifix and entered Fountains. The interest of the passage lies not in the suspicious similarity of the incident to one in the life of St Bernard,[7] but in the approach Haget made to the cistercians for advice. His counsellor was not the abbot, not even a monk, but 'a certain lay-brother of singular grace and purity called Sunnulphus'.[8] It was Haget's custom, apparently, to visit him often for discussion and counsel, and to invite his prayers. *Homo simplex et illiteratus*, Sunnulphus was yet a man of great spiritual knowledge and wisdom, possessing, it would

---

[1] *Ibid* p 117.

[2] 'Haec de se sanctus domnus, non sine lachrimis, nobis aliquociens referebat.' *Ibid* p 122.

[3] 'Nihil', ait 'in omni vita mea expertus sum quod huiusmodi dulcedini valeam adaptare'. *Ibid* p 120.

[4] *Ibid* pp 120–1.   [5] *Ibid* pp 121–2.

[6] *Ibid* pp 118–20.   [7] *Vita Prima*, bk I, ch 3.

[8] 'inter quos conversus quidam singularis gratie et puritatis enituit, Sunnulphus nomine; homo simplex et illiteratus, sed Dominus erudierat eum. Habebat, pro codice, conscientiam; spiritum sanctum pro eruditore; et legens in libro experientiae, crescebat cotidie in scientia sanctorum; habens etiam spiritum revelationis. Huic servo Dei familiaris admodum fuit sanctus abbas Radulphus, etiam dum adhuc in armis agebat; et multociens Fontes accessit, gratia eum visitandi ut se orationibus eius commendaret. Multa nobis narrare consuevit digna relatu, de sanctitate et sobrietate viri, de gravitate silentii, de maturitate in gestu et morum disciplina; quam alacer in exhortando, quam efficax in consolando, quam dulcis in collatione, quantoque semper cavebat studio, ne unquam otiosum verbum illi ex ore proflueret.' *Memorials* I, p 118.

seem, the spirit of prophecy. How exceptional Sunnulphus was,[1] how Haget came to have access to him, how normal such contacts were are questions which cannot be considered here, but taken just as it stands the incident serves to emphasise the spiritual richness of a house like Fountains in the last quarter of the twelfth century. However large the community, whatever prosperity it enjoyed, the presence in it of men like Sunnulphus, the attraction it exercised on men like Haget, indicate that the springs of primitive cistercian spirituality had not run dry a century after the monks of Molèsme had established themselves in the wilderness of Cîteaux.

In other circumstances, however, such richness could be dangerous arising as it did from the untutored individuality of men like Sunnulphus:

Outdoor rustic people have not many ideas, but such as they have are hardy plants, and thrive flourishingly in persecution. One who has grown a long time in the sweat of laborious noons, and under the stars at night, a frequenter of hills and forests, an old honest countryman, has, in the end, a sense of communion with the powers of the universe, and amicable relations towards his God...he knows the Lord. His religion does not repose upon a choice of logic; it is the poetry of the man's experience, the philosophy of the history of his life. God, like a great power, like a great shining sun has appeared to this simple fellow in the course of years, and become the ground and essence of his least reflections ...here is a man who has his own thoughts, and will stubbornly adhere to them in good and evil.[2]

It was not, of course, of Sunnulphus that Robert Louis Stevenson was writing, but the cap fits. Whatever superstructures might overlay it the essence of cistercian spirituality was to be found in the individual experience of the holy. Men like Sunnulphus and Haget knew the Lord. He had become the ground and essence of their least reflections, and in the time of Stephen of Lexington there were fewer men around than there had been fifty years before capable of supplying the orthodox theological guidelines for such reflection.[3] It is, of course, impossible to be dogmatic in the absence of conclusive evidence, but it may at least be

---

[1] See the continental examples of men like Sunnulphus given by Lawrence, p 165, referring to S. Roisin, *L'hagiographie cistercienne dans le diocèse de Liège au xiii*[e] *siècle* (Louvain 1947).

[2] R. L. Stevenson, *Travels with a Donkey in the Cevennes*, Folio Society (London 1967) pp 119–20.

[3] The field, of course, was not entirely barren, but men like Stephen of Sawley were very much the exception in the thirteenth century, see A. Wilmart, 'Les méditations d'Etienne de Salley sur les Joies de la Vierge Marie', in *Auteurs Spirituels et Textes Dévots du Moyen Age Latin* (repr Paris 1971) pp 317–60.

suggested, in the context of his time and his career, that the heresies Stephen of Lexington indicted were not so much formal creeds or defined practices as aberrations from the strongly ascetic, personal cistercian way of life, occurring in the absence of sound, informed spiritual direction, and allowed unaccustomed licence by the decay of discipline and authority within the Order.[1] Stephen of Lexington's letter to John of Pontigny leaves little doubt that he saw a close relationship between these phenomena. This was the basis on which his campaign for the organisation of cistercian studies rested, and while it is impossible to indicate any definite connection it is not, perhaps, entirely without significance that the most serious trouble over heresy within the Order preceded the establishment of the house of studies at Paris, and that all reference to heresy vanishes from the statutes not long after the inception of the first cistercian master in theology in 1256.

It is paradoxical that an Order which could so categorically deny its members the right to 'make books',[2] and whose most eminent spokesman could declare 'a monk's duty is not to teach, but to lament',[3] should have depended so much on the recruitment of men of letters for its health and well-being. Though they might not have cared to recognise it cistercians had always been led by an élite who combined, and needed to combine, great spiritual and intellectual qualities. When, in the thirteenth century, formal legislation was proposed to encourage and organise study it was out of necessity, not jealousy or academic rivalry, and the innovation was new only in form not in substance. Had Stephen of Lexington's proposals not been implemented there would indeed have been 'peril and scandal', not so much from the appearance of coherent heretical doctrines or practices in cistercian cloisters as from the uncontrolled growth of that individualism which formed the basis of the cistercian ideal. Such individuality, of course, need not

---

[1] It is worth noticing, in connection with Haget's spiritual experiences, that when Hugh of Kirkstall interrogates him about their precise form he never allows himself to speculate or embroider: 'Quaesivi ab eo de dulcedine quae ei videbatur; cuius speciem saporis praeferret. Si quid mellis haberet simile, vel cibi alicuius corporalis? At ille; "Nihil", ait, "in omni vita mea expertus sum quod huiusmodi dulcedini valeam adaptare"' (*Memorials* I, p 120).

'Sed quis timor, aut qualis timor ille? "Nihil", ait, "terribilius, nihil hoc timore horribilius excogitari, audirive potest" (*ibid* p 121).

'Sciscitatus sum ab eo sub quo scemate vel forma, haec facta fuit revelatio. At ille, "Nihil", ait, "ibi formatum, nihil figuratum apparuit, et tamen vidi in visione beata tres Personas in Unitate. Vidi, inquam, et cognovi, Patrem ingenitum, Filium unigenitum, et Sanctum Spiritum ab utroque processum" (*ibid* p 121).

[2] See above, p 97, n 6.   [3] Quoted Lawrence p 176.

have been either harmful or vicious, but, lacking control, it might have luxuriated into all kinds of eccentricity, heresy amongst them, and in that age of authority and centralisation any divergence in observance and expression was viewed with suspicion. In the circumstances of the mid-thirteenth century the continued integrity of the cistercian life and ideal depended, as Stephen of Lexington saw, upon the creation and adoption of a structure of studies by the Order: Sunnulphus might have 'conscience for his code, the Holy Spirit as his master, and grow in holy wisdom by his study of the book of experience', but such a curriculum was no longer adequate in the age of Aquinas.

REFORMATIO REGNI:
WYCLIF AND HUS AS LEADERS OF
RELIGIOUS PROTEST MOVEMENTS

by MICHAEL WILKS

IN May 1382 William Courtenay, archbishop of Canterbury since the murder of his predecessor Sudbury during the Peasants' Revolt the previous year, declared it to be a matter of frequent complaint and common report that evil persons were going about his province preaching without authority, and spreading doctrines which threatened to destroy not only ecclesiastical authority but civil government as well. They were the adherents, he was informed, of a certain teacher of novelties at Oxford, named John Wyclif, whose sect broadcast the seeds of pestiferous error so widely in the pastures of Canterbury that only the most savage hoeing would root them out.[1] The chroniclers hastened to confirm this account. According to their accounts, by 1382 Wyclif had been able, through his writings and the preaching of his followers, to seduce the laity, including great lords and members of the nobility, over a great part of the realm. Even members of the clergy and scholars were not free from infection. Thus Knighton commented that – at least in the area around Leicester – every other person one met was a Lollard.[2] Thirty years later it is the same story in Bohemia. As the carthusian prior Stephen of Dolany complained, despite the condemnation of Wyclif's teachings at the university of Prague in 1403, the Wycliffites swarmed everywhere: 'in the state apartments of princes, in the schools of the students, in the lonely chambers of the monks, and even in the cells of the Carthusians'.[3]

---

[1] *Fasciculi Zizaniorum*, ed W. W. Shirley, RS 5 (London 1858) p 275; [D.] Wilkins, *Concilia* (London 1737) III pp 158 and 172.

[2] [Henry] Knighton, *Chronicon*, ed J. R. Lumby, RS 92, 2 vols (London 1889–95) II p 191; compare pp 176, 183, 185; *Eulogium Historiarum*, first continuation, ed F. S. Haydon, RS 9, 3 vols (London 1858–63) III pp 351, 354–5; compare [Thomas of] Walsingham, *Historia Anglicana*, ed H. T. Riley, RS 28, 2 vols (London 1863–4) I p 325; II pp 50, 53; *Chronicon Angliae*, ed E. M. Thompson, RS 64 (London 1874) p 396. Although outdated in some respects, the best survey of this material is still H. L. Cannon, 'The Poor Priests: A Study in the Rise of English Lollardy', *Annual Report of the American Historical Association for 1899* (Washington 1900) I pp 451–82.

[3] Cited H. B. Workman and R. M. Pope, *The Letters of John Hus* (London 1904) p 11.

Yet I do not need to remind this audience that Courtenay's action in and after 1382 destroyed Wyclifism as a movement for the next generation. Whilst making allowance for the events culminating in the Oldcastle Rising of 1414, it is still true to say that Lollardy was in effect driven underground in England for the rest of the medieval period. In Bohemia, under the inspiration of Wyclif's teachings, the Hussite reform movement succeeded in creating a national church-state which was to triumph over all the forces of christian universalism – pope, emperor and general council – so that it may fairly be said that the Reformation began in Bohemia a century before the rest of Europe.[1] Why? What was the essential difference which made Wyclifism an abject failure in England and an astonishing success story in Bohemia?

It is now nearly half a century since Workman published the magisterial two volumes which remain the authoritative account of Wyclif's life.[2] An enormous amount of more recent scholarship, particularly in the past two decades, has produced a bewildering variety of different interpretations (and permutation of other people's interpretations) on individual points. But it now seems to be generally accepted that the reasons for Wyclif's failure must be sought in a radical phase of his career, beginning about 1379 and continuing with increasing intensity until his death at the end of 1384.[3] It is agreed that the years immediately following 1379 were a time when Wyclif committed two acts of indescribable folly and suffered one piece of appalling bad luck. He resolved his earlier doubts about the remanence of bread and wine in the eucharist, and was so elated by his newfound certainty that he flung discretion to the winds and published the *De eucharistia*. The work followed the usual pattern of being made up of a series of very repetitive lectures already given in the schools at Oxford, and this had been enough to cause many former friends and supporters, who had warmly applauded his demands for reform of the clergy, to refuse to follow him into outright heresy on the matter of the sacraments. Since many of these former supporters were friars,

---

[1] F. Zilka, 'The Czech Reformation and its Relation to the World Reformation', *Slavonic and East European Review*, VIII (London 1929-30) pp 284-91; compare F. Kafka, 'The Hussite Movement and the Czech Reformation', *Journal of World History* (=*Cahiers d'histoire mondiale*), v (Paris 1960) pp 830-56.

[2] [H. B.] Workman, [*John Wyclif: A Study of the English Medieval Church*,] 2 vols (Oxford 1926).

[3] For example J. H. Dahmus, *The Prosecution of John Wyclif* (New Haven 1952) p 81; [K. B.] McFarlane, [*John Wycliffe and the Beginnings of English Nonconformity*] (London 1952) pp 96-7; compare M. Hurley, '*Scriptura Sola*: Wyclif and his Critics', *Traditio*, XVI (New York 1960) pp 275-352.

Wyclif was led to retaliate against this apostasy by launching into one of the most vigorous denunciations of the mendicant orders made by a secular master during the fourteenth century.

Wyclif's position was now extremely precarious. Condemned by the Barton committee at Oxford for heresy, suspended from teaching duties, and excommunicated, Wyclif published a defiant manifesto against his enemies in May 1381, and appealed to the government for protection. But the outbreak of the Peasants' Revolt at the end of the month made it impossible for the government to intervene on behalf of anybody accused of stirring up sedition, and it was not long before Wyclif and his remaining followers were being openly accused of having fomented the Revolt itself by their teachings. Forced out of Oxford, Wyclif retired to his parish of Lutterworth in time to escape the further condemnation of his teachings at the Blackfriars council of 1382 and Courtenay's subsequent purge of the university. His remaining years in retirement were a sad epilogue in which, ill and perhaps partly paralysed, he occupied himself with writing even more vitriolic attacks against his opponents, and with the production of enormous numbers of pamphlets, tracts and sermons for use by a steadily dwindling number of lollard preachers.

The implication of all this is that it was Wyclif's heresy, particularly in the matter of the eucharist, which is the key to his failure. Much has been made of the point that it was precisely on the question of denying transubstantiation that Hus refused to follow Wyclif, as if to suggest that Hus deserved to succeed, where Wyclif failed, for having been more orthodox than his master. Although Hus, most unfairly, paid the supreme penalty which Wyclif for not very obvious reasons somehow escaped, the Hussite movement is made to appear as a movement of religious dissent to be contrasted with the deliberate heresy of Lollardy. But this line of argument, it seems to me, is unfruitful. Heresy was a by-product of the Wycliffite system, a symptom rather than a cause; ultimately it was irrelevant in determining the success or failure of the movement either in England or Bohemia – and it does not therefore really matter from this point of view whether Hus *was* more orthodox than Wyclif. Wyclifism was above all a political movement, whose significance both in England and in Bohemia would be determined by political factors, by the policies pursued by political leaders, and by the interaction of political circumstances.

In the first place, the English bishops did not need an open declaration by Wyclif that his theories would involve a drastic reinterpretation of eucharistic doctrine, nor his enmity with the friars, nor his alleged complicity in the Peasants' Revolt, in order to secure his condemnation. Although the two hearings held at St Paul's by Wyclif's ecclesiastical superiors – one in February 1377, and the other in January 1378 – had proved abortive, partly due to government intervention and partly to the violence of the London mob, nevertheless the fact remained that the reception of Gregory XI's bulls of May 1377 meant that Wyclif's teaching on lordship, dominion and grace, and on the validity of papal and episcopal jurisdiction, had been pronounced a matter of error by the supreme authority in the Church.[1] Henceforth it was papal policy that the influence of his theories was to be stamped out, and Wyclif himself was ordered to be put in prison in chains or cited to the papal court itself. The legal process was in fact extremely slow, and technically was never completed. But this does not alter the point that from 1377 onwards the bishops had unassailable legal justification for acting against Wyclif and his followers whenever they deemed it expedient to do so. That the bishops did not deem it expedient to act in haste, but allowed Wyclif enough rope to hang himself several times over by the further elaboration of his principles over a period of four and a half years, should not be allowed to conceal the fact that it was the political character of Wycliffite theology which was so obnoxious, and was indeed the root cause of all the trouble.

There is one other preliminary consideration. It would give a false impression to suggest, as some recent commentators have done, that Wyclif suddenly lurched into heresy on the sacraments on the rebound from these early attempts to secure his condemnation. That he now took a positive delight in emphasising the more radical aspects of his system of thought, and that his language became increasingly vigorous and vindictive, is not in doubt. But it was essentially a matter of emphasis, of tilting the balance, of elaborating and applying the principles which he had already laid down in his philosophical works some ten or twenty years before. Wyclif said nothing after 1378 that reasonably astute opponents like William Woodford, William Binham, Uthred of Boldon or John Cunningham, and particularly Adam Easton, were not perfectly capable of deducing for themselves during the early 1370s.

The guiding principle of Wyclif's philosophy was the theme of double substances and the need to combine them in christian teaching,

[1] Walsingham, *Historia Anglicana*, 1 pp 353ff.

whilst recognising that each substance retained a fundamental independence, integrity and identity, and that there could be a conversion from
one to another without denying the reality – without annihilating –
the former. God and man; the whole and the part; universal and
accident; the divine and the natural; sacred scripture and human tradition; faith and reason; Augustine and Aristotle; papal power and civil
government; headship and community; *societas Christiana* and pagan
polis; *corpus Christi* and eucharistic bread – the proper relationship
of all these things was susceptible in Wyclif's eyes to the techniques
which he had evolved in dealing with the philosophical problem of
insolubles. In a sense they were all aspects of the same central issue
of how the apparently opposed and contradictory characteristics of
divine and natural substances could be brought together in harmony
and the contradictions 'solved' by equivocation. To take a simple
example. In *c* 1370 Wyclif wrote a short work on the nature of man,
De compositione hominis, the purpose of which was on the surface to
make the quite unremarkable point that man was a combination of
matter and form, natural and divine elements, in other words body and
soul. Either part could exist in isolation (*per se intrinseco*),[1] just as man
before baptism was pre-eminently body, and after death was pre-
eminently soul, but for most of his life was a combination of two
distinct parts neither of which ever totally surrendered its individual
identity. Each part, he wrote, has its own life and its own substance:
'quia partes...habent vitam propriam et propriam quiditatem'.[2]
There is a double nature, one divine and the other natural, both of
which for practical purposes act together as one.[3]

The immediate application of the principle was in christology, since
Christ, Wyclif argued, was the supreme expression of dual substances
as God and man. By the incarnation God had demonstrated that man
should play an equal part with God in earthly affairs – and he assidu-
ously attached the phrase *Deus et homo* to every mention of Christ's

[1] *De compositione hominis*, 4, ed R. Beer, W[yclif] S[ociety] (London 1884) p 73.
[2] *De compositione hominis*, 4 p 58.
[3] *De compositione hominis*, I p 11; compare 2, p 35, 'homo est duae substantiae vel naturae'.
Wyclif does of course emphasise that these are essentially theoretical distinctions, and
that in practice the two natures should be taken together – each in isolation would be
incomplete – so that it is possible to describe both together as a complete third nature:
'ut quilibet homo est natura spiritualis cui accidit esse animam; est iterum natura vel
essentia corporea cui accidit esse corpus humanum; et haec duo incommunicabiliter
sunt distincta; et est tertio natura ex corpore et anima integrata quae distingwatur ab
utraque...Nec est negandum quin omnis persona hominis sit tres naturae, duae
incompletae et tertia integra'. His immediate application of this is to the two ends
of human life, p 13.

name to remind his readers of the principle. But he was already aware that this could be directly transposed into political terms, 'nam homo est pars populi'.[1] Like the Greek thinkers, he saw society as the individual writ large, and realised that the same scheme of double quiddities must apply to the Church, at once a heavenly *corpus mysticum* and a conglomeration of natural human communities, a universal society (a society having the nature of a universal) and a collection of national semi-sovereign states. And when he came to write his eucharistic theory he was at pains to point out that he was saying nothing new, but was simply adopting the same principle of double substances. 'Sacramentum altaris', he wrote in 1382, 'est verus corpus Christi et verus panis *sicut Christus est verus Deus et verus homo.*'[2] There was here a conversion, a switch of attention, from the corporeal *substantia panis* to the spiritual *substantia Christi* – but like the Church itself, the eucharist was and remained on earth a combination of the two quiddities, divine and natural, after the manner of man himself: 'Hoc dicit pro pane et vino, et sic *duplicis substantiae* totum fibaret hominem, scilicet hominem exteriorem et hominem interiorem, corpus et anima.'[3]

One may remark in parenthesis that if Hus was as good a *Wiclefista* as he claimed to be, then the question of whether he actually followed Wyclif into eucharistic heresy, as the Council of Constance accused him of doing, becomes a relatively minor issue. Once Hus had adopted Wyclif's philosophical principles, once he had accepted his definition

---

[1] *De compositione hominis*, 5 p 92. The work was specifically written to serve as an introduction to his discussion of lordship and obedience: 1 pp 1–2, 'Tria movent ad tractare materiam de compositione hominis...Tertio quia antecedit ad tractatum humani dominii, cum relatio non potest cognosci nisi per notitiam sui principii subiectivi. Nec sciri potest quomodo homo naturaliter dominetur atque servat sibiipsi...nisi praecognoscatur quomodo homo est duarum naturarum utraque, secundum quas relatio servitutis et dominii in eodem supposito congregantur'.

[2] S. H. Thomson, 'John Wyclif's "Lost" *De fide sacramentorum*', *JTS*, XXXIII (1932) pp 359–65 at p 363; compare p 364, 'sic constat in sacramento altaris. Ibi est forma vel substantia Christi humanitatis spiritualiter, et forma vel substantia panis corporaliter'. For the correlation between eucharist, *Ecclesia* and the nature of Christ, see, for example, *De Ecclesia*, 1, ed J. Loserth, WS (London 1886) p 8; *De eucharistia*, 9, ed J. Loserth, WS (London 1892) p 325.

[3] *De fide sacramentorum*, p 365; *De eucharistia*, 4 p 100, 'Et sic conversio illa non destruit naturam panis, nec mutat naturam corporis inducendo in materiam aliam quidditatem, sed facit praesentiam corporis Christi et tollit principalitatem panis'; cf. 3 p 82, 'potest ergo dici quod panis et vinum convertuntur principaliter in corpus Christi et sanguinem ...nec panis aut vinum deterioratur sed melioratur...manet namque utraque natura'. Both substances co-exist, but they are looked at in different ways, and by consecration attention is switched from one to the other, in the same way that the stars are still present but are ignored and not seen when the sun comes out: 5 pp 130, 137; 7 p 231.

of the *Ecclesia* – which he undoubtedly did[1] – then only by the grossest inconsistency could Hus have refused to accept a double-substance theory of the eucharist, the idea that after consecration you could eat your bread and still have it. The truth of the matter is that Hus saw the point and simply stopped short without committing himself. But in this he was merely following in his predecessor's footsteps. Wyclif himself had already worked out his eucharistic theory ten years before he wrote the *De eucharistia*, and simply refused to write it up because he was well aware that it would have disastrous effects on his friendship with many of the friars.[2] Later, when he had parted company with the mendicants, he bitterly reproached himself for this act of intellectual cowardice – and was all the more vicious towards the friars in consequence for failing to reciprocate. But during the 1370s Wyclif dissembled on the eucharist, pretending to agree with Woodford that he was always changing his mind and really did not know what he did think.

All this meant that when Wyclif began to write his great *Summa theologiae* in 1373, which was carefully planned and eventually reached to fourteen volumes, he decided to leave the theology out for as long as possible, and concentrate on its legal and political implications. Following Aquinas's four-fold classification of law, he produced *De dominio divino* on the eternal law by which God regulated himself; *De mandatis divinis*, the divine law for men; and correspondingly the *De statu innocentiae* outlining man's basic rights under natural law: and then proceeded to show how the divine and the natural came together in human law, in three volumes of the *De dominio civili*. The way in

---

[1] Compare M. Spinka, *John Hus' Concept of the Church* (Princeton 1966) pp 253–6, and G. Leff, *Heresy in the Later Middle Ages* (Manchester 1967) pp 638–9; 'Wyclif and Hus: A Doctrinal Comparison', *BJRL*, L (1967–8) pp 387–410 at 403ff, both of whom broadly accept the view of de Vooght that Loserth had been wrong to regard Hus as a slavish imitator of Wyclif and that Hus refused to follow him into error: for example P. de Vooght, 'Jean Hus et ses juges', *Das Konzil von Konstanz: Beiträge zu seiner Geschichte und Theologie*, ed A. Franzen and W. Müller (Freiburg, Basle, Vienna 1964) pp 152–73; and see also S. H. Thomson in the introduction to his edition of *Hus, Tractatus de Ecclesia* (Boulder, Col., and Cambridge 1956) pp viii–x, xxxiii. The continuing debate is well summarised by H. Kaminsky, *A History of the Hussite Revolution* (Berkeley and Los Angeles 1967) pp 35–7, who rightly follows R. Kalivoda, *Husitská ideologie* (Prague 1961) pp 151–91, in accepting the basic identity of doctrine between Wyclif and Hus. See now also F. Smahel, '*Doctor evangelicus super omnes evangelistas*: Wyclif's Fortune in Hussite Bohemia', *BIHR*, XLIII (1970) pp 16–34 at pp 26–8.

[2] G. A. Benrath, *Wyclifs Bibelkommentar* (Berlin 1966) pp 266–71, indicates that Wyclif had already accepted the principle of remanence in his *Postilla super totam Bibliam* and was dubious then about the accepted theory of transubstantiation. In the *De eucharistia*, 2 p 52, Wyclif says himself that his theory is a logical extension of his philosophical work on the question of annihilation.

which man and God acted together to interpret divine law was further treated in a separate volume, the *De veritate sacrae scripturae*, completed in 1378 but conceived six years earlier.[1] But if Wyclif's treatment of scripture was ostensibly Augustinian (the *De veritate* is supposedly modelled on Augustine's *De doctrina christiana*) his treatment of papal and royal government was distinctly Aristotelian. The *De officio regis* was written for the new king Richard II, and the *De potestate papae* to complement it, written for the new pope Urban VI. Wyclif not only professed to tell them how to govern, but in the *De Ecclesia* combined Augustine and Aristotle, again within a Thomistic framework, to emphasise the dual nature of the christian society over which popes and kings should act together in harmony. This completed the overtly political sections of the work, and by 1379 Wyclif had no option but to pass from the *corpus mysticum* to the *corpus verum* and expound much the same principles in terms of the eucharist. Finally the *Summa* was rounded off with a trilogy, three short and hurriedly written books on the subject of heresy, books which tend, understandably, to be much more autobiographical than the others.

Although, therefore, there was the closest of links between Wyclif's politics and his theology, this order of writing meant that Wyclif – convinced of the need for a great renewal of christian life and an extensive re-structuring of the christian society – was obliged to produce a design for an essentially political reformation with no more than a suggestion that doctrinal reform would follow once the new political order had been achieved. Unlike the movement led by Hus, in which the question of the eucharist was present from the beginning, and became for many of Hus's colleagues a symbol of the political movement itself, Wyclif's demand for a general *reformatio Ecclesiae* was a predominantly political one in the first instance, and may bear comparison with the *reformatio orbis* demanded by the Staufen emperors in previous centuries, and the course which the Reformation took in England during the sixteenth century.

Wyclif appears to have derived the actual term *reformatio* from Grosseteste,[2] who had used it in the sense of a correction of sinners

---

[1] Even the *De logica*, ed M. H. Dziewicki, WS (London 1893–9), appears to have envisaged the application of his philosophical principles to Biblical studies: 1 proem. (1 p 1), 'Motus sum per quosdam legis Dei amicos certum tractatum ad declarandum logicam sacrae scripturae compilare'; compare W. Mallard, 'John Wyclif and the Tradition of Biblical Authority', *Church History*, xxx (Chicago 1961) pp 50–60 at p 56.

[2] *Epistola* 127, ed H. R. Luard, *RS* 25 (London 1861) p 360, but cited by Wyclif in its version as a separate work *De cura pastorali*.

(meaning, of course, the correction of sinners by their bishops and clergy). But he linked this up with his own conception of a universal deformation – a *deformitas Ecclesiae*[1] – a world which had, he said, suddenly seemed to go mad under the impact of increasing papal and episcopal tyranny. 'I say "suddenly seemed" to be deformed,' he commented, 'since it has only just been realised, now that I have pointed it out.'[2] But in fact it was a process which had been going on for a long time, and had passed the point of tolerability in 1200 under the papacy of Innocent III. The beginning of the thirteenth century was in his eyes a climacteric moment in human affairs, initiating a period of permanent crisis. Wyclif saw the history of the Church, in Joachimist fashion, as having passed through three ages, each one worse than the one before, and each with its appropriate allocation of ecclesiastical jurisdiction between lay rulers and papacy. In the first age of true apostolicity, the age of innocence which the *Ecclesia primitiva* had enjoyed down to the fourth century, all governmental power and jurisdiction had been in the hands of lay priest-kings, and the clergy had contented itself with its duties of preaching true doctrine and administering the sacraments. But with the Donation of Constantine – the *donatio*, or rather *dotatio*, *Constantini* by which Constantine had embraced Christianity and married the papacy, granting it an endowment or marriage settlement of secular power – there had begun a second age of partnership between pope and lay ruler, a *dualitas*, in which ecclesiastical jurisdiction was shared between them, as depicted in the good old law of Gratian's *Decretum*. It was always therefore a matter of some importance for Wyclif to distinguish the true popes who came before 1200 from the tyrannical popes who came afterwards. On one occasion he goes to considerable lengths to demonstrate by quoting chronicles that Nicholas II was an earlier pope than Innocent III, and was therefore all the better for this priority.[3] But with Innocent there began the third, last and worst age, the age of Antichrist (the age, he added later, of the mendicant orders whom Innocent had instituted as pseudo-apostles) in which the popes had endeavoured to take all power into their own hands, to claim a plenitude of power, and make themselves into the real king in every kingdom. This was a characteristic, he commented, which had become markedly worse since the popes moved to Avignon. There was now an age of confusion, in which both jurisdictions, temporal and spiritual, had been fused

[1] For example *De Ecclesia*, 11 p 292.
[2] *De Ecclesia*, 12 p 265.   [3] *De eucharistia*, 5 pp 140–1.

together in the claims of the papal monarchs, aided and abetted by a satellite clergy in every realm.

Wyclif therefore conceived his reformation as a revolution in the traditional sense, which one still finds used in English thought by Locke and Burke, as a revolving or turning back to a past ideal situation.[1] The new order would essentially be a re-forming or recreation of the apostolic Church, a new age in which the tyrant-priests would be deprived of their wealth and political power by the lay rulers, and redeemed as new men into a primitive purity. Moreover, it was this insistence on the need for a great rebirth, for a *renovatio*, for the need for the clergy to be born again as new men and to undergo – so to speak – a process of baptism and emerge as *novi homines*, which explains Wyclif's obsessive demands for the confiscation of clerical wealth. It was not that Wyclif objected to property ownership, to wealth as such: otherwise it would hardly have been logical to require the pauperisation of the clergy in order to hand over their burden of sin to the laity. But for him the possession of wealth and political power by the clergy was a symbol of their status as alienated beings. It denoted that they were men who had become divorced from their rational, right-thinking christian selves, and were no longer their true selves but *possessionati*, men possessed by a diabolical other identity, which was reflected in their lust for power and property. Similarly his constant attacks on the clergy for seeking material comforts to the exclusion of spiritual virtues was an expression on a different level of the ancient notion that the clergy had become animal men as distinct from truly human, rational men: they were not themselves at all, and it was small wonder that they had become mad, the stuff of which tyrants and heretics were made, and that their only salvation lay in conversion to their true, ideal identities. The real purpose of dispossession was symbolic, a sign that the clergy were reborn as right-willing beings, had become themselves as they ought to be.

It was this deep sense of clerical self-alienation which goes far to explain why Wyclif looked to the king as the means of generating the reformation.[2] In the fashion of a Waldensian or Spiritual writer, he

---

[1] V. F. Snow, 'The Concept of Revolution in Seventeenth-Century England', *HJ*, v (1962) pp 167–74.

[2] See further my 'Predestination, Property and Power', *SCH*, II (1965) pp 220–36. For the importance of the idea of the *voluntas inordinata* in Wyclif's theory see now F. de Boor, *Wyclifs Simoniebegriff: Die theologischen und kirchenpolitischen Grundlagen der Kirchenkritik John Wyclifs* (Halle 1970), espec pp 64ff.

stipulated against the existence of an actually existing present Church of wrong-willing beings, an *Ecclesia malignantium*, the true reality of an *Ecclesia* of the just, the community of right-willing selves which was present with, or rather, in God – the *res publica* of the righteous. Only when the clergy shed their selfishness, their self-interest, and sought to identify themselves with their public selves in the *respublica Dei*, could there be a rebirth of apostolicity. And it was this abstraction, the *communitas iustorum* – the true State – which it was the function of the king to represent on earth. In order to achieve his true self, his public identity – in order to identify himself with the *respublica* of the just – every individual had to become a king's man, owing allegiance only to the king, in the first instance Christ, the heavenly king, and in practice his vicar, the lay ruler. And it was this conception of society as a heavenly *congregatio*, an abstract entity – in modern terms, a sovereignty – given a visible embodiment in the king, which enabled Wyclif, with devastating logic, to demand the dissolution of the religious orders in England by the monarchy. Sovereignty, as Bodin later pointed out, cannot recognise the existence as independent entities of any other corporate bodies; and Wyclif in his own way was making exactly the same point. It is sometimes suggested that Wyclif was trying to create his own order of friars, a preaching order modelled on the Franciscans, but the real purpose of his urge for the creation of an *ordo Christi* was to make all men equal as subjects under the king. It was to be an order to end all orders, an end to the divisive effects of independent ecclesiastical corporations, and to bring all together in unity under the crown. The new order in society, born out of the reformation, would mean a new order of political beings, of all men as citizens, giving obedience to the lay prince as both priest and king.

This is not to suggest, as some scholars have tended to do, that Wyclif did not seek to create his own sect, his own band of poor priests, of wandering preachers who would seek to instil into the community at large the principles of right living, and who would endeavour in their own lives to emulate the righteousness of their ideal identities. Wyclif saw himself as the prophet of the new age:[1] he sometimes liked to picture himself as the only sane person in a world

---

[1] *De vaticinatione seu prophetia*, 1, ed J. Loserth, *Opera Minora*, WS (London 1913) p 165, 'spectat ad officium doctoris evangelici prophetare'; and note his comparison of himself with St Paul and his sufferings, *De eucharistia*, 9 pp 294–5. He had already pointed out in the *Postilla* that a prophet would need to secure the help of lay lords to protect him from the persecution of evil priests, Benrath, p 89 n 212.

full of madmen,[1] and to harp upon his loneliness as the burden which a prophet had to bear. But he also conceived it his duty (again there are analogies with Joachism and Franciscan Spiritualism) to prepare the way through a group of itinerant priests whose preaching would usher in the new era, and whose suffering under persecution would only serve to emphasise their Christ-like character. That they were always a small number does not seem to be in doubt (although their opponents tended to see them lurking behind every bush), but Wyclif went out of his way to emphasise that they were a few speakers of truth, a minority pitted against the possessioners,[2] a saving remnant of the faithful. Some of them would appear to have been friars, but we know virtually nothing about them, and little is to be gleaned from Wyclif's oblique references except the fact of their existence, and that they considered themselves as forming a *fraternitas* or order. What can now be said with confidence, however, is that this select band of true priests, *viri apostolici*, was not a creation of Wyclif's later years when he had no other means of spreading his views, but was an integral part of his scheme for a *reformatio* in the years before 1378 – the earliest references do in fact date back to as early as 1372/3.[3] He seems to have viewed them as a species of Platonic philosopher guardians whose function was to guide kings and other lords in the way of truth, an academy of consultants to government, whose knowledge of righteousness, he once said, would give them more real power in government than a bad pope.[4] They were, in other words, the true rulers of the

---

[1] For example *De apostasia*, 13, ed M. H. Dziewicki, WS (London 1889) p 173, 'nunc Ecclesia nostra occidua in qua sunt multi maniaci'.

[2] For example *De Ecclesia*, 15 p 357, 'ideo propter multitudinem, propter famam et propter terrorem istorum satellitum exterriti sunt pauci simplices dicere veritatem'. Although only a year or so later (1379–80) he was claiming that 'certe sumus quod plures nobiscum sunt quam cum illis', *Responsiones ad Strode* (*Opera Minora*) p 198.

[3] See the numerous instructions on preaching given to the simple followers of Christ living an apostolic *vita* in the *Postilla*: Benrath, espec pp 179–90, 341–6; compare B. Smalley, 'Wyclif's *Postilla* on the Old Testament and his *Principium*', *Oxford Studies presented to D. Callus* (Oxford 1964) pp 253–96 at pp 280–1. As pointed out by W. Mallard, 'Dating the *Sermones Quadraginta* of John Wyclif', *Medievalia et Humanistica*, XVII (Boulder, Colorado 1966) pp 86–105 at p 99, there is a passage in a sermon (iv 59 p 462) firmly datable to 19 October 1376 which suggests that there was a recognisable group in existence: 'Et licet scribae nostri dicant praedicantes religionem istam esse blasphemos atque haereticos, destructionem Ecclesiae machinantes, tamen visis miraculis veritatem nostri ordinis confitentur'. It may perhaps be suggested that the series of sermons on the Ten Commandments (iv 35–45) of the spring of 1377, some addressed 'vestrae fraternitati', and which seem to have been given to mixed audiences in different places, may have been intended for a group or groups of adherents.

[4] *De blasphemia*, 2 p 37, 'Sacerdos enim mundo incognitus, qui similius sequitur Christum in moribus, habet potestatem regendi et aedificandi Ecclesiam excellentius, quia non

community, even if the community ignored their existence – again a very Platonic sentiment. But that he handpicked men of high quality and capacity may perhaps be indicated by the rapid promotion of the Oxford Lollards once they had recanted and come to terms with the ecclesiastical authorities.

Wyclif never made any secret of the fact that he hotly resented his own lack of ecclesiastical preferment, and one can appreciate the hostility of the ecclesiastical establishment towards a renegade priest whose early career seems to have been as an exponent of the hierocratic theme.[1] Nevertheless it is a little surprising that one who enjoyed the protection of Gaunt should not have secured more advancement during the mid-1370s, unless he himself came not to desire it, and preferred to see himself in the role of adviser behind the throne, the *specialis clericus* of the king. Yet it is difficult to tell whether Gaunt ever regarded Wyclif as anything but a propagandist and pamphleteer, who was useful to him in the incessant guerilla warfare which the English government carried on against the hierocratic tendencies of the bishops in a continuous struggle to secure control of the English clergy and to turn the *ecclesia Anglicana* into a proprietary church. It was traditional royal policy to regard the bishops as organs of government, and the Hundred Years War was emphasising the usefulness of the clergy in acting as expounders of government policy and whipping up support for campaigns against France.[2] If Gaunt was in favour of reform, it was essentially because he sought to strengthen this traditional royal control of the clergy. For this purpose Wyclif was useful. But he and his movement were not essential – as was to be demonstrated by the fact that between 1380 and the early fifteenth century the English government did come to exercise a very firm control over its bishops without Wycliffite assistance.[3]

But what Wyclif meant by reform was, as we have seen, something far more fundamental. He wanted a virtual refoundation of the *ecclesia Anglicana*, a clergy stripped of political character and reduced to naked

consistit regimen Ecclesiae in spoliatione...sed in meritoria operatione...Sic quod melius foret Ecclesiae non esse papam vel praelatos huiusmodi, sed, abiecta tota traditione caesarea, sacerdotes pauperes docere nude et familiariter legem Christi'; cf. 1 p 9, 'Unde potens est Deus illuminare et exercitare mentes paucorum fidelium qui constanter detegant et moneant, si digni sumus, ad destructionem huius versutiae Antichristi'.

[1] Compare Wilks, *SCH*, v (1969) pp 69–98.
[2] H. J. Hewitt, *The Organisation of War under Edward III* (Manchester 1966) pp 160–5.
[3] E. F. Jacob, *Henry Chichele and the Ecclesiastical Politics of his Age* (Creighton Lecture: London 1951) pp 2–3.

essentials, and he argued that no really effective reform could take place unless this was done first, a going back to the beginning and starting again. From this point of view, however, Gaunt proved to be far more dangerous to Wyclifism than Courtenay. He was a man of government, a statesman, in the sense in which these terms were later to be applied to Sir Robert Peel as a man who put the stability and political advantage of the realm above matters of principle, and beyond considerations of personal advantage. The crucial period was from 1377 to 1379, years in which Gaunt did to a very large degree have command of the government and become the *rex incoronatus* that his enemies at St Albans always accused him of being. The death of Edward III put a minor on the English throne: Richard II was ten years old in 1377. The outbreak of the Great Schism in 1378 effectively meant the immediate removal of papal control in England, and, incidentally, halted the process against Wyclif himself. Gaunt had a virtually free hand: for Wyclif it was the supreme opportunity, the very conditions most favourable for the implementation of the *reformatio* programme.

But neither Gaunt nor the English government generally saw it in these terms at all. To them the schism meant a splendid opportunity to embarrass the French by choosing to support Urban VI against his Avignonese rival. And having once chosen him, the government became obsessed by the unlimited opportunities for treason now open to the clergy in favour of Clement VII – there was constant alarm that the clergy in coastal areas might be acting as French spies[1] – and reacted by insisting all the more firmly on the necessity for obedience to Urban VI. Wyclif, of course, did his best in the circumstances. He talked half-heartedly about *noster Urbanus*, and even pretended to believe for a time that Urban (a quite incredible suggestion when one remembers what Urban VI was really like) might be the longed-for *papa angelicus* who would inaugurate the new age.[2] But it was a poor

---

[1] Compare Hewitt, *Organisation of War*, pp 165–8.

[2] For example *De simonia*, 5, ed S. Herzberg-Fränkel and M. H. Dziewicki, WS (London 1898) p 67, 'O quam gloriosum foret exemplar Ecclesiae si Urbanus noster VI renuntiaret omnibus mundi divitiis sicut Petrus, ita quod in Urbano I et VI compleatur circulus quo clerus religione Christi relicta in saecularibus evagatur'. But note 7 p 93, 'Tria autem remedia ex Dei gratia coniecturo. Primum quod Deus irradiet mentem papae exempli gratia Urbani VI quod...conquasset omnes huiusmodi symonias: sed illud foret inopinatum et immensum miraculum'; and by *De blasphemia*, 1 pp 7–8, he has decided that nothing is to be done but wait for Urban to die and hope for a better replacement: see the passage beginning 'O si regnum nostrum post mortem Urbani sexti non foret seductum per satrapas, sic quod liberet se a tali capite et generatione hac pessima'.

strait to be in for one arguing that the English church could manage without popes at all.

Similarly the minority of Richard II only served to convince Gaunt that the *stabilitas regni* was the prime consideration.[1] He would defend Wyclif against the bishops, since he was well aware that the prosecution of Wyclif was an oblique attack on his own position: but Wyclif was still to him just one more episode in the interminable series of political contests which he waged against the hierocrats, and in which the waging tended to be more rewarding than the winning. Overall Gaunt was prepared to come to an accommodation with the bishops in the interests of maintaining stable government during the minority (even indulging in a series of diplomatic absences when necessary), and he ultimately preferred to work with a relatively moderate primate like Sudbury (who became royal chancellor in 1380) in order to maintain the functioning of government, rather than plunge the realm into the sort of turmoil that a Wycliffite reformation would have engendered. As Wyclif complained, in a very revealing passage written in late 1378 or early 1379,[2] he was encountering all the arguments against sudden change which it seems in the nature of bureaucracies to produce automatically: that the *reformatio* would produce too much upheaval; that it might not even then succeed; or that if it could be achieved, now was still not the right time to attempt it. It might be the right thing to do, but the present difficult circumstances made it inadvisable to act within the foreseeable future. He was meeting the normal responses made by any bureaucracy to a reformer who wanted to change things and do it in a hurry. In other words he found that the trouble with fourteenth-century government was that it had become, by medieval standards, a highly efficient administrative machine, a bureaucratic organism, encouraging the spread of an implicit assumption that it was the running and smooth functioning of the existing machinery which mattered more than a reassessment of the purpose for which the machine existed. Moreover the highly factional nature of English politics in the 1370s and 1380s[3] meant that the lay lords, the aristocracy, whom Wyclif saw as a key factor in the *reformatio*, were far more interested in which faction controlled the machine than in asking what it was supposed to be doing. But above all the Aristotelian

---

[1] According to Wyclif, Gaunt thought that an action imperilling the realm was worse than deflowering the king's daughter: *De Ecclesia*, 12 p 266.

[2] *Responsiones ad Strode*, pp 193–200.

[3] R. H. Jones, *The Royal Policy of Richard II: Absolutism in the Later Middle Ages* (Oxford 1968).

revolution, the growth of an increasingly secularised outlook, had created a great deal of confusion in the minds of contemporaries about the proper relationship between the civil and spiritual ends of society. And when ends are uncertain, there is a tendency to concentrate on maintaining existing arrangements and present equipment, without too much questioning of why the equipment is there and why it exists in that form. Much of the trouble which the controlling forces in the English government found with Richard II was that he proved to be a terrible nuisance, a man who wanted to clarify the purpose of government, to restate, to redefine its nature and function as the king's government, instead of allowing the machine to carry on running as it was, and by itself.

Wyclif's reformation then was a scheme for a revolution, but a revolution which was to be imposed from the top downwards. It was to be literally a *coup d'état*, an act of State, undertaken by the government itself under the guidance of a small élite of right-minded theologians who knew what should be done better than anybody else. The preaching campaigns which Wyclif insisted upon to support the revolution were designed to do precisely that, to provide popular support, not to make the reformation an act carried out by the people themselves. There is nothing in the instructions which Wyclif gave his preachers to suggest other than that the preaching to the laity was to be instruction of the most elementary kind. The reformation was to be a revolution by the head itself.

But what if the head refused to act? We have very little idea of what Wyclif was *doing* between 1379 and 1381: he virtually disappears from view. All we know is that he wrote rather less than usual: it is the one relatively unproductive period in an otherwise incredibly productive literary career. But there is a very significant change between one end of this period and the other. In 1379 Wyclif remarks that he has told the people that the Gospel work of reform would have to go forward slowly. He was still convinced that the king could, he said, bring the reformation about immediately by direct legislative action: but he seems to have accepted that the government had no intention of doing so.[1] In his analysis of kingship, however, Wyclif had accepted that a king who became a tyrant ceased to wield valid governmental power and could be replaced by community action. He had further accepted

---

[1] *Responsiones ad Strode*, pp 197–8, beginning 'Unde in vulgari consuluit quod istud generaliter non fiat subito sed prudenter sicut coeperat paulative' (where he is employing a favourite device of referring to himself in the third person).

the traditional notion that *inutilitas*, uselessness, was to be classified as a species of tyranny, and that the people could move when the ruler failed to carry out his duty of good government. He himself had witnessed the power of the London mob at the hearings of 1377 and 1378. Early in 1381 Wyclif wrote that the faithful few could do little by themselves against the might of clerical power, and would be better advised to retire from public life.[1] But, he added, it would be another thing if the people would rise up under their leadership. If the king will not act, he threatened, there will be a rising of the people under prophetic leadership; refusing to pay taxes, especially tithes; and making new appointments to public offices by popular election.[2] I am prepared to disturb the public peace, he declared on more than one occasion at this time,[3] but this may be justified on the grounds that the clergy have already upset the good order of the realm. If the realm is soon in turmoil, it will have been the fault of the clergy for creating the conditions of disturbance: disorder breeds disorder.[4]

Like other shrewd observers (but unlike the government) Wyclif may simply have been aware of popular discontent – there had been a number of minor outbreaks before 1381 – and was using this as means of threatening Gaunt and trying to force him into action. If there was to be a popular rising, he was not averse to claiming the credit for it in advance. But when the so-called Peasants' Revolt did break out at the end of May,[5] it seems to have been sparked off by nothing more than opposition to a second collection of poll taxes – or perhaps resentment at the virginity tests carried out by the royal officials allegedly in order to assess how many members of a family were eligible for tax. Since it is not my purpose to attempt to investigate the economic causes of the Revolt of 1381 (except to note that professor Postan recently declared that he could not explain the Revolt in terms of oppression and economic distress, because condi-

---

[1] *De blasphemia*, 1 pp 8–9, 18, 'Et tantum inveterata malitia invaluit quod unius simplicis momentanea rebellio parum proderit, cum satraparum suorum persecutione sit statissime extinguendus'.

[2] *De simonia*, 7 p 93; 8 pp 101–3.

[3] *XXXIII Conclusiones*, 25 (*Opera Minora*) p 55, citing Matt. 10: 34, 'Unde doctor christianus non omitteret propter perturbationem pacem talem prudenter dissolvere'; and the similar passages in *De vaticinatione*, 2 pp 170 and 174, where he again uses Christ's remark about bringing a sword, not peace, in order to answer accusations of disrupting the peace, adding 'Sufficeret enim pars regni quae est iam toxice in manu mortua per se debellare vel in iusta causa resistere'.

[4] *De simonia*, 4 p 44.

[5] [C.] Oman, [*The Great Revolt of 1381*] (2nd ed with introduction by E. B. Fryde: Oxford 1969); [R. B.] Dobson, [*The Peasants' Revolt of 1381*] (London 1970).

tions had been steadily improving, and that the primary cause might well be seditious preaching),[1] let me instead simply call your attention to certain aspects of the Revolt.

In the first place the Revolt was remarkably well organised on a local community basis; it had no difficulty in finding leaders of considerable ability, some of them priests like Ball, others lay priest-kings like Wraw and Litster, and the rebels seemed to know in advance whom they wanted as leaders; and the attack on London was a brilliantly co-ordinated movement, particularly bearing in mind that the initial target of the revolt was not London but Canterbury. We get that remarkable long march of the Revolt from London to Canterbury and back again, not only to pick up recruits on the way, but also to act as a sort of political Canterbury pilgrimage, a travelling classroom for the purpose of teaching the masses on the way the purpose, aims and methods of the Revolt.

The Revolt was more of an urban movement than a rural one – unlike most English popular risings, which used the green lanes and hollow ways of the countryside, it spread along the roads from town to town – and the towns and roads were the pulpits of the poor preachers;[2] and because it was urban, it was often the ecclesiastical centres – like St Albans and Bury St Edmunds – which suffered most. Courtenay himself certainly had no doubt that the movement was primarily aimed against the clergy.[3] And of course the most important victim of the rising was the archbishop of Canterbury, Sudbury – who apparently made the ludicrous mistake of threatening the mob with the pope, and promptly lost his head. After the Revolt had collapsed, Wyclif politely expressed his regrets that the archbishop should have been killed: if there were bad bishops, it was better to preach against

[1] M. M. Postan, *Cambridge Economic History of Europe*, I (2 ed, Cambridge 1966) pp 609–10.

[2] See the statute of 1382 against unlicensed preachers 'in certain habits under the guise of great holiness' who move from county to county and from town to town, preaching not only in churches but also in churchyards, fairs, markets and other public places: *Rotuli Parliamentorum*, III pp 124–5; and the mandate against lollard preaching issued by the bishop of Worcester on 10 August 1387, which refers to them preaching publicly in churches, graveyards and on the streets, and privately in halls, rooms, gardens and enclosures: Wilkins, *Concilia*, III pp 202–3. For Swinderby's wayside pulpit of mill-stones, Knighton, II p 192.

[3] [M. E.] Aston, ['Lollardy and Sedition, 1381–1431'], *PP*, XVII (1960) pp 1–44 at pp 5, 37; Dobson, p 71; compare Walsingham, *Chronicon Angliae*, pp 310–11. For the way in which the Revolt was seen as a vindication of Courtenay's warnings against Wyclif, see J. H. Dahmus, *William Courtenay, Archbishop of Canterbury, 1381–1396* (Pennsylvania and London 1966) pp 70–3.

them and ostracise them rather than indulge in bloodshed.[1] But since Wyclif had remarked that amongst the ranks of the possessed, Sudbury was the archdemon,[2] one need not perhaps take this too seriously.

None of this demonstrates that Wyclif or the Wycliffite preachers were in any degree responsible for the Revolt. On the other hand it does demonstrate that their opponents were perfectly entitled to suggest that they were, and the accusation was duly levelled.[3] But more to the point is Wyclif's reaction afterwards. Not only did he express sympathy for the rebels,[4] and for the conditions which led to the rising – again emphasising that the clergy were mainly to blame for heavy taxation[5] – but, whilst he condemned the Revolt, the only real reason that he gives is that the rebels went about it the wrong way. They had the right idea, but they just carried it out improperly: 'licet maiores bonos instinctus habuerint, non plene fecerunt ad regulam'.[6] The fatal flaw in the movement was that it acted against the clergy without the authority of parliament, of the lay lords who made up the *communitas regni* together with the king. It should have been an act, he writes, of the *totum regnum* undertaken with full public authority.[7] If one recalls that the rebels had made considerable efforts to suggest that they were acting on royal authority; that every care was taken not to harm the members of the royal family; and that the London rebels dispersed as soon as Richard II took over the nominal leadership of the Revolt, then it may be suggested that it is a matter of considerable significance that Wyclif condemned the Peasants' Revolt because, although it tried, it *failed* to be a revolution from above.

I hope I have now said enough to suggest the real answer to my original question: why did a Wycliffite movement under Hus's command succeed where Wyclif failed? Hus had nothing more to say

[1] *De blasphemia*, 5 p 76; *XXXIII Conclusiones*, 22 p 49.

[2] *De blasphemia*, 13 p 194.

[3] Aston, pp 2–5, 36; Oman, pp 19–21, 101; Fryde, p xxxvii; Dobson, pp 367, 373–8; compare N. Cohn, *The Pursuit of the Millennium* (London 1957) p 413: all agree that Wyclif was innocent of the charge of complicity, however damaging the revolt undoubtedly was for the future of the lollard movement. Similarly Workman, II pp 236–41; McFarlane, pp 99–100.

[4] *De blasphemia*, 13 pp 197–8. Compare J. Stacey, 'The Character of John Wyclif', *London Quarterly and Holborn Review*, CLXXXIV (London 1959) pp 133–6 at p 134.

[5] *De blasphemia*, 6 p 83; 13 pp 190, 198; 14 p 214; 17 p 267; *Responsiones ad Strode*, pp 198–200.

[6] *De blasphemia*, 13 p 190.

[7] *De blasphemia*, 13 p 197, 'Tertio deficit populus in modo agendi multiplici...et tertio quia exspectari debet totius regni exhortatio sive consilium': the *totum regnum* should have acted 'in parliamento publico', 17 p 269.

than Wyclif about the need for a *reformatio regni*: if anything, he said considerably less; but there was no essential difference between his and Wyclif's scheme for reform. It is true that he succeeded to a well-established and flourishing native reform movement, and enjoyed a very great measure of popular support. But it is arguable at least, in the light of the rising of 1381, that Courtenay and the chroniclers were right to maintain that a reformation of the clergy would have gained massive popular support in England. The essential difference in Bohemia, however, is that the Czech reformation at a crucial period did take on the character of a revolution from above.

The Czech reform movement had grown up to a large degree under royal protection, first from Charles IV and subsequently from Wenceslas, although it can hardly be said to have been state-orientated until after 1400 when the influx of Wyclif's writings provided the Czechs with a groundplan for a national church-state under royal control – a feature which does much to explain why the writings of an obscure Oxford don of twenty years before proved so acceptable in Bohemia. But Wenceslas (who, ironically enough, was soon to be deprived of his claim to Roman emperorship on the grounds that he was *inutilis*, useless) had learned from his contest with John of Jenstein during the 1380s and early 1390s that a king could gain control of his clergy and create a proprietary church if he was prepared to act sufficiently vigorously against his primate. At various times Wenceslas imprisoned the archbishop of Prague, confiscated his estates, killed one of his officials, and eventually forced the archbishop into resignation.[1] It is perhaps significant that one of Hus's earliest writings as a royal pamphleteer deliberately reminds the Czech clergy of Wenceslas's treatment of Jenstein.[2]

Wenceslas saw in Hus and the growing Wycliffite movement in Bohemia the means of recovering his position after the civil war of 1399–1403 and of making himself supreme in his own kingdom. Whilst it suited him, Wenceslas played the part of Wyclif's ideal

---

[1] See now R. E. Weltsch, *Archbishop John of Jenstein, 1348–1400: Papalism, Humanism and Reform in Pre-Hussite Prague* (The Hague and Paris 1968). A convenient survey of Wenceslas's struggle with the higher nobility during the 1390s, which involved a further contest between the king and bishop John of Litomysl, is provided by F. Dvornik *The Slavs in European History and Civilization* (New Brunswick, N.J, 1962) pp 183–8.

[2] [*Mistra Jana Husi,*] *Korespondence [a Dokumenty]*, ed [V.] Novotný (Prague 1920) pp 3–4. The tract is written in the form of a letter from Wenceslas to Boniface IX, dated August 1402, in which the king supposedly threatens to throw his opponents into the Vltava, as had happened to Jenstein's vicar-general, John of Pomuk, in 1393.

king, and converted the Czech reform movement into a *reformatio regni* for the benefit of the Bohemian monarchy. In the five years after 1408 Wenceslas deliberately and no doubt cynically used the Hussites to make himself master of *studium*, *sacerdotium* and *regnum*. The decree of Kutna Hora in January 1409 not only gave the Czechs control of the university of Prague, and encouraged the removal of the anti-Hussite German masters, but the effect was to make Wenceslas the real rector and regulator of the university. Wencelas's seizure of archbishop Zbinek's estates and revenues in 1409 and 1410, and his expulsion or imprisonment of all clergy who observed the archbishop's interdict in 1411 – all actions undertaken ostensibly in support of Hus himself – forced Zbinek into death in exile, and enabled the king to appoint his own physician (Albik) as archbishop of Prague. And in 1413, on the plea of ensuring adequate Hussite representation on the city council of Prague, Wenceslas transferred all appointment of councillors to the crown, and gained control over the government of his capital.[1]

Yet that Wenceslas was acting solely for his own royal advantage is made abundantly clear by his treatment of Hus himself over the affair of the indulgences for the Neapolitan crusade of 1412. When Hus preached against the indulgences – and thus imperilled Wenceslas's policy of maintaining good relations with pope John XXIII – Wenceslas decided that Hus had outlived his usefulness and had to be silenced. Hus was driven out of the capital into exile in southern Bohemia (Kozí Hrádek) for eighteen months: he was not recalled even though the question of the indulgences became a dead letter within a month of his departure. Hus had served the royal purpose, and could be dispensed with as soon as the royal supremacy was established. It was almost certainly Wenceslas who engineered Hus's departure for Constance, partly through Henry Lefl of Lazany, the lord of Krakovec, a leading member of the royal council, at whose castle Hus was invited to reside in the summer of 1414, and from which he left for Constance;[2] and partly through the king's brother Sigismund, who encouraged Hus

---

[1] For these events see now [M.] Spinka, *John Hus: [A Biography]* (Princeton 1968); also P. de Vooght, *L'Hérésie de Jean Huss* and *Hussiana* (Louvain 1960).

[2] This supports the testimony given at Constance by the Prague inquisitor, Nicholas of Nezero, according to which Wenceslas obliged Hus to go to the council: Spinka, *John Hus' Concept of the Church*, p 353; *John Hus*, p 220. This statement has been generally decried as being part of evidence obtained under duress and contradicting earlier testimony, and on the grounds that Wenceslas would never have done this for the reason stated by Nicholas, to clear his realm of suspicion of heresy. This does not necessarily clear Wenceslas of blame, although his reasons may have been very different from that given by the bishop.

to take his case to Constance, and whose safe-conduct ensured that Hus never returned.[1] One would very much like to know how far the Czech clergy at Constance who acted as Hus's accusers were acting under royal instructions.

But it is not my intention to open the case of Hus here. My purpose is simply to emphasise that, as Wyclif himself had always stressed, a *reformatio* could only succeed – and subsequently in Bohemia *did* succeed – when it was seen as a revolution from the top downwards. In a sense the real heir of Wyclif in Bohemia was not Hus, but Wenceslas. It was Wenceslas rather than Hus who in the end proved that Wyclif was right: that a reformation has to be an act by the head. But England had to wait for a century and a half after Wyclif's death for a king who was capable of understanding the point and of putting it into effect.

[1] For Sigismund's invitation, Novotný, *Korespondence*, p 197. The safe conduct had been offered to Hus before he left Krakovec, since he refers to it on 1 September, although it was not actually issued until 18 October, when Hus had already set out (on 11 October). The document was ambiguously phrased so that it was not clear whether it covered Hus at Constance itself or on a return journey see F. Palacký, *Documenta Magistri Joannis Hus* (Prague 1869) p 238; [M.] Spinka, [*John Hus at the Council of Constance*] (New York and London 1965) pp 89–90. Hus later accused Sigismund of acting like Pilate in betraying him to his Czech enemies: Spinka, pp 259–60, 286; compare *John Hus' Concept of the Church*, pp 331–7; *John Hus*, pp 222–37. Sigismund's sincerity in the matter of the safe conduct is defended by de Vooght, *L'Hérésie*, pp 325–8, 334–5.

BISHOP BUCKINGHAM AND THE LOLLARDS OF LINCOLN DIOCESE

by A. K. MCHARDY

THE first case of lollardy in which Buckingham is known to have acted concerned William Swinderby, the hermit of Leicester. Swinderby's story is well known,[1] and needs no re-telling here. What should be noted as important for our purpose is the timing of his prosecution: the first inhibitions and citations against him were dated 5 March 1382.[2] Thus Buckingham took action before additional powers were obtained from the lay arm and before the Blackfriars council itself met, though it may be conjectured that when he acted he had the forthcoming meeting of the council in view. Buckingham issued the commission to Swinderby's two judges on 12 May 1382 when he was in London for the council, and published the sentence against him on 11 July.[3] On the following day he passed on to his archdeacons the council's condemnation of Wycliffite opinions,[4] though the decrees had already been published in the diocese, at Oxford, on 15 June 1382.[5]

This year, 1382, marked an important stage in the development of the lay power's interest in heresy.[6] On 26 June a letter patent gave archbishop Courtenay and his suffragans power to arrest and imprison heretics without invoking the lay arm.[7] Buckingham did receive a copy of this letter at some time, as will be seen, but he did not invoke it in his next known action against a heretic.

This was John Corringham, vicar of Diddington, a village five miles

---

[1] His trial in Lincoln diocese, drawn largely from Buckingham's Memoranda Register, is described in [K. B.] McFarlane, [John] Wycliffe [and the Beginnings of English Nonconformity] (London 1952) pp 121–5.

[2] [Lincolnshire Archives Office,] Reg[ister] 12 [Register of John Buckingham (Memoranda)], fols 236v, 242.

[3] Reg 12 fol 243v; [Chronicon Henrici] Knighton [Monachi Leycestrensis], ed J. R. Lumby, RS 92, II (1895) p 197.

[4] Reg 12 fols 239v–240v; printed, Knighton II, pp 167–70.

[5] McFarlane, Wycliffe pp 109–10.

[6] For discussion see [H. G.] Richardson, ['Heresy and the Lay Power under Richard II'] EHR, LI (1936) pp 7–8.

[7] C[alendar of] P[atent] R[olls], Richard II, 1381–5, 6 vols (London 1895–1909) II, p 150.

south-west of Huntingdon. Corringham the heretic seems to have eluded the scrutiny of historians so far; that he did not elude the vigilance of his bishop may have been because on the road northwards from Diddington the next village is Buckden which was the site of an episcopal manor house. The vicarage of Diddington was in the gift of the warden and scholars of Merton College, Oxford,[1] and Corringham had been a fellow of Merton, where he was almost certainly a contemporary of Mr John Aston, one of Wycliffe's leading disciples.[2] Moreover, his uncle, Roger Corringham, was a fellow of the Queen's College during some of the years when Wycliffe rented rooms there.[3]

On 9 March 1384 Buckingham issued a commission to the official of the archdeacon of Huntingdon, the rural deans of Huntingdon and St Neots, the rector of Southoe and the vicar of Buckden which are the two parishes adjacent to Diddington. He informed the commissaries that Corringham had been excommunicated for his many contumacies, excesses and errors, which he had publicly preached and taught; the commissaries were to see that he abjured these conclusions before the multitude of the faithful during solemn mass, and the ceremonies were to take place in St Mary's church, Huntingdon, on the Sunday following the receipt of the order, and then in the churches of Diddington, St Neots and Southoe on successive Sundays. The five commissaries were to send Buckingham a written report by 17 April 1384.[4]

The first part of Corringham's recantation closely followed that made by Swinderby nearly two years earlier.[5] Then come his nine unorthodox conclusions.[6] The first and second of these were Wycliffite conclusions condemned at the Blackfriars council: that the true body of Christ was not in the sacrament of the altar, and that all priests should be allowed to preach the word of God without need of papal or episcopal licence.[7] Conclusion no. 3: that just as it was lawful for two men to be priests at the same time, so two could be pope simultaneously; no. 4: that the antipope was the helper of pope Urban VI; no. 5: that the devil was his helper and God's helper also; no. 6: the form of the Norwich crusade was contrary to scripture; no. 7: that

---

[1] *The Early Rolls of Merton College*, ed J. R. L. Highfield, *OHS*, new series, XVIII (1964) p 45.

[2] [A. B.] Emden, [*A Biographical Register of the University of*] *Oxford* (Oxford 1957–9) I, pp 494, 67.

[3] *Ibid* I, pp 494–5; McFarlane, *Wycliffe* p 19.   [4] *Reg 12* fols 271v–272.

[5] See *Reg 12* fol 243v; printed in *Fasc[iculi] Ziz[aniorum]*, ed W. W. Shirley, *RS* 5 (1859) p 337.   [6] *Reg 12* fol 272; for text see appendix.

[7] *Reg 12* fol 240; printed in *Fasc Ziz* pp 278, 280.

neither the bishop of Norwich nor any other crusader was permitted to kill a heretic or schismatic; no. 8: killing for self-defence was unlawful: a person in danger of his life should rather allow himself to be killed; no. 9: everyone who either granted or paid a subsidy to the king for wars outside the realm was *ipso facto* excommunicate.

Corringham's conclusions merit some further consideration. Only two of them, as we have seen, were taken over directly from Wycliffe; two others might be said to stem from the Wycliffite doctrines that God should obey the devil and that no pope after Urban VI should be recognised.[1] Corringham's dislike of the Norwich crusade was shared by his former colleague, John Aston, who preached a sermon against the project at Gloucester on 21 September 1383.[2] But the group of beliefs as a whole is both individual and strongly political, and illustrates clearly the impact of national and international events on the mind of one man.

Corringham's recantation seems to have marked a genuine change of heart, for his later life was impeccably orthodox. On 28 January 1388 he exchanged Diddington for the rectory of Rossington in Yorkshire,[3] and from then on his career in Church and State was one of uninterrupted progress until he died in November 1444, a canon of Windsor and the first known registrar of the Order of the Garter.[4]

The first lay heretic against whom Buckingham acted was Thomas Compworth, an esquire of Thrupp in the parish of Kidlington, immediately north of Oxford. In the story of Crown–Church action over heresy his case is important because it was the first in which Buckingham invoked powers newly granted by the crown, a fact mentioned both in Buckingham's register and in the chronicle account. Compworth was said to have preached heresy for many years; he also refused to pay tithes to his rector, the abbot of Osney.[5] He was an elusive man to bring to justice. Buckingham's first mandate to discipline him of which we have knowledge was dated 26 August 1385, and was addressed to John Belvoir, Thomas Brandon and John Bottlesham; they were to make enquiries and to proceed against Compworth on account both of his heresies and his non-payment of tithes.[6] A second commission dated 30 August 1385, was addressed to four *magistri*, John

[1] *Ibid* pp 278, 279.   [2] *Knighton* II, p 178.
[3] *CPR*, Richard II, 1385–9, 6 vols (London 1895–1909) III, p 398.
[4] Emden, *Oxford* I, p 494.
[5] The proceedings against Compworth are described at length in *Historia* [*Vitae et Regni*] *Ricardi II* [*Angliae Regis a Monacho quodam de Evesham consignata*], ed T. Hearne (Oxford 1729) pp 67–9.   [6] *Reg 12* fol 310.

Thomas rector of Pickworth (Lincs) a relation of Buckingham,[1] Thomas Fulford rector of Whitchurch (Berks), Geoffrey rector of Stanton St John (Oxon) and Henry Fowler bachelor in laws, ordering them to arrest Compworth and imprison him in Banbury castle. As authority for such action Buckingham incorporated in his directions the letter patent of 26 June 1382 giving archbishop Courtenay and his suffragans power to arrest and imprison heretics.[2] The letter, though not addressed to Buckingham, and described as being 'recently' received – probably an elastic expression[3] – was clearly regarded by him as providing authority for the imprisonment of Compworth. On the same day a separate commission was issued to proceed against Compworth's accomplices and supporters.[4] After being excommunicated on 18 October 1385[5] Compworth was forced to submit just before Christmas, and the Oxford doctors who tried him ordered him to pay £40 compensation to the abbot of Osney for withholding tithes.[6]

At about the same time Buckingham was taking action against a Leicestershire bailiff who was probably a heretic though never described as such. This was William Whytsyde, of Ashby de la Zouche (Leics), who was signified as an obdurate excommunicate on 19 September 1385.[7] He seems to have been captured quickly and put in the king's gaol at Leicester, but the keeper allowed him to wander about the town as he pleased. He frequented mass and other divine offices in churches, and infected the faithful sheep of the bishop's flock with his own 'disease', which may well have been heresy. An order from Buckingham, dated 7 November 1385, was sent to the abbot of St Mary de Pratis, the rural dean of Leicester, and to all parochial clergy of the deanery: they were to excommunicate William and his adherents, citing them to appear before Buckingham's commissaries at a given day and place; and further, they were to warn the warden of the king's gaol at Leicester to keep Whytsyde in prison, and if, after three days, Whytsyde was not more strictly kept, the gaoler himself was to be excommunicated.[8] There seems to have been no immediate repentance on Whytsyde's part, for he was still unreconciled to the church on 1 January 1386.[9]

During the next few years Buckingham is not known to have dealt with any individual heretics; nor to the best of our knowledge did he

---

[1] Emden, *Oxford* III, pp 1861.   [2] *CPR 1381-5*, p 150.   [3] *Reg 12* fols 311r-311v.
[4] *Ibid* fols 310v-311.   [5] PRO MS C85/108/13.
[6] *Historia Ricardi II* p 69.   [7] PRO MS C 85/108/14.
[8] *Reg 12* fol 315v.   [9] PRO MS C85/108/17.

receive any new powers[1] or commissions from the crown to deal with heresy: the migration of Mr Nicholas Hereford to Nottingham caused attention to be focused on heresy there. But the great increase in lollardy which Henry Knighton complained of at this time[2] did not go unnoticed by Buckingham, who in the spring of 1388 issued two un-headed and undated mandates against admitting unlicensed preachers.[3]

More important was the renewed activity of the lay power after the Merciless Parliament. There was issued, starting on 30 March 1388, a series of commissions ordering the searching out of heretical writings.[4] Two of the series concerned Lincoln diocese. On 23 May 1388 an order was issued to a group consisting of two clerics and two laymen, headed by Mr Thomas Brightwell doctor of theology and dean of Newark College, Leicester, a former fellow of Merton and an erstwhile sympathiser with Wycliffe's ideas.[5] It directed them to seize and bring before the council any books containing the heresies of Wycliffe, Nicholas Hereford, John Aston and their followers; and to prohibit by proclamation the holding of such heresies or the ownership of any books containing them. The two clerical members were empowered to arrest, examine, and imprison suspects. An identical commission was issued to William Ownby, Buckingham's suffragan bishop, on 30 September 1388.[6]

In these two commissions the council is seen acting (as it did, of course, in other dioceses) against heresy in general.[7] It may be seen in Buckingham's jurisdiction proceeding against an individual in the person of Thomas Latimer of Braybrooke (Northants), one of Richard II's chamber knights, who on 2 May 1388 was summoned before the council to be examined for heresy.

Latimer was also lord of the manor of Chipping Warden (Northants), and it was perhaps as a result of these enquiries about him that the activities of John Woodward came to light. John Woodward junior,

---

[1] Individual letters patent granting the right to imprison heretics were sent to seven bishops of the southern province, the first being issued to the bishop of Coventry and Lichfield on 21 May 1386. Richardson, p 9.

[2] *Knighton* II, p 260.

[3] Probably 25 March and 10 May. *Reg 12* fols 349v, 350.

[4] Richardson, pp 10–12.

[5] Emden, *Oxford* I, pp 266–7; the other members of the commission were William Chisulden a prebendary of Newark College, Richard Barewe knight, and Robert Langham. *CPR 1385–9*, p 468.

[6] *Ibid* p 550.

[7] On 23 May 1388 commissions similar to that issued to Brightwell and his colleagues were addressed to groups headed by the chancellor of Salisbury cathedral and the prior of Thurgaton (Notts). *CPR 1385–9*, p 468.

of Knebworth, was a chaplain staying in Chipping Warden and preaching heresy and making converts. When this came to Buckingham's notice he ordered William Sligh, vicar of Blakesley (Northants) and rural dean of Brackley, to cite Woodward to appear before him or his commissaries at Sleaford on 18 December 1388.[1] On Tuesday 8 December Sligh, with a chaplain, William Stoke, rode into Chipping Warden to deliver the summons. Tuesday was market day, and the assembled crowd gave them a rough reception. They fled to the church for safety, but they were dragged out, and Stoke was wounded and the churchyard polluted by his blood. The crowd then seized their horses and cut off their tails. And Latimer, far from having been cowed by his appearance before the council, brought an action against the rural dean, alleging that Sligh made seven attempts to serve the summons on Woodward on successive Tuesdays, so that market trade was disrupted and he, as owner, lost his profits.

Buckingham's mandate to excommunicate the offenders, to discover their names and cite them to appear before masters Thomas Brandon, John Bottlesham and Richard Kyllom in Sleaford church twelve days after the citation had been served was dated 20 December 1388.[2] When he issued this mandate he did not know who the miscreants were, but he later discovered the names of forty-five of Woodward's supporters and signified them to the chancery as being excommunicate. This was before 8 March 1389 when a mandate for their imprisonment was issued to the sheriff of Northampton.[3] On 10 March 1389 Buckingham again called to trial those who attacked the rural dean, but nothing is heard of the case thereafter.[4]

Though there followed, it seems, a lull in Buckingham's activities against heretics, lollardy was by no means eradicated from the diocese, as archbishop Courtenay's visitation of Leicester in October 1389 was to show.[5] Early in 1392 Buckingham issued yet another mandate against the admittance of unlicensed preachers. This time, however, he was concerned with one particular place for his mandate to the archdeacon of Huntingdon, his official and the parochial chaplain at North Mimms (Herts) concerned illegal preaching in North Mimms church.[6]

[1] This episode is largely drawn from the typescript of K. B. McFarlane's lectures on the lollard knights.   [2] *Reg 12* fol 357.
[3] *CCR, Richard II, 1385–9*, 6 vols (London 1914–27) III, pp 667–8.
[4] *Reg 12* fol 357v.
[5] [*The*] *Metropolitan Visitations* [*of William Courtenay Archbishop of Canterbury 1381–1396*], ed J. H. Dahmus (Illinois 1950) pp 164–7.
[6] Probably issued on or about 12 January 1392. *Reg 12* fol 388.

Bishop Buckingham and the Lollards of Lincoln diocese

The final coven of heretics to concern Buckingham was at Northampton. When archbishop Courtenay made his visitation of St James's abbey, Northampton, on 5 and 6 November 1389, he heard, it would seem, no rumour of heresy in the town. We may doubt his wisdom in summoning to Northampton from Leicester an anchoress called Maud who had been accused of heresy and who came to make her submission to him,[1] for from our vantage point we can see that there was always a risk in encouraging heretics, even those who were contrite, to move about the country. It was not, however, until 1393 that lollardy in Northampton began to plague the ecclesiastical or civil authorities. According to one townsman, Richard Stormsworth, the root of the trouble was the heretical tendency of John Fox who was elected mayor in the autumn of 1392. There were lollard demonstrations in the town on 26 December 1392 and 12 January 1393,[2] and Buckingham took action. In a mandate issued on or about 20 January 1393 to a group of unnamed commissaries he complained that he had heard of various evildoers running about in the town of Northampton pretending to be priests and preaching. Their sermons, moreover, contained erroneous enormities against the faith. These men were to be prohibited from preaching, and, if after three warnings on successive Sundays they did not desist, they were to be excommunicated and cited to appear before him in fifteen days.[3] It was probably when issuing one of the three warnings that Buckingham's commissaries were, according to Stormsworth, openly defied by mayor Fox and one of his supporters, Mr William Northwold, on Sunday 9 March 1393.[4] On the 24th of the following month John Fox was deposed from the mayoralty by the lay power, and the townsmen told to choose a successor. Not long afterwards, Fox was arrested and imprisoned at Nottingham, while his rival, Stormsworth, succeeded him in office, but only for a brief period.[5]

Buckingham seems to have made no further moves, until on 3 August 1393 he issued a fresh mandate to a group of six men. They were headed by his suffragan William Ownby ('*Pisenensis*') with whom were associated the abbot of St James's, Northampton, the archdeacon of Northampton Thomas Butler, brother William Beauford a Carmelite friar and doctor of theology, Mr Eudo Zouch doctor of laws and canon of Lincoln, and the rector of Towcester (Northants) parish church Mr Robert Palmer. The commissaries were to call together the upright

---

[1] *Metropolitan Visitations* p 169. [2] McFarlane, *Wycliffe* pp 141–2.
[3] *Reg 12* fol 398. [4] McFarlane, *Wycliffe* p 142. [5] *Ibid* p 144.

men of the place and enquire into the names of all those, of either sex, who were preaching, teaching, holding or sympathising with heresies. They were to make their report to the bishop by 8 September.[1] But before then conditions in the town had become so serious that Buckingham himself intervened. According to the report which he later sent into chancery, it was as though the greater part of the town had been infected by this heretical poison. His own commissaries were in such grave peril from the lollards that once with great difficulty they fled for their lives to the vestry of All Saints' church. In an effort to prevent the situation becoming even worse, Buckingham went to the town and on 5, 6, and 7 September 1393 held an enquiry in All Saints' church, questioning the more upright and worthy people both of Northampton itself and of neighbouring places. This inquisition brought to light the activities of Anna Palmer, an anchoress living in a house next to St Peter's church. She was the main receiver of lollards in her house at night, especially Thomas Patteshull, John Chory, Simon Colyn, John Wolf, and two chaplains John and Thomas Wheelwright, the principal lollards who held secret conventicles and illicit congregations. The whole group privately and publicly held and taught articles which Buckingham listed in an appendix to his report. A further result of the inquisition was that Anna was also suspected of incontinence. Buckingham caused her to be summoned before him to answer those charges. When she appeared she openly referred to her bishop as anti-Christ and his clerks as anti-Christ's disciples,[2] sentiments previously expressed in a sermon at Northampton by William Northwold.[3] The articles against her were read out in English by Buckingham's chancellor, but she said proudly and impudently that she did not want to answer them, save the charge of incontinence, which she denied. This refusal brought her under deep suspicion of heresy, error and lollard depravity; and so, because of her intransigence and lest she infect others of the faithful, she was ordered to be detained in the episcopal prison at Banbury until she should return to the bosom of the Church. She remained in prison throughout the winter of 1393–4. On 26 March 1394 a writ of *venire faciatis* against her was issued to Buckingham, returnable by 3 May before the king and council in chancery; he was not only to

---

[1] *Reg 12* fol 406. Buckingham also addressed a letter in similar terms under his privy seal to one of the commissaries, almost certainly his suffragan, on 8 August 1393, *ibid* fol 406.

[2] [Lincolnshire Archives Office], *Reg[ister] 12B*, [*Register of John Buckingham (Royal Writs)*] fol 64.

[3] On 9 March 1393, *The Peasants' Rising and the Lollards*, ed E. Powell and G. M. Trevelyan (London 1899) p 50.

send her to London for examination but was to show also the cause of her capture and detention.[1]

Another religious woman who was ordered to be imprisoned was Agnes Nowers, an apostate nun, who was wandering about in the town of Northampton associating with lollards. Her arrest was ordered in a mandate issued by Buckingham on 20 September 1393.[2] Buckingham also gave orders for Anna Palmer's associates to be arrested, along with Thomas Peyntour of Northampton and Henry Tolvylle of Buckinghamshire. The men were lodged in Northampton castle to await trial, either by the bishop or his commissaries, or before the king and council, and mainperned for each other on 13 March 1394.[3] Possibly John Chory and John Wolf speedily returned to the fold, but on 9 November 1394 Simon Colyn, Thomas Patteshull, the two Wheelwrights, John and Thomas, along with the chaplain Richard Bullock were signified as being obdurate excommunicates.[4] The group discovered by Buckingham was not identical with that accused by Richard Stormsworth of promoting heresy in the town. Richard Bullock was mentioned also by Stormsworth, and Simon Colyn may possibly be identified with the runaway apprentice James Collin named in Stormsworth's petition; but of Thomas Compworth, Nicholas Weston[5] and William Northwold Buckingham made no mention.[6]

Though the ultimate fate of Anna Palmer and her associates at the hands of the council is not known, we do have a record of the list of charges against them which Buckingham forwarded to the lay authorities, and they merit examination for the light they throw on a phase of heretical belief. There were fifteen in all, not set down in any apparently logical order, and here they will be discussed in the order which best illustrates their place in the development of lollard thought.[7]

One article listed in the charges was to a great extent the same as a conclusion of Wycliffe's condemned in 1382,[8] namely, that a priest in mortal sin had no power to consecrate the sacrament of the eucharist or of baptism, though the assertion that a chaplain who did so was the devil was strong language. A similar vehemence is to be found in the article attacking the veneration of images and crucifixes. But the attack itself was no new thing. Wycliffe had taken the same line, and hostility

---

[1] *Reg 12B* fol 64. [2] *Reg 12* fol 406v.
[3] *CCR 1392–6* p 260. [4] PRO MS C85/109/38.
[5] Signified as an apostate friar by the prior of the carmelite convent, Northampton. No date. PRO MS C81/1793/29.
[6] McFarlane, *Wycliffe* p 141. [7] *Reg 12B* fols 64–64v. For the text see appendix.
[8] *Fasc Ziz* p 278.

to images was a well-established strand in heretical thought by this date.[1] Mocking of images and indeed image-breaking had been a feature of heresy at Leicester since 1382.[2] The Northampton group gave it as their opinion that there was as much merit in kissing the stones lying in the field as in kissing the feet of the crucifix in church, or in putting lights or gifts before images. They shared Wycliffe's dislike of pilgrimages, as did other lollards,[3] believing that when, as a penance for sins, pilgrimage was prescribed there was more merit in expending the cost of the journey on the poor, than in undertaking the penance enjoined. In the same article stood their assertion that after AD 1000 Satan was loosed from his bonds; all born after that date who were regarded as saints by the orthodox were on the contrary believed by these lollards to be so diabolically infected that they rather thought them damned than saved, and they called them the millennial saints (sanctos millenos). The next article was about St Thomas of Canterbury and other saints adored by pilgrims in different parts of England. The lollards suspended all belief in their sanctity.

The Northampton lollards maintained, further, that it was unlawful for priests to accept stipends for celebrating divine offices; and oblations made for marriages and burials they accounted simony. Payment for celebrating services had long been disliked; Swinderby and lollards in Leicester at a later date had all condemned them, while oblations for burial of the dead were mentioned particularly by the lollards brought before Courtenay in 1389.[4] Anna Palmer and her friends condemned the giving of alms to the able-bodied; sturdy beggars had also been condemned at Leicester, as Knighton records for the year 1382.[5]

Other conclusions forwarded to the council were severely critical both of the papacy and of the ownership of property by the Church. Not the man generally called pope but whoever because of sanctity was close to God in this life, they maintained, was confirmed as pope; he alone had power to grant relief from the pain and guilt of sins. Because in the time of St Silvester the Church was dowered with simony it remained poisoned to that day, and so they despaired of the power of the pope and of other prelates. Thus they placed no faith in indulgences

---

[1] For discussion and references see J. M. Russell-Smith, 'Walter Hilton and a Tract in Defence of the Veneration of Images', *Dominican Studies*, VII (London 1954) pp 180–214.

[2] *Knighton* II, pp 182–3. *Metropolitan Visitations* p 164.

[3] H. B. Workman, *John Wyclif* (Oxford 1926) II, p 18; *Fasc Ziz* pp 364 (1395), 409–10 (1399).

[4] Compare Swinderby, 1382, *Fasc Ziz* p 339; *Knighton* II, pp 174, 262; *Metropolitan Visitations* p 164.

[5] The Leicester lollards, 1382. *Knighton* II, p 175.

granted by the pope even for alms given to charitable causes. Faith in papal power had been severely shaken by the great schism as well as by Wycliffe's writings.[1] The Donation of Constantine had been attacked by Wycliffe on several occasions, and the Wycliffites who were mentioned by Henry Knighton under the year 1388 also said there had been no true pope since St Silvester.[2]

Perhaps more radically, they disclaimed the need for any material church, which they called 'Caym's castle';[3] they said it was sufficient that every Christian should keep God's commands in bed or field, adoring Him secretly, and not with public prayers, lest they should be reckoned pharisees. The attack on church revenues leads naturally to the attack on church buildings. This had already been done, albeit hesitatingly, at Leicester in the 1380s[4] and was linked at Northampton with the derogatory language used of friar's property.

Nor did the Northampton group see the need for an order of priests, for the members held that every Christian is permitted to inform his brother about the ten commandments and the gospels so that he knows and preaches them, and further that the head of every household should be responsible for himself and for the deeds of his family. The depreciating of the clergy had as its counterpoise the exalting of the laity, whose claims to be able, even if unlettered, to preach, teach, and act as priests had been put forward at Leicester in 1389.[5]

The last four points to be mentioned are less easily placed in an historical context, though it would be rash to claim that they were, even for their period, unique. The Northampton lollards affirmed that a chaplain was not bound to say matins or the canonical hours either before or after celebrating mass unless he wholeheartedly wished to, nor did he need to confess, save to God alone, before celebrating. If anyone heard mass while in a state of mortal sin, that mass would be to their damnation. If anyone committed a mortal sin, forgot about it and died unconfessed, he was damned for that forgotten sin even if he sought God's mercy, for it was not in God's power to save him by mercy. The innocent were gathered neither into hell nor heaven after

---

[1] For scepticism about the value of indulgences see *Metropolitan Visitations*, p 164; Wycliffe's views on the papacy are described in H. B. Workman, *John Wyclif* II, pp 73–82.
[2] For references see Gordon Leff, *Heresy in the Later Middle Ages* (Manchester 1967) II p 528; Compare *Knighton* II, p 260.
[3] For explanation see p 143 n 3 below.
[4] 'Non potius orandum est in ecclesia quam alibi.' *Knighton* II, p 262.
[5] *Metropolitan Visitations* p 164.

death but into a place between, there to await the scrutiny of the last judgement. It should be noted that the articles made no mention of transubstantiation, tithes, or excommunication; and far from regarding confession as useless the Northampton group evidently considered it essential. On those points, therefore, the opinions held were uncharacteristic of lollard thought.

To sum up, we have seen that the greater number of the beliefs held by the Northampton heretics derived more or less directly from Wycliffe. There is striking similarity with beliefs known to have been embraced at Leicester; at least eleven, just over two-thirds of the articles, approximate so closely to beliefs described by Henry Knighton as existing in Leicester or discovered there by archbishop Courtenay as to suggest a 'family resemblance'. This is scarcely surprising: Leicester was the earliest centre of popular heresy, and its comparative proximity to Northampton would have made evangelisation easy. Yet the beliefs of the Northampton lollards had a flavour all their own. Their chief characteristics were pessimism about many people's chances of salvation, and a strength, even violence, of language, which was to become more common in the fifteenth century.[1]

They also show how quickly certain ideas, especially about liturgical change and the role of the laity, had developed. From Miss Wood-Legh's work on the statutes of perpetual chantries one can see that the clergy in late medieval England were widely regarded as being greedy, lecherous, quarrelsome, and lazy.[2] They were indispensable, however, since only they could perform the miracle of the mass, and only through the mass could the faithful lay hold on salvation. The writings of Wycliffe took away the central role of the mass by disbelieving its supernatural element and by stressing instead the place of the Bible, and they removed the protection of monopoly which all priests, however unsatisfactory, had possessed. Once these twin foundations of the ecclesiastical position were gone the whole structure of religious life was vulnerable. The erroneous beliefs of the Northampton lollards show clearly that the logical conclusions of Wycliffe's ideas, with their far-reaching liturgical, administrative and social consequences, were being grasped and propagated within a decade of his death.

---

[1] For example, in 1420 William Taylor said that the prayers of priests were of no greater value than the lowing of oxen or the grunting of pigs. J. A. F. Thomson, *The Later Lollards* (Oxford 1965) p 25. See also McFarlane, *Wycliffe* pp 184–5.

[2] K. L. Wood-Legh, *Perpetual Chantries in Britain* (Cambridge 1965) especially chapter x.

APPENDIX

A. Conclusions and articles to be publicly renounced by John Corringham, rector of Diddington, 1384. *Reg* 12 fol 272.

In sacramento altaris non videtur corpus christi verum set signum tantum eiusdem ac species et figura nec est christus in e[o]dem sacramento ydemptice vere realiter et in presencia personali.

Item quod liceat sibi et alii cuicumque presbitero predicare verbum dei absque auctoritate sedis apostolice vel episcopi loci seu alia de qua sufficienter constet.

Item quod ita est l[icit]um quod quod (*sic*) duo simul existancium obtinentes dignitatem papalem quorum uterque simul sit papa sicut est licitum quod duo sint simul presbyteri et sacerdotes.

Item quod antepapa est coadiutor domini nostri pape Urbani sexti.

Item quod diabolus est coadiutor eius et eciam dei.

Item quod non licet iuxta sacram scripturam domino episcopo Norwycensi exequi negocium cruciate in forma sibi commissa.

Item quod nullo casu liceat ei nec alicui in negocio cruciate proficiscenti occidere scismaticum vel hereticum.

Item quod nulli liceat pro defensione sue persone non valens[1] mortem aliter evitare interficere aliquem volentem eum occidere set tenetur permitere se interfice[2] ab eodem.

Item quod omnes et quicumque concedentes aut solventes Regi subsidium pro guerris extra regnum Anglie faciendis sint eo ipso excommunicati.

B. Articles said to be held by Anna Palmer, Thomas Patteshull, John Chory, Simon Colyn, John Wolf, John Wheelwright chaplain and Thomas Wheelright chaplain, lollards of Northampton, 1393. *Reg* 12B fols 64r/v.

IN PRIMIS DICITUR quod prefata Anna et ceteri supradicti dicunt palam et expresse quod Innocentes ad dominum migrantes nec in inferno nec in paradiso post decessum collocantur set in medio loco sunt examen extremi iudicii expectantes.

Item quod cuilibet christiano sufficiens est dei mandata servare in cubili vel in campo deum secrete adorare, nec in domo materiali publice precibus incumbere, ne phariseis se conformans ypocrita computetur, nec ecclesia materialiter constructa apud illos pro sacra ecclesia reputatur ymmo quedam domus materialis et apud quosdam constructa castellum 'caym'[3] vocatur.

Item qui proximus est deo in hac vita sanctitate causante papa confirmatur,

---

[1] Correctly 'volens'.   [2] Correctly 'interfici'.

[3] Property held by the friars. The word 'caym' was formed from the initial letters of the Carmelites, Augustinians, the Jacobites (Dominicans) and the Minorites. *Select English Works of John Wyclif*, ed T. Arnold (Oxford 1871) II, p 348n.

nec papa quem nos dicimus summum pontificem pontificem (*sic*) potestatem habet a pena et culpa veniam peccancium concedendi. Et quod tempore sancti Silvestri pape erat universalis ecclesia simoniace dotata. Et sic usque in hodienum diem residet toxicata et ideo de potestate pape et aliorum placitorum[1] eis omnino desperatur.

Item cum iniungatur alicui nomine penitencie propter peccata peregre proficissi[2] affirmant illi lollardi magis meritorium quantitatem summe illius in peregrinacionis itinere expendende fore pauperibus erogande quam penitenciam sibi pro commissis iniunctam peragere iuxta (fol 64v) canonis instituta. Et dicunt quod post annum millenarium a nativitate domini sathanas erat solutus a nexibus et omnes quos postmodum natos reputamus fore sanctos taliter credunt diabolice infectos quod cicius credendos est illos fore dampnatos quam salvatos et huiusmodi sanctos vocant sanctos millenos.

Item sanctum Thomam Cantuar' vel alium sanctum quem peregrini in partibus anglicanis adorant pro sancto affirmare omnino indubio suspendunt nec credunt articulos fore licitos nec divine comnendabiles voluntati pro quibus sanctus Thomas persolvit tributum condicionis humane.

Item affirmant quod capellanus non tenetur matutinas et horas canonicas dicere ante celebracionem divinorum neque postea nisi ex mera sua voluntate eiusdem capellani nec indiget confiteri nisi soli deo ante celebracionem.

Item si sacerdos sit in mortali peccato caret potestate sacramentum Eukaristie et baptismi consecrandi et idem capellanus diabolus est.

Item quod ita meritorium est ut eis videtur ostulare[3] lapides in campo iacentes sicut pedes crucifixi in ecclesia vel aliquas ymagines in ecclesia cum luminibus adorare vel munera eis offerre.

Item quod oblaciones facte in sponsalibus et sepulturis mortuorum sunt subtrahende eo quod in simoniam penitus redundant.

Item quod si aliquis commiserit aliquod peccatum mortale et illud oblitus fuerit et inde obierit non confessus licet misericordiam dei pecierit dampnatus est pro illo peccato mortali oblito et quod non est in potestate dei ipsum salvare per misericordiam.

Item quod non est licitum sacerdotibus fore stipendiarios pro celebracione divinorum.

Item quod est licitum cuilibet christiano informare fratrem suum in decem mandatis et sanctis evangeliis ut ea sciat et predicet et quod quilibet paterfamilias respondebit pro se et commissis familie sue.

Item dicunt ut dicitur quod est cassum dare alicui mendicanti elemosinam nisi solummodo claudis et curvis et cecis que fuerint debiles aut paralitice iacentes et quod omnes contribuentes huiusmodi elemosinam sunt fautores et susten-

---

[1] Correctly 'prelatorum'.   [2] Correctly 'proficisci'.
[3] Correctly 'osculare'.

tatores dictorum mendicancium in peccatis et qui ita dat elemosinam servit diabolo.

Item affirmant ut dicitur quod si aliquis in mortali peccato existens audieret missam quod illa missa erit sibi in dampnacionem.

Item dicunt ut dicitur quod omnes indulgencie concesse a domino papa in remissionem peccatorum vel ad relevacionem alicuius hospitalis seu alterius loci propter elemosinas dandas et querendas per questores sunt false casse et vane, et in cupidinem redundant absque salute anime quia questores et receptores huiusmodi elemosinarum inde superbiose et delicate vivunt et nullum aliud bonum inde provenit.

SOME ASPECTS OF LOLLARD
BOOK PRODUCTION

by ANNE HUDSON

IT has recently been observed that 'the corpus of surviving lollard literature is regrettably small, and it is to be found in the volumes of Wyclif's so-called English writings and a few other printed and manuscript works'.[1] To one concerned to re-edit the vernacular lollard literature the position seems otherwise: the corpus is formidably large, the printed material inadequately represents the state of the texts so edited, and there are a large number of other works still in manuscript. The printed material, if grouped together, would extend to perhaps five bulky volumes, in all about 2400 pages; a rough estimate of the vernacular texts now known suggests that this is perhaps only a fifth of the evidence available.[2] Moreover, the editors were ignorant of a large number of the manuscripts of the works they printed, and hence could not assess the circulation of the texts: to give an example, Arnold used only one manuscript of what I shall call the standard lollard sermon-cycle, with fitful reference to three others, whereas now thirty manuscripts are known, together with a further three containing a modified series based on the original set.[3] It is also impossible from the existing printed editions to gain any picture of the views of the lollard authors: only extensive

---

[1] [J.] Crompton, ['Leicestershire Lollards'], *Transactions of the Leicestershire Archaeological and Historical Society*, XLIV (Leicester 1968–9) pp 14–15.

[2] The main printed material is contained in [T.] Arnold, [*Select English Works of John Wyclif*], 3 vols (Oxford 1869–71) and [F. D.] Matthew, [*The English Works of Wyclif hitherto unprinted*], Early English Text Society Original Series 74 (London 1880). For a survey of the other published writings see the bibliography by E. W. Talbert and S. Harrison Thomson in *A Manual of the Writings in Middle English 1050–1500*, II, ed J. Burke Severs (Hamden Conn. 1970) pp 521–33; the list of manuscripts, and of works unprinted, there given requires considerable amplification. For continued help with the paleography, and for knowledge of some of the manuscripts here considered, I am indebted to the great kindness of Dr Ian Doyle.

[3] The sermon-cycle was printed by Arnold in vols I–II of his edition; for full consideration of the nature of this cycle see my article in *Medium Ævum*, XL (Oxford 1971) pp 142–56. The modified series is found most completely in Trinity College Dublin MS C.1.22 and in part in St John's College Cambridge MS G.22 (fols 1–78v) and Cambridge University Library MS Add. 5338; isolated phrases from the cycle version are incorporated into new and longer sermons.

commentary will reveal the implications of remarks made and vocabulary used.

It is, of course, a regular feature of investigation of suspected Lollardy that English books are mentioned; regularly the commission requires that the contents of a suspect's house be examined for ownership of books, and the abjuration commonly includes the forfeiture of such books and the promise that, if books, or information about them, subsequently come to the notice of the penitent, they will be passed on to the diocesan authorities.[1] It is clear, furthermore, that the market for lollard books was good and was also well supplied. Amongst the early suspects of Lollardy are a number of *parchemyners* and scribes, and the quality of the early manuscripts, in particular, attests to their excellence.[2] Even in the later period, whilst it is true that the adherents of Lollardy were mostly of low social status, literacy was obviously important and widespread: the situation mentioned in bishop Blythe's register at Salisbury in 1498 can be frequently paralleled 'we and eyther of vs hath holden company beyng present with them sundry tymes at the techyng and redyng of their erroneous opinions and bokys'.[3] The tradition had persisted since 1414, when *plures libros Anglicos* had been seized in Colchester, where they had been read *infra mansiones*, 'tam per diem quam per [noctem] secrete et aperte, aliquando ad invicem et aliquando per se'.[4] Whilst it is true that ownership of the Wycliffite Bible was not confined to lollard sympathisers but extended to people of such unimpeachable orthodoxy as Henry VI, and whilst it is possible that the Bible translations may also have been copied by orthodox scribes (a possibility quite credible for the vast majority that lack the

---

1 References are too numerous to be given in full; for the early period see *Calendar of Patent Rolls 1385–9* (London 1900) pp 427, 430, 448, 468 etc.; for a later form, including the terms of abjuration, the procedural material recorded in Worcester, *Register Polton* pp 111–12 and in BM MS Harley 2179 fols 157v–159 is typical. Suspicion of all English books is not uncommon: see, for instance, Wells, *Register Stafford* for 1441, ed T. S. Holmes, *Somerset Record Society*, XXXI–XXXII (London 1915–16) II, p 267.

2 For instance William Perchemener and Michael Scryvener, both of Leicester, mentioned in Courtenay's register in 1389, J. H. Dahmus, *The Metropolitan Visitations of William Courtenay Archbishop of Canterbury 1381–1396* (Urbana 1950) pp 164–7; for further early copying in Leicester see further below. For lollard manuscripts of fine quality see, for instance, BM MS Egerton 617–18, Cambridge University Library MSS Dd.1.27 and Mm.2.15 of the Wycliffite Bible, BM MSS Royal 18 B. ix and Additional 40672 and Christ's College Cambridge MS 7 of the sermon-cycle, or Bodleian MS Bodley 143 of the Glossed Gospels; the list could be considerably extended.

3 Salisbury, *Register Blythe* fol 71, the abjuration of two women from the parish of St Giles in Reading. For the later period see J. A. F. Thomson, *The Later Lollards 1414–1520* (2 ed Oxford 1967).

4 PRO K.B.9. 204/1 nos 10–11.

distinctively Wycliffite prologue), the number of surviving manuscripts remains astonishing: over 235 are now known.[1] Even when one
comes to the sermon-cycle, a work that cannot have been unwittingly
copied by orthodox scribes, the thirty manuscripts that survive would
be hard to equal from other middle English prose works of comparable
length. It is, moreover, clear from the textual relations of the manuscripts that this can be only a small proportion of the original number.

The nature of lollard books can only be roughly assessed from episcopal and chancery records. Three types are regularly mentioned:
schedulae, *quaterni* and *libri*, clearly in ascending order of size; in
English the equivalents appear as *rollis*, *quairis* and *bookis*.[2] So far as
I am aware, no example of a *schedula* survives in its original form,
though documentary evidence of some is available, and it is possible
to suggest that some surviving texts originated in this form. Of the
first, the so-called 'Twelve Conclusions of the Lollards', or the lists
of anti-mendicant complaints scattered round London by Patteshull,
an apostate friar, in 1387 are more obvious examples.[3] The second is
possible with the vernacular version of Wyclif's confession, with the
short text 'Answeris to hem þat seien we schulden not speke of Holy
Writte', and may account for some of the shorter items found in
lollard anthologies such as Trinity College Dublin MSS C.3.12 and
C.5.6.[4] The *schedulae* were obviously ephemeral documents, of the
same kind as the *bills* copied by Thomas Ile of Braybrooke in 1414 and
distributed round Leicester by William Smith.[5] One use for them is

[1] Ownership of Bible manuscripts is dealt with by M. Deanesly, *The Lollard Bible*
(Cambridge 1920) pp 319–50. The most recent list of manuscripts is by C. Lindberg,
'The Manuscripts and Versions of the Wycliffite Bible; a preliminary survey', *Studia
Neophilologica*, XLII (Uppsala 1970) pp 333–47.

[2] See the commission and abjuration mentioned above, p 148 n 1, also Lincoln, *Register
Repingdon* 15, fol 152v and Chichele's *Register*, ed E. F. Jacob, Canterbury and York
Society (London/Oxford 1943–7) III, p 198; for the English form see Chichele's *Register*
III, p 207 and Ely, *Register Grey*, fol 133.

[3] H. S. Cronin, 'The Twelve Conclusions of the Lollards', *EHR* XXII (1907) pp 292–304;
for Patteshull see Walsingham, *Historia Anglicana*, ed H. T. Riley, RS 28 (1863–4) II,
pp 158–9; the documents nailed to the door of St Paul's by Hereford and Repingdon
in 1382 – D. Wilkins, *Concilia Magnae Britanniae et Hiberniae* (London 1737) III, p 165 –
and Aston's schedule of the same year – *Fasciculi Zizaniorum*, ed W. W. Shirley, RS 5
(1858) p 329 – must also have been of this form. Compare also Lincoln, *Register Repingdon* 15, fol 173.

[4] The appearance, out of context, of Wyclif's shorter confession in Bodleian MS Bodley
647, fols 63v–64v, suggests such circulation; the short text, in all about 24 lines, appears in
BM MS Harley 2322, fols 87–8, and Bodleian MS Add.B.66, fols 90–90v; many of the
texts from the Trinity College Dublin MSS were printed by Arnold, III, and by
Matthew but a number of short items from the end of each were unaccountably
omitted.   [5] PRO K.B.9.204/1 nos 130 and 141.

shown by an episode in the career of William Taylor when, before Chichele's convocation in 1421, he 'extraxit de sinu suo quasdam auctoritates et dicta in quadam papiri cedula scripta'.[1] Of the *quaterni* a single example has survived, and is now preserved in Durham University as MS Cosin V.iii.6; it is a quire of eight leaves, the hand dating from before or about the year 1400, containing a dialogue between a knight and a clerk on the subject of civil and ecclesiastical jurisdiction. Its survival intact, with only interleaving to distort the original format, makes it possible to appreciate episcopal concern about these apparently trivial documents.[2] Again it seems likely that works now surviving only in composite manuscripts may originally have circulated as *quaterni*: some of the many tracts that provide lists of biblical and patristic texts on such lollard subjects as images, pilgrimages and the eucharist may well have started life in this form.[3] It seems likely that such compilations were intended for use in the centres of lollard instruction of which the documents provide evidence.[4]

The books are, of course, both the most frequent survivals and the most interesting, not merely from their content but also from the implications of their relationship and appearance. They can, I think, be divided into two groups that I shall call 'official' and 'peripheral', a tendentious division that I shall hope to justify. The 'official' group is the easier to characterise: the texts that fall into it are preserved in a relatively large number of manuscripts of expensive type, are often set out for reading aloud, and are usually corrected, even in the most minute and immaterial detail. The most obvious member of this group is the Wycliffite Bible, with its ramifications of version and revision; but this is a separate topic which I do not wish to deal with here.[5]

[1] Chichele, *Register* III, p 67.

[2] For discussion of this manuscript, its form and content, see my article 'A Lollard Quaternion', *Review of English Studies*, new series XXII (Oxford 1971) pp 435-42.

[3] For instance texts on images in Bodleian MS Eng.th.f.39, fols 1-8, 37-8, Trinity College Cambridge MS B.14.50, fols 34-5, BM MS Additional 24202, fols 24r/v, 26-8v; on pilgrimages in Eng.th.f.39, fols 12v-14v; on the eucharist in Trinity College Dublin MS C.5.6, fols 145-6v and Cambridge University Library MS Ff.6.31(3), fols 27v-35v. The material on the necessity of preaching found in Bodleian MS Laud Misc. 210, fols 168-74v, and in Durham University MS Cosin V.v.1. fols 175v-9v, may well be of the same type.

[4] For instance a letter of Alexander [Tottington], bishop of Norwich 1407-13, written into a precedent roll, BM MS Additional 35205, m.xiv^d; compare also the material cited by Crompton p 19. I have deliberately excluded from consideration here the question of Latin writings produced by lollard centres.

[5] Most recent discussion, and bibliography, is to be found in S. L. Fristedt, *The Wycliffe Bible Part II*, Stockholm Studies in English, XXI (1969).

The others in this category are the Gospel commentaries, extensive and not yet edited,[1] the sermon-cycle to which I shall return, and a small group of shorter tracts including *Vae Octuplex* and *Of Ministers in the Church*.[2] Paleographically many of the manuscripts of these works date from the end of the fourteenth or early years of the fifteenth century, and the richness of their production and the organisation that must lie behind their corrected texts suggest composition before the Oldcastle rebellion. To these points I will return. The 'peripheral' group is more amorphous, but the texts that belong here share certain features: they are preserved in only a small number of manuscripts, less than six, those manuscripts are usually of poorer quality, with little sign that they were intended for public reading, and with scant trace of systematic correction. Their content is extremely varied, from material based on, though not straightforwardly translated from, Wyclif's Latin works, such as the *Tractatus de Regibus* in Bodleian MS Douce 273 (fols 37v–53), dependent upon the *De Officio Regis*, or the dialogue between *Reson* and *Gabbyng* in Trinity College Dublin MS C.5.6 (fols 154v–61), drawn from the first part of the *Dialogus*, to more extreme diatribes against ecclesiastical abuses, such as the long text, purporting to be a report of a sermon against the mendicants, preserved in Cambridge University Library MS Dd.14.30(2).[3] In date these texts are more difficult to assess: there is rarely internal evidence for composition and equally rare is external dating, such as is available for *The Lanterne of Liȝt*;[4] the actual surviving manuscripts range in

---

[1] The nature of these has been surveyed by H. Hargreaves, 'The Marginal Glosses to the Wycliffite New Testament', *Studia Neophilologica*, XXIII (1961) pp 285–300.

[2] These two were printed by Arnold II, pp 379–423; of the first fourteen manuscripts are now known, of the second seventeen. The two are related to, though not translations of, Wyclif's expositions of Matt. 23 and 24, *Opera Minora*, ed J. Loserth, Wyclif Society (London 1913) pp 313–82. Apart from these, and leaving aside commentaries on certain canticles, prayers and creeds printed by Arnold III, pp 5–116, almost none of the works printed so far is known to survive in more than six manuscripts (the one exception is Arnold III, pp 188–201 found in seven).

[3] Unfortunately, the manuscript is defective at both ends; but sufficient of the conclusion remains for an assessment of the work's nature to be made. The relevant material is (fol 100v) 'Now sires, þe dai is al ydo and I mai tarie ȝou no lenger, and I haue no tyme to make now a recapitulacioun of my sermoun. Neþeles I purpose to leue it writun among ȝou, and whoso likiþ mai ouerse it...And certis if I haue seid ony þing amys, and I mai now haue redi knowleche þerof, I shal amende it er I go; and if I haue such knouleche herafter, I shal wiþ beter will come and amende my fautis'.

[4] Edited L. M. Swinburn, EETS, OS 151 (1917); a second manuscript, BM MS Harley 6613, and the print of [1530?] by Redman should be added. The evidence for dating, between 1409 and 1415, is summarised on pp viii–xiii. The dating of most vernacular lollard works from internal evidence is very difficult, because the abuses mentioned are normally persistent and not isolated ones.

date through the fifteenth century. Obviously, when so many manuscripts were destroyed by ecclesiastical authorities, it would be unwise to argue simply from the chance survival of manuscripts, but the nature as well as the number of them distinguishes the two groups: whereas the first group is the result of organised production, the second seems the chance outcome of individual, and often idiosyncratic, interest.[1]

From the viewpoint of the movement's history as a whole, the 'official' group of texts is the more important; to illustrate its interest I should like to deal more extensively with the standard sermon-cycle. This has been available to critics for the last hundred years in the edition of Arnold, but the deficiencies of that edition have hidden its importance. In the first place it was presented as part of the 'English Works' of Wyclif himself, and has, therefore, been treated as if belonging to the heresiarch's thought, a part that can safely be ignored as a pale reflection of views expressed with more sublety and cogency in Latin. The evidence in favour of Wyclif's authorship of the cycle, or indeed of any English works, is very poor: in only one manuscript of the cycle is Wyclif's name attached by the medieval scribe, and the manuscript is textually not a good one.[2] The evidence against Wyclif's authorship is much more convincing: references are found to events after Wyclif's death which, since the cycle is quite certainly to be regarded as a single unit and not as the chance outcome of the assembly of a number of texts, must settle the issue.[3] This is not to say that the cycle has nothing to do with Wyclif: a number of the sermons draw on ideas found in the Latin sermon for the corresponding occasion and are, therefore, clearly the work of someone acquainted with

---

[1] A case in point would be BM MS Additional 24202, containing, amongst other items, tracts against miracle plays, printed in *Reliquiæ Antiquæ* ed T. Wright and J. O. Halliwell (London 1841-3) II, pp 42-57, against dicing, on tithes, on the duties of priests, and a section of a longer treatise against the religious orders.

[2] In Bodleian MS Douce 321, fol 65v, appears the rubric 'Expliciunt tam epistole quam Euangelia Dominicalia secundum exposicionem Doctoris euangelij'; this manuscript, probably of the early fifteenth century, was in quality over-estimated by Arnold (I, pp xiii, xviii-xix) as a full collation reveals. Wyclif's name appears also in New College Oxford MS 95, but not attached to these sermons. In Corpus Christi College Cambridge MS 336, p 475, the Ferial set ends with the enigmatic note 'Expliciunt euangelia ferialia secundum M.J.' by the original scribe. The evidence of Netter (cited by Arnold, II, p v) is probably to be ascribed to his knowledge of some relationship between the vernacular sermons and Wyclif's own, but cannot on its own account be regarded as decisive.

[3] For evidence that the cycle must be considered as a unit see the article mentioned above, p 143 n 3; these arguments must be taken to modify the discussion of

Wyclif's own work.[1] The second, and more serious, deficiency of the old edition is Arnold's lack of interest in anything beyond the provision of a bare text: to this end he printed, without emendation even when manifestly corrupt, a single manuscript, giving only the sketchiest list of some other manuscripts and adding virtually no commentary to his text.[2] As a result, amongst other things, he missed certain clear implications of the manuscripts. The sermon-cycle as Arnold printed it falls into five sets: sermons, 294 in all, for the Sunday Gospels, the *Commune* and *Proprium Sanctorum*, Ferial Gospels and the Sunday Epistles, in that order. Only one other surviving manuscript preserves that precise order, though two others, lacking one or more sets, agree as far as their limited material allows.[3] A wide number of permutations is found amongst the other manuscripts. More far-reaching are two re-organisations, one intercalating the sermons on the Sunday Epistle and Sunday Gospel to form a complete dominical cycle, found in five manuscripts,[4] and a second intercalating Sunday Epistle, Sunday Gospel and Ferial Gospel for the ensuing week to form a single sermon-cycle for the liturgical year, an arrangement found in three extant manuscripts.[5] The fact that each of these re-organisations occurs more than once suggests a clear motivation in the use to which the sermons were to be put. This is borne out by the fact that the groups of five and three manuscripts involved in these particular arrangements are not textually closely related; they are not, in other words, copies made

E.W. Talbert, 'The Date of the Composition of the English Wyclifite Collection of Sermons', *Speculum*, XII (1937) pp 464–74, and M. W. Ransom, 'The Chronology of Wyclif's English Sermons', *Washington State College Research Studies*, XVI (1948) pp 67–114.

[1] *Sermones* I–III, ed J. Loserth, Wyclif Society (London 1887–9) contain Wyclif's Latin sermons on the Sunday Gospels, *Commune* and *Proprium Sanctorum* and Sunday Epistles; it should be noted that no Latin source is available for the lengthy vernacular Ferial set and that many of the English Sunday Epistle sermons bear no relation to the Latin work for the equivalent occasion.

[2] Arnold printed MS Bodley 788; in his list of other manuscripts known to him (I, pp xvii–xx) he admitted that he had not seen all, and had only examined most cursorily. Somewhat fitfully, he records identification of patristic references in the text, but many allusions pass unremarked.

[3] The single manuscript in complete agreement is Leicester Wyggeston Hospital 10.D.34/6, unknown to Arnold; Trinity College Cambridge MS B.2.17 agrees in the order of the first four sets but lacks the last, whilst Corpus Christi College Cambridge MS 336, wanting sets 1 and 5, contains sets 2, 3 and 4 in that order.

[4] Namely Bodleian MS Douce 321, BM MS Cotton Claudius D.viii, Robert Taylor MS Princeton (once Wrest Park 32), Lambeth MS 1149 and Bodleian MS Don.c.13.

[5] The arrangement is found complete in BM MS Royal 18 B.ix and, though now mutilated by later loss of leaves, St John's College Cambridge MS C.8; BM MS Harley 2396 contains this arrangement for the period between Advent and the fourth Sunday after the octave of Epiphany.

from a single exemplar in each case.[1] It seems likely that a patron, or group of sympathisers, seeking a copy of the cycle, would be given the option of three basic 'patterns' for the manuscript to be made. Liturgically, of course, each pattern is quite comprehensible.

In the production of the manuscripts, once the basic pattern was selected, considerable care was taken. Of the thirty surviving manuscripts, no two are in the same hand. Yet twenty-seven share certain common features: they are most scrupulously rubricated and a rigid division is observed between the underlining in red of the gospel or epistle text that forms the basis of the sermon and the absence of such underlining for other biblical texts incidentally quoted; they are corrected, by the original scribe or another, even in matters of quite insubstantial kind, such as the omission or inclusion of the definite article.[2] It is noticeable, also, that such correction is systematic and not random: when a correction appears at a certain place in one manuscript, it is very unusual for that correction not to appear at the same place in others. One manuscript contains the note 'Ista euangelia dominicalia corriguntur per primum originalem'.[3] The three exceptional manuscripts reinforce the case: one appears to be an unfinished product, incompletely rubricated and not yet fully corrected, a second is an idiosyncratic attempt to incorporate the Sunday Gospel sermons into larger tracts, and the third is a late copy, plainly from its size and hand designed for private use only.[4] The large majority of manuscripts, however, appears to be the product of an organised attempt to supply books of lollard instruction, a supply that must have been closely

[1] This is particularly obvious in the case of the first arrangement: discrepancy in ordering, resulting from two faulty but independent attempts at alternation, are found in the Taylor manuscript and in Bodleian MS Don.c.13; similarly, the text of Lambeth MS 1149 is very closely related to that of BM MS Additional 40672, itself having the five sets separate.

[2] Vernacular manuscripts of this period rarely show this combination of care for the accuracy of the text together with attention to its appearance. The quality of lollard manuscripts even aroused comment from an investigating authority in the case of John Galle, priest of London, in 1428, found to possess 'quidam liber in vulgari de evangeliis bene scriptus' (Chichele, Register III, p 190); compare also the Pauline epistles 'in amplo volumine' recorded in J. Fines, 'Heresy Trials in the Diocese of Coventry and Lichfield 1511–12', JEH, XIV (1963) p 165.

[3] Leicester Old Town Hall MS 3, fol 216v; the claim cannot fully be justified until further work has been done on the text, but the correction has certainly been carefully done.

[4] The first is Trinity College Cambridge MS B.14.38, the second Sidney Sussex College Cambridge MS 74; for its text see E. W. Talbert, 'A Fifteenth-Century Lollard Sermon Cycle', University of Texas Studies in English (1939) pp 5–30, the third New College Oxford MS 95.

supervised. Amongst the scribes involved, one at least can be found at work on another lollard manuscript, a copy of the later Wycliffite version of the Gospels translation.[1] It is likely that, as work on the bulk of manuscripts proceeds, more such overlapping will be found. The question, of course, immediately arises of the whereabouts of the places in which this supervised copying took place. Linguistically, the scribes show considerable variation: phonology and morphology obviously did not come under the close scrutiny to which matter and even syntax were subjected. Most scribes can, however, be localised by their language as coming from the East Midlands, in its widest sense.[2] Oxford is an obvious suggestion, but is both linguistically improbable and inherently unlikely since the Wycliffite ideas, before they left Oxford, were almost exclusively the property of men whose written language was Latin.[3] Much more probable, both linguistically and historically, is the area between Northampton and Leicester, an area which includes Braybrooke and in which a number of copyists are known to have worked, men such as Thomas Ile, William Smith, Michael Scryvener and Thomas Scot.[4] It is perhaps not insignificant that two of the manuscripts of this sermon-cycle are now at Leicester.[5] Documentary evidence for such a centre, as opposed to evidence for individual scribes, is lacking at present, but this may well be attributable to the skill of the lollards in covering their tracks rather than to the

---

[1] The hand of BM MS Harley 2396 appears in part of Gonville and Caius College Cambridge MS 179/212, containing a fragment of the Gospels in the later Wycliffite version.

[2] Exceptions are the scribe of Bodleian MS Don.c.13, clearly a northerner, and that of Trinity College Cambridge MS B.14.38, who must have come from the south-west. I am grateful to professor McIntosh for discussing linguistic questions about these manuscripts with me.

[3] The English dialect of Oxford can be roughly gauged from the evidence presented by S. B. Meech, 'Nicholas Bishop, an exemplar of the Oxford dialect of the fifteenth century', *Publications of the Modern Language Association*, XLIX (Menasha 1934) pp 443–59. The evidence concerning the preaching expedition of Hereford, Aston and others in the Winchester diocese in 1382 makes no mention of written material: see *Wykeham's Register*, ed T. F. Kirby, Hampshire Record Society (London 1896–9) II, pp 337–8.

[4] For the relevant period the persistence of Lollardy in Northampton and Leicester is well established: for Northampton in 1389 by the Courtenay register (above, p 148 n 2) p 169, for 1392–3 by Lincoln, *Register Buckingham* 12, fols 398, 406, and the document printed by E. Powell and G. M. Trevelyan, *The Peasants' Rising and the Lollards* (London 1899) pp 45–50, and for 1416 by Lincoln, *Register Repingdon* 15, fol 176v; for the Leicester material see the article by Crompton. For Braybrooke, and its lord Sir Thomas Latimer, see K. B. McFarlane, *John Wycliffe and the Beginnings of English Nonconformity* (London 1952) pp 146, 173 and 178. Note also the mention of Thomas Scot of Braybrooke, *scriveyn*, in the 1414 return, PRO K.B.9.204/1 no 111.

[5] Namely Leicester Old Town Hall MS 3 and Leicester Wyggeston Hospital MS 10.D.34/6.

fact that none existed. It will be remembered that Nicholas Faulfiš and his friends obtained copies of some of Wyclif's Latin works on a visit to Braybrooke in 1407.[1]

The numbers of vernacular lollard manuscripts surviving do much to explain the constant concern of the bishops about the *schedulae*, *quaterni* and *libri*, whilst the wide distribution that the sermon-cycle must have achieved may also explain the recurrence of certain specific ideas in different areas of the country. In the Salisbury diocese there seems to have been a particularly good supply of lollard writings, to judge by the series of references running throughout the fifteenth century. In 1416 is recorded a mandate to seek out 'libros suspectos in lingua vulgari Anglicana conscriptos', in 1418 John of Bath was interrogated before the next bishop, John Chaundler, 'super certis articulis in quibusdam libris Anglicis secum inuentis' and quotations from his books are given; in 1428 it is reported that William Fuller, *alias* Heede, kept 'libros tractatus articulos et opuscula' containing heresies and errors.[2] Under Aiscough, bishop from 1438 to 1450, a number of heretics were apprehended; almost all of them admitted to possessing forbidden books, whilst one of them, John Piers, *alias* John Fyncaisshe, of Netheravon used one of his *quaterni* to refresh his memory in the course of interrogation 'Also y haue bileued diuers other articles and opynyons conteyned in a quaier in English writen to the whiche y refferre me'.[3] In 1478 brief reference to books is again found, but the importance of them reappears in the series of investigations under bishops Langton and Blythe from 1490 to 1498. 'One suspecte boke of commaundementis' contained material against the worship of images, a claim that can certainly be borne out from extant lollard literature; 'a suspecte boke conteynyng errours and heresies' included the claim that laymen could preach.[4] The importance of written material in the persistence of Lollardy is seen in the story of the 'redyng of...erroneous opinions and bokys' mentioned earlier; it also explains the claim of Thomas Boughton of Hungerford that 'sith the tyme of my first acqueyntaunce with the said heretikes, I haue had

---

[1] See A. B. Emden, *A Biographical Register of the University of Oxford to A.D. 1500*, II (Oxford 1958) p 670.

[2] Hallum, *Register*, fol 127; Chaundler, *Register* pt II, fols 17v–18; Nevill, *Register* pt II, fol 77v, with which compare the acknowledgement of a man from Devizes, fol 57v, that he 'was woned an vsed to here in secret place, yn holkys and hyrnes, the redyng of the byble yn Englyssh'.

[3] Ayscough, *Register* pt II, fol 52v; further confessions appear on fols 52v–54v.

[4] Beauchamp, *Register* pt II, fol 17v for 1478; Langton, *Register* pt II, fols 35 and 38v, compare also fols 36 and 40v.

a great mynde to here sermouns and prechynges'.[1] The contents of the lollard books that survive give some colour too to the assertion of Joan Baker, this time from the London diocese, a woman probably associated with a group having a considerable library of heretical tracts, that 'she cold here a better sermond at home in hur howse than any doctor or prist colde make at Poulis crosse or any other place'.[2]

[1] Above, p 148 n 3. Blythe, *Register*, fol 74v.
[2] Guildhall, London, *Register Fitzjames*, fol 27; for the group see Trinity College Dublin MS D.3.4, fols 122v–124v.

A SERMON BY JOHN LUKE
ON THE ENDING OF THE
GREAT SCHISM, 1409

by MARGARET HARVEY

IN 1409[1] the council of Pisa, called by the cardinals in defiance of two rival popes, attempted to end the thirty-year-old Great Schism by deposing both rivals for heresy and schism. On 26 June 1409,[2] the cardinals unanimously elected as pope Peter Philargi of Candia, cardinal 'of Milan', and amid general rejoicing he took the name Alexander V.[3] The schism seemed over, provided that all the powers of Europe were prepared to acknowledge the new pope. Some time after the new election but before 27 July 1409, master John Luke who was at the council as a theologian, probably representing Oxford university, preached a sermon before the new pope, praising his election and hopeful of his role in the unity of the Church. Luke gave an elaborate justification of the deposition for heresy and schism of Gregory XII (the Roman pope, whom the English thought was the true one). It is with this sermon that I am concerned in the present paper.

John Luke,[4] a former fellow of Merton College and in 1408 a priest and bachelor of theology, was a protégé of Robert Hallum, bishop of

---

[1] I must thank professor H. S. Offler for his kindness in reading a draft of this paper and helping me to wrestle with the transcript of the manuscripts. I also thank Mr Gerald Bonner and *Etudes Augustiniennes* for helping in the hunt for St Augustine. I have not seen A. Brüggen, 'Die Predigten des Pisaner Konzils', Theology Dissertation in typescript (Freiburg 1963).

[2] For definitive sentence see [J.] Vincke, 'Acta [Concilii Pisani]', *Römische Quartalschrift* XLVI (Rome 1941) pp 295–8, with references there.

[3] Vincke, 'Acta', p 308.

[4] All information about Luke comes from [A. B.] Emden, [*Biographical Register of Oxford Graduates to 1500*,] 3 vols (Oxford 1957–9), under Luke, unless otherwise stated. Dr Emden did not know of this sermon, nor of the following references to Luke's presence at Pisa: gave his opinion as a Bachelor of Theology of Oxford on deposition of the popes: Stiftung Preussischer Kultur-besitz, Depot der Staatsbibliothek, Berlin, Ms Theol Lat fol 251, fol 30v; Vatican Library Mss Vat Lat 4172, fol 241; Vat Lat 4171, fol 119; Vat Lat 4904, fol 31; Ottobon 111, fol 246. He was said to be a proctor for Oxford University: Bodleian Library Oxford, Ms Canonici Pat Lat 205, fol 4 (called Wyk); Vatican Archives Arm 54, 34, fol 123 (called Unli).

Salisbury, who led the English delegation to the council. On 28 May 1409 Peter Philargi had assembled about a hundred theologians at the council and asked them whether, on the evidence before them, the popes merited deposition. The theologians agreed unanimously that they did, and John Luke was among those consulted.[1] There is no evidence of any writing of his however, apart from this sermon, and that does not give one great enthusiasm for reading anything else. The sermon is not of very high quality, but it is nonetheless of interest for two main reasons. Firstly it is by an Englishman, and so far very little is known about English activity at Pisa. Secondly it gives a theologian's viewpoint, when much else that we know was written by canon lawyers. In its small way then this sermon gives a glimpse of the achievement of an Oxford theologian of the early fifteenth century.

I know three fifteenth-century manuscripts of the sermon, all in the Vatican. One of these (Vat Lat 4192) copies another (Vat Lat 4000) and the third (Vat Lat 7305) is so closely related that one is in effect dealing with a single exemplar.[2] In each manuscript there is a sermon headed *Sermo habitus in Concilio Pysano*[3] followed by another headed *Alius sermo habitus in eodem*, and the second has at the end *Johannes Luck Anglicus*. There is no reason to doubt and good reason to support Luke's authorship of the second sermon. It has typically English quotations from Grosseteste, and also unacknowledged quotations from the sermon on the schism delivered in Oxford in 1395 by Nicholas of Fakenham.[4] Fakenham's sermon follows Luke's in all three manuscripts.

[1] Mansi XXVII cols 399–401.

[2] [Vatican Library Mss Vat Lat] 4000, fols 112v–19; 7305, fols 163v–72v; 4192, fols 143–50v. 4000 and 7305 depend on the same exemplar for their material on Pisa. 7305 is the better text. It did not copy 4000, which has lacunae which do not exist in 7305. Nor did 4000 copy 7305 I think, but certainty would need a more detailed comparison of both Mss. Both are mid-fifteenth century, see J. Vincke, *Schriftstücke zum Pisaner Konzil, Beiträge zur Kirchen- und Rechtsgeschichte*, III (Bonn 1942) p 15. 4192 is late fifteenth century and copies 4000 for its Pisa material (they have the same lacunae). All Mss contain the sermon preached in 1395 in Oxford by Nicholas of Fakenham (see Emden under 'Fakenham'). Except where Mss disagree I quote from 7305.

[3] An Ascension Day sermon (16 May 1409). The text is Acts 1:6 but the sermon is not that by Gerson for this date, see J. Gerson, *Oeuvres Complètes*, ed M. Glorieux, V (Paris 1963) pp 204–17.

[4] For use of Grosseteste see below. The Fakenham sermon was edited by F. Bliemetzrieder, 'Traktat des Minoritenprovinzials von England Fr Nikolaus de Fakenham (1395) über das grosse abendländische Schisma', *Archivum Franciscanum Historicum* I (Quarrachi 1908) pp 577–600; II (1909) pp 79–91. Luke quotes word for word from Fakenham on the miseries brought by twins: 'ex lege nature...contristata', *ibid* I p 582, with further reminiscences, in 7305 fol 164.

A sermon by John Luke

Luke's sermon was probably delivered a few days before 27 July 1409, because there is a reference in it to people who (wickedly) wish to be confirmed in titles to benefices, however obtained,[1] and begging the pope not to be a party to such a move. This was a question about which a decree was passed on 27 July, giving a general confirmation of titles granted to supporters of the council before a certain date.[2] It is possible of course that Luke was speaking after the decree was passed and introduced the reference to titles because he disagreed with the council's decision or thought that some people were taking wrongful advantage of it. There is however another piece of evidence which suggests a date before 27 July. This is a reference to the need and power of the pope to bring back the erring by using the sword of the Spirit '"in alligando reges eorum in compedibus, et nobiles eorum in manicis ferreis" [Ps. 149: 7–8]. Reges dico Neopolitanum et Ungarie cum sibi similibus ut reducantur ad ovile Christi.'[3] The king of Hungary was Sigismund who held aloof from Pisa.[4] In July 1409 there were two claimants for the title king of Naples. One was Ladislas of Durazzo, who opposed the council. His rival was Louis of Anjou, and it is most unlikely that Luke would have suggested an attack on him. He supported Pisa[5] and on 25 July he came in person to the council to gain its blessing for his claim.[6] He was actually present at the session of 27 July when the decree on titles to benefices was passed,[7] and Alexander V subsequently confirmed his title to Naples.[8] Luke could hardly have suggested that Louis needed bringing back to the flock of Christ. He might have called Louis's rival king of Naples however, before Louis came to Pisa, though it seems unlikely that he would do so afterwards, even though the pope did not officially name Louis king of Naples until 19 August. So in the absence of more conclusive evidence some time just before 27 July looks the most probable date for the delivery

---

[1] 7305 fols 171–171v 'Ergo [Alexander V] ecclesie universalis scilicet reformacio…quia multi iniquitatis filii ut per te et sacrum concilium in tantum innituntur ut confirmentur quasi in verum in suis titulis beneficorum sive iuste sive iniuste possidencium. Quod secundum videre meum necnon multis fidelium non est [Ms esse; 4000 est] reformacio ecclesie sed dissipacio ecclesie et deformacio'.

[2] Vincke, 'Acta', p 318 and references there.

[3] 7305 fol 172.

[4] On 8 June 1409 the cardinals agreed to recognise Sigismund's brother Wenceslaus as King of the Romans if one of them became pope – [N.] Valois, [La France et le Grand Schisme d'Occident] (Paris 1902) IV, p 64 n 1. They tried to persuade Sigismund to support them but during the council he kept aloof (ibid pp 74–5).

[5] Valois IV, pp 117–23.

[6] Valois IV, pp 119–20.   [7] Vincke, 'Acta' p 318; Mansi XXVI col 1234.

[8] Valois IV, p 120.

of the sermon. The sermon was delivered in the presence of the pope since he is referred to, for instance in the discussion of titles 'quod absit quod hoc proveniat a te, Pater Sancte'.[1]

The sermon follows a traditional pattern,[2] but it is too complicated to discuss fully in a short paper. I have therefore picked out the most interesting points, at risk of losing some of Luke's subleties in the process. With the text 'Fiat pax in virtute tua' (Ps. 122:7), Luke sets the theme. The pope he says is the corner-stone on which break up all heresies, especially the heresy of having several popes.[3] Alexander is Peter, the firm rock. Just as the rock who is Christ the corner-stone makes all one, so his vicar the pope unites all those things which have been so long divided.[4] Then follows a commentary on a prophecy of Zechariah (11:8 ff) to show that the wicked, avaricious popes, Benedict XIII and Gregory XII, had been neglectful shepherds, who had not kept their promises to make union. Zechariah had said 'Woe to the idol shepherd that leaveth the flock. The sword shall be upon his arm...and his right eye shall be utterly darkened.' This applies to those relatives and counsellors who had advised continuing the schism (pope Gregory's nephews had been severely criticised).[5] The 'right eye' included John Dominici, a particularly hated adviser of Gregory.[6] Gregory and Benedict might say that they had called councils of their own but their insincerity is clear – deeds speak louder than words. One of the charges against the popes at Pisa was that their councils were hollow shams forced on them by the calling of Pisa.[7]

---

[1] 7305 fol 171v. The text is from Ps. 122 (Vulgate 121): 7.

[2] On sermon-making in general see T.-M. Charland, *Artes Praedicandi*, Publications de l'Institut d'Etudes Mediévales d'Ottowa VII (Paris/Ottowa 1936). A recent and helpful book on English sermons is J. W. Blench, *Preaching in England in the late fifteenth and sixteenth centuries* (Oxford 1964) especially Chapter 2, pp 71ff for construction of sermons.

[3] 7305 fols 163v–64. 'Fitque lapis angularis per quem saxa et parietes diversarum heresum [4000 heresim] maxime de multiplicatione summorum pontificum, omni bone policie repugnante ex illo philosophico "tantum unus princeps" 12° metaphysice intitulato, confringantur' [Ms. confringatur; 4000 gitur]. The reference is Aristotle, *Metaphysics*, XII, 1076a.

[4] 7305 fol 164. 'Videlicet ut sicut petra qui est Christus lapis angularis facit utraque unum [Eph. 2:14], sic proprietate nominis vicarie fecit utraque unum que multis temporibus, de quo dolendum est, fuerunt nimis divisa.'

[5] 7305 fol 165. 'Id est, vindicta super cognatos eius et super filios consiliatorios eius, si introduxerunt ipsum ad istud pestiferum scisma continuandum.'

[6] 7305 fol 165. 'Id est falsi consiliarii, ut Jo. Dominici, ecclesiastici.' On Dominici see *Lexikon für Theologie und Kirche*, v (Freiburg 1960) under 'Johannes.'

[7] 7305 fol 165. 'Sed forte obicit hic Gregorius sive Petrus de Luna vel aliquis nomine eius, quod non stat per eos quin unio sit facta, dicendo "Domine, Domine, nonne

The theme then is clear. Papal schism is heresy, but a properly constituted pope should be a centre of unity. The rival popes are utterly wicked, because they have prolonged the schism and they and their supporters merit divine punishment. Luke is in fact much more concerned to condemn Gregory than Benedict, since he clearly thought that Gregory was in the true line of succession, so despite a few references to Benedict the sermon is really aimed at Gregory.

The sermon proper then begins. There are three parts with the usual division of the words of the text and a justification of the division. The first part is a discussion of 'the virtuous action of true peace' because the text says *fiat pax*. Luke's intention is to show that unity ought to exist in the church because it must reflect the unity of God and the natural appetite for unity which the world therefore displays. The discussion of divine unity includes ideas on divine illumination from pseudo-Dionysius's *De divinis nominibus*[1] and Grosseteste's commentary thereon[2] with examples of the essential unity of numbers[3] and of God thought of as a circle with its centre everywhere and its circumference

---

misi litteras pro unione fienda etc. faciendo concilia etc." Hic respondeo secundum sententiam salvatoris...[Matt. 7:21]...Immo facta plus instruunt quam verba. Sic [4000 si] enim homo realius concedit terram per cartam vel sesinam quam per verbum, sic enim concedit nobis deus multa que dicit in facto etsi nunquam vociferet nobis.' See article 30 against the popes (Vincke, 'Acta', p 283) for the charge that their councils did not fulfil the oath of 1406.

[1] 7305 fol 165v. 'Unde ille magnus Dyonisius, qui a beato Paulo per triennium didicit alta misteria, ponit in libro suo "De Divinis Nominibus" Capitulo 2 [? Mss have X°] et 3° eandem sententiam: declarans quomodo raciones ydeales in Deo se habent ad creaturas ad extra per modum principii'. This seems to be a paraphrase from chapters 2 and 3 of *De Divinis Nominibus*, see *Dionysiaca* I (Paris 1937) pp 57–144. Some examples are from Chapter 5, *ibid* pp 343–6.

[2] 7305 fol 165v. 'Et inde philosophi dicunt quod genus est materia quia continet in se omnes formas de sua potentia productibiles. Correspondenter Deus unit in se omnes creaturas non sic quod sint multe existencie ad intra, sed omnia sunt ibi unum [Mss. unde] esse, una vita, ut dicit beatus Augustinus 6 de t' capitulo 21 (=Augustine, *De Trinitate* IV, I, 3. *Corpus Christianorum*, Series Latina, L, Pt 16 (Turnholt 1968) p 162). 'Unde venerabilis Lyncolniensis in exposicione textus beati Dyonisii parte 3ª sic scribit "Deus est eo(?) accipiens et praeaccipiens, totum esse in se ipso in eternis racionibus simul eternaliter habens, et antequam in seipsis sunt omnia, totum esse omnium habens, inde producens esse eorum in se ipsis".' The commentary is still in Ms, see Merton College, Oxford, Ms. 86 fol 191 (not quoted exactly). See also S. H. Thompson, *The writings of Robert Grosseteste* (Cambridge 1940) p 79. See L. E. Lynch, 'The doctrine of divine ideas and illumination in Robert Grosseteste, Bishop of Lincoln', *Medieval Studies*, III (New York, Toronto 1941) pp 161–73.

[3] 7305 fol 165v. 'in unitate preexistit omnis numerus uniformalis vel [4192 et] simplex. Omnes enim numeri quantumcumque magni simplicitantur in unitate ex qua originaliter effluunt.'

nowhere.[1] Examples from the natural world include the prevalence of spheres among the heavenly bodies,[2] the way raindrops gather into one,[3] or bees elect one king.[4] Hence, says Luke

merito magis Angelus Corrario hoc appeteret effectualiter, tanto vinculo iuramenti indissolubili astrictus. Et quia hoc non facit, iusto Dei iudicio, exigente suo demerito, auctoritate generalis concilii Pysis, per sententiam diffinitivam, ab officio papatus est depositus, necnon ut hereticus a singulis fidelibus censendus.[5]

Correr's great sin, his heresy, as the council of Pisa also judged, was to have broken the oath made in the conclave in 1406, and renewed on his election, that he would use all reasonable means to end the schism.[6]

Luke then undertakes to justify, in twenty points from scripture and other authorities, the definitive sentence of 5 June 1409, by which Gregory was deposed. He points out that an argument from God's authority is needed here, since it is from God that the authority of the general council comes.[7]

The second part of the sermon is a discussion of *pacis inclusio*, because the text joins *fiat* to *pax*. This is a discussion of the true peace of mankind to show that it must come from union with God and charity or one is separated from Father, Son and Holy Ghost 'qui enim in ea [pace] inventus non fuerit...alienus fit a spiritu sancto quia non invenitur in caritate, quem passum credo nimis difficilem pro utroque

---

[1] 7305 fol 165v. 'Deus [Mss dra], ut dicit quidam Doctor, est quidam circulus intelligibilis cuius centrum est ubique et circumferencia nusquam.' The doctor may be a reference to the 24 Masters, see C. Baemker, 'Das psuedo-hermetische Buch der XXIV Meister', *Beiträge zur Geschichte der Philosophie und Theologie des Mittelalters*, xxv (Munster 1927) p 208. But this notion was a commonplace, see D. Mahnke, *Unendliche Sphäre und Allimittelpunkt. Beiträge zur Geneologie der Mathematischen Mystik* (Halle 1937). I owe the first reference to Dr R. W. Hunt and the second to Dr Timothy Merritt.

[2] 7305 fol 166v. 'Ex hoc namque appetitu mundi istius elementa etsi contraria et repugnantia indissolubili concordia mundum componunt et celum quod continet universa corporaque celestia, videlicet sol, luna et sydera, que formata sunt in figuras spericas et rotundas, que est omnium capacissima et pulcherrima et contra omnes casus munitissima, non habens angula, prominencia pungitiva, nec depressionis cavitatem sordes colligentem.'

[3] 7305 fol 166v. 'Unde et gutta pluvie fluida [4000 plivie fluiuda] in spericam figuram se colligit ex unitatis appetitu.'

[4] 7305 fol 166v. 'Apes gregantes [Mss. greganti] volant et regem sibi preficiunt et unde hoc nisi amore unitatis', see Aristotle, *De Animabilibus* Bk 9, 40 (625a, b).

[5] 7305 fol 166v.

[6] M. Souchon, *Die Papstwahlen in der Zeit des Grossen Schismas* (Braunschweig 1898) 1, pp 285–95.

[7] 7305 fol 166v–7. '...sicut in aliis generibus omnia sunt reducibilia ad unum primum, quod est metum et mensura omnium aliorum, sic in genere notitie hominis fides est primum, et correspondenter omnes loci argumentorum reducuntur ad unum primum

contendente.'[1] The third part deals with the results of peace, since the text concludes *in virtute tua*. This is a discussion of the strength of the papacy and the bonds which unite the mystical body of Christ which is the Church.[2] The great numbers at the council revealed the presence of the Holy Spirit, as did the fact that the pope had been elected 'nedum auctoritate Generalis Concilii et sic Spiritus Sanctus, verum eciam a singulis Cardinalibus nullo discrepante'.[3] This was a veiled reference to arguments before the conclave about how the pope should be elected.[4]

Luke then makes a plea for consideration of the common good in reformation, and then after a long discourse to show that the papacy controls both swords,[5] he asks the pope to use the sword of the spirit against dissenters. He concludes with a eulogy of Alexander V as a unifying force.

A most interesting feature of the sermon is the twenty points justifying the sentence of deposition against pope Gregory. In the first ten points Luke attempts to show that there is excellent scriptural warrant for ejecting the wicked. Where the accusations are specific

qui est locus ab auctoritate. Quamvis enim locus ab auctoritate humana sit debilissimus, tamen locus ab auctoritate Dei est primus et validissimus, gratia cuius ut verissime speratur et creditur processit auctoritas generalis concilii contra te, o Angele.'

[1] 7305 fol 170v. 4000 has 'quem passim credo nimis defecilem'.

[2] 7305 fol 170v. 'Et bene "virtute tua" id est fortitudine vicaria cum uterque gladius, spiritualis scilicet et materialis, auctoritative et nutu tuo resideat in manu tua'. The mystical body has a fourfold union 'conformitas naturalis, communio sacramentalis, connexio caritatis et consumacio felicitatis' [7305 has confirmitas naturalis and 4000 has confirmacio felicitatis]. 'Conformitas nature' is the reflection of the divine image which gives nature an urge to be conformed to its original and this is the origin of natural affection. The sacraments of the Church form a bond between the faithful. Charity makes all one mystical body. 'Consumacio felicitatis' is the sharing of one spirit. See H. de Lubac, *Corpus Mysticum; L'Eucharistie et l'Eglise au Moyen Age*' (2nd ed Paris 1949) especially pp 116–35, for late medieval use of the mystical body.

[3] 7305 fol 171. 'Totum istud [4000 illud] factum [Ms factam], videlicet generalis concilii infuisse a Spiritu Sancto. Primo quo ad [Mss quantum quo ad] concursum populi concurrentis Pysis "ex omni nacione que sub celo est" [Acts 2:5] et hoc miraculose. Et quo ad medium ut constat in assumpcione vestra...'

[4] M. Harvey, 'Nicholas Ryssheton and the Council of Pisa, 1409.' *SCH*, VII (1971) pp 205–6.

[5] 7305 fol 171v. 'Ad hoc [reformation] enim fortis es, ut predixi, cum uterque gladius tam materialis quam spiritualis gladius sit Petri et per consequens tui nomine et officio... Materiali autem gladio utuntur principes ecclesie per manum et ministerium principum secularium qui ad nutum et disposicionem principum ecclesie gladium quem portant debent evaginare et in locum suum remittere [John 18:11]...Unde principes seculi quicquid [Ms quitquit, 4000 quicquic, 4192 corr] habent potestatis a Deo ordinate et dignitatis recipiunt ab ecclesia. Principes vero ecclesie nichil potestatis aut dignitatis recipiunt ab aliqua seculari potestate sed immediate a Dei ordinacione.'

they refer to the breaking of the oath and prolonging schism.[1] A few examples will show the kind of thing said:

We are to withdraw from every brother that walketh disorderly (2 Thess, 3:6) as Angelo Correr did 'Cum ergo predictus Angelus ambulat inordinate et non secundum tradicionem apostolicam, quia causat scisma in ecclesia militante, sequitur quod omnes Catholici sicut et de facto faciunt instinctu spiritus sancti debent se ipsos subtrahere ab eodem'.[2] Because of a moderate sin, Paul, an individual, resisted Peter to whom he was subject (Gal, 2:11). 'A pari vel forciori cetus verorum Cardinalium cum omnibus Catholicis prelatis fecit sicut et debuit resistendo predicto Angelo cum est... plus reprehensibilis quam Petrus.'[3] Hosea (2:2–3) told the sons to judge their mother for her adultery,

O fideles Cardinales qui diu laborastis pro unitate ecclesie cum fidelibus episcopis et prelatis, iudicate, ymmo Sancto Spiritu cooperante iam iudicastis matrem vestram ecclesiam scilicet predictum Angelum scismaticum nedum fore deponendum, sed esse precisum tamquam hereticum et heresiarcham, ut membrum putridum pro proprio abiciendum et abiectum propter fornicaciones et adulteria spiritualia, avariciam, symoniam et inordinatissimas translaciones episcoporum et ineptissimas promociones ymmo pocius prophanaciones novorum Cardinalium contra votum proprium et solempne iuramentum.[4]

The promotion of new cardinals was called profanation in the council charges against Gregory.[5]

Luke goes on to point out that, according to the *Decretum* the pope can be deposed for heresy, and prolonged schism, according to saint Jerome, is tantamount to heresy. In fact the *Glossa* on the *Decretum*

---

[1] The points not quoted in the text are: 1. Correr did not humble himself (Matt. 18:4, 6) therefore he is not the greatest in the Kingdom and ought to be deposed. 2. He did not do the works of the Father and ought not to be believed (John 10:37). 3. In Luke 13:7 the fig-tree, human nature, was cut down because it did not do good works (Gregory the Great, Homily 31, *PL* 76 (1878) col 1228). The dressers are the cardinals, bishops and doctors who succeed the apostles. 7. If the cardinals and faithful prelates had not rooted out Antichrist the fate predicted in Mic. 3: 9, 10, 12 might have befallen. 8. Jeroboam was punished (1 Kings 13:33–4). 7305 fol 168...'Cum ergo predictus Angelus Corrario propter symoniam vel carnalem [Ms Cardinalem] amorem vel preces dominorum fecit saccerdotes excelsorum [Ms excellorum] de novissimis populis, videlicet inhabiles Cardinales, Episcopos et alios inferiores ad pluralitatem beneficorum, sequitur quod domus eius, hoc est ipse, iusto Dei iudicio per generale concilium eversa est...' 9. The cursed fig-tree (Matt. 21:18–22) is Correr who made promises but perpetuated schism. 10. Hos. 4:6 shows that knowledge without good result makes the sin worse. Correr did not have heavenly knowledge.

[2] 7305 fol 167v.

[3] 7305 *ibid*. The omitted passage seems to read 'quodammodo in similem'.

[4] 7305 *ibid*. Mss have 'spiritalia avarioram'.   [5] Vincke, 'Acta', pp 274, 284.

says that the pope can be accused of any notorious crime and condemned by the cardinals. 'Sed scisma generale est heresis valde gravis et scandalum tocius ecclesie destructivum, ergo propter tale scisma Papa debet accusari et condempnari a fideli cetu Cardinalium cum cunctis fidelibus episcopis et prelatis. Quod et factum est ipsi in hoc iuste convicto.'[1]

The gravity of the notorious crimes is then spelled out. Gregory was elected primarily to restore unity and when he failed to do so, out of self interest, he already ceased to be pope.[2] If he could he would have killed the defecting cardinals so he is a murderer. This repeats a charge against the pope that he wanted the cardinal of Liège alive or dead.[3] He made unqualified cardinals out of his relatives and others contrary to his oath.[4] He is a heretic. Proof of this is 'hic hefuga est hereticus manifestus quia docet dogma falsum, sacre scripture contrarium, publice edoctum et pertinaciter defensatum', which is heresy according to the definition of saint Augustine and Grosseteste.[5] The heresy is that

in facto docet quod iuramentum voluntarium atque scientificum non obligat. Ymmo quod licitum est transgredi manifeste hominum iuramentum, et

---

[1] 7305 fol 168v. 'Papa potest deponi propter heresim ut testatur *Decretum* XL di. *si Papa* [=di. 40 c.6] et secundum glosam ibidem de omni crimine notorio Papa potest accusari et a Cardinalibus condempnari...Minorem testatur beatus Jheronimus xxiiii q. iii capitulo *inter schisma* [=C.24 q. 3 c. 26] et capitur ex omelia super epistolam ad Galathas [recte Ad Titum 3:10 see *PL* 26 (1884) col 598]. 12° Jheronimus xxiiii q. prima capitulo *non afferamus* [=C.24 q. 1 c. 21] permagnam [Mss permagnum] diffinit gravitatem scismatis excellere ydolatriam. Cum ergo Papa potest deponi propter ydolatriam, a fortiori propter scisma generale, quod gravius est peccatum'. For di. 40 c. 6 and gloss see B. Tierney, *Foundations of the Conciliar Theory* (Cambridge 1955) pp 9, 65–6 and 251 where the *glossa ordinaria* is cited in full. The second citation of Jerome is really Augustine, *De Baptismo* II 6, 9, *PL* 43 (1865) col 132.

[2] 7305 fol 168v. 'Cessante causa principale cessat effectus vel cessare debet, secundum principale iuristarum. Et causa principalis quare Angelus Corrario fuit assumptus in Romanum pontificem fuit hoc, quod faceret [Ms facere, 4000 corr] omnem diligenciam sibi possibilem ad faciendum unionem ecclesie. Et nedum iam sed continue pertinaciter retrocessit et retrocedit et scisma continuat [Ms continat], propter affectionem carnalem vel commodum temporale vel stercora huius mundi'.

[3] 7305 fol 168v. Num. 35: 30–3 and Exod. 21: 12, 14–16, give the penalty for homicide. 'Sed Angelus Corrario fecit homicidium in quantum in se fuit Cardinalium, prodiciose ponendo insidias armatorum in camera sua et locis propinquis'. See Vincke, 'Acta' p 279 for charge at Pisa.

[4] 7305 fol 168v. The wickedness of making unsuitable prelates is testified by '*de Electionibus*, capitulo *Nichil* in antiquis' (=Decretals I tit. 6 c. 44), and by Grosseteste 'in sermonibus' (7305 only). No doubt this is 'Dominus Noster Jesus Christus', see E. Browne, *Fasciculus Rerum Expetendarum...*(London 1690) II pp 251ff.

[5] 7305 fols 169–9v. For Augustine see *Decretum* C. 24 q. 3 c. 31. Matthew Paris reports (*Chronica Majora* s.a. 1253 RS 57e (1880) p 401), that Grosseteste declared 'heresis est sententia humano sensu electa, scripture sacre contraria, palam edocta, pertinaciter defensa'. I owe this reference to professor Offler.

pertinaciter ymmo incorrigibiliter hoc defendit. Quia mallet incarcerare, ymmo occidere, fideles Cardinales si esset in potestate eius (quod absit) quam errorem huiusmodi revocare vel ab ipso aliquatenus resilire.[1]

The facts were true, but whether this refusal to keep the oath was heresy in the traditional sense seems open to question. Luke however had more incontrovertible proof of Gregory's heresy. He quotes Matthew 18:15-17, and goes on

Ecce quam plane ab auctoritate illius textus et scripture sic probatur et declaratur Angelum Corrario censendum de facto esse hereticum. Quod, salva reverencia iuristarum, nesciunt ex scriptis suis hoc fundare. Sic patet quod scriptura est efficacius fundamentum Generalis Concilii ad fundandum ipsum esse hereticum quam aliquod ius humanitus adinventum, saltem pure et auctoritative. Unde frater peccans in singulos Cardinales fuit Angelus Corrario in hoc quod noluit facere quod vovit et promisit. Secundo adhibuerunt duos testes vel tres, quia omnes et singuli requisierunt ipsum de voto suo et iuramento. Et tercio dixerunt ecclesie, ex hoc quod notificaverunt per eorum litteras et nuncios satis solempnes: que omnia recusavit, quare ut ethnicus et publicanus ab omnibus est censendus et per consequens scismaticus notorius, hereticus et heresiarcha.[2]

Luke was not the first to use the text of Matthew: it was a commonplace.[3] He obviously thought this one of his best points however, though his earlier use of the canon law does not suggest very wide knowledge of what he was criticising. The hit at the lawyers is typical from a theologian of this period. This theological argument however still does not avoid the problem of equating wickedness with heresy, which is a notable extension of the traditional definition.

Essentially, nonetheless, Luke's position is moderate. Perhaps the most interesting aspect of the sermon is his ideas on unity with the references to pseudo-Dionysius and Grosseteste. But Luke probably shared his interest in these matters with many Oxford contemporaries,[4] and he may even have borrowed ideas from Richard Ullerston's *Petitiones* written at Hallum's request in 1408 as a reform programme for Pisa.[5]

[1] 7305 fol 169v.
[2] 7305 fol 169. Ms *auctoritive;* 4000 corr.
[3] See for example discussion by Ockham, *Dialogus de potestate Pape et Imperatoris*, I, 6, 92, ed M. Goldast, *Monarchia* II (1614) pp 610-11. I owe this reference to professor Offler.
[4] J. A. Robson, *Wyclif and the Oxford Schools*, Cambridge Studies in Medieval Life and Thought, new series 8 (Cambridge 1961) pp 26ff.
[5] For 'Ullerston' see Emden. The *Petitiones* are printed in H. von der Hardt, *Magnum Oecumenicum Constantience Concilium* (Frankfurt 1700) I cols 1126ff. Passage on unity cols 1128-31.

For the rest, although Luke says that a council derives its powers from the Holy Spirit, he is stressing that Gregory, by his heresy, had already ejected himself before the council met. The only proper thing for Christians to do was to desert him. The definition of heresy may be weak, but Luke tried hard to make it stick because it was the heresy rather than Gregory's other crimes or the power of the council, which was the really important point.

THOMAS RUDBORNE, MONK OF WINCHESTER, AND THE COUNCIL OF FLORENCE

by JOAN G. GREATREX

ONE of the ways in which historians show their wisdom is by their reluctance to make general, definitive pronouncements. Is there anyone among us, for example, who can say with certainty that the spirit of ecumenism abroad today is deeper and more prevalent than in any preceding age? The history of ecumenical councils is the history of the Church's constant striving to reconcile heretics and end schism. Furthermore, it is surely not true to say that concern for the unity of Christendom has been confined in the past only to the small group of council delegates who for spiritual, theological and often, unfortunately, political reasons were, so to speak, professionally involved. However, before I am anathematised for expounding on a negative generalisation let me hasten to draw your attention to the ecumenical interests of Thomas Rudborne, O.S.B.

This side of Rudborne's character has apparently escaped the notice of historians because it is tucked away in the middle of his *Historia Maior* which is a fairly lengthy history *cum* chronicle of his own monastery, Winchester, intermingled with the *gesta* of some of the Saxon and early Norman kings. Neither M. R. James and Claude Jenkins, who give a fairly detailed description of this volume[1] in their catalogue of the manuscripts in Lambeth Palace Library, nor Wharton, who printed a large portion of it in his *Anglia Sacra*,[2] have made any comment on the five folios devoted to the council of Florence.[3]

Their unexpected intrusion into an account of the first Crusade in the chapter on William Rufus may possibly be likened to the 'this reminds me' approach to history, for some of Rudborne's frequent digressions can, I think, be explained in this way; however, others seem to have resulted from the possession or acquisition of particular writings such as the book of the privileges of the Church of Durham which he

---

[1] It is numbered 183, and is a volume containing 218 folios which measure 12 inches by 7¾ inches. [2] I, pp 179–285.

[3] Folios 160ᵛ to 162ᵛ according to the pencilled enumeration at the top of each folio.

borrowed from bishop Robert Neville[1] and which led to a lengthy note
De dignitate prioris Dunelmensis ecclesie.[2]

On the other hand I would suggest that the case of the council of
Florence is rather different, and to support this view there are at least
two reasons.

In the first place, as far as I have been able to ascertain, no other so-
called digression contains information of such recent origin. According
to Wharton who cites internal evidence as proof,[3] Rudborne wrote the
Historia in 1454, a mere fifteen years after the council; thus we have
what amounts to contemporary, almost 'hot off the scriptorial writing
board' news for some of his readers, especially if copies found their
way to some of the smaller and remoter English religious houses.

That Rudborne himself had an eager and inquiring mind is clearly
shown by his inclusion of some thirty folios of information on the
Holy Land, providing a sufficiently detailed description of the major
towns, the countryside and crops, and the religion and customs of the
inhabitants to satisfy even the most apprehensive would-be pilgrim or
crusader. This section is introduced with the explanation: 'here we
must insert what has been written by the venerable father and lord
James of Vitry, patriarch of Jerusalem in his book *De Conquestu Terre
Sancte*, and also by brother Burchard of the Order of Preachers in his
book *De Terra Sancta*'.[4] These are the sources for the lengthy section
which follows beneath the heading, 'Incipit divisio terre sancte per
loca et provincias secundum Jacobum de Vitriaco et Brocardum'.[5] The
reliability of these two thirteenth-century writers may be questioned
although Sir Steven Runciman says that the letters of James of Vitry
are one of the main sources for the fifth Crusade;[6] and even though
most of the Holy Land was in infidel hands during his term of office
as bishop of Acre and Jerusalem, and much of his history is taken from
William of Tyre,[7] he must have had first hand familiarity with both
land and people. It is probably true, as Wharton affirmed,[8] that
Rudborne never saw the writings of James but was content to transcribe

---

[1] Bishop of Durham, 1438 to 1457.   [2] Fols 112r/v.

[3] I p xxvii. 'Dedicata est Ecclesia Wintoniensis anno CLXIX. IV. Cal. Novembr. A
prima fundatione et dedicatione Winton. ecclesis fluxerunt anni MCCLXXXV.'
This statement is accepted by A. F. Pollard in *DNB*.

[4] *Historia Maior*, fols 134r/v, my rendering of Rudborne's words.

[5] Fol 135r.

[6] *A History of the Crusades*, III, *The Kingdom of Acre* (Cambridge 1954) p 483.

[7] According to A. Stewart in his translation of *The History of Jerusalem by Jacques de
Vitry*, Palestine Pilgrims' Text Society, XXXI (London 1896) p v.

[8] I, p 267; ipse [Brocardus] Vitriaci librum nunquam vidit.'

lengthy passages from Brocardus, or Burchard, who in turn had copied freely and sometimes verbatim from the bishop. Thus, where Burchard has written 'Dicit enim venerabilis pater...Jacobus de Vitriaco',[1] Rudborne, in taking the same passage from Burchard, has truthfully added 'et eciam...frater Brocardus'.[2] Without further painstaking investigation it is impossible to know which of these two authorities is finally responsible for any particular statement in this part of Rudborne's work; but it is worth noting that the opinions presented are both intelligent and remarkably tolerant in respect of the faith and practices of the followers of Islam. In fact, the behaviour of the latter presents a striking contrast to that of the Christians in the Holy Land: 'in rei veritate peiores sunt nostri Latini quam ceteri habitatores'.[3]

This surprisingly unprejudiced comment is followed by the remark which forms the connecting link between the crusades and the council of Florence. The Greeks, who are also to be numbered among the inhabitants of the Holy Land, so the passage continues,[4] are Christians but schismatics despite the efforts of pope Gregory X (at Lyons in 1274). Then Rudborne breaks in with 'set pro hoc ulterius notandum, quod'[5] in the year of our Lord 1437 pope Eugenius IV transferred the council of Basel with the consent of his clergy to Ferrara.[6] The account that follows is for the most part in accordance with the findings of Fr Gill in his excellent work on the council of Florence.[7]

This brings me to the second point on which my argument rests. If Rudborne's description of the council is not actually in his own words it is unusual for him not to give the source from which he has drawn. However, there may be a clue provided in the list of four names of the English representatives at this council, three of whom do not seem to have been previously noted by historians. They are all Carmelites and *magistri*: Walter Hunt, the only one who is known to have attended and to have been 'one of the chief exponents of the Latin view';[8] John Kylynghal or Kenynghale, the English prior provincial during the period of the council; and John Thorpe and his brother William. Let us pause for a moment to meet the three Carmelites whose presence at Ferrara and Florence has now come to light.

[1] *Columna Epithoma Historiarum* (Lübeck 1475) I, fol clxxx, c 11.
[2] Fol 134v.   [3] Fol 160v.
[4] *Ibid*. The words are from Burchard.   [5] *Ibid*.
[6] *Ibid*. The English paraphrases the Latin.
[7] [J.] Gill, [*The Council of Florence*] (Cambridge 1959).
[8] James Tait in *DNB*. See also [A. B.] Emden, [*A Biographical Register of the University of Oxford to A.D. 1500*], 3 vols (Oxford 1957–9) II.

John Kenynghale, the provincial, has been located by Dr Emden[1] at the carmelite house in Oxford in 1428, and is known to have been at the council of Basel in 1433, and to have visited the Roman curia several times on behalf of his good friend the Carmelite, Thomas Netter. He died at Norwich in 1451. There is nothing in this information to contradict Rudborne.

John Thorpe was prior of the Cambridge convent[2] between 1410 and 1411, and is described by John Bale, himself an erstwhile Carmelite, in his interesting catalogue of English carmelite writers, *Anglorum Heliades* as *doctor ingeniosus*.[3] Little else is known about him except that he died in 1440 at Norwich.

Bale does not seem to have been aware that the two Thorpes were brothers. They were both present, as was Kenynghale, at the diocesan synod in Norwich in 1428 before which William White was accused of the lollard heresy.[4] Emden notes that William Thorpe was at the Oxford house in 1414, and was prior of the Norwich convent for a time in the 1420s and vicar provincial in England in 1432. He was also at the General Chapter of the Carmelites in Rome in 1446.[5] Bale, in *Anglorum Heliades*, has only a passing reference to William to the effect that 'scripsit super cronicos Anglie reducterum Librum unam et alia quedam'.[6]

There is more plentiful information about Walter Hunt, the *doctor insignis*,[7] who was widely regarded as one of the leading theologians of his day. Among his writings listed by Bale *que iam habemus*[8] are the *Acta Conciliorum* (or *Acta Ferrariae et Florentiae*) and the *De Processu Sacri Concilii*. Unfortunately these works appear to have been lost since the publication of Bale's catalogue in 1559.[9]

It would seem possible, if not highly probable, that Rudborne either had access to one or both of these books (which could easily have been completed by 1454),[10] or that he was in personal contact with one of these four Carmelites through the carmelite convent in Winchester. It is true that nothing is known to suggest the connection of any of them with the Winchester house, but a school of philosophy was

[1] *Ibid.*
[2] A. B. Emden, *A Biographical Register of the University of Cambridge to 1500* (Cambridge 1963).   [3] BM MS Harley 3838 fol 98r.
[4] *Fasciculi Zizaniorum* ed W. W. Shirley, *RS* 5 (1858) p 417.
[5] Emden, III.   [6] Fol 205r.
[7] BM MS Harley 1819. *Codex chartaceus...in quo continentur collectanea Joannis Balaei*, fol 67r.   [8] *Anglorum Heliades*, fol 105r.
[9] J. Bale, *Illustrium Maioris Britannie Scriptorum Summarium* (Ipswich 1548) VIII, p 39.
[10] Hunt was alive until 1478.

flourishing there in this period,[1] and one can safely assume that these men were in great demand as speakers after their return from Italy.

To return to Rudborne's failure to state the source of his information about Ferrara–Florence. If he had heard from an eyewitness rather than read the report of the council proceedings he might well have forgotten all else in his haste to write everything down while his memory remained fresh. Furthermore, because his book was written primarily for his benedictine brethren he might well have thought it unnecessary to give any references for the benefit of readers who knew him and would have known any carmelite connexions that he might have had.

There is one additional fact in Rudborne's account which does not appear to have been mentioned elsewhere. According to Fr Gill 'the imposing embassies that it had been proposed to send to Ferrara never left England'[2] because convocation pleaded the usual burdens of poverty, famine, plague and taxation. Rudborne provides a further reason. Apart from the Carmelites, none of the English doctors were there because, and here I translate and paraphrase from Rudborne, they could procure neither a safe conduct nor a route free from danger in the face of much opposition especially on the part of the duke of Burgundy who at that time was particularly hostile to the English kingdom. However the pope wrote to that duke to obtain a safe conduct on behalf of the [four] Englishmen.[3]

A reading of the five folios now under scrutiny leaves the impression that Rudborne was concerned to improve the knowledge and understanding of his readers. He stressed the rightful place of the council of Florence as the latest and most important of the truly ecumenical or universal councils which had been recognised by both the Eastern and Western Churches. He went on to explain that the failure at Lyons to end the schism a century and a half before had been due to the fact that the Greek delegation had not been empowered to make any decisions in the name of the Greek Church.[4] At Florence, on the other hand, the Greeks were fully represented by both patriarch and emperor, and only three of the Greek prelates refused to sign the articles of union. The great majority felt themselves compelled to return to the Roman obedience by the convincing arguments of the Latin theologians whom

[1] D. Knowles, *The Religious Orders in England*, II (Cambridge 1955) p 145. The history of the Carmelites in England has yet to be written, but the task may be at present an impossible one in view of the scanty materials available. Knowles mentions one unpublished MA thesis (Manchester, 1933): M. E. Turner, 'Some aspects of the English Carmelites in the first half of the fifteenth century.' Unfortunately this MS has recently been lost!   [2] Gill, p 133.   [3] Fol 162 v.   [4] Fol 162r.

they were unable to refute.[1] He concludes that never, since the first separation of the Eastern from the Western Church had there been *tanta et talis unio*[2] as at Florence. This last statement seems to imply that the words were written only a short time after the council was over; that this council like its predecessor at Lyons would prove to be a dead letter must still have been a depressing fact of the unknown future.

Finally, let us turn to a charming incident in this section of Rudborne's volume in which we have a vivid illustration of the type of attitude on both sides which has bogged down ecumenical discussions from that day to this. Burchard, the source for this paragraph, claimed to have overheard the following protest from a Greek patriarch: 'We are desirous of returning to the Roman obedience but I marvel greatly that their bishops and archbishops, who are inferior prelates should try to compel me, who am patriarch, to do obeisance to them and kiss their feet, *ad quod me credo non teneri.*'[3]

---

[1] Fol 162v. Gill states that the Latin spokesmen quoted from the Greek as well as the Latin fathers to support their case, Gill, Chs VI–VIII.

[2] Fol 162r.   [3] Fol 163r.

JULIUS II AND THE SCHISMATIC
CARDINALS

by WALTER ULLMANN

IT would seem that in the assessment of the forces prevalent on
the eve of the Reformation too little attention has been paid to the
determined steps which a number of cardinals initiated in 1511 when
they took it upon themselves to convoke a general council at Pisa. The
cardinals and the ensuing council have never had a good press. In fact
there seems a unanimous condemnation of their initiative: they were
labelled schismatics paradoxically because they tried to prevent a
schism; they had proved themselves, so it was alleged, as mere instruments of French expansionist policy and had acted against the interests
of papacy and Church prompted as they were by personal considerations and animosity against Julius II. It seems almost 'heretical' to
question this general verdict.

Yet as far as I can see no detailed investigation has been undertaken
to arrive at a more equitable and balanced verdict which, moreover,
takes into account the actual and juristic background of the cardinals'
initiative. The purpose of this communication is to invite attention to
some features which do not seem to be adequately appraised or even
analysed. And these features belong almost wholly to juristic categories
of thought in conjunction with the reality of the situation. The cardinals
moved entirely within the juristic thought pattern. Three points must
be made straight away. First that before his election Pope Julius II
had entered into the by then quite common electoral capitulations in the
conclave and promised under oath that among other things he would
convoke a general council within two years of his election.[1] What
distinguished this capitulation from most previous ones was that the
College of Cardinals insisted on Julius II repeating his promise *after*
his election which he did; he also solemnly declared in his function as
pope that neither he himself not anyone else could absolve him from

---

[1] For these capitulations see [O. Raynaldus,] *Ann[ales] Eccl[esiastici]* (ed Bar-le-Duc 1877)
XXX, p 537: anno 1511 no 3, where the relevant parts of the capitulations are given
verbatim. For the general juristic problems caused by these capitulations see W.
Ullmann, 'The legality of the papal electoral pacts' in *Ephemerides iuris canonici*, XII
(Rome 1956) pp 212ff.

the obligation sworn to.[1] For just under eight years following his election there is no evidence whatsoever that Julius took any steps towards implementing the promises given under oath. The second point is that the whole pontificate of Julius was overshadowed by a tension between him as pope and the College of Cardinals, amongst whom – and they were the articulate, learned and also independently-minded – there were outspoken opponents of the monarchic idea of the papacy as represented by Julius's manner of government and his aims. He made not only no concessions to the prevailing mood amongst the more educated and critically inclined clerical and lay sections, but also adopted a veritably retrograde policy which showed him a mixture of a crafty and at times violent renaissance prince and a wily medieval pope. The third point is that amongst the cardinals there were men who as far as one can judge by their deeds, were perfectly aware of the needs of the time and who sensed the perilous nature of the policies pursued by this renaissance pope.[2] What a small section of the cardinals realised was that if nothing concrete was done to quell the spiritual unrest, decomposition, demoralisation and protest of contemporary Christendom, if in other words some effective measures were not taken at least to initiate a 'reform in head and members', a complete cataclysm could hardly be avoided. Moreover, amongst these far-sighted cardinals were some who were quite outstanding as canonists, such as Johannes Antonius de s. Georgio who in his lengthy and somewhat diffuse commentary (written before he had become a cardinal) faced the question crucial at the time – what to do with a pope whose government proved deleterious to the cause of Christendom, who refused to summon a general council and who could be shown to be suspected of heresy by his actions, teachings and the scandal he inflicted upon Christendom.[3]

[1] See especially *Ann Eccl* p 397a, 1503, no 6: 'Ego Julius secundus electus...praemissa omnia et singula promitto, iuro et vovo...et sub poena periurii et anathematis, a quibus nec me ipsum absolvam nec alicui absolutionem committam.'

[2] This present communication deals with Julius as pope, and not with the man who in so magnificent a manner had largely made Rome what it has become. It will be recalled that it was Julius II who granted Henry VIII the dispensation from the marriage impediment, see *Ann Eccl* p 402a–b, 1503, no 22 where the papal decree is dated 26 December 1503.

[3] See Johannes Antonius de sancto Georgio, *Commentaria super decretorum volumina* (ed Lyons 1522) hereafter Songiorgio, ad D.a.c.1, *Dist* 17, no 3, fol 66ra, and *Dist. ead.c.*1 (Synodum) no 5, fol 66va. The extremely detailed presentation by Sangiorgio would warrant a study of its own. He devotes no fewer than six folios to the question of pope and general council. On him see [F. J.] Schulte, [*Geschichte der Quellen und Literatur des canonischen Rechts*](Stuttgart 1877) II, pp 338–41; A. van Hove, *Prolegomena ad Codicem Iuris*

Julius II and the schismatic cardinals

That the government of Julius II caused serious apprehension in the College of Cardinals was therefore comprehensible, especially when his total inability as well as unwillingness to enact any of the necessary reformatory measures was considered. In view of the papacy's immediate past record there was considerable justification for the cardinals insisting upon the implementation of the electoral capitulations. To them therefore the general council appeared as the only appropriate forum to enact on a universal and comprehensive scale the *reformatio in capite et membris*. But Julius would have none of this. A man of iron will, pertinacity, and stubbornness Julius preferred petty Italian power politics to any attempt at an improvement of the spiritual, disciplinary and moral standards of which contemporary Christianity was ostensibly in need. This is not to say that his restoration of some order in the papal state was not a considerable achievement but is simply to point out the singularly one-sided interest which he displayed as pope. The other side of his interest – regeneration and rebirth on not only artistic and architectural levels – was conspicuously absent, and if he ever realised the need for this regeneration or rebirth, he never showed it in his public or official acts. Assuredly, there was more of a military commander and a king in him than of a pontiff.[1] Perhaps not so manifest as in recent pontificates nepotism of cardinalitian appointments still reached quite respectable dimensions: no fewer than four members of his family (the della Rovere) received the cardinal's hat in successive creations. Julius's over-all governmental concept culminated in the restoration of the papacy as a universal power: once more it was to be the nerve-centre of the christian world.[2] The means to achieve this end were the full deployment of papal-monarchic powers based on the traditional petrinological argument. That neither the plan nor its

---

Canonici (2 ed Mechlin-Rome 1945) p 498. He was created a cardinal by Alexander VI in 1493, having been appointed an auditor of the Rota by Innocent VIII in 1481 (see A. Cerchiari, *Capellani papae et apostolicae sedis auditores* (Rome 1926) II, p 69). He was professor of Roman and canon law at Pavia and was one of the most outstanding jurists of the late fifteenth and early sixteenth centuries. He died in March 1509 (see Schulte, p 339).

[1] One can hardly disagree with [L.] Pastor's judgment, see his [*Geschichte der Päpste im Zeitalter der Renaissance*] (Freiburg 1895) III, p 526. See further the unnecessarily reticent view of G. Schwaiger on Julius II in *L[exikon für] T[heologie und] K[irche]* V (Freiburg 1963) p 1205: 'hinter der gewaltigen politisch-militärischen Tätigkeit trat das geistliche Wirken sehr stark zurück.' Here are good bibliographical details.

[2] Once more we can cite Pastor's view, III, p 527: 'Der Hauptgedanke: die Weltmacht des Papsttums neu zu beleben, dem heiligen Stuhl durch einen festgefügten Staat Unabhängigkeit und Ansehen zu verschaffen, stand von Anfang seiner Regierung an unverrückt vor der Seele des neuen Papstes.'

execution met with the support of the College of Cardinals, would not seem surprising. Indeed, some of the alert and reflective cardinals felt not only justifiable apprehension, but also alarm on account of the policy consistently pursued by Julius. The view which Luther – in common with many other contemporaries – formed of this pope when on a visit to Rome during Julius's pontificate, may well have reflected the sentiment of a great many non–Italians: 'a blood-sucker', 'a cruelly violent animal'.[1]

The dichotomy between promise and achievement can hardly have been more obvious than in this pontificate. It is not difficult to visualise how agonising the situation must have been for these members of the curia who realised the need for drastic measures. That both the French king Louis XII and the German emperor-elect Maximilian – for reasons which may well have been different from those which prompted a number of cardinals to leave the curia – displayed animosity against the pope by 1510 and early 1511, no doubt weighed heavily with the faction of cardinals who now began to take matters into their own hands. Even by contemporary standards the situation had indeed reached intolerable dimensions on account of the military policy of Julius who by 1510 was not merely the nominal, but the real supreme commander of the army in the field. Nevertheless, with his permission five cardinals left the curia: they had clearly sensed the futility of acting as advisers of the pope who had threatened some of the independently-minded cardinals with ecclesiastical censures and had actually incarcerated some of them. There can be no doubt that contact was established between the French king and those cardinals who had left the curia, yet it would be erroneous to see in this contact anything more than a diplomatic *rapprochement* strongly reminiscent of the situation exactly a century earlier. Indeed, the situation in 1407 culminating in the secession of a number of cardinals from both popes and resulting in the Council of Pisa in 1409, provided the men of the early sixteenth century with a pattern, even in regard to the locality. It is not generally known that the cardinals who seceded in 1407 obtained the opinion of some very eminent jurists, such as Antonius de Butrio (canonist) and Paulus Castrensis (civilian):[2] exactly the same procedure was followed by the cardinals in 1511.

[1] Quoted from *Reallexikon für Theologie & Kirche*, ed A. Hauck, IX (Tübingen 1907) p 624.

[2] See the latter's *Consilia* (ed Frankfurt 1582), *cons* 419 by him himself (fol 216va); no 420 by Antonius de Butrio (fol 218ra); and no 421 by two other Bolognese doctors. Nor is it generally known that Baldus de Ubaldis dealt at some length with the with-

Julius II and the schismatic cardinals

On 16 May 1511 nine cardinals of whom the outstanding Carvajal[1] was clearly the leader issued their summons for a general council to be opened on 1 September at Pisa. These cardinals were by no means all French – only two of them were ostensibly so – and it would be a somewhat *simpliste* assumption and facile explanation to say that they were the tools of Louis XII or of Maximilian. That there had been negotiations between the two rulers and the cardinals their convocation edict explicitly mentions; it goes even so far as to say that both Louis and Maximilian had agreed through their proctors to their step. But before initiating this fateful measure the cardinals had – like their predecessors of a century earlier – consulted some of the most eminent jurists: Phillipus Decius,[2] Jason de Mayno,[3] Franciscus Curtius and Paulus Picus[4] were some of those who initially advised the cardinals on the legality of convoking a general council. Only the *consilium* of the first-mentioned is known, though to the best of my knowledge it has never been properly analysed.[5] An analysis of their convocation edict shows that the cardinals relied entirely on the juristic advice proffered by these outstanding canonists and civilians. Neither the iurists nor the cardinals considered that this convocation of a general council constituted a schismatic action or turned them into schismatics.

The main points in the cardinals' summons were first that because the pope had neglected to implement the promise to convoke a general council, the duty to do so developed upon them in order to deal with the sorry state of the Church and to effect a reform in head and mem-

---

drawal of the French king from the anti-pope Benedict XII in 1397; see Baldus, *Lectura in decretales* (ed Venice 1615) ad *Extra*: 1.iii.25 (Olim), fols 53rb–53va. See further [Petrus de] Ancharano, [*Consilia*] (ed Lyons 1539) *cons* 281, fols 116ra ff which is a very subtle and lengthy treatment of the juristic points raised by the cardinals who had receded from both obediences; see further Domenicus Geminianus, *Consilia* (ed Lyons 1533), *cons* 88, fols 51ra–vb.

[1] On him see [C.] Eubel, [*Hierarchia catholica medii aevi*] (Münster 1914) II p 22 and III p 4; further J. Wodka in *LTK*, II (1957) pp 959–60: cardinal since 1493 and curial legate in Germany in 1496 and 1507–8.

[2] For him see [F. C.] Savigny, [*Geschichte des römischen Rechts im Mittelalter*] (Heidelberg 1850) VI, pp 374ff; Schulte, II, pp 361ff and [M. P.] Gilmore, [*Humanists and Jurists*] (Cambridge, Mass. 1963) pp 73ff. See also M. Ascheri, *Un Maestro del 'Mos italicus': Gianfrancesco Sannazari della Ripa* (Milan 1970) pp 27–9.

[3] See Savigny, VI, pp 397–418, Gilmore, pp 68–72 with further literature.

[4] See Savigny, VI, p 381.

[5] See Pastor, III, p 649 (a mere mentioning); [H.] Jedin [*Geschichte des Konzils von Trient*] (Freiburg 1949) p 86 (only a few lines) (Engl transl 1957, at p 106). Jedin also refers to an anonymous *consilium* which he himself had discovered in Rome, Vatican MS Bibl Barb Lat 843; see furthermore J. Hefele-H. Leclercq, *Histoire des conciles* (Paris 1917) VIII, p 316, and for a very brief summary, Gilmore, pp 75–7.

bers.[1] Moreover, the Council of Constance in the decree *Frequens* had stipulated that a general council should be held every ten years, and though the present pope had sworn to convoke one within two years he had done nothing in this direction. The cardinals considered him 'nedum negligens in praecepto ecclesiae et concilii set et voti et iuramenti huiusmodi transgressor'. In so far they merely re-echoed Julius II's own words.[2] By his unwillingness to convoke the council the pope had adversely affected the well-being of the Church: the duty to convoke it developed upon them.[3]

It is difficult to see in these statements of the cardinals anything that formally or constitutionally could be called schismatic, since there was no suggestion whatsoever that the cardinals (or for that matter Louis or Maximilian) considered a separation from the Roman Church or from the pope.[4] On the contrary, as the second point in their documents makes amply clear the cardinals had so little intention of being the agents of a schism that they humbly and most respectfully invited the pope to give his assent to the council envisaged and convoked, and to honour it either by his own personal presence or by his legates.[5] By no stretch of imagination could this be seen as a schismatic step nor as one that showed any disrespect to the pope. Throughout their lengthy document there is no indication that the cardinals viewed Julius as anything else but the lawful pope whose wrath in case of independent action they nevertheless had cause to fear, as they also made abundantly clear when they explained the reason why their convocation was not issued from the curia but was nailed on the church doors at Modena, Reggio, Parma, and so on: the pope, they said, had thrown some cardinals into the dungeons and had imprisoned others

---

[1] See *Ann Eccl* xxx, p 538: 'pro vera pace christianorum fundanda et sufficienti bello contra infideles et pro extirpatione haeresum et errorum in diversis mundi partibus superiorum negligentia pullulantium et similiter schismatum ac divisionum necnon potissime pro reformatione morum universalis ecclesiae in capite et membris plurimum collapsorum ac emendatione criminum gravissimorum notoriorum, continuorum aut incorrigibilium universalem ecclesiam scandalizantium'.

[2] See above, p 178 n 1.

[3] See *Ann Eccl* xxx, p 538b.

[4] The statement by [J. J.] Scarisbrick, [*Henry VIII*] (London 1968) 26, that Louis XII summoned a schismatic general council to meet at Pisa in May 1511 'which would have on its agenda nothing less than the deposition of Julius himself' does not seem accurate.

[5] *Ann Eccl* xxx, p 538b: 'Quapropter cum omni reverentia et humilitate ac instantia sanctissimum dominum nostrum Julium papam nomine quo supra supplicamus et per viscera misericordiae Dei nostri requirimus, ut huic vocationi concilii pro dictis causis assentire dignetur et illud personaliter vel per legatos suos honorare et confirmare.'

contra ius gentium – these were notorious facts, they maintained, which caused them to be apprehensive of their safety, hence the unusual method of publication.[1]

What must be stressed is that there is no shred of evidence that the cardinals intended to charge the pope with any particular crime or offence. All they did was what the pope should have done. In so far the nine cardinals did not go beyond what the moderate section of canonists had held to be legitimate. In any event the juristic problem raised by their convocation of a general council was certainly not that of pope versus council. Because of the gravity of their step they wished to be assured of its legality, and that was why they sought the expert opinions of famous jurists. As a matter of fact, one of their own colleagues who had died only two years previously, the already mentioned Johannes Antonius de s. Georgio, had advocated a scheme of things which was fully embraced by the great Jason de Mayno in his *consilium*. The late cardinal had maintained[2] that if the pope's conduct had caused scandal, the cardinals *quasi ex necessitate* were entitled to convoke a general council. And once they had convoked the council and assembled together, they should request the pope to be present and authorise the council as a general council. Only if the pope were to refuse he could then be treated as someone suspected of heresy and be deposed. The essential point of cardinal Sangiorgio was that a pope could be charged and condemned and deposed only for heresy: for no other crime could he be brought to trial.[3] Jason de Mayno literally followed the cardinal's

---

[1] *Ibid* p 539a: 'Quia tutum non esset nobis procuratoribus dictam convocationem concilii et protestationem in praesentia sanctissimi domini nostri facere, qui sanctae universalis ecclesiae cardinales fratres suos et ecclesiam universalis principes carceribus aliquando mancipandos minari fecit oratoresque principum contra ius gentium detineri, prout notorium est et pro notorio allegatur, ideo decrevimus per affixionem huiusmodi schedulae.'

[2] I am unable to understand the statement by Jedin, p 87 (Eng trans p 108) that 'Sangiorgio blieb bei Julius II.', because he had been dead for two years by the time the cardinals convoked the general council; he died on 14 March 1509, see Schulte, above p 178 n 3 and Eubel, II, p 22, n 3.

[3] See Sangiorgio, fol 66ra: 'Satis videtur cum papa ex hoc videtur scandalizareuniversalem ecclesiam, poterunt cardinales quasi ex necessitate convocare concilium ...ubi congregati fuerint (possint) rogare papam ut adsit et auctorizet congregationem, quod si fecerit monendus erit ut se corriget...quod si neque venire neque auctorizare voluerit vel se corrigere recusaverit tamquam suspectus de haeresi poterit deponi, c.si papa (=*Dist.* xl.c.6).' About the provenance of this chapter in Gratian see W. Ullmann, 'Cardinal Humbert and the ecclesia Romana' in *Studi Gregoriani*, IV (Rome 1952) pp 111ff; here also further literature. In another place Sangiorgio declared that in case of scandal caused by the pope, the council could well proceed against him 'non intelligo ad iudicandum eum, sed ad monendum et inducendum eum ad correctionem, quia a nemine excepta causa haeresis iudicari potest' (fol 66va, no 5).

exposition by copying his words in his own *consilium* and adding that such a solemn and charitable exhortation issued formally by a general council could not fail to produce the desired result.[1] Since the nine cardinals adopted a point of view which was wholly consonant with the most moderate section of canon lawyers, it is hard to understand why they should have attracted the opprobrious charge of being schismatics. What needs stressing is that both Sangiorgio and Jason rejected the standpoint put forward by the *glossa ordinaria*[2] which was generally accepted. These two jurists restricted the accountability of the pope before a general council to matters of heresy, while Phillipus Decius adopted the view of the *glossa* and held that for *any* notorious crime the pope could be charged and condemned by a general council. The *glossa ordinaria* (based as it was on Huguccio)[3] as well as the common opinion maintained that incorrigibility and negligence (*contumacia*) of the pope amounted to heresy and therefore was a chargeable crime.[4]

That Pisa was chosen as the locality of the forthcoming general council had again its explanation in the model situation of exactly a century earlier. Indeed, Antonius de Butrio and Panormitanus had already pointed out that nobody had ever charged the cardinals who had left Gregory XII, with the crime of schism. And Gregory XII's case was not at all unlike that of Julius II: he too had sworn in conclave and repeated the promise under oath as pope that he would renounce the papacy and would not create new cardinals in order to bring the schism to an end – and yet did neither. That the pope could not absolve himself from the oath he had taken, was common opinion which Julius himself had endorsed.[5] By not adhering to his own promises the

---

1 See Jason de Mayno, *Consilia* (ed Frankfurt 1609) IV, *cons.* 95, pp 349ff at no 41, p 356b: 'Item per concilium generale poterit fieri charitativa admonitio et exhortatio papae circa eius correctionem denuntiando ei qualiter pernicioso vitae suae exemplo universam ecclesiam scandalizaret et conturbaret. Quae exhortatio sic a tota ecclesia facta cum tanta sollenitate et auctoritate non est dubium quin magna virtutis et efficaciae esset ad animum papae in bonum convertendum.'   2 On *Dist.* xl, c. 6.

3 See further Baldus, *Lectura ad tres priores libros decretalium* (ed Venice 1615) ad *Extra*: I.iii.25, no 22, fol 53vb: after referring to Huguccio 'quod papa potest removeri propter notorium crimen enorme. Tene menti.' The outstanding Ludovicus Romanus Pontanus held in his *Consilia* (ed Frankfurt 1577) *cons.* 523, no 15, fol 285rb that 'papa stans in crimine notorio scandalizante totam ecclesiam desistere nolens incidit in suspicionem haeresis...potest ut haereticus condemnari atque consequenter deponi a papatu.'

4 See *gl. ord.* ad *Dist.* xl, c. 6. [Phillipus] Decius in his [*Consilium*], ed in Melchior Goldast, *Monarchia Romani imperii* (Frankfurt 1668) II pp 1767ff at p 1771, no XIII, lines 25ff: 'Illa enim incorrigibilitas seu contumacia dicitur haeresis secundum glossam, et tali casu non requiritur quod sit haereticus proprie.' See also Ancharano above, p 180 n 2.

5 See above, p 178 n 1. See further Antonius de Butrio, *Commentaria ad decretales* (ed Lyons 1556) ad *Extra*: I.ii.1, no 10, fol 9vb: 'Et papa astringitur voto et iuramento ac promis-

pope had given an example which all too easily could influence lower placed officers and hence all Christians: 'scandalum generatur mentibus laicorum dicentium, Ubi est deus clericorum?'[1]

A difficult juristic point was this: could the cardinals who convoked the general council be said to constitute the majority of the College of Cardinals and represent its opinion? That numerically they did not form the majority of the College, could hardly be disputed. But did they render themselves culpable of the charge of causing a schism by wilfully setting aside the majority view? There was general agreement that in case of need the College itself was entitled to summon a general council. Certainly, the present contingency of only nine cardinals issuing an invitation to a council was not provided for in law.

Decius devoted a great deal of space and argument to this intricate problem. The argument by which he chose to solve it, was not unlike the one which canonists of an earlier generation had advocated in settling a similar question. In their manner he operated with the analogy of a cathedral chapter. If, so it was pointed out, the bishop was negligent or remiss in his duties, the cathedral chapter stepped into his place, and if the chapter itself was negligent, the right to act devolved upon the individual canons.[2] As a matter of fact, the great civilian Paulus Castrensis had dealt with exactly the same problem in his *consilium* on the situation in 1407-9.[3] His conclusion appeared to be directly applicable to the contingency in Julius II's pontificate. Decius

---

sione nec ab illis stante vinculo seipsum absolvere potest...ex quibus patet Gregorium XII qui in conclavi ante papatum tamquam cardinalis et post papatum promisit, iuravit et vovit renuntiare pro sedando schismate quod duraverat XXX annis...quod et publicavit per universum orbem, suo astringitur iuramento et voto et promissione... cardinales pene omnes ab eo de Luca recesserunt Pisas.' Cf. further Panormitanus, *Super quinto libro decretalium* (ed Lyons 1512) ad *Extra*: v.xxxix.44, no 5, fol 248ra, as well as Decius in *Cons.*, p 1772, no XVII, lines 30ff. The latter pointed out that the oath came within the precincts of divine law, from which, by general consent, the pope could not dispense.

[1] Decius, p 1770, lines 3-5.
[2] *Ibid*, p 1774, no XXVI, lines 58ff. For earlier similar views see [B.] Tierney, [*Foundations of conciliar theory*] (repr Cambridge 1969) pp 127ff.
[3] See Paulus Castrensis, *Consilia* (ed Frankfurt 1582) I, *cons.* 419, who went even so far as to say that 'si cardinales persistant in eius obedientia [Gregory XII] videntur eius esse fautores et participare in crimine praestando ei auxilium et favorem'. See also Antonius de Butrio, *cons.* 420, fol 217rb who held a similar opinion. Cardinal Zabarella had indeed envisaged the possibility of a divided College of Cardinals in which case he counselled recourse to the emperor, obviously an advice that could not be adopted in the present instance, see his *Consilia* (ed Lyons 1552), *cons.* 150, fols 90vb–92rb, at no 5, fol 91ra: 'ipse [imperator] repraesentat totum populum christianum' with a reference to the *lex regia*. About Zabarella see W. Ullmann, *The Origins of the Great Schism* (repr London 1967) pp 191ff.

therefore held that in the interests of the universal Church even individual cardinals were entitled to convoke a general council 'propter negligentiam papae et collegii cardinalium'.[1] And the negligence of the pope was amply proved by his failure to convoke a council as he had promised to do within two years after becoming pope. Nor was any further admonition necessary, because where a promise remained unfulfilled after the appointed time no special admonition was called for.[2]

There was another argument according to which individual cardinals were entitled to proceed to a convocation of a general council. Negligence on the part of the pope redounded to the detriment of the universal Church, and hence the summoning of a council could be viewed as a defensive measure. This indeed was a standpoint that was closely linked with the whole question of negligence of a superior, even if he were pope. For if he proved himself to be a *malus praelatus* even an excommunicated individual was entitled to take the necessary steps to remove him – 'ubi agitur de repellendo de malo praelato, dicitur defensio necessaria, ideo etiam excommunicatus admittitur'. The conclusion which Decius reached – and indeed he was able to muster the common opinion in his favour[3] – was that individual cardinals were fully entitled to act where the defence of the Church was concerned. Hence they could from the strictly legal standpoint speak on behalf of the whole College of Cardinals which as a legal corporation was impeded in its actions and consequently incapable of expressing its own point of view.[4] 'Totum ius collegii in ipsis [cardinalibus] residere videtur.'[5] And lastly, according to the commonly accepted

---

[1] Decius, p 1775, lines 12ff and lines 23ff: 'Quia collegium deprehenditur in negligentia, haec provincia ad cardinales deferri videtur, ut omnes doctores tenent.'

[2] Decius refers to Baldus, *Lectura in Codicem* (ed Venice 1615), v.i.2, fol 149vb, but this appears hardly relevant, as Baldus dealt here with the unfulfilled promise to marry within two years, in which case no special warning was necessary.

[3] See for instance, Panormitanus, [*Super primo libro decretalium*] (ed Lyons 1512) ad *Extra*: I.v.2, no 9, fol 77ra: '...quaeritur numquid ius universitatis possit remanere in uno solo omnibus aliis mortuis vel privatis...tota potentia collegii residet in isto solo ...iste tamen solus non poterit seipsum eligere'. See also Petrus de Monte, *De potestate pontificis*, ed in *Tractatus universi iuris* (ed Venice 1579) XIII, 1, fol 147va: 'ius universitatis potest esse in uno residente.' This standpoint had already been clearly expressed by the gl. ord. on *Extra*: I.v.2, s.v. 'Pauciores'. For Petrus de Monte compare also A. Black, *Monarchy & Community* (Cambridge 1970) pp 58, 62ff.

[4] See further the gl. ord. on *Extra*: I.v.2; and Panormitanus, no 5, fol 76vb.

[5] Furthermore, the right of the College of Cardinals could devolve on one cardinal only, as the corresponding *universitas* in Roman law also could consist of one member only, according to Decius, p 1775, no XVIII, lines 51, 55ff referring to *Dig.* 3.4.7 §2: 'ius omnium in unum reciderit et stet nomen universitatis.'

doctrine, one sole remaining member of a chapter can elect the prelate, and hence 'in uno solo cardinali ius collegii residere potest et ipse poterit papam eligere'.

These were some of the main points made by contemporary *lumina iuris* whom the cardinals had consulted. It will be readily seen that from the formal and juristic standpoint the charge of having caused a schism could not be made against the cardinals. They had powerful doctrinal support and had not even adopted the commonly accepted viewpoint of the *glossa ordinaria*: they limited the case of an accusation of the pope to that of an alleged heresy, a charge which they had not raised. In their edict there was therefore no suggestion that they would proceed to an election of another pope or that they would take measures which could conceivably be construed as schismatic.

Paradoxically enough, the most convincing vindication of the cardinals' step came from the pope himself. There can be no doubt that he was galvanised into the very action and procedure which formed the case of the cardinals. The edict now issued by Julius II completely changed the situation and gravely affected the standing of the cardinals who had taken the initiative. Two months after the cardinals had despatched their edict, Julius II issued on 25 July 1511 the decree (dated 18 July 1511) by which he summoned a general council (the Fifth Lateran Council) for 19 April 1512 at the Lateran. In order to defuse the – admittedly dangerous – situation Julius attempted to wrest the initiative from the cardinals and did what he should have done some time within the preceding eight years.

What strikes the reader of this papal communication[1] is that Julius was far more concerned with attacking the cardinals than with the question of how to effect some concrete 'reform in head and members of the Church', a terminology which is conspicuously absent in this document. Instead, the cardinals were called 'sons of darkness' who had 'mendaciously acted as true schismatics'. Their envisaged council was no more than 'a schismatic conventicle'[2] or a synagogue of Satan provoking a malignant schism – *pessimum noviter pullulans schisma*.[3] The cardinals had neither the power to convoke a general council nor a legitimate cause. In any event, Pisa was a notoriously unsafe place. Again and again, Julius (and those cardinals who had remained with him) returned to the charge and accused their opponents of treasonable and schismatic conduct: the papal edict declared that they took the step 'ad scindendam et scandalizandam universalis ecclesiae unitatem',[4]

---

[1] *Ann Eccl*, pp 540b–545b.   [2] *Ibid* p 543b.   [3] *Ibid* pp 543b, 544a.   [4] *Ibid* p 543b.

hence their proposed measure was pronounced totally invalid 'ne cancerosus morbus invalescat'. Severe sanctions were threatened against individuals, groups and localities willing to render any help to the schismatic cardinals. In contrast to the lengthy and diffuse vituperations and condemnations of the cardinals the papal document becomes rather economical, if not tantalisingly vague, when it approaches the reason for convoking the general council: all the edict said was that the council would do everything to exalt and preserve the unity of the Church and activate its reform so that heresies and schisms were to be extirpated.[1]

In the annals of the medieval papacy it is indeed rare to find a document which in so one-sided a manner and without giving the cardinals accused and convicted of the crime of schism a chance to defend themselves, so completely disregarded fundamental principles of law applicable to the lowliest villein, a feature that was pointed out by cardinal Jacobazzi at the time.[2] Yet from the purely formal and constitutional standpoint the summoning of a general council was the master stroke of the experienced, shrewd and ruthless diplomat that Julius II had proved himself throughout his pontificate. Clearly, there was a very real dichotomy between the constitutional position of the pope and his undoubted right (and duty) to convoke a general council on the one hand, and the reasons which prompted him to act, that is, the action of the cardinals on the other. Their alleged schismatic action was the reason for the pope's summons – nevertheless, according to the solid body of established juristic theory and the opinion of the most outstanding jurists as well as according to the cardinals' own intentions the charge raised against them stood on extremely shaky foundations.

There is need for a more balanced assessment of the cardinals' step than it has so far received. For, as pointed out, on any strict analysis they could not be stigmatised as schismatics, because one of the pre-suppositions of schism in the juristic sense was absent: the essence of the crime of schism was rupture of the unity of the Church by separating parts of the Church from the pope, that is, withdrawal of obedience from him.[3] But this was precisely not the case here: on the contrary the cardinals had invited the pope to confirm and attend the council.

---

[1] *Ibid* p 544b.

[2] In his lengthy work *De concilio*, lib. vii, art. 1, ed in *Tractatus universi iuris* (Venice 1584), XIII-1, fol 302.

[3] Gratian, XXIV.i.34; also Panormitanus in the heading on the *gl. ord.* on *Extra*: v, 8.

Nor had they, as already mentioned, created or intended to create an anti-pope. But Julius II was all out to smash the initiators of the Pisan Council as well as the conciliar idea itself with the help which conciliarism provided. Indubitably, the cardinals had forced his hand. The question was not simply council versus pope, but whether the council summoned by the pope or that initiated by the cardinals was to be the instrument by which reform was to be carried out. The pope spoke vaguely of a 'reformatio morum tam ecclesiasticorum quam saecularium personarum'[1] – an unobjectionable and laudable aim, but hardly one that touched the core of the matter – and as the first sessions of the Fifth Lateran Council proved, nothing of any consequence in the direction of reform was in fact enacted. The pope merely used the device of a general council to render harmless the intentions of the cardinals. The design of the cardinals to effect the 'reformatio in capite et membris' – and this is one of the crucial points – was brought to naught by the papal summons. But from the formal juristic standpoint the papal action cornered the cardinals: for by continuing to pursue their plan *after* the papal summons had gone out, they now formally and constitutionally began to become schismatics.

This indeed was also the opinion of contemporaries who had displayed great sympathy with the cardinals' cause. For instance, cardinal Jacobazzi[2] in common with many others held that while before the papal summons the cardinals could not possibly be called schismatics,[3] their standing afterwards assumed an entirely different complexion: they now had become schismatics *vere et proprie*.[4] Julius II knew how to derive the greatest profit from his constitutional position and relentlessly drove home his undoubted right which he used to the fullest possible extent and advantage: in the early autumn of 1511 he set the cardinals a term within which they had an opportunity of recanting. When the ultimatum expired, in public consistory on 24 October 1511

---

[1] *Ann Eccl*, p 544.

[2] For Jacobazzi see W. Ullmann in *Medieval Studies presented to Aubrey Gwynn*, ed J. A. Watt, J. B. Morrall, F. X. Martin (Dublin 1961) p 360, n 4, with further literature.

[3] See *De concilio*, no 80, fol 302vb: 'Non videntur dicendi schismatici [cardinales] quia nullam scissuram in ecclesia fecerunt...cum ergo per discessum ipsorum cardinalium adhuc nulla reperiatur illicita divisio per inobedientiam ab unitate ecclesiae, sequitur quod adhuc praedicti cardinales non possunt dici schismatici.'

[4] *Ibid* no 82, fol 303ra: 'Vereor si post intimatum concilium per sanctissimum dominum nostrum ad quem hoc spectat, se non subiecerunt voluntati eius, et a suis coeptis non destiterint volendo a seipsis concilium tenere et antipapam erigere, quod tunc erunt vere et proprie schismatici, quia tunc quicquid fecerunt, ambitiose factum esse ostenderent.' See also *ibid* no 87, fol 303rb. Jedin has rightly stressed the importance of Jacobazzi's standpoint, p 89 (Eng trans p 107).

the chief actors amongst them were excommunicated and deprived of their cardinalate.[1] Herewith the cardinals were publicly exposed as seditious schismatics. The first session of their council did not take place until 5 November 1511 – the delay was caused by a number of factors of which the papal summons, the lukewarm support by Louis XII and the detached attitude of Maximilian were in the foreground – and it was a council without a constitutional head and entirely in the hands of formally condemned schismatics who had been excommunicated in a juristically unimpeachable manner.

In a word, the situation had changed quite drastically by the autumn of 1511. Considering the profound issues at stake, was the display of legal formalism really sufficient and adequate to stem the rapidly advancing tide of a far more serious schism, the contours of which could clearly be discerned on the not too distant horizon? Assuredly, the College of Cardinals had, as also in previous pontificates, shown considerably greater awareness of the very pressing needs of the time than the papacy – one has but to recall the high-powered commissions of cardinals appointed by Pius II and Alexander VI and their terms of reference – but what does strike the distant observer is the conspicuous and fundamental divergence in the juristic and theological approach to the issues at stake. Frequently enough do we obtain just more than a mere glance in the protagonists of either side of some deep-seated aversion from the other's point of view.[2]

What must be emphasised is that the jurists were quite ostensibly aware of the necessity for some quick, drastic and effective measures if the collapse of a united and uniform Christendom was not to come about. They certainly had their ears more to the ground than their theological colleagues. What is particularly interesting and what also needs to be stressed is that the jurists did not employ any new arguments, still less propound radical solutions, but entirely relied on established doctrine and the more recent exposition of the constitutional law of the Church. Here we find a feature which is not at all unfamiliar to those who have some acquaintance with the development of juristic themes in the Middle Ages. What fifteenth and early six-

[1] *Ann Eccl*, pp 553–7, with testimonies of eye witnesses and actual texts of sanctions promulgated.
[2] See, for instance, Decius, no XI, p 1770, lines 50ff: 'Non curandum est quod theologi aliter dicant, quia in ista materia magis standum est doctoribus canonum quam theologiae magistris, quia hoc non exigitur de articulis fidei, sed de moribus et integritate vitae, quo casu magis credendum est professoribus canonum.' See also no XII, p 1771, lines 20ff expressing a similar point of view.

teenth-century jurists advocated was merely a practical application of already accepted doctrine – this indeed is a parallel case of the conciliar theme itself which, as has been shown by one of my pupils, was virtually as old as canonistic doctrine itself was.[1] Here we have exactly the same situation: in themselves perfectly harmless juristic theses gained the greatest topical significance when applied to a concrete situation. Apparently when set forth in lectures, glosses, commentaries and books, these themes were considered innocuous and abstract enough, but once applied to a real contingency, they assumed an unexpectedly dangerous complexion. Yet looking at the scene as the fateful second decade of the sixteenth century opens, one can hardly resist the temptation to think that they might well have offered some solution of the crucial problems besetting contemporary Christendom. One can go further and say that juristic doctrine in the fifteenth and early sixteenth centuries attempted to accommodate the law to the exigencies of the time by simply adapting well-worn abstract themes to reality. And in this canonistic jurisprudence showed itself fully alive to its vocation and mission as a social science.

On the other hand, the theologians showed themselves, as their numerous statements amply prove, wholly impervious to the exigencies of the time. There is no doubt that the papal convocation edict was inspired by one of the greatest theologians of the time – and one who was unsuccessfully to confront Luther only six years hence: Thomas de Vio, commonly known as Cajetan. His mastery of theology was never in doubt;[2] what might legitimately be doubted was whether the theological arguments as set forth by him, were suitable and relevant at this particular juncture of time. His theology showed an inflexibility and rigidity that admitted of no adjustment or accommodation to newly emerging problems. It was a regurgitation of stale hierocratic themes and axioms which bore little relation to the changing conditions of the time. The very able and eloquent Dominican General proved himself a highly gifted pupil of Bernard of Clairvaux and of Innocent III but nevertheless had not their sense of realism.[3] His bitterness about the canonists was proportionate to the contempt in which the latter held the former. It was the unyielding dogmatic position concerning the pope which acted as an additional solvent of the one and universal Church. The theological stance not inconsider-

[1] See Tierney, especially pp 96ff.
[2] See Scarisbrick, p 166: 'probably the most considerable Catholic theologian of the century.'   [3] See also the assessment by Jedin, p 91 (Eng trans p 114).

ably contributed to the cataclysm which paradoxically enough it was designed to avoid. Neither legal formalism nor old-fashioned hierocratic arguments were adequate means to effect a cure of the endemic disease from which contemporary Christianity suffered. These ills could not be cured by stigmatising cardinals as heretics, merely because they proposed to do what the pope had failed to do. Nor were the craftiness of Julius II, his political sagacity, astuteness and alertness, his reliance on the conservatism of the curia and the theologians apt to ward off the clearly discernible break-up of Christendom. What would seem to me a very necessary research task is the detailed analysis of the part which the professional theologians and the professional jurists played on the eve of the Reformation.

The year 1511 with its dramatic and swiftly following events would seem to assume profound significance in the involved and complex contingencies on the eve of what technically and from the medieval standpoint was a schism. We should not forget that it was also in the same summer months of 1511 that the emperor-elect Maximilian made determined attempts to become pope himself.[1] That the convocation of the Fifth Lateran Council was nothing but a manoeuvre on the part of the pope, can hardly be disputed. Its early sessions, still in his pontificate, demonstrated this, and they also demonstrated that contemporaries had looked through this manoeuvre – the pamphlet *Julius exclusus e coelis* was a persuasive pointer.

Above all, could the hierocratic theme of papal monarchy still make much impact in the early sixteenth century? Was not this the very age in which constitutionalism, that is, the restriction of monarchic prerogatives, had already made great strides? Once again, it would seem that the jurists – and they were civilians as well as canonists – were on the whole more alive to the constitutional needs of the period than their theological colleagues. And the jurists among the cardinals incurred the charge of being schismatics because *inter alia* they advocated a governmental scheme that appeared better attuned to the social and legal needs than the theologians cared to admit. The problem besetting christian society as seen by the jurists was in other words not so much a matter of faith as one of law and order.[2] Great issues seem to be telescoped within the few summer months of 1511. Was not the papal endeavour to re-establish papal monarchy, not with the help of

[1] See Pastor, III, p 564; more recently H. Wiesflecker, 'Kaiser-Papst Plan Maximilians i.J.1511' in *Mitteilungen des Instituts für österreichische Geschichtsforschung*, LXXI (Vienna 1963) pp 311–32.
[2] See Decius above, p 190 n 2.

jurists, but with the help of theologians, anachronistic in the situation of the early sixteenth century? Did not this papal intention contribute to a still greater alienation of currently critical opinion from the papacy and all it stood for? Did not papal intransigence prove itself to be a factor which unwittingly but all the more potently promoted schismatic aspirations? Insistence on outworn principles of government can hardly be called a sign of prudence, wisdom or statesmanship.[1]

Yet contemporaries who across the Alps watched the situation from the distance, could not but see a confirmation of their deep apprehension concerning the state of the Church, the papacy and officially endorsed theology. It was perhaps not so much the fact of the pope excommunicating and deposing eminent cardinals – the most intimate counsellors of the pope, always designated as *partes corporis nostri* [*papae*] – as the manner in which the punitive measures were taken against them and still more the reason for invoking the heaviest sanctions which must have been grist to the mills of the critics of the papacy. The policy of Julius II and the pitiable performance of both the Pisan and the Lateran councils could not but fail to impress the in any case critical contemporaries: Luther – soon to join the ranks of heretics and schismatics – can be cited as a witness for the general feeling of frustration and disillusionment at the efforts – unsuccessful as they were – to lift the universal Church out of the quagmire into which it had fallen.[2]

[1] There was of course consistency in Julius II's basic aims. Two years earlier, on 2 July 1509, he had issued his decree *Suscepti regiminis*, ed in *Bullarium* [*Magnum Romanum*] (Lyons 1692) I, pp 511–12, in which any appeal to a general council against a decree or law by whomsoever initiated, made the appellant at least suspected of heresy. This, incidentally, is still the law in the modern *Codex iuris canonici* (c.2332). But this decree of Julius II was an extension of Pius II's decree *Execrabilis* of 18 January 1459: it was the first time that an appeal from a decree or verdict of the pope to a general council incurred the penalties of the crime of *lèse-majesté* (ed in *Bullarium*, I, p 386).

[2] See his *Resolutiones* (ad annum 1518) in conclusio 89, *WA* (1883) I, p 627, lines 27ff. 'Ecclesia indiget reformatione, quod non est unius hominis, pontificis nec multorum cardinalium officium sicut probavit utrumque novissimum concilium, sed tocius orbis, immo solius Dei.' On this see esp C. Stange, 'Luther und das Konzil von Pisa von 1511' in *Zeitschrift für systematische Theologie*, X (Tübingen 1933) pp 681ff at pp 685–8, 709–10.

LINCOLNSHIRE 1536:
HERESY, SCHISM OR RELIGIOUS
DISCONTENT?

by MARGARET BOWKER

THE Pilgrimage of Grace has received much attention: besides the massive study of the Misses Dodds, both professor Knowles and professor Scarisbrick have devoted many detailed pages to it,[1] and its importance as a challenge to the Henrician régime is not in question.[2] What continues to perplex generations of scholars is why an outbreak of this kind should have occurred in the autumn of 1536, and whether the explanations for it should be primarily (though not necessarily exclusively) sought in the fields of administrative, economic, social or religious history. If religion is the key, is the Pilgrimage best understood as a rebellion by 'conservative' catholics who disliked the recent religious innovations, or of progressives who sought for further and more far-reaching reforms? Is it a heretical or schismatic movement or neither? The problem was clearly stated in a paper to this society by professor Dickens,[3] and it has been the subject of local studies and detailed papers ever since.[4] These studies have focused attention on the importance of regional differences in the Pilgrimage. They have shown clearly that our understanding of it will not be advanced further unless we are prepared to attend to these differences, and to the whole structure of local politics which accompanied them. This is no easy task, since it requires a knowledge of local families, of their fortunes and misfortunes, which few have achieved. But a notable exception must surely be Mr Mervyn James whose article in *Past and Present* on the

---

[1] [M. H. and R.] Dodds, [*The Pilgrimage of Grace 1536–1537 and the Exeter Conspiracy 1538,*] 2 vols (Cambridge 1915). [D.] Knowles, [*The Religious Orders in England, the Tudor Age*] (Cambridge 1959) pp 322ff. J. J. Scarisbrick, *Henry VIII* (London 1968) pp 338ff.

[2] For a short narrative and selection of documents on it, together with a map see A. Fletcher, *Tudor Rebellions* (London 1968) pp 21–47, 118–34.

[3] [A. G.] Dickens ['Secular and Religious Motivation in the Pilgrimage of Grace'] *SCH*, IV (Leiden 1968) pp 39 ff.

[4] Notably, Christopher Haigh, *The Last Days of the Lancashire Monasteries and the Pilgrimage of Grace* (Manchester 1969). R. B. Smith, *Land and Politics in the Reign of Henry VIII: the West Riding of Yorkshire 1530–46* (Oxford 1970). [C. S. L.] Davies, ['The Pilgrimage of Grace Reconsidered',] *PP*, XLI (1968) pp 54ff.

Lincolnshire Rebellion indicates just how rewarding this approach may be.[1] He has shown that the Lincolnshire gentry who participated in the rebellion were far from being the intimidated and powerless group which they have been made out to be, and that, on the contrary, they had the power to suppress the rebellion which they did not choose to use. Their complicity can be explained if we look at their fortunes and religious affiliations: both would suggest that they were denied the offices they sought, and had reached the dangerous position of having to weigh the various consequences of trying to achieve by connivance the perquisites of power denied them by policy.[2]

Yet the gentlemen, however much they connived in the rebellion and however important they were in its ultimate leadership, did not actually start it. Similarly, a concentration on the gentlemen does not in itself account for the role of the clergy in the rebellion. The occasion for the rebellion and the nature of its support is much more closely related to the clergy than has been hitherto realised, arising particularly from the activities of three quite separate sets of commissioners who were working in the shire in the autumn of 1536. It is of some import-ance to be clear what precisely these so-called commissioners were doing, and on whose authority they were acting.

It is usually stated that there were three sets of *royal* commissioners in Lincolnshire in October 1536.[3] Certainly there were three sets of people charged with doing different things, subsidy commissioners, commissioners for the suppression of the monasteries, and men charged with enforcing the Ten Articles and the subsequent Injunctions. But not all of these worthies were 'royal' commissioners. The collec-tion of the subsidy rested on a parliamentary commission[4] and some ambiguity surrounds the precise authority enjoyed by the men enforcing the Ten Articles and the Injunctions. No record exists of the precise nature of their commission. One deponent referred to them as the bishop's commissaries,[5] another referred to their valuation of benefices[6] and another to their carrying 'the king's writings' at the sight of which 'they put off their caps and bade God save the king'.[7] An unknown correspondent writing to Lord Chancellor Audley

[1] [M. E.] James, ['Obedience and Dissent in Henrician England: the Lincolnshire Rebel-lion 1536',] PP, XLVIII (1970) pp 3ff.   [2] Ibid p 32.
[3] Dodds, 1 p 91 follows F. A. Gasquet, Henry VIII and the English Monasteries (London 1893) p 45. I am exceedingly grateful to professor Elton for his help in untangling these commissions, and with the whole paper.   [4] 26 Henry VIII, c. 19.
[5] L[etters and] P[apers, Foreign and Domestic of the Reign of Henry VIII,] ed James Gairdner, XI (London 1888) no 853.   [6] PRO E.36/118 p 7.
[7] LP XI, no 970.

refers to their visiting 'by virtue of the king's writ',[1] and William Morland, the monk of Louth Park who was prominent among the leaders of the rebellion, testified that John Frankish who was visiting Louth had, among his books, a royal commission.[2] The Injunctions themselves envisaged enforcement on a deanery basis[3] and it is clear that this was what was happening in Lincolnshire in September and October 1536.[4] But the earliest circular letter to bishops which has survived and which ordered them to go from place to place reading and declaring the Articles and Injunctions, and which required them to see that religious superiors and secular priests did the same, is dated 19 November 1536.[5] Longland appears to have acted well before November in the diocese of Lincoln. There survives in his register a commission to John Rayne ordering him to enforce the orders abrogating holidays which appear in both the Articles and Injunctions. It is dated 3 September 1536.[6] By 20 September 1536 Rayne was at work visiting the deanery of Bolingbroke, not merely enforcing the abrogation of holidays but the articles and Injunctions as well,[7] and by October, other deaneries in the archdeaconries of Lincoln and Stow were expecting him or one of his colleagues.

There would seem therefore, to be a suggestion, which will recur in our story, that at the sparking point of the trouble was an *episcopal* commission empowered by an ecclesiastic, John Longland, a man usually thought of as a conservative in religious affairs.[8] It may have been Longland's speed in enforcing religious change which was the occasion for the rising, and which prompted the belief which was held as far afield as Yorkshire, that it was the bishop of Lincoln who was the 'beginning of the trouble'.[9] Certainly Longland was included in the list of 'heretic bishops' named by Thomas Bradley in his testimony, along with the archbishop of Canterbury, Thomas Cranmer, and the bishop of St David's, William Barlow.[10] In any event, whatever his convictions, Longland appears to have acted in advance of some, if not all, of his fellow bishops, and let loose in the shire a dangerous amount of episcopal and governmental activity, which was cumulative

---

[1] *Ibid* no 585. [2] LP XII (1) no 380.
[3] [H.] Gee and [W. J.] Hardy, [*Documents Illustrative of English Church History*] (London 1896) p 269. [4] LP XI no 975. [5] LP XI no 1110.
[6] L[incoln] R[ecord] O[ffice], Register 26 fols 276–76v. Gee and Hardy, p 271; for a discussion of the attitude of the articles to saints days, see below, pp 208ff. The letter for the abrogation of holidays appears to have been issued at Chertsey, 11 August 1536. Chichester Record Office, Register Sampson, Ep/1/1/6 fo 3. I am grateful to Mr Stephen Lander for this reference. [7] Dodds, I, p 91. [8] James, p 19.
LP XI no 705. [10] *Ibid* no 828 (v).

in its effect. Throughout the last week of September 1536, while Rayne was visiting the deanery of Bolingbroke, John Pryn in his capacity as official of the archdeacon of Lincoln and his registrar Peter Effard had been visiting the archdeaconry of Lincoln and proving wills in it. Pryn and Effard were engaged in routine activities, but it so happened that they reached Caistor on 23 September, Louth on 26 September, and Alford the following day.[1] They were, therefore, in advance of the bishop's commissaries, and Effard at least appears to have been responsible for spreading rumours about the commissaries. William Morland said that it was Effard who had reported that the chalices were to be taken from parish churches and that there should be only one parish church within a radius of six or seven miles.[2] Effard was a respected citizen of Lincoln with much diocesan experience behind him. He had also been mayor of Lincoln in 1531 and his words may well have carried weight.[3] At any rate, a clerk in his office appears to have helped in writing the rebels' petition[4], and his presence in Caistor and Louth in the week before the arrival of the episcopal commissaries served to increase rumour rather than allay it. By the time the bishop's officers arrived gossip was rife, but their arrival was inopportune for another reason as well: by Monday 2 October when the rising began the commissioners for the subsidy and those charged with the suppression of religious houses were in very close geographical proximity. Those responsible for the suppression had reached Legbourne priory, one of the bishop's commissaries had reached Louth which was only a few miles away, while on 3 October, the subsidy commissioners and the bishop's commissaries were both due at Caistor. The coincidence in time and place of these commissions, following an archidiaconal visitation, provoked fears of various kinds, particularly fear for property; they also served to bring together the leaders of local communities, especially the clergy, with the result that fears could be exchanged and rumour spread; a hostility to one commission might be thought to be a hostility to all.[5]

It was in the interaction of opposition to three quite different stimuli that the rebellion took both its origin and its colour. It began and remained an amalgam of different interests – a difference not lost on the government; the king shrewdly told the commons that 'we wonder at your madness in trying to make us break the laws agreed

---

[1] LRO LCC fols 167–72v; Vij. 1 fols 96, 154–5v.   [2] LP XII no 380.
[3] J. W. F. Hill, *Tudor and Stuart Lincoln* (Cambridge 1956) p 25.
[4] PRO E.36/118 p 9: one Surdon of Lincoln 'clarke to Peter Afford Registrer of the Arsedeconrye of Lincolne' (*sic*) was accused.   [5] Dodds, I, pp 90–1.

to by the nobles, knights and gentlemen of this realm, *whom the same chiefly toucheth*'.[1] Yet though these differences figure so strongly in the rebellion, it is possible to detect certain pressure groups whose grievances prompted specific demands, notably the gentlemen, the clergy and the religious. The interest in the subsidy and the statute of uses was clearly gentle in origin, and the commons were said hardly to have understood these issues.[2] It is true that they were of importance in providing the occasion for gentlemen with a grievance of earlier origin to participate and connive in the rebellion as Mr James has shown. But there were other issues involved as well, like that of the examination of the clergy, of first fruits and tenths and of the threat to the plate of parish churches. These were not so obviously prompted by gentle interest. To the king, at least, though the part played by the local gentry was important, the part played by the clergy and religious was equally so. This is shown clearly in his treatment of offenders: no priest or religious was included in the list of sixty-three men who, though condemned to death for their part in the rising, were not executed.[3] Priests and religious appear to have enjoyed little mercy. Even Robert[4] Yule, rector of Sotby, who was said to have been old and blind and had held his benefice since 1508 was executed. It was never alleged, and can hardly be supposed that a man without sight or youth played a very active part in the rebellion, but he had retailed rumour and was tactless enough to say that the king's council were 'false harlottes in devising of false lawes' and had been led astray by Thomas Cromwell.[5] In part his seemingly savage treatment and that of many others like him may reflect the hostility of the king to clergy of doubtful loyalty; friends advised William Morland to flee after the rebellion 'thinking that priests should be worst handled of all others'.[6]

The severity which marks the treatment of the religious and seculars who took part in the rebellion may indicate an appreciation on the part of the king, or his advisers, of the critical part played by parish priests and monks in the rising. Is it possible to discover what that part was, and why they, like the gentlemen, had reached a position in which rebellion alone provided a possible remedy for grievance? Is it

---

[1] LP XI no 780 (italics mine). [2] LP XII (1) no 70.
[3] LP XII (1) no 581. [4] His name is sometimes given as Thomas.
[5] PRO E.36/118 p 5; LP XI no 973; XII (1) nos 70, 581; LRO Register 23, fol 130v.
[6] LP XII (1) no 380. The king in his own hand appears to have noted in connection with the part taken by a friar in Hallam's rebellion that 'this knave is to be taken and, well examined, to suffer'. *Ibid* no 370.

true of the clergy, as it was of the gentry, that economic and social advantage mingled with religious grievance, or were they genuinely interested in advancing or hindering religious reform? Were they concerned with such basic matters as heresy and schism, or can a religious protest be found in their actions? It is these questions which I would like to consider here. They do not admit of an easy answer, because the clergy and religious, with a few exceptions, did not give very full testimony under examination. But if their depositions and those of their companions are compared with what we know of them from diocesan sources, then their role becomes clearer and more explicable.

Several rebels referred to the large number of priests who participated in the Lincolnshire rising; one deponent thought that there were 'seven or eight hundred' priests at Louth with the vicar of Louth prominent among them.[1] George Huddiswell thought that there were a great number of priests at Caistor and estimated that it could have been eight score.[2] John Overy of Louth seemed to think that 'the priests were the occasion of this business'[3] and it is clear from other depositions that they did provide many of the leaders: Robert Brom-wight of Nether Toynton[4] was said 'to procur and sett forward the Commons beyng amongst them hymselffe with wepon and in harnes'.[5] The vicars of Hainton and Halington were also thought to have been 'great procurers of the Commons to the Assemble (sic)'.[6] The vicars of Alford, Louth and Gaiton were prominent in urging the rebels forward[7] and the rector of Biscethorpe, John Lyon, was 'very busy to procure the people forward' as was the rector of Snelland.[8] The 'busiest' of them all was William Morland alias Borroby, formerly a monk of Louth Park.[9] Often it was the priest who 'caused the common bell to be rung'[10] and who thereby brought his parishioners running from their houses: William Wilson of Alford said that 'the first stirring of the town was by the ringing of the common bell, which he thinks was done by the vicar who had been at Louth on 2 (October) and there promised to ring it'.[11] The vicar of Louth confirmed that all the priests, who had come to Louth on 2 October to meet the bishop's commissary, had promised to ring the bells and in so doing raise the county.[12] But their part did not end there. Priests gave money and religious provided

[1] LP XI no 854. [2] Ibid no 853. [3] Ibid no 972. [4] LRO Register 25 fol 23.
[5] PRO E.36/118 p 4 (LP XI no 975). [6] Ibid p 5. [7] LP XI nos 854, 972.
[8] PRO E.36/118 p 6 (LP XI no 975). [9] LP XI nos 568, 975, XII (1) no 380.
[10] PRO E.36/118 p 2. [11] LP XI no 967.
[12] LP XII (1) no 70.

food for the pilgrims,[1] and abbots and monks, as well as parish priests, were to be seen unusually attired in harness.[2]

It is hardly surprising that the clergy and religious played such a prominent part in leading and sustaining the rebellion. They were the natural leaders of the local community particularly in villages where there was not a prominent gentleman in residence. What is interesting, however, about their participation in the events of 1536 was that it was not unbeneficed clergy who appeared to be active but the beneficed and the religious. This fact can be perhaps best explained by the changes that had occurred in the archdeaconry of Lincoln between 1500 and 1536. At any time before 1536 it would have been highly irregular for a religious to involve himself in local affairs; the suppression of the lesser houses provided the occasion for their doing so for a number of reasons: the ex-religious either found himself a member of the village with little else to do, or he had chosen to pursue his religious vocation in another house which had not as yet been suppressed. In the event of his continuing as a religious it was likely that his separation from the world would have undergone a shock and he would have become rudely aware of the necessity of safeguarding the possibility of a continuing religious life by political means. As Sir William Fyrffax put it in a letter to Cromwell: 'The houses of religion not suppressed make friends and "wag" the poor to stick in this opinion, and the monks who were suppressed inhabit the villages round their houses and daily "wag" the people to put them in again'.[3] This aptly describes the position in Lincolnshire: the monks of Louth Park, which had been suppressed, appear to have stayed in the neighbourhood. William Morland was at Keddington a mere three miles from his old house and at least three of his former brethren were near at hand to assist him in the rebellion.[4] The monks of Kirkstead, which had not been suppressed, were said to have helped the rebels;[5] three, whose part was prominent enough for them to be executed, had been monks of Vaudey.[6] The most distinguished of the monastic participants was Matthew Mackerell, the abbot of Barlings who was variously accused of supplying the rebels with food and shelter, aiding and encouraging them and of allowing his monks to ride in harness with them.[7] But he was a suffragan bishop of York and was commissioned to act in the

[1] LP XI nos 805, 828, 853, 967, 968, 972, 975; XII (1) no 70.
[2] PRO E.36/118 pp 1, 2, 10.
[3] LP XII (1) no 192.   [4] LP XI no 974; XII (1) no 380.
[5] LP XI nos 828, 975.   [6] LP XI no 828; XII (1) no 581.
[7] LP XI nos 805, 827, 828, 967; XII (1) no 70.

Lincoln diocese in 1535.[1] Suffragans did not play a prominent part in diocesan affairs,[2] but it was usual for them at Michaelmas to hold ordinations.[3] On 24 September 1536 the bishop conducted ordinations in person and it looks as though Mackerell was at Barlings devising ways and means of disposing of the wealth of the house before the king could do so.[4] In any event he was at his house, possibly unexpectedly at this particular time in the year, when the rebellion broke out. Similarly the parochial clergy appear to have been resident in 1536 on a scale hitherto unprecedented.

In 1500 when the vicar general visited the archdeaconry of Lincoln just over one quarter of all the incumbents of parishes were not residing in them.[5] A similar proportion were non resident some years later when the bishop visited deaneries in the archdeaconry.[6] But when Pryn and Effard visited deaneries in the archdeaconry on behalf of the archdeacon between 1533 and 1536, the pattern had changed. Only just over one seventh of all incumbents were non resident;[7] a few like Geoffrey Smythwhyte rector of Greetham were pluralists and resided in another benefice[8] and there were some who were absent because they were acting as chaplains to great men or because they were away at university.[9] But it would seem that for many the legislation of 1529 had had its effect. It forbade the holding of cures in plurality by any whose income from a single cure exceeded £8, but royal servants, chaplains and scholars were exempted.[10] As a result, those with an adequate stipend could no longer hope to augment it further and had to confine their energies to one parish at a time. This in its turn made them more vulnerable: to lose their one benefice was to lose all, and it may be exactly this vulnerability which explains their fears in 1536.

This fear was most vividly expressed in the words attributed to the rector of Conisholm: Morland reported that he had said on the Saturday before the insurrection 'They will deprive us of our benefices

---

[1] *Chapter Acts of the Cathedral Church of St Mary of Lincoln 1520–36*, ed R. E. G. Cole, LRS, XII (1915) p xv.

[2] [M.] Bowker, [*The*] *Secular Clergy* [*in the Diocese of Lincoln 1495–1520*] (Cambridge 1968) pp 23ff. Compare James, p 20. Mr James suggests Mackerell was 'a more familiar representative of authority than the absentee bishop'. The phrase is more appropriately applied to the bishop's chancellor and vicar general, John Rayne. (James, p 14 where his name is incorrectly given as Robert.)

[3] LRO Register 26 fols 26–53 suggest that Michaelmas ordinations were usual but not invariable.　　　　[4] LRO Register 26 fol 53; LP XII (1) no 702.

[5] LRO Vj.5 *passim*.　　　　[6] Bowker, *Secular Clergy*, p 90.

[7] LRO Vij.1 *passim*.　　　　[8] *Ibid* fol 87v.

[9] See for example, LRO Vij.1 fols 88v, 89, 146v, 147v.　　　[10] 21 Henry VIII c. 13.

because they would have the first fruits, but rather than I will pay the first fruits again I had liever lose benefice and all!'[1] A similar fear of deprivation lies behind the words of the priests of Louth who said 'that they woldnott be so orderyd ne yet examyned of ther Abillyte in lernynge or otherwyse in keping of cure of Sowle'.[2] Much the same fear seems to have prompted the widespread belief that parish churches which were close to one another were to be pulled down thereby giving less chance of employment.[3] It is all too easy to attribute these fears to the lack of education and financial resources of Lincolnshire priests at this time. But it would not appear that they were either ill-educated or underpaid. The evidence suggests that Longland and his deputies went to considerable trouble to test the learning of the clergy, and records of ordination examinations survive: a tiny note in the margin of Longland's ordination lists indicates both who was examined and by whom. These notes commence in 1525[4] when only a few ordinands were marked out as having been examined; by 1533 nearly all were so noted and a picture of comprehensive examination emerges for the years 1535 to 1543/4.[5] Obviously few of those holding benefices in 1536 had been ordained as late as 1533, and the canonical requirements for an ordinand which were to be tested were not as exacting as those suggested by the contemporary humanist.[6] Yet it would seem that a bishop who was evidently careful at the level of ordination was likely to be equally careful before institution; the only complaint made by parishioners at visitation which reflects on the education of the clergy was made against the rector of Manby who was said in 1537 not to have taught either the children of the parish, or their parents, the Our Father, the *Ave* or the Creed; the rector may well have been conservative in his sympathies, and his failure may not have been one of ignorance.[7] The income of the dissident parish priests was also adequate in comparison with other incumbents, and averaged £8 net; it is also noteworthy that over half of those actually accused by anyone for their part in the Lincolnshire rising were rectors and were thereby protected by their glebe from a rise in the price of food.[8] Fear of deprivation does not seem, therefore, to have been prompted by

---

[1] LP XII (1) no 481. [2] PRO E.36/118 p 8.
[3] LP XI nos 828 (xiii), 967, 970, 973; XII (1) nos 70, 380.
[4] LRO Register 26 fol 31. [5] *Ibid* fols 35–63.
[6] Bowker, *Secular Clergy*, pp 42ff. [7] LRO Vij. 1 fol 156.
[8] Notably the incumbents of Belleau, Belchford, Biscethorpe, Conisholm, Donington on Bain, Farforth, Gaiton, Harrington, Hatton, Maningsby, Rothwell, Scartho, Snelland, Sotby, Stewton, South Somercotes, Thoresway Welton.

greater personal inadequacy: when we make an examination of incumbents those who actually took part in the rising do not appear to have belonged to the least privileged group of beneficed priests. Under normal circumstances they could have expected to have kept their livings for as long as they wished. What, then, made the circumstances of 1536 so different, so abnormal, that they had reason to fear?

Clearly two factors had created a new situation: the act for the payment of first fruits and tenths,[1] and the threat of examination implicit in the Injunctions. The act allowed to the king the first fruits from every benefice during the first year of incumbency; it thereby put a considerable financial premium on enforcing mobility between benefices. If incumbents could be moved from one benefice to another the king would profit, just as Henry VII had moved bishops for the same purpose. The only difficulty was to see that they did in fact move even when the king was not patron of the living. An examination was the perfect device. Clearly any religious injunction which had to be explained to the parishioner by his priest could potentially involve a commissary in the examination of that priest in order to ascertain that he was able to instruct the parish. In a situation in which a parish priest knew that the king had something to gain from depriving a man of his cure, and the priest concerned could not rely on the learning, such as it was, which took him through ordination and institution, to weather the examination, any royal injunction which required a visitation for enforcement was a threat, especially in the circumstances which obtained in Lincolnshire in 1536.

Local priests tended to look to a nearby religious house for a title at ordination, and perhaps, later, for a benefice.[2] Certainly if the ordination lists for the diocese for the period 1514–20 are studied the houses of Legbourne, Bardney, Barlings, Louth Park, Kirkstead, Welhow, and Revesby were responsible for giving titles to some sixty local ordinands and to only six candidates who came from outside the diocese.[3] The removal of Welhow, Louth Park and Legbourne from the scene would have had made some impact on those who owed them a title. Still more would it have affected those who owed to them, or to houses which, like them, were in the course of being suppressed, a cure. Once again it is significant that of the thirty-two beneficed priests who are named as taking part in the rebellion a high percentage owed their livings to these houses: eleven had been appointed by

[1] 26 Henry VIII c.3.
[2] Bowker, *Secular Clergy*, p 61.   [3] LRO Register 25 *passim*.

religious houses which were suppressed or in the process of being so, or which were taking part in the rising.[1] A further nine owed their patronage to houses or religious corporations whose loyalty by this date was dubious, like the college of Tattershall which was said to have helped the rebels, or Trentham which was ultimately suppressed in March 1537.[2] A further five owed their livings to gentlemen who were themselves implicated in the rising.[3] If there were to be a deprivation of livings, many priests in Lincolnshire, as elsewhere, would have to find new patrons. The problems of doing so were always great[4] but they were rendered more difficult by the influx of the religious on to the benefice market. Theoretically if pluralism had declined, the problem of getting a benefice should also have declined and the drop in the number of ordinands which marks Longland's episcopate should have accelerated this process.[5] But at precisely the moment when the pressure should have eased the religious were looking for benefices.[6] William Morland the former monk of Louth Park was honest enough to admit that he hoped for a benefice as a result of the examination of some of the incumbents of the diocese and their subsequent deprivation; he said he was 'right glad' on hearing of the proposed examination 'thinking he might happen to succeed to the room of some of the unlettered parsons'.[7] This comment shows clearly that though gentlemen, commons, religious and seculars made common cause in the Lincolnshire rising, their interests remained subtly different. The seculars were obviously concerned about first fruits and the threat of examination, and their fears found expression in the reported grievances. But the rising would not have achieved even a semblance of unity had clerical agitation and support stopped at these issues. A wider base had to be found to link churchmen and bind them more closely to the commons.

[1] Namely Alford, Cockerington, Elkington, Gaiton, Halington, Saleby, Snelland, Scothern, Sotby, North Somercotes, Welton. LRO Register 23 fols 67, 126, 128, 130, 130v, 146v, 148v; Register 27 fols 21v, 59v, 83v; Vij 1, fol 149v.

[2] Namely, Biscethorpe, Donington on Bain, Hainton, Hatton, Louth, Miningsby, Rothwell, Tetney, Nether Toynton. LRO Register 23 fols 36, 91, 103, 143v; Register 25 fols 16, 23; Register 27 fols 51, 53, 59.

[3] Namely Belchford, Belleau, Conisholm, Farforth and Harrington. LRO Register 27 fols 25, 46v, 55v, 57v, 60v. [4] Bowker, *Secular Clergy*, pp 70ff.

[5] LRO Register 26 *passim*; between 1530 and 1536 an average of sixty-five men were ordained priest in a year compared with an average of one hundred and twenty-six between 1514 and 1520.

[6] For a discussion of the fate of the religious of the diocese see G. A. J. Hodgett, *The State of the Ex-Religious and Former Chantry Priests in the Diocese of Lincoln 1547–74*, LRS, LIII (1958) pp xiff. [7] LP XII (1) no 380.

The threat to church plate was precisely that link. It was reported by Philip Trotter 'that the beginnynge of thys mater was by Reason of a noyse that the Ornamentes of ther churchys shuld be taken ffrom them by the kinges commandemente'.[1] Other participants in the rising were of a similar opinion.[2] Simon Malteby rector of Farforth after meeting the bishop's commissary at Bolingbroke told his neighbours 'that churche goodis shuld be taken from them and he said ther was dyvers challyces made of tyne which sholdbe delyvered to them in exchange for ther sylver chalices and the sayd silver chalices to be had to the kinges visitors'.[3] One of the earliest reports which the king received of the rising and which came from the subsidy commissioners contained the rumour that there was a fear that 'all jewels and goods of the churches to be taken away'.[4] This rumour served to create common ground between the secular clergy and the religious: if the king was taking the spoils of the monastic houses, then it was easy to suppose that he might proceed to parish churches. Just such an assumption lay in the comment attributed to one John Benson, 'Surely,' he said, 'these abbeys shall be put down and the jewels of the church shall be taken away.'[5] But the supposed threat to church goods also linked the grievances of the parish priests with the commons at large. It was improbable that the commons would have been gravely concerned about an attempt to exact first fruits from the clergy, but a threat to the parish churches was another matter. Clearly the commons of Louth who had spent so much on their church were very concerned to protect its treasures, and the guard placed upon the church on Sunday 1 October indicates their concern. But it was not only the men of Louth who valued their church.[6] Had that been the case the rebellion might have started and ended in Louth alone. If bequests are studied, it becomes clear that the great majority of testators left money to the parish church as well as leaving money for tithes and mortuary. Three quarters of the wills dated 1530 which have survived for Lincolnshire contain a bequest to the parish church, and a quarter contain bequests to other churches in addition to the parish church, quite apart from bequests to the cathedral church of Lincoln.[7] The men of Louth, therefore, were by no means alone in their concern for the treasures of their church.

Quite why the commons supposed plate and church treasure were in

[1] LP XI no 828 (2); PRO S.P/1/109, fol 2.
[2] LP XI nos 828(1), 853, 854, 967, 968, 970, 972, 973; LP XII (1) no 170.
[3] LP XI no 975 summarises the statement contained in PRO E.36/118 p 7.
[4] LP XI no 534.   [5] LP XII (1) no 70.   [6] Davies, p 70.
[7] Lincoln Wills 1505–1530, ed C. W. Foster, LRS, x (1918) pp 170–210.

danger it is hard to know. It was perhaps inferred from the valuation of church property, both secular and religious, and its dramatic consequences in the subsequent suppression of certain houses.[1] Certainly any kind of assessment seems to have been viewed with the utmost suspicion. Morland found among John Frankish's books 'a book of reckonings' which he attempted to keep from the flames to which the remaining volumes of the unfortunate commissary had been assigned. But the commons called him 'a false perjured harlot' for his pains, since he was told that by 'saving of that book' he had saved 'the thing which should do unto them most tene'.[2] In fact the book was unlikely to have been more than a valuation of benefices, necessary for the levy of first fruits, but in the excitement of the moment it was easy for confusions to arise. Clearly Morland, who had been given the books to read, had not seen fit to destroy it for the simple reason that he was not very concerned about first fruits; but all too easily an illiterate mob could conclude that the book contained the information necessary for the confiscation of the treasure bequeathed to the parish by local families for generations.

So far then we can detect amongst the parochial clergy in Lincolnshire a discontent which arose mainly as a result of legislation and of a visitation which might be regarded as a threat to their livelihood. Among the religious much the same fears were at work, but the ex-religious had less to lose from rebellion. For both groups the protest was ultimately directed against the legislation which had been facilitated by the break with Rome; this legislation owed its ultimate origin to a change in the source of ecclesiastical authority, but it was mainly economic in its initial effects. How far, if at all, did the Lincolnshire insurgents, and particularly the secular priests and religious perceive that the root of their discontent lay in the fact of schism? Were there those who saw that, stretching beyond their immediate fears for their livelihood, lay greater questions which hung over religious faith itself?

In the circumstances of 1536 I would suggest that it was still very difficult to be sure whether religious faith was in question; it took a degree of sophistication to see that implicit in the orders abrogating holidays was a new attitude to the saints. Saints might be prayed to and invoked:

[1] For the exact order of events see Sybil Jack 'The Last Days of the Smaller Monasteries in England', *JEH*, XXI, 2 (1970) pp 97ff.
[2] LP XII (1) no 380, see also James p 15 note 54. Tene = teen, meaning 'hurt' (OED).

as our devotion doth serve us; so that it be done without any vain superstition, as to think that any saint is more merciful or will hear us sooner than Christ... And likewise we must keep holy-days unto God, in memory of him and his saints, upon such days as the church hath ordained their memories to be celebrate, except they be mitigated and moderated by the assent and commandments of us the supreme head to the ordinaries, and then the subjects ought to obey it.[1]

The novelty of this article lay primarily in two things: first, in the assertion that saints were not more merciful than Christ, which ran contrary to popular piety, and second, in that the power to mitigate and moderate holiday was vested in the supreme head. But it was one thing to detect this difference and isolate it, it was another to take issue with the effect of the article which proved in fact to be the curtailment of holidays. The men of Louth, Horncastle and Caistor were said to have wanted 'to keep holidays as before' but none is reported to have touched on the root of the grievance in terms of authority.[2]

Mr James has suggested that the clergy detected in the articles a 'changed role which the new religious trends required of the priesthood' and the 'devaluation of important aspects of traditional religion apparent in the Articles and visitation Injunctions'.[3] He particularly suggested that the clergy would have noticed with distaste the shift from what he regards as the ritualistic functions of the priest, celebrating the mass, visiting the sick and hearing confessions, to the more evangelistic role implicit in the injunctions to preach and teach.[4] If this is in fact so, the clergy and religious kept quite unusually silent about it. Not one of them, for example, complained about having to preach, and the only suggestion that has come down to us that the rebel priest disliked the emphasis on the evangelical devices of preaching and of teaching by means of books in the vernacular comes from Thomas Kendall the vicar of Louth. He wanted to 'put down schismatic English books, which deceived the unlearned'.[5] He was probably referring to the English New Testament and to Frith's book both of which Frankish had in his possession and which the Louth mob burned.[6] But it is clear that the offending books were burned before they had been read; Morland testified that he had asked the commons not to burn them before they knew what was in them, and to that end

[1] Thomas Fuller, *The Church History of Britain* (London 1837) II, bk v, cent XVI, pp 86–7.
[2] LP XI no 553.   [3] James, pp 14–5.   [4] James, p 15.
[5] LP XI no 970.   [6] LP XI no 828 (1).

six 'who were learned' were appointed 'to look what was in the books'. But before the six had had time to do their homework 'those who were on the cross looking on the other books upon the hideous clamour of those beneath flung all the books down, and every man below got a piece of them and hurled them into the fire'.[1] The story is not denied by any other deponent and has the graphic quality of truth about it. With the sole exception of Thomas Kendall, it would not appear that either the commons or the priests were concerned with the books because they represented a shift in faith, or a change in the sacerdotal role. Rather it would appear that these actions were those of a vindictive and largely uninformed mob who expressed their anger against the bishop's commissary by burning his luggage.

Thomas Kendall knew better; but this was not unexpected. He was a theologian from the university of Oxford and, perhaps significantly, no other rebel priest had his theological qualification. It is hardly surprising, therefore, that Kendall emerges as the leader of a very small band of priests who were concerned with the preservation of the essentials of the old faith. Professor Dickens has suggested that 'The Lincolnshire men showed no interest in Papalism'. He suggested that 'throughout the voluminous Lincolnshire records the Royal Supremacy is mentioned only once, and then reported as actually accepted by the insurgents'.[2] Mr Davies accepts professor Dickens' arithmetic and like him contrasts the shire sharply in this respect with Yorkshire where the whole question of the 'cura animarum' was debated.[3] Professor Dickens is right in referring to the acceptance of the supremacy by George Huddyswyll, who reported that the men of Caistor 'will take the king to be supreme head of the Church' but I venture to think he is wrong in suggesting that this was the *only* view of the supremacy which was expressed. Again Thomas Kendall clearly knew that the supremacy was the source of the trouble: he proceeded circumspectly, however, and asserted under examination that men had 'long grudged that the king should be Head of Church'.[4] On examination he could not state precisely the names of those who 'grudged at the King's supremacy', and he confined his remarks to the highly ambiguous assertion that he had counselled the rebels 'not to meddle with the king, but only for the repression of heresy and maintenance of the Faith'.[5] But what was heresy? Another Lincolnshire priest, who

---

[1] LP XII (1) no 380.   [2] Dickens, p 51.   [3] Davies, p 63.
[4] LP XII (1) no 970; James has also remarked upon the doctrinal commitments of Kendale (James, p 16).   [5] LP XII (1) no 70.

was not a graduate, had his ideas on this matter. When the rebels seemed to have won ascendancy in the shire he showed his colours for 'he dyd byde the bedis the nexte Sonday after (the) insurrection and prayed for the poope of Roome with the... Cardinalles'.[1] Clearly he may have been invoking the wrath of the Almighty upon the papacy, but if that had been the case it was sufficiently in accord with the royal will not to have been a matter of report. There appears to be no evidence in Lincolnshire that books about the supremacy were circulating[2] but this did not preclude discussion, not least because the parson was required to preach about it. One such sermon seems to have provoked the wrath of the parish and to lend some support to Kendal's contention that Lincolnshire men begrudged the king his title.

Nicholas Leach was rector of Belchford and a bachelor of arts; he was also the brother of William Leach who took a prominent part in leading the rebellion.[3] Nicholas said that he had not conferred with anyone before or after the rebellion about 'the authority of the bishop of Rome, but preached against it and persuaded the people that they might work upon the days abrogated by the king; *for which cause he feared he might be slain by the commons*'.[4] He was not slain by the commons but in fact led them, and though his testimony was clearly an attempt to save his own neck, it would seem that his defence was inherently contradictory. If his own view of the supremacy and of saints days and that of the commons were at odds, we would expect him to have enjoyed at best a secondary role in the rebellion and certainly not to have emerged as a leader. I would suggest, therefore, that to the protest of many priests and religious which took the form of a thinly veiled concern for livelihood, we must add that of a few who saw that the supremacy lay at the heart of the trouble. There were also a few who saw that the threat to the old faith did not end with the supremacy.

Mr Davies has suggested that 'the failure of the Ten Articles to mention four of the seven sacraments could seem significant as a pointer to drastic change in the future'.[5] Once again if this is so the Lincolnshire clergy were silent about it. Only Kendal latched on to the most significant part of the Ten Articles, which concerned Justification and Purgatory, and indicated the headway which Lutheran ideas had made. He testified that men 'grudged at the new erroneous

[1] LP XI 975; PRO E.36/118 p 7.
[2] Compare LP XII (1) no 370.   [3] LRO Register 27 fol 57v.
[4] LP XII (1) no 70 (XI) (italics mine); Longland was concerned about preaching against the papacy, see LP IX no 349.   [5] Davies, p 69.

opinions touching Our Lady and Purgatory'.[1] More widespread were fears about the mass. In fact the article about the mass is ambiguous enough to be interpreted in either a Lutheran sense or a traditionally catholic one; the Real Presence is upheld and only a person already familiar with the language of Lutheran debate would recognise the possibility of a Lutheran interpretation.[2] But these were not the subtleties which concerned the Lincolnshire clergy. They were shocked at the way in which the commissioners treated the sacrament at the suppression of Hagneby, and the parson of Nether Toynton wanted the sacrament carried before the pilgrims. The protest, such as it was, was not directed against novelty but irreverence.[3]

It would be a mistake to cast the priests of the shire in the role of martyrs for the old faith; the crown of martyrdom sits uneasily on the head of Nicholas Leach. A mere year before he led the pilgrims he had been reported for his negligence in looking after his parish.[4] Simon Malteby who interceded for the bishop of Rome had been with the mob who had urged the commons to kill the bishop's chancellor John Rayne; he was known for his incontinence and was probably only spared execution because his patrons were the Thimilbys whom the king singled out for mercy.[5] Thomas Beche the rector of Welton who gave money and encouragement to the rebels[6] was suspected for incontinence,[7] and the part of Thomas Ratford rector of Snelland and a former canon of Welbeck was none too creditable;[8] when the gentlemen and commons met in the chapter house at Lincoln to consider the king's reply to their grievances and part of the letter was omitted since it was deemed to be inflammatory, Ratford saw an opportunity to make trouble and prove himself as good as the next man. He said 'the letter was wronge Redd and wold have had the letter hym self saing he colde Rede yt as well as the best of them'.[9] Only Kendal emerges with dignity from the affair. The Lincolnshire clergy were not of the stuff of Robert Aske.

What then are we to make of the Lincolnshire rising which served as the signal for the Pilgrimage of Grace? Much research obviously remains to be done; the part played by the commons and the religious

---

[1] LP XII (1) no 70.
[2] For a discussion of these articles see A. G. Dickens, *The English Reformation* (London 1964) p 175; compare P. Hughes, *The Reformation in England* (London 1956) I, pp 350ff.
[3] LP XII (I) no 70; PRO E.36/118 p 10.   [4] LRO Vij. 1 fol 92.
[5] LP XI nos 672; 975; LRO Vij. 1 fols 149v, 154.   [6] LP XI no 968.
[7] LRO Vij. 1, fol 149.   [8] LRO Register 23 fol 67.
[9] PRO E.36/118 p 6.

orders and the precise importance of regional differences would still repay detailed study. But Mr James has shown that the Lincolnshire gentlemen connived at, or participated in, the rebellion because their expectations of advancement had been blocked – either because their religious views cut them off from the source of patronage, or because those closer to the court were deemed more suitable recipients of the most coveted prizes. This, it may be argued, was neither a protest against schism or heresy but a protest against a loss of power in which religion was only one factor among many. If we accept Mr James's analysis of this group, and move to the other, and perhaps more important, group which provided the leaders of local society, the clergy, whom he has only touched upon cursorily, we find some of the same factors at work. There was fear among the clergy. This fear was aggravated by the vulnerability brought them by the decrease in pluralism, the presence of ex-religious waiting vulture-like for their benefices, and it was increased further by the Act for First Fruits and Tenths, and the visitations conducted before, and then necessitated by, the Ten Articles and Injunctions. They had reason to believe that their bishop was thorough: his treatment of ordination candidates suggested that. He also appeared to be enforcing the Articles and Injunctions with some speed. They had no reason to suppose that he would treat them gently, and their fears were increased by the rumours spread by Peter Effard the archdeacon's registrar. But the problem for the clergy was to get enough support, and this support was forthcoming partly at least because the presence of the subsidy commissioners made the gentlemen susceptible. The fear that the valuations of livings would result in plunder of church plate seemed all too likely, judging by the fate of the monasteries, and this served to agitate the commons.[1] The clergy rose to the occasion. Some of their number went further and saw that the source of the trouble was in the change in the precise location of authority within the Church. For the rest the protest was against religious legislation which had far reaching economic consequences. It was one in a long series of fights for parsons' freehold, but, in this instance, against a prince who saw the Church as a milch cow.

[1] Davies, p 58 suggests other causes for their disgust.

THE FAMILY OF LOVE AND THE
DIOCESE OF ELY

by FELICITY HEAL

FEW of the major heretical movements of continental Europe
have found permanent homes in England. One of the periods
when it seemed most likely that they might do so was the years
between the Henrician reformation and the growth of native separatism towards the end of the sixteenth century. The persecution of
continental anabaptists, sectaries and spiritualists in their native lands
forced many of them into exile in England; an exile which they often
used to continue their evangelistic work, as well as to maintain their
own versions of the radical reformation.[1] They found a ready reception
for their beliefs among certain sections of the population of south-east
England; notably, but not exclusively, the artisans. Devout but ill-
disciplined study of the Bible, the lack of protestant preachers, and the
social dislocation of Tudor England, all facilitated the missionary work
of the radicals. A majority of the preachers were Netherlandish by
origin, and continued to look to the Low Countries as the source of
their inspiration; none more so than one of the most interesting of the
spiritualist sects, the Family of Love.

The Family sprang exclusively from the revelations of Henry
Niclaes, a mercer for many years resident in Emden, who believed
himself to be divinely inspired and to have been granted the same
charismatic powers of leadership as the greatest of the Old Testament
prophets.[2] His message was set forth in a large number of pamphlets
which were both mystical and often profoundly mystifying to the
non-believer.[3] These were disseminated by the elders of the church,

---

[1] [G. H.] Williams, [*The Radical Reformation*] (London 1962) pp 401–3; pp 778–90.
Mennonite Encyclopaedia, II, pp 215–20.

[2] The basic account of Niclaes and his sect is still [F.] Nippold, ['Heinrich Niclaes und
das Haus der Liebe',] *Zeitschrift für die historische Theologie*, XXXII (Gotha 1862). I
would like to thank Mr Tom Scott for his help in translating this article. Other accounts
are in R. M. Jones, *Studies in Mystical Religion* (London 1909); *DNB*, under Nicholas
and Vitels; [J.] Ebel, ['The Family of Love: Sources of its History',] *Huntington Library
Quarterly*, XXX (California 1967).

[3] Nippold located twenty-six works that can be attributed positively to Niclaes. Of the
works translated into English in the sixteenth century the *Evangelium Regni* (Amsterdam? 1574?) was most widely known and distributed.

first in handwritten form, and later in print. Niclaes consciously
eschewed preaching and public proclamation of the word in order to
avoid persecution, and urged upon his followers obedience to the
magistrate and conformity with the religious ceremonies established
by law, since they were matters of total indifference to the godly.
His ideas were spread by the written word, and by the personal contacts which his elders achieved when they undertook missionary
journeys on his behalf. Niclaes's central experience was that of illumination by the spirit of love, that is of the godhead personified as love
in-dwelling in man. Those who, like H.N., as he was usually known,
perceived this in-dwelling love, were illuminate with him, and were,
to use the phrase his enemies most frequently assailed, 'godded with
God'. Since the movement was founded upon a spiritualist conception
of inner light it inevitably had antinomian and indifferentist tendencies, though its followers rarely seem to have deserved the epithet
'libertine' which was often applied to them, and Niclaes stressed
that his revelations fulfilled the law rather than overthrowing it.
On such controverted doctrines as the nature of Christ, the status of
the persons of the Trinity, adult baptism and the interpretation of
scripture, Niclaes claimed to have new and exclusive revelation: in
practice, however, his ideas have close affinities with those of some
other Low Countries sects, particularly the followers of David Joris,
and the Melchiorite strain of anabaptism.[1]

The Family of Love did not survive for long in the Netherlands:
even before Niclaes's death in about 1580 many of its most influential
supporters had deserted the prophet, and it soon lost its independent
place among the competing Dutch sects.[2] In England, however, it
seems to have maintained an attenuated existence for the better part
of a century, and it is often alleged that some of its members, as
well as its spiritualist ideas, were absorbed into the Quaker movement.[3]
The date at which the teaching of the Family first spread to England
is very difficult to establish: it has been claimed that Niclaes made a
first missionary journey to England under Edward VI, and that he
may have become a member of the Dutch strangers' church in London.[4] Missionising efforts by the radical reformers were certainly

---

[1] Williams, pp 778–80.   [2] Nippold, p 379.   [3] Ebel, p 340.
[4] The evidence for Niclaes's visit under Edward is that many dissensions rent the strangers'
church at this period, and that Martin Micronius, pastor of the church, had personal
knowledge of the work of H.N., and attacked it briefly in his work on ceremonies,
written several years after his return to the continent. T. Fuller, *The Church History of
Britain*, IV (London 1837) pp 409–10.

becoming common by this date: David Joris, for example, attempted to visit England as early as 1535, only to be turned back by news of persecution.[1] However, no evidence can be adduced from H.N.'s writings of a visit at this early date, and it would probably be more compatible with his style of evangelising if his influence was at first indirect. If he did visit England in person it seems more likely that his journey took place under Elizabeth, when the initial conquests had already been made. The Dutch strangers' congregation was certainly disturbed by conflicts with the radicals, but the main crisis concerned Arian interpretations of the nature of the Trinity, which were never accorded a central position in Niclaes's theology.[2]

Even in the later 1550s and 1560s there is little tangible evidence that the Family had gained a sure footing in England. The main difficulty is to establish the date at which the later leader of the movement, Christopher Vitels, became a convert, for it was Vitels who translated the writings of H.N., and thereby made it possible to build an English movement. Vitels was originally from Delft, but had been resident in England since the reign of Henry VIII, and had always favoured radical ideas.[3] During Mary's reign he went on missionary journeys in the East Anglian area, preaching and disputing with orthodox protestant leaders. Henry Crinel, a protestant from Willingham in Cambridgeshire, heard him dispute at Colchester with a militant preacher of the gospel named John Barry.[4] Vitels argued against the divinity of Christ, as well as upholding adult baptism, and used the Bible so effectively that Barry was reduced to astonished silence. At some later time Vitels visited Cambridgeshire, visiting Willingham on the edge of the Isle of Ely, and staying at Balsham in the south-east of the county with one W.H., who was later described as 'a flat Arian'.[5] In 1560 or 1561 his preaching attracted the attention of the ecclesiastical authorities, and he was required to recant his 'Arian' doctrines at Paul's Cross.[6] Although it is not unlikely that Vitels already knew something of the work of Niclaes during his

[1] Williams, p 402.

[2] Micronius to Bullinger: *Original Letters Relative to the English Reformation*, II, ed H. G. Robinson, Parker Society (Cambridge 1847) pp 574-5.

[3] [J.] Rogers, *An Answere [unto a Wicked and Infamous Libel made by Christopher Vitel...]* (London 1579).

[4] [W.] Wilkinson, *A Confutation [of Certaine Articles Delivered by (H. Niklaes) unto the Family of Love]* (London 1579).

[5] *Ibid* fol 30.

[6] [J.] Rogers, *The Displayinge [of an Horrible Secte...naming themselves the Family of Love]* (London 1578).

first missionary journeys – for example, he praised a great doctor from beyond the sea to Crinel – his preoccupations at this time do not seem to be identical with those of the master, and can perhaps be better associated with some form of spiritualist anabaptism. This impression is reinforced by the fact that his contact at Balsham, W.H., never adopted the ideas of the Family, and in the mid-1570s confessed to views very similar to those which Crinel had attributed to Vitels.

The other early evidence for the existence of the Family outside the Dutch congregation is also difficult to interpret. John Rogers, one of the anti-familist writers, printed a confession supposedly made by two members of a Surrey branch of the sect before William Moore, JP, in 1561.[1] The two men described in considerable detail a flourishing congregation, with contacts as far away as the Isle of Ely, whose beliefs and organisation are largely compatible with the spiritualist ideas of H.N. They were aware of other congregations with the same beliefs, and it was from one of these in the Isle of Ely that they found a bride for one of the brethren.[2] Two problems arise from this confession: one is that the men failed to mention H.N. and his doctrine, but spoke of being instructed exclusively from the Bible; this is a surprising omission in view of their frankness upon all other issues. The other is that members of the Family of Love, replying to Roger's attack in 1579, denied that the Surrey men were part of their sect, and even questioned whether the examination could have taken place as he claimed. Vitels himself was more guarded about the Surrey men: he did not disown them as members of the Family, but insisted that they knew very little of the writings of H.N.[3] Close affinities between the various branches of anabaptist and spiritualist doctrine seems to have been a characteristic of English radicalism under Edward and Mary, and it is perhaps plausible to suggest that it was only some time after the beginning of Elizabeth's reign that the Family of Love became identifiable among the rest, and that the doctrines of H.N. gained much favour.[4]

Nothing is known of the Family in England between the early 1560s and 1574, but during this time a number of converts must have been made, and Vitels must have emerged as the leader of the English movement and translator of the master's works. Most of the major

[1] *Ibid* appendix.
[2] Thomas Chandler married a bride from the Isle of Ely, but divorced her a year later because they proved incompatible.
[3] Rogers, *The Displayinge* (2 ed London 1579), Rogers, *An Answere*.
[4] Williams, pp 778–9.

writings were printed in English at Amsterdam in 1574 or 1575, and this was also the period when the Family in England began to issue some of its own propaganda and demands for toleration.[1] Between 1574 and 1580 the movement apparently increased in strength and gained more converts, until the government eventually initiated a full attack which drove the sect more effectively underground. The clandestine nature of the Family inevitably means that there is little evidence upon its local activities available even in the few years of relative security, and that even less derives from non-hostile sources. However, in Cambridgeshire the sect was particularly strong, and it is possible to garner some interesting information from that locality about its size, structure, membership and beliefs.

The initial missionary endeavours of Vitels in the Isle of Ely and at Balsham have already been mentioned. These two areas became the main centres of familist activity in the diocese of Ely, and one must presume that they were thoroughly evangelised by preachers of the sect in the 1560s. William Wilkinson, a Cambridgeshire puritan, who wrote one of the attacks on the Family, describes their preachers thus: 'some of them be weavers, some basketmakers, some musitians, some botlemakers, and such other lyke that by travailing from place to place do get their lyving. They whiche amongest them beare the greatest countenaunce are such as, havyng deceived some Justices of Peace...where they dwel, have gotten licences to trade for corne up and downe the countrey'.[2] Only one of these itinerants is known to us by name: one of the earliest preachers of the sect was Allen, a weaver, who may possibly have influenced the Surrey congregation, and who encountered trouble from the JPs of Cambridgeshire for possessing copies of the work of H.N.[3] The itinerant elder, who had renounced all worldly possessions, and lived by the aid of the faithful, was considered by Niclaes as the main exemplar in his church, and it was no doubt the fervent devotion of a few men such as Vitels and Allen that really won converts to H.N.'s cause.

It is, however, from the settled congregations under their own illuminate elders that most of the evidence for the Family derives. The

---

[1] *A Brief Rehearsal of the Belief of the Good-Willing in England...set forth in 1575*; *An Apology for the Service of Love* (both published London 1656).

[2] Wilkinson, *A Confutation*, fol 31.

[3] Rogers, *An Answere*; Wilkinson, *A Confutation*, fol 61v. It is difficult to be sure that these two Allens can be identified. Roger's Allen seems to have been the leader of the Surrey sect, and if it can be proved that they were not closely linked with the Family we may merely have two sectaries with the same name.

Balsham group emerged from obscurity when, in 1574, they aroused the suspicions of the parish by their private assemblies. On 13 December of that year six men from the village, accompanied by Robert Sharpe, parson of Strethall in Essex, presented a confession of their orthodoxy to Andrew Perne, dean of Ely and rector of their parish.[1] The object of their confession was to assure the authorities that their conventicles had no subversive purpose: they therefore laid great stress upon their loyalty and conformity, and insisted that the meetings were only intended to improve their own knowledge of scripture. They also felt compelled, or were persuaded, to deny doctrines which were specifically familist in origin, such as the resurrection of the soul but not the body, and they even avowed that 'we do knowe and allowe of no revelations in theis our daies...but such as god hath sett forthe and expressed in his written worde in the old and newe Testaments'. Perne accepted their submission at face value, despite the known willingness of the Family to lie for their faith, and appended his signature to the document. The men assured him that no more meetings would be held, and that they would consult him on all difficult matters of scripture, but they can have had little intention of keeping faith, and those who were still alive in 1580 were imprisoned rather than deny H.N. a second time.[2]

The leaders of the Balsham group were two of the Lawrence family, and Edmund Rule, though it is not known whether any or all of them were considered to be illuminate elders of the sect. It is tempting to identify Rule as the elder who debated with William Wilkinson under the illuminate name of Theophilus, and who was alleged by him to be one E.R., but Rule claimed to be illiterate in 1574, and the identity of the initials is probably therefore no more than coincidence.[3] He was one of only two Balsham men who made marks on the confession, the other four could all sign their names, and were sufficiently prosperous to have been properly educated. Their wills show that they were of yeoman stock, and the Lawrences, for example, were quite substantial tenant farmers, which suggests that the common sneer of their enemies that the sect were of mean condition has little foundation.[4] The six men who signed the confession were the core of the Balsham group: they came from families who were inter-related, and clearly belonged

[1] [London, Inner Temple], Petyt MS 538/47, fol 492.
[2] [Cambridge] Gon[ville] and Caius Coll[ege] MS 53/30, 2nd pt, fol 73.
[3] Wilkinson, A Confutation, fol 56v.
[4] Camb[ridge] Univ[ersity] Arch[ives], Ely Cons[istory] Court Will Reg[isters] R, fols 196–7; T, fols 289v–90.

to the same social class. A further five men are known to have sympathised with them, either from the evidence of local wills or from the more detailed investigation which was held in 1580.[1] This probably does not exhaust the list of local supporters, and the Balsham men may also have been active in spreading the teaching of H.N. in the surrounding deanery of Camps, and the neighbouring parts of Suffolk.[2] Much of the activity of the Family in the diocese of Norwich seems to have centred in the area of Bury St Edmunds, and the presence of the parson of Strethall, just across the border into Essex, among those testifying before Perne in 1574 suggests the influence of the sect there as well.[3]

At the other end of the diocese of Ely, in the northern part of the Isle, familism was probably an even more important force. The testimony of the Surrey sectaries would suggest that there had been organised congregations in this area since the Marian period, but for many years they escaped the attention of the episcopal authorities and apparently lived unmolested. Richard Cox, the first Elizabethan bishop of Ely, was publicly alerted to the danger in the Isle by the issue in 1579 of William Wilkinson's 'A Confutation of Certain Articles...delivered unto the Family of Love'. This was dedicated to the bishop and alleged that the numbers of the sect in the diocese increased daily, and that the Isle was particularly infested with the heretics.[4] To this alarm was added the exhortation of the privy council who, concerned at the spread of H.N.'s books, and the discovery of familists among the Yeomen of the Guard, urged Cox to hunt out any sectaries in his diocese.[5] As a result of these warnings a full-scale investigation began, and a group of men and women from Wisbech were examined before the bishop between 3 and 5 October 1580.[6]

The examination was intended to include ten people, but one, Thomas Pierson 'yeoman, and the welthiest of the company... conveyed himselfe away as it is thought to London'. The rest were mainly artisans and tradesmen from the town, the leading figure being

---

[1] The wills of John Diss, Leonard Durgeon and William Cornell are all witnessed by one of the Lawrences or Edmund Rule. Camb Univ Arch, Ely Cons Court Will Reg T, fol 268; V, fols 154, 329.

[2] J. Strype, *Annals of the Reformation...* (Oxford 1824–40) II, ii p 266. BM Lansdowne MS XXIX, 39; XXXIII, 20, 22. *APC* nos XI, pp 138–9.

[3] Petyt MS 538/47, fol 493.

[4] Wilkinson was given some encouragement with his book by Cox, who added a recommendation at the beginning of the volume. Wilkinson, *A Confutation*. Gon and Caius Coll MS 53/30, fol 52v.

[5] *APC* nos XII, pp 211–12.   [6] Gon and Caius Coll MS 53/30, fols 126v-9.

John Bourne, a glover. He was examined particularly thoroughly and persuaded to recant his errors before the rest were required to surrender, and then revealed to the investigators the places in his house where the works of H.N. were concealed. All this would suggest that he was the elder of the Family, and fortunately this can be corroborated by the separate testimony of his apprentice, Leonard Romsey. Romsey was not one of those examined in 1580, but at some later time he found his allegiance to the sect was damaging, and dictated a voluntary, somewhat sensational, account of their activities to one of the local ministers.[1] It was Bourne who had first recruited Romsey, who guided him though the writings of H.N., and who supervised the activities of the rest of the Family. Bourne's devotion to the sect is suggested by his avowed intention to leave his trade and become an itinerant elder, though, perhaps as a result of the persecution of 1580, he never carried out this project.

Many of the rest of the Wisbech group seem to have been personal friends and contacts of Bourne's, though Margaret Colville, who came from one of the leading gentry families in the Isle, consorts oddly with the town artisans. They all followed their leader readily enough in recanting their beliefs: Margaret Colville, and an old man called George Reeve, who were disposed to argue on such theological points as the resurrection of the body, were quickly reduced to silence and confusion by the blandishments of Richard Greenham and William Fulke, who had accompanied Cox as theological experts. Bonds were taken for the good behaviour of all the suspects, though this does not seem to have deterred most of them from returning to the Family once the period of persecution had passed. The examination of the Wisbech group was followed by a more comprehensive search for the Family of Love throughout the diocese, Cox being assisted in this work by lord North and two other local JPs.[2] Fifty-seven suspects were discovered, examined and, wherever possible, persuaded to recant. Only a minority were willing to suffer imprisonment for their views: five, including Edmund Rule of Balsham, recanted after one night in prison, and a further ten, including the two Lawrences, and others from Balsham and the nearby villages, were willing to remain in gaol for a longer period.

When the Wisbech group are added to the rest it would appear that

[1] PRO SP 12 cxxxiii, 55. The document is undated, and is filed under 1579, but this is almost certainly a mistake, since Romsey mentioned the events of 1580.
[2] Gon and Caius Coll MS 53/30, 2nd pt, fol 73.

there were about sixty sympathisers and members of the sect in the diocese of Ely, though in most cases we do not even know their names. Others were probably overlooked, as Romsey's subsequent confession would suggest, and as is also indicated by the presentation of a Downham man, Robert Becke, before the Consistory in 1581 on suspicion that he favoured the sect.[1] Yet when this is taken into account the Family of Love still scarcely presented the great threat to the security and morality of the nation portrayed by its detractors. It was, in a small sense, a thriving organisation, which maintained itself partly because of the translation of H.N.'s works, the sheer bulk of which were a source of great wonder to some of the Family.[2] The power of the written word was sustained by the itinerant preachers, and perhaps also by a network of contacts between the settled congregations. The converted were encouraged to believe, in Romsey's words, 'that in all contries of Christendome there is an infinite number of this opinion'. At a more practical level, the Wisbech group was aware that there were members of the Family at court: this had a value both in sustaining morale, and in providing information about the actions of the government. Romsey had prior knowledge of the persecution of 1580 because the Yeomen of the Guard were able to send information to the Wisbech group, and also to suggest to them how they should behave.[3] The morale and cohesion of the Family were also strengthened by the use of the so-called 'Book of Life'. Both Bourne and Romsey believed that their names had been conveyed to H.N. himself, and written in his book of the elect, and every time Bourne recruited a new member he transmitted the name to the Netherlands for approval. In practice this probably meant that some intermediary such as Vitels approved the name, and it cannot be demonstrated that the 'Book of Life' actually existed, though the tradition that it was kept was still current in the seventeenth century.[4] Romsey also suggests that the movement was sustained by apocalyptic visions of the establishment of the kingdom of David and the reign of Love: belief in the spiritual triumph of their faith played a role in sustaining most of the persecuted sects, though the Family was always predominantly quietist, and it is unlikely that it often surrendered itself to millenarian visions.

[1] Ely Diocesan Records, D/2/10a, fol 145v. The case was referred to the bishop.
[2] *A Supplication of the Family of Love...examined and found to be Dangerous* (Cambridge 1606) p 29. [3] PRO SP 12 cxxxiii, 55.
[4] The author of *A Supplication* claimed that the book still existed and that if it were examined it would disprove the Family's claims to be few in number and very poor.

After 1580 the Family of Love probably ceased to expand and gain many new recruits; though the effects of the government campaign of that year, which included a proclamation banning the books of H.N., are difficult to determine, the sect obviously had a more difficult time as it became more clandestine. Most of the leaders in Wisbech and Balsham adhered to their views: in such of their wills as survive there is no mention of the established church, and their supervisors and witnesses are usually drawn from the tight-knit circle of the sect.[1] The only notable defector seems to have been Thomas Pierson, the yeoman who fled to London to avoid persecution. The dedication of his will, a model of devout piety, runs thus: 'as towchinge my sowle, I comit the same unto the infinite mercies of god almightie my Saviour and Redemer, By whose death and passion only I hope and truste to be saved, under the lawes of whose moste holie churche I protest myself unto the worlde to die, an humble and true repentaunte person for my sinnes committed'.[2] Lesser defections, such as Romsey's, were no doubt common in the face of persecution. The suppression and death of the first generation of the leaders of the movement, and loss of contact with the Netherlands, made the organised survival of the Family more difficult, as did the growth of native separatism with its counter-attractions. Moreover, the puritan preachers conceived it as their particular duty to attack Niclaes's doctrine, and to persuade members of the Family to repentance: Wilkinson, John Rogers and John Knewstub all wrote passionately against the Family, and Richard Greenham and Knewstub were active in searching out its members after 1580.[3] It may not be a coincidence that Pierson left a bequest to the energetic puritan rector of Wisbech, Matthew Champion. Despite these difficulties, however, the Family of Love maintained an attenuated existence until the civil war, and in the remote Isle of Ely it may have had adherents at an even later date. Evelyn described a group of the Family, who presented a plea for toleration to James II, as 'a sort of refin'd Quakers, but their numbers very small, not consisting... of above three score in all, and those chiefly belonging to the Isle of Ely'.[4]

[1] Camb Univ Arch, Ely Cons Court Will Reg S, fol 259; T, fols 83v–4v; V, fol 224r/v.
[2] PCC 86 Woodhall.
[3] APC nos XII, p 317.
[4] A. C. Thomas, 'The Family of Love or the Familists', Haverford College Studies, XII (Fifth Month 1893) p 25.

THE QUEST FOR THE
HERETICAL LAITY IN THE
VISITATION RECORDS OF ELY IN
THE LATE SIXTEENTH AND EARLY
SEVENTEENTH CENTURIES

by MARGARET SPUFFORD

A tradition existed, and perpetuated itself, amongst the relatively humble Congregationalists of Cambridgeshire that Francis Holcroft, their evangelist, was working on old-established foundations when he gathered in his church in the 1650s and 1660s. Calamy said that he 'fell in with the Old Brownists'.[1] Robert Browne, the arch-separatist, spent nine years evangelising in Cambridgeshire and Norfolk, after taking his degree in 1572–3 and spending a little while in the model puritan household of Richard Greenham, rector of Dry Drayton in Cambridgeshire, before leaving for the continent in 1581.[2] The Brownists were not the only separatists who might have existed in the diocese of Ely in the late sixteenth century; the Family of Love is known to have taken firm root there, and a portion of the Letter Book of bishop Cox of Ely,[3] is taken up with the examination of nearly seventy of its adherents in October, 1580.

The obvious way to see whether this theory of the seventeenth-century nonconformists that the roots of their belief ran back to forbears in the sixteenth century, and particularly to Robert Browne's activities, is to see whether these supposed forbears and their opinions left any trace in the regular diocesan visitations conducted in the sixteenth century by the bishop of Ely, and in the cases he conducted by virtue of his office, in his consistory court, against parishioners in spiritual and moral error. Ely was fortunate to have a man of the calibre of bishop Cox as its head during the Elizabethan settlement. As well as becoming a leading exponent of the *via media* himself by the 1570s, anathematising papist and puritan alike, he was resident in

---

[1] *Calamy Revised*, ed A. G. Matthews (London 1934) p 272.
[2] *Alumni Cantabrigienses*, ed J. Venn, 1 (Cambridge 1922) p 237.
[3] G[onville and] C[aius College] MS 53/30, fols 126 v–29 r, particularly, fols 72 v–3 r.

his diocese, and according to Mrs Felicity Heal, who is the authority on his rule,[1] he rarely left his local manors after 1566, except on formal business as a prince of the Church. At least five of his visitations were conducted partly by Cox in person. I hoped therefore that the visitation records of a bishop as zealous as Cox for sound reform and conformity should mirror any turbulence caused by Robert Browne's teachings, and be aware of the growth of any strong heretical feeling amongst the laity. But, as Mrs Heal has written 'The clergy occupied such an important part in the records of Cox's episcopate that it is difficult to avoid the feeling that the laity were somewhat neglected, and that there was a tendency to underestimate the degree of independent thought of which they were capable, and the importance of increased literacy, and of the dissemination of the Bible'. The only visitation articles which survive from Cox's episcopate, dated by Mrs Heal to 1567 or 1570, show that this was indeed so.[2] Elementary religious instruction, punctual attendance at church, and morality, were to be the objects of enquiry amongst the laity, with the single exception of 'whether there be any persons that...presume to exercise any kind of ministry in the church of God without imposition of hands, and ordinary authority'. Much emphasis was laid by Cox on the residence of the clergy, preaching at least quarterly, the acquisition of the prescribed books by every church, and the regular catechising of the laity. But apart from noticing absenteeism from church, as Mrs Heal says, there is no evidence in bishop Cox's 'letters or his records that the independent rôle of the laity, or their support for puritanism, were important matters for him'. The morals of the laity, on the other hand, took a great deal of the attention of Cox and his officials. There were odd presentations for non-reception of communion, as well as absenteeism, but the vast bulk of the office cases dealt with, were made up of one sort of licentious living or another. Adultery, fornication, pre-marital pregnancy, the odd case of bigamy, failure to marry after betrothal, or once married, to co-habit with one's spouse, together with a bit of scolding, backbiting, and brawling between neighbours made up the vast mass of the consistory court's

[1] All my general statements on bishop Cox are drawn from Mrs Heal's unpublished Cambridge PhD thesis 'The Bishops of Ely and their Diocese during the Reformation Period: Ca. 1515–1600'. I am extremely grateful to Mrs Heal for allowing me to use her work, and quote her, in this generous way.
[2] Dated by Frere to 1571. W. H. Frere, *Visitation Articles and Injunctions of the period of the Reformation*, III (London 1910) pp 296–302. See particularly articles 4, 5, 18, 20, 24, 30, 33.

business.[1] Only 37 out of 346 cases in a register of excommunications made in the diocese between 1571 and 1584[2] were based on doctrine, or failure to communicate, or to attend church. The minds and opinions of the laity, the people of God, did not seem to Cox and his ecclesiastical officials to have merited any attention.

The point is made with force when the names of the fifteen men and women who were imprisoned as members of the Family of Love at the end of 1580 are considered.[3] Cox had personally visited at least some of the deaneries in his regular visitation of the year before,[4] but there is no trace of a single one of these people in the returns for any of the parishes concerned, even Balsham or Shudy Camps, which respectively produced six and five obdurate members of the Family of Love for Cox and his commission to imprison in the following year. This neglect is even more curious in the case of Balsham where Andrew Perne, rector of Balsham and dean of Ely, as well as five times vice-chancellor of the university, master of Peterhouse, and master-trimmer of sails to whatever ecclesiastical wind blew, had carried out his own investigation into a small group of six suspects in 1574.[5] Three of Perne's suspects cleared in 1574, appeared again as obdurate in 1580. Their existence must have been well known; but the visitation of 1579 showed no care to investigate their opinions. Other matters preoccupied the churchwardens more. At Cottenham, for instance, four couples had begotten children before wedlock, the schoolmaster had no licence, and Thomas Hawkins would not pay 16*d* for church repairs and maintain his part of the churchyard wall. Perhaps worst of all was the case of William Starling who 'misbehaved himself in church by sleeping...and being rebuked by one of the questmen, he did give him froward answers'. But no-one thought to mention that John Essex had odd opinions, although Cox imprisoned him at the end of 1580 as a member of the Family.[6]

The late sixteenth-century visitation returns and court books are so disappointing, as a guide to the opinions and state of religious feeling amongst the laity, or even as a guide to the growth of a specific

---

[1] I have based this conclusion on detailed analyses of C[ambridge] U[niversity] L[ibrary] E[ly] D[iocesan] R[ecords], B/2/4 (Cox's second visitation, 1564); B/2/6 (Office Court Book 1567–8); D/2/8 (Office Court Book 1568–70); D/2/10 (Office Court Book 1576–9 and Visitation, 1579).

[2] CUL EDR B/2/9. Noticed and briefly commented on by Patrick Collinson, *The Elizabethan Puritan Movement* (London 1967) p 40.

[3] GC MS 53/30, fol 73^r. [4] CUL EDR D/2/10 fols 150 ff.

[5] John Strype, *The Life and Acts of M. Parker* (London 1711) pp 472–3.

[6] CUL EDR D/2/10 fols 176–7.

heresy, that I have examined one seventeenth-century episcopal visitation in great detail, hoping that such an analysis would give some insight both into the truth of this dismissal of episcopal visitations as a source of information for this type of enquiry, and, if it proved true, into the reasons for the failure of visitations of this period to reflect anything other than the state of morals amongst ordinary parishioners.

I have chosen for this purpose, the visitation made by bishop Wren in 1639.[1] The choice was made on three grounds. Bishop Mathew Wren was Laud's most trusted trouble-shooter; he had been posted to one of the most difficult dioceses in the country, Norwich, to deal with the puritans there, even against the express wishes of Elizabeth of Bohemia, who wished to put in her own nominee. In Norwich he was outstandingly successful by Laud's standards. The degree of this success may be gauged by the boat loads of puritan emigrants he was responsible for launching, and the puritan lecturers he was responsible for exiling. When Wren was moved to Ely, in 1638, he was presumably moved, not only because it was a diocese of greater standing and revenue, but also because trouble was known to be brewing there. His visitation of 1639 ought therefore to reflect any trouble which did exist, particularly since he already knew his diocese. He had not been only a scholar, and then fellow of Pembroke,[2] but had also been vicar of Teversham in 1615.[3] Secondly, lists survive of the names of the churchwardens and questmen in each parish who were responsible for the presentments upon which the visitation rested.[4] It is therefore possible in this particular instance, to examine the sympathies of many of the active laity in the parishes, upon whose attitude Wren depended, for the excellent reason that a large part of the petition made to parliament in 1640 against the 'Tyranicall courses and Administrations of Dr Wren, Bishop of Ely' survives.[5] It is ruined by wet, and wear and tear, but all the same, 500 odd names can be recovered from it.

---

[1] CUL EDR B/2/52.

[2] [P. A.] Welsby, *Lancelot Andrewes [1555-1626]* (London 1964, first published 1958) pp 47-8.   [3] *DNB*, xxi (1937-8) p 1009.

[4] CUL EDR B/2/50 fols 1-22. This document is in fact a list of the names of the wardens and questmen for the diocese in 1637 and 1638, produced for the metropolitical visitation of 1638, but B/2/51, a similar list for the episcopal visitation of 1638-9, seems to contain only the names of the 'new' wardens and questmen of 1638 in B/2/50, together with some additional 'assistants', who were often the wardens or questmen of 1637. I have therefore taken B/2/50, to cover the lay officials of both 1637 and 1638 in my analysis.

[5] W. M. Palmer discusses this document, London, British Museum MS Egerton 1048, and prints the articles complained of against Wren in his *Episcopal Visitation Returns for Cambridgeshire* (London 1930) pp 72-5.

Although the names of the petitioners were organised by hundreds, the parishes from which the most prosperous of them came can frequently be identified by comparison with the nearest lay subsidy covering the same areas as the petition, which was taken in 1641.[1] Over a hundred of the petitioners of 1640 can be identified in this way. Some villages produced only one or two signatories from amongst their wealthiest inhabitants who paid taxes; but nine villages stood out because they produced five or more petitioners. These petitioners, incidentally, wanted no further reformation within the church. They asked specifically that parliament should not only redress the wrongs done them by bishop Wren, but should also 'be further pleased for the cleerer manifestation of God's glorie and the propagation of his holie word in the puritie thereof to abolish the government of bishops...and that a government according to the Holie Scripture maie be established in this Kingdome'. So there was no question in the minds of these men that they wanted a total abolition of episcopal and traditional church government.

There can be no doubt that considering Mathew Wren's known attitudes, that if the episcopal visitation is a revealing document for our purposes, his visitation of 1639 should show, unmistakably, the presence of strong puritan feeling, at least in those nine villages which a year later came out so strongly in favour of the abolition of the episcopate. He asked specifically, at his visitation, whether there were any 'abiding in the Parish' who do 'at any time preach or maintain any heresie contrary to ye faith of Christ'; whether there were any who affirmed that the form of consecration of bishops, priests and deacons, or the government of the church, was unlawful or antichristian; or whether any had been to unlawful assemblies, conventicles, or meetings.[2] Wren, unlike Cox, was well aware that the opinions of the laity were of importance. His visitation returns should surely pick up just those parishes where a year or so later, so many signatories were found to petition for 'government according to the Holie Scripture'. But they do not do so; or at least do so for only one of the nine parishes concerned. Wren wanted, in general, the communion tables to be removed to the east end of the chancel, away from their previous, apparently universal, position in the nave. He also wanted steps to be made up to them, and for them to be railed. There was no

[1] PRO MSS E.179/83/411; E.179/83/407; E.179/83/408.
[2] Chapter 1 of 'Articles to be Inquired of Within the Diocese of Ely', ed W. M. Palmer, *Documents relating to Cambridgeshire Villages* (London 1926) p 44.

doubt about the strength of feeling against these 'innovations' at Toft. There, the curate was presented for administering the last Easter communion in the body of the church, the parish clerk, William Aungier, for being responsible for moving the communion table back from its 'new' position behind the rails so that communion could be administered in the position that the laity had presumably come to accept since bishop Cox had persuaded them into it at the Elizabethan settlement. A whole group of parishioners connived at this, and were presented. But none of the other eight parishes appeared in this way. At Melbourn, where the earliest baptist church in Cambridgeshire was founded under the Commonwealth by a farmer, Benjamin Metcalfe, all that appeared in the visitation was that John Scruby refused to kneel at the altar rails to receive communion, and Timothy Atkin irreverently called a court leet after service. The visitation is scarcely an accurate guide to the under-lying ferment in Melbourn, where, in 1640, eleven named ringleaders, one of whom had been a churchwarden in the previous year, of a mob of a hundred or so, first beat up, and then ran out of town, the sheriff's collectors of ship money.[1] Later in the year, five men signed the petition for the total reform of church government.

A careful examination of the visitation entry shows that a detail in the return for a parish will often confirm previous suspicions, raised by other firm evidence, but that visitation entries taken alone are in no way reliable or clear guides to the state of feeling, and doctrine, as opposed to morals, in a parish.

The reason why the visitation records are such unreliable guides to doctrinal deviations in a parish becomes plain when the opinions of the churchwardens, who were responsible for drawing up the *comperta*, on which the episcopal official's proceedings were based,[2] are examined. In the deaneries concerned, Barton, Chesterton, Bourn and Shingay, men who were petitioners in 1640 seem to have made up something like a seventh of the adult male population.[3] The nine villages which so

---

[1] A. Kingston, *East Anglia and the Great Civil War* (London 1902) p 21.

[2] Dorothy M. Owen 'Episcopal Visitation Books', *History*, XLIX (1964) p 186. I would like to acknowledge my indebtedness to Mrs Owen, the Ely Diocesan Archivist, for much general help and time spent assisting me, although the opinions expressed here in no way necessarily coincide with hers.

[3] This is a very rough estimate, based on a comparison between petitioners, and numbers of householders in the same areas in the hearth-tax. It cannot be pushed far, both because it ignores any growth of population there may have been between the 1630s and 1660s, and because some householders in the 1660s were women, who were naturally ineligible for lay office. Moreover, the number of office holders for any parish was

clearly wanted a reform in church government had fifty-eight men who held office as churchwardens or questmen in 1637–8. No less than twenty-two of these, well over a third, signed the petition demanding 'government according to the Holie Scripture'. Those of the parochial laity who wanted a further reformation in the Church, or even a complete break with tradition, therefore had a deliberate policy, or were naturally drawn, to take up office in their parishes. The figures are adequate proof that this is so. It is therefore no longer surprising that the visitations based on returns made by men who were often of puritan disposition, did not uncover the puritanism which men like Mathew Wren were so eager to destroy. If Nicholas Grey at Bassingbourn, where Holcroft 'gathered' his first church, and Benjamin Metcalfe, later founder of a baptist church at Melbourn, and Richard Staploe at Eltisley, which was the base from which the General Baptist churches in Cambridgeshire were evangelised, were questmen or churchwardens in 1637 and 1638, it is not surprising that their parishes did not appear as centres of potential puritan revolt in Wren's visitation of 1639. It was hardly in their interests to call their bishop's attention to their own activities, which they sincerely considered to be godly.

It is not possible to make any generalisation on the accuracy with which episcopal visitations elsewhere reflect doctrinal change amongst the laity. We can only say that in the 1630s, in the diocese of Ely, puritans who wanted further reform, within or even outside the established church, filled a high proportion of lay parochial offices, and that the visitations drawn up on the presentations they made are unrevealing for that reason. We can probably extrapolate backwards in time, at least in this diocese, and say that Elizabeth puritans, and even separatists may well have been active in the same way. Visitation records[1] are no guide to the opinions or doctrines of the laity in the late

relatively static, while some Cambridgeshire villages were over four times the size of others. It also ignores the shocking state of the petition. Even if as many as a third of the 'petitioners' names are missing, however, petitioners would only have made up a fifth of householders.

[1] As a further test of visitation records, I have covered the three visitations made in the time of Lancelot Andrewes, who held Ely from 1609 to 1618. Andrewes was Wren's patron, and when he moved from Ely to Winchester, formulated anti-puritan articles for his new diocese (Welsby, *Lancelot Andrewes*, pp 13–18). He is scarcely likely to have favoured any puritans or separatists in Ely. But the visitations of 1610–11 (EDR B/2/31 fols 56–106) 1615–16 (EDR B/2/33) and one described as of 1617 (EDR B/2/37, in which most of the actual proceedings date from 1619) are as inconclusive as those of Cox or Wren. There are odd hints, which would possibly be confirmatory, if there was firm supporting evidence. But there are no clear indications, any more than there

sixteenth and early seventeenth century; possibly because the laity had such a formative hand in their composition, as well as because in the sixteenth century at least, the very subject of parochial doctrine below the level of the gentry, appeared to lack importance to the episcopate.

were, with one exception, in 1639, that any of the Cambridgeshire villages was a nursery of active puritanism, even though other evidence suggests that it certainly existed. Puritanism, separation and heresy simply do not appear as issues which can be detected in the visitations, except by the gift of hindsight, although some excommunicant people were, no doubt, classifiable as puritans, separatists and heretics.

'DENS OF LOITERING LUBBERS': PROTESTANT PROTEST AGAINST CATHEDRAL FOUNDATIONS, 1540–1640

by CLAIRE CROSS

IN *A View of Popishe Abuses* which enlarged upon the corruptions remaining in the English church, already itemised by protestant radicals in *An Admonition to the Parliament* of 1572, the writer dwelt at some length upon the iniquities of cathedral foundations.[1]

We should be too long to tell your honours of cathedral churches, the dens aforesaid of all loitering lubbers, where master dean, master vicedean, master canons or prebendaries the greater, master petty canons or canons the lesser, master chancellor of the church, master treasurer, otherwise called Judas the pursebearer, the chief chanter, singingmen, special favourers of religion, squeaking choristers, organ players, gospellers, pistellers, pensioners, readers, vergers etc. live in great idleness and have their abiding. If you would know whence all these came, we can easily answer you, that they came from the pope, as out of the Trojan horse's belly, to the destruction of God's kingdom. The church of God never knew them, neither doth any reformed church in the world know them.[2]

Protests of this sort produced no noticeable reforms and understandably during the archiepiscopate of Whitgift the puritan campaign against cathedrals intensified. The 'Petition to Parliament for the succession and restoring of Christ to his full regiment', composed probably in 1587, denounced cathedrals considerably more violently, comparing them to 'the sinful houses of friars that were some time amongst us'.

These are indeed very dens of thieves, where the time and place of God's service, preaching and prayer, is most filthily abused in piping of organs, in singing, ringing, and trouling[3] of the psalms from one side of the choir to another, with squeaking of chanting choristers, disguised, (as are all the rest) in

---

[1] Both these pamphlets have been reprinted in *Puritan Manifestoes*, [ed W. H. Frere and C. E. Douglas] (London 1954). This is the edition referred to here, but the spelling has been modernised.   [2] *Puritan Manifestoes*, p 32.
[3] 'To troul' is defined as 'to utter volubly' in S. Johnson, *A Dictionary of the English Language*, II (London 1820) p 887.

white surplices, others in cornered caps and filthy copes, in pistelling and gospelling with such vain mockeries, contrary to the commandment of God and true worshipping of God, imitating the manners and fashions of antichrist, the pope, that man of sin and child of perdition, with his other rabble of miscreants and shavelings...These unprofitable members, for the most part dumb dogs, unskilful sacrificing priests, destroying drones, or rather caterpillers of the Word, they consume yearly, some £2500, some £3000, some more, some less, whereof no profit, but rather great hurt cometh to the church of God and this commonwealth. They are dens of lazy, loitering lubbards, the very harbourers of all deceitful and timeserving hypocrites.

Rising to a climax of indignation, the anonymous writer called for a complete overthrow of cathedrals, or at the very least, for these loiterers to be driven out and be replaced in each foundation by five learned preachers who could minister to adjoining parishes.[1]

Behind this strident, and repetitious, invective, Elizabethan puritans were asking fundamental questions which perhaps have never received sufficient attention either at that time or since. In a protestant church could largely unreformed cathedral foundations be justified on theological grounds? In a national church where a majority of the parochial clergy lived in relative poverty could the comparatively lavish endowment of cathedral establishments be justified on economic grounds? The state of English cathedrals between 1540 and 1640 certainly entitled conscientious protestants to question their present purpose.

English protestants in the second half of the sixteenth century had good reason for seeing cathedrals as anachronisms from a remote past. Professor Brooke has pointed out that by the Norman Conquest cathedral chapters had already lost their primary purpose of acting as centres from which to missionise the surrounding countryside. They had had to discover a new reason for existing, and had transformed themselves into the liturgical centre of the diocese.[2] Now this change in its turn had become outdated: few convinced protestants would defend the ceaseless performance of the *Opus Dei*. Only if cathedrals had, at the Reformation, been turned into powerhouses of protestant preaching could their objections have been partially satisfied.

In many ways it is difficult to understand why cathedral foundations were not more drastically pruned during the Henrician and Edwardian

---

[1] *The Seconde Parte of a Register*, ed A. Peel, II (Cambridge 1915) p 211. Spelling modernised.

[2] C. N. L. Brooke, 'The Earliest Times to 1485' in *A History of St Paul's Cathedral*, ed W. R. Matthews and W. M. Atkins (London 1957) pp 9–10.

Reformation, and the changes that did come about seem to have happened at least partly by accident. The dissolution of the monasteries affected immediately the eight English monastic cathedrals, Canterbury, Durham, Winchester, Worcester, Ely, Norwich, Rochester and Carlisle. The government of Henry VIII assumed the necessity for their continuance in a modified form, and indeed founded new episcopal sees based on new cathedral foundations of which five, Oxford, Bristol, Chester, Gloucester and Peterborough, survived. These foundations and refoundations show evidence of some new thinking, most significantly in the size of their establishments which were much smaller than those of medieval English secular cathedrals. At Canterbury, Durham and Winchester the state made provision for a dean and twelve prebendaries as well as lesser officials. A dean and six prebendaries was the average size of the cathedral establishment of the newly created sees, while the crown allowed the former monastic cathedral of Carlisle only four prebendaries in addition to the dean. Interestingly, some churchmen begrudged the provision of cathedral establishments even on this scale. In 1539, when the bill was being drawn up to create the new cathedral foundation at Canterbury, Cranmer wrote to Cromwell protesting that the £40 set aside for the annual stipends of the eight prebendaries was much too lavish. He objected to prebendaries largely on moral grounds: they 'spent their time in much idleness, and their substance in superfluous belly cheer'. 'Wherefore,' he continued, 'if it may so stand with the king's gracious pleasure, I would wish that not only the name of prebendary were exiled his grace's foundations, but also the superfluous conditions of such persons.' He suggested that the money set aside for the Canterbury prebendaries could be far better spent upon scholarships for students at Oxford and Cambridge.[1]

The government did not take Cranmer's advice. Henry, presumably, wished his new foundations to appear like the cathedrals of the past. It may be that the Henrician government still regarded cathedral prebends as a proper reward for government servants and was unwilling to deprive itself of a useful form of patronage. Even when these qualifications have been made it is still difficult to see why the old secular cathedrals, St Paul's, York, Lincoln, Bath and Wells, Chichester, Exeter, Salisbury, Lichfield and Hereford emerged from the revolutionary decades of the latter part of the reign of Henry VIII and of his

[1] *Cranmer's Miscellaneous Writings*, ed J. E. Cox, Parker Society (Cambridge 1846) pp 396–7.

son virtually unscathed. At the beginning of the reign of Elizabeth (and these establishments then underwent no major change before the Civil War) Lincoln still had a dean and fifty-two prebendaries, Bath and Wells had fifty prebendaries while Salisbury had forty-five. The six other cathedrals of the old foundation retained establishments ranging from a dean and thirty-one prebendaries to a dean and twenty-four prebendaries. The crown had taken some spoils. At York, for example, the prebend of Bramham, annexed to the priory of Nostell, and that of Salton which had become attached to the priory of Hexham, fell to the king when the two priories were dissolved and in addition the crown confiscated the two richest prebends of the see, that of Masham, worth £136 and that of South Cave, worth £87 annually as well as the revenues of the treasurership which had been valued at £220, the richest office in the minster.[1] Lincoln similarly lost its treasurership and five of its richer prebends.[2] Yet considerable wealth still remained with these cathedrals of the old foundation which could well have been taken, it seems, without much opposition. The state had to a varying extent modified cathedral chapters, but the changes had not been nearly radical enough to satisfy Elizabethan protesters. This may have been a case when the state was content to countenance the status quo, perhaps largely for reasons of patronage, when even quite moderate church reformers would have preferred wholesale change.

The basic protestant objection to cathedral chapters was that they continued to exist in this at best half-reformed state. As Elizabeth's reign progressed fundamental changes which would have led to the abolition of chapters or drastic curtailment of the numbers of prebendaries appeared increasingly unlikely. In consequence protesters tended to concentrate upon individual abuses within the prebendal system. From the twelfth century onwards reformers in England had complained because so few prebendaries resided in cathedrals and instead left their duties to be performed by vicars.[3] Now protestants attacked prebendaries for living idly in cathedral closes when they could have been directing their energies to preaching in parishes throughout the diocese. If York can be taken as a test case, the records

[1] These, and all subsequent valuations, unless otherwise stated, are taken from *Valor Ecclesiasticus temp. Henr. VIII*, ed J. Caley, 6 vols, Record Commission (London 1810–34).

[2] B. Willis, *Survey of the Cathedrals of Lincoln, Ely, Oxford and Peterborough*, II (London 1730) pp 95, 141, 176, 209, 245, 252.

[3] The whole question of residence in English medieval secular cathedrals is discussed at length in K. Edwards, *The English Secular Cathedrals in the Middle Ages* (revised ed Manchester 1967) especially p 35.

do not in fact show any noticeable increase in residence: two, three or sometimes four canons, including usually one of the four great officials, resided at the beginning of the sixteenth century, normally three or four at the end.[1] Yet while only this very small number technically resided and participated in a set number of services, many more prebendaries than might be supposed kept up a formal attachment to the minster. The York chapter act books unfortunately only begin to record attendance at chapter meetings in 1565. Usually about half a dozen canons went to a particular chapter meeting, though a record number of thirteen appeared for no obvious reason on 16 January 1568. Nevertheless, this could mean, as in the year which ran from Martinmas 1567 to Martinmas 1568, that fifteen prebendaries, that is exactly half the chapter, attended at least one chapter meeting during the year.[2] In addition, the vicars choral, all ordained clerics, were present in considerable numbers in the minster. Theoretically until the Reformation there had been a vicar choral for every prebendary, that is an establishment of thirty-six, but the falling revenues of the vicars choral had meant that this number could not be maintained in the early sixteenth century. After the abolition of chantries, since most vicars choral seem to have supplemented their incomes as vicars with the holding of a chantry priest's place in the minster, the number of vicars diminished rapidly. Even so, there were between nine and eleven vicars choral in the Elizabethan period.[3] When a dozen or so choirmen and boys as well as the cathedral servants are counted in, an unsympathetic observer could conclude with reason that the minster overflowed with functionaries, some, like the dean and most of the prebendaries, with high academic qualifications, most of whom could have been far more profitably employed elsewhere.

Allied to this charge of idleness against cathedral clergy was that of luxurious living and again the reformers had much substance in their protests. Not all prebends were rich ones. The Henrician government endowed the prebends of the cathedrals of the new foundation with a relatively moderate sufficiency: the prebendaries of Durham seem to have received most with £32 5s 10d a year each; the prebendaries of Carlisle had a little over £22 each, the prebendaries of Chester,

---

[1] These remarks are based on the rolls of the minster chamberlain, ninety-four of which have survived sporadically for half years between 1480 and 1679. York, Minster Library MS E. 1. 46-138.

[2] Chapter Act Book, 1565-1634. York, Minster Library MS H.4 fols 1-377.

[3] York, Minster Library MS H.4 fols 35r, 117r, 180v, 210v and see F. Harrison, *Life in a Medieval College* (London 1952) especially parts five and six.

Bristol, Gloucester and Ely exactly £20, while at Norwich and Peter-borough they had only £7 16s 8d.[1] The cathedrals of the old founda-tion displayed no such uniformity: the best prebend at Lincoln was worth £68 16s 0½d, the worst nothing at all; at St Paul's the prebends varied in value from £46 to £5 6s 8d a year; at York the prebendary of Wetwang enjoyed £82 11s 3d (according to the *Valor* valuations, by 1559 the richest prebend remaining in any English cathedral) while the prebendary of Tockerington only had £2 17s 1d annually. The possession of a prebend usually entitled its holder to protest residence and the financial advantage to those who did so could be very consid-erable. Both the chamberlain's account rolls survive at York for the half years which ran from Whitsun to Martinmas 1578 and from Martinmas to Whitsun 1578-9 and they make it possible to calculate the income Matthew Hutton received from minster funds alone in that particular year. As dean he had £308 10s 7½d on the *Valor Ecclesiasticus* valuation which was likely to be an underestimate by this date, as was the income of £32 13s 4d from his prebend of Osbaldwick. His prebend allowed him to take up residence, which he did for the whole year: his quotidian payments for the year totalled £27 14s, much more importantly his share of the common fund again for the whole year amounted to £88 1s 4d. His gross income from the minster, therefore, reached at least £456 19s 3½d.[2] He also, incidentally, held prebends at Southwell and St Paul's as well as the rectory of Settrington in Yorkshire until he became bishop of Durham in 1589. Prebendaries who did not possess one of the four major cathedral offices could not hope for wealth on this scale: nevertheless, at least some could live comfortably. In 1593 William Goodwin was prebendary of Bole from which he drew, on the *Valor* valuation, £17 17s 1d. He resided from Whitsun 1593 to Whitsun 1594 and his quotidian payments together with his shares of the common fund came to £109 2s 5d, a total income from the minster of £126 19s 6d: he held in addition the Yorkshire rectories of Etton and Stonegrave.[3]

[1] For Durham, Carlisle, Chester and Bristol see B. Willis, *Survey of the Cathedrals of York, Durham, Carlisle*, I (London 1727) pp 222, 285, 329, 760. For Ely and Peterborough see B. Willis, *Survey of the Cathedrals of Lincoln, Ely, Oxford and Peterborough*, II (1730) pp 346, 503. For Gloucester see T. D. Fosbrooke, *An Original History of the City of Gloucester* (London 1819) p 219. For Norwich see F. Blomefield, *An Essay towards a Topographical History of the County of Norfolk*, IV (London 1806) p 566.

[2] Chamberlain's Rolls, York, Minster Library MS E.1, VII, 93, 93b. *DNB*, XXVIII, pp 357-8 under 'Matthew Hutton'.

[3] York, Minster Library MSS E.1, VII, 96; E.1, VIII, 103. *DNB*, VII, pp 150-1 under 'William Goodwin'.

'Dens of loitering lubbers'

So critics of cathedral luxury may not have indulged in wild exaggeration when they alleged that cathedral clergy consumed annually 'some £2,500, some £3,000.'[1] On the *Valor* valuations, the four great dignitaries at York after the Reformation, the dean, the precentor, the chancellor and the subdean together with the succentor were paid £540 2s 4½d: the total annual value of the thirty remaining prebends came to £861 12s 8½d. The common fund of the minster had an endowment estimated to bring in annually £439 2s 6d while the vicars choral had a more modest annual income of £136 5s 3d. The total income from these four sources was £1,977 2s 10d on the Henrician valuation: by the middle of Elizabeth's reign the clergy of York minster could collectively have been enjoying well over £2,000 a year. To protestants the scandal was worst compounded in that at York, and probably at most other cathedrals, by far the greatest part of the cathedral revenues came from impropriate rectories: cathedral prebendaries literally lived at the expense of parochial clergy. Whitgift in 1589 answered the puritan call for an educated preaching minister in every parish by the flat statement that many parish livings had not adequate revenues to maintain a university-trained cleric.[2] With the amount of impropriations since the Reformation in the possession of bishops and deans and chapters part of the remedy for this problem lay within the church's own control if it had wished, and been allowed, to resolve it.

Visually cathedral establishments shocked more radical protestants with their reminders of an unregenerate catholic origin and, with its approval of more elaborate ceremonial especially in cathedrals, the Arminian movement in the earlier part of the seventeenth century added to this offence. Pastorally cathedrals offended by retaining well educated clergy who many protestants felt could be better employed ministering to parochial cures. Economically cathedrals caused real resentment by drawing the greater part of their revenues from impropriate livings. It is not surprising that so few bewailed the demise of deans and chapters in 1649: what is surprising is that the cathedral foundations, restored in 1660 exactly as they had been in 1640, were not reformed until the reign of Queen Victoria.

[1] See p 232 n 1.
[2] J. Strype, *The Life and Acts of John Whitgift* (London 1718) pp 280–1.

THE ANGLO-GALLICANISM OF
DOM THOMAS PRESTON, 1567–1647

by MAURUS LUNN

GALLICANISM – the name given to the general theory that the Church, especially the Church in France, is free from the jurisdiction of the pope, while remaining Roman and Catholic – is familiar to most historians. The existence of such a thing as Anglo-Gallicanism, on the other hand, seems scarcely credible. Post-Reformation English Catholics present the image of a persecuted and retiring group of people, who, in order to preserve their corporate identity, became more Italianate in their culture than the Italians and in their theology more papalist than the popes; and of the majority of English Catholics this was true. But throughout their history there runs a thin red line of dissent, which passes from the Appellant priests in the late sixteenth century, via Blackloism in the seventeenth, to Charles Butler, Joseph Berington and the Catholic Committee at the dawn of emancipation.[1] Gallicanism, and perhaps its English counterpart, were given a death-blow by Napoleon's application of papal authority to the French bishops. But Anglo-Gallicanism was an unconscionably long time dying, for at Downside in the early nineteenth century William Bernard Ullathorne, later bishop of Birmingham, was taught theology from Gallican textbooks.[2] In this tradition a prominent part, in terms of impact and literary output, was played by another Benedictine, Thomas Preston, *alias* Roger Widdrington.

Very little can be said about his life, since almost half of it was spent uneventfully in prison.[3] A Shropshire lad, born Roland Preston in 1567, he studied at Oxford and at the English College in Rome, where he sat at the feet of the Jesuit Gabriel Vasquez, whose doctrine of

---

[1] J. H. Pollen, *The Institution of the Archpriest Blackwell* (London 1916); *The Wisbech Stirs, 1595–1598*, ed P. Renold, Catholic Record Society, II (London 1958); R. I. Bradley, 'Blacklo and the Counter-Reformation: an enquiry into the strange death of Catholic England', *From the Renaissance to the Counter-Reformation*, ed C. H. Carter (London 1965) pp 348–70; B. Ward, *Dawn of the Catholic Revival in England, 1781–1803* (London 1909).

[2] W. B. Ullathorne, *Autobiography* (London 1891) p 46.

[3] [W. K. L.] Webb, ['Thomas Preston O.S.B., *alias* Roger Widdrington (1567–1640),'] *Biographical Studies*, II (London 1954) pp 216–68.

Probabilism he was to adopt in his books. After ordination he became a benedictine at Monte Cassino in 1591, adopting the name Thomas. There, says father Augustine Baker, for his erudition in canon law and his reputation as a good monk, he was made professor of theology. He remained in Italy until 1602, when he was one of the first two English Cassinese monks to be sent on the mission to England, where three Anglo-Spanish monks had just arrived.[1] After the dissolution of Mary Tudor's re-foundation of Westminster Abbey, English monastic life had lapsed completely, until, from the 1590s, Englishmen studying for the secular priesthood in Rome and Valladolid had started leaving their colleges in increasingly large numbers in order to enter Italian and Spanish monasteries. On being given special papal permission to go to England as missionaries, they formed a link with the last surviving member of Westminster Abbey, Dom Sigebert Buckley, with whose help they revived what they thought had been the autonomous pre-Reformation English Benedictine Congregation, although they saw it through tridentine spectacles. The English Benedictines flourished exceedingly in the years that followed, so that they became second only to the Jesuits among the regular clergy in numbers and influence. Although they wavered at first, the majority of the English Benedictines became firmly anti-Gallican.[2] But in their origins they sided actively with the Appellants against the Jesuits, and therefore it was to be expected that a pioneer of the benedictine movement such as Thomas Preston would sympathise with the Appellants' Gallican sentiments.

The history of Anglo-Gallicanism repeats itself, and the point to which it returns after every digression is the oath of allegiance.[3] In appearance the oath was a test of the loyalty of Catholics to their sovereign in temporal matters, like the 'Declaration of Allegiance' which in January 1603 thirteen Catholic priests offered to make to

---

[1] D. M. Lunn, 'The Origins and Early Development of the Revived English Benedictine Congregation, 1588–1647,' unpublished Ph.D. thesis (Cambridge 1970).

[2] M. Lunn, ['English Benedictines and the Oath of Allegiance, 1606–1647,'] R[ecusant] H[istory], x (London 1969) pp 146–63.

[3] J. de la Servière, De Jacobo I, Angliae Rege, cum Cardinali Roberto Bellarmino...disputante (Paris–Poitiers 1900) especially pp 32 et seq; L. Willaert, 'Négotiations politico-religieuses entre l'Angleterre et les Pays-Bas catholiques (1598–1625)', RHE VI–IX (1905–1908) especially VI (1905) pp 822 et seq and VIII (1907) pp 90 et seq; D. H. Willson, 'James I and his Literary Assistants', Huntington Library Quarterly, VIII (San Marino, California 1944) pp 35–57; C. J. Ryan, 'The Jacobean Oath of Allegiance and the English Lay Catholics', Catholic Historical Review, XXVIII (London 1942) pp 159–83; T. H. Clancy, Papist Pamphleteers (Chicago 1964) especially Ch IV.

The Anglo-Gallicanism of dom Thomas Preston, 1567–1647

Queen Elizabeth.[1] Parliament, however, had begun in February 1606, following the discovery of the Gunpowder Plot, to debate articles for 'the better discovering and repressing of Popish Recusants', and in May the act embodying the new oath received King James's formal assent.[2] Anyone who took the oath declared that James was lawful king and that no pope had authority to depose him or to command Catholics to take up arms against him. So far a Catholic might, with a bit of mental gymnastics, have taken the oath, since nothing was affected except his temporal allegiance to his king. But, next, a juror would have to say, 'I do further…abjure as impious and heretical this damnable doctrine and position…that princes which be excommunicated or deprived by the Pope may be deposed or murdered by their subjects or by any other whatsoever'. It was just the one word 'heretical' which altered the whole meaning of the oath and turned it into a theological matter. For a Catholic it meant consigning those popes and respected theologians, who had defended the papal deposing power, to eternal perdition. It also meant that James and his parliament had the right to determine matters of orthodoxy. Clearly, by the use of such terminology, James intended to provoke a battle among the English Catholics between those who would and those who would not take the oath.

The king was rewarded by more than a local battle. Much to his initial delight the 'Schoolmaster of the Realm'[3] started a battle of the books which penetrated into every corner of Europe and brought some of the best minds of the age into the opposing ranks. Pope Paul V opened the battle in the same year by condemning the oath. Shortly afterwards the aged head of the English Catholics, George Blackwell, was captured and imprisoned, taking the oath and inviting his clergy to follow him. Cardinal Robert Bellarmine SJ, the most celebrated Catholic controversialist of that age, wrote to Blackwell, urging a retractation. In 1608 James himself published a reply to Bellarmine and the pope, and waited impatiently for a reply. This came quickly and

---

[1] C. Dodd [vere Hugh Tootell], *Church History of England*, 3 vols (Wolverhampton 1737–42) II pp 292–3; Preston, *A New-Yeares Gift for English Catholikes* (London 1620) pp 11, 33, 34; M. Lunn, *RH* x (1969) p 146. For similar contemporary declarations see R. G. Usher, *The Reconstruction of the English Church*, 2 vols (New York 1910) II, p 103; T. H. Clancy, 'English Catholics and the Papal Deposing Power, 1570–1640', *RH* VI (1962) pp 207–8; J. Bossy, 'Henri IV, the Appellants and the Jesuits', *RH* VIII (1965) pp 97–8.

[2] J. R. Tanner, *Constitutional Documents of the Reign of James I, 1603–1625* (Cambridge 1961) pp 82–3, 86 et seq.

[3] D. H. Willson, *King James VI and I* (London 1963) Ch XVI and pp 228–42.

devastatingly from Bellarmine and gave the signal for a host of lesser combatants to join in the fray, so that in 1611, for example, no less than eleven books were published on the controversy.

It was in this year that there appeared a book with the title *Apologia Cardinalis Bellarmini pro Jure Principum* by an author who called himself Roger Widdrington, 'an English Catholic'. Another misleading detail was the false imprint, 'Cosmopoli, apud Theophilum Pratum', together with the Jesuit ornament, thus intentionally giving the impression that it was printed abroad and by the Jesuits. In fact it was printed in London by Government order.[1]

King James was highly pleased, and English Catholics thought that it was even more effective than the only other recent publication of a similar sort by a Catholic, William Barclay's *De Potestate Papae* (1609).[2] Part of the sensation was caused by the fact that no one believed that Roger Widdrington, a roughneck Catholic squire from Northumberland, was capable of writing the book, although he may have given his name willingly and acted as a purveyor of books for Preston.[3] Suspicion soon fastened on Preston, despite the fact that he was living in the Clink prison, ostensibly suffering horribly for his faith. In fact his presence there was nothing but an elaborate smokescreen put up by himself and the Government, for he lived more comfortably than he would have done in any monastery, with a well-stocked library, a personal valet, a maid-servant to cook for him and keep his rooms tidy, permission to go out when he wished and (eventually) a royal pardon.[4] Early in 1612 George Abbot, the archbishop of Canterbury, revealed Preston to be 'Widdrington', although Preston continued to deny it and to use the

1 Webb, *Biographical Studies*, pp 228–30. For a register of Preston's published writings and their full titles see [A. F.] A[llison] and [D. M.] R[ogers], *A Catalogue of Catholic Books in English Printed Abroad or Secretly in England, 1558–1640* (Bognor Regis 1956) nos 660–78. To this should be added William Howard [*vere* Preston], *A Patterne of Christian Loyaltie* (London 1934). This is no 13871 in A. W. Pollard and G. R. Redgrave, *A Short-Title Catalogue of Books Printed in England, Scotland, and Ireland and of English Books Printed Abroad 1475–1640* (London 1926). The *Apologia* was re-printed in M. Goldast, *Monarchiae S. Romani Imperii...*, 3 vols (Frankfort 1668) III, pp 688–763, and at Frankfort, 1613 and 1621 according to C. Sommervogel, *Bibliothèque de la Compagnie de Jésus*, 10 vols (Brussels–Paris 1890–1901) I, col 1225.

2 A and R, no 69; *Calendar of State Papers, Venetian, 1610–13* (London 1864) XII, p 136: Marc' Antonio Correr to the Doge and Senate, 2 April 1611; A[rchives of the] A[rchbishopric of] W[estminster, Series A] 10, fol 277: G. Birkhead to T. More, 10 August 1611; AAW *ibid* fols 233 and 275.

3 E. L. Taunton, 'Thomas Preston and "Roger Widdrington",' *English Historical Review*, XVIII (1903) pp 16–19; Preston, *Supplicatio* (1616) p 24; AAW 11, fol 329: A. Champney, Sorbonne, to T. More, 17 July 1612; *ibid* fols 7, 325, 331, 351 (on Widdrington's chaplain).   4 Webb, *Biographical Studies*, pp 226–38.

pseudonym. There can, however, be no doubt that he wrote the 'Widdrington' books,[1] although at times he may have had literary helpers.[2]

So much for the authorship of the *Apologia Cardinalis Bellarmini pro Jure Principum*. The title, too, caused a mild sensation, although its purpose was misunderstood. Bellarmine was angered by what he thought – or affected to think – was a mere hoax, designed to make it seem to the ignorant that he had written a book against himself.[3] In fact the title contained an allusion to a book called *The Protestants Apologie for the Roman Church*, a highly successful attempt by a Catholic author, who called himself John Brereley, to convict the Protestants, from their own writings, of pro-Catholic sentiments.[4] Preston adopted the same method. He dug up arguments from Bellarmine's other works which supported the Widdringtonian position, and for the rest he argued that the Jesuit's proofs for the papal deposing power were so unconvincing that they amounted to self-refutation. Preston, therefore, refused to join in the sterile exchange of invective between the cardinal, the king and their men, for he hardly quoted Bellarmine's latest challenge. Preston knew his Bellarmine better than that, plainly admired him and caught from him his courtesy in debate.

Professor Charles McIlwain has called Preston's book

a typical statement of the position of moderate Catholics who were willing to submit to the oath as merely civil...clear and comprehensive...one of the most powerful arguments that appeared, answering Bellarmine's arguments for the indirect power step by step in excellent latin and with the citation of many authorities, fully up to the level of the better-known work of Barclay, and possibly more important for us because the author always has the oath in mind and applies his theory more concretely to the situation in England.[5]

The launching-pad of Preston's argument was in fact the oath and in particular the word 'heretical'. He started with the difficulty that he

---

[1] AAW 11, fol 123: Birkhead to More, 21 March 1612; Stonyhurst MS, Anglia A. VII, fol 84: Preston, petition to Parliament, [1646].

[2] For example Dr William Gabriel Gifford, O.S.B. (AAW 11, fol 531: John Mush to T. More, 17 October 1612). But see Silos Abbey Archives, General Series XII, fol 565: Gifford to Alonso Barrantes, [July 1614]; Vatican Archives, Nunziatura di Francia 56, fols 299, 323v: Ubaldini to Millini, 3 May 1616, and to Borghese, 26 July 1616; *ibid* Fondo Borghese I, 902, fols 125, 155: Borghese to Ubaldini, 8 April and 22 August 1616.

[3] Bellarmine, *Examen ad Librum Falso Inscriptum, Apologia Card. Bellarmini pro Jure Principum, etc. Auctore Rogero Widdringtono Catholico Anglo*... Rome – printed, not published – 1612); partly printed in X-M. Le Bachelet, *Auctarium Bellarminianum* (Paris 1913) p 360. See also James Brodrick's interpretation in his *The Life and Work of Blessed Robert Francis Cardinal Bellarmine, S. J., 1542–1621*, 2 vols (London 1928) II, p 255.

[4] A and R, nos 131–3; Preston, *Apologia Cardinalis Bellarmini* (1611) pp 25, 188, 203; *Supplicatio* (1616) pp 11–12.

[5] *The Political Works of James I*, ed C. H. McIlwain (Cambridge, Massachusetts 1918) p lxxiii.

could not follow King James in calling the doctrine of papal deposing power heretical and still remain a Catholic. He argued instead that the doctrine was neither heretical nor, as against the papalists, of faith; it was merely probable, by which he meant that it was doubtful or debatable. Therefore, because the question was still under discussion, the Catholics might have the benefit of the doubt and could take the oath with an easy conscience. The cleverness of his method was that of a conjuror. By concentrating the attention of his readers on his attack against the pope's triple crown, he distracted their attention from the fact that the king's theological plaything had quietly disappeared. By showing that the deposing power was not of faith, he also demonstrated that it was not 'heretical'. Preston thus drew the poison from the oath and the heat from the controversy. Historians have not given him enough credit for this nor for the (initial) independence of his judgement from both pope and king. But do his arguments stand up to scrutiny?

These arguments relied on Probabilism, the system of moral theology based on the principle that, if the lawfulness of an action is in doubt, it is permissible to follow a minority opinion, which favours liberty, even though the opposing opinion, favouring the law, be more probable and therefore safer. In the seventeenth century Probabilism, which could be reduced to the maxim, 'It is probable, for it has one sound author to support it', tended towards laxity, but it had its good points as a practical guide to ethics and it remained almost without opposition until Blaise Pascal started writing the *Lettres Provinciales* in 1656, when it collapsed in a gale of laughter. Hedged about with safeguards, it was later rehabilitated and is now the dominant moral system in the Roman Catholic Church.[1]

In order, therefore, to show that there was a probable opinion in favour of taking the oath, all Preston had to do was to point to himself as the one learned and reputable theologian needed to make this action lawful. But this was not necessary. He could, it is true, produce only a few English Catholic authorities who openly supported the oath itself, although he claimed a lot of silent support.[2] But he could cite a host of learned men who opposed the big obstacle to taking the oath, namely the deposing power. Preston's erudition was immense, and everything was grist to his mill, scripture, patrology, canon law, historians and medieval scholastics but mainly the modern theologians

---

[1] T. Deman, 'Probabilisme', *DTC*, XIII, cols 417–619; B. Pascal, *Les Lettres Provinciales*, ed H. F. Stewart (Manchester 1920) pp xxvi–xxxvi and 45–67.
[2] *Apologia Cardinalis Bellarmini* (1611) pp 2–3. See also *A New-Yeares Gift* (1620) pp 4–13; *A Copy of the Decree* (1614) p 12.

and controversialists. Ironically, the authors he owed most to were Spanish Jesuits, such as Francisco Suarez, Gabriel Vasquez and Juan Azor, because they were Probabilists; they were the best Catholic theologians of the age; and some of them had taught him in Rome. Less surprisingly, he relied heavily on the Gallicans, Jean Quidort de Paris, Pierre Pithou and many others.[1] But more effective than the citing of many authors was his use of the example of contemporary France. In France, he said, the pope tolerates those Catholics who propose the equivalent of Widdringtonism and admits them to the sacraments. Why, asked Preston, should there be one law for the powerful French Catholics and another for the leaderless English? The French, he added, thought that the English Catholics were fools to risk losing goods and life for the sake of a debatable doctrine. The existence of strong French public opinion was, therefore, Preston's weightiest proof that there was a solid probable argument against the deposing power and in favour of the oath.[2]

Having made this point, however, Preston still had to get round the difficulty of the papal pronouncements, especially Paul V's two condemnations of the oath. This Preston did by making the distinction in canon law between pronouncements which laid down the law and had to be obeyed, and those which merely pointed to an existing law, which law in some cases might need further clarification by canonists and theologians. Paul V's pronouncements, Preston said, were examples of the latter type. They left the matter still open to dispute. With regard to papal censures made later against himself Preston was to show ingenuity amounting to sophistry in claiming that none of them applied to himself. He swallowed the most indigestible of papal thunderbolts as if, says Matthew Kellison (one of his adversaries) he had the all-consuming stomach of an ostrich.[3]

Preston was a good logician, better as biblical exegete than many of his contemporaries, and a master of restrained irony. On the other hand

[1] Preston defended his use of Gallican writers in *A Cleare, Sincere and Modest Confutation ...of T. F.* (London 1616) pp 73–134.

[2] *Apologia Cardinalis Bellarmini* (1611) pp 26–9; *Strena Catholica* (1620) pp 267–8, 271, 280; *Responsio Apologetica* (1612) pp 84–5; with Thomas Green O.S.B., *Appellatio* (1620) pp 2 and 10.

[3] *Apologia Cardinalis Bellarmini* (1611) pp 171–2. This position is more fully developed in *Disputatio Theologica* (1613) pp 288, 316–21; *Discussio Discussionis Decreti Magni Concilii Lateranensis* (1618) Preface; *Last Reioynder* (1619) pp 559–60; *An Adioynder* (1620) p 97. Kellison's statement, from *The Right and Iurisdiction of the Prelate and the Prince* (1617) – A and R, nos 427–8 – is quoted by T. H. Clancy in *New Catholic Encyclopaedia* (1967) 761.

much of his success in getting support among the English Catholics[1] was caused partly by the fact that Probabilism was an easy doctrine to defend, since it put all the *onus probandi* on its opponents. It is not difficult to see, moreover, how Widdringtonism could lead to laxity. Finally, the promise shown in the *Apologia Cardinalis Bellarmini* was not fulfilled. He produced, it is true, almost a book every year until 1621, taking on all comers, most of them Jesuits. But his language fell from the elevated tone of his first work,[2] and he indulged against Jesuits and others a bad taste for intrigue.[3] His political position became steadily more absolutist[4] and his attitude to the oath less impartial,[5] no doubt under pressure from the government, although financially he remained independent.[6] Three times he was threatened by Rome with removal of his priestly faculties, and each time he made a feigned submission, but his books were put on the *Index Librorum Prohibitorum*.[7] In 1634 he published his last book, *A Patterne of Christian Loyaltie*, under the name of a young Catholic layman called William Howard.[8] Attempts were made by the papal envoy, Gregorio Panzani, to reconcile him and to modify both the oath and the papal condemnations of it, but in vain, since neither Charles I nor Urban VIII could change what their predecessors had solemnised.[9] Preston lived on in the Clink, dying in 1647 at the age of eighty.[10]

---

[1] C. Dodd, *Church History of England*, ed M. A. Tierney, 5 vols (London 1839) IV, p clxx: Birkhead to More, 30 May 1611; *Guido Bentivoglio Diplomatico*, ed R. Belvederi, 2 vols (Ferrara 1949) II, p 362: Bentivoglio to Borghese, 11 July 1615.

[2] See for example *Responsio Apologetica* (1612) pp 146–51; *Disputatio Theologica* (1613) 11.

[3] Webb, *Biographical Studies*, pp 249–55. For intrigues among his Cassinese brethren see *Spicilegium Benedictinum*, 5 vols (Rome 1896) II, pp 5–12: D. Codner to G. Law, 23 December 1636.

[4] *Responsio Apologetica* (1612) pp 72–6; *Supplicatio* (1616) pp 1–3, 44, 105.

[5] *Responsio Apologetica* (1612) pp 146, 151; *A New-Yeares Gift* (1620) pp 141–7.

[6] Abbey of S. Pietro, Perugia: 'Cong. Cass. SS': papers of Gregory Law, fol 535: arrangements concerning Nicholas Fitzherbert's will, 1613–18; Rome, Congregation of Propaganda, 'Scritture originali riferite nelle Congregazioni Generali' 409, fols 167, 170v: D. Codner, petition to Propaganda, [c. September 1645]. For an example of Government pressure on Preston see *Calendar of State Papers, Domestic, Charles I, 1633–4*, 23 vols (London 1858–97) VI, pp 577–8: archbishop Laud to Preston, [April 1634]. [7] M. Lunn, *RH* x (1969) pp 152–4.

[8] For Preston's authorship see Stonyhurst MS, Anglia A. VII, 84: Preston, petition to Parliament, [1646]; Vatican Archives, Nunziatura d'Inghilterra 3A, fols 39–40: diary of Gregorio Panzani, 27 December 1634. For the identity of William Howard see R. E. Grun, 'A Note on William Howard, Author of "A Patterne of Christian Loyaltie"', *Catholic Historical Review* XLII (1956–7) pp 330–40.

[9] G. Albion, *Charles I and the Court of Rome* (Louvain 1935) pp 251–86.

[10] E. Gattola, *Historia Abbatiae Cassinensis*, 4 vols (Venice 1733) II, p 752: a circular from Andrea Arcioni, abbot of Monte Cassino, dated 17 June 1647.

HENRY IV AND
THE HUGUENOT APPEAL FOR A
RETURN TO POISSY

by W. B. PATTERSON

WHEN the queen mother, Catherine de Medici, summoned protestant and catholic spokesmen to a conference at Poissy, in 1561, the religious situation in France was still remarkably fluid. Religious ideas of an innovative and reformist character had long had an appeal in French intellectual circles, but it was only recently that Protestantism in France had begun to take on the appearance of an organised religious movement. The persecution of Protestants had been severe at times, but neither systematic nor continuous, and the bulk of French Protestants was inclined to be conciliatory. Even the question of whether they could be considered heretics was still somewhat open, as the council of Trent had not yet concluded its sessions. Thus the time must have seemed propitious to the queen, then enjoying real political power in France for the first time, to attempt to reconcile the theological differences which were dividing her subjects, and to restore the religious unity of the realm.[1]

The actual conference fell a long way short of fulfilling her hopes. At its opening on 31 July 1561, with only catholic ecclesiastics present, the young king, Charles IX, and the chancellor, Michel de l'Hôpital, stressed the need for reforming what was amiss in the French Church and for restoring conditions of peace and unity in the nation. The chancellor affirmed that these matters need not be left to a general council, composed for the most part of strangers to France, but should be dealt with by those who knew French problems best. When the protestant representatives were finally brought in, on 9 September, they stood at one end of the room, looking rather like the accused at the bar of justice. Their spokesman, however, the Genevan theologian Théodore de Bèze, put forward the protestant case with such vigour that the catholic theologians, including the great ecclesiastical

---

[1] Lucien Febvre, *Au Coeur religieux du XVIe siècle* (2 ed Paris 1968) pp 3–70; Samuel Mours, *Le Protestantisme en France au XVIe siècle* (Paris 1959) pp 101–36; [Jean] Heritier, *Catherine de Medici* (London 1963) pp 145–72.

statesman, the cardinal of Lorraine, found themselves strenuously defending traditional practices and beliefs. Once, the presiding officer was so shocked by de Bèze's views on the eucharist that he declared that such remarks were not fit for the ears of the Most Christian King. By the end of September the prelates had had enough, declaring that their canons forbade them to confer with such men. In the conference's final phase, discussions were continued by a smaller group under the queen's supervision until the middle of October, but without any definite result.[1]

The failure of the colloquy of Poissy was only one aspect of the more general failure of the government's policy of conciliation, and in less than a year the religious wars had begun which were to wrack French society and institutions almost to the end of the century.[2] Yet Poissy was not forgotten. Among some of the Huguenots the idea of resuming the abruptly concluded discussions between Catholics and Protestants had a powerful appeal. It seemed to substitute rational for irrational procedures in the resolution of France's religious problems and to hold out the promise that through a specifically French conference a settlement could be found in which the interests of the Protestants would be adequately represented. If the circle of those who kept the idea alive had been confined to theologians and political commentators, the appeal for a return to Poissy might have been an interesting but largely irrelevant item in the flourishing marketplace of ideas in late sixteenth and early seventeenth-century France. But as shrewd and hardheaded a politician as Henry of Navarre was deeply attracted to it, and in his hands this irenical and somewhat utopian idea came surprisingly close to being realised.

It was the huguenot soldier and diplomatist, Philippe Duplessis-Mornay, who made the explicit suggestion to Henry, in 1580, that he take the initiative in convening a conference between Catholics and Protestants.[3] It was not to be concerned with the whole of France, however, only with Béarn, Henry's hereditary territory on the Spanish border, where the exercise of the catholic religion had been forbidden under the terms of a reformation carried out by Henry's

[1] Philippe de Félice, 'Le Colloque de Poissy, 1561.' *Bulletin de la Société de l'histoire du protestantisme français*, CVII (Paris 1961) pp 133–45; Joseph Lecler, *Toleration and the Reformation*, 2 vols (London 1960) II, pp 55–67.

[2] Heritier, *Catherine de Medici*, pp 188–210; [Georges] Livet, *Les guerres de religion* [(1559–1598)] (Paris 1966) pp 7–25.

[3] [Philippe Duplessis]-Mornay, *Mémoires et correspondance*, 12 vols (Paris 1824–25) II, pp 94–9; [Raoul] Patry, *Philippe du Plessis-Mornay: [Un Huguenot homme d'état (1549–1623)]* (Paris 1933) pp 20–54.

mother.[1] King Henry III of France was now demanding that Catholics be given the freedom to exercise their religion there. To refuse, as Mornay pointed out, would allow the king to say that Navarre was asking for something for his protestant followers in France which he was unwilling to allow his catholic subjects in his own territories. But rather than grant the request outright, Mornay urged that the king of Navarre convene a conference or council at which representatives of both religious traditions would participate, in order to give his people satisfaction. Théodore de Bèze might be among the French Protestants invited, and catholic spokesmen from abroad were to be allowed to enter under sufficient guarantees for their protection. It is clear from Mornay's description of such a conference that he expected that once the authority of the Scriptures for faith and practice had been established the protestant spokesmen would have little difficulty in defending successfully the reformed character of the Church in Béarn against catholic objections. But the king of France, he argued, could hardly find anything to object to in this procedure, since it would be following the example of the colloquy of Poissy, and in any case the settlement could then be submitted to a free council.

Henry did not take up this suggestion for Béarn, but he made the call for a council a prominent feature of his campaign for political support in the struggle against the Catholic League. The League had entered a new phase on the last day of December 1584 with the signing of a treaty involving Spain, the French family of Guise, and the cardinal of Bourbon, commiting them to the extirpation of Protestantism in France and the exclusion of the heretical Henry of Navarre from the French throne. On 31 March 1585 they issued a manifesto declaring their opposition to Henry and their determination to defend Catholicism.[2] The answer by Navarre's party was a *Remonstrance* to France, written by Mornay. The Guises, it said, were seeking power only for themselves and were using religion as a pretext. The present king, Henry III, would be able to see through their nefarious plans. They claimed to desire 'only one religion in France', which was, said the *Remonstrance*, 'the common hope of all men of good will, and of all Christians.' But what means did they advocate? Only force and violence, and these had long ago been shown to be ineffectual in matters of conscience.[3] As for the succession to the throne, why did

---

[1] Nancy L. Roelker, *Queen of Navarre: Jeanne d'Albret, 1528–1572* (Cambridge, Mass, 1968) pp 265–78.
[2] Patry, *Philippe du Plessis-Mornay*, pp 99–100.
[3] Mornay, *Mémoires et correspondance*, III, pp 49–51, 55–7.

this matter so concern them, as the present king was young and well. If, however, the king were to die childless and Henry of Navarre was his successor, what then? To expect the king of Navarre to renounce the faith in which he had been brought up would be to require of him an inconstancy quite unworthy of a king of France. But Henry was 'ready and will always be ready to receive instruction from a free and legitimate Council, and to abandon error, when it will be shown to him'.[1]

The *Remonstrance* was followed by a *Declaration* of the king of Navarre, on 10 June 1585, in which Henry affirmed his commitment to the christian faith, and more specifically to the word of God contained in the Old and New Testaments, to the creeds, and to the decisions of 'the most ancient, celebrated, and legitimate Councils'.[2] If a 'legitimate and holy council' were assembled, he was ready to acquiesce in its decisions. He was not the first to complain of abuses in the Church which needed reforming, nor did this make him a heretic or an enemy to the Church. The need for reformation had been a common cry for 500 years. The kings of France had not only exhorted the popes and other christian princes to reform the Church by means of a general council, they had, on their own authority, called councils for the reform of the Gallican Church. He urged the king to have 'a free and legitimate Council' convened.[3]

This call for a council was reiterated by Henry in the summer and autumn of 1585. In a letter to Henry III on 21 July he affirmed his willingness to abide by the decisions of a free council.[4] He developed his ideas in detail to the faculty of theology at the Sorbonne, the traditional home of conciliar theory, in a letter of 11 October 1585. Here he declared that France had the choice of either a civil war or a council, either the extermination of one party by the other or the reunion of the two parts of the realm in one. If the latter were followed, all Christendom might be drawn together as a result. His own preference was for a council, such as had been held in the past by their advice and guidance.[5] In the same month he sent another message to Henry III, regretting that the king seemed to be following the course advocated by the League, but assuring him that he and his followers were ready to heed the decisions of a council.[6] Mornay accompanied this with a

---

[1] *Ibid* pp 59–60, 62–3.   [2] *Ibid* p 90.   [3] *Ibid* pp 90–3.

[4] Henri IV, *Les plus belles lettres [de Henri IV]*, ed Philippe Erlanger (Paris 1962) p 26.

[5] *Ibid* pp 28–32.

[6] Mornay, *Mémoires et correspondance*, III, pp 195–8; Patry, *Philippe du Plessis-Mornay*, pp 108–12.

letter of his own, observing that when councils have been assembled, 'opinion has finally yielded to knowledge, darkness to light, verisimilitude to truth, sophistry to reason'.[1]

By March 1589 the League and the king of France were bitter enemies, the result of the overbearing manner of the leaguer chiefs in their relations with the court. This had led, in the preceding December to the assassination of the duke of Guise, by order of Henry III, who hardly bothered to deny his complicity.[2] While these sombre events were taking place, the three estates of the realm had been in session at Blois, and were no doubt profoundly shocked. Writing to them on 4 March, Henry of Navarre stressed the need for a peaceful solution to the problems of France. Force had achieved nothing. He and his followers had had to endure the assaults of ten armies in the past four years, but they were still standing firm. There was, however, a peaceful course which could be followed, namely the convening of a free council. 'Instruct me,' he invited, 'I am not opinionated.'[3] He would not only embrace truth when he was shown it, but he felt sure that his party would do so as well. This was the way of peace and union, of obedience and order, of concord and national strength. In the meantime he would see to it that Catholics in his own realms were not constrained in the free exercise of their religion and that the Catholic Church was under his protection in the cities which he controlled.[4]

The delineation of the project for a council in manifestoes and despatches from the headquarters of Henry of Navarre in 1585 and afterwards provides the context for understanding the well-known *Declaration* of the new king Henry IV on 4 August 1589. The enmity between Henry III and the League had led, almost inevitably, to an alliance between the kings of France and Navarre. In fact, the reconciliation between the two, on 30 April 1589, had been very cordial, and they had kept in close touch in the following months.[5] The assassination of Henry III on 1 August, by a catholic zealot, not only brought Henry of Navarre to the throne, but gave him the opportunity of gaining the late king's supporters in the continuing war with the League. Henry IV's *Declaration* would seem to be aimed at them as well as at moderate Catholics throughout the realm. The heart of the

---

[1] Mornay, *Mémoires et correspondance*, III, p 202.
[2] [Hardouin de] Péréfixe, *Histoire du roy Henry le Grand* (rev ed, Amsterdam 1664) pp 95–105; Heritier, *Catherine de Medici*, pp 452–6.
[3] Mornay, *Mémoires et correspondance*, IV, pp 325, 327.
[4] *Ibid* pp 328–31, 340.   [5] Patry, *Philippe du Plessis-Mornay*, pp 154–62, 171–2.

document was in two promises. Henry vowed that he would 'maintain and preserve in our realm the Catholic, apostolic, and Roman religion in its entirety, without innovating or changing anything in it'. In addition, he stated that in accordance with 'the open declaration made by us before our advancement to this crown, we are altogether ready, and desire nothing more than to be instructed by a good, legitimate and free Council, general or national'. He promised that he would see that such a council were convened in six months, or sooner if possible.[1]

Since the war showed no signs of ending after Henry's accession, it is perhaps not surprising that such a council failed to materialise within the stated period of six months. In November 1590, however, a declaration was written on this subject. The king, it said, had found his realm full of ills and dissensions upon his accession.[2] Differences in religion had been the cause of bitter divisions and these had led to a contest of arms which threatened to extinguish all religion, of whatever kind. He was therefore determined to reunite the hearts and wills of his subjects and lead them back to the true service of God by composing their differences in religion. After long and mature deliberation 'with the princes of our blood, cardinals, officers of our crown, notables and great personages of our counsel, of our courts of parlement and others of this realm,' he had resolved to endeavour with all his power to procure a general council, in which could be determined all the differences in religion which had for so long tormented christendom.[3] He asked for the support of all christian princes and states concerned about the hardening of the religious schism. Such a council ought not to be denied, in view of the circumstances in which ecumenical councils had been called in the past. Moreover, this was not a case simply of winning back some individual or diocese to the Church, but 'of several kings, princes, republics, entire nations, of an infinite number of learned persons; and, in sum, of several millions of souls'. These men could be convinced, taught, and set on the right path by a general council; they could never be so won over by inquisitions or battles.[4]

If, however, 'by human malice,' it proved impossible, despite all he could do, to bring about this universal good, 'so much desired by all Christians', the king intended 'to convoke a national Council in

[1] Mornay, *Mémoires et correspondance*, IV, p 381; J. H. Mariéjol, *Histoire de France*, ed E. Lavisse, VI, pt I (Paris 1911) p 304.
[2] Mornay, *Mémoires et correspondance*, IV, p 493.   [3] *Ibid* p 496.
[4] *Ibid* p 497.

our realm, free, holy, and legitimate, in order to be instructed thereby,'
and to compose the religious differences among his subjects, cutting
'the root, insofar as we are able, of the troubles, miseries, and calamities
of this realm'.[1] If, because of some unanticipated difficulty, even
this should be impossible, he would make provision, within a year,
for the convening of 'some holy and notable ecclesiastical assembly
of the most holy, learned, wise, and serious persons of the realm'.
In the meantime, Catholics and Protestants were guaranteed the
exercise of their religion on terms earlier agreed to with Henry III.
The king hoped that this would dispose them to 'the true reconciliation of differences such as we are proposing'.[2]

This formulary, drawn up by Mornay, was approved in the king's
council, and ordered sent to the parlement at Tours in order to be
registered there. The order, however, was countermanded, and the
declaration was never issued. Apparently some of the king's catholic
counsellors felt that the specific guarantees to Protestants in the document went too far.[3] The high-water mark in the campaign for a
national or general council had been reached. The idea survived for
another twenty years, and even enjoyed a considerable vogue, but
Henry IV's apparently firm promise to see that a general or national
council was convened never came this close to fulfilment again.

The circumstances of the king's 'conversion' could, however, be
taken as fulfilling some of his announced intentions. By the spring of
1592 some of the more moderate Leaguers were prepared to accept
Henry IV, but only on the condition that he receive instruction with
the intention of entering the Roman Catholic Church – a condition
which Henry seems to have accepted.[4] In spite of the risk of losing his
protestant allies at home and abroad the king proceeded with this
plan in the following year. On 15 July 1593 he assembled a group of
bishops at Mantes and discussed matters of doctrine with them, making
it clear that what he wished to do was to make a general profession
of his adherence to the catholic faith. He evidently did not require
much instruction, as he made his formal abjuration of Protestantism
at the abbey of Saint-Denis on 28 July.[5] He had thus received instruction, which he accepted, at the hands of an ecclesiastical assembly,

[1] *Ibid* p 497.   [2] *Ibid* pp 498–503.
[3] *Ibid* p 504; Patry, *Philippe du Plessis-Mornay*, pp 194–9.
[4] Patry, *Philippe du Plessis-Mornay*, p 219.
[5] Charlotte Arbaleste, Mme de Mornay, *Mémoires*, ed Mme de Witt, 1 (Paris 1868)
pp 262–6; Jacques Bongars, *Lettres Latines* (Paris 1668) pp 244, 248, 285, 288 – letters to
Camerarius in Nuremberg, July–November 1593.

but without, of course, allowing the representatives of the protestant churches to be heard. In fact, however, he did hear their representatives at Mantes in the autumn of the same year, but by then the question of the treatment to be accorded Protestants in France was a more pressing subject for discussion than the king's own doctrinal beliefs.[1]

But this did not mark the end of Henry's interest in the project of a council. In the September following the ceremony at Saint-Denis, Mornay, dismayed by the recent turn of events, went to see the king at Chartres. Henry spent some three hours with him, going over the reasons for his actions. He had found himself 'on the edge of such a precipice,' he said, that he had little other room for action. He declared, however, that 'his heart would remain always the same towards the Religion and those who made profession of it'.[2] As for the problem of religious differences in the realm he considered that it was serious largely because of the animosity of preachers. But he hoped that one day, by his authority, he would be able to compose these differences. It was Mornay who then brought up the subject of a council, and went over some of the difficulties in the way. Mornay argued that before 'the reunion of religions and the extinction of schism in France' could be achieved, two things had to happen: the king had to be absolutely established in his state and 'liberty restored to the Gallican Church'. Otherwise the pope would be able to prevent the convening of a national council in France, which was, Mornay thought, 'the most certain way to proceed, by the public discussion of the religions, to reach an accord on the difference between them'.[3]

If the king was still interested in this possibility, even after his conversion, so were a good many of his subjects. The 1590s saw, in fact, an outpouring of literature, by Protestants and by moderate Catholics, stressing the right of the Gallican Church to settle its own affairs, and pointing to the broad areas of belief and practice on which Catholics and Protestants in France were already in agreement.[4] To Protestants like Jean Hotman de Villiers or Jean de Serres it appeared that fairly minor adjustments to the two traditions would enable all Frenchmen to worship God in a single national church. Henry IV

[1] Patry, *Philippe du Plessis-Mornay*, pp 241–54; Mme de Mornay, *Mémoires*, I, pp 269–71.
[2] Mme de Mornay, *Mémoires*, I, p 267. 'The Religion' was the term normally used by Huguenots to denote their protestant faith.
[3] Mme de Mornay, *Mémoires*, I, pp 267–8.
[4] Corrado Vivanti, *Lotta politica e pace religiosa in Francia fra Cinque e Seicento* (Turin 1963) pp 132–291.

interested himself in these proposals, and perhaps encouraged them. They were considerably less appealing to official synods of the reformed Churches, which apparently feared that the court was working covertly to win Protestants in France back to the Roman obedience.[1] The edict of Nantes, in 1598, was not a step directly towards the reconciliation of Catholics and Protestants, but by guaranteeing the right of Protestants to exercise their religion under specified conditions, it at least gave them a secure position in French society from which they might negotiate a religious settlement with their catholic fellow-countrymen.

About 1600, the same year in which Duplessis-Mornay was humiliated in a theological disputation with the bishop of Evreux at the court at Fontainebleau, Madame de Mornay felt that there was a change in Henry's attitude towards his former co-religionists.[2] The king apparently made it clear to Protestants in the court circle that he wished them to be converted to Catholicism. He spoke sometimes to catholic associates as if he were a zealot for the advancement of the Roman Church. Mornay dropped from the king's favour, and never recovered his former position of prominence. Yet Madame de Mornay also reported that the king sometimes spoke warmly of the prospect of a national council, to which some protestant ministers would be invited, where the differences in religion in France would be settled.[3] Mornay himself was so sufficiently convinced that a council might still be forthcoming that he drew up a memorandum on the subject in June 1600, stressing the need for the provinces of the French reformed Churches to keep themselves informed about developments in this direction.[4]

The project for a council even enjoyed something of a revival at court in 1607 and 1608. It was in early December 1607 that Théodore Agrippa d'Aubigné, the soldier, poet, and former huguenot associate of Henry of Navarre, paid a visit to Paris and learned from a group of protestant ministers that the city was buzzing with rumours of an accord between the two religions. On visiting the court he was sent by Henry to cardinal du Perron, with whom he discussed the possible basis of an agreement. The cardinal seemed determined that if satisfaction could not be obtained from Rome, the matter would have to be

[1] Livet, *Les guerres de religion*, pp 47–50.
[2] Mme de Mornay, *Mémoires*, I, pp 368–78; Patry, *Philippe du Plessis-Mornay*, pp 381–93.
[3] Mme de Mornay, *Mémoires*, I, p 393.
[4] Mornay, *Mémoires et correspondance*, IX, pp 393–6.

settled in Paris.[1] The protestant pastor Daniel Chamier learned in January 1608 from the bishop of Aire that there was now more talk at court than ever of a conference between Catholics and Protestants, and that the king himself had broached the subject to him.[2] Chamier finally obtained an interview with the king on 12 March 1608, at which this project was discussed. Henry apparently said that he would give his arm to be able to reunite his subjects in the same faith. For the purpose of such a reconciliation he had in mind to assemble a council, and he needed the assistance of the Protestants. Chamier assured him that the pastors would give such a project every support as they had formerly done at the colloquy of Poissy.[3] Two days later Chamier also spoke to the chancellor, who indicated his firm support of the project for a council. Chamier agreed to back the plan with his efforts and prayers, but expressed the hope that the catholic representatives not be allowed to thwart such a worthy design, as had happened at Poissy.[4]

The moderate Catholic Pierre de l'Estoile, who recorded in his *Journal* with evident enthusiasm the moves made in these years towards a religious reconciliation, also sounded a note of pessimism in the autumn of 1608. Commenting on a protestant treatise on the proposed national council, he expressed regret that it was not likely to be well-received by all readers, since whatever was avowed by one side would be infallibly rejected by the other.[5] L'Estoile's gloomy forecast seemed borne out by the unsuccessful negotiations of the last years of the reign of Henry IV.

The failure of such an ambitious project is not surprising; the fact that it engaged for such a long time the attention of one of Europe's dominant political figures is perhaps more so. What, precisely, had he hoped to achieve? There were, it seems, three phases in what might be called Henry's conciliar diplomacy. In the first, from 1585 to 1600, Henry had put forward the project of a national council, with the stated objective of achieving a religious settlement in France, on the basis of the liberties of the Gallican Church. The more urgent objective was to frame a platform on which could be united two rather divergent groups, the Huguenots on the one hand and the moderate Catholic,

---

[1] Théodore Agrippa d'Aubigné, *Mémoires* (Amsterdam 1731) pp 156–61; [Daniel] Chamier, *Journal* [*de son voyage à la cour de Henri IV en 1607*], ed Charles Read (Paris 1858), pp 40, 306–8.   [2] Chamier, *Journal*, pp 44–5.
[3] *Ibid* pp 57–61.   [4] *Ibid* pp 61–2.
[5] Pierre de l'Estoile, *Journal pour le règne de Henri IV*, ed André Martin, II (Paris 1958) pp 373, 377.

Gallican, *politique* party on the other. It was this combination of supporters which enabled him to defeat the ultramontanist Catholic League and to lead France out of the chaos of the civil wars. From 1600 to about 1607 the situation had changed. Henry had established himself securely on the throne, and had given some satisfaction to both his catholic and protestant subjects – to the former by his conversion, to the latter by the edict of Nantes. But the king was still under considerable pressure from the forces of ultramontanist Catholicism – the papacy, catholic powers abroad, catholic zealots at home – and hesitated to give the impression that he was moving towards apostasy. Thus the project for a council languished. But beginning in about 1607 and continuing to the end of his reign Henry was engaged in forming an international alliance of states, mostly protestant, for a war against the Habsburg monarchy, the war which the catholic Ravaillac prevented by his act of violence in 1610.[1] In forming this anti-Habsburg alliance Henry had served as godfather and protector to the protestant union of states, formed in 1608. Along with this revival of the old huguenot alliance went a revival of the old huguenot project of a return to Poissy. No doubt the king wished to see a *rapprochement* between French Catholics and Protestants at home much as he wished to see such a *rapprochement* abroad.

Yet, in the end, there is an element of idealism in the project which does not seem to be entirely accounted for by Henry's political motives. Henry's adviser, Sully, spoke of the king's 'grand design' for a European peace – a plan which, it has been claimed, was more Sully's invention after the king's death than it ever was Henry's.[2] Henry's earliest biographer, Péréfixe, spoke of the king's desire for a christian commonwealth of Europe, free from political and religious dissensions.[3] The visionary element which these two observers saw in Henry of Navarre was evidently that which also caught Mornay's eye. Underneath the pragmatist and the witty aphorist, there was something of the prophet.

---

[1] L. Anquez, *Henri IV et l'Allemagne, d'après les mémoires et la correspondance de Jacques Bongars* (Paris 1887) pp 121–32; Roland Mousnier, *L'Assassinat d'Henri IV: 14 Mai 1610* (Paris 1964) pp 1–6, 101–22, and *passim*.
[2] *Sully's Grand Design of Henri IV*, ed David Ogg (London 1921) esp pp 3–12.
[3] Péréfixe, *Histoire du roy Henry le Grand*, pp 445–6, 511–12.

ORTHODOX AND CATHOLICS IN THE SEVENTEENTH CENTURY: SCHISM OR INTERCOMMUNION?

by K. T. WARE

EVENT OR PROCESS?

FOR use on the first Sunday in Lent, the service books of the Greek Orthodox Church include a special office known as 'The *Synodikon* of Orthodoxy', which contains no less than sixty anathemas against different heresies and heresiarchs.[1] Yet in this comprehensive denunciation there is one unexpected omission: no reference is made to the errors of the Latins, no allusion to the *Filioque* or the papal claims, even though more than a third of the anathemas date from the eleventh to the fourteenth centuries, a time when doctrinal disagreements between East and West had emerged clearly into the open. This omission of the Latins is an indication of the curious imprecision which prevails in the relations between Orthodoxy and Rome. It is altogether obvious that an estrangement has long existed between the Greek East and the Latin West. What is much less obvious is the precise point at which this estrangement evolved into a definitive schism, into a clear and final breach in sacramental communion. The division between the two halves of Christendom did not occur as a single event, accomplished once and for all at a specific moment in history: it was, on the contrary, a gradual, fluctuating, and disjointed process,[2] stretching over a remarkably extended period.

Despite the reappraisal of the history of the schism, following on the researches of Dvornik, Runciman, and others, it is still not generally realised how complicated this gradual and disjointed process was, and how slow in coming to its final conclusion: perhaps, indeed, the process never has been finally concluded. Long after the anathemas of

---

[1] For the text of the *Synodikon*, see Τριῴδιον κατανυκτικόν (Apostoliki Diakonia, Athens 1960) pp 144–51. Compare also J. Gouillard, 'Le Synodikon de l'Orthodoxie: édition et commentaire', *Travaux et Mémoires*, II (Centre de recherche d'histoire et civilisation byzantines, Paris 1967) pp 1–316.

[2] I take this phrase from Fr Gervase Mathew, OP: see *The Eastern Churches Quarterly*, VI, 5 (Ramsgate 1946) p 227, and compare [G.] Every, [SSM,] *Misunderstandings [between East and West]*, Ecumenical Studies in History, No 4 (London 1965) p 9.

1054, long after the sack of Constantinople in 1204, long after the formal repudiation of the Union of Florence in 1484, Greeks and Latins continued in practice quietly to ignore the separation and to behave as if no breach in communion had occurred. Instances of *communicatio in sacris* are especially abundant in the seventeenth century, and if we are to speak of a 'final consummation' of the schism, perhaps this should not be placed earlier than the years 1725-50.

In the relations between Old and New Rome a recurrent pattern may be distinguished. A sharp dispute occurs between the two, leading to acute tension and even to mutual excommunications; yet on neither side are these excommunications treated as conclusive, and within a few decades the dispute is ignored or forgotten. In 863-7, for example, we see pope Nicolas I seeking to assert supreme jurisdiction over the East; his claim was rejected at Constantinople by patriarch Photius; communion was broken off, and in his encyclical letter of 867 to the other eastern patriarchs,[1] Photius accused the West of heresy concerning the procession of the Holy Spirit. In this way the traditional causes of disagreement between East and West – the *Filioque* and the papal claims – had already emerged plainly and unambiguously as early as the middle of the ninth century, and had led to an open breach in ecclesiastical relations. Yet the schism was very far from complete. Ten years later, when Photius returned to the patriarchal throne for a second period of office (877), he was in communion once more with the Roman see. Neither he nor the popes who succeeded Nicolas I withdrew explicitly from the positions adopted by the two sides in 863-7, but both parties abstained prudently from pushing the argument to its logical conclusion. Rome did not press her claim to jurisdiction in the East, while Constantinople suffered the charge of heresy to lie dormant. Although the basic grounds of disagreement remained unresolved, each side was content to pass them over in silence for the time being.

The conflict in the middle of the eleventh century was equally indecisive. In the summer of 1054, when cardinal Humbert and patriarch Michael Cerularius anathematised one another, each was at pains to restrict the scope of his excommunication: Humbert directed his anathema against Cerularius and his followers personally, not against the Greek Church as such, while Cerularius and the synod at Constantinople were equally careful to excommunicate Humbert but not the pope or the Roman Church.[2] Admittedly, since the

---

[1] For the text, see *PG* 102 (1860) cols 721-41.
[2] See *PL* 143 (1853) cols 1004B; *PG* 120 (1864) col 748B.

papacy took no steps whatever to disown Humbert's action, his excommunication and the reply of Cerularius came to acquire a wider application, involving not only the two protagonists as individuals but also their Churches. Yet in 1089, when the emperor asked the synod at Constantinople why the pope's name was not commemorated in the diptychs, the bishops in their answer made no reference to the anathemas of 1054, but chose to regard the estrangement as something existing *de facto* but not *de jure*. 'Not by a synodical judgement and examination', they stated, 'was the Church of Rome removed from communion with us, but as it seems from our want of watchful care (ἀσυντηρήτως) the pope's name was not commemorated in the holy diptychs.'[1]

Recognising the inconclusive nature of the 1054 quarrel, several recent writers have drawn attention to the effect of the Crusades, and more especially the sack of Constantinople in 1204, in widening the division within Christendom. Sir Steven Runciman, for example, treats the events of 1204 as marking the 'final consummation' of the schism, if not juridically, then at any rate psychologically. 'The Fourth Crusade', he observes, 'could never be forgiven nor forgotten by the Christians of the East. Thenceforward there was definite schism between the Greek and the Latin Churches.'[2] But the rift was not as absolute as might at first appear. When Greeks and Latins met at the council of Ferrara–Florence in 1438–9, from the outset they treated one another as members of the same Christian Church, albeit mutually alienated. Neither side required the other to do penance as schismatics or heretics, and then to undergo a formal ceremony of reconciliation to the Church. Each acted towards the other as if there were a schism *within* the Church, not a schism by one or other party *from* the Church. 'Let the heavens rejoice and let the earth be glad', stated the preamble to the decree of union promulgated on 6 July 1439. 'For the wall, which divided the Western and the Eastern Church, has been removed from our midst (*sublatus est enim de medio paries, qui occidentalem orientalemque dividebat ecclesiam*).'[3] The 'wall', be it noted, is *inside* the Church. The decree does not say that the East has hitherto been separated from the communion of the Catholic Church and is now being received back: neither side is 'received back', for

---

[1] Greek text in W. Holtzmann, 'Die Unionsverhandlungen zwischen Kaiser Alexios I. und Papst Urban II. im Jahre 1089', *Byzantinische Zeitschrift*, XXVIII (Leipzig 1928) p 60: cited by G. Every, *The Byzantine Patriarchate 451–1204* (2 ed, London 1962) p 180. [2] *The Eastern Schism* (Oxford 1955) p 151.
[3] Text in J. Gill, *The Council of Florence* (Cambridge 1959) p 412.

both are already within. The reunion council, on this interpretation, did no more than render explicit an underlying unity which had never been wholly destroyed.

But what of the events which followed the fall of the Byzantine empire? In 1484 a synod was held in Constantinople, attended by the four eastern patriarchs, at which a special service was drawn up 'for those who return from the Latin heresies to the Orthodox and Catholic Church'. The convert was required to renounce the 'shameful and alien dogmas of the Latins', to pronounce anathema on all who add *Filioque* to the Creed, and to repudiate the Union of Florence; he also promised to 'abstain completely from Latin services'. After this he was anointed with the holy chrism (μύρον).[1] Here, it may well be thought, was an official and definitive severance of communion. The Greeks treated the Latins as heretics, who could be admitted to the sacraments only after a formal abjuration of errors and chrismation. From the Latin viewpoint the Greeks were now schismatics, perhaps also heretics, for they had expressly rejected the dogmatic decisions of the ecumenical council of Florence. It was, surely, no longer a question of mere estrangement but of open division.

Yet the historical reality turns out to be more complicated. Despite the Greek synod of 1484, despite a constant flow of polemical literature from either side – but more especially from the Greeks – in actual practice relations between Catholics and Orthodox often continued to be extraordinarily amicable, above all during the years 1600–1700. In the many regions of the Levant where members of the two Churches dwelt side by side, if there was sometimes tension on the local level, more frequently there was friendly cooperation, and not only co-operation but intercommunion. Within the Venetian dominions it was the normal policy of the Latin authorities to do everything possible to encourage harmony between their catholic and orthodox subjects; within the Ottoman empire, servitude to the infidel made Greeks and Latins alike more conscious of the common heritage which they shared as Christians.

Writing at Rome in the 1640s, the Greek Catholic Leo Allatius remarked of the contemporary situation:

[1] The text of this service is given in I. N. Karmiris, Τὰ Δογματικὰ καὶ Συμβολικὰ Μνημεῖα τῆς 'Ορθοδόξου Καθολικῆς 'Εκκλησίας, ΙΙ (Athens 1953) pp 987–9. Orthodox writers occasionally describe the synod of 1484 as 'ecumenical', see, for example, G. A. Rallis and M. Potlis, Σύνταγμα τῶν θείων καὶ ἱερῶν κανόνων, V (Athens 1855) p 143, but it should more correctly be styled 'local', compare P. N. Trembelas, Δογματικὴ τῆς 'Ορθοδόξου Καθολικῆς 'Εκκλησίας, Ι (Athens 1959) p 136, n 53.

Orthodox and Catholics: schism or intercommunion?

The Greeks show no abhorrence for intermarriage with the Latins; they frequent the Latin churches, they attend the divine offices, the church sermons, and all the other functions of the Latins, and they entrust their sons for education at Latin hands...Greeks with Latins, and Latins with Greeks, attend worship and celebrate services indiscriminately (*promiscue*) in the churches of either rite.[1]

Allatius is not always a reliable witness, but in this instance there is plentiful evidence to show that he was not exaggerating.[2] There were not only mixed marriages between Greeks and Latins: in many Greek islands there were also mixed churches, with parallel naves and two adjacent sanctuaries, one for the Greek and the other for the Latin rite.[3] Roman Catholics were accepted as godparents at orthodox baptisms, and *vice-versa*. Latin missionaries from the west, in the absence of a bishop of their own Church, behaved towards the local orthodox hierarch as if they recognised him for their ordinary, seeking faculties from him, asking formally for permission to work in his diocese. The orthodox authorities on their side welcomed the Jesuits and other religious orders as friends and allies, and even took the initiative in summoning them to undertake pastoral duties among their flocks. With the blessing of the Greek bishops, catholic priests preached in orthodox churches, heard the confessions of orthodox faithful, and gave them holy communion. When Greeks wished to embrace Roman Catholicism, the Latin missionaries usually rested content with a secret act of submission, and instructed their converts to receive the sacraments as before at orthodox altars. In the light of all this, the question can scarcely be avoided: How far is it legitimate to speak of a definitive schism or irrevocable breach between Orthodoxy and Rome in the seventeenth century?

Needless to say, local conditions varied considerably, and relations were not uniformly cordial. Contacts were closest in the Ionian and Aegean islands. Outside the Turkish empire, on the other hand, in Russia there was no cordiality at all: so consuming was the hatred felt by orthodox Russians for catholic Poles, particularly after the Polish

[1] *De Ecclesiae Occidentalis atque Orientalis Perpetua Consensione* (Cologne 1648; photo-graphic reprint with new introduction by K. T. Ware, Gregg International Press, Westmead 1970) cols 979–80, 1059.

[2] A vast inventory of acts of *communicatio in sacris* during the seventeenth century is supplied by [P.] Grigoriou-Garo, Σχέσεις [καθολικῶν καὶ ὀρθοδόξων] (Athens 1958). The main evidence is briefly summarised by [Timothy (K. T.)] Ware, *Eustratios Argenti: [A Study of the Greek Church under Turkish Rule]* (Oxford 1964) pp 17–23, 36–7.

[3] See A. K. Sarou, Περὶ μεικτῶν ναῶν ὀρθοδόξων καὶ καθολικῶν ἐν Χίῳ, in 'Επετηρὶς 'Εταιρείας Βυζαντινῶν Σπουδῶν, XIX (Athens 1949) pp 194–208; Grigoriou-Garo, Σχέσεις, pp 25–6, 34–41, 57.

incursions in the 'Time of Troubles' (1601–13), that during the first half of the seventeenth century catholic converts to Orthodoxy were not only chrismated by the Russians but rebaptised. In the eastern Mediterranean during the seventeenth century there were few if any instances of such intense hostility, but widespread anti-Latin feeling was displayed on occasion in Constantinople, in Jerusalem, and on the Holy Mountain of Athos. Yet when full allowance is made for all the exceptions, the fact remains that in the years 1600–1700 vast numbers of Catholics and Orthodox, educated clergy as well as simple believers, acted as though no schism existed between East and West.

THE JESUITS AND THEIR 'TROJAN HORSE' POLICY

Some of the most striking examples of catholic-orthodox cooperation are to be found in the story of the jesuit missions in the Levant during the seventeenth century.[1] The Jesuits could have chosen to treat the Orthodox strictly as schismatics or even heretics, refusing all collaboration and common worship with them, aiming simply to win over individual Greek converts whom they would then place in self-contained communities, under their own immediate care and wholly independent of the orthodox congregations. This, with certain qualifications, was normally the course recommended by the Holy Office and the Congregation of the Propaganda at Rome.[2] The practice of

---

[1] For contemporary accounts of these missions, see [François] Richard, [SJ,] *Relation [de ce qui s'est passé de plus remarquable à Sant-Erini isle de l'Archipel, depuis l'établissement des Pères de la Compagnie de Iésus en icelle]* (Paris 1657); the anonymous report dating from 1643 and perhaps by Fr Mathieu Hardy, SJ, entitled 'Relation [de ce qui s'est passé en la résidence des Pères de la Compagnie de Jésus establie à Naxie le 26 Septembre de l'année 1627'], ed [V.] Laurent, [*Echos d'Orient*], XXXIII (Paris 1934) pp 218–26, 354–75, and XXXIV (1935) pp 97–105, 179–204, 350–67, 473–81; [A.] Carayon, [SJ,] *Relations inédites [des Missions de la Compagnie de Jésus à Constantinople et dans le Levant au XVIIe siècle]* (Paris 1864). Compare [H.] Fouqueray, [SJ,] *Histoire [de la Compagnie de Jésus en France des origines à la suppression (1528–1762),]* 5 vols (Paris 1910–25) especially III, pp 200–15, 606–35; IV, pp 315–62; V, pp 341–89. There is much valuable material in the series of articles by V. Laurent, 'L'âge d'or des Missions latines dans le Levant (XVIIe–XVIIIe siècle)', *L'Unité de l'Eglise* (Paris) issues for 1934–5. For the work of the Capuchins in the Near East (who were usually more cautious and reserved than the Jesuits in the matter of *communicatio in sacris*), see Fr Hilaire de Barenton, FMC, *La France catholique en Orient durant les trois derniers siècles* (Paris 1902).

[2] See the articles by [W.] de Vries, SJ, 'Das Problem der "communicatio in sacris cum dissidentibus" im Nahen Osten zur Zeit der Union (17. und 18. Jahrhundert)', *Ostkirchliche Studien*, VI (Würtzburg 1957) pp 81–106; 'Eine Denkschrift zur Frage der "communicatio in sacris cum dissidentibus" aus dem Jahre 1721', *Ostkirchliche Studien*, VII (1958) pp 253–66; '"Communicatio in sacris": An Historical Study [of the Problem of Liturgical Services in Common with Eastern Christians Separated from Rome']', *Concilium* IV, 1 (London 1965) pp 11–22.

the Jesuits, however, was very different. Arriving in the Levant, they found the directives from the authorities in Rome strangely irrelevant and inapplicable to the local situation. Deeply impressed by the extent to which the christian East agreed with Catholicism, impressed also by the warm friendship which many Greeks showed towards them, they found it difficult to treat the Orthodox simply as aliens, as schismatics or heretics whom they must shun. In all essentials, so the Jesuits felt, the Greeks were brother Catholics – albeit Catholics who had drifted into certain errors and corruptions from which they required to be purged gently. Most of the Jesuits were devoted priests, with a strong pastoral conscience. Seeing the neglect and spiritual poverty from which the simple Greek believers suffered, and finding that their own ministrations were eagerly welcomed, they strove at once to render what help they could, without waiting for a formal 'reconciliation' of the Greek East to Rome. As in China, they displayed a remarkable flexibility and readiness for adaptation; but in the Levant this policy of accommodation could of course be carried much further, since those among whom they worked were fellow Christians.

It goes without saying that the ultimate aim of the Jesuits was to secure the full submission of Greek Orthodoxy to the Holy See – to reestablish the Union of Florence which, in their view, remained still theoretically in force, although unjustifiably repudiated in practice by the Greeks. But they were shrewd enough to realise that they could achieve more by pastoral collaboration than by polemics, more by courtesy and conciliation than by an aggressive proselytism. Instead of engaging in the kind of negative apologetics which underlined the points of divergence between East and West, they strove to win the confidence and affection of the Greeks, to infiltrate among them, and so to work upon them *from within*. Deliberately they adopted a 'Trojan horse' policy, not creating a Greek catholic community distinct from and in rivalry to the Greek orthodox, but fostering a catholic nucleus inside the canonical boundaries of the orthodox communion. This nucleus, so they hoped, would slowly grow until it was in a position to take over the leadership of the eastern patriarchates and to proclaim organic unity as a *fait accompli*.

It was a policy which came very near to success. In the initial stages most Orthodox overlooked the long-term aims which inspired jesuit friendship, and they gladly accepted western help without inquiring into its ulterior motives. Jesuit sermons were received with enthusiasm. On his first arrival at Smyrna in 1624, Fr Jérôme Queyrot,

SJ, was at once invited to preach in the Greek church of St George, and this he continued to do regularly on festivals and during Lent. He was also allowed to teach the catechism to Greek children: at the end of each class he took care to insert a prayer for the pope, which he made all the children recite together.[1] Probably this particular detail escaped the notice of the orthodox authorities. Ironically, when the Jesuits in Smyrna encountered opposition and hostility, it came not from the 'schismatic' Greeks but from their own catholic colleagues, the Capuchins. In the ensuing quarrel between the two groups of Latin religious, the Greek metropolitan Iakovos intervened vigorously on the jesuit side, and even wrote an appeal to Louis XIII of France. In his letter to the French king, he terms the Jesuits 'able teachers, zealous for the salvation of souls'. 'Since their establishment in our most holy archdiocese,' he continues, 'they have not ceased to help all kinds of Christians, alike by the good example of their life, by their preaching in our church, and by the instruction which they give to the children of our rite... These reverend fathers work much for the good and the salvation of Greeks, Latins, and Armenians.'[2] Clearly the Greek metropolitan looked on the Jesuits, not as enemies who had come to steal his sheep, but as trusted helpers in his pastoral tasks.

The same attitude was displayed by the orthodox authorities elsewhere. In 1630 the Greek metropolitan Ieremias of Naxos gave formal permission in writing, authorising the Jesuits to deliver sermons and hold catechism classes throughout his diocese. His successor Makarios renewed the authorisation but thought it wiser not to put it in writing. The Jesuits were clearly regarded as the best preachers in the island: it was members of the Society of Jesus, rather than the Greek clergy, who were asked to deliver the address at great feasts when the churches were packed with worshippers, and the Jesuits were regularly invited to preach in the Greek cathedral at liturgies celebrated by the metropolitan himself.[3]

The western missionaries were in demand not only as preachers but as confessors. A jesuit priest on Santorini claimed to have heard the confessions of some 400 Greeks in the space of four years;[4] another in

---

[1] Fouqueray, *Histoire*, IV, pp 344–5.
[2] 'Brième relation [de l'établissement des Pères de la Compagnie de Jésus en la ville de Smyrne...'], in Carayon, *Relations inédites*, pp 174–5: compare Fouqueray, *Histoire*, V, p 367.
[3] 'Relation', ed Laurent, XXXIV, pp 350–1, 353–4: compare the letter of Fr Mathieu Hardy in Carayon, *Relations inédites*, p 116.
[4] Richard, *Relation*, p 127.

Naxos spoke of confessing 600 Greeks in a much shorter period.[1] One reason for their popularity – or so the Jesuits themselves claimed – was that, unlike the Greek clergy, they did not demand money from their penitents![2] Now the hearing of confessions is manifestly a more delicate matter than the preaching of sermons: it is one thing to deliver a sermon to schismatics, but quite another to pronounce absolution on someone who chooses to remain formally in schism. Yet the Jesuits adopted an exceedingly lenient view. As a general rule they put no questions to their Greek penitents concerning the Church of Rome; still less did they demand of them any explicit abjuration of schism or act of submission to the Holy See. So long as they detected no evidence of active personal hostility against the papacy, they prudently refrained from inquiring into the dogmatic convictions of the Greeks who came to them for absolution.

Being human, the Greek clergy must sometimes have resented the popularity of the Jesuits, yet in many cases they displayed no signs of jealousy. One Jesuit recounts how, while he was talking to a village priest on the island of Naxos, a woman came up and asked the Greek *papas* for confession. 'Here is the confessor,' the Greek at once replied, pointing to the Jesuit, 'here is the father, make your confession to him': and he promptly withdrew, leaving her in the care of the Latin missionary.[3] This ministry of confession was normally performed with the knowledge and tacit consent of the local orthodox bishop, and sometimes, as at Smyrna, Aegina, and Naxos, with his explicit authorisation.[4] The Jesuits acted as regular confessors at the orthodox convent of St Nicolas in Santorini.[5] Sometimes Greek clergy and even bishops went to Latin priests for confession.[6]

Cases where western missionaries administered holy communion to Greek faithful are understandably less frequent. Because of their superior education and pastoral training, the Jesuits were in demand as preachers and spiritual fathers, but for holy communion the Greeks naturally tended to go to their own parish priests, who would administer the sacrament to them in the familiar way under both kinds. On occasion, however, acts of intercommunion certainly occurred. The

---

[1] Grigoriou-Garo, Σχέσεις, p 83.
[2] 'Relation', ed Laurent, XXXIV, pp 359–60.
[3] 'Relation', ed Laurent, XXXIV, p 357.
[4] 'Brième relation', pp 172–3; Fr F. Richard, SJ, in Grigoriou-Garo, Σχέσεις, p 83; Laurent, 'L'âge d'or', *L'Unité de l'Eglise*, No 72 (1935), p 477.
[5] Grigoriou-Garo, Σχέσεις, p 34.
[6] For examples, see Richard, *Relation*, p 135; Grigoriou-Garo, Σχέσεις, p 97.

dominican liturgist Jacques Goar, resident in Chios from 1631 to 1637, relates one such instance:

> If the [Greek Orthodox] bishops and parish clergy learn that some of the sheep in their flocks have turned aside to the pastures of the Latin Church and are receiving communion there, they are not in the least annoyed. On the contrary, they issue no public condemnation of such a course, thus by their silence implicitly commending it. I add, not something which I witnessed, but something which I myself did: with my own hands, publicly in the presence of all and in the sight of the church, I gave holy communion – under one kind – to some Greek deacons; and when their bishop learnt about it, he made no protest whatever.[1]

At Corpus Christi processions, the Orthodox behaved with marked reverence towards the Latin sacrament. The Chian Jesuit Andrea Rendi recounts how in 1630 the Greek metropolitan with another orthodox bishop went specially to a house from which they could conveniently observe the procession, while in front of the building they posted three priests in vestments, to cense the blessed sacrament as it passed.[2] On the predominantly orthodox island of Andros, the Greek bishop himself took part in the Latin Corpus Christi procession, accompanied by his clergy in full vestments, with candles and torches.[3]

So delighted were the orthodox authorities with Latin ministrations that they did not merely wait passively for the missionaries' arrival but actively encouraged them to come. In 1615 patriarch Theophanes of Jerusalem, after meeting the Jesuits during a visit to Constantinople, begged some of them to accompany him on his return to the Holy City: he promised them quarters in one of the Greek monasteries, which they could use as a centre for pastoral work among the Orthodox. The plan came to nothing, not because of orthodox hostility, but because of opposition from the Franciscans in Jerusalem, who had no wish to see the Jesuits established there.[4] In 1628 a former abbot from that stronghold of traditional Orthodoxy, the Holy Mountain, called on the officials of the Propaganda in Rome and requested a priest, to open a school on Athos for the monks.[5] In 1644

---

[1] Allatius, De...Perpetua Consensione, cols 1659–60; compare S. Salaville, Studia Orient-alia Liturgico-Theologica (Rome 1940) pp 54–61.

[2] Grigoriou-Garo, Σχέσεις, p 107.

[3] Hilaire de Barenton, La France catholique, p 175. For other examples, see Richard, Relation, pp 309–12; 'Relation', ed Laurent, xxxiv, pp 198–9; Grigoriou-Garo, Σχέσεις, pp 83, 112, 116.

[4] Fouqueray, Histoire, iii, p 618.

[5] G. Hofmann, 'Athos e Roma', Orientalia Christiana, xix (Rome 1925) pp 5–6, 29–31; Grigoriou-Garo, Σχέσεις, pp 163–74.

Orthodox and Catholics: schism or intercommunion?

the Greek patriarch of Antioch Euthymios asked the Jesuits to found a house in Damascus,[1] while in 1690 metropolitan Damaskinos of Aegina wrote directly to pope Innocent XI, with a request for two Jesuits to undertake pastoral work within his diocese.[2]

Père Besson spoke no more than the truth when he observed in his book *La Syrie sainte*: 'The Greeks and the Syrians open their houses to the apostolic men; they open even the doors of their churches and their pulpits. The parish priests welcome our assistance and the bishops beg us to cultivate their vineyards.'[3]

LATIN INTERPRETATIONS OF THE 'GREEK SCHISM'

Such are not the relationships which we should expect between two Christian communities divided by schism, and it may well be asked how the canonists and theologians on either side defended these acts of *communicatio in sacris*.

On the Greek side there seems to have been little or no attempt at theoretical justification. The official theology of the Greek Church throughout the seventeenth century remained fiercely polemical: though influenced by the thought forms and terminology of Latin scholasticism, it never ceased to chastise the Latins for their doctrinal deviations, treating them not just as schismatics but as heretics. If the Greek bishops acted differently in practice, this was not because of any special theory concerning the incomplete nature of the schism, but simply because of urgent pastoral necessity. They and their flocks were fighting for survival under the rule of a non-christian government; their own clergy were almost entirely simple and ill-educated; in desperate need of qualified preachers, catechists, and confessors, they turned naturally to the Latin missionaries.

The Latin missionaries, for their part, were likewise influenced by pragmatic considerations. The attitude of the Turkish authorities made it difficult for them to do otherwise than adopt the method of secret conversions. Religious minorities in the Ottoman empire were organised in a series of self-contained *millets* or 'nations'. There was a 'Roman' – that is, Greek Orthodox – *millet* under the patriarch of Constantinople; there were Armenian and Jewish *millets*; there were catholic communities of the Latin rite, which enjoyed the protection

---

[1] Fouqueray, *Histoire*, V, pp 382–3.
[2] G. Hofmann, 'Byzantinische Bischöfe und Rom', *Orientalia Christiana*, LXX (Rome 1931) pp 19–20.   [3] J. Besson, SJ, *La Syrie sainte* (Paris 1660), p 11.

of the western catholic powers, especially France. But there was no Greek Catholic or 'Uniate' *millet*. What, then, were the Jesuits to do with their Greek converts? They could admit them to the Latin rite, but this had two grave disadvantages: it made the act of conversion more difficult, since it required the Greek convert to adopt unfamiliar forms of worship; and it provoked Turkish suspicions, since a growth in the Latin rite implied an extension of the influence of the western powers within the Ottoman dominions. If they were to avoid trouble with the authorities and possible expulsion, the Jesuits had really no alternative to the 'Trojan horse' policy: they had to tell their Greek proselytes to remain outwardly where they were. The directives concerning *communicatio in sacris* from the authorities in Rome failed to take account of the concrete practicalities of the local situation.

But the Latin missionaries were not merely opportunists, for they were prepared to offer a reasoned defence of their conduct. The form which this theoretical justification took can best be illustrated from two books: *Quaestiones morales...de Apostolicis Missionibus* by the Theatine missionary Angelo Maria Verricelli, published at Venice in 1656; and *De Ecclesiae Occidentalis atque Orientalis Perpetua Consensione* by Leo Allatius, published at Cologne in 1648. The first provides a rationale of the missionaries' policy from the standpoint of canon law, the second from that of church history and theology.

Verricelli takes as his basis the decree *Ad evitanda scandala* of pope Martin V (1418),[1] which he considers applicable to the situation of the Greeks.[2] On this basis he argues that *communicatio in sacris* with heretics and schismatics is permissible, provided that the persons in question have not been excommunicated *publice et nominatim*.[3] Heretical hierarchs, even those who are 'notorious', retain power of jurisdiction, so long as they have not been condemned by name; *a fortiori* the same is true of mere schismatics.[4] Since the four eastern patriarchs and the Greek hierarchy in general have not been condemned *publice et nominatim*, they are to be treated as true bishops of the Church, endowed with genuine spiritual authority, and common worship with them is not excluded.

Verricelli proceeds to give specific examples of what he has in mind. A catholic priest may attend a schismatic Greek liturgy, vested

---

[1] Mansi, xxvii, cols 1192D–93A. For the importance of this decree for the question of *communicatio in sacris*, see de Vries, '"Communicatio in sacris": An Historical Study', p 13.

[2] *Quaestiones*, p 207.

[3] *Quaestiones*, p 138.

[4] *Quaestiones*, pp 139, 465.

in a cope.[1] A Catholic may request the sacraments of confession or communion from a schismatic Greek priest, even *extra mortis articulum*.[2] A Greek, converted to Catholicism, may continue to receive the sacraments from schismatic and heretical Greek clergy.[3] A Catholic may receive ordination from a Greek bishop, even from one who is a 'notorious heretic or schismatic', provided that the hierarch in question has not been excommunicated *nominatim*.[4] A Greek priest, converted to Catholicism, need not mention the name of the pope when celebrating mass, but may continue to commemorate a bishop or patriarch who is a 'notorious heretic'.[5]

Here, then, is a church lawyer fully prepared to justify, on canonical grounds, all that the Latin missionaries were doing in the Near East. Admittedly, Verricelli speaks of the Greek Orthodox as schismatics and heretics,[6] but the cumulative effect of his recommendations is that in practice they are to be treated as nothing of the sort. It is significant that Verricelli's book appeared at Venice, where the writ of the Inquisition did not run. It is doubtful whether such a work could have been published at Rome, with the blessing of the Holy Office and the Propaganda.

Allatius goes much more deeply into the whole question than Verricelli. Passing beyond the level of canon law, he raises the basic issue of principle: Has there ever been, and does there exist today, a complete schism between the christian East and Rome? During the middle years of the seventeenth century, precisely at the time when Allatius was writing, western scholars were beginning to formulate what may conveniently be styled the 'standard view' of the eastern schism. This 'standard view' is set forth succinctly by a personal friend of Allatius, the French Oratorian Jean Morin, in the opening pages of his monumental *Commentarius de Sacris Ecclesiae Ordinationibus*.[7] In this work Morin was concerned to prove that, ever since the start of the schism, Rome had never called in question the validity of schismatic Greek ordinations; and it was therefore important for him to

---

[1] *Quaestiones*, p 145.
[2] *Quaestiones*, p 152. But Verricelli admits that others hold an opposite view on this point, and he only defends his opinion as *probabilis*.   [3] *Quaestiones*, p 753.
[4] *Quaestiones*, pp 492–3. Compare the truly Machiavellian schemes of Thomas à Jesu, *De Procuranda Salute Omnium Gentium* (Antwerp 1613) pp 293–7.
[5] *Quaestiones*, p 148.
[6] Verricelli in fact inclines to the view that the Greeks in general are to be considered schismatics rather than heretics; individual Greeks may be tainted with heresy, but this cannot be affirmed of the Greek nation as a whole (*Quaestiones*, pp 634–5).
[7] First edition: Paris 1655.

establish precisely when the schism had in fact begun. He had little doubt about the exact date, 1053, and about the identity of the two chief culprits: Photius and Cerularius. 'The first seeds of the secession of the Greek Church from the Latin', he writes, 'were sown around the year 866... Photius was the first Greek who dared to accuse the Latin Church of errors in the faith, thus advancing the banner of schism and pointing the way for others to follow.' Pope John VIII, 'acting somewhat remissly', in 879 consented to the restoration of Photius to the patriarchal throne; and so, for the time being, the further evolution of the schism was halted. Disagreeing with Baronius, Morin evidently thinks that there was no 'second Photian schism', but that East and West remained in communion until Cerularius closed the Latin churches in Constantinople in the middle of the eleventh century. 'One hundred and eighty-seven years after the seeds were first sown by Photius, open schism broke out in the year of salvation 1053... Such is the date which we must assign to the schism.'[1]

Apart from the question of the 'second Photian schism', where Morin anticipates the conclusions of Dvornik, this is very much the view of the schism which prevailed generally until the second world war, and which still persists in the popular textbooks: a preliminary conflict under Photius in the 860s; a final breach under Cerularius in 1053–4. Allatius, by contrast, presents an account of East–West relations that is incomparably more subtle and more carefully qualified. The incidents of Photius and Cerularius he sees as important, but in themselves totally inconclusive. His main thesis, clearly indicated in his title *De Ecclesiae Occidentalis atque Orientalis Perpetua Consensione*, is that there never has been a 'final breach': the Western and Eastern Churches remain essentially united in a single faith. 'Greeks and Latins', so he argues, 'approve and reject the same things, and with united mind they pronounce the same concerning the dogmas of the faith. Their religious experience springs from one source, and both alike interpret it identically'.[2]

According to Allatius, there have been quarrels and misunderstandings between individuals on either side, but no act of complete schism formally and irrevocably committing the two Churches as

---

[1] *Commentarius*, p 3. On the views of seventeenth-century historians concerning the date of the schism, see the valuable discussion in Every, *Misunderstandings*, pp 15–24.

[2] This particular statement comes, not from *De...Perpetua Consensione*, but from another book on the same subject, in which Allatius collaborated with Bartold Nihusius and Abraham Ecchelensis: *Concordia Nationum Christianarum...in Fidei Catholicae Dogmatibus* (Mainz 1655) p 721.

Orthodox and Catholics: schism or intercommunion?

such. Particular Greeks have been hostile to the Holy See, as were Michael Cerularius or Mark of Ephesus; particular Greeks have misinterpreted the *Filioque*, as did Photius, or they have propounded heretical theories about the divine light, as did Symeon the New Theologian or Gregory Palamas.[1] But these hostile attitudes and doctrinal misconceptions are not to be attributed to the Greek Church and nation at large. Adducing a wealth of evidence from the period after 1054, Allatius maintains that there have never been lacking Greeks who remained well-disposed towards Rome; and he points to the friendly contacts which exist in his own day. Neither in 1054 nor at any other time has there ever been a 'complete consummation' of the schism.

As Allatius puts it in one of his other works:

Individual persons, although holding office in the Greek Church, do not constitute the Greek Church. Nor, because various heresies have arisen and spread within that Church, is she herself to be considered heretical...The Greek Church as a whole, whether in her professions of faith or in the service books read continually in her public worship, has never professed any heresy condemned by the councils and the Church of Rome...Because certain individual Greeks have endeavoured to spread some ancient or freshly invented heresy, and have inveighed against the papacy in their published writings, it does not therefore follow that the Greek Church is separated from the Church of Rome: this would only be the case if the heresy in question were universally adopted and outwardly professed by all alike; and this, you will find, has never happened on the occasions when certain individuals have launched attacks against the Roman Church.[2]

The standpoint of Allatius is concisely summarised by his younger contemporary, Nicolo Papadopoli: 'There are many schismatics in Greece, but Greece itself has never been schismatic.'[3] With this may be compared the statement of Carlo Francesco da Breno, in his manual for Latin missionaries in the Near East, published in 1726. 'Is the Eastern Church schismatic?' he inquires, and replies: 'Considered in itself it is not really schismatic, although there are many schismatics within it' (*non esse secundum se spectatam reipsa Schismaticam, etsi in ea multi Schismatici sint*).[4]

---

[1] For the views of Allatius on Hesychasm, see his *De Symeonorum Scriptis Diatriba* (Paris 1664), pp 151–79; *De...Perpetua Consensione*, cols 802–40.
[2] *Ioannes Henricus Hottingerus Fraudis, & Imposturae Manifestae Convictus* (Rome 1661) pp 6–7. Compare *De...Perpetua Consensione*, col 711.
[3] *Praenotiones Mystagogicae ex Jure Canonico* (Padua 1697) p iv.
[4] *Manuale Missionariorum Orientalium*, 2 vols (Venice 1726) I, p 83: compare G. Borgomanero, 'Gli apologisti della dottrina cattolica contro i Greci nel secolo XVII. Il P. Carlo Francesco da Breno', *Bessarione*, 3rd series, VIII (Rome 1910–11) p 292.

THE SEQUEL: INCREASING HOSTILITY AND
RENEWED FRIENDSHIP

Such, then, were the friendly contacts existing between Orthodox and Catholics during the seventeenth century; and such was the theoretical justification provided by contemporary catholic scholars for the acts of *communicatio in sacris* which took place daily throughout the Levant. In the first part of the eighteenth century, however, relations deteriorated markedly. Instances of joint worship and sharing in the sacraments, which around 1650 were a commonplace, had virtually ceased a hundred years later. By 1750 the separation between East and West had come to possess a sharpness and a finality which in 1700 it still lacked.

On the orthodox side, the man most responsible for the growth in hostility was Dositheos, patriarch of Jerusalem for nearly forty years (1669–1707), an able and tireless foe of Rome, inspired by a passionate aversion for the Jesuits and all their works.[1] On the catholic side, a rigorist approach to *communicatio in sacris* came to prevail more and more. The authorities at Rome, who had always looked with reserve on jesuit leniency, grew increasingly severe in their directives as the eighteenth century proceeded. On 5 July 1729 Propaganda issued a general prohibition, excluding all common worship in terms of the utmost strictness. On 10 May 1753 the Holy Office published another general prohibition, insisting that the decree of Martin V, *Ad evitanda scandala*, applied only to civic cooperation and not to *communicatio in sacris*.[2]

But the most decisive single factor in the deterioration of relations was probably the schism in the patriarchate of Antioch from 1724 onwards.[3] The western missionaries had found Syria and the Lebanon a particularly fruitful field, and nowhere else in the Levant did they succeed in making so many secret converts, including several patriarchs of Antioch. But the eventual outcome belied the jesuit hopes. Instead of securing the reconciliation of the entire patriarchate *en bloc* to the papal obedience, they succeeded only in producing a schism: in 1724 rival patriarchs were elected, the one looking to Rome and the other to Constantinople, and thenceforward the faithful were divided into two opposed flocks. This incident not only caused great local bitterness but led to widespread alarm throughout the orthodox

[1] See Ware, *Eustratios Argenti*, pp 31–2.
[2] See de Vries, '"Communicatio in sacris": An Historical Study', pp 18–19.
[3] See Ware, *Eustratios Argenti*, pp 28–30, for further details and bibliography.

world. Many Greeks realised for the first time the way in which friendship with the Latins was leading to secret conversions; they were terrified that what had happened in Antioch would occur elsewhere, and so they broke off friendly contacts with the Latin clergy. The schism of 1724 made them view the Latins, no longer as fellow-workers whose collaboration they could sincerely welcome, but as enemies dedicated to the subversion of their Church. Anti-Latin feeling came to full development in 1755, when the patriarch of Constantinople, together with his colleagues of Alexandria and Jerusalem, laid down that Latin converts were to be received henceforward by rebaptism, and no longer by chrismation, as in the regulations of 1484.[1]

By the nineteenth century acts of shared worship had become little more than a dim and distant memory for both Catholics and Orthodox. In 1862 Dom Jean-Baptiste Pitra, the future cardinal, prepared a perceptive memorandum on *communicatio in sacris* with the Orientals.[2] He was well aware of the intercommunion which had existed between Greeks and Latins some two centuries previously, and he cited the *De...Perpetua Consensione* of Leo Allatius and the reports of the jesuit missionaries, as well as interesting evidence from Kerkyra (Corfu) in 1724. But he went on to insist that the situation had altered. The precedents adduced from the seventeenth and early eighteenth centuries, so he argued, now possessed no more than a 'speculative value'; such practices he considered out of the question in the mid-nineteenth century.

Yet even in Pitra's day the sacramental severance was not total, for Latin canon law has never ceased to permit a Catholic, if in danger of death and cut off from his own Church, to receive orthodox sacraments.[3] And had Pitra been writing, not in 1862 but in the years following the second Vatican council, his conclusions would necessarily have been different. The decrees of Vatican II 'On Ecumenism' and 'On Eastern Catholic Churches', both dated 21 November 1964, together with the supplementary 'Ecumenical Directory' issued in May 1967, have greatly enlarged the possibilities of *communicatio in*

---

[1] See Ware, *Eustratios Argenti*, pp 65–78. The 1755 measure did not apply to Russia, which ceased to rebaptise Latin converts from 1666–7 onwards. Since the end of the last century, the 1755 decision has fallen largely into disuse, but it has never been formally revoked and is still occasionally applied.

[2] Memorandum to cardinal von Reisach, in A. Battandier, *Le Cardinal Jean-Baptiste Pitra* (Paris 1893) pp 435–9. This reference was kindly supplied to me by Br George Every.

[3] See *Codex Juris Canonici Pii X Pontificis Maximi iussu digestus* (Rome 1949) §882; C. Journet, *The Church of the Word Incarnate*, 1 (London 1955) p 508.

sacris with the Orthodox. The reaction of many Orthodox to these decisions has been guarded, but on 16 December 1969 the synod of the Russian Church declared that 'if...Catholics ask the Orthodox Church to administer the holy sacraments to them, this is not forbidden'. The Russian resolution has been vigorously attacked by the synod of the Church of Greece, but the ecumenical patriarchate has maintained a discreet silence and issued no condemnation. It appears that catholic-orthodox relations are entering upon another period of flexibility, reminiscent of the seventeenth century. Let us hope that the establishment of closer contacts will not lead to a fresh schism among the Orthodox, such as occurred at Antioch in 1724.

THE EMERGENCE OF SCHISM IN SEVENTEENTH-CENTURY SCOTLAND

by GORDON DONALDSON

IT is perhaps debatable whether the Reformation itself had involved schism, or at any rate whether those who took part in it thought that it did. It is true that in 1555, on the insistence of John Knox when he was in Scotland on a visit from Geneva, some of the reforming party were prevailed on to give up attending 'that idol', the mass,[1] and that before he left Scotland Knox administered the Lord's Supper after the reformed model.[2] It is true, too, that from this time or shortly thereafter Protestants began to gather together for worship, hardly in secret – for the government's policy was not repressive – but at least without official recognition. These 'privy kirks', which existed before there was 'the face of a public kirk' and had their preachers, elders and deacons,[3] were parallel to the congregations which English exiles were organising on the continent in the same years, and parallel, too, to the much more secret congregations which then existed in London. In the 'First Bond' of December 1557 a few notables renounced 'the congregation of Satan' and pledged themselves to work for the erection of a reformed Church, but, as they followed this with a supplication that the 'common prayers' should be read every Sunday in all parishes, it is evident that the aim was to reform the whole Church, not to separate from it.[4]

In England the tradition of the 'privy kirk' survived, or at any rate was soon revived, for the first separatists from the Elizabethan establishment were 'zealous Londoners' who 'remembered and followed the precedents of Marian days'.[5] But the Scots, although they may have themselves been schismatic while the Church was still unreformed, were of opinion that separation from a reformed Church – and such they deemed the Church of England to be – was not justified. The English separatists, on their side, failed to understand

---

[1] [John] Knox, [History of the] Reformation in Scotland, ed W. Croft Dickinson, 2 vols (Edinburgh 1949) I, pp 120–1.   [2] Ibid p 121.
[3] Ibid I, p 148; II, p 277. Works of John Knox, ed David Laing, 6 vols (Edinburgh 1846–64) IV, pp 129–40; VI, p 78.   [4] Knox, Reformation in Scotland, I, pp 136–8.
[5] M. M. Knappen, Tudor Puritanism (Chicago 1939) p 212.

the Scottish attitude: because they thought the Church of Scotland represented their own ideal and, as they put it to Knox, 'we desire no other order than you hold',[1] they expected sympathy and support. But they got neither. In 1568 some of them went to Scotland, evidently with the encouragement of bishop Grindal, much as in our day Maoists might be encouraged to go to China. Scotland, it turned out, did not come up to their exacting standards, and they were soon back home, drawing from Grindal the apt comment: 'The Church of Scotland will not be pure enough for our men. They are a wilful company. God grant them humble spirits.'[2] Worse was to come, for Knox formulated his considered opinion in a letter which roundly condemned secession: 'I cannot allow those that obstinately do refuse to hear the message of salvation at such men's mouths as please not us in all things... I wish your consciences had a better ground... God forbid that we should damn all for false prophets and heretics that agree not with us in our apparel and other opinions, that teacheth the substance of doctrine and salvation in Christ Jesus'.[3] This episode constituted something of a prologue to much that was to follow: but the Scots on the whole were long to adhere to the anti-separatist position which Knox had taken up so emphatically in 1568.

It is hardly surprising that the visit to Edinburgh in 1584 of Robert Brown, the English Separatist, was not a success. As he 'held opinion of separation from all kirks where excommunication was not rigorously used against open offenders not repenting', he had the effrontery (or the courage) to tell some members of the presbytery of Edinburgh that 'the whole discipline of Scotland was amiss and that he and his company were not subject to it'.[4]

John Penry, another English Puritan, spent a good deal of time in Scotland between October 1589 and August 1592. Although he was less radical than Brown, his visit was not a success either. He was at first 'well entertained' by the ministers and appeared at 'public assemblies', but a divergence soon became apparent. One of the books published for him was produced 'without the privity of the ministers',[5] and he clearly had serious differences of opinion with some of

[1] [Peter] Lorimer, [*John Knox and the Church of England*] (London 1875) pp 298–300.

[2] Edmund Grindal, *Remains*, ed William Nicholson (Parker Society, Cambridge 1843) pp 295–6.

[3] Lorimer, pp 298–300.

[4] [David] Calderwood, [*History of the Church of Scotland*,] ed T. Thomson and D. Laing, 8 vols (Wodrow Society, Edinburgh 1842–9) IV, pp 1–3.

[5] *Calendar of State Papers relating to Scotland [and Mary, Queen of Scots]*, x, ed W. K. Boyd and H. W. Meikle (HMSO 1936) no 391.

them, for some years later, when king James accused John Davidson, one of the more extreme of the ministers, of speaking 'anabaptistically' and having had 'too much acquaintance with Mr Penry', Davidson replied that 'he was no Anabaptist, and agreed not with Mr Penry'.[1] The Scottish ministers seem to have done little to intercede for Penry with king James when the English ambassador, ultimately with success, pressed for his banishment from Scotland,[2] and their attitude to him contrasts with the appeal they supported for the release of Udall and Cartwright and other more orthodox English Presbyterians.[3] But Penry, elusive as ever, successfully evaded banishment for a time, and if he was lurking underground it may be that he found some Scottish friends to shelter him.[4] The king later bracketed Brown and Penry together as 'brainsick and heady preachers',[5] and most of his subjects would probably have concurred.

Long before Penry's visit, the Scottish Presbyterians had found themselves in a situation which might have justified them in going into schism had they been so minded. They were, of course, stronger than their English brethren, and had a weaker executive to contend with, so they had shown little hesitation in disregarding the magistrate. Echoing the familiar English phraseology about 'reformation without tarrying', they pronounced that 'discipline and government...hath the command and power given to use it...without tarrying for any authority or command of men'.[6] By 1582-3, their presbyteries, organised in pursuance of this policy, were in a fair way to taking over ecclesiastical administration from the bishops in some parts of the country. It was all strictly illegal, and their proceedings were presently to be described as the erection of 'that form lately invented in this land, called the presbytery, wherein a number of ministers of a certain precinct and bounds, accounting themselves all to be equal, without any difference, and gathering unto them certain gentlemen and others of his Majesty's subjects, usurped all the whole ecclesiastical jurisdiction and altered the laws at their own appetite'.[7] The reaction came in the shape of the so-called 'Black Acts' of 1584, which reaffirmed episcopal authority and referred contemptuously to 'the pretended presbyteries'.[8]

This meant, so the Presbyterians said, that 'our whole form of

---

[1] Calderwood, v, p 698.   [2] *Calendar of State Papers relating to Scotland*, x, no 454.
[3] *Ibid* nos 574, 587.   [4] *Ibid* no 499.
[5] James VI, *Basilicon Doron*, ed J. Craigie, 2 vols (Scottish Text Society, Edinburgh 1944–50) I, p 15.
[6] Calderwood, IV, p 229.   [7] *Ibid* p 259.
[8] *Acts of the Parliaments of Scotland*, III (Record Commissioners, Edinburgh 1815) p 312.

spiritual government, grounded upon the Word of God...is altogether cast down'.[1] Some of them fled to England – a curious refuge for Presbyterians, as their adversaries did not fail to point out.[2] Their main reason for flight was fear for their lives and liberties, and they admitted that their bodies as well as their consciences had been brought into 'hazard and danger' by the 'Black Acts'.[3] But they shuffled a bit in their explanations, and argued that they were of more use alive than dead to a church which, they said, was 'like to be overthrown':[4] 'albeit it was good for us to have suffered all extremities, and to be dissolved from these bodies of clay and be with Christ, yet was it meet for the kirk that we should preserve ourselves for the comfort thereof'.[5] The really conclusive fact about their outlook is that they came back from England as soon as a political change ensured their physical safety but before the obnoxious legislation had been repealed. This would seem to absolve the exiles from any schismatic intent, but even if it does not, the attitude of the Presbyterians who remained in Scotland was a clear affirmation of a refusal to break the unity of the Church. Thus the ministers of Berwickshire, although they declared themselves opposed to 'the tyrannical supremacy of bishops and archbishops over ministers', nevertheless conformed.[6] Even a minister who told king James to his face that he considered him a persecutor who maintained 'the tyranny of bishops, and absolute power', did not offer to leave his parish.[7] The dissidents had actually given a formal undertaking to refrain from any proceedings which might be deemed schismatic: 'They shall abstain from all faction, privy preachings by [apart from] the common order, in public or private places, or any such quiet conventicles.'[8]

In the later years of the sixteenth century the Presbyterians were in the ascendant, and the ecclesiastical system was largely, though not entirely, shaped according to their proposals. At the beginning of the seventeenth it was evident that the tide was turning against them and that they would again find themselves in opposition. As the king began to tamper with the times and places appointed for meetings of the general assembly, anxiety grew, and when the assembly appointed for Aberdeen in July 1604 was prorogued to July 1605 and then prorogued indefinitely, the Presbyterians felt impelled to make a stand. Therefore nineteen ministers who had gathered at Aberdeen in July 1605 insisted

[1] Calderwood, IV, p 75.   [2] Ibid p 90.
[3] Ibid p 104.   [4] Ibid p 104.
[5] Ibid p 103.   [6] Ibid pp 604–5.
[7] Ibid p 486.   [8] Ibid p 350.

on constituting an assembly and, when charged in the king's name to disperse, appointed another meeting for the following September. These ministers would have been horrified at the idea that they were guilty of schism, but king James, who referred to their assembly as a 'conventicle',[1] put his finger with characteristic precision and prescience on the way in which their action showed the way to schism and anticipated the technique by which later secessions were to take place. An official 'Declaration of the king's proceedings' demanded 'what might let [hinder] as many general assemblies to be convened at any time, in diverse places...as there are several numbers of nineteen ministers throughout the country?' and added that if there was nothing to hinder such an outcome, then 'there should be at one instant far more general assemblies in Scotland, one against another, than ever there were popes in one time in our adversary church'.[2] The king put a similar question more directly to the presbyterian leader: 'Whether think ye that where a few number of eight or nine, without any warrant, do meet, wanting the chief members of an assembly, as the moderator and scribe, convening unmannerly without a sermon,... can make an assembly or not?'[3]

Within another five years the king had succeeded in prevailing on the Church to accept a modified form of episcopal government. But there was no schism in consequence. Although many ministers, especially in the southern half of the country, were resolutely opposed to bishops – forty-two of them signed a protest against episcopacy presented to parliament in July 1606 – not one resigned his charge.

As yet there had been no question of the imposition of liturgical requirements or of changes in public worship, but when such matters did become an issue feeling was much more profoundly stirred than it ever had been over the presbyterian–episcopalian controversy. The revival of disputes even brought a renewal of the challenge to episcopacy, for John Scrimgeour, minister of Kinghorn, deprived for nonconformity, protested that the archbishop of St Andrews could not depose him, because he had received his admission from the synod of Fife, 'and for anything you do, I will never think myself deposed from it': the archbishop replied that he did not deprive him of his ministry, but only inhibited him from the exercise of it, and affirmed that Scrimgeour could be readmitted without reimposition of hands[4] – one way of anticipating and preventing schism. In the main, how-

---

[1] *Ibid* VI, p 583; VII, p 311.   [2] *Ibid* VI, pp 427–8.
[3] *Ibid* p 573.   [4] *Ibid* VII, p 423.

ever, the argument on polity which arose from the liturgical innovations centred on the location of supreme power in the Church. In 1617, when it was proposed that the king, with the advice of a competent number of the ministry, should be authorised to make laws for the Church, a protest was signed by fifty-six ministers.[1] Then, when the government's liturgical requirements took shape as the Five Articles of Perth and these were passed by an assembly in 1618, the opposition condemned the assembly as 'unlawful';[2] but no one proposed to proceed to schism by calling a rival and 'lawful' meeting.

Yet in the years that followed, there was a tendency towards separatism such as had never existed before since the 'privy kirks' of the 1550s. In 1620 there were 'private meetings of some good Christians in Edinburgh' which the town's ministers called 'privy conventicles'.[3] Now, the term 'conventicle' had a long history in England as descriptive of a gathering of dissidents, and in Scotland at the time of the Reformation an indignant Roman Catholic had referred to 'the private conventicles of schismatics and heretics'.[4] At the same time, the word could still be used in 1621 of more innocent 'privy conventicles and meetings' which were designed merely for lobbying parliament.[5] But the participants in the religious 'conventicles' of 1620 were dubbed 'Brownists, Anabaptists, Schismatics, Separatists', and they were accused of bringing in an English preacher called Mr Hubert.[6] The king even charged the conventiclers with assuming the name of 'the Congregation' which had been used by the revolutionaries before 1560.[7] Reports appeared in 1624 of 'divers sects' in Edinburgh, such as 'Brownists, Waderdowpers [or Watterdippers][8] and such like', with their 'private conventicles', and a private conventicle was defined as 'a private meeting of men and women to a private religious exercise in time of public sermon' – not a bad definition of separatism.[9] These varied accusations were on the whole denied.[10] One Edinburgh man, accused in 1624 of keeping a Brownist minister in his house to teach and keep conventicles, denied that the Brownist had ever

[1] *Ibid* p 256.
[2] *Ibid* pp 339, 428.   [3] *Ibid* p 449.
[4] Ninian Winzet, *Certane Tractatis* (Maitland Club, Edinburgh 1835) p 44.
[5] Calderwood, VII, p 472.
[6] *Ibid* p 449.   [7] *Ibid* p 612.
[8] The variants appear in Calderwood, VII, p 620 and VIII, p 123. 'Watterdippers' suggests those who practised baptism by immersion, but Mr David Murison, editor of the *Scottish National Dictionary*, states that 'Waderdowper' is the Dutch 'weder-dooper', literally 'again-baptizer', that is Anabaptist.
[9] Calderwood, VII, p 620.   [10] *Ibid* VII, p 614; VIII, p 123.

taught in his house.[1] Perhaps the most significant denial came from another Edinburgh burgess: 'I never separated myself from the kirk and never thinks to do. I know there is no man nor woman but they are sinful, nor any kirk so pure but there are some faults in it. As for myself, I had rather live in the Kirk of Scotland than in any other kirk.'[2] This is the authentic voice of what long continued to be the prevailing Scottish attitude – a willingness to acquiesce in much that a man did not approve of, rather than abandon the Church. This was emphatic enough, and when the archbishop of St Andrews spoke of a 'schism' or 'a great rent in the church' he meant only deep disagreement.[3] However, the protests were so forceful that the obnoxious Five Articles were not strictly enforced, and any possibility there may have been of real schism was extinguished for the time being.

After a spell of leniency, extending through the early years of Charles I, pressure intensified in the 1630s on those who were not disposed to conform, and it built up until it reached its climax with the Prayer Book of 1637. Yet schism or even conventicles seem barely to have been regarded as possibilities. This is clear from the attitude of Samuel Rutherford, one of the most extreme and vocal of the recalcitrants. Rutherford was minister of the parish of Anwoth, in Galloway, until July 1636, when he was dismissed by the bishop and banished to Aberdeen. Now, Rutherford was, or at any rate believed he was,[4] the only minister in all Scotland who had not merely been deprived of his living but had been forbidden to preach at all. But, hard feelings apart, he took a very gloomy view of the position and prospects of the Church of Scotland. As far back as 1630 he had come very near to rejecting it as no longer part of Christ's Church. He referred at that time to some English Puritans who had left for New England, and, using his customary erotic imagery, he went on to say that 'Our Blessed Lord Jesus, who cannot get leave to sleep with His spouse in this land, is going to seek an inn where he will be better entertained'. Probably by 'this land' he here meant England, but he goes on to say, in this letter to one of his female correspondents, that in Scotland 'Christ is putting on his clothes, and making him [ready], like an ill-handled stranger, to go to other lands. Pray Him, sister, to lie down again with His beloved.'[5] At a later stage Rutherford took a sympathetic interest in the fortunes of some Scotsmen who were ministers

[1] *Ibid* VII, p 603.   [2] *Ibid* p 603.   [3] *Ibid* pp 545, 563.
[4] [Samuel] Rutherford, [*Letters*,] ed A. A. Bonnar, 2 vols (Edinburgh 1863) I, p 249.
[5] *Ibid* pp 63–4.

in Ireland and who, when ousted by the bishops, set out for America but were driven back by the weather:[1] he said, 'my soul is grieved for the success' – he means non-success – 'of our brethren's journey to New England'.[2] He told the wife of the provost of Kirkcudbright, 'Try your husband afar off to see if he can be induced to think upon going to America'.[3] This was in 1635, and in 1637 he did not rule out emigration as a solution of his own difficulties: 'If I saw a call for New England, I would follow it.'[4]

Yet even Rutherford never quite came to the point either of emigration – which in the circumstances would have implied a separatist attitude – or of schism within Scotland itself. In 1632 he wrote: 'It is our Lord's wisdom that His Kirk should ever hang by a thread: and yet the thread breaketh not.'[5] His attitude seems to be summed up in his own picturesque phraseology to the effect that although – as he never wearies of saying – the Church of Scotland is a harlot, heading for the brothel of Rome,[6] and although at one point he even calls her 'this apostate kirk', which 'hath played the harlot with many lovers',[7] yet the harlot was still his mother: 'We have cause to weep for our harlot-mother; her Husband is sending her to Rome's brothel-house...Yet...this Church shall sing the Bridegroom's welcome home again to His own house';[8] again, 'there is no question but our mother-church hath a Father, and that she shall not die without an heir'.[9] There is more about 'our mother-church' in the same vein, but less tastefully put.[10]

One of Rutherford's contemporaries was Robert Baillie, a much more moderate man, and one more disposed to conform. In January 1637, when the Prayer Book was imminent, he wrote, 'I am resolved, what I can digest as any ways tolerable with peace of conscience, not only in due time to receive myself, but to dispose others also, so far as I can in word and writ, to receive quietly the same.'[11] When he wrote, 'I look for the most pitiful schism that ever poor kirk has felt', he probably meant no more than controversy,[12] but he seems to have feared that others might be less accommodating than he was, because in that same month of January he was asking for 'some good treatises of Brownism', by which he apparently meant works refuting 'separation', for, as he explained, 'I fear to have too much use of such pieces.'[13]

[1] Ibid pp 170, 228, 232. [2] Ibid p 194.
[3] Ibid p 145. [4] Ibid p 376 [5] Ibid p 93.
[6] Ibid I, pp 242, 261, 265, 370, 446; II, p 50. [7] Ibid I, p 392.
[8] Ibid II, p 50. [9] Ibid p 82. [10] Ibid p 112.
[11] [Robert] Baillie, [Letters and Journals,] ed David Laing, 3 vols (Bannatyne Club, Edinburgh, 1841–2) I, p 2. [12] Ibid p 5. [13] Ibid p 12.

The emergence of schism in seventeenth-century Scotland

The National Covenant, the great manifesto of the opposition, opened up the possibility of a real division, and in April 1638, a few weeks after it had been signed, there were rival communion services in Glasgow, one, in the cathedral nave, where the communicants knelt, and the other, in the crypt, where they sat. Baillie saw this as 'a proclamation of red war among the clergy of that town'.[1] Had the Covenant not been followed so soon by the collapse of the king's system, there might well have been schism, and had the Covenanters then been crushed men such as Rutherford might well have gone to America like Scottish Pilgrim Fathers.

Later in 1638, when the Glasgow assembly abjured episcopacy and cast out the liturgical innovations, the Presbyterians were again in the saddle and it was the turn of the Episcopalians to be under pressure. But they had no more taste for schism than the Presbyterians had had under similar circumstances. It is true that nine bishops fled to England, much as Presbyterians had done in 1584. But the reason was – and again there is a parallel to the presbyterian exiles of 1584 – that at home the bishops were not safe from rude handling, if no worse, and one bishop who did not escape actually suffered a fourteen months' imprisonment. But it is more significant that five bishops carried their conformity so far as to abjure episcopacy, and four of them, apparently quite happily, returned to the office of a parish minister.[2]

But the National Covenant was itself to prove a source of discord. With the passage of time, it was political rather than ecclesiastical issues which proved divisive, but there are indications of other factors. At a time of close collaboration between Scottish Presbyterians and English Parliamentarians, some Scots became acquainted as never before with the ideas of English Separatists. Orthodox Presbyterians of course detested them. Robert Baillie condemned Brownism as 'democratic anarchy',[3] he lamented the growth in England of Brownists, Separatists, Anabaptists, Antinomians and Independents,[4] and he put in hand a refutation of some of their tenets in a work to be called *The Mystery of Brownism*.[5] This never saw the light of day under that title, but no doubt it provided the matter for his *Dissuasive for the*

[1] *Ibid* p 63.
[2] James Fairlie, bishop of Argyll, became minister of Lasswade; John Abernethy, bishop of Caithness, became minister of Jedburgh; Alexander Lindsay, bishop of Dunkeld, became minister of St Madoes; Neil Campbell, bishop of the Isles, became minister at Campbeltown. George Graham, bishop of Orkney, abjured episcopacy but retired from active life. [3] Baillie, II, pp 115, 194.
[4] *Ibid* I, pp 293, 311; II, pp 27, 111, 117, 320. [5] *Ibid* II, pp 71, 76.

Errors of the Time (1645), which he expected to bring 'a shower of Independents about my ears'.[1] Rutherford, as it happened, was in print on the subject before Baillie. In 1640 he had written: 'As for separation from a worship for some errors of a church, the independency of single congregations, a church of visible saints, and other tenets of Brownists, they are contrary to God's word. I have a treatise at the press in London against these conceits.'[2] This was *A peaceable and temperate plea for Paul's presbytery in Scotland*, published at London in 1642. Rutherford's condemnation of 'separation from a worship for some errors of a church' reflects the classical Scottish view. However, while he saw a simple issue between Presbyterianism and Separation, Baillie was more perceptive, for he detected a danger that Presbyterianism itself might slide towards Independency if too much power should be vested in congregations, and for that reason he opposed any proposal that congregations should elect their ministers: this was 'too near the main foundation of Brownism – the divine right of the church, that is the parish, to elect, admit, depose, excommunicate their ministers and elders, of which right neither prince nor presbytery nor assembly can deprive them'.[3] That was written in December 1639, and it must remain uncertain whether Brownist influence had anything to do with the agitation which actually led to the abolition of patronage ten years later. At any rate, the Brownism which Baillie so detested in England did show signs of spreading to Scotland, as an unexpected and to most Scots unwelcome by-product of the association which produced the Solemn League and Covenant. As early as 1643 Baillie remarked that 'rigid Brownism', had appeared in the south-west of Scotland and 'avowed Brownism' in Aberdeen.[4] There is not much other evidence at this stage, but already in 1641 a somewhat cryptic act of the general assembly had instructed ministers to avoid 'all meetings which are apt to breed error, scandal, schism',[5] and in August 1647 the assembly found it necessary to pass an act against 'vagers [wanderers] from their own ministers',[6] which must mean that there were separatists of a kind, in the sense of people who repudiated the concept of the strict adherence of all the inhabitants of a parish to their parish church.

It may be, therefore, that the rigidity of the presbyterian system was shaking somewhat loose when the political divisions arose which

---

[1] *Ibid* p 327.   [2] Rutherford, II, p 304.
[3] Baillie, I, p 241.   [4] *Ibid* II, p 54.
[5] *Acts of the General Assembly of the Church of Scotland* (Church Law Society, Edinburgh 1843) p 47.   [6] Baillie, III, p 15.

led to the first real schism in post-reformation Scotland. In 1648 the royalist majority in the Scottish parliament approved the Engagement whereby the Scots undertook to invade England on behalf of Charles I, and the majority in the general assembly opposed it. After the failure of the expedition to England the extremists gained control, and several ministers who had supported the Engagement were deposed – eleven in the synod of Perth and Stirling and eighteen in Angus and Mearns.[1] Yet royalist opinion grew after the execution of Charles I, and when it was proposed that the Scots should commit themselves to support Charles II, after he had agreed to take the covenants, the mind of the assembly had changed. The majority now supported 'Resolutions' to the effect that all who were willing to fight for king and country should be permitted to do so, irrespective of their past records, but a minority supported a 'Remonstrance' (17 October 1650) against the admission of 'Malignants' or former Royalists to the army and against the agreement with a king whom they suspected of insincerity.

When the Resolutions were formally approved by the general assembly in July 1651, between twenty and thirty ministers[2] protested against the lawfulness of the meeting. Thus the minority, from being known as Remonstrants, became known as Protestors.[3] The assembly deposed three of the leaders of the protesting party and suspended another.[4] In October the leading Protestors summoned their brethren from 'sundry parts of the country' to an 'extra judicial meeting' at Edinburgh. They spent much time in prayer, fasting and confessing their sins, but they also challenged the general assembly's authority. They repudiated the commission appointed by the 1651 assembly and resolved to restore that appointed by its predecessor, in which their views had prevailed and which they therefore recognised as 'lawful'. Sixty-six ministers are said to have been present at that meeting in October 1651, and when the next assembly, in 1652, was in turn rejected, the rejection was signed by sixty-seven.[5] The intention of the dissidents to protest against yet another assembly, in 1653, was fore-stalled by the action of Cromwellian troops in dissolving it.

The political wranglings which had thus split the assembly had

---

[1] *Ibid* pp 91, 97; [W. Law] Mathieson, [*Politics and Religion in Scotland,*] 2 vols (Glasgow 1902) II, pp 112–13.

[2] Figures vary from 21 to 28 [Archibald] Johnston [of Wariston, *Diary*] *1650–54*, Scottish History Society, 2 series, XVIII (Edinburgh 1919) p 93.

[3] *Ibid* p 146n; compare Mathieson, II, pp 165–6.

[4] Rutherford, II, pp 357, 375.

[5] Mathieson, II, pp 165–6; Johnston, *1650–54*, p 181.

repercussions at other levels. When Baillie wrote in July 1652 of 'a clear beginning of a schism',[1] he was thinking especially of recent happenings at presbyterial level. The Remonstrants had for a time had their own army – the 'holy army' as it was called[2] – and the ministers in it described themselves as 'the presbytery of the western army':[3] this would seem to have been the first appearance of anything like a schismatic presbytery, a presbytery claiming independence of the officially authorised church judicatures, but it was a special case in that it was a non-territorial presbytery. However, in June 1652 the presbytery of Dumbarton was so openly split that a section of it proposed to ordain a minister without the concurrence of the rest of the members,[4] and in July the majority of the presbytery of Glasgow, led by Patrick Gillespie, who had been deposed by the previous assembly, voted against sending commissioners to the current assembly.[5] Six months later, ministers who had seceded from the presbytery of Glasgow claimed to constitute a rival presbytery, and Baillie observed that Gillespie had 'his separate presbytery'.[6] In the presbytery of Stirling, three ministers formed a schismatic presbytery; three or four more, who stood by the decisions of the general assembly, formed the legal presbytery; and three more were 'neutral and abstained from both'.[7] This goes some way to justify king James's taunt in 1605 that if authority should be disregarded there might be more assemblies at one time 'than ever there were popes at one time in our adversary kirk'. The presbyteries of Lanark and Linlithgow also divided, though the former subsequently reunited.[8]

Divisions spread from the presbyteries upwards to the synods as well as down to the congregations. 'The brethren of the protesting judgement in the synod of Perth' desired that the synod would declare that certain of the acts of the assemblies of 1651 and 1652, censuring those who would not acknowledge those assemblies, should be of no force within the bounds of the synod, and that the synod would declare two ministers capable of voting in presbytery and synod despite their deposition by the 'pretended assembly'.[9] The synod of Glasgow divided in April 1653,[10] and when an 'anti-synod met synodically

[1] Baillie, III, p 191.
[2] J. Nicoll, *Diary of public transactions and other occurrences*, ed D. Laing (Bannatyne Club, 1836) p 39.   [3] Baillie, III, p 122.
[4] *Ibid* p 186.   [5] *Ibid* p 194.
[6] *Ibid* pp 203, 211.   [7] *Ibid* p 257.
[8] *Consultations of the Ministers of Edinburgh*, ed William Stephen, 2 vols, *Scottish History Society*, 3 series, vols I, XVI (1921–30) II, p 3.
[9] Rutherford, II, p 405.   [10] Baillie, III, p 215.

very frequent at Glasgow' and appointed a committee for purging the synod and presbyteries of ministers not in agreement with it, the 'other part of the synod' retaliated, for it was determined to have its purging committee 'as well as they'.[1]

The attitude of the Protestors, reduced to the simplest terms, was that they would not accept majority rule. Already in 1655 Baillie observed that 'our brethren regard little either presbyteries or synods when opposed to their desires'.[2] But worse was to come, when they 'proceeded further to declare the body of our presbyteries, synods and congregations to consist of a plurality of corrupt members' and therefore 'refused openly submission to the sentences of any of our kirk judicatories';[3] and 'when they are censured, they deny subordination, avowing themselves to be right and their censurers wrong'.[4] They were quite candid about it: one minister opposed the resumption of meetings of the general assembly because his party would find itself in a minority: as the Church, he said, was 'in a troubled state, and the plurality thereof corrupt, we conceive it [an assembly] ought not to be granted without security to the godly'.[5] By a process of reasoning which has puzzled later historians as it puzzled contemporaries, the Protestors managed to pay lip-service to Presbyterianism and did not formally renounce its principles, however much they ignored them in practice. One writer has remarked that 'though devoted to Presbytery in the abstract, they allowed themselves great latitude as members of a Presbyterian Church' and that 'they revolted against a system of ecclesiastical government which they still asserted to be divine'.[6] Much the same point had been made by Baillie two and a half centuries earlier – 'they seem to be for the thing in general, but not for submission to our judicatures'.[7]

Contemporaries were in no doubt that it all amounted to schism, and when the ministers of Edinburgh in 1657 deplored 'what scandal there is given to the whole Church by their schism'[8] they were using the word as we should use it. They had reflected earlier on the whole problem of schism and on the differences, as they thought, between the Scottish situation and the English. In England, they reasoned, there might have been a case for separation, because there had been persecution and there had been errors in 'the worship and ordinances of God',

---

[1] *Ibid* p 254.   [2] *Ibid* p 284.
[3] *Ibid* p 305.   [4] *Ibid* p 379.
[5] *Consultations of the Ministers of Edinburgh*, I, p 351.   [6] Mathieson, II, p 170.
[7] Baillie, III, p 300.   [8] *Consultations of the Ministers of Edinburgh*, I, p 274.

but they firmly believed that there was no case for separation in 'a church so constituted and reformed in all the ordinances of Christ as the Church of Scotland'.[1] If there was anything more in this pronouncement than national conceit, it suggests a belief that separatism could be more easily justified by differences about worship than by differences about polity. This would, of course, be related to earlier statements about the greater cause for separation in England than in Scotland, though such statements are nevertheless somewhat ironical. It must be recalled that in 1618, although there had been those who characterised as 'unlawful' the general assembly which had passed the Five Articles, no schism had then followed. Now schism did follow, though the differences which were splitting the Scottish Church were political rather than ecclesiastical at all; and, besides, most of the later secessions in Scotland arose from disputes not about worship but about Church–State relations. However, the Edinburgh ministers were on perfectly sound ground when they reaffirmed that the essence of Presbyterianism was subordination to presbyteries, from which, in the event of grievance, appeal must be made to the synod and thence to the general assembly,[2] and when they denounced the proceedings of the Protestors as 'destructive of the visible kirk' and 'destructive of the government of the kirk'.[3]

This was a serious charge, but, if it was justified even in relation to what was happening in presbyteries and synods, it is evident that at parish level there were those who formally renounced all pretence of presbyterian principles and turned to something more like Independency. This, no less than the schisms in presbyteries and synods, was a novelty, and it did not arise, any more than they did, from the differences about worship which some had always held to provide some ground for separation. Possibly it would be fair to conclude that political divisions went deeper than ecclesiastical divisions, but this might be to ignore three other factors which caused schism to deepen and spread. For one thing, schism at congregational level was facilitated, if not indeed for the first time made possible, by the abolition of patronage in 1649 – a step which, as Baillie had foreseen ten years before, might open the way to Brownism. Secondly, there was the readiness of the Cromwellian administration to support the extremist minority of Protestors or schismatics. As Baillie put it: 'When a very few of the Remonstrators or Independent party will call a man, he gets a kirk and the stipend, but when the presbytery, and well near

---

[1] *Ibid* p 42.   [2] *Ibid* pp 90–1.   [3] *Ibid* p 269.

the whole congregation, calls and admits, he must preach in the fields, or in a barn, without stipend.'[1] In the parish of Douglas, in 1656, the Protestors incited some of the elders to put up a rival nominee for the parish and bring him to the church; when refused entry, he preached on a hill-side to a small number of the members, and they, by appealing to the army, got support to declare him minister of the parish.[2] At Lenzie, when the presbytery admitted James Ramsay, the 'dissenting brethren' procured an order from the English forbidding the presbytery to give any ordination without their approval.[3]

A third factor which intensified the drift to separatism was the influence of English Independency. The earliest hint of a link between the Protestor standpoint and Independency is to be found in January 1651: the Remonstrants' 'holy army', besides having its own presbytery, also contained 'a seed of hyper-Brownism'.[4] It was not purely a matter of English influence: once patronage was abolished, the transition from the Protestor position to Independency was not a difficult one at congregational level, and some were quite conscious of its logic: it was their principles as Protestors that had led them to separate from the Church of Scotland and deny its constitution.[5] The trend towards something like a 'gathered congregation' can be seen in Glasgow in 1653: 'they are moving to celebrate a Communion here...They will exclude such multitudes for one cause or for another that the end will be the setting up of a new refined congregation of their own adherents.'[6] But even earlier, in 1652, the minister of Stonehouse in Lanarkshire was said to be 'embodying in a church so fast as he can, and celebrating the Communion to his proselytes'.[7] This minister was subsequently translated from Stonehouse to East Kilbride, where he formed another Independent congregation. When he was accidentally killed in 1656, Johnston of Wariston – who persisted in reconciling the Protestor standpoint with theoretical adherence to Presbyterianism – was exultant: 'God has blasted the only two gathered congregations in Scotland.'[8] There were, however, other instances. Some people in Fenwick, in Ayrshire, had declared in favour of 'separation', and the dissidents in Lenzie proclaimed themselves Sectaries.[9] The main centre

---

[1] Baillie, III, p 244. [2] *Ibid* p 248.
[3] *Ibid* pp 215–17. [4] *Ibid* p 127.
[5] *Consultations of the Ministers of Edinburgh*, I, pp 269–70.
[6] Baillie, III, p 200. [7] *Ibid* p 187.
[8] [Archibald] Johnston [of Wariston, *Diary*,] *1655–1660*, ed James D. Ogilvie, Scottish History Society, 3 series, XXXIV (1940) p 35.
[9] Baillie, III, pp 193, 215–17.

of separatism seems, however, to have been in Aberdeen, where Baillie had noted 'avowed Brownism' as early as 1643. In 1652, when Wariston said that colonel Lockhart had 'gathered a congregation', apparently in Edinburgh, he added that there was danger of the same thing happening in Aberdeen,[1] and it is evident that provost Jaffray had a separate congregation there.[2] Wariston himself received a letter from Jaffray and three others, in name of a larger number, 'wherein they declare their judgment against the constitution and government of this kirk'.[3] When, in 1653, the ministers of Edinburgh had commented on 'the way of separation from this church, to which the inclination of some is working, and into which several already have involved themselves', they made special mention of 'some of our Christian brethren and friends in Aberdeen'.[4] In 1654 it was noted that 'almost all in both Colleges [of Aberdeen], from Remonstrators, have avowedly gone over to Independency and Separation'.[5]

One characteristic of some leading separatists is specially worth noting. Provost Jaffray, the Independent leader in Aberdeen, had been a prisoner in England and had learned English ways. Lockhart, who founded the separatist congregation in Edinburgh, was an agent of the Cromwellian government. And Johnston of Wariston has a significant remark about another of the collaborators with the English, Sir John Swinton, who said that he repented of 'leaving ordinances and engaging to the Englishes',[6] by which he seems to have meant that his understanding with the Cromwellian administration had involved abandoning the worship of the Church of Scotland. It is plain that there was a strong English flavour about the whole separatist movement, at any rate among its leaders, though no doubt they found ready followers among disgruntled Protestors. The direct influence of chaplains to the occupying forces and of itinerant English preachers must not be left out of account.

It would appear, further, that the presbyterian schism led in some places not only to separation but to Quakerism, which also filtered into Scotland from England in the 1650s. Its history can be traced from 1653, when meetings were held at East Kilbride and Glassford in Lanarkshire and at Kirkintilloch, which lies between Glasgow and Stirling – in other words, in areas where the presbyterian schism had made its

---

[1] Johnston, *1655–60*, p 169.   [2] *Ibid* p 171.
[3] *Ibid* p 173, compare p xlvi.
[4] *Consultations of the Ministers of Edinburgh*, I, p 38.
[5] Baillie, III, p 242, compare pp 364–5.   [6] Johnston, *1655–60*, p 304.

mark. Moreover, provost Jaffray of Aberdeen, who had formed his separatist congregation in 1652, passed over to Quakerism ten years later.[1]

While schism in several forms had thus unquestionably emerged in Scotland in the 1650s, it did not have a continuous history thereafter, at least if we discount the persistence of the numerically insignificant Quaker testimony. Episcopacy was of course restored in 1661, but the objectors were no more ready to form a rival church now than they had been in the early years of the century, for, now as then, no changes of any substance were made in the forms of public worship, and it was such changes, rather than episcopacy, which had caused men like Rutherford to come so close to a schismatic point of view in Charles I's reign. The appetite for schism would seem still to have been very limited, and adherence to the national Church showed far more vitality than might have been expected after the experience of the 1650s. There were men who were firmly presbyterian in their prin-ciples and were ready to refuse to give an undertaking to do nothing to overturn episcopacy, but they saw the presbyterian–episcopalian issue as one within a single church and were prepared to continue their work within the episcopalian establishment just as their fathers and grandfathers had done. When one of them said that, although he was a Presbyterian, 'I will not separate from the Church of God',[2] he was expressing Samuel Rutherford's belief that the harlot-mother was still a mother. Even when a large number of presbyterian ministers assembled together in the late 1670s, they made it clear that their meeting was for consultation only: they were neither constituting a general assembly nor providing for presbyterian ordinations, which would have *ipso facto* created a schismatic church.[3] It would seem to need some ex-plaining why even Protestors, who had been ready enough to separate from the Presbyterian Church of the 1650s, were much less ready to separate from the Episcopalian Church of the 1660s and 1670s. It was not until about 1680 that some of them – and even then only a very

---

[1] There is a brief account of early Quakerism in Scotland by W. H. Marwick, *Short History of Friends in Scotland* (Edinburgh 1948) pp 1–3. Dr Nuttall has drawn my attention to additional material in the Swarthmore MSS in the Library of the Society of Friends at Friends House, Euston Road, NW1, a calendar of which he compiled in 1951 under the title *Early Quaker Letters*. There is information about baptist churches in Scotland both in this collection and in the Clarke MSS (Worcester College, Oxford), 27, fol 133. See W. T. Whitley, *A Baptist Bibliography*, 2 vols (London 1916–22).

[2] Robert Wodrow, *History of the Sufferings of the Church of Scotland*, 2 vols (Edinburgh 1721) I, p 189.

[3] *Ibid* p 436 and Appendix LXIX.

small number – repudiated the establishment and made provision for their own ordinations.[1]

It is hard to believe that the idea of adherence to the national Church took a new lease of life, and some other explanation must be sought. It is probably to be found in the government's attitude and measures. In the 1650s there had been no penalties for separation – indeed, the government of that period instead rather encouraged the separatists. After the Restoration, on the contrary, the firm measures of the government gave little scope for conventicles, let alone a schismatic church, and a realistic outlook must take account of this. The bold words used nearly a century earlier about discipline and government having the command and power given to use them without tarrying for any authority or command of man seem to have been forgotten. It is a singular commentary on much that had happened before, and perhaps an indication of a certain hollowness in a lot of the rationalising that had been going on, that when schism first became serious again it was the result not of any reconsideration of attitudes to the Church but of a change in the law, when all repressive measures were suddenly removed by James VII in 1687. Although the Presbyterians detested toleration, few of them were prepared to refuse it when it was offered to them. And since that date – 1687 – there has never been a time when there have not been congregations and organisations outside the Scottish establishment.

[1] *Ibid* II, pp 133, 222 and Appendix CXXI.

RELIGIOUS PROTEST AND URBAN AUTHORITY: THE CASE OF HENRY SHERFIELD, ICONOCLAST, 1633

by PAUL SLACK

THE trial of Henry Sherfield, the puritan recorder of Salisbury, before Star Chamber in February 1633 was one of the most famous in that court's last years; and his offence, 'unlawfully, riotously and prophanely' smashing the window in St Edmund's church which contained pictures of the Creation, is one of the best-known cases of puritan religious protest in the years preceding the Civil War.[1] But the background to the trial, and in particular the local tensions which lay behind it, have never been thoroughly explored. Yet Sherfield's case, like the contemporary churchales controversy in Somerset, provides an example of that important amalgam of local and national issues which shaped the English Revolution.[2] It also illuminates the social and political conditions which moulded Puritanism in an urban setting.

The facts of Sherfield's case were simple enough. In January 1630 the select vestry of St Edmund's parish, Salisbury, authorised him to remove a painted window and to replace it with plain glass, because, according to the vestry minute, it was 'very darksome whereby such as sitt neere to the same cannot see to reade in their bookes'.[3] But the

---

[1] There is a good summary of the trial in [S. R.] Gardiner, [History of England from the Accession of James I to the Outbreak of the Civil War] (London 1883–4) VII pp 254–8. The trial proceedings were printed in The Proceedings in the Star Chamber against Henry Sherfield Esq. (London 1717), and in various collections of state trials, including [S. Emlyn, A Complete Collection of] State Trials (3 ed London 1742) I pp 399–418, which is the account referred to here. Sherfield's case was one of those brought against Laud at his own trial: The Manuscripts of the House of Lords, XI (new series) Addenda 1514–1714 (London 1962) pp 402, 419, 458; W. Prynne, Canterburies Doome (London 1646) pp 102–3, 491, 494–5.

[2] See T. G. Barnes, 'County Politics and a Puritan Cause Célèbre: Somerset Churchales, 1633', TRHS 5th Series IX (1959) pp 103–22.

[3] [H. J. F. Swayne,] Churchwardens' Accounts [of S. Edmund and S. Thomas, Sarum 1443–1702] (Salisbury 1896) p 190. The churchwardens of the parish of St Thomas had removed a similar window with the approval of the subdean in 1583: ibid p 294. On the

major reason was the fact that the window was superstitious, absurd and idolatrous: the painter had

> put the Form of a little old Man in a blue and red Coat, for *God the Father*, and hath made seven such Pictures; whereas *God* is but One in Deity;... and in one Place he hath represented God the Father creating the Sun and Moon with a pair of Compasses in his Hand, as if he had done it according to some Geometrical Rules.

One woman had been found by the rector 'bowing to the Window'; a recusant stranger and his servant 'did kneel down and pray before' it. The window had been a 'Cause of Idolatry to some ignorant People'.[1]

When he heard of the vestry's order, the bishop forbade the window's destruction, but in October 1630 the child of the sexton saw 'a Man all in black' attacking it 'with a black Staff with a Pike in the End of it'. The incident became still more dramatic when 'the Staff broke, and he fell down... and lay there a quarter of an Hour groaning', and 'afterwards kept his House for a Month'. The offender, other witnesses testified, was Henry Sherfield. Complaint was made to the bishop's chancellor and Sherfield was prosecuted by the Attorney General in Star Chamber. He was fined £500 and ordered to make public acknowledgement of his offence before the bishop, although Laud, Neile, Wentworth and Cottington had pressed for a higher fine and his dismissal from his place as recorder.[2]

There were clear political reasons why this banal, somewhat ludicrous case should come before so illustrious a court and so eminent a set of judges. Sherfield had been MP for Salisbury in the parliaments of the 1620s, and had there been successively a fierce antagonist of Buckingham, an opponent of Montague and Arminianism, and a critic of the raising of tonnage and poundage. He was also the step-father of Walter Long, one of the leaders of the parliamentary opposition imprisoned with Eliot in 1629.[3] It is no surprise that Laud and archbishop Neile, himself criticised by Sherfield in debates on Montague's book, should wish to discredit so distinguished an opponent. For them two general issues were also involved. The first was the usurpation by the vestry of St Edmund's of the bishop's prerogatives.

St Edmund's window itself, probably fifteenth century in date, see G. M. Rushforth, *Medieval Christian Imagery* (Oxford 1936) p 151. (I am grateful to Dr P. A. Newton for this reference.)

[1] *State Trials* pp 399–400, 404, 405.   [2] *State Trials* pp 399–418 *passim.*

[3] PRO MS SP 16/55/64; Gardiner VII p 49; D. H. Willson, *The Privy Councillors in the House of Commons 1604–1629* (Minneapolis 1940) p 188; *House of Commons Journals* I pp 858, 921, 927; *The Manuscripts of the House of Lords* XI p 206; *DNB* under Sherfield

Sherfield and the other vestrymen claimed the church as a lay-fee in their control; indeed they even seem to have been able to choose their own puritan ministers in 1623 and 1641.[1] The bishops naturally agreed with Wentworth that such independent vestries should be reduced 'into Order and Obedience', and with Cottington that the implications were far-reaching: even if the window was 'scandalous', he argued, Sherfield had 'touched upon the Regal Power, and encroached upon the Hierarchy of the Bishops'.[2]

The second issue was what Laud, in one of his most famous speeches, alleged to be the presumption and arrogance of common lawyers like Sherfield: 'There was a time when Churchmen were as great in this Kingdom as you are now;...there will be a Time when you will be as low as the Church is now.' As if to prove his point, the two chief justices successfully urged a mild punishment on Sherfield which would leave him in his place as recorder; for Sir Thomas Richardson he was 'a grave Bencher, and a learned Man', for Sir Robert Heath 'a Gentleman of reputation'. Both judges were soon themselves to lose royal and Laudian favour.[3]

But local issues were as important in this trial as general principle or prejudice. Chief Justice Heath had advised Sherfield in the negotiations leading to the Salisbury charter of 1630; and in this he had been associated with another of Sherfield's judges, Philip, earl of Pembroke and Montgomery, the town's high steward, who declined to give any sentence in the case. In 1631 both Heath and Pembroke were again involved in correspondence with the town over its constitutional conflict with the bishop and the close.[4] This was a vital struggle for the liberties of the town and Sherfield's case played an important role in it. The charter of 1630 had confirmed the separation of the town from the bishop's jurisdiction, first achieved when Salisbury was incorporated in 1612. Immediately the bishop and cathedral chapter protested to the Privy Council and tried to obtain representation on the city's commission of the peace, 'for the better government of the sayd City and countenancing of the Churches Authority'. The king and Laud supported the bishop, as they did in similar conflicts elsewhere, and the

---

[1] *VCH Wiltshire* VI pp 151-2; *Churchwardens' Accounts* pp 173, 212. On select vestries, see C. Hill, *Society and Puritanism in Pre-Revolutionary England* (London 1964) p 435.

[2] *State Trials* pp 414, 408-9.

[3] *State Trials* pp 414, 409, 411; Gardiner VII pp 320, 361.

[4] S[alisbury] C[orporation] M[uniments], N101, letter to Heath of ? Jan 1627/8, letter of 30 Dec 1631; Add. 1, document 15Q; Tin Box 9, document 16. I am indebted to the Town Clerk of Salisbury for permission to consult and to quote from the archives in his care.

issue was finally decided in favour of the close in 1637.[1] But at the time of Sherfield's trial the struggle was at its height. In 1631 the town was compelled to defend itself to the king against charges of 'inconformitie to the state government and of Puritanisme', while the close could attack the recorder as a 'factious man'.[2] Sherfield's action had provided an ideal weapon for the ecclesiastical authority in Salisbury to use against the secular.

The ecclesiastical authority may itself have been divided, however. The bishop, John Davenant, was scarcely the Laudian ideal. He was already at odds with the king and Laud for preaching on predestination, and he was also in conflict with his dean and chapter over patronage within the close.[3] As a moderate Calvinist, his religious sympathies might have been expected to lie with Sherfield. Certainly in November 1629 he was addressing the recorder as his 'very loving friend' and assuring him that he 'hartily wished the orderly government and prosperous estate of the Cittie'.[4] It may be that he was pushed into taking action against Sherfield by his energetic chancellor and an already offended Laud. It is noticeable that in March 1633 the dean was writing to Secretary Windebank, hoping that Davenant might 'be encouraged and confirmed in his Resolution' to make Sherfield submit publicly, and it appears that in the end the bishop allowed Sherfield to tone down the wording of his submission.[5] Davenant was caught between the Scylla of the local interests of his dean and chapter on the one hand and the Charybdis of Laudian principles at court on the other. Sherfield was similarly caught, in his major role as representative of

1 R. Benson and H. Hatcher, *Old and New Sarum or Salisbury* (London 1843) p 377; Salisbury Diocesan Archives, Papers on disputes between the bishop and the town, document 15; *Calendar of State Papers, Domestic, 1637* pp 1, 4, 78, *1638–9* pp 122–3; PRO PC 2/46 pp 246–7, PC 2/47 p 404. For similar disputes in other cities, see Claire Cross, 'Achieving the Millennium: the Church in York during the Commonwealth' in *SCH* IV (1967) p 128; C. Hill, *Economic Problems of the Church* (Oxford 1956) p 9; W. T. MacCaffrey, *Exeter 1540–1640* (Cambridge, Mass. 1958) pp 218–20; and for the earlier history of this dispute in Salisbury: F. Street, 'The Relations of the Bishops and Citizens of Salisbury (New Sarum) between 1225 and 1612', *Wiltshire Archaeological and Natural History Magazine*, XXXIX (Devizes 1916) pp 319–61.
2 SCM N101, letter of 30 December 1631; Tin Box 4, document 19; Salisbury Diocesan Archives, Papers on disputes between the bishop and the town, document 16.
3 Gardiner, VII p 137; D. H. Robertson, *Sarum Close* (London 1938) pp 177–85.
4 SCM, letter of 30 November 1629 in a bundle of 'Law Papers in Chancery on the Charters'.
5 It was Dr Lynne, the chancellor, who informed the Privy Council of Sherfield's offence and he was prominent in finding witnesses against him: *Acts of the Privy Council 1630–1* p 204; *State Trials* p 403. On Sherfield's submission, compare the various proposals and drafts in PRO SP 16/232/56, 233/88, 89, 236/33, 75.

secular authority in a cathedral city as well as in the minor one of iconoclast in a parochial church.

If bishop and chapter were, as ever, divided, so too – and more seriously – was the town council. There Sherfield was the most eminent member of a small, but temporarily dominant, puritan oligarchy. He had been elected recorder in 1623 against the wishes of the old guard in the town, but by 1630 he was, with other puritan aldermen, in complete control.[1] Those who were suspected of icono-clasm with him, aldermen like Bartholomew Tookye and Henry Pearson, were members of the same puritan group; so were those who appeared for him at his trial, notably the energetic ex-mayor John Ivie and Peter Thatcher, rector of St Edmund's.[2] The chief men in this urban oligarchy, Sherfield, Thatcher, Tookye, Pearson, Ivie and John Dove were all members of St Edmund's vestry and were all 'commonly reputed and taken to be such persons as doe impugne and oppose Episcopall Jurisdiction'.[3] Those who survived, especially Ivie and Dove, were leaders of the commonwealth party in Salisbury during the Civil War.

While they owed their cohesion as a group to their control of St Edmund's vestry, within the town council they met with strong opposition. At this time they were trying to remodel both the govern-ment and the society of Salisbury by instituting an ambitious and expensive programme to relieve and discipline the poor. The scheme involved interference with private interests in the town in order to provide employment for the poor and also the establishment of a municipally owned brewery whose profits should be used for the benefit of the destitute. The aim was a typically puritan one, 'to reform the drunkenness, idlenes, running to the Alehowse...which have been and are the bane of our poore in Sarum', and the scheme met with what Thatcher described as the 'violent opposition of such turbu-lent spirits as made their own gayne the only levell of their actions'.[4] The opposition included both the dean and chapter and a sizeable minority within the council, led by the brewers whose economic

---

[1] Further elaboration on the statements made in this and the following paragraph and full references may be found in my chapter, 'Poverty and Politics in Salisbury 1597–1666' in *Crisis and Order in English Towns*, ed Peter Clark and Paul Slack (London 1972).

[2] *Acts of the Privy Council 1630–1* p 204; *State Trials* p 404. The account in *State Trials* gives the name 'John Joye'; it is clear from the MS notes on the trial in PRO SP 16/211/20, however, that this is a misreading of 'John Ivye'.

[3] PRO SP 16/183/58.

[4] PRO SP 16/527/4. John Ivie described the poor relief scheme and the opposition it encountered in his tract. *A Declaration* (London 1661).

interests were at stake. It is significant therefore that the one major Salisbury figure to give evidence against Sherfield was a brewer, Thomas Hancock, who said he had been the only man to oppose the order in St Edmund's vestry against the offending window. Seven years earlier the Sherfield clique had tried to vote him off the commission of the peace because of his opposition to the poor scheme; twelve years later two of his relations were suspected of royalism during the Civil War.[1] The prosecution of Sherfield could find support from the conservative opposition within the Salisbury council, as well as from the cathedral close; and his trial was one stage in the process by which local factions hardened into two opposing parties.

But Sherfield's trial also revealed the popular hatred of the puritan magistrates among those outside the political nation and divorced from its concerns. Their attempts to govern what they regarded as the 'great unjust rude rabble'[2] inevitably met with opposition from below. The depositions taken before Sherfield's trial are full of complaints that the justices bound over to appear before Quarter Sessions any who ventured to accuse them or their allies before the ecclesiastical courts.[3] They had tried to exclude from the town a rival jurisdiction which offered a traditional and alternative channel for litigation. They had similarly encroached on the preserve of ecclesiastical discipline by summoning before them those causing an affray in St Edmund's church over disputed seating arrangements, just as later in 1633 the mayor sent a child to the workhouse for hanging a pair of horns outside a gentleman's door, calling its mother 'hussye, baggage and a Rebell rogue'.[4] They also offended against traditional popular *mores*: the wife of one councillor 'would not weare a kercheif when she was churched', complained a witness.[5] And their justice was self-interested and partial. A woman who wished Sherfield had broken his neck in his fall was threatened with a whipping by the keeper of the workhouse; she asked the bishop's chancellor to protect her. Elizabeth Bowen, daughter of the sexton, was threatened with the same penalty by Sherfield himself for giving evidence against him. The popular

---

[1] PRO SP 16/183/58; SCM Council Ledger C fol 299r; *House of Lords Journals*, VII p 485.
[2] Ivie, *A Declaration* p 19.
[3] PRO SP 16/183/58. The following paragraphs are based on these depositions.
[4] PRO SP 16/540/93. The JPs also had recusants and separatists presented before them, as the town clerk pointed out in Sherfield's defence: *State Trials* p 404; for actual cases, see SCM S162, 12 July 1630, 5 December 1631, 9 May 1632 (accounts of monthly meetings of overseers of the poor before the justices).
[5] On puritan opposition to wearing the veil and to the whole ceremony of churching, see Keith Thomas, *Religion and the Decline of Magic* (London 1971) pp 38, 60–1.

attitude towards Sherfield and the puritan élite was summed up in the outburst of Nicholas Pitt, who was said to have asked 'a miserable poore person, having vile torne clothes on his backe', 'Hath Mr Recorder beheaded and broken so many neckes and couldst not thou gett noe clothes amongst them?'

Particular discontent arose out of Ivie's and Sherfield's attempts to control the town during the chaos caused by the plague of 1627. John Bowen, the sexton of St Edmund's, had then been deprived of his wages by the vestry because of 'disorder in his place to Mr Thacher' and had been replaced by John Nicholas, one of Thatcher's puritan clients. Bowen regained his office after the epidemic but only held on to it through the support of the bishop. He now attacked Nicholas's wife as 'a factious and seditious person and altogether adhering to such as effect Schismes and ready to oppose the discipline of the Church'. Bowen's own wife was the chief witness against Sherfield. Another was Thomas Lord, who had criticised Ivie's attempts to regulate the relief of the sick poor in 1627 and been presented before Quarter Sessions for doing so.[1] The trial of Sherfield provided an outlet for grievances such as these. The disaffected within Salisbury seized on the opportunity to bring down the recorder.

Sherfield's case, therefore, exemplifies the isolated and precarious position of a puritan urban oligarchy, endeavouring to impose order and discipline in the face of opposition not only from vested interests and higher authorities but also from below. And it was this latter threat which the other members of the Salisbury oligarchy stressed in their recorder's defence. Sherfield, they said, had brought the city 'to the present good estate...which they feare through his dishearteneinge will sodanly returne to the former extremities of Beggery and disorder'.[2] The earl of Dorset, one of his judges, also saw the problem of government in its local context: he opposed a harsh sentence

to avoid the Tumults of the rude ignorant People in the Countries where this Gentleman dwelleth, where he hath been a good Governour,...and hath punished Drunkenness and other Disorders; and then such Persons shall rejoice and triumph against him, and say, This you have for your severe Government.

The Attorney General might urge that 'when private Persons, or a Vestry, will take upon them Reformation,...it is the Highway to pull all out of order'; and it might be thought that 'New England

---

[1] *Churchwardens' Accounts* p 186; Ivie, *A Declaration* p 22.
[2] SCM Tin Box 4, document 19.

were the fitter place for Him...for it must be new or it will not please him'. But in his own local community, it was Sherfield who was the representative of authority and the guardian, so it seemed, of social order. In that context, the charge that 'he is an Encourager and Maintainer of all such as are ill affected Persons to their Government, and Contemners of their Authority', was completely misplaced.[1]

The trial of Sherfield was a concerted attempt to demolish a major pillar of strict puritan magistracy, not only by those who hated the Puritanism, but also by those excluded from or oppressed by the magisterial rule. 'The Defendant's witnesses', said his counsel, 'are Justices of the Peace, and such as have been Mayors of the city...; but the other Witnesses are poor People, and silly Women led by Mr Chancellor.'[2] In fact Sherfield's opponents were the real iconoclasts. The radical protest in Sherfield's case was against the puritan idol, the 'Man all in black', not against the 'little old man in blue' in a painted window.

[1] *State Trials* pp 415, 407; PRO SP 16/232/107; *State Trials* p 403.
[2] *State Trials* p 404.

SWEDENBORGIANISM: HERESY, SCHISM OR RELIGIOUS PROTEST?

by W. R. WARD

THE separation of Methodism from the Church of England has become one of the famous chestnuts of ecclesiastical history; despite the allegations of excited high-churchmen and Tractarians at the time, it was not well described in terms of heresy or schism, and embodied a great many other things besides religious protest; moreover it was a separation which has never been quite complete. The case of Swedenborgianism is interesting not only in its own right, but as showing that the issue between the Methodists and the Church was not a bi-partite affair, that there were other possibilities within and between them both, and it illustrates the curious mixture of spiritual and social factors which underlay the religious fragmentation of the late eighteenth and early nineteenth centuries.

Emmanuel Swedenborg, who died in London in 1772, had had a distinguished career as a scientist and a public servant of the Swedish monarchy. He had attempted as a scientist to demonstrate the spiritual basis of the material universe, and he retained his scientific interests even when in 1745 he gave up his diplomatic career to fulfil a divine mission to expound the Scriptures in the light of a series of visions and a vivid intercourse with the world of spirits. Swedenborg offered not a new revelation, but a true interpretation of the old one, based on the assumption that each part of the Scripture had a spiritual as well as a natural sense, and that the former had been revealed to him by what he called 'correspondencies' which had been lost since the time of Job. The doctrine of the Trinity he regarded as a piece of tritheism, and redemption was not an atonement to justice, but a process of bringing 'the hells into subjection, and the heavens into order and regulation, thus preparing the way for a new spiritual church'.[1] The accomplishment of this redemption began in 1757 and the new church, consisting of true believers of whatever denomination, was laid up in the new heavens in its internal form; at the last judgement the new earth, the New Jerusalem Church in its external form, would become apparent.

[1] E. Swedenborg, *The true Christian religion* (London 1874) para 115.

Swedenborg's doctrines attracted a good deal of ridicule among the orthodox. Bogue and Bennett, the historians of dissent, tried to be kind, commenting upon his writings, 'What reasonable man can hesitate to say that they afford evidence that he was insane? His was, indeed, no ordinary insanity, but that of a devotional and philosophic mind which often appears greatest when in ruins.'[1] John Wesley enjoyed himself hugely at Swedenborg's expense. 'Anyone of his visions puts his real character out of doubt. He is one of the most ingenious, lively, entertaining madmen that ever set pen to paper. But his waking dreams are so wild, so far remote both from Scripture and common sense, that one might as easily swallow the stories of "Tom Thumb" or "Jack the Giant-killer".'[2] After reading Swedenborg's *Theologia Coelestis* he added: 'It surely contains many excellent things. Yet I cannot but think the fever he had twenty years ago, when he supposes he was "introduced into the society of angels", really introduced him to the society of lunatics; but still there is something noble, even in his ravings.'[3] This last concession was important, for Wesley did not disguise the attraction which Swedenborg had for him. Like the evangelicals in other ways, Swedenborg witnessed to the apologetic difficulties in which the eighteenth-century churches had been placed, and to the anxieties which were abroad that neither the old orthodoxies nor the old mechanisms of religious establishment were reproducing the faith from generation to generation at a popular level. Swedenborg shared with them an intense devotion to the person of Jesus, and an affection for informal methods.

Indeed, the first important disciple of Swedenborg in England was Thomas Hartley, rector of Winwick in Northamptonshire (not Lancashire as stated in Cross's *Dictionary of the Christian Church*),[4] a friend of the countess of Huntingdon and other evangelicals, and a man in whose mystical and millenarian tendencies Wesley found much to commend as well as to condemn.[5] The most important translator of Swedenborg's works was John Clowes, a pupil of John Clayton, a member of Wesley's Holy Club, and subsequently a fellow of the Manchester collegiate church. A relative of the Byrom family, Clowes was presented to the rectory of St John's, Deansgate, Manchester, in

[1] D. Bogue and J. Bennett, *History of Dissenters* (2 ed by J. Bennett, London 1833) II, p 458.
[2] *Journal of John Wesley* [ed Nehemiah Curnock] (London 1938) V, p 354.
[3] *Ibid*, V, p 440. Wesley wrote a full scale review of Swedenborg's works in 1783 in the *Arminian Magazine*, VI (London 1783) pp 437–680.
[4] *The Oxford Dictionary of the Christian Church*, ed F. L. Cross (London 1957) p 1310.
[5] L. Tyerman, *Life and times of John Wesley* (London ed 1890) II, pp 518–24.

1769, when it was built by Edward Byrom. In 1780 Clowes formed a small society which in due course translated and published the entire Swedenborg corpus, and he defended the doctrines not only in the pulpit, but against his bishop,[1] and in the press against Methodists, Unitarians and Independents.[2] Moreover in somewhat the Methodist manner he gathered informal groups in his own house, for the study of the new doctrines on an undenominational basis, linked up with similar groups in principal towns elsewhere, began itinerant evangelism in the industrial villages round about, and gave active support to the Sunday schools, as a portent of the descent of the New Jerusalem from heaven.[3]

It was this point which gave the first trouble. The Swedenborgians, like the Methodists, had to face the question whether their status in the Church was tenable. The London society which had met in the Temple from 1783 broke up on this issue in 1787. One party, finding that the Society made limited progress, held that they could do better by public preaching, or as it was put, with ominously orthodox overtones, in Swedenborgian terms, by bringing the external church at once into agreement with the internal church as it existed in the hearts of believers. Clowes came down to London to save the day for the majority, arguing from Swedenborg's exposition of the apocalypse that the New Church should abide in the old until it grew to maturity, and that the authorities of the established Church would in the end revise their liturgy in a way palatable to Swedenborgians. The minority, however, were not to be restrained, and withdrew under the leadership of Robert Hindmarsh, the son of one of Wesley's preachers, who had himself been converted in a revival at Kingswood school, and who now brought in his father and subsequently a second Methodist preacher as ministers of the first Swedenborgian congregation.[4] This association did not last long, for Hindmarsh was a troublesome character, and in 1789 was expelled with five others on the ground of

[1] [A] *memoir of* [*the late Rev.*] *John Clowes* [*A.M. written by himself*] (Manchester 1834) p 43.

[2] For example, [J. Clowes] *A dialogue between a Churchman and a Methodist on the writings and opinions of Baron Swedenborg* (London 1802); J. Clowes, *A letter to Rev. John Grundy* (Manchester 1813); J. Clowes, *A letter to the Rev. W. Roby, containing some strictures in passages of his lectures in which he speaks of. . .Emmanuel Swedenborg* (Manchester 1819); J. Clowes, *A letter to Rev. W. Roby. . .in reply to his pamphlet. . .entitled Anti Swedenborgianism* (Manchester 1819).

[3] *Memoir of John Clowes*, p 47: [Theodore] Compton, *Life* [& *correspondence of Rev. John*] *Clowes* (3 ed London 1898) pp 30, 46.

[4] [Robert] Hindmarsh, *Rise and progress* [*of the New Jerusalem Church in England and America and other parts*] (London 1861) pp 53–5; *Journal of John Wesley*, v, 258–60.

lax views of the conjugal relationship, views charitably described by the *DNB* as 'perhaps only theoretical'.

But for the Swedenborgians as for the Methodists, the question would not be settled by what happened in London, but by what happened in the more dynamic circumstances of the North, and under social more than religious pressures. In the early 'nineties as the Manchester Methodists were concluding that they must establish a status independent of the Establishment, by having their preaching at church hours, and receiving the sacrament from their own preachers, the great majority of the Manchester Swedenborgians resolved to come out too, and in 1793 opened a chapel of their own in Peter Street, taking as their minister the Reverend William Cowherd, Clowes's curate. The language of the new congregation was significant; they spoke of themselves as 'so disaffected to a separation, that they wish not any longer to separate their outward profession from their inward sentiments',[1] and they gathered numerous congregations among the disaffected of South Lancashire and Yorkshire. After the war, as Manchester was moving towards Peterloo, the pressures were even greater. It is probable that, even then, the Peter Street congregation was what it is revealed to have been a little later by the Manchester marriage registers,[2] namely, more nearly the religious expression of an occupational group than any other church in the town, its mainstay consisting of Failsworth silk weavers, the hard-pressed labour force of an industry which failed to hold its ground on the northern fringe of the town. The Reverend Joseph Proud, an ex-General Baptist Minister, now a Swedenborgian, then laid it down that 'the church on earth must be a distinct, visible, external church, seen and known to be such in the world,' while even Clowes concluded 'that the present distresses of the times are awful symptoms of the decay and dissolution of the old Christian Church, and announce with a loud voice...that the coming of the Lord is at hand, for the establishment of his predicted New Church'.[3] If social schism must take the true church into secession, it exerted a psychological pressure which made Cowherd an extreme example of the doctrinaire churchman of the day. Before long he had seceded again, and established a new congregation in which teetotallism was *de rigueur* and a vegetarian diet was

---

[1] Hindmarsh, *Rise and progress*, p 146.

[2] I am indebted to the Registrar-General for permission to examine the 1837–50 registers in the Manchester Register Office.

[3] Compton, *Life of Clowes*, pp 66, 166.

made a condition of communion so strict, his enemies averred, 'that many individuals of his Society, particularly weakly females, fell sacrifices to the task imposed on them'. Equally doctrinaire, the congregation he left behind, abandoned his reformed anglican liturgy as an old garment, 'to be seen clothed in their proper New Jerusalem attire.'[1]

The schismatic Swedenborgians, who in Manchester were organised under the name of Bible Christians, took up the cause of radical reform with enthusiasm, and when at the time of Peterloo the official denominations did their best to stamp out radicalism in the Sunday Schools, the Bible Christians incurred violent unpopularity with the press, by endeavouring to capture the undenominational tradition for themselves, in Manchester, Oldham and elsewhere, by organising Union Sunday Schools. The one they established in connexion with Christ Church, Hulme, lasted at least fifty years and claimed later to be the first scientific institution established in England for the working-classes.[2] The leading figure here was James Scholefield, a poetaster and lively autodidact, who violently attacked the reactionary attitudes of official Methodists and evangelicals,[3] and in 1823 opened his own chapel in Every Street, Ancoats, a building which ultimately became part of the University Settlement. It was no doubt the founding of this congregation, and the Swedenborgians' reputation for liturgical innovation, which led to a report in the *Supporter & Scioto Gazette* in far-off Chillicothe, Ohio, that ' a new society of Christians has been formed at Manchester, England, who profess as one of their leading tenets, to wear sky-blue stockings and orange coloured shoes'.[4] From Every Street Scholefield dispensed radical politics (he was a friend of Cobden and took an active part in the Chartist Convention), vegetarian recipes, 'Scholefield's Cholera Mixture', and an undertaking service for those it failed to cure.[5] At the time of the religious census in 1851

[1] Hindmarsh, *Rise and progress*, pp 147–8.
[2] J. Scholefield, *Letters and tracts on religious subjects* (Manchester 1827–41); *Manchester City News*, 15 December 1883.
[3] J. Scholefield, *A reply to the 'Address to the labouring classes of Manchester & Salford'; together with remarks on the subject of the Auxiliary Bible Society* (Manchester, 1821); *Manchester Observer* p 944.
[4] *Supporter and Scioto Gazette*, 25 November 1824. I owe this reference to the kindness of my colleague, Mr D. J. Ratcliffe.
[5] See for example J. Scholefield, *Odes to the sun and moon in which are shown the unchange-ableness of deity* (Manchester 1832); J. Scholefield, *An address to the members and friends of the Bible Christians assembling at Christ Church Every Street, Manchester* (Manchester 1845).

Christ Church, Ancoats, still had a congregation,[1] but the family tradition was that before his death Scholefield declared, 'Make what use you can of the chapel, girls. Use it for a circus if you can – after all it's round. It has served its turn as a chapel.'[2] Manchester Corporation closed his burial ground in the course of sanitary improvements in 1855, and apart from educational effort continued in other forms, the Vegetarian Society which has survived to our own days, and the services to radical and teetotal causes of Joseph Brotherton, member of Parliament for Salford, 1832–57, and minister of a Bible Christian congregation there, not much remained.

For some years after Peterloo, however, it seemed likely that things might turn out otherwise, for if Swedenborgianism was by no means disentangled from the establishment, it was intermingled with various forms of evangelicalism. Clowes ministered among Methodists and on occasion preached from a Methodist pulpit. After Wesley's death substantial Methodist secessions to the Swedenborgians were expected, and later the Primitives also suffered losses in the same quarter.[3] One Swedenborgian missionary, John Parry, a former Methodist New Connexion preacher, succeeded in 1819 in seizing a Wesleyan pulpit from the minister at Adwalton, near Leeds, and looked to methodist societies to foster the growth of the New Church, as Clowes looked to the establishment. In 1821 Swedenborgianism was reported to be displacing Independent Methodism at West Houghton, and in 1822 to be infecting Methodism near Accrington. In 1823 the essence of a confused situation was displayed in microcosm at the village of Embsay near Skipton. Here there was a Union Chapel in which the pulpit was occupied in turn by the Wesleyans, the Primitives and the Calvinists, and it is not surprising that the trustees were prevailed upon to admit the Swedenborgian missionary into the cycle.[4] It is commonly said that evangelicalism represented a revival of orthodoxy, but at the grass-roots it was a very undenominational kind of orthodoxy. The history or even the cataloguing of the Union Chapels has not been attempted, and within the larger communities the situation was still open enough for Swedenborgianism to retain a cross-bench status. The bigots of the 'thirties and 'forties, evangelical,

---

[1] PRO MS H.O. 129/21/473.1.1.13.

[2] Mary D. Stocks, *Doctor Scholefield* (Manchester 1936) pp 8–9.

[3] *Memoirs of the first forty-five years of the life of James Lackington. By himself* (London ed 1794) p 310; J. Macdonald, *Memoirs of the Rev. Joseph Benson* (London 1822) p 228; John Walford, *Memoirs of the life and labours of Hugh Bourne* (London 1855–6) II, 7.

[4] Hindmarsh, *Rise and progress*, pp 326–7, 336, 339–40, 362, 368, 396–7.

Tractarian and Buntingite, had to exclude a great deal from the traditions they claimed to defend.

Yet the social fabric did not collapse, even in the Peterloo crisis, and Robert Hindmarsh, like evangelicals of England and Germany, was able to construct a conservative vision of salvation from the East, believing that the Holy League and the new Prussian liturgical reforms were founded on New Jerusalem doctrines.[1] Moreover the Swedenborgians, like old-style Wesleyans, never all felt the compulsion to secede from the Establishment. Clowes retained his living till he died in 1831 at the age of 88, and in the annual conferences at Hawkstone (the former seat of the cross-bench evangelical brothers, Sir Richard and Rowland Hill) he established a continuing forum for the Swedenborgians who did not wish to secede, and some who did. His bishop took his part against his anglican critics, and if in controversy he was in the odd stance of defending a denomination to which he did not belong, and in important respects disapproved of, his position was by no means insupportable, and in various ways resembled that of the old evangelicals. For if Swedenborgianism was heresy, it was abused rather than condemned; if it was schism, it was never all schismatic; and though it embodied, and felt the pressure of violent social protest, it did not cut all its roots in the old establishment or the religious quest of the eighteenth century.

[1] Martin Brecht, 'Aufbruch und Verhärtung. Das Schicksal der nach Osten ausgerichteten Erweckungshewegung in der nachnapoleonischen Zeit'; paper presented before Commission Internationale d'Histoire Ecclésiastique Comparée (Moscow 1970); Robert Hindmarsh, *Remarks on the Holy League* (Manchester 1816).

AN IRISH HERETIC BISHOP:
ROBERT CLAYTON OF CLOGHER

by A. R. WINNETT

IN 1735 a great change took place in Cork society. Hitherto, wrote John Boyle, fifth earl of Cork and Orrery, 'we trembled at a bumper and loath'd the Glorious Memory. We were as silent and melancholy as captives and we were strangers to mirth'. But now, he went on, 'we sing catches, read *Pastor Fido* and talk love.'[1] The change was due to the death of Peter Browne, bishop of Cork and Ross, and the advent of his successor, Robert Clayton. Browne, according to Harris, was 'an austere, retired and mortified man',[2] but Clayton was a man of the world and given to social life. Browne had written treatises against drinking in memory of the dead (his inclusion of the toast to the memory of king William in his condemnation led to his being regarded by some as a Jacobite) and against the drinking of healths: the former was a blasphemous profanation of the Lord's Supper, and the latter a pagan custom and a cause of intemperance.[3] Under the more relaxed rule of Clayton glasses could be raised unaccompanied by troubled consciences.

There was a more important respect in which Clayton presented a contrast to his predecessor in the Cork bishopric. Browne was the champion of an uncompromising orthodoxy and a determined opponent of all forms of Arianism, including the semi-Arianism of Dr Samuel Clarke. His doctrine of analogy was an instrument employed for the exposition and defence of the two great mysteries of the Gospel, the Trinity and the Person of Christ.[4] Clayton, so far from enjoying a reputation for orthodoxy, lived the latter part of his life, and finally died, under the suspicion of grave heresy, and his heretical

[1] Letter to Thomas Southerne, 20 March 1736-7, in *The Orrery Papers*, ed Emily C. Boyle (London 1903) I, pp 206-7.
[2] *The Whole Works of Sir James Ware, revised and improved by W. Harris* (London 1764) I, p 541.
[3] On Browne see [C. A.] Webster, [*The Diocese of Cork*] (Cork 1920) pp 303-17.
[4] Browne's two major works were *The Procedure, Extent and Limits of the Human Understanding* (London 1728), and *Things Divine and Supernatural conceived by Analogy with Things Natural and Human* (London 1733).

propensities were not without justification linked with his friendship with Samuel Clarke.

Robert Clayton was born in Dublin in 1695, the son of John Clayton, dean of Kildare and minister of St Michael's, Dublin. He was educated at Westminster under Zachary Pearce, and at Trinity College, Dublin, of which he became a fellow.[1] He belonged to the wealthy Clayton family of Fulwood in Lancashire and was possessed of a considerable personal fortune. He conferred part of his patrimony upon his three sisters, and marrying Catherine, daughter of chief baron Donnellan, he presented his wife's dowry to her sister. It was Clayton's generosity which was an indirect cause of his ecclesiastical preferment. Visiting London soon after his marriage he was appealed to for financial help by an impoverished scholar, who brought a recommendation of his case from Samuel Clarke. Clayton gave him £300, an action which led to a close friendship with Clarke, and the two would meet to discuss together some of the currently disputed questions of theology. In the development of Clayton's theological opinions it is impossible not to discern the influence of Clarke. Clarke spoke in high terms of Clayton to queen Caroline, whose favourite and mistress of the robes, lady Sundon, was a cousin by marriage of Clayton,[2] and this twofold royal interest made his nomination to a bishopric almost certain. In 1730 he was consecrated bishop of Killala, whence he was translated in 1735 to Cork and Ross. Further advancement came to him ten years later with his appointment to the see of Clogher.

In 1751 Clayton became the centre of a theological controversy arising from the appearance of a small volume entitled *An Essay on Spirit, wherein the Doctrine of the Trinity is considered in the Light of Nature and Reason*. This anonymous work, stated on the title-page to be by 'a clergyman of the Church of Ireland', was on its publication generally believed to be by Clayton, but Andrew Kippis in his account of Clayton in *Biographia Britannica* says that its author was a

[1] The fullest account of Clayton's life is in [Andrew] Kippis, [*Biographia Britannica*] (2 ed, London 1778–84) III, pp 620–8. See also Webster, pp 318–20, and *DNB*, art. Clayton, Robert.

[2] See Katherine Thomson, *Memoirs of Viscountess Sundon* (London 1847) II, ch 1 for letters written by Clayton to Lady Sundon. These letters reveal his ambition and worldly attitude to ecclesiastical office. 'It has not been customary for persons either of birth or fortune to breed up their children to the Church...the only way to remedy which is by giving extraordinary encouragements to persons of birth and interest whenever they seek for ecclesiastical preferment, which will encourage others of the same quality to come into the Church and may thereby render ecclesiastical preferments of the same use to their Majesties as civil employments.' Letter of 19 March 1730–1.

young clergyman of the Clogher diocese, who showed it to the bishop, expressing a fear as to the consequences of publishing it under his own name, whereupon the bishop, 'with that romantic generosity which marked his character, readily took the matter upon himself', and prefixing a dedication to George Stone, the primate, arranged for its publication, not avowing it as his own but allowing it to pass as such.[1] It is difficult to assess the truth of Kippis's statement as to the origin of the *Essay on Spirit*. One may ask with Dr D. A. Chart whether a bishop, however great his 'romantic generosity', would place his position and prospects in jeopardy to safeguard an obscure young clergyman,[2] though a few years later Clayton was to place himself at serious risk by committing his views to print under his own name. The author of the *Essay*, writing a year or two after its publication, gave as the reason for its anonymity, that 'theological disputants very seldom treat one another with that politeness or even candour which ought to be expected from a liberal education, and he had a mind to disengage his subject from all personal reflections and personal altercations'.[3] In some of the replies to the *Essay* Clayton is named as its author. One of these was by Thomas Knowles, 'addressed by permission to the Lord Archbishop of Canterbury', and the ascription in it of the *Essay* to Clayton elicited from the author of the *Essay* the somewhat inconclusive comment, 'I own that I cannot but be surprised to find that Dr Herring should lend his name to such a piece of impoliteness'.[4] The *Gentleman's Magazine* for January 1752 described the *Essay* as 'written as supposed by Dr Clayton, bishop of Clogher',[5] but a correspondent in the May number gave it as his opinion that in view of its contents the bishop could not have written it and that it must be the work of a papist seeking to injure the Church of Ireland.[6] A bookseller's advertisement of 1757 lists the *Essay* among the works by Clayton,[7] and it was included under his name in the 1759 single-volume edition of the *Vindication of the Histories of the Old and New*

---

[1] Kippis, III, p 623. J. B. Leslie, *Clogher Clergy and Parishes* (Enniskillen 1929) p 19 suggests that the author, who wrote under Clayton's direction, may have been a certain John Hawkshaw, but he gives no reasons.

[2] *History of the Church of Ireland*, ed W. Alison Phillips (Oxford 1933) III, p 231.

[3] *Some Thoughts on Self-Love, Innate Ideas, Free Will, etc, occasioned by reading Mr Hume's Works* (Dublin 1753) p 47.

[4] *Ibid* p 53. [5] *Gentleman's Magazine* (London 1752) p 13.

[6] *Ibid* p 159.

[7] Back page of *The Bishop of Clogher's Speech* [*made in the House of Lords in Ireland for omitting the Nicene and Athanasian Creeds out of the Liturgy,*] 'London, printed for R. Baldwin and M. Cooper, in Paternoster Row, 1757.'

Testament. There is a similarity of ideas and argument between the *Essay* and Part III of the *Vindication*, and its language and style resemble those of Clayton's undisputed works. Kippis asserts that Dr Bernard, dean of Derry, Clayton's nephew by marriage and his executor, was one of the few who knew the true authorship of the *Essay* and that he authorised Dr Thomas Campbell to disclose that Clayton was only its 'adopted father'.[1] Nevertheless Campbell in his *Philosophical Survey of the South of Ireland*, published in 1777, refers to Clayton without qualification as the author of the *Essay*, adding that 'he was a disciple of Dr Clarke, to whom they say he owed his preferment'.[2] The balance of evidence on the whole supports Clayton's authorship of the *Essay on Spirit*, but in any case there can be no doubt that he fully identified himself with its contents.

The dedicatory preface addressed to primate Stone, and acknowledged by Kippis as the work of Clayton, is a plea for religious toleration and a charitable attitude to religious differences. After observing that many Christians might well have been Jews or Muslims had they been born elsewhere, the author continues:

If it pleases the Almighty to endow one man with a better understanding, or greater natural abilities of any kind, than his neighbour, or to appoint the place of his birth where he has better opportunities of being informed in true religion ...these are blessings for which he ought to be thankful to his Creator, but are far from being any reason why he should bear an ill-will to those persons who have not received the same advantages from Providence; or why he should not live in a kind and neighbourly manner with them, though he thinks them in an error with regard to their religious principles.[3]

Theologically the *Essay* represents an extreme form of subordinationism, the Father alone being truly God and the Son and Spirit possessing only the delegated rank of godhead:

There can be but one God, that is, one supreme intelligent Agent; which one God may, however, create an infinite series of spiritual agents in subordination to one another, some of which may, by an authority communicated to them from the supreme God, act as Gods, with regard to those inferior beings who are committed unto their charge.[4]

---

[1] Kippis, III, p 623.
[2] *A Philosophical Survey of the South of Ireland* (London 1777). Thomas Campbell was successively curate 1761, prebendary 1772 and chancellor 1773 of St Macartan's cathedral, Clogher.
[3] *Essay on Spirit* (2 ed, London 1751) pp xxxvii, xxxviii. An earlier edition appeared the same year in Dublin, and a third edition in Dublin the following year.
[4] *Ibid* pp 113–14.

These subordinate beings are angels, and the author employs an ingenious method of scriptural exegesis to identify the angel of Jehovah, Wisdom, the *Logos* and the Son of God with the archangel Michael.[1] A similar mode of exegesis is employed to show the identity of the Holy Spirit with the angel Gabriel.[2] The author considers it more befitting to God's perfection that he 'should choose to govern this universe by a gradual subordination of beings, one superior to another, rather than to be the sole Director or Governor of every the most minute affair',[3] and he justifies the worship paid to the Son and Spirit on the ground that 'such adoration or worship, not being paid them on their own account but on account of the authority which hath been delegated unto them, terminates in the one only and supreme God'.[4]

As was to be expected the *Essay* met with a hostile reception from the upholders of orthodoxy. Warburton described it as 'made up out of the rubbish of old heresies, of a much ranker cast than common Arianism', observing that what would be heresy in an English bishop 'in an Irish 'tis only a blunder.'[5] A stream of books and pamphlets in reply to the *Essay* issued from the press during the next few years, and among their writers were William Jones of Nayland, Thomas Randolph, president of Corpus Christi College, Oxford, and Thomas McDonnell, fellow of Trinity College, Dublin. Some of these replies were answered in turn by the author of the *Essay*.[6] For Clayton the association of his name with the *Essay* meant his being passed over for the archbishopric of Tuam, vacant in 1752 by the death of Dr Josiah Hort, for which his name had been put forward by the lord-lieutenant, the duke of Dorset.[7]

In the Dedication prefixed to the *Essay on Spirit* Clayton had advocated a change in the form of subscription required of the clergy, and he returned to this in a speech to the Irish House of Lords in February 1756. The occasion was his introduction of a bill 'for more effectually uniting His Majesty's Protestant subjects and for explaining an Act for the uniformity of public prayers'. What the bill proposed was the amendment of the Declaration of Assent and the removal of the Nicene

---

[1] *Ibid* pp 44–71. The identity of Christ with Michael is held to-day by the Jehovah's Witnesses. [2] *Ibid* pp 73–82.
[3] *Ibid* p 85. [4] *Ibid* pp 83–4.
[5] Letter to Hurd, 18 November 1751, in John Nichols, *Literary Anecdotes of the Eighteenth Century* (London 1812–15) II, p 231.
[6] See appendix to this paper for a list of works appearing in connection with the controversy over the *Essay on Spirit*.
[7] Kippis, III, p 624; R. Mant, [*History of the Church of Ireland*] (London 1840) II, p 615.

and Athanasian creeds from the Prayer Book. Clayton urged that the wording of the Declaration be so altered that assent was given not to all things contained in the Prayer Book but only to their *use*. Those who could not entirely approve of the things themselves, he held, might in perfect honesty agree to their use for the sake of peace and uniformity.[1] The proposal concerning the creeds was the replacement of the Nicene and Athanasian creeds, where they are ordered in the Prayer Book, by the Apostles' creed. Clayton did not in his speech explicitly reject the consubstantiality of the Son as taught in the Nicene creed but he regarded it as a 'metaphysical point of theology not plainly revealed in the scriptures' and therefore not an article of faith.[2] On the Athanasian creed he was more severe. He abhorred its damnatory clauses, and maintained that the statement of the creed asserting the co-equality and co-eternity of the Persons was inconsistent with the 'priority of order and dignity' existing between the Persons.[3] Although rejecting the Athanasian authorship of the creed he took the opportunity of attacking the character of Athanasius, whom he represents as ambitious and unscrupulous, getting himself illegally consecrated, and after being dispossessed forcing his way back into the bishopric 'over the murdered corpses of his antagonists and wading into his cathedral through seas of blood'.[4] The bill was defeated by twenty-six votes to four.[5]

In 1752 Clayton published part I of his *Vindication of the Histories of the Old and New Testament*, written in answer to the objections of lord Bolingbroke. Part II followed in 1754 and Part III in 1757. In Part III he once more treated of the Trinity and the Person of Christ, largely reproducing the ideas earlier put forward in the *Essay on Spirit*. Clayton's Arian sympathies are here quite explicit, and for him Arianism, or at least a subordinationist doctrine of the Trinity, is the only alternative to Sabellianism on the one hand and a virtual tritheism on the other. He rejects what he terms the 'Athanasian explanation of the doctrine of the Trinity' as contrary both to scripture and to common-sense. Christ is not 'a composition of two parties, perfect God and perfect Man', but 'an intermediate Being, as the term Mediator naturally implies'.[6] Clayton interprets the Nicene creed in a way that approaches as nearly as possible to Arianism. He points

---

[1] *The Bishop of Clogher's Speech*, p 9. Clayton pointed out that in the Act of Uniformity itself assent was demanded only to the *use* of all things in the Prayer Book.

[2] *Ibid* p 12. [3] *Ibid* p 24. [4] *Ibid* p 20.

[5] 2 February 1756, *Journals of the House of Lords* (Dublin 1779–1800) IV, p 47.

[6] *A Vindication of the Histories of the Old and New Testaments, in three Parts* (London 1759) p 387.

out, for instance, that the Son is declared to be not *monoousios* but *homoousios* with the Father, that is, 'not one and the same individual substance but of the same kind of substance with the Father, as a human son, although a distinct and separate existence, is of the same kind of substance with his natural father'; that *homoousios* does not mean equality with the Father in power and glory; and that the derivative nature of the Son's deity implies his inferiority to him who has deity in himself.[1] Clayton considers the term Son of God as applied to Christ. When Christ is said to be 'the Son of God before all worlds' it must be understood to signify not 'the manner of his production into existence' but only God's special love and affection towards him.[2] Though men and angels are called in scripture sons of God, Christ has a better title than the rest to be so called, as 'he was the first, and therefore probably the most perfect and complete, production of God's creative power'. Christ is also called Son of God because as a glorified preexisting spirit he 'submitted himself to descend from heaven and have himself conveyed by the wonderful power of God into the womb of the Virgin'.[3] As in the *Essay on Spirit* Christ is identified with the angel of Jehovah and the archangel Michael.[4] Michael is represented in scripture as the chief adversary of Satan, and this conflict culminates in the passion of Christ.[5] Clayton's teaching on the redemptive work of Christ interprets it as a victory over Satan won by Christ's obedience unto death;[6] as the suffering of an innocent Person which wins a corresponding reward from God, 'a kingdom for himself and glory for us';[7] and as 'the sacrifice of the Son of God to rectify [the world's] moral constitution'.[8] He rejects, however, the notion of satisfaction as resting upon a false premise, namely, 'that God could not forgive the trespasses against himself, and so remit the penalty if he pleased, without any other satisfaction but that of his own goodwill'.[9] Finally Clayton adopts a minimising interpretation of justification by faith. Faith corresponds to intention in morality, so that where the will exists to do good but the ability is lacking, 'there my faith will supply the want of works, which is the sole instance that can possibly be put wherein we shall be saved by faith alone'.[10]

The influence of Clarke is plainly seen in Clayton's trinitarian and christological doctrine, and in one respect Clayton went further than Clarke. Clarke explicitly repudiated the notion that Christ was a

[1] *Ibid* p 431. [2] *Ibid* p 442. [3] *Ibid* p 443.
[4] *Ibid* pp 453–8. [5] *Ibid* pp 485–8. [6] *Ibid* p 487.
[7] *Ibid* p 491. [8] *Ibid* p 497 [9] *Ibid* p 491.
[10] *Ibid* pp 500–1.

creature and he could therefore claim that his teaching could not properly be described as Arian,[1] but Clayton asserted the creaturehood of Christ, both by identifying him with the archangel Michael and by expressly declaring him to be 'the first, and therefore probably the most perfect and complete, production of God's creative power'. Clayton's position was in effect a union of Arianism with the earlier angel-christology which Martin Werner finds present in the New Testament.[2]

The views of Clayton expressed in Part III of the *Vindication* moved his fellow-bishops to action, and the king was petitioned with the object of his ordering the lord-lieutenant, now the duke of Bedford, to take steps for Clayton's prosecution. A meeting of bishops was held at the primate's house to prepare the case against him and Clayton was cited to appear before an ecclesiastical commission, but on 26 February 1758, before the commission sat, he died of a nervous illness thought to have been brought on by the shock of the prosecution and probable loss of his bishopric.[3] Queen Caroline, who might have protected him, had died, and it was said that he felt deeply his abandonment by the king. Clayton, whose death took place at his house in St Stephen's Green, Dublin, was buried in the churchyard of Donnybrook.[4]

Clayton is chiefly remembered as an exponent of Arian theology and as a bishop whom only opportune death saved from almost certain condemnation for heresy, but there are other grounds for according him a place in the history of eighteenth-century Ireland. He was a man of versatile mind and wide interests, which were recognised by his being admitted to the fellowship both of the Royal Society and of the Society of Antiquaries. His scientific bent is evident in the astronomical and geological discussions in Part II of the *Vindication* and in the references to his own observations of rocks and plants in

---

[1] Clarke taught the eternity of the Son, but held that scripture gave no support to the doctrine of his oneness with the Father. 'They are both worthy of censure: both they who on the one hand presume to affirm that the Son was made out of nothing, and they who on the other hand affirm that he is the self-existent substance.' *The Scripture Doctrine of the Trinity* in *Works* (London 1738) IV, pp 205-6.

[2] *The Formation of Christian Dogma*, trans S. G. F. Brandon (London 1957) pp 120-30.

[3] Kippis, III, p 627; Mant, II, 617-18. According to Burdy, Clayton asked a lawyer whether he thought he should lose his bishopric. When told, 'My lord, I believe you will', Clayton replied, 'Sir, you have given me a stroke I'll never get the better of.' Mrs Clayton is said to have warned her husband of the consequence of publishing his opinions. [S.] Burdy, [*Life of Philip Skelton*], ed Norman Moore (Oxford 1914) p 138.

[4] [W. Maziere] Brady, [*Clerical and Parochial Records of Cork, Cloyne and Ross*] (London 1864) III, pp 77-8.

Cork and Clogher.[1] In 1753 he edited *A Journal from Grand Cairo to Mount Sinai and back again*, 'translated from a MS written by the Prefetto of Egypt'. This ran into several editions, in Dutch and German as well as English. It was included in John Pinkerton's *A General Collection of Voyages* (London, 1808–14). Clayton had artistic tastes and great social gifts.[2] His generosity was well known. As a member of the Linen Board he sought to procure employment for the poor of his diocese.[3] One of his clergy in Clogher was Philip Skelton, far removed from him in doctrinal conviction. When Clayton and he met they invariably fell to arguing, but their personal relationship appears to have been on the whole cordial.[4] If lapidary tributes are not always a reliable source of information concerning those whom they commemorate, there is no reason to doubt what was said of Clayton on his tombstone in Donnybrook,

> He lived esteemed by good men,
> He died regretted by many.[5]

APPENDIX

BIBLIOGRAPHY OF THE CONTROVERSY ARISING FROM 'AN ESSAY ON SPIRIT'

A. WORKS BY THE AUTHOR OF THE 'ESSAY' (= ROBERT CLAYTON?)

1 *A Sequel to an Essay on Spirit, addressed to his Grace the Archbishop of Canterbury* (London 1752).

2 *A Defence of an Essay on Spirit* (London 1752). [Contains answers to 6, 7 and 8.]

3 *Some Thoughts on Self-Love, Innate Ideas, Free Will, etc, occasioned by reading Mr Hume's Works* (Dublin 1573). [Attacks 12 and defends anonymity of the *Essay* against 15.]

4 *The Doctrine of the Trinity as usually explained inconsistent with Scripture and*

---

[1] *Vindication*, pp 326–7.
[2] 'He eats, drinks and sleeps in taste. He has pictures by Carlo, Morat, music by Corelli, castles in the air by Vitruvius.' *Orrery Papers*, I, p 206. The horse-races and balls under the bishop's patronage in Killala are described by Mrs Delany. *Autobiography and Correspondence of Mary Granville, Mrs Delany* (London 1862) I, p 373.
[3] Burdy, p 139.
[4] Skelton felt gratitude to Clayton for his living of Pettigo and so refused to write against him. Clayton invited Skelton to preach a visitation sermon and is recorded as dining with him in Pettigo. Burdy, pp 115–17.
[5] Brady, III, p 78.

Reason, in a Letter to the Author of the late Vindication of the Doctrine of the Trinity (London 1754). [Reply to 19. This is attributed to Clayton, though on p 1 the author professedly distinguishes himself from the author of the *Essay*.]

5 *Some Remarks on Dr McDonnell's Essay towards an Answer to the Essay on Spirit* (Dublin 1754). [Reply to 22.]

B. WORKS BY OTHERS, MOSTLY CRITICAL OF THE ESSAY

6 *A Letter to the Right Reverend the Lord Bishop of Clogher occasioned by His Lordship's Essay on Spirit* (London 1752). [See 2. Attributed to Richard Moseley. This and 13 are written from a theological standpoint similar to that of the *Essay*. The author criticises the *Essay* on various secondary points of doctrine, but chiefly because it clothes simple truths in 'metaphysical garb' and 'metaphysical jargon'.]

7 *An Answer to an Essay on Spirit in a Dissertation on the Scripture Expressions, Angel of the Lord and Angel of Jesus Christ* (Dublin 1752). [See 2.]

8 Henry, Samuel. *A clear Vindication of the true eternal Godhead of Jesus Christ and of the Holy Ghost, in opposition to the Notions published in a late pamphlet, entitled an Essay on Spirit* (Waterford 1752). [See 2.]

9 Kirkby, John. *An effectual and easy Demonstration of the sacred eternal and co-equal Trinity of the Godhead* (London 1752).

10 *A friendly Conference between Matter and Spirit, being a complete Illustration of a Treatise entitled An Essay on Spirit* (Dublin 1752).

11 *A modern Preface put into plain English by Way of Abstract for the Use of the Poor and made plain to vulgar Capacities* (Dublin 1752). [A satirical attack.]

12 *The genuine Sequel to an Essay on Spirit* (London 1752). [See 3. Purports to be written by the author of the *Essay* but in fact ridicules it.]

13 *A second Letter to the Right Reverend the Lord Bishop of Clogher, being an Answer to the Defence of an Essay on Spirit* (London 1753). [See 6. Attributed to Richard Moseley.]

14 A Friend of the Established Church. *A plain and proper Answer to the Question, Why does not the Bishop of Clogher, supposing him to be the Author of an Essay on Spirit, resign his Preferments* (London 1753). [Attributed to Frederick Toll, vicar of Dogmersfield. The author is sympathetic to Clayton, maintaining that he is no more dishonest than other clergy who subscribe to the Prayer Book and Articles. Subscription imposes an intolerable burden on the clergy.]

15 Knowles, Thomas. *An Answer to the Essay on Spirit* (London 1753). [See 3.]

16 Jones, William. *A full Answer to the Essay on Spirit* (London 1753). [By Jones of Nayland.]

17 Rudd, Sayer. *The Negative on that Question, Whether is the Archangel Michael our Saviour, examined and defended, in a Letter to the Lord Bishop of Chloger (sic)* (London 1753).

18 Scott, John. *The holy scriptural Doctrines of the Trinity and the Godhead of Jesus Christ* (London 1754).

19 Randolph, Thomas. *A Vindication of the Doctrine of the Trinity from the Exceptions of a late Pamphlet entitled An Essay on Spirit* (Oxford 1754). [See 4.]

20 A Layman. *A moral Discourse on the Attributes of God, or a short Review of the Christian Religion occasioned by a small Book entitled An Essay on Spirit* (London 1754). [On the title-page attributes the *Essay* to 'a certain Right Reverend Prelate in a neighbouring Kingdom', though on p 1 professes to acquit him of being the author. The writer of the pamphlet believes in the pre-existence of souls, for which he claims the authority of Origen.]

21 A Gentleman. *Observations on the Essay on Spirit* (Dublin 1754).

22 McDonnell, Thomas. *Essay towards an Answer to a Book entitled An Essay on Spirit* (Dublin 1754). [See 5.]

23 McDonnell, Thomas. *A short Vindication of the Passages in the Essay towards an Answer to the Essay on Spirit, as remarked on by the Author of that Essay* (Dublin 1754). [Reply to 5.]

24 Watson, George. *The Doctrine of the everblessed Trinity proved in a Discourse on the eighteenth Chapter of Genesis* (London 1756). [The writer refers to 'the miserably deluded, still persisting, and to the great scandal of the Christian Church and hierarchy, yet unexcommunicated author of the *Essay on Spirit*'.]

THE ARIAN SCHISM IN IRELAND, 1830

by J. M. BARKLEY

I N Irish Presbyterianism Henry Cooke is commonly regarded as the champion of orthodoxy. Was it not he who drove the Arians out of the Synod of Ulster in 1830? The purpose of this paper is not to examine the theological issues involved, but rather to try to discover the real cause of the schism.[1]

The Reverend J. Smethurst (Moreton Hampstead) visited the North of Ireland during the autumn of 1821. The traditional picture is that of Cooke routing the unitarian Smethurst in Killyleagh (where Cooke was minister) and pursuing him from place to place in his zeal for orthodoxy. This, however, fails to take into account an important aspect of Smethurst's campaign. He writes,

I feel persuaded that there is considerable inquiry on religious subjects amongst the Dissenters in the North of Ireland, and that liberal opinions are fast gaining ground amongst them...One of the greatest obstacles in the way of their doing so, is the view they have been accustomed to take of the Christian religion, as being a system upheld solely by its union with the secular power. If they could see it free from this connexion, they would view it in a far more favourable light, and the most formidable of their prejudices would be removed. Even amongst the Dissenters the natural tendency of the most remote connexion of this kind is too obvious to escape notice. The Presbyterian Church of Ireland has long been considered as a sort of demi-establishment. And though its connexion with the civil power is not so close as that of the Church of England, yet the union, as far as it goes, is no less injurious.[2]

From this it is clear that, as well as unitarianism, political issues figured prominently. J. S. Porter, Cooke's son-in-law, in his *Life of Henry Cooke* freely admits this,

He [Smethurst] assailed the doctrine of the Trinity...insulted Trinitarians.. and he generally concluded his addresses with a few touches advocating advanced liberal views, which most thoughtful men would call revolutionary. He was

---

[1] R. G. Crawford, 'A critical examination of nineteenth century non-subscribing presby-terian theology in Ireland', PhD thesis (1944) Queen's University, Belfast.
[2] 'Unitarian Fund Report, 1822', *The Christian Reformer* VIII (London 1822) p 220.

at first successful. His free theology, and still freer political creed, attracted the multitude, especially those who retained or had imbibed the spirit of '98.[1]

When one finds historians of the arian controversy completely ignoring this aspect of Smethurst's meetings, he may be forgiven for thinking a reassessment necessary.

THE POLITICAL BACKGROUND

From the Restoration religious life in Ireland flowed in three distinct and clearly defined streams – Anglicanism, Presbyterianism and Roman Catholicism. The Presbyterians, having suffered many indignities at the hands of the Stuart kings, naturally supported king William in 1688–90. Not that this availed them much. 'Disappointed of receiving immediate legal toleration as reward for their services during the revolution', writes professor J. C. Beckett, 'the Irish Presbyterians made two further attempts during the reign of William III to secure their position by an act of Irish Parliament. Though both of these attempts had the sympathy of the king... they failed, and the failure was due to the opposition of the established church in Ireland.'[2] This meant that the Irish political scene consisted in playing off the Protestants (that is, Anglicans) against the Romanists, and vice versa, with the Presbyterians in between in a sort of independent no man's land, yet suffering under the disabilities of the law.

Henry McCook, for such was his name, was born at Grillagh, Maghera, on 11 May 1788.[3] At the time, Presbyterians and Roman Catholics suffered under the yoke of oppression, and unable to endure this any longer many of them joined together to form the United Irishmen in an attempt to obtain justice and liberty by constitutional means.[4] In 1795–6, as a result of suppression and persecution, the United Irishmen became a revolutionary movement, and by 1797, because of the barbarities of the king's forces, Ulster was on the

---

[1] [J. L.] Porter [*Life and Times of Henry Cooke*] (Belfast 1875) p 51. For the Rebellion of 1798 see below.

[2] J. C. Beckett, *Protestant Dissent in Ireland, 1687–1780* (London 1948) p 31.

[3] Porter pp 1–2. [J. and S. G. McConnell] *Fasti* [*of the Irish Presbyterian Church*] (Belfast 1936–43) p 195. Both Porter and McConnell treat Cooke as the younger son of John Cooke and Jane Howe, but R. L. Marshall, 'Henry Cooke' (MS unpublished lecture) makes out a good case for his being the illegitimate son of the local lord of the manor, Colonel William Melevera, and Mrs McCook (née Howe) who worked in the house.

[4] A. T. Q. Stewart, 'The transformation of presbyterian radicalism in the north of Ireland, 1792–1825', MA thesis (1956) Queen's University, Belfast. R. B. McDowell, *Irish Public Opinion, 1750–1800* (London 1944).

brink of revolution. The rebellion came the following year. The Tipperary militia, led by Englishmen, came to Maghera to punish the rebels. They occupied the kirk. John Glendy, the minister, who had baptised Henry, had to flee to America. Watty Graham and Billy Cuddy, the elders, were not so fortunate. They were hanged on the spot. Others were flogged to death. All round the McCook's home burned the homes of Presbyterians and Roman Catholics who had dared to claim rights as freemen. These days made a deep impression on the boy of ten. 'On the morning of the 5th of June', he wrote later, 'when returning home after passing the night in a cave among the mountains, I saw the soldiers burn Watty Graham's house. It was then and thus I learned my political principles.'[1]

The attitude of Presbyterians to Roman Catholics may be illustrated from the atrocities of the years before the rebellion. When 1,400 Roman Catholics were burned out of their homes in County Armagh, the Presbyterians of Belfast, Carnmoney and Templepatrick sheltered them in their homes, and, to quote one of their own historians who lived through the events, 'made a stock-purse, and by weekly allowances, in proportion to the numbers of the exterminated families, supported them till they could procure work or settlement'.[2]

On the issue of Catholic Emancipation the Synod in 1813 called for 'the abolition of political distinctions on account of religious profession',[3] and the plea for emancipation was supported by every presbytery in the Synod with the exception of Ballymena.[4]

Neither is it without significance that it was at this time that Presbyterians were first called 'Blackmouths'. When demythologised, this was a term of political abuse, applicable to rebels or potential rebels against the establishment. Its very use testifies to the radicalism of the Presbyterians and their desire for political democracy.[5]

This was a grave situation for the Ascendency and it became official government policy to encourage conservative elements in the Synod. Castlereagh wrote to the prime minister, Addington, in 1802:

---

[1] Porter, p 12.

[2] F. Plowden, *An Historical Disquisition concerning the rise, progress and effects of the Orange Societies in Ireland* (Dublin 1810) p 66. This was the origin of the 'Glasgow Irish' for when it was impossible to incorporate such numbers into their industry the Presbyterians of Belfast wrote to their co-religionists in Glasgow to help them out. This they did by organising work for these Roman Catholic refugees in Glasgow and Paisley. See F. Plowden, *History of Ireland from the Union, 1801–1810* (Dublin 1811) I, intro and p 67.

[3] R[ecords of the] G[eneral] S[ynod of] U[lster, 1691–1820], (Belfast 1890) III, p 397. If after 1820 *RGSU* with year.   [4] [The] N[orthern] W[hig] 24 April 1829.

[5] R. L. Marshall, 'Blackmouth', *The Presbyterian Herald*, no 26 (Belfast 1945) pp 14–16.

J. M. BARKLEY

In such a body as the presbyterians of Ireland, who...have partaken so deeply first of the popular and since of the democratic politics of the country as to be an object much more of jealousy than of support to the government, I am of opinion that it is only through a considerable internal fermentation of the body...that it will put on a different temper and acquire better habits.[1]

In other words, if the Ascendency was to survive, a policy of 'internal fermentation' or tory infiltration within the Synod was necessary. Such was the opinion of Castlereagh, who had been born and baptised within Presbyterianism but had forsaken it for political gain.

GOVERNMENT PRESSURE ON THE PRESBYTERIANS

As a result of the rebellion, Pitt determined to unite the parliaments, and in spite of tremendous opposition the Act of Union was passed in 1800, after much 'jobbing' and 'dirty work' to use the terms of the viceroy, Lord Cornwallis.[2]

A 'Plan for strengthening the connection between the Government and the Presbyterian Synod of Ulster' was prepared by Castlereagh.[3] Its ministers from the time of William III (although there were several breaks) had received the *Regium donum*. This had been distributed among them in equal shares by an agent of their own appointment, Robert Black (Derry), a tory. In the proposed Plan, the architects of which were Castlereagh and Black, congregations were to be classified into three groups and the fund was to be administered from Dublin Castle. The Synod resisted the classification, but Castlereagh remained adamant.[4] The purpose behind this is revealed in a letter from the duke of Portland to the lord-lieutenant, 'a principal object in increasing and remodelling their allowance was to make them more dependent, and render them more amenable to government'.[5]

This aim was evident in two things. (i) One of the provisions of the Scheme was that each application had 'to be accompanied by a certificate signed by two magistrates, stating, that the memorialist has taken

---

[1] Castlereagh to Addington 21 July 1802, [*Memoirs and Correspondence of*] *Castlereagh* (London 1848–53) IV, p 224. [J.] Jamieson [*History of the Royal Belfast Academical Institution*] (Belfast 1959) p 38.
[2] *Correspondence of Charles, first Marquis Cornwallis*, ed C. Ross (London 1864) III, pp. 100–2.
[3] *Castlereagh* III, pp 172–4.
[4] [J. S.] Reid [*History of the Presbyterian Church in Ireland*] (London 1853) III, pp 512–15. Reid only completed two volumes, the third was edited by W. D. Killen from papers Reid had collected.
[5] Duke of Portland to the lord-lieutenant 31 August 1799. *Castlereagh* II, p 384.

and subscribed before them the oath of allegiance',[1] and (ii) no endowment was granted to the congregation of second Keady, of which
Dr William Steel Dickson, formerly a United Irishman, was now
minister.[2]

Another aspect of the government's approach to the Presbyterians
concerned university education. Cornwallis, writing to the duke of
Portland, in 1799, says,

> It has long been considered that the establishment of a second university in
> this kingdom, and especially in the province of Ulster, so as to assist the educa-
> tion of dissenters, and to promote an emulation in the University of Dublin,
> would be of great public benefit.[3]

Nothing came of this, any more than of Fitzwilliam's promises in
1795,[4] yet collegiate education played a prominent role in the arian
controversy. The Belfast Academical Institution, founded in 1810,
was built by public subscription, and had both school and collegiate
departments. Its aim, to quote William Drennan, one of those responsible for its foundation, was 'to diffuse knowledge as one of the
necessaries rather than the luxuries of life'.[5] In 1815, after a conference
between representatives of the Synod and the Institution, the Synod
decided to recognise the classes in the College.[6] Hitherto, students,
with a few exceptions, had received their higher education in the
university of Glasgow. Now they were to receive this at home, and
everyone hoped for great things from the new arrangement. 'Reflect-
ing the liberal spirit then so characteristic of Belfast', writes professor
T. W. Moody, '"Inst" was based on the principles of united or non-
sectarian education. Students were admitted and professors appointed
without regard to their religion, and professors were pledged not to
interfere, directly or indirectly, with the faith of their students. The
presence of divinity professors was not inconsistent with this system,
for they were appointed and remunerated by their respective churches,
and they taught only members of their own communion. Besides the
presbyterian bodies the local catholic bishop was invited to appoint a
divinity professor; though he did not do so (in view of the existence of
Maynooth, established in 1795) he was friendly to the Institution and

---

[1] *RGSU* III, pp 270–2. Castlereagh to Addington 21 July 1802. *Castlereagh* IV, pp 223–6.
[2] Reid, p 519, n 66.
[3] Cornwallis to Duke of Portland, 29 July 1799. *Castlereagh* II, pp 364–5.
[4] *RGSU* III, pp 192–3. Reid III, pp 491–3.
[5] Jamieson, pp 203–7.   [6] *RGSU* III, p 421.

allowed catholic students, including one or two who were destined for Maynooth to attend it.'[1]

The address at the opening of the Institution in 1814 was given by Dr William Drennan, who personified the spirit of presbyterian radicalism.[2] At a public dinner, on 16 March 1816, several politically 'objectionable' toasts were honoured.[3] The Institution had received an annual grant of £1,500, and this was now withdrawn. The tory attitude to the Institution may be summed up in the words of Castlereagh to Peel, then chief secretary, 'a bastard Institution, ostensibly for academical purposes, but in fact establishing a junta which might be turned to oppressive and mischievous ends'.[4]

The first attack on the Institution, in which both Presbyterian and Roman Catholic co-operated, was not theological, but political, when, in 1817, Dr Black, the confidant of Castlereagh, gave voice to his master's threats to withdraw the *Regium donum* if the Synod permitted its students to attend the Institution.[5] The tory aim was not simply to drive a wedge between the Synod and the Institution, but to bring about a separation.

The Westminster *Confession of Faith* had been adopted as a doctrinal standard in Irish Presbyterianism *c* 1647, and in 1698 it was enacted that those entering the ministry should subscribe it.[6] To solve the first non-subscription controversy, 1719–26, when all parties were orthodox but some objected to 'man-made' documents as doctrinal standards, the Synod had placed all the nonsubscribers in one presbytery, that of Antrim,[7] but the ministers of each body interchanged pulpits and there was full inter-communion. Within the Synod itself, although the law of subscription had been reaffirmed in 1705, 1720 and 1784, it was more honoured in the breach then the observance.[8] The crunch came when the Reverend William Bruce, of the presbytery of Antrim, was appointed professor of Latin, Greek and Hebrew in the Institu-

---

1 T. W. Moody, 'Higher Education', *Ulster since 1800*, second series, ed T. W. Moody and J. C. Beckett (London 1957) p 194. Words in brackets added.

2 Jamieson, pp 203–7.

3 Porter, p 54. Reid III, p 537.

4 Castlereagh to Peel 9 November 1816. London, British Museum MS Add. 40181, fol 214. This letter (fols 211–24) outlines Castlereagh's attitude to the Institution and its relation to the Synod.

5 Reid III, pp 539–41.

6 P. Adair, *A true narrative of the rise and progress of the Presbyterian Church in Ireland*, ed W. D. Killen (Belfast 1866) p 135. *RGSU* I, p 34.

7 *RGSU* II, p 96.

8 *RGSU* I, pp 100, 521–2; III, p 63. Reid III, pp 446–8.

tion.[1] Cooke maintained that he had been elected by arian influence.[2] In his campaign against Smethurst Cooke reveals that he is convinced that Arians are 'politically dangerous'. As radicals in theology tended to be radicals in politics, a revival of Arianism would produce a revival of radicalism.[3] This he also applied to the Institution.

The political overtones of the conflict were soon recognised, as the survey of the situation in the Synod of Ulster in *The Christian Reformer* shows,

The unchristian and hateful temper of the majority in the Synod of Ulster has, we believe, been nurtured by the Orange faction in Ireland. Lords and lordlings in Ireland have turned fanatics and have set up a crusade against common sense and the rights of conscience. Theirs is the true popery.[4]

EVENTS IN THE SYNOD OF ULSTER

At the meeting of Synod in Newry, in 1822, Cooke launched his attack on Arianism, but it aroused no immediate response.[5] 'The Bible', he declared, 'has taught me to approach my Redeemer as "God manifest in the flesh", "God over all, blessed for ever", and to regard the Holy Spirit not as an inferior created agent or mere attribute. The Bible has taught me that the Father, the Word, and the Holy Ghost are one God.'[6] He concluded,

In my opposition to the appointment of Arian professors I seem this day to stand alone. Yet I am not alone. Men may draw back in fear but God and truth are with me. I believe, too, that the hearts of many of my brethren are with me. I know that the great body of the presbyterian laity are with me. They will never quietly look on while the enemies of every doctrine they hold sacred are here, as elsewhere, scaling the walls, and entering the inmost chambers, and occupying the highest towers of their Zion.[7]

The reference to arian professors shows that he was definitely attacking the Institution, and events were to show that Cooke's confidence in the Church at large was not misplaced doctrinally.

At Newry Cooke proclaimed the theme of his campaign, Arianism is contrary to evangelical doctrine, therefore Arianism must be destroyed or it will destroy us. This was the note which he struck relentlessly in the months and years that followed as he preached throughout

[1] B[elfast] N[ews] L[etter] 6 November 1821; *Commercial Chronicle* 24 November 1821.
[2] Reid III, pp 552–3.   [3] *NW* 27 October 1825.
[4] *The Christian Reformer* XIII (London 1827) p 376.
[5] Porter, p 57.   [6] *Ibid* p 56.   [7] *Ibid* p 57.

the province and in his speeches in the Synod.[1] The Synod meeting in Armagh, in 1823, shows that Cooke has now become the leader of a 'party', and the following year, at Moneymore, he was elected Moderator.[2] In 1824, both the Synod and the Institution adopted a diplomatic attitude in their relations, because of the prospect of a commission to enquire into the state of Irish education. The Institution needed the support of the Synod if the government grant was to be restored, and the Synod hoped that this provision would include endowment of their divinity chair.[3] The Synod passed a unanimous resolution in support of the Institution,[4] and in these circumstances Cooke himself proposed an overture stating the terms on which he and his 'party' could support it. This was seconded by William Porter, clerk of Synod and an Arian,

That whenever the Moderator of this Synod shall be called on to vote at the election of a Professor in the Belfast Institution, he shall, in due time, convene the General Synod's Fixed Committee; and cause to be laid before them, the names of the several candidates, with their recommendatory testimonials; and shall afterwards communicate to the electors, the opinion of the Committee.[5]

Commenting on his action, a year later, Cooke said that he hoped this plan 'might save the Institution from being overwhelmed by an Arian deluge and at the same time gain for it through the synod's recommendation the countenance and support of government'.[6]

The Institution, at its annual meeting, a few days later welcomed both the resolution and the overture, although one of the managers insisted that 'this is not a seminary alone for presbyterians but for protestants and catholics likewise'.[7]

As moderator, Cooke was called upon to give evidence not only to the commissioners on education, but also before select committees of both houses of parliament inquiring into the state of Ireland. From London he wrote to his wife, 'I have been very unfortunate, for Lord Roden, Colonel Forde, etc., are at Cheltenham, so that the poor parson of Killyleagh is here without any of his natural protectors'.[8] It is significant that the 'poor parson of Killyleagh' should find his 'natural protectors' in two prominent protestant-ascendency tories, when carrying out his duties as moderator of Synod.

[1] The Christian Moderator (London 1826) p 111.   [2] RGSU 1824, p 10.
[3] [H. Cooke,] I[llustration and] D[efence of the Rev. Mr] C[ooke's] E[vidence] (Belfast 1825) p 23.   [4] RGSU 1824, pp 21–2.
[5] RGSU 1824, p 31.   [6] IDCE, p 23.
[7] NW 8 July 1824.   [8] Porter, p 65.

When extracts from Cooke's evidence on catholic emancipation became public in April, *The Northern Whig*, representing the liberal presbyterian viewpoint, in an editorial reminded him that the Synod had officially declared itself in favour of emancipation in 1813 and that there had been no withdrawal.[1] But the bitterest and most prolonged criticisms concerned his evidence regarding the Institution. Even *The Belfast News Letter*, which would have agreed with his views on emancipation, 'begged totally to differ from Mr Cooke respecting the alleged tendency of the Belfast Academical Institution to dessiminate the principles of Arianism. We hold the direct contrary to be the fact.'[2] Denials were also issued by the Joint-Boards of the Institution, the faculty and the students.[3] Cooke fought back by presenting himself to the public as the champion of orthodoxy fighting against the soul-destroying demon of Arianism.[4] By presenting the issue as a confrontation between orthodoxy and Arianism he created an *odium theologicum*. This was recognised,[5] but the net result was that at the Synod in Coleraine, in 1825, Cooke emerged victorious.[6]

However, on 5 July, it became clear that the Institution would not submit tamely to the Synod's dictation.[7] Indeed, during the year such a reaction set in, probably caused by his own extremism, that following the meeting of Synod in Ballymena, in 1826, Cooke's hopes lay in ruins.[8]

In view of the multitude and severity of the attacks upon him and the Ballymena debacle it is perhaps not surprising that Cooke took ill. He went to Dublin for medical advice, and spent some time recuperating in the homes of Lord Roden and Lord Mountcashel.[9]

The Institution's correctness and impartiality in theological matters was vindicated in the majority report of the commissioners,[10] but two of the five, in a minority report, did recognise that the appointment of arian professors gave some cause for anxiety.[11] It was ironical, therefore, that the Report provided the opportunity for the renewal of hostilities in the Synod. In their evidence both William Porter and

---

[1] *NW* 14 April 1825.   [2] *BNL* 20 April 1825.
[3] *NW* 21, 28 April 1825; *BNL* 22, 26 April 1825. Some of Cooke's critics were in fact as orthodox as himself, for example, James Thompson, professor of mathematics (*IDCE* p 29), Samuel Edgar, professor of divinity of Secession Synod (Edgar to Hinks 14 May 1825, *RBAI* papers), and Samuel Hanna, professor of divinity of Synod of Ulster (*IDCE* p 33; *BNL* 10 June 1825).
[4] *NW* 12 May 1825. *BNL* 27 May 1825.   [5] *NW* 12 May 1825.
[6] *RGSU* 1825, pp 30–1.   [7] *NW* 7 July 1825.
[8] *NW* 6, 13, 27 July 1826; James McKnight to Miss Barber 26 August 1825. MS Pres. Hist. Soc., Belfast.   [9] Porter, pp 93–4.
[10] *Fourth Report [of the Commissioners of Irish education inquiry]*, HC 1826–27 (89) XIII, pp 3–26.   [11] *Fourth Report*, pp 27–9.

Henry Montgomery had avowed themselves Arians, and the former had asserted that Arianism was gaining ground 'amongst the thinking few'.[1] These statements formed the basis of attack when the Synod met at Strabane in 1827.[2]

In a highly pietistic speech, Cooke introduced a new feature. He called for a separation in the Synod, 'Let us withdraw from them, let us divide the flocks'.[3] Then he gave notice that 'he would next day propose a measure for the separation of the Synod'.[4] Further details need not detain us, except to say that the separation finally took place in 1829, when the non-subscribers (not all of whom were Arians) withdrew and formed the Remonstrant Synod in 1830.[5]

COOKE'S PRIMARY MOTIVE

In the events outlined there appear to be two turning points. The first was the meeting at Killyleagh in 1821, and the second the year 1826–7. Let us look at the former.

In Killyleagh, Archibald Hamilton Rowan, lord of the manor, and the people were to a man Presbyterians. Rowan had been implicated in the '98 rebellion and had been driven into exile.[6] The majority of the people also had been implicated in the rising, but, unlike him, they were conservative in theology. Rowan's younger son, Captain Sydney Hamilton Rowan, on the other hand was a tory, and rejected the revolutionary politics of '98.[7] As a ruling elder, he had been instrumental in bringing Cooke to Killyleagh in 1818 and was 'one of his most attached friends'.[8]

This kinship was natural not only because of Cooke's orthodoxy, but because of his political principles. His son-in-law writes,

Cooke's political principles were formed at a very early period, and never changed. The effects produced upon his mind by the dark scenes of '98...led him to regard with the strongest feelings of horror the revolutionary sentiments and acts of the United Irishmen. Everything tending to disturb settled government or excite popular passions, he looked upon as radically wrong.[9]

[1] *Fourth Report*, pp 136, 49, 137.   [2] *NW* 5 July 1827.
[3] *NW* 12 July 1827.   [4] *NW* 12 July 1827.
[5] *RGSU* Cookstown 1829, pp 5–30.   [6] Porter, pp 49, 110.
[7] Porter, p 118.   [8] Porter, p 49.
[9] Porter, p 223. Porter's account of his father-in-law is somewhat glorified, and what is stated follows the information he supplies. On the other hand if Cooke was, in fact, the son of Colonel William Melevera his attitude is more easily explained, because the colonel was assassinated along with a number of the Tipperary militia when serving eviction notices c 1800.

In passing, it may be noted that this explains why throughout Cooke's career the principles of social justice which inspired the minister who baptised him or the plight of presbyterian farmers like Watty Graham had no place. Instead his friends were the Castlereaghs, the Rodens, the Donegalls, the Downshires, the Mountcashels, the Batesons, the Ernes, and others like them.

When Smethurst came to Killyleagh, in 1821, proclaiming the benefits of unitarianism and political radicalism, the captain and the minister were present. At the close of the meeting, the captain challenged the speaker and placed Cooke in the position of having to reply, which he did 'next Sunday'.[1] The importance of the meeting, as of Smethurst's whole visit, was to convince Cooke that Arians were politically dangerous.[2] This raises the issue of the primary motive for Cooke's attack first on Smethurst and then on the Institution – was it theological or political?

On the theological side, it may be argued that Cooke, before 1821, had participated in what he calls 'Arian ordinations'.[3] That in the Synod when the Reverend James Elder (Finvoy) moved that subscription to the Westminster *Confession of Faith* be obligatory in 1824, 1825 and 1826, he had not Cooke's support.[4] Indeed, in 1826, saying that 'there were things in the Westminster Confession of Faith to which neither he nor any other member of the house could subscribe',[5] he moved an amendment,

That a Committee be appointed to draw up a condensed view of the doctrines of the Westminster Confession of Faith...with a view to the consideration, acceptance, and signature of Candidates for license and ordination; and for exhibiting to the world a brief summary of the doctrines of this Church, and a testimony to the doctrines of the Lord Jesus Christ.[6]

In his evidence before the commissioners, in 1825, Cooke said that 'the majority would be favourable to a subscription that did not go all the length of the Westminster Confession, in particular details, but should be at the same time evangelical'.[7]

When the legislation of 1827–8 was being discussed in the Synod of 1829, Robert Gray (Scriggan) suggested that the real object of the overtures and the theological examinations committee was to drive

[1] Porter, pp 52–3. [2] Jamieson, p 38.
[3] Porter, pp 37–8. [4] *RGSU* 1824, p 24; 1825, p 30; 1826, p 38.
[5] *BNL* 7 July 1826. [6] *RGSU* 1826, p 38.
[7] *Fourth Report*, p 155.

the Arians out of the Synod.[1] This Cooke vehemently denied, saying, 'It is well known I have ever been of opinion as an individual that examination and subscription of the Westminster Confession of faith joined with the pacific act would be a more efficient way of effecting our great object. To this end the Synod, I hope, will yet come.'[2]

When we turn to the Presbytery of Dromore, we find that the formula of subscription is, 'We believe the Westminster Confession of Faith contains the essential doctrines of Christianity and as such we subscribe it.'[3]

To this, Cooke took no exception prior to 1821, but on 22 August 1822 he gave notice that at the next meeting he would move, 'That the formula of subscription to the Westminster Confession of Faith in this Presbytery be the Synod's formula, subject to the provisions of the Pacific Act (of 21 June 1720).'[4]

Cooke's reference to the Synod's formula is rather fanciful in that only five of the fourteen presbyteries – Belfast, Dromore, Route, Tyrone and Dublin – required subscription.[5] Also, in the Presbytery of Belfast there are sixteen variations in the formula during the years 1774–1800,[6] and in the Dromore Presbytery it could be argued that subscription was not always required. The minute of Cooke's installation reads,

Mr Simpson from Belfast Presbytery, Mr White from Bangor Presbytery and Mr Glendy from Templepatrick Presbytery were invited to sit with us with which request they complied.
Appeared on the part of the Congregation of Killyleagh as commissioners Mr Sidney Rowan and Mr McEwen who confirmed the report made at the last Presbytery of paying to Mr Cook £100 per annum during his ministry in their Congregation.
Installation at Killyleagh Mr White preached the sermon and Mr McCance installed.[7]

There is no reference here to Cooke's having subscribed. The same is true in the presbytery's report to Synod, although the same report, as do the presbytery minutes, records that this was done by William

---

[1] BNL 25 August 1829. The BNL gives Robert Gray as minister of Dungiven in error for Scriggan. See Fasti, p 203.   [2] BNL 25 August 1829.
[3] Minutes of Presbytery of Dromore 6 May 1823. MS Box 59 Church House, Belgast.
[4] Minutes of Presbytery of Dromore 22 August 1822. Words in brackets added. See RGSU I, pp 521–2.   [5] Reid, p 550, n 10.
[6] Minutes of Presbytery of Belfast, 1744–1800. MS Pres. Col., Belfast. J. M. Barkley, The Westminster Formularies in Irish Presbyterianism (Belfast 1956) pp 13–14.
[7] Minutes of Presbytery of Dromore 8 September 1818.

Craig (Dromara) and Samuel Crory (Drumlough). Indeed, it is possible that Cooke had never signed the Westminster Confession prior to his installation in May Street, Belfast, in 1829.[1] Be this as it may, when his proposal was not adopted by the Presbytery of Dromore, Cooke, in 1823, refused to license students although they had signed the presbytery's formula.[2]

The reference to the Pacific Act in the Presbytery in 1822 and in the Synod in 1829 reveals that there was a greater consistency in Cooke's theological outlook than some of this critics have been prepared to admit. Alongside this, however, we have to place two things: (a) That Cooke in his evidence before the Commissioners, in 1825, showed clearly that he regarded Arianism as a dying cause.[3] What he feared was its revival. Why? (b) That in his denial of the accusation of Gray in 1829 that the aim was to drive out the Arians, Cooke said the policy adopted was not his 'as an individual', declaring, 'I have yielded my opinion to wiser and better men'.[4] Who were these men? Was Lord Mountcashel one of them?

While there is no reason to doubt Cooke's theological integrity, as some have done,[5] the evidence is rather against his primary motive being theological.

Turning to the political side, it may be argued that Cooke's whole campaign began because of the rejection by the tory captain of, what Latimer calls, the 'humanitarianism' of Smethurst.[6] That, as we have seen above, Cooke, as moderator, when in London missed 'his natural protectors', Lord Roden and Colonel Forde. To this we must add the evidence of Cooke's letter to Peel, the British home secretary, on 20 July 1825.[7] As Irish chief secretary, 1812–18, Peel had been closely associated with Castlereagh in the issue of the relationship of the

---

[1] *RGSU* III, pp 330, 336, 365. 1830, p 9. Cooke was licensed by the Presbytery of Route (July 1807), ordained in Duneane by the Presbytery of Ballymena (13 November 1808), installed in Donegore by the Presbytery of Templepatrick (22 January 1811) and in Killyleagh by the Presbytery of Dromore (8 September 1818). It has not been possible to trace the Route minutes, but none of the others record his subscribing or report it to the Synod. At his installation in May Street by the Presbytery of Belfast (24 November 1829) his subscription is recorded, and this was duly reported to Synod.

[2] Minutes of Presbytery of Dromore 6 May 1823.

[3] Porter, p 36. *Fourth Report*, p 146. *First Report of the Commissioners of education in Ireland* HC 1825 (400) XII, p 821.

[4] *BNL* 25 August 1829.

[5] J. Jamieson, 'The influence of the Rev. Henry Cooke on the political life of Ulster', M.A. thesis (1952) Queen's University, Belfast, p 78.

[6] W. T. Latimer, *A History of the Irish Presbyterians* (Belfast 1893) pp 192–3.

[7] Cooke to Peel, 20 July 1825. BM MS, Add 40380 fols 147–51.

Institution and the Synod and in the withdrawal of the grant from the former. Cooke acknowledges that he is writing privately out of his 'attachment to His Majesty's government and the interests of religion', and refers Peel to 'Lord Dufferin and Lord Roden to both of whom I have the honour of being a little known'. He continues,

Experience has established the Institution as an adequate literary seminary, but has raised many suspicions and much decided opposition upon grounds partly political and chiefly religious. As matters now stand a dissolution of connection between the synod of Ulster and the Belfast Institution seems to me to be a matter that can either be avoided or accomplished.

He presents the Presbyterians as 'nine-tenths' in agreement with the doctrines of the Established Church and loyal to the tory government.[1] In the letter Cooke is looking for guidance as to his course of action for 'we have been told on the one hand that government wished us to continue the connexion and control the Institution, on the other hand we have been told that government wanted us to dissolve all connexion and in that event we might have a presbyterian college erected somewhere in Ulster'.

In this letter, written behind the back of the Synod, Cooke offers himself as the government's agent and ally in the Synod, and so links himself definitely with the tory and protestant-ascendency interest.

Peel, in his reply, did not commit himself, pointing out that the question of the Institution was about to be the subject of a special inquiry. At the same time, he did not reject Cooke's offer.[2]

When one adds to this the evidence, given below, concerning Lord Mountcashel's recommendation 'to bring about a separation', it becomes clear that while Cooke was sincere in his orthodoxy his primary motive, even though he may not always have been aware of it, was political.

REFORM OR SEPARATION

The second turning point occurred during the year 1826–7, because at the Synod in 1827 Cooke first called for 'separation'. Why?

Admittedly, Cooke in his evidence before the Commissioners, in 1825, did refer to 'separation'.

---

[1] Porter admits the inaccuracy of this when he says, 'During the first quarter of the present century, nine-tenths of the Presbyterians of Ireland were Whigs', p 224.
[2] Peel to Cooke, 14 August 1825. BM MS Add 40380, fols 178–9.

The subject of subscription and separation from the Arians has often formed matter of deep consideration to many members of the Synod of Ulster. I confess I am favourable to both. I feel myself a member of a church openly tolerating what I consider erroneous doctrines. But alas! where should I retire into greater purity...I have therefore, with others, laboured to reform rather than abandon a church I acknowledge in some degree corrupt.[1]

In 1827, 'reform' has been abandoned for 'separation', as is evident not only from his speech in the Synod but from his letter to the Reverend J. Johnston (Tullylish),

My Dear Sir,
  ...You should come to Synod; as some of us intend most decidedly to attempt a separation from the Arians. Why are we with them? or they with us? Their stronghold the B.A.I. will not be endowed. They have got, I hear, a flat refusal. I would that Bruce, Hincks, McEwen, and Montgomery would withdraw, and leave the ground for better men, and it would, I have good reason to believe, be endowed before 12 months. They will not do this I fear. So as they made their bed with dogs, they must sleep with the fleas. I wish them more wisdom, and better company.

Yours truly,
H. Cooke[2]

Cooke, as we have seen above, had taken ill following the Synod in 1826, and had spent part of the time recuperating with Lord Mount-cashel. In a letter to Porter, Cooke's son-in-law, Mountcashel writes, 'I strongly recommended him to bring about a separation, this he afterwards effected; and I have always thought that the course he adopted was in a great degree prompted by my advice'.[3]

Here, again, the evidence points to Cooke taking his directions from a member of the ascendency.

FURTHER CONSIDERATIONS

The conclusion that Cooke was primarily politically motivated is strengthened by two further considerations.

Firstly, at a great protestant meeting at Hillsborough, in 1834, to oppose the repeal of the Union, presided over by the earl of Hillsborough, when the speakers included the marquis of Downshire, Colonel Forde, the marquis of Londonderry, Lord Arthur Hill, Lord

---

[1] *Fourth Report*, pp 826-7.
[2] Cooke to Johnston, 9 June 1827. MS Pres. Hist. Soc., Belfast.
[3] Porter, p 110.

Clanwilliam, Sir Robert Bateson, Lord Castlereagh, Lord Roden, and others, Cooke said,

Were they [Presbyterians] for a Repeal of the Union on the walls of Derry? (Cheers) Were they Repealers when they manned the walls of the maiden city, and pointed guns on the Popish invader, and drove the pusillanimous James and his army beyond the Boyne? (Great cheering) Our Protestant forefathers would not Repeal the Union, neither will their Protestant sons (Applause)... Presbyterians have been falsely represented as being unfriendly to the sister country. I stand here as a Presbyterian...and I say that they are friendly to the Established Church of Ireland (Loud and continued cheering).[1]

Following a hint that if the Union was repealed 'we will all be robbed of our liberties, if not of our lives',[2] he published the banns for a marriage of the Presbyterian Church with the establishment.[3]

In 1867, at a protestant meeting at Hillsborough, opposing the Irish Church Bill, and surrounded by the same exalted company, Cooke declared, 'It is now more than thirty years since I stood on a platform in this very field, and proclaimed the banns of holy marriage, intellectual and spiritual, between the Presbyterian Church and the Established Church'.[4]

From this it is clear that Cooke's basis for Church union was not biblical and theological, but a political anti-Catholicism.

Secondly, we have his attitude in the General Assembly, in 1843. Though Presbyterians numbered almost half of the whole protestant population in Ireland, there was only one Irish presbyterian member of parliament. That year the Assembly resolved,

That...this Assembly earnestly recommends to her members such a united and faithful discharge of their duty, as Christian electors, as shall most effectually secure a full and adequate representation of the principles and interests of Presbyterianism in the British Legislature.[5]

Because Cooke 'felt that the motion was...a reflection on the conduct and policy of his political friends',[6] he withdrew from the Assembly, and did not enter it again until the resolution was rescinded in 1847.[7] Here again Cooke's ecclesiastical behaviour was politically conditioned.

---

[1] [The] G[reat] P[rotestant] M[eeting in County Down] (Ballymena 1834) pp 12–13.
[2] GPM, p 13.   [3] GPM, p 16.
[4] The Great Protestant Demonstration at Hillsborough (Belfast 1867) p 20.
[5] Minutes of the General Assembly, Belfast 1843, p 224.
[6] Porter, pp 392–3.   [7] Porter, p 395.

CONCLUSION

With hindsight, of course, it is possible to see how the schism could have been avoided and the heresy of Arianism allowed to die out within Irish Presbyterianism. It is also possible to see the disaster which inevitably follows making religious orthodoxy and the policy of one particular political party synonymous. At the same time, it should not be forgotten that within seven years, after the schism had taken place, the Synod of Ulster had made unqualified subscription to the Westminster *Confession of Faith* obligatory,[1] whereas within a quarter of a century the Remonstrants, because they had no doctrinal standard, found themselves rent asunder.[2]

[1] *RGSU* 1836, p 45.
[2] *The Christian Unitarian*, I–III (Belfast 1862–4); Remonstrant Synod papers. MSS Clerk of Synod, Minutes of Remonstrant Synod, 1853–60.

PROTEST AND SCHISM
IN NINETEENTH-CENTURY
GERMAN CATHOLICISM:
THE RONGE–CZERSKI MOVEMENT,
1844–5

by WAYNE DETZLER

FROM the seclusion of Upper Silesia a suspended priest published his protest against the powerful bishop Wilhelm Arnoldi of Trier. The peasants' poverty was compounded by exploitation. Virgins were robbed of their purity. The superstitions of the common folk were fanned into flames of fanaticism.[1] Guilty alone for this massive oppression was bishop Wilhelm Arnoldi of Trier. As defender of the oppressed, the priest Johannes Ronge emerged, who had been exiled to the Silesian mining hamlet of Laurahuette a scant six months before.

The occasion of Ronge's open letter was the display of Christ's seamless robe at Trier in the autumn of 1844. Thrice previously the sacred garment had been shown for the edification of the faithful. In 1585 it was put on display to prompt giving toward the restoration of the churches of Trier. After the Thirty Years War, in 1651, the robe was again presented to the public eye. Having been returned to Trier from the safety of Augsburg following the Napoleonic threat, the tattered relic was again exposed to the view of Catholics in 1810.[2]

As a rising tide of Hermesianism licked at the foundations of Roman Catholicism in Germany, the ultramontanists cast about for materials to build a spiritual dyke.[3] On 2 May 1837 Edward Michelis, the faithful

---

[1] Johannes Ronge, *Offenes Sendschreiben an den Herrn Wilhelm Arnoldi, Bischof zu Trier* (Laurahuette 1844). Within two months 12,000 copies of Ronge's letter had been circulated, and 50,000 copies were printed in all.

[2] [Heinrich] Schmid, *Geschichte der Katholischen Kirche [Deutschlands von der Mitte des 18. Jahrhunderts bis in die Gegenwart]* (Muenchen 1874) p 611.

[3] The Hermesian party in the Roman Catholic Church of Germany was named after professor Georg Hermes of Muenster who attempted to reconcile catholic theology with Kant. Some of Hermes's writings were placed on the Index by pope Gregory XVI in 1835. The ultramontanists sought to defend the Church of Rome against the two-headed monster of Hermesianism and nationalism.

secretary to the imprisoned archbishop of Cologne Droste-Viscering, corresponded with Anton Joseph Binterim. Binterim was a staunch supporter of curial Catholicism and parish priest at Bilk. Michelis urged the priest to revive the practice of pilgrimages.[1] In this atmosphere the display of the holy coat was conceived by bishop Arnoldi of Trier to be a great demonstration of the loyalty of the common man to the Church of Rome. Arnoldi hoped it would forever seal the coffin of nationalistic and rationalistic revolt.[2]

Success quickly crowned Arnoldi's plan. Heinrich Brueck, the historian of nineteenth-century Catholicism, acclaimed the pilgrimage as a 'grossartige und herrliche Manifestation des katholischen Bewusstseins' ('a great and glorious manifestation of catholic consciousness').[3] Statistics serve only to confirm Brueck's analysis. Between 18 August and 6 October 1844, 1,050,833 pilgrims filed past the ancient robe.[4] A steady stream of Germans shuffled through the cathedral daily from 2 am until 11 pm.

Some of the pilgrims actually experienced healing as they viewed the robe. The most notable of these was the grand niece of archbishop Droste-Vischering. For three long years she had been crippled by a scrofulous, or tuberculous, tumour on her knee. While peering at the robe the girl suddenly screamed: 'I can stand on my feet!'[5] Eighteen instances of healing were recorded during the display. But sceptical surgeons noted that sixteen of the patients were women who probably suffered from psychosomatic sickness.[6]

The popularity of the pilgrimage to Trier and the real or imagined benefits arising from it awakened doubts regarding Ronge's attack on bishop Arnoldi. Why should the suspended Silesian impugn the prelate's person and practice? Were the people actually exploited, seduced, or aroused to fanaticism?

Some of these questions find answers in the autobiography which Ronge wrote about a year after his open letter to bishop Arnoldi. Ronge recounted the rise of scepticism and doubt in his attitude toward the Church. After studying at the university of Breslau, he entered a seminary at Breslau in December 1839. Regarding his seminary experience, where he 'received indelibly the stamp of bondage', Ronge later wrote: 'The confidence which I had thus far felt

---

[1] Schmid, *Geschichte der Katholischen Kirche*, p 610.   [2] *Ibid* p 628.

[3] Heinrich Brueck, *Geschichte der Katholischen Kirche in Deutschland im neunzehnten Jahrhundert* (Mainz 1889) II, p 516.

[4] Schmid, *Geschichte der Katholischen Kirche*, p 612.

[5] *Ibid* p 614.   [6] *Ibid* p 615.

for my spiritual teachers was destroyed when I saw them in close proximity, and when I perceived how religion was perverted in order to oppress and subjugate the people.'[1] Ronge castigated the catholic clergy for hypocrisy, oppression of the German people and the division of their land into lay and clerical 'castes'.

Scarcely a year after entering upon a curacy at Grottkau Ronge first employed his pen to publish his complaint. The bishop of Breslau, count Sedlnitzky, was set aside because of his moderate position on the volatile question of mixed marriage between Protestants and Catholics. Two names emerged as candidates for the bishopric: Dr Joseph Ignatius Ritter and canon Knauer. Dr Ritter, a former Hermesian professor of ecclesiastical history at Bonn, had recently become a convinced curial supporter. He was the administrator of the Breslau diocese. Canon Knauer, a kindly octogenarian, was distinguished only by his colourless senility and fidelity to Rome. The chapter of Breslau chose Knauer, and Rome waited a year before confirming the appointment.[2]

Strengthened by the Breslau affair in his hatred of the hierarchy Ronge rushed into print with an article assailing the curia. Under the title 'Rome and the Chapter of Breslau', Ronge wrote a stinging critique for publication in the nationalistically inclined *Saechsische Volksblaetter*.[3]

Immediately seventy catholic clergymen submitted a petition demanding the dismissal of Ronge. They complained that his hair was too long and his cassock too short. Meanwhile the mayor of Grottkau together with thirty-eight citizens requested Ronge's retention as curate at Grottkau. When the case came before Dr Ritter he was only too ready to banish the troublesome curate to the mountains of Upper Silesia. Ronge was suspended from all priestly duties.[4]

Dr Ritter hoped he would never again hear from the revolutionary, and bishop Knauer sought only the placid enjoyment of his bishopric. Ronge, however, would not be muzzled. He had been in Laurahuette little more than a year when the open letter to bishop Arnoldi brought fame and infamy. The clearly inflammatory brief – only one page in length – proved to be the catalyst which unleashed a flood of pamphlets. Whilst many nationalists rushed to Ronge's side, the Church excommunicated him on 30 November 1844. In December 1844 he

---

[1] Johannes Ronge, *The Autobiography and Justification of Johannes Ronge (the German Reformer)*, translated from the 5th edition by John Lord (London 1846) p 4.
[2] *Ibid* pp 27–32.   [3] *Ibid* pp 28–9.   [4] *Ibid* p 55.

struck again urging German Catholics to sever ties with Rome –
'Lossagen muss sich die deutsche Nation von jenem italienischen
Bischof' ('the German nation must declare itself free from that Italian
bishop'). He urged ecclesiastical independence upon his fellow Germans and Catholics. The details of this proposed deliverance included
the abolition of auricular confession and the celibacy of the clergy
and the permission of mixed marriages between Protestants and
Catholics.[1]

An anonymous pamphlet appeared early in 1845 asserting that the
Roman hierarchy fostered superstition, belief in miracles and the
intellectual slavery of the faithful.[2]

One of Ronge's staunchest supporters in the rebellion against
Rome was Franz Schuselka of Sudeten Germany, who published an
account of Ronge's triumphal tour of Weimar in November 1845.
God has sent Ronge to awaken the German people to a 'new Christian
consciousness'. Through Ronge, the reformer, all dangers would be
overcome and all hopes fulfilled.[3]

Robert Blum, the theatrical cashier who achieved fame in the 1848
revolution, also identified himself with Ronge. Ronge's protest to
bishop Arnoldi had 'loosened the tongues of millions, whose souls
were full of rage over the mockery of common sense at Trier'.[4]

As the nationalists and rationalists rose to Ronge's defence, so
Roman Catholic spokesmen stood with bishop Arnoldi. Joseph Heinrich, a Silesian priest, wrote that Ronge's open letter was rather a bad
joke than a masterpiece of enlightenment.[5]

A Roman Catholic jurist, Mauritius Moritz, justified the pilgrimage
to Trier from the standpoints of reason, revelation and the social
effects. Although relics awaken worship in man, God alone performs
the miracles. After all, had not the woman been healed of her haemor-
rhage by touching the hem of Christ's robe? God could certainly work
wonders through the same seamless garment.[6]

Bishop Arnoldi was portrayed in glowing terms by another catholic
author, Lucilius Lucianus Christhold. The bishop was the paragon and

---

[1] Johannes Ronge, *An Meine Glaugensgenossen und Mitbuerger* (Altenburg 1845) pp 4, 6–9.
[2] *Die Wunder zu Trier oder Arnoldi und Ronge, ein Wort der Belehrung und Warnung fuer
das deutsche Volk* (Dortmund 1845) p 11.
[3] Franz Schuselka, *Ronge in Weimar den 14., 15. und 16. November 1845* (Weimar
1845) p ix.
[4] Heinrich Schmid, *Geschichte der Katholischen Kirche*, p 627.
[5] Joseph Heinrich, *Sendschreiben an Johannes Ronge zur Widerlegung* (Breslau 1844) p 4.
[6] Mauritius Moritz, *Die Verehrung heiliger Reliquien und Bilder, und das Wallfahrten nach
der Lehre der Katholischen Kirche* (2 ed, Aschaffenburg 1845) p 24.

personification of a faithful Catholic, dedicated pastor, brilliant philosopher, and patriotic German.[1]

From Halle the noted jurist and Dante scholar Johann Heinrich Carl Witte penned a pamphlet in opposition to Ronge. The reformer from Laurahuette was 'ein rechtes Kind des neunzehnten Jahrhunderts' ('a true child of the nineteenth century'). As a rationalist and suspended priest Ronge actually had no right to speak out against the bishop, the Church, and the pilgrims. Of the open letter to bishop Arnoldi, Witte wrote disparagingly: 'It would, in fact, be a difficult riddle to solve, should one attempt to express more nonsense in the same number of words.'[2]

Whilst Ronge's fame rose to the accompaniment of the pamphleteers' debate, another revolutionary movement was emerging northeast of Poznan. In the city of Schneidemuehl, a curate named Johann Czerski led his congregation in open opposition against catholic authority. On 19 October 1844 the Schneidemuehl congregation determined to declare its independence from the Roman Catholic Church and become an independent community. A week later they submitted a creed to the Ministry of the Interior at Bydgoszcz, the capital of a Prussian province bearing the same name. On the positive side, the Schneidemuehl creed advocated mass in the vernacular, the right of intermarriage between Protestants and Catholics and the sacrament in both kinds. Negatively, the invocation of the saints, auricular confession, clerical celibacy and the subjection to the papal primate were rejected.[3]

Czerski, the Schneidemuehl priest, had passed through stages of development in his revulsion against Rome which closely resembled those of Ronge. After attending schools in Bydzoszcz, the aspirant to the priesthood enrolled in the episcopal seminary at Poznan. There he commenced to doubt the dogmas of the Church which he compared with the Bible. His scepticism was further nurtured by reading Paulo Sarpi's *Istoria del Concilio Tridentino*, a clearly critical account of the Council of Trent. From the seminary Czerski proceeded to a curacy at Poznan cathedral, which he deplored as the 'Hauptsitz des hier-

[1] Lucilius Lucianus Christold, *Nothwendige und gruendliche Vertheidigung des Hochwuerdigen Bischofs Arnoldi zu Trier wegen der ihm zum Vorwurfe gemachten Ausstellung des heiligen Rockes* (2 ed, Leipzig 1845).

[2] Johann Heinrich Friedrich Karl Witte, *Der Heilige Rock, Ronge und Czerski* (Breslau 1845) pp 18, 20-1.

[3] *Offenes Glaubensbekenntnis der christlich-katholischen Gemeinde zu Schneidemuehl, in ihren Unterscheidungslehren von der roemisch-katholischen Kirche, das heisst Hierarchie* (Berlin 1845) pp 3, 7-17.

archischen Priesterregiments' ('the headquarters of the hierarchichal priestly regimen'). Most of the anti-catholic ideas embodied in the Schneidemuehl confession germinated there. Like Ronge, Czerski was also suspended from his duties as a priest. Unlike Ronge, however, the cause was lust rather than liberalism. Czerski was cohabiting with a woman. (Czerski preferred to call his relationship a *Gewissensehe*, a 'marriage of conscience'.) After being suspended for one month, a second offence brought transference from the cathedral at Poznan to a less prominent post in Schneidemuehl.[1]

The schism at Schneidemuehl freed Czerski to marry. Before Christmas 1844 he sought permission from political authorities to take Marianne Guttkowska, a gentle, blonde daughter of a Polish landowner, as his wife. After having been sent from one ministry to another, governmental approval for the marriage came on 29 December 1844. Two months passed, however, before a clergyman could be persuaded to perform the ceremony. On 21 February 1845 the protestant pastor Gruetzwacher united Czerski and Marianne in marriage. The simple ceremony was performed in Czerski's apartment, which also served as the place of worship for the Schneidemuehl congregation. The bridegroom had been excommunicated by catholic authorities four days before the marriage. To the excommunication Czerski replied in tones reminiscent of Martin Luther: 'Cast your thunders of excommunication after me, stir up the funeral pile, forge the chains, *here I stand, and can do no other. God help me! Amen!*'[2]

Although Czerski led only a local movement and his writings were few in comparison with Ronge, he was subjected to predictable criticism. The main fuel for attack on Czerski was, of course, his illicit premarital relationship with Marianne. The marriage and excommunication had not only alienated the parents of both the bride and bridegroom. Czerski's own father died as a result of the excitement.[3]

Another catholic critic, Bertholdi, attacked Czerski for doctrinal diversion. He had violated the clear teaching of the Church by denying the authority of tradition and the invocation of the saints. Furthermore

[1] R. Johann Czerski, *des Stifters der ersten christlich-katholischen Gemeinde zu Schneidemuehl, Leben und Wirken* (Jena 1845) pp 5–8, 9, 11–13.

[2] J. Czerski, *Religious Movement in Germany, and Extensive Secession from Popery. Justification of my Secession from the Roman State Church. A Public Letter to All who Can and Will Hear, See, and Examine* (London 1845) p 21.

[3] Johann Czerski, *Stifter der neuen Gemeinschaft, dargestellt nach seinem eigenen Bekenntnis* (Magdeburg 1845) p 10.

he had subverted the celebration of the Sacrament by abolishing both auricular confession and absolution.[1]

The confluence of the Ronge and Czerski streams of revolt occurred at Easter 1845 in Leipzig. A congregation sympathetic to Ronge had been constituted at Breslau, and it issued a call for a council to be convened in Leipzig on 23 March. Ronge called Easter 1845 the 'resurrection festival of the free Christian church in Germany'.[2] Twenty-one congregations were represented at Leipzig, and the motto of the meeting was 'freedom'. Every congregation was to enjoy unbridled liberty and independence in its formulation of the nature of Christianity. To preclude restrictions, a minimal doctrinal statement was accepted which referred to God as creator, sustainer and ruler of the world. Jesus Christ was not declared to be divine, and the Holy Spirit was only named. The triune nature of God was conspicuous by its absence. Ronge and Czerski appeared only briefly in Leipzig before rushing off to Halle and a triumphal reception sponsored by protestant dignitaries and professors of the university.[3]

In many ways the council at Leipzig was the apex of the revolutionary movement in nineteenth-century German Catholicism. The impress of liberalism was affixed to the loose confederation of congregations. The name agreed upon by the delegates was as broad as the confession of faith. They were to call themselves German-Catholic Churches.

With the coming of summer 1845 the German-Catholic Churches began to show symptoms of mortality. In Mannheim and Heidelberg the congregations were extended toleration.[4] In Saxony the German-Catholic clergy were granted permission to perform the sacraments and bury the dead. Communicants were excused from the payment of church taxes.[5]

The most obvious symptom of decline within the German-Catholic Church was a tendency to internal schism. On 23 June 1845 *The Times* reported that Czerski's followers had changed their name to the

[1] H. Bertholdi, *Das Schneidemuehler Glaubensbekenntnis und roemischer Gegner in Posen* (Danzig 1845) pp 9–10.

[2] *Ronge und Czerski zur Kirchenversammlung in Leipzig* (2 ed, Leipzig 1845) p 8.

[3] *Die deutsch-katholischen Deputirten in Halle. Ein Gedenkblatt an die Feier vom 27. Maerz 1845, den zu Leipzig Concil entsandten deutsch-katholischen Deputirten zu Ehren in Halle veranstaltet und Adresse an Saemmtliche freie katholische Gemeinden und Katholiken Deutschlands* (Halle 1845) pp 4–5.

[4] *The Times*, 19 December 1845.

[5] *Die Verhandlungen ueber die Deutsch-Katholiken in der gegenwaertigen Standesversammlung Sachsens* (Leipzig 1846) Appendix.

'German Apostolic Catholics', and in Berlin the congregation led by Pribil assumed the title of 'Catholic German Protestants'.

In October 1845 Ronge asked Ignatius Heinrich Wessenberg, the controversial reforming priest of Constance, to sanction the German-Catholic Church and join the movement. Although Wessenberg deplored the display at Trier, he refused resolutely to lend his name to a new sect.[1]

At the end of 1845 the communicants of the German-Catholic Church numbered 60,000, but they were hopelessly scattered by schism.[2] They represented theological positions as diverse as Czerski's orthodoxy and Ronge's rationalism.

The death knell tolled when the revolution of 1848 erupted. As Samuel Cheetham put it: 'the pole of light of the German-Catholic Church vanished in the telluric fires of the Revolution of 1848'.[3] Ronge fled to England in 1849, and Czerski had been a long-forgotten man when death overtook him on 22 December 1893.

A post-mortem examination of the German-Catholic Church reveals three basic contributors to its demise. First, the movement failed to lay firm foundations of doctrine. In writing of his tour through Germany prior to 1848, the Swiss Evangelical J. H. Merle d'Aubigne noted that the German-Catholic Church had failed to return to the creeds which primitive Catholicism and Protestantism held in common.[4]

An anonymous pamphlet, *Eiliges Sendschreiben an die geehrten Mitglieder der neukatholischen Kirche in Deutschland*, warned that the German-Catholic Church was in danger of falling into rank rationalism. The reformers had rejected catholic claims that there is no salvation outside the Church of Rome. The movement failed, however, to recognise that apart from faith in Jesus Christ there is no truly Christian Church.[5]

In explaining the essence of the German-Catholic Church Friedrich Ferdinand Kampe boasted of the freedom which congregations enjoyed. No creeds circumscribed the communities. By 1850 philosophical socialism had replaced religion. The essence of the German-

---

[1] Schmid, *Geschichte der Katholischen Kirche*, p 639 n.

[2] *Ibid* p 652.

[3] Samuel Cheetham, *A History of the Christian Church since the Reformation* (London 1907) p 422.

[4] J. H. Merle d'Aubigne, *Germany, England, and Scotland; or, Recollections of a Swiss Minister* (London 1848) p 57.

[5] *Eiliges Sendschreiben an die geehrten Mitglieder der neukatholischen Kirche in Deutschland* (Magdeburg 1846) p 9.

Catholic Church was the sanctification of socialism and the universal brotherhood of man.[1]

To the absence of doctrinal definition must be added a second weakness in the German-Catholic Church. Neither Johannes Ronge nor Johann Czerski possessed sufficient personal magnetism to mould a movement capable of surviving in an atmosphere of unbounded liberty. Born of negativism and schism, the German-Catholic Church was doomed to division and defeat. The Roman Catholic Church had been rejected, but no purer church was created to fill the vacuum.

For the historian a third failure is of supreme significance. The German-Catholic Church failed to build a bridge between the liberal tendencies prominent in nineteenth-century Germany and the increasing influence of the ultramontane movement.[2] The popular German-Catholic Church died and disintegrated, leaving only a trail of polemic pamphlets.

[1] Friedrich Ferdinand Kampe, *Das Wesen des Deutschkatholicismus mit besonderer Ruecksicht auf sein Verhaeltnis zur Politik* (Tuebingen 1850) p 320.
[2] Friedrich Heyer, *The Catholic Church from 1648 to 1870*, translated by D. W. D. Shaw (London 1969) pp 149–50.

'GOD AND MAMMON'
RELIGIOUS PROTEST AND EDUCATIONAL CHANGE IN NEW ENGLAND FROM THE REVOLUTION TO THE GILDED AGE

by KEITH HAMPSON

I hasten at the start to point out that I am not an ecclesiastical historian, but a historian of America who is interested in church history since the field in which I work – educational history – desperately needs to be studied in a wider historical context. Then, as now, educational ideas, and the functions people ascribe to education, cannot be dissociated from the political, social, and economic background. Of all the many factors bearing upon the evolution of education in New England from approximately the 1780s to the 1880s religion was in several ways of central importance. Most studies have been interested in the religious nature of the mass of colleges founded from 1780 to 1860.[1] My interest here is entirely different. Although the rhetoric naturally changed in emphasis, it seems to me that right from the seventeenth century to the late nineteenth century religious forces in New England, but of course not just there, used schools and colleges as cardinal agencies in efforts to restrain secularism and a growing materialism.

'Where a Selfish, covetous spirit and Love of this world prevails, there the Love of God decayeth', declared the puritan divine William Russell.[2] In puritan New England men were expected to practise industry and thrift, and God's favour would bring material rewards. What mattered was not wealth *per se*, but one's attitude towards it. Avarice and the excessive pursuit of wealth were condemned as morally wrong and against the public good.[3]

[1] See D. G. Tewksbury, *The Founding of American Colleges and Universities before the Civil War; with Particular Reference to the Religious Influences Bearing Upon the College Movement* (New York 1932); and *The Colleges and the Public, 1787–1862*, ed T. R. Crane (New York 1963).

[2] Quoted in [R. L.] Bushman, [*From Puritan to Yankee: Character and the Social Order in Connecticut, 1690–1765*] (Cambridge, Mass, 1967) p 188.

[3] In 1639 Robert Keayne was accused by the elders of the First Church in Boston of excessive profit making, which it was maintained was not only a crime but a sin; see *The Apologia of Robert Keayne*, ed B. Bailyn (New York 1965).

By the end of the seventeenth century New England ministers were deeply worried over the state of the 'new Zion' as rapid economic expansion produced disputes over trade, currency, and land titles, rife speculation and gambling, intemperance and ostentation. The root of the trouble was clear: growing worldliness. Equally disconcerting, and related to the breakdown in spiritual standards was the potential collapse of the social order. Growing opportunities for the acquisition of riches blurred traditional social gradations. A man was tempted to rise out of his station, to kick against social and political restraints.

Puritan ministers waged a counter-offensive throughout the century. In this fight against the Anti-Christ, they held up the example of an idealised version of society during the earliest years of settlement. But at the close of the seventeenth century there was a growing gap between these idealised standards and reality. It was clear that New Englanders were 'much more concerned about getting Land and Money and Stock than they be about getting Religion revived'.[1]

The Great Awakening of the 1740s was in large part a reaction to this: an attempt to return to the standards of an earlier, more virtuous generation. During the Awakening, James Davenport, for example, made bonfires of symbols of worldliness such as wigs and fine clothes. But despite their earlier hopes, the Awakening ceased to appeal to conservatives once they saw the logical results. It exacerbated political and social disharmony and ultimately undermined religious harmony, too. However, because of the denominational rivalry it engendered, the Great Awakening promoted a notable expansion of higher education: each sect needed to ensure a supply of trained ministers. They had to take in a fairly wide range of students because of the need for fees, but their basic intention was always to form 'a succession of sober, virtuous, industrious citizens', 'checking the course of a growing Luxury' by 'forming youth to the knowledge and exercise of private and public virtue'.[2]

If the civil leaders ignored the appeals from the Jeremiahs to protect congregational orthodoxy and lead a crusade for traditional moral standards, other means had to be found to awaken the people to a

---

[1] Bushman, p 189. See [J. P.] Greene, ['Search for Identity: An Interpretation of Selected Patterns of Social Response in Eighteenth Century America'], in *Journal of Social History*, IV (Berkeley 1970) pp 189–220.

[2] Quoted by Greene, p 213. See B. McAnear, 'College Founding in the American Colonies, 1745–75', in *M[ississippi] V[alley] H[istorical] R[eview]*, XLII (New Orleans June 1955) pp 24–44. See also, *The Great Awakening: Event and Exegesis*, ed D. B. Rutman (New York 1970).

life based on the scriptures. Otherwise a decline into total dissolution could not be arrested. 'Empires', it was explained at a college commencement in 1770, 'proceed, in fatal round, from virtuous industry and valour to wealth and conquest; next to luxury, then to foul corruption and bloated morals; and, last of all to sloth, anarchy, slavery and political death.'

This became even more pressing with the onset of the American Revolution. Certain groups realised that it might not be what it had seemed in theory. It might be dangerous discarding traditions. How was the imperial disengagement to be prevented from turning into political radicalism or undermining social stability? Because without question there had been some dramatic, and unanticipated social consequences of the Revolution. To those already established it was highly disturbing to watch the 'sudden appearance of new men everywhere in politics and business'. It was 'Whiggism run mad'.[1] Concern of course reached its peak when social turbulence broke into Shay's Rebellion in 1786. The drafting of a new federal constitution in 1787 was a direct consequence.

'The principal cause of all the evils we now experience', it was repeatedly affirmed, was the 'luxurious living of all ranks and degrees'. The remedy in Richard Henry Lee's judgement was the moral regeneration of the country. However, so many of the objections about political developments in the post-war years were not directed in the first instance at actual constitutional arrangements, but towards the character defects of those gaining power, 'specious, interested, designing men'.[2] The constitution was seen by its proponents as an instrument to keep their world in proper check and balance, control remaining in the hands of those best equipped to exercise it. Government was regarded as 'a complicated science, and requires abilities and knowledge of a variety of other subjects, to understand it'. Too many of those seeking power were 'men without reading, experience or principle'. The good ruler needed enlightenment and special training.[3]

Without such men in charge the country would slide into a moral decline, since 'government will partake of the qualities of those whose authority is prevalent'. Unfortunately, the years from 1783 to 1787

---

[1] [G. S.] Wood, [*The Creation of the American Republic, 1776–87*] (Chapel Hill 1969) pp 115, 476; William Goddard, *The Prowess of the Whig Club* (Baltimore 1777) quoted by Wood, p 477.

[2] Benjamin Austin, in the *Boston Independent Chronicle*, 6 December 1787; Charleston, *Columbian Herald*, 23 September 1785, quoted by Wood, pp 477, 484–5.

[3] Hartford, *Connecticut Courant*, 20 November 1786.

suggested that the feared decline had already begun. 'Virtue, I fear', wrote George Washington, 'has in great degree taken its departure from our land.' This was all the more galling because the Revolution had been seen by many as more than just a change from colony to nation. It had a strong moral dimension. It had been a purifying process: a casting off of the Old World. America was once more a beacon for mankind, truly a 'City upon a Hill'. This could never be if it fell into 'licentiousness' or anarchy and, so many also thought, if it were ungodly. The excesses of the French Revolution seemed to prove the wisdom of such thinking. Without Godliness there would be anarchy.[1]

Hence, education was not only important, but had to be ideally of two types. 'An attachment to the laws may be formed by early impressions upon the mind', it was frequently suggested. Education could train youth to have obedience to authority and respect for their betters. It could confine and channel the direction of social mobility. Hopefully, it could enable the public to recognise who would make 'good' rulers, and reject the non-experienced and unprincipled. As governor Caleb Strong told the Massachusetts legislature, 'the whole of education is necessary in Republican Governments – they depend for their support upon the enlightened and affectionate attachment of the people – there is no ground to expect they will be preserved unless youth are trained to knowledge and virtue'.[2]

The 1780s and 1790s were notable for prolific essay writing on the need for schooling in the new republic. The American Philosophical Society offered a prize for the 'best system of liberal education and literary instruction, adapted to the genius of the Government of the United States'. Although schemes varied tremendously, the overriding aim was to establish a 'foundation of virtue', and so 'keep the people steady'. As the famous Land Ordinance of 1787 declared, 'Religion, morality and knowledge being necessary to good government and the happiness of mankind, schools and the means of education shall be forever encouraged'.[3] Of the fourteen new state constitutions

[1] John Dickinson, *Letters of Fabius*, quoted in Wood, p 507; George Washington to John Jay, 18 May 1786, quoted by [D. H.] Fischer, [*The Revolution of American Conservatism*] (New York 1965) p 379.

[2] *Essays on Education in the Early Republic*, ed F. Rudolph (Cambridge, Mass, 1965); T. Post, 'Historical Address', in *Centennial of Lennox Academy* (Lennox 1903) p 11.

[3] *Connecticut Courant*, 4 July 1791; George Cabot to Rufus King, 14 August 1795, quoted in Fischer, p 4; 'North West Ordinance', Article 3, in *Documents of American History*, ed H. S. Commager (5 ed New York 1949) p 131.

written prior to 1800, seven had articles calling for public aid for education. At the same time, though, there had to be some provision of a high moral and intellectual calibre for training men to lead the country altruistically. By establishing Harvard in 1636, and requiring certain towns to provide Latin grammar schools to feed it students, the Puritans had created just such a special educational level, training Godly leaders, men of 'sound doctrine' for pulpit and public service.

Public education, provided by towns as required by law, had proved unpopular, however. In 1790 only 30 of the 227 towns required to possess a Latin grammar school did in fact do so, despite the heavy penalties threatened by the laws. Consequently, grandiose schemes for a national system of education were emotionally and practically non-starters. Moreover, the old public school system had proved wholly unsuitable for rural areas; and it was, of course, from these back-country areas that Shay's Rebellion had sprung. As a result a new, non-public but highly flexible pattern of secondary education was evolved in the 1780s with the growth of academies.[1]

This movement gained its impetus from the Phillips family of Massachusetts, who in 1778 founded the Phillips Academy, Andover, and followed this in 1781 with the Phillips Exeter Academy in New Hampshire. Samuel Phillips, Jr, felt there was a pressing need for an improvement of schooling because he was so distressed at 'the present degeneracy which has increased upon us with such rapidity; bringing very frequent instances of the decay of virtue, public and private, the prevalence of public and private vice, the amazing change in the tempers, dispositions and conduct of people in this country within these thirty years. The trouble [he declared] is owing to the neglect of good instruction.' Hence the '*principal duty* of the Instructors [in the Phillips academies was] to regulate the Tempers, to enlarge the Minds, and form the Morals of the Youth committed to their care'.[2]

All academies followed the pattern set by Phillips at Andover. They were private foundations; policy lying in the hands of a board of independent trustees. There was no public control of the conduct or content of instruction, but being non-profit making legislators were ready to give them incorporated status, and to aid some with public funds by means of land grants and tax exemptions. Their great con-

[1] R. Middlekauff, *Ancients and Axioms: England* (New Haven 1963) pp 129–30.
[2] Undated MS of Samuel Phillips, Jr, quoted by [C. M.] Fuess, [*An Old New England School*] (Boston 1917) p 56; Constitution of Phillips Academy, reprinted in [T. R.] Sizer, [*Age of the Academies*] (New York 1964) pp 79–89.

venience lay in not involving communities in the commitments, especially financial, that the compulsory grammar school system had entailed. By not needing a large tax base for their maintenance, but charging their pupils fees, academies could also be established in small rural towns, pupils who came from outside the immediate vicinity being boarded out with families in the town.[1]

It is unfortunate that most readily available material on these schools comes from the later years of their existence, from the 1830s to 1850s. In this period their catalogues presented a wonderful range of subjects to be taught. As a result the nature of the early phase of the movement has been to some extent misunderstood. They were much more special-ised, élitist, classically based and religious – in fact direct descendants of the Latin grammar schools, with the same college-preparatory function – than historians have realised.

An examination of the charters of incorporation of academies founded around the turn of the century shows that they differed little in their main objective from the Phillips foundations. Of course, any balance of subject matter could be struck, so flexible was the system, but in 1820 an Andover pupil had to have completed thirteen classical and two mathematical courses plus lessons in writing and singing in order to gain a diploma. Diversification and change of emphasis in the curriculum ultimately came, more elsewhere than at Andover, but of greater significance was the tone and wider operations of the academy. As John Phillips stressed

above all it is expected that the attention of Instructors to the *disposition* of the Minds and Morals of the Youth under their charge, *will exceed every other care*; well considering that tho' goodness without knowledge, as it respects others, is weak and feeble, yet knowledge without goodness, is dangerous; and that both united, form the noblest character; and lay the surest foundation of useful-ness to mankind.

His main concern was the inculcation of proper attitudes since 'at an early period in life, the mind easily receives and retains impressions'.[2] Academies *as conceived by their founders* did not herald the dawn of secular utilitarianism in education. These schools were dedicated to 'advancing the interest of the *great Redeemer*', with the specific hope that many pupils would be 'devoted to the sacred work of the Gospel ministry'.[3] Rather than being a follow-on from the short-lived

[1] Sizer has a useful introduction.
[2] Fuess, p 171; Constitution of Phillips Exeter Academy, reprinted in [L. M.] Crosbie, [*The Phillips Exeter Academy, A History*] (Norwood, N.H., 1923) p 308; Act of Incor-poration, in Crosbie, p 311.   [3] Crosbie, pp 304, 308.

'God and Mammon'

'English' school in Benjamin Franklin's academy in Philadelphia in the 1750s, the Phillips Academy was an attempt to keep coming generations *out* of the hands of free thinkers and secularists, especially at a time when Jeffersonian Republicans were very sympathetic to Deism.[1] Given the orthodox Congregationalism of most academies, and the social and political leanings of their founders, it is not unreasonable, I think, to suggest that they originated as a protest against the trends of the time. In other words, there was a body of devout men of wealth who believed that a society of moral habits, stable institutions and order presupposed a thoughtful electorate brought up on sound moral precepts and rulers educated in the learned languages and the Bible.

During the years of the French revolutionary wars in particular, such men as these, of a Federalist disposition, genuinely feared what they believed to be the Jacobinism of the Jeffersonian Republicans, and even after the peaceful transfer of power to Jefferson in 1800, in large part hounded from office, they continued to get increasingly worried at the rate and tendency of social change. When the new economic forces, with new men in their train, finally came into their own during the administrations of Andrew Jackson, the gap between the way they thought society *should* function and the realities of what De Tocqueville called an age of individualism had become acute. In particular, it seemed to them that these new men were more concerned for their own interests than for the public welfare.

It was in this period, 1826 to 1835, that the greatest expansion of academies took place. This was a period of economic growth after the depression following the war of 1812, but there is a strong possibility that many foundations were part of a reaction by those men who perceived in the Jeffersonian and Jacksonian eras a threat to their sort of society. It is, I think, indicative that the years between 1815 and 1830 also saw the birth of almost a dozen religious benevolent societies: the American Education Society, the American Bible Society, the American Sunday School Union, the American Home Missionary Society, the American Tract Society. These societies sought not only to guide men along God's narrow path but also to direct their social and political conduct along the way. They were, announced the Home Missionary Society, 'equally indispensable to the moral advancement and the political stability of the United States'. They were certainly

---

[1] *Benjamin Franklin on Education*, ed J. H. Best (New York 1965). For Jefferson's deism and Republican support for dissenting sects see L. K. Kerber, *Federalists in Dissent* (Ithaca 1970) p 53.

357   12-3

anti-Jackson. Their historian, in fact, has maintained that they were all launched by the well-to-do to bridge the gap between themselves and the poor and counter the threats to social equilibrium posed by irreligious democrats.[1]

My study of the founding of academies is not complete but many of the founders were certainly, like the Phillips family, among the élite of their communities, and politically and religiously they were conservative. Some academies were founded directly by churches, sometimes town meetings voted to buy some shares, but even so, the initiative usually sprang from the efforts of groups of devout laymen, notable citizens of the town. The impetus, in short, for these private schools came from men who as 'rulers' of the colonial period had, for similar reasons, tried, but failed, to impose *public* schooling.

So successful for opening up educational opportunities in rural areas, academies were impractical for the industrialising areas of New England. So impending, it was thought, was the degeneracy of character in these cities that recourse was made once more to publicly maintained secondary schooling. As early as 1824, a conservative member of the Massachusetts legislature attacked academies for being too exclusive. Degraded members of society who most needed schooling, he argued, were not likely to volunteer for it, even if they could afford it. So he called for the direct re-involvement of the state and a revival of compulsory public schooling. The function of a city public school was as the Boston school committee explained in 1853:

> to take children at random from a great city, undisciplined, uninstructed, often with inherited stupidity of centuries of ignorant ancestors; forming them from animals into intellectual beings; and so far as a school can do it, from intellectual beings into spiritual beings.[2]

Recent work throws doubt on the view that the establishment of public high schools was part of a democratic reform movement, a victory of newly enfranchised classes supported by humanitarian intellectuals against élitism and entrenched religion, and has suggested that the promoters of local high schools were generally the most affluent citizens, who viewed the extension of educational opportuni-

---

[1] By 1850 there were about 1000 academies, including some 800 non-incorporated ones; see Sizer, p 12; C. S. Griffin, 'Religious Benevolence as Social Control 1815-60', in *MVHR*, XLIV (December 1957).

[2] James G. Carter, *Letters to the Hon. William Prescott LL.D. on the Free Schools of New England with Remarks upon the Principles of Instruction* (Boston 1824). For the School Committee quotation I am indebted to professor Michael Katz.

ties partly as a means of sustaining economic prosperity, but most importantly as a corrective for the moral and cultural disintegration of life in an industrial city. The innate passions of a child, liable to be whetted by city life, had to be controlled. 'The love of gain and love of place', and 'continual excitement for wealth': these Horace Mann, from 1837 to 1848 the secretary of the newly created Massachusetts Board of Education, wanted to replace by more honourable values. The public common school was the means to raise the tone of the community, 'to elevate the sentiments, the taste, and the manners of the pupils'.[1]

Nevertheless, mass common schooling was only one antidote for the malaise. To check the falling off of virtue and arrest the collapse of society required the right sort of leaders. Seeing themselves as a natural aristocracy, New England Federalists had argued that 'the grand secret of forming good government is to put good men into the administration: for wild vicious, or idle men, will ever make a bad government, let its principles be ever so good'. Attitudes such as this survived in New England long after the Federalist party had died. Following the Civil War many such men possessed a strikingly high degree of optimism about creating a better Union, in much the same way that their puritan ancestors had seen the Commonwealth of Visible Saints, and their immediate predecessors had regarded the Revolution. Their object, said James Russell Lowell in 1865, was 'to make the world ready for the true second coming of Christ'. Most had been in reform movements before the war, attacking, for example, the increase in drinking and gambling, and calling for the abolition of slavery, the prime symbol of America's moral failure. They were amenable to these perfectionist reform movements associated with revivalism because of a kind of prior value orientation. They had long denounced the pursuit of material goals. They were individuals who held unusually high expectations of their society, and who had a long-developed sense of self-identity with its fortunes. They measured the present against an idealised conception of the past: the rhetoric of the eighteenth century Jeremiahs had gained a life of its own.[2]

Their hopes in the 1870s for a rebirth of the nation under their own

---

[1] See M. Katz, *The Irony of Early School Reform* (Cambridge, Mass, 1969).

[2] Pelatiah Webster, *The Weakness of Brutus Exposed* (Philadelphia 1787), quoted by Wood, *American Republic*, p 508; [James Russell] Lowell, [*The Writings of James Russell Lowell*] (London 1890) v, p 310; see T. L. Smith, *Revivalism and Social Reform: American Protestantism on the Eve of the Civil War* (New York 1965), and J. L. Thomas, 'Romantic Reform in America 1815–65', in *American Quarterly*, XVII (Philadelphia 1965) pp 658–81.

guidance were soon shattered, however. They not only failed to elevate the level of politics, but were in large measure forced reluctantly out of office-holding by the bosses of the Republican party. Some moved vigorously into extra-party movements, tariff and civil service reform, for example: others into a plethora of social reform agencies. But there was always an assumption on the part of these gentlemen reformers that real improvement could only come if they, the 'Best Men', were in charge. They shared the Federalists' general attitudes about the organisation of society and the nature of political leadership, holding to a concept of stewardship first subscribed to by John Winthrop and Cotton Mather: that the people should participate in the choice of 'rulers', but only the 'better sort' should be chosen; once in office they were really accountable only to God for the way in which they exercised their talents. Cotton Mather had described the political system of Massachusetts Bay as 'a *speaking* Aristocracy *in the face of a silent* Democracy'. Only in the post Civil War era the Democracy was not silent, the new leaders seemed prepared to sacrifice the public good for private gain, and many of the old aristocracy, out of frustration, were not bothering 'to speak', even though they totally lacked confidence in the new leadership. How then in this Gilded Age were they to keep their values alive and their class as a whole active politically?[1]

The majority of Americans were succumbing to the materialism of the age and greedily scrambling for profit and status. Standards in business and politics were declining, the latter was being put to the service of the former, ignorant foreign voters in the cities were being used to keep corrupt 'bosses' in power. The new tycoons, moreover, lacked not only moral scruples but culture and taste. Nor was this the only cause for concern. Earlier fears of the new, propertyless city proletariat sharpened in the last quarter of the century. They were clearly suspect in exercising sound political judgement, while their envy of their wealthy neighbours promised to strain social harmony. Class conflict, was, in fact, not long in erupting into violence with the railway strikes in 1877 and the Haymarket bomb outrage in 1886. Moreover, ethnic and national groups showed a disturbing unwillingness to shed old world customs.

[1] Cotton Mather, *Magnalia Christi Americana* (Hartford 1820), quoted by Fischer, p 4. Various views of the Gilded Age can be found in *The Gilded Age*, ed H. Wayne Morgan (rev ed Syracuse 1970). On the reactions of patricians, see G. Blodgett, *The Gentle Reformers* (Cambridge, Mass, 1966) ch II, and J. G. Sproat, '*The Best Men*': *Liberal Reformers in the Gilded Age* (New York 1968).

'God and Mammon'

If you believed with James Russell Lowell in 1886 that 'it is moral forces that, more than all others, govern the direction and regulate the advance of our affairs, and these forces are as calculable as the Trade Winds or the Gulf Stream', then you felt that they could be taught in schools. Public education had once found some of its staunchest promoters amongst New England patricians, as we have seen. Many, it is true, still felt disquiet at the growth of catholic parochial schools and were concerned that all urban immigrants pass through the 'Americanising' experience of the common school. But secular and commercial forces had gained a strong hold on American education by this time. In the 1880s protestant and catholic spokesmen attacked the 'truly Christless and Godless' schools at a time when a 'spirit of unstableness and change' was the predominant 'spirit of our age and country'. In the public high school, manual training was taking over from mental training. Higher education, too, was expanding fastest in vocational directions with the growth of the technical and agriculturally orientated land-grant universities. American students, wrote Thomas Hughes in 1870, were being 'trained more into competitive money-making machines than into thinking cultivated men'. Yet there was a general apathy regarding the quality of learning because of the dream of rapid wealth.[1]

The common public school was most certainly not purveying the traditional liberal education of a gentleman. To train a cultivated élite, James Russell Lowell's 'sounder thinking men' who would 'accommodate the conduct of communities to ethical laws' and act as a counter-force against the rise of Mammon and the gospel of wealth, American patricians rejected the public schools and the surviving, somewhat rundown academies. Instead, they established a special college-preparatory system based on the English public schools. Removed from the cities and immigrant-filled schools, free of worldly temptations, these schools offered the traditional curriculum (even though, declared the headmaster of St Paul's School, the classics were 'unpopular in an age the drift of which is materialistic') in a religious and cultivated environment. They set out 'to emancipate us...from making selfish indulgence and money-getting our chief business in this world'.[2]

---

[1] Lowell, vi, p 171; B. J. McQuaid, 'Religion in Schools', in *The North American Review*, cxxxii (Boston 1881) pp 332–44; Thomas Hughes to Fanny Hughes, 9 October 1870, quoted in E. C. Mack and W. H. G. Armytage, *Thomas Hughes* (London 1952) p 182.

[2] Lowell, v, p 195; H. A. Coit, 'An American Boys' School: What it Should Be', in *The Forum*, xii (New York September 1891) p 5; H. A. Coit, *School Sermons* (New York 1909) p 240.

Endicott Peabody, the founder of Groton School in 1884, felt that ideally the home 'is the natural place for a boy to live in', but a city environment was now clearly not 'conducive to either the physical or moral health of a growing boy'. This, then, he maintained, was 'the chief reason for the modern boarding school;...established chiefly for, and patronised largely by the city boy'. The condition of the cities, the rampant lawlessness, indeed the general condition of American society worried him greatly. He despaired of the prevailing values of his day: in January 1897 he was enthusiastic that Rainsford, the minister of Trinity Church in the heart of New York's financial district, had 'spoken out' against 'the lavish display of the millionaires'. Believing, therefore, that 'the real question is whether the country will care for honesty first or prosperity first', Peabody launched a school which he hoped would instil in his pupils 'a quest for morality'.[1]

It was a classical school, but above all he wanted a boy to have religion 'implanted in his life', to be constantly present as a conditioner of attitudes and values, not merely a thing of outward manifestation. The grouping of the school buildings, explained bishop Lawrence of Massachusetts, the president of the school trustees, 'fitly expresses the character of Groton school, the Christian faith at the heart and centre of a home for the moral, intellectual and physical development of such boys as may dwell here'. The chapel was 'the most beautiful of all the buildings and will dominate the group, as it is intended that the spiritual life shall dominate the development of the boys character'.[2]

Peabody 'encouraged the boys to show their religion in moral conduct and service'. His pupils were 'missionaries' for a better America: benevolent paternalists who were to govern for the good of the governed. The danger, he told his wealthy Social Register pupils, was that 'you will be decent, you will be as wealthy as you can, you will enjoy life, in a rational sort of way, and let it go at that...you will live and let live. And so a man easily drops into this pleasant and material kind of life, and – the years go by.' A Grotonian was expected to serve, 'to minister to others', and in particular to his country; a

---

[1] [Endicott] Peabody, 'The Boy and The Boarding School', in *The New York Times* 26 September 1908; Peabody to bishop J. Atwood, 28 June 1897 and 17 February 1908, Endicott Peabody Papers, Houghton Library, Harvard University.

[2] Peabody to Atwood, 20 January 1888; William Lawrence, 'The Sermon Preached at the Consecration of St John's Chapel, Groton School, on Saturday, 13 October 1900', in [The] *Consecration of St John's Chapel*, [*Groton School, Groton, Massachusetts*] (Boston 1900) p 9; Peabody, 'The Aim of Groton School', in *The Church Militant*, III (Boston April 1900) p 3.

philosophy summed up by a favourite sermon text, Matthew chapter 20, verses 26–8, 'whosoever shall be great among you let him be your minister; even as the Son of Man came not to be ministered unto but to minister, and to give his life a reason for many'. In short, Peabody believed that the noblest fulfilment of one's religious duty was through public service. Thus life would be 'more than simply cakes and ale; life [would] seem a wonderful, glorious opportunity leading forward and up, higher and higher still, unto Christ, who stands ready to receive and crown his work'.[1]

More than a dozen boarding schools were launched on the same path during the closing decades of the century. By chapel sermons, compulsory athletics, school newspapers, and a whole maze of customs and rituals it was hoped that boys would be so steeped in the school's ideals that these ideals would always be their natural mainspring of conduct, whatever their wealth and whatever temptations the world put in their way. They would know instinctively that one way was right, the other wrong. As Horace Taft, the founder of The Taft School explained, these schools were not established 'simply to give a boost to a few individuals in the struggle for wealth and influence', although, as sociologists have pointed out since, they did precisely that. Taft founded a boarding school, in fact, because he believed that 'many parents fail in the contest they must wage against modern luxury and materialism'. He chose as his school's motto 'not to be ministered unto but to minister', because he believed that 'the main object of a school of this kind should be to have the spirit that boys will live this great text into their lives'.[2]

They were, in short, an attempt to counter prevailing social trends and perpetuate the standards of an earlier day; a protest against the increasing dominance of a plutocracy subscribing to a very materialist philosophy. Economic and social change and politics needed to be controlled by time-honoured values. One way of attempting this was to take future leaders of society and business, isolate them from the temptations of a material, city life, and inculcate sound habits and ideals that would stay with them throughout life. Then the school could create 'a spirit of duty and self-sacrifice', and

---

1 Peabody to Father Sill [headmaster of Kent School], 10 January 1907; Peabody, 'A Sermon preached at the Consecration of St John's Chapel, Groton School on Sunday, 14 October 1900', in *Consecration of St John's Chapel*, pp 35–6, 29.
2 [Horace Dutton Taft,] 'Sermon', 6 January 1935; H. D. Taft, *Memories and Opinions* (New York 1942) p 260; 'Sermon', 22 September 1935. Horace Taft's papers are in the school archives.

together with the college make men recognise 'an aim higher than money-getting'.[1]

In conclusion, let me emphasise that I am not seeking to maintain that all educational developments throughout this period were caused solely, or even primarily, by men of a conservative and religious temperament. I am simply drawing attention to an overlooked aspect ot human motivation, one which was also important outside education, in certain reform movements, for example. That is, the *failure* of important groups to make a successful adjustment to the conditions of abundance which were so central to American development. They continued to subscribe to an idealised set of values, in origin religiously based, which led them to protest against the moral ramifications of the exploitation of abundance as practised by successive generations of Americans. They sought to change educational forms each time they realised that they had ceased to be instruments for the dissemination of old standards and had instead become agents for better achieving material ambitions, at the cost of higher ideals, of failing to lay hold of progress and use it for conforming society to the will of God. As the first president of the new university of Minnesota so effectively explained the fear in his inaugural:

We are so busy with farms and merchandise; we so dote upon our great mills and factories, and warehouses, we are so engrossed with cent per cent, and the fluctuations of the exchange; we fall down and worship so many 'gods of gold and silver, of brass, of iron, or wood and of stone', that we forget the highest life of men and society.[2]

---

[1] Le Barron R. Briggs, *School, College and Character* (Boston 1901) p 11. The concern of the pre-Civil War colleges for the moral ends of knowledge, embodied in the 'liberal' curriculum and collegiate principle, continued after the war more than has usually been recognised, see G. E. Peterson, *The New England College in the Age of the University* (Amherst 1964), but on the survival of the older concepts in juxtaposition with new German ideas in the universities there is as yet no satisfactory study.

[2] See D. M. Potter, *People of Plenty: Economic Abundance and the American Character* (Chicago 1954). W. W. Folwell, 'Inaugural 1869', in *University Addresses* (Minneapolis 1909).

REASON AND EMOTION IN WORKING-CLASS RELIGION, 1794-1824

by STUART MEWS

IN the last decade considerable attention has been paid to Methodism, revivalism, and the development of working-class consciousness in early nineteenth-century England. The purpose of this paper is to add a few footnotes and caveats to some of the assertions which have been made about these topics. The assertions on which I wish to comment can be divided into two groups. The first includes the view widely accepted by sociologists and social historians that in so far as working-class people resort to religion in periods of rapid social change, the religious style which they adopt tends to be of an highly emotional type.[1] Hence the numerical success of Methodism in the lower if not the lowest regions of the social scale is attributed to the prominence which it gave the experiential dimension of religious commitment.[2] On the other hand a religious system like Unitarianism which was theologically highly rational and stressed the intellectualist dimension is dismissed, almost on *a priori* grounds from having any popular appeal. K. S. Inglis after claiming that before 1850 the Unitarians were 'uninterested in evangelizing the masses', quotes G. M. Trevelyan to the effect that theirs was 'a faith likely to be taken up by the mill-owner but not by his workmen'.[3] According to E. P. Thompson 'it seemed too cold, too distant, too polite and too much associated with the comfortable values of a prospering class to appeal to the city or village poor'.[4] The first area in which I wish to submit new evidence is concerned therefore with the general relationship between working-class religion and reason and emotion.

The second topic concerns the internal dynamics of Methodism itself. Methodism was subject to considerable structural strain in the

---

[1] [E. P.] Thompson, [*The Making of the English Working Class*] (revised Pelican ed London 1968) ch 2; Liston Pope, *Millhands and Preachers* (New Haven 1942); H. Richard Niebuhr, *The Social Sources of Denominationalism* (New York 1929).

[2] Thompson, p 31. On the experiential and other dimensions of religious commitment see Charles Y. Glock and Rodney Stark, *Religion and Society in Tension* (Chicago 1965) ch 2.

[3] *Churches and the Working Class in Victorian England* (London 1963) p 13.

[4] Thompson, p 31.

period after Wesley's death. The source of this strain is usually located in the disputes over the roles and statuses of the travelling preachers and the people in the area of church polity, and over the question of normative religious behaviour. In the latter case stress is usually laid on the opposition of the ministerial leaders of the connexion to the more wild and extravagant forms of revivalism which were manifesting themselves particularly in the Potteries and Cornwall, and threatening the routinisation and stabilisation of the denomination. At this point scholarly consideration of methodist dissension usually stops. On the question of methodist doctrine, recent historians have either failed to consider the possibility of doctrinal dissent and theological confusion[1] or have asserted that the great strength of Methodism lay in the consensus reached in theology. 'Doctrinally', J. D. Walsh has remarked, 'Wesleyan Methodism was solid.'[2]

The assertions contained in both these groups of statements can be backed by very substantial evidence and it would be foolish to attempt to refute them. However there is value in filling out and slightly modifying our picture of the religious situation in the early nineteenth century by considering some of the evidence which does not quite fit in with these assertions. One standpoint from which certain features of early nineteenth-century religion can be reconsidered is that of the development of popular Unitarianism.

One of the less important but by no means insignificant religious movements of the early nineteenth century was the development of a popular Unitarianism, in some cases through a process of the apparently spontaneous evolution of ideas, in several instances carried through by people who had been influenced at some stage by Methodism. One of the minor religious heroes of the period was Richard Wright (1764–1836), the chief evangelist of popular Unitarianism. Son of a Norfolk agricultural labourer, Wright's spiritual pilgrimage took him from Calvinism, through Arminianism, to Unitarianism. During his Arminian stage the Wesleyans heard of his zeal and made use of him in their pulpits though he never actually joined them.[3] Soon he was called to Wisbech as one of the ministers of a little group

[1] Robert Currie, for example, does not deal with theological controversy before the 1870s: *Methodism Divided. A Study in the Sociology of Ecumenicalism* (London 1968) pp 112ff.
[2] 'Methodism at the End of the Eighteenth Century', *A History of the Methodist Church in Great Britain*, ed Rupert Davies and Gordon Rupp, I (London 1965) p 287.
[3] [Alexander] Gordon, [*Addresses Biographical and Historical*] (London 1922) ch x: 'Richard Wright and Missionary Enterprise', p 318.

of Johnsonian or Sabellian Baptists, his two co-ministers being John Johnson, the founder of the sect and Samuel Fisher.[1] In 1794 Wright found a final spiritual resting-place in unitarian beliefs and was put out by the Johnsonian Baptists, though it seems that many members of his Wisbech congregation went with him and continued to support him. Wright had now achieved spiritual and mental peace, but with all the ardour of the young convert, wanted to spread his new faith. Unfortunately for the would-be evangelist, English Unitarianism which had recently possessed all the confidence of a self-proclaimed social, intellectual, political and theological élite was going through an acute crisis of identity at the end of the eighteenth century.[2] Even without this development, Wright would have had difficulty in gaining support for his proposition. 'I had learned', he revealed later, 'that Unitarians were found chiefly among the more opulent and well educated parts of society, and heard it asserted that Unitarianism neither was nor could be the religion of the common people, of the poor and unlearned.' Against this view Wright contended that as Unitarianism was true, it must be able to be popular, and that 'it was better suited to them [the poor] than any other religious system'.[3] However it was not until twelve years after his commitment to Unitarianism that the appropriate machinery was set up to enable him to fulfil satisfactorily his missionary ambitions.

Chiefly responsible for setting in motion the discussions which were to culminate in the establishment in 1806 of the Unitarian Fund for Promoting Unitarianism by means of Popular Preaching was another young man who shared Wright's lowly social origins, his relentless quest for truth, and his sense of responsibility for the poor and un-learned. This was David Eaton, a native of Brechin in Scotland, who after an unusually deprived childhood which included playing the fife at the age of nine for a Scottish regiment raised for the American war, found his way to York where he was apprenticed to a shoemaker. He was, it seems, always of a pious disposition, and in York attended methodist services. However he was working ferociously hard from 4 am to 12 pm in order to support the almost destitute members of

---

[1] On the sect see: *History of a Forgotten Sect of Baptised Believers Heretofore known as 'Johnsonians'*, ed Robert Dawburn (London and Wisbech n.d. 1914?). On Fisher see: Edward Deacon, *Samuel Fisher, Baptist Minister of Norwich and Wisbech, England, 1742–1803* (Bridgeport, Conn. 1911), and Thompson, pp 129ff.

[2] H. L. Short, 'Presbyterians under a New Name', *The English Presbyterians* by C. G. Bolam, Jeremy Goring, H. L. Short and Roger Thomas (London 1968) pp 235ff.

[3] *A Review of the Missionary Life and Labors of Richard Wright written by himself* (London 1824) p 27.

his family, and not surprisingly his health collapsed. When he re-covered he found a new employer who introduced him to a small congregation of Baptists who were groping their way towards a new and more satisfying interpretation of their beliefs. When he joined them he made the 'amazing discovery' that the doctrines of the Trinity and the Atonement were not to be found in the New Testa-ment.[1] Up to this time the congregation had been supplied with a Calvinist preacher by the countess of Huntingdon though they found 'the expense very heavy'.[2]

In a pamphlet published in 1800 Eaton chronicled the restless and anguished quest of the little society:

At seasons, indeed, we felt transported with joy at the prospects of the elect, and our hearts bounded with gratitude to God, from the consideration of our being the objects of his eternal love; but for a large portion of our time, our experience did not at all answer these views, by reason of which our minds were often a prey to gloom and heaviness, and we were often led to question our-selves whether we really were of the elect.

...When our passions were warmed and affected by hearing sermons or by other means, our hearts were filled with joy; but when we were dull and languid, they were oppressed with sorrow; and as clouds and darkness often surrounded us, we were often subject to the most alarming doubts and fears.[3]

They tried to convince themselves that the Lord was simply testing his people, but this brought them no comfort. Either in a fit of depression, or because the expense had become too heavy, they broke with lady Huntingdon and dismissed her preacher.

The next stage in their pilgrimage was reached when they became acquainted with the writings of John Johnson, the founder of the little sect through which Richard Wright had progressed to Unitarianism. They discovered that Johnson had proved that both the Calvinists and the Methodists were essentially wrong: 'Such assertions, supported as they seemed to be, excited in our uneasy minds the most painful alarms, and stirred within us every source of anxiety.' Being unable to fault the logic of Mr Johnson, they decided to follow him in the hope that he would eventually be able to deliver them from their spiritual turmoil. However, it was not long before this prophet was found to be wanting. They discovered that Johnson believed that when Christ-

---

[1] Letter of introduction from Mrs Cappe to Mrs Lindsey, 6 May 1802, C[hristian] R[eformer], xv (Hackney 1829) pp 346–7; Robert Aspland, 'Biographical Sketch of the late Mr David Eaton', ibid pp 227ff.
[2] David Eaton, Scripture The Only Guide To Religious Truth. A Narrative of the Proceedings of the Society of Baptists in York (York 1800) p 14.   [3] Ibid p 15.

ians had received the spirit of justification they should 'wait and expect the same effusions of the spirit that the first Christians enjoyed'. Johnson had written that the early Christians had not been anxious about the fate of their souls but had concentrated on following their calling. 'As these considerations did not at all agree with our feelings... we were led to conclude that we were not real Christians.'[1]

They had now reached a point of such suspicion of false prophets that they resolved to continue their search through the Bible alone. 'The measure of leaving all men and their books, and betaking ourselves to the reading of the Scriptures as our only guide is to us one of the most memorable events of our lives; an event which even at this distance of time, we contemplate with the warmest gratitude.'[2] Though Eaton stresses that at the time they did not know that 'there was a Unitarian in the world besides themselves' they reached that position through the unaided study of the Bible.

Unfortunately Eaton had some sort of disagreement with the other members of the society – it seems that he became too liberal even for them – and left for London in 1802. For some years he had wanted to spread his new beliefs through popular preaching, and had written to several unitarian leaders though without securing any support. Gradually he cultivated his contacts: Robert Aspland, an ex-Baptist who was minister of the important Gravel-pit chapel, Hackney, William Vidler, a bricklayer's son who had founded the leading unitarian journal, and John Simpson, a General Baptist minister who had formerly been a Wesleyan travelling preacher. All three were men of great zeal and individuality. Simpson had been an intimate friend of John Wesley himself who on hearing of his difficulties on the subject of the influence of the Holy Spirit warned him, 'Samson, the Philistines are upon thee – escape for thy life!'[3] Vidler has been described as having a 'fine physiognomy surmounting a corporal bulk of wellnigh elephantine proportions'. Once when he had squeezed into a narrow pulpit, his exertions during the sermon so swelled his body that it was impossible to get him out, and there he stayed until

[1] *Ibid* pp 17–19.
[2] *Ibid* p 22. The psychological problem of the proof of election is of course the key to the argument deployed by Max Weber in *The Protestant Ethic and the Spirit of Capitalism* (Eng trans London 1930). The York baptist incident is but one of many examples of the breakdown of the psychological adequacy of the Calvinist system in the late eighteenth century. See also *Max Weber on Religion*, ed Stuart Mews (forthcoming).
[3] R. B. Aspland, *Memoir of the Life, Works and Correspondence of the Rev Robert Aspland* (London 1850) p 195.

after the afternoon service when it is presumed that he delivered a more temperate address.[1]

These three men and a Mr Marson joined with Eaton in writing a manifesto 'An Address to unitarian Congregations', outlining a plan for the popular preaching of Unitarian beliefs, which was published in Vidler's *Universalist Miscellany* in September 1805. Some of the unitarian leaders expressed their theoretical approval but felt that there were many practical objections. Underlying these objections seems to have been the deeply-rooted belief that Unitarianism was not, and could not be a popular religion. Moreover the unitarian leader, like the whig politicians, were wary of appealing to the people in the years after the French Revolution.[2] The Priestley riots of 1791, if taken at their face-value, had shown that there was no love lost between the common people and the 'Aristocracy of Dissent'.[3] Thomas Belsham, the most influential unitarian leader of the day, declined to serve on the committee, his opposition being ascribed to an 'almost constitutional distaste to popular movements'.[4] Like the middle-class radical reformers whose views many Unitarians shared, they felt it safer and more seemly to create an informed and favourable public opinion, and for this purpose the Unitarian Book Society was regarded as quite adequate. Unitarians were already suspected for their advanced political views, would not their attempts to win the masses be misinterpreted? The denomination wanted peace. The ministers of the unitarian chapels which had recently been presbyterian were more interested in quietly cultivating their flocks, a 'practical and negative style of preaching' predominated; there was a general feeling that 'bolder measures would inflame prejudice'[5] and possibly result in legal reprisals. The proposal that laymen without formal education should be employed as missionaries shocked the older ministers.[6] Six months after this forward movement had been launched Aspland reported his regret that 'the Society is regarded by some of our Unitarian brethren with a dubious sort of feeling, bordering upon suspicion and dislike. They think we shall degrade the Unitarian cause, and put ourselves on a level with the Methodists.'[7]

The suspicion that a popular Unitarianism might take on those

[1] Gordon, p 333.   [2] Thompson, p 78.

[3] G. Kitson Clark, *The Making of Victorian England* (London 1962) p 159; R. B. Rose, 'The Priestley Riots of 1791', *PP* xviii (November 1960) pp 68–88.

[4] Gordon, p 299.

[5] David Eaton, 'Account of the Rise and Progress of the Unitarian Fund', *M[onthly] R[epository]*, xx (Hackney 1825) p 338.   [6] Aspland, p 196.   [7] *Ibid* p 198.

characteristics of Methodism which were objectionable to men of good taste was dispelled through the labours, writing and temperament of the most devoted and successful of the missioners Richard Wright. More pleasant to listen to than to look at, Wright was an ugly little man, addicted to his pipe, who combined a precise mind, a remarkable coolness and composure, with a tremendous physical stamina. Walking at the rate of thirty or forty miles a day, he preached throughout Britain from Aberdeen to Cornwall and from Milford Haven to Yarmouth. Shortly after he commenced his full-time labours for the Society he was requested by the unitarian reviewer of one of his books to publish a selection of his missionary addresses especially on 'the subjects of *death* and *judgment, heaven* and *hell*, which are the favourite topics of popular missionaries, and which have been so extravagantly and mischievously treated as to lend the sober quiet part of our people to think that a missionary must necessarily be a melancholy fanatic!'[1] But neither the style nor the content of Wright's addresses could be described as fanatical. 'It was gradually that I acquired a compressed, plain, rather argumentative style, which I think not altogether without clearness and strength... I think that I never used any low or disgusting language in preaching. In addressing congregations of illiterate people, I have frequently adopted a familiar and colloquial style, and have found it to have a good effect.'[2] In the open air he had preached to congregations ranging from 500 to 2000 but had always taken pains to ensure that 'no tumult or disorder was likely to be produced by it'. In all his preaching he had avoided saying anything about politics.[3] He avoided embarrassing the 'large and genteel congregations' of older-established Unitarians by not visiting them until asked.

In neither his nature nor his views could Wright be described as fanatical. In fact much of his time was to be spent in opposing and being opposed by religious enthusiasts. He had come into contact with a particularly bizarre form of fanaticism early in his days at Wisbech. A certain William Daken from Northamptonshire had come to sell some goods at the market. In a long private conversation he revealed to Wright that he was none other than Jesus Christ, a claim which was fully believed by two disciples who accompanied him. His message to the world was that all Christians should abstain from sexual intercourse and all men should grow beards.[4] When rational argument had

[1] *MR*, VI (1811) p 615.   [2] Wright, pp 139ff.   [3] *Ibid* p 147.
[4] 'Fanaticism further exemplified in the case of William Daken and others', *CR*, IV (1818) p 88.

failed, Wright could only remark: 'If it be allowed that the Spirit teaches by inward suggestions and impulses, and by applying passages of Scripture in a peculiar sense to the mind, who is to draw the line between what the Spirit dictates, and what is mere fantasy and imagination?'[1] It was Richard Wright's mission to attempt to save men from the dangers of fanaticism by explaining the power and place of reason in religion at a time when different regions of the country were being swept by waves of revivalism and millennialism. Against them Wright proclaimed:

Reason and revelation are both gifts of the same lord; consequently they cannot clash with each other...Those who decry reason that they may exalt revelation, and would build faith on its ruins, whatever may be their intentions do great injury to Christianity. So far as they succeed in leading others to suppose that revelation is inconsistent with reason, and that the Gospel contains irrational doctrines, they strengthen the hands of its opponents, and render its truth and authority questionable...To build faith upon the ruins of that reason, is substituting religious frenzy in the place of real christianity, and opening the door for every extravagance, absurdity, and corruption of the gospel to enter. ...Those who lay aside the use of reason in religious matters level themselves so far as religion is concerned with infants, idiots, and maniacs, but as they do it voluntarily, in them it is criminal.[2]

Though he abstained from politics, nevertheless there were social and political implications in his message. 'Who have been the persons,' he asked, 'in all ages, that have been opposed to the use of reason in religion? They have been either mercenary priests and designing men, who have felt it their interest to keep the people in ignorance or mental bondage; or persons who see themselves enslaved to a particular creed or system and determined to maintain notions which would not bear the test of reason.'[3]

The place given to reason and the opposition to emotionalism in Wright's teaching and writing had two effects. In the first place it commended him to the leaders of Unitarianism who shared his abhorrence of enthusiasm. The second consequence was the implacable opposition in many but not all places of the promoters of enthusiastic religion such as the Methodists but especially the disciples of Joanna Southcott who were then at the height of their influence. At Mirfield

[1] *Ibid* p 90. For another example of a returned 'Jesus' in this period see P. G. Rodgers, *Battle in Bossenden Wood, The Strange Story of Sir William Courtenay* (Oxford 1961).
[2] R. Wright, *Sixteen Unitarian Missionary Discourses* (Liverpool 1817) pp 20ff.
[3] *Ibid* p 33.

he debated with the Southcottians until 1 am. At Wakefield the methodist preacher joined with the Southcottians in attempting to defend
the deity of Christ.[1] In many places, however, Wright was invited to
preach either by Methodists or ex-Methodists. On the north Lincolnshire marches near the mouth of the Humber he met a group of
Methodists who had been put out of their society for expressing doubts
about eternal punishment, doubts which had apparently arisen through
a methodist preacher who was secretly a universalist.[2] He was invited
to Thorne in Lincolnshire by a group of New Connexion Methodists
who had also given up the doctrine of endless punishment. In 1812 he
preached the full unitarian message in the methodist chapel at New-
castle under Lyme with the full knowledge of the trustees. It seems that
once Methodists started having doubts about any one of their doctrines,
the way was open for Wright to win them gradually to Unitarianism.
After a tour of Cornwall in the wake of the great methodist revival of
1814, Wright remarked: 'The Methodists have in a considerable
degree, prepared the way for the Unitarians. Among the Methodists
there are Universalists and persons whose enquiries go beyond the
system of their party.'[3]

Wright's value was soon appreciated by the leaders of Unitarianism.
Shortly after the first unitarian societies composed mainly of ex-
Methodists, had been founded in Cornwall in 1811 as a result of one
of his visits, the Cornish methodist writer Samuel Drew initiated a
pamphlet skirmish with one of the leaders of the congregation at
Flushing, Thomas Prout.[4] When he had exhausted the scriptural and
philosophical arguments Drew revived an old jibe by drawing a
comparison between Thomas Prout and Tom Paine to the effect that
Unitarianism was disruptive of the social order. But Unitarians were
no longer prepared to take such language lying down, and when news
came in the following year, 1814, of the wild revival in Cornwall –
news which was given considerable coverage in the *Monthly Reposi-*

---

[1] Wright, pp 212, 216, 358; Richard Wright, 'A conversation between Mr Wright and
a Preacher of Joanna Southcott's', *CR*, 1 (1815) pp 65ff. On the Southcottians see
J. F. C. Harrison, *Robert Owen and the Owenites in Britain and America* (London 1969).
[2] Wright pp 66ff.
[3] ['Messrs Wright and Cooper's] Missionary Tour in Cornwall', *MR*, x (1815) p 770.
Whilst the Methodists with their stress on experience were opposed to the rationalism of
the Unitarians, on another level they had in common a whole-hearted Arminianism
and were both opposed to the old Calvinist orthodoxy.
[4] *The Life, Character, and Literary Labours of Samuel Drew, AM*. By his eldest son (London
1835) pp 257ff; Samuel Drew, *Scriptural and Philosophical Arguments to prove the Divinity
of Christ, and the Necessity of his Atonement* (London 1813).

tory[1] – the Unitarians took the opportunity to counter-attack. One of the most distinguished unitarian preachers Dr Lant Carpenter preached and published two powerful sermons against the 'fallacious confidence of those who mistook wild ecstacies for promises of acceptance'. He was particularly scathing about the kind of last minute repentance summed up in the rhyme:

> Between the stirrup and the ground,
> He mercy sought, and mercy found.[2]

Apparently these strictures were taken very seriously by influential Wesleyans, some of whom had privately beseeched him not to publish them. Lant Carpenter had previously supported the Strangers' Friend Society, a benevolent institution largely controlled by Methodists.[3]

In the following year an anxious Richard Wright undertook his second missionary tour in Cornwall. 'This I deem one of the most important missions I have ever engaged in', he reported.[4] At Falmouth he found that the little congregation, most of whom 'were formerly Methodists and were excluded merely on account of their opinions' was standing firm and making progress despite considerable opposition. 'Several of them have suffered loss in their trade, as well as reproach, by becoming Unitarians.' Here Wright preached in the market square to an audience of 500 which included two Jews 'who are said to be men of considerable learning, especially one of them, who is from Morocco, and was in Moorish dress'. Gradually Wright progressed through Cornwall visiting the towns and villages until at last he reached Redruth 'the centre of what is called the late revival among the Methodists, which appears from what I have heard, to have been a scene of great extravagance and absurdity'. He preached twice in the streets of Redruth drawing a crowd of 5000 to the first service and 1000 to the second. Altogether on his preaching tour Wright claimed to have been heard by 10,000 people.[5] It would seem that the men of Cornwall like the men of Athens were ready to hear any new thing.

---

[1] A long letter describing the rise and progress of the revival written by William Henshaw, the methodist preacher at Plymouth Dock, to William Bramwell, one of the leaders of Wesleyan revivalism, was reprinted in the *MR* IX (1814) pp 377–8.

[2] Carpenter quoted this verse in 1822 from the tombstone of a profligate drunkard who died by falling off his horse, but it sums up a view of salvation to which he was just as opposed in 1814: J. Estlin Carpenter, *James Martineau. Theologian and Teacher* (London 1905) p 114.

[3] *Memoirs of the Life of the Rev. Lant Carpenter, LL.D.* Edited by his son, Russell Lant Carpenter (Bristol and London 1842) pp 196–8.

[4] 'Missionary Tour in Cornwall', p 718.   [5] *Ibid* p 770.

Reason and emotion in working-class religion, 1794–1824

For twelve years from 1810 to 1822 Richard Wright walked and preached covering an average of 3000 miles per year. In various parts of the country he founded small unitarian congregations, often persuading groups disenchanted with the doctrinal position of their own denomination to join him. The largest such accession was probably the General Baptists of Kent and Sussex who were ripe for the harvest having never been Calvinists and always having had antitrinitarians amongst them.[1]

When Wright looked back upon his missionary labours in 1824 he believed that he had accomplished his object. He had demonstrated that Unitarianism could be the religion of the common people: 'The success of Unitarianism has been chiefly among the common people. Many new congregations have been formed, the bulk of whose members are unlearned and working people. Such persons when instructed in the Unitarian doctrine, I found among the most active and efficient promoters of it.'[2] As evidence of the intellectual ability and capacity of working men he cited Eaton's account of the development of doctrine at York, and John Ashworth's description of the evolution of the methodist unitarian movement in north-east Lancashire.[3]

The methodist unitarian movement, which so delighted Wright when he visited it in 1818 was another seemingly spontaneous development by a group of workingmen. Consideration of its origin brings us to the second set of questions about the extent of theological dissension within Wesleyan Methodism. Dr Walsh's view that Methodism was doctrinally solid at the end of the eighteenth century has already been noted, but whilst he may be correct this situation does not seem to have prevailed into the nineteenth century. T. G. Osborn, a Victorian historian of Methodism, and himself a member of one of its most eminent families, claimed in 1898 that the years from 1805 to 1808 were a period of 'special dangers' for the doctrinal integrity of Methodism which were very keenly felt.[4]

These dangers reached flashpoint in 1806 when Joseph Cooke was expelled from the Wesleyan ministry because of his unsound views on the witness of the Spirit. This doctrine was one of the distinctive features of methodist theology. When John Wesley referred to 'our

---

[1] Wright, p 220. [2] Ibid p 440.
[3] John Ashworth, Ten Letters, giving an Account of the Rise and Progress of the Unitarian Doctrine at Rochdale, Newchurch-in-Rossendale, and Other Places formerly in connection with the late Joseph Cooke (Rochdale 1817).
[4] 'Two Old Letters', [Proceedings of the Wesley Historical Society], 1 (London 1898) p 101.

doctrines' he was calling attention not to a complete scheme of christian doctrine, but to certain specific doctrinal emphases which constituted a theology of christian experience to which he believed Methodists were called to bear witness through their writings and sermons, and to exemplify in their spiritual experience. When Cooke called into question the accepted interpretation of one of the key items in the methodist plan of salvation, he could hardly expect to escape unscathed.

Cooke's troubles seem to have begun when he became second minister of the large Rochdale circuit in 1803. Some of his sermons disturbed members of the societies at Rochdale, Bacup and Newchurch. They were unable to meet him in argument but felt instinctively that he was not preaching good Methodism. One of his initial opponents at Newchurch was a young local preacher, John Ashworth, who was later to succeed to the leadership of the small secession.[1]

After his expulsion Cooke published two sermons from his Rochdale period which provide a sample of the state of his beliefs at the time. Perhaps because he spent the early years of his ministry in the hot-house atmosphere of Cornish Methodism (his first three circuits were Redruth, Penzance and St Austell), followed by a term in the more sober Burslem circuit where he married a woman 'of refined and literary tastes, with strong doctrinal feelings',[2] he came to distrust what E. B. Pusey later called 'justification by feeling'.

Let us...take care how we believe, or say, that any man is a child of God, merely because he professes to have such a joyful assurance; for though he should be able to tell us the time when, and place where, he received that assurance, nay, though we should be present with the man when he professes to receive it; we have after all nothing but the man's word for it....We have no right to consider any man a child of God, any farther than his conduct bespeaks him such.[3]

Cooke seems to have felt a particular concern for those Methodists whose hearts were strangely unwarmed in spite of their will to believe. This, of course, as H. R. Niebuhr has pointed out is a particular problem for the second generation members of any revivalistic movement. To his congregation, Cooke could only say:

[1] On Cooke and Ashworth as Methodists see [William] Jessop, [*An Account of Methodism in Rossendale*] (Manchester 1880).
[2] [H.] McLachlan, [*The Methodist Unitarian Movement*] (Manchester and London 1919) p 4.
[3] Joseph Cooke, *On Justification by Faith and the Witness of the Spirit* (Rochdale 1806) p 23.

Reason and emotion in working-class religion, 1794–1824

Some of you have believed...but others, who have as truly believed, and consequently are as really justified, are still afflicted, tossed with the tempest, and not comforted...You have heard tell of those who have heard a voice, or seen a sight, or had some extraordinary impression made upon their minds, by which they have been satisfied that God had pardoned them. Perhaps so. But what is that to you? Is any voice or sight, or impression, more to be depended upon than the plain positive declaration of Jehovah to, and by his servants; he that believeth shall be saved, or shall not come into condemnation.[1]

Clearly Cooke had in mind a group of Methodists who were going through the same psychological terrors as David Eaton's flock of Calvinistic Baptists in York. But in Methodism such teaching was bound to be challenged and Cooke was compelled to appear before the conference of 1805. He was prepared to admit that his teaching was contrary to that of the young Wesley, but claimed that it was consonant with the views of the aged Wesley and of John Fletcher. At any rate he seems to have satisfied the conference for the time being. Whilst he did not give an explicit undertaking that he would not make his new views known, there was an implicit understanding to that effect, or so the members of the conference believed.[2] However Cooke maintained that he had been misunderstood, and to enable a correct assessment of his views to be more widely known, he published two of his sermons in 1806. It was not so much what he said as the way he said it which gave offence. It was plain that the 'style and manner of expression was unmethodistical',[3] and Cooke was once more referred to the conference.

This time there was no argument. Several of the preachers 'heartily deprecated any debate in the Conference upon their system of doctrines'.[4] As Edward Hare, Cooke's successor at Rochdale and resolute wager of war by pamphlet, remarked there was nothing to debate: Cooke wanted Methodism to change, not himself.[5] The president of the conference, Adam Clarke, one of the connexion's greatest scholars, who was himself in later years to be rebuked by the conference for heretical beliefs, refused to allow Cooke to defend himself by quoting

---

[1] *Ibid* p 13.

[2] McLachlan, pp 10–11; G. Smith, *History of Wesleyan Methodism*, II, 5 ed (London 1872) p 433.

[3] Benjamin Goodier, 'Narrative of the Expulsion of Mr Cooke, of Rossendale, by the Methodists', *CR*, IV (1818) p 60. On the important place of language and expression in religious groups, see Sven Wermlund, 'Religious Speech Community and Reinforcement of Belief', *Acta Sociologica*, III (Stockholm 1958) pp 132–46.

[4] Joseph Cooke, *Methodism Condemned by Methodist Preachers* (Rochdale 1807) p 37.

[5] *Genuine Methodism Acquitted, and Spurious Methodism Condemned* (Rochdale 1807) p 87.

Wesley, on the grounds that he would lift convenient passages out of their true context. After a discussion with a committee of preachers and the refusal by Cooke of a day to think the matter over, he was expelled from the Wesleyan ministry.

In itself this would not have been particularly serious. But it seems that Cooke was not the only heresy-case under consideration in 1806. Adam Clarke had told his wife that there were 'two or three knotty cases in reference to charges of false doctrine'. Later he reported:

We have now got through all the characters except —'s for Pelagianism, and —'s for denying the direct witness of the Spirit. Mr — has had the questions proposed to him which were sent to Mr —, and has answered all to the perfect satisfaction of the Conference. Mr —, who was under the same accusation, has had the same questions put to him, and has not answered to their satisfactions...The brethren are so incensed against evasive answers on this subject, that every man has Argus eyes...There is the utmost need to take heed to our doctrines.[1]

If the modern historians of Methodism have not taken this doctrinal threat seriously, Adam Clarke and the conference certainly did. 'Socinianism,' he wrote, 'and every other isms, equally as bad, are gaining strength and boldness. As a body, we cannot stand and speak with our enemies in the gate, much less turn the battle to the gate.' He believed that more consideration must be given to providing the preachers with a training which would 'cause them all to preach the same Gospel, and prevent the great doctrines of Methodism from being forgotten'. 'Have not a few of our young men fallen into heterodox opinions, or at least been charged with them, for want of some general and uniform instruction in sound Methodistical Theology?'[2] On the other hand Thomas Coke believed that the setting up of a theological institution could open the door to Unitarianism which had made so much headway in the dissenting academies.[3]

Meanwhile the conference would do what it could. Before being admitted into full connexion every preacher had now to testify

[1] J. W. Etheridge, *The Life of the Rev. Adam Clarke, LL.D.* (London 1859) p 212. For further information about the preacher charged with Pelagianism (probably John Burdsall) see 'Two Old Letters' which includes a letter of 1805 from Thomas Coke: 'Pelagianism has certainly gained the ascendancy in the minds of one or more of the Preachers who laboured last year in Cornwall' (p 103).

[2] *Observations on the Importance of Adopting a Plan of Instruction for those Preachers who are admitted upon trial in the Methodist Connexion* (London 1807) pp 6, 9.

[3] See the letter from Coke to Addington in G. Pellew, *Life and Correspondence of the Right Hon. Henry Addington, first Viscount Sidmouth,* III (London 1847) p 47.

explicitly as to his belief in the main methodist doctrines. A course of sermons was ordered to be preached upon them by Joseph Benson, Adam Clarke and Jabez Bunting (who being then stationed in Manchester had taken a keen interest in the controversy between Cooke and Hare in Rochdale). Finally the conference requested Coke, Clark and Benson to draw up a comprehensive list of the distinctive doctrines of Methodism and their basis in Scripture and the writings of Wesley.[1]

The doctrines of Wesleyanism were now more rigidly defined than ever before. They were considered 'as immutable as the rock from which they all proceed. The maxims and opinions of men may fluctuate and change, and the systems popular in one age may be exploded in another; it is not so with the evangelical truths which have distinguished Methodism in all its progress. Hence, however urged by circumstances, we are resolved never to sacrifice one iota of Sacred Truth to the caprice of the age and the relaxed opinions of many so called Christians.'[2] Hence it also can be seen that at the same time that the Wesleyans were being accused by revivalists such as Hugh Bourne of deserting 'primitive' Methodism, they were in the doctrinal sphere in fact re-affirming their loyalty to it. It may be that a clearer appreciation can be gained of the difficulties facing Methodism in the early nineteenth century if it is recognized that Wesley's heirs had to contend not only with a violent and exaggerated revivalism but also with a threat from the other flank, from Unitarianism, Socinianism, Pelagianism, Arianism.

When Joseph Cooke left Methodism a 'considerable secession' took place from the main Wesleyan chapel in Rochdale.[3] In Newchurch-in-Rossendale another thirty or forty were led out in the following year by John Ashworth. For a time they constituted a lively little circuit which was used as a base for missioning the surrounding towns and villages of Padiham, Burnley, Todmorden and Haslingden. Then in 1811 disaster threatened when Cooke died. Though he had moved far from Methodism he had not yet got as far as Unitarianism. This was a stage which his followers had to reach for themselves. Within three years of Cooke's death dissension broke out both within the congregation at Rochdale and between a faction there and the society at Newchurch.[4] From 1814 this latter cause became the centre of the

---

[1] *Articles of Religion Prepared By Order of the Conference of 1806*, Publications of the Wesley Historical Society, no 2 (London 1897).
[2] Address to the Irish Conference in the *Minutes* of 1806 quoted in preface to *ibid* p 5.
[3] Jessop, p 188.   [4] McLachlan, p 37.

Cookite sect, and the little band who sustained it was described by John Ashworth, who now took over the leadership, in the following way: 'Our number in Newchurch was small; our circumstances mean: most of us being parents of large families; and to a man we had all to procure our bread by our hand labour; provisions at this time were extremely dear, and work was so ill to get, that some of us had not full employment.'[1] Ashworth himself was described as a 'clothier, a manufacturer of blankets and course woollens. He made use of a contrivance to suspend a book before him at the loom so that he could read and weave at the same time'.[2] Ashworth was clearly something of a bookworm, and under his guidance the little congregation began to develop and extend the ideas of their founder. First to go was the doctrine of original sin. A year was spent in puzzling about the divinity of Jesus: 'Perhaps at that time we might have been called Sabellian.' At this point in their thinking Cooke passed away, and it was under Ashworth's leadership that they relinquished the doctrine of the divinity of Jesus Christ.[3] This step was decisive and dangerous. It gave great offence and aroused much opposition. They still owed over half the money spent on their £500 chapel, and they could only appeal for help outside the Rossendale Valley: 'Such generally has been the badness of trade, and the consequent poverty of our circumstances.' By the time of the application for a grant from Lady Hewley's Trust in 1815 their numbers had increased so that they could count on 200 in the afternoon and somewhat less in the morning.[4] In the year 1815 this little company which had not previously known of the existence of a body of Unitarians and which had fought-out its faith by prayerful, diligent study of the Scriptures found itself on the edge of a wider fellowship of churches.

[1] Ashworth p 13. On the general question of the standard of living of handloom weavers, see Duncan Bythell, 'The Handloom Weavers in the English Cotton Industry during the Industrial Revolution: Some Problems', *Ec.HR* xvii, 2 (December 1964) pp 339–54. On the situation in Rossendale: G. H. Tupling, *The Economic History of Rossendale* (Manchester 1927).

[2] 'Communication from Dr John Thompson [of Halifax relative to a church of Unitarian Christians at Newchurch']], *MR* x (1815) p 316.

[3] Letter to the trustees of Lady Hewley's Fund from the Newchurch society quoted in *ibid* p 314. It would seem that this process of theological rationalisation took place at a time when they believed their economic situation to be worse than usual. Scholars who have related theological development to social and economic factors have usually noted the opposite process. Max Weber, for example, held that 'it is far easier for emotional rather than rational elements of a religious ethic to flourish in such circumstances': *The Sociology of Religion* (Eng trans London 1965) p 101.

[4] 'Communication from Dr John Thompson', pp 314–15.

Most of the methodist unitarian members (as they now began to call themselves) were weavers or colliers. In some places they had the help of men who were somewhat better off. In Rochdale James Taylor who ministered to the remnant of Cooke's flock 'is in pretty good circumstances. His father keeps a farm, and conducts a woollen dye-house; at one or other of these James constantly works'.[1] In Todmorden the most famous member of the society was John Fielden, a mill manufacturer, who was to become the champion of the hand-loom weavers and factory reformers.

The Methodist Unitarians did not have any of the Wesleyan leadership's inhibitions about politics. John Ashworth and many of his flock supported the Chartists' demands. At Oldham in 1816 William Browe, a leader, trustee and local preacher, was chairman of the Oldham Union Society formed to fight in conjunction with the Hampden Club for the reform of parliament. In 1832 John Fielden at Oldham and James Taylor at Rochdale were radical candidates in the general election.[2] The Methodist Unitarians cannot be accused of the 'chiliasm of despair'. Through their Sunday schools which taught writing when the Wesleyans had given it up, the little libraries attached to their chapels, and the opportunities which they provided for theological adventure, it is not surprising that they helped to produce, and attracted, men of independent and radical political views.

Benjamin Goodier, who became minister of the Oldham chapel, has described spending a night with John Ashworth in 1815:

about nine o'clock when the sun had set, and the people could not see to work, six or seven of them came to see and converse with their preacher; most of them were without hats and coats, with their aprons and clogs...on, and one of them was 'smoking his pipe'. They were all serious, and engaged in religious conversation with great readiness. Religion with them is an affair of the heart and life not merely as with many, a speculative inquiry.[3]

The Methodist Unitarians had not exalted reason in the place of emotion. They believed that their beliefs and practices were the logical conclusion of the unaided study of the Bible. But they retained many of the characteristics of the working-class Methodist: 'their earnest

---

[1] *Memoir of the Rev. Benjamin Goodier* (Liverpool 1825) p 76.
[2] McLachlan, ch VII. On Unitarianism and politics in Oldham see A. Marcroft, *Historical Account of the Unitarian Chapel, Oldham* (Oldham 1913), A. Marcroft, *Landmarks of Local Liberalism* (Oldham 1913) and on the political situation there: John Foster: 'Nineteenth-Century Towns – A Class Dimension', in *The Study of Urban History*, ed H. J. Dyos (London 1968) pp 281–300.   [3] *Memoir of Goodier*, pp 76ff.

praying ways, their love of vigorous, unconventional, extempore preaching, their capacity for being wrought up into fervour and enthusiasm.'[1]

It is not surprising that Richard Wright had a special place in his heart for the Methodist Unitarians. Together with Eaton's little baptist society in York they exemplified his conviction that Unitarianism was the logical conclusion of the workingman's spiritual quest. In this he was at one with Herbert Marsh, bishop of Peterborough, one of the earliest English students of German biblical scholarship, who had predicted that if the children of the common people were to be educated as Joseph Lancaster desired, and were to have the naked Bible placed in their hands, as the Bible societies wished, they could become Unitarians. 'I am inclined to think', Richard Wright remarked, 'his lordship will be found correct.'[2]

Whether in fact the provision of working-class education, or the distribution of Bibles contributed to the alienation of the people from the orthodox denominations is a debatable question. What is certain is that despite Richard Wright's earnest hopes, and despite the anxious forebodings of some of the orthodox, they were not to be won in any large numbers by institutionalised Unitarianism. But this is to look beyond the period under consideration, and to launch into deep and dangerous waters.

[1] Brooke Herford, *Travers Madge, A Memoir* (London 1868) p 23.
[2] Wright, p 441.

A. H. CLOUGH: A CASE STUDY IN VICTORIAN DOUBT

by P. G. SCOTT

IN 1868, F. W. Farrar addressed the Church Congress in Dublin on the reasons why young men were increasingly alienated from the church: 'the alienation of the most highly educated', he declared, 'is as much an intellectual as the alienation of the uneducated is a moral and social phenomenon'.[1] The emphasis we have inherited on the intellectual difficulties in religious belief felt by Victorian doubters of the upper-middle classes has obscured the extent to which their alienation, like that of the uneducated, was part of a broader shift in attitudes. This change of attitudes could precede disengagement from institutional religious allegiance by many years, and had little to do with specific intellectual difficulties. Discussion in terms of 'difficulties' caused by geology, biblical criticism, and so on, may be the way doubters chose to explain their detachment from the Church, and only one cause among many of that detachment.

Arthur Hugh Clough, one of the Victorian doubters of the early 'forties, has very commonly been used as an 'exhibit at the inquest on early Victorian faith':[2] in his life, the distinction between a growing scepticism in general attitudes, and the clean break of institutional disengagement, can be clearly seen, and in his life also the importance of social and psychological factors in unbelief is well documented, as is the relative unimportance of the intellectual causes usually given for early Victorian doubt.

Clough was born in 1819, which puts him in the same generation of Oxford liberals as Jowett, Stanley, Matthew Arnold, and J. A. Froude. He was a prize pupil of Dr Arnold at Rugby in the eighteen-thirties, and was undoubtedly deeply influenced by Arnold's personality. A contemporary of Clough's at Rugby described 'the almost feminine expression of trust and affection with which he looked up to Arnold in answering his questions and hanging on his words'.[3]

[1] F. W. Farrar, 'The Church and her younger members', *Fortnightly Review*, n.s. IV (London 1868) p 573.
[2] T. E. Welby, *Back Numbers* (New York 1929) p 109.
[3] [William Gover], in *The Parent's Review*, VII (London 1896) p 133.

It is common to describe Clough at this period of his life as a fervent young believer, and to refer to the pious letters of exhortation which he wrote to his brother George, who had been sent, not to Rugby, but to the evangelical King William's College, on the Isle of Man.[1] Yet Arnold's teaching in the classroom introduced Clough to the new historical scholarship of Germans such as Niebuhr and Bunsen,[2] and Arnold's preaching in the pulpit laid considerable emphasis on the possibility of religious doubt as well as on the need for faith. 'More surely than the winter is now coming on', Arnold proclaimed to the Rugby boys, 'will your hearts be hardened by the coming years'; 'it may be that our faith may fail,... our hearts will ever be whispering, what if it be all but a cunningly devised fable? What if there be no resurrection, no Christ, no God?'[3] Nor did Arnold assume that his school congregation consisted of those who found it easy to believe: he spoke of 'those of you who are waiting but have not yet seen the dawn; who pray, but pray with effort; who believe, yet are full of unbelief'.[4] Without going so far as to agree with the verdict of *The Record* that Arnold's theological opinions were 'other than fitted to lead [his pupils] to a simple knowledge of the way of faith',[5] one may remember that Arnold was an Oriel Noetic as well as a head-master. Clough as a schoolboy already felt his evangelical contemporaries to be hypocritical (he calls them 'the Pyms' in his letters),[6] and the piety of Clough's Rugby letters is minimal by comparison with that of a fellow-prefect H. W. Fox, one of the Pyms, who recorded that *The Dairyman's Daughter* had been 'an especial means of grace' to him.[7] Even during Clough's schooldays, particularly in the last year, he felt isolated from his fellows: 'I do confess', he wrote, 'that I have not one real friend in the School'.[8] It is clear too that even while at Rugby, Clough saw himself as a failure in religious terms. In an unpublished poem 'The Vernal Equinox', dating from March 1837, he contrasts the way that the equal balance of darkness and light in nature will lead on to the triumph of light, with the grimmer out-come of the 'vernal equinox' of boyhood:

[1] For example, *Correspondence* [*of Arthur Hugh Clough*, ed F. L. Mulhauser] (Oxford 1957) I, p 21–2.
[2] *Correspondence*, I, p 34.
[3] T. Arnold, *Sermons*, III (London 1834) pp 23, 384.
[4] T. Arnold, *The Christian Life, its hopes, its fears, and its close* (London 1842) p 444.
[5] *Brief Observations on the Political and Religious Sentiments of the Late Rev. Dr Arnold...* (London 1845) p 19.   [6] *Correspondence*, I, p 30.
[7] George Townshend Fox, *A Memoir of the Rev. Henry Watson Fox* (Brighton 1850) p 29.
[8] *Correspondence*, I, p 46.

A. H. Clough: a case study in Victorian doubt

> Alas, with us it is not so;
>   The fury of that fiercer storm,
> Those bitterer blasts that ever blow
>   O'er boyhood's frail and shrinking form –
> Not sure, alas, the triumph there, –
> There *must* be fear, and *may* despair,
> Oft falls it ne'er to rise again;
> No spring, no summer cometh then.[1]

Before Clough left Rugby, his ideas were already hostile to simple faith, though he felt the imperative of faith very strongly.

Clough went on from Rugby to Balliol as a scholar, and his tutor was W. G. Ward: it seems extremely unlikely that Clough was ever drawn into the whirlpool of Tractarianism, and there is little evidence of more than formal contact with Newman. Ward's main influence on Clough was in strengthening the attitude of sceptical enquiry fostered by Arnold's historical teaching, and asked for also by Scott's lectures at Balliol on Roman history.[2] In particular Ward drew on the writings of the utilitarian, John Stuart Mill, to challenge orthodox belief. Ward destroyed much of Clough's belief, without being able to turn him into a Tractarian, and later wrote of Clough, 'I fear that, from my own point of view, I must account it the great calamity of his life that he was brought into contact with myself'.[3]

Alongside such an intellectual influence, one may set the equally disturbing one of finding that the forces of truth and falsehood, good and evil, by no means corresponded to the divisions between the church parties in Oxford: such recognition must turn one against close involvement with any religious group. Clough's hero Philip Hewson, in his poem *The Bothie*, published in 1848, discusses religious belief with his Oxford tutor, who advises conformity, using the common Victorian analogy of life as a battle, and the Church as a single army, in which the great Field-Marshal's dispositions must be obeyed. Philip retorts that

> If there is battle, 'tis battle by night: I stand in the darkness...
> Yet is my feeling rather to ask, Where *is* the battle?
> Neither battle I see, nor arraying, nor King in Israel,

[1] Oxford, Bodleian MS Eng Misc c 359, fols 150–1; quoted by permission of Miss K. Duff and the Keeper of Western MSS. Professor F. L. Mulhauser had made an independent attribution of this poem to Clough, and is including the full text in his forthcoming edition.

[2] Geoffrey Faber, *Jowett, a portrait with a background* (London 1957) p 134.

[3] Wilfrid Ward, *William George Ward and the Oxford Movement* (London 1889) p 109.

Only infinite jumble and mess and dislocation,
Backed by a solemn appeal, 'For God's sake, do not stir there!'[1]

Philip, of course, is a fictional character, not Clough himself, but he has Clough's characteristic habit of mind, and surely expresses a reasonable reaction to the controversies of Oxford in the forties. W. J. Coneybeare saw reaction to party strife as a chief cause of unbelief: 'the highest ranks and most intelligent professions are influenced by sceptical opinions...this state of affairs has been directly caused by the dissensions of the Church'.[2]

The result of these very general intellectual influences, and of the party conflicts of Oxford, was in Clough's case first of all a near-breakdown. In the summer of 1840, his sister recorded, 'he was the most depressed and least able to work. His health suffered, he lost his hair, he was feverish and disquieted and often shut himself up from his family.'[3] This fever and disquiet, though, was not the cause of his leaving Oxford or the Church: he soon came to suspend his judgement on all disputed points, to attempt what he called a religion of silence.[4] He wrote in 1844:

Without the least denying Xtianity, I feel little that I can call its power. Believing myself to be in my unconscious creed in some shape or other an adherent of its doctrines I keep within its pale: still whether the Spirit of the Age whose lacquey and flunkey I submit to be, will prove to be of this kind or that kind I can't the least say. Sometimes I have doubts whether it won't turn out to be no Xty at all.[5]

Rather similarly, he wrote to his sister in 1847:

What is the meaning of 'Atonement by a crucified Saviour'? - ... the Evangelicals gabble it, as the Papists do their Ave Mary's - and yet say they know; while Newman falls down and worships *because* he does not know and knows he does not know.

I think others are more right, who say boldly, we don't understand it, and therefore we won't fall down and worship it...Until I know, I wait.[6]

Clough's attitude in the forties was what would later be called agnostic, and can be summed up in the first line of a poem of 1847:

[1] *Poems [of Arthur Hugh Clough*, ed H. F. Lowry, A. L. P. Norrington, and F. L. Mulhauser] (Oxford 1951) p 170: on the night-battle, see R. M. Gollin, '"Dover Beach": the background of its imagery', *English Studies*, XLVIII (Amsterdam 1967) pp 493–511.
[2] W. J. Coneybeare, *Essays Ecclesiastical and Social* (London 1855) p 163.
[3] *Correspondence*, I, p xix.
[4] *[Selected] Prose [Works of Arthur Hugh Clough]*, ed B. B. Trawick (Alabama 1964) p 287.
[5] *Correspondence*, I, p 141.   [6] *Correspondence*, I, p 182.

A. H. Clough: a case study in Victorian doubt

'Why should I say I see the things I see not?'.[1] He had already given up regular private prayer in the crisis of 1840–1. His attitude was not caused by specific intellectual difficulties, for indeed he seems to have had very few. He found no challenge to his faith, for instance, in the writings of D. F. Strauss on the historicity of the gospels:

> Matthew and Mark and Luke and holy John
> Evanished all and gone!...
> The place of worship the meantime with light
> Is, if less richly, more sincerely bright.[2]

Nor did Clough find, as J. A. Froude or F. W. Newman found, Christianity morally repugnant. He wrote to his cousin Margaret: 'A great many intelligent and moral people think Xty a bad religion – I don't; – but I'm not sure, as at present preached, it is quite true.'[3] Clough was the archetypal Victorian doubter in that he had 'kept all commandments from his youth / Yet still found one thing lacking – even Truth'.[4] His development to this state of agnosticism was gradual, and only in the most general sense an intellectual development: it was more a change in the way he held his beliefs than any definite repudiation of specific points.

By contrast, Clough's successive resignations of his Oriel tutorship and fellowship in 1848 were decisive acts, by no means passive. It seems very likely that if Clough had not been an Oxford don he would never have felt the need to make a clean break with institutional religion. Clough's stated reason for resigning was that he no longer wished to be considered by others as believing in the XXXIX Articles. Provost Hawkins of Oriel attempted to counter his decision to resign with such standard works of apologetics as Paley's *Natural Theology* or Butler's *Analogy*, but Clough replied that 'I do not fancy the books which you speak of exactly fit to meet the doubts with which young men now are familiar'.[5] Clough's objection was not to individual articles, but to the idea of articles at all: he felt his appearance of continued conformity to be a sham, and he 'deeply repented of ever having submitted' to making his subscription.[6] There was not much difference between his beliefs in 1848, and his beliefs at any time since 1841, nor were his ideas to develop much further before he

---

[1] *Poems*, p 21.   [2] 'Epi-Strauss-ium', *Poems*, p 49.
[3] *Correspondence*, I, p 304: on ethical repugnance to orthodoxy see Howard Murphy, *American Historical Review*, LX (New York 1955) pp 800–17.   [4] *Poems*, p 409.
[5] *Correspondence*, I, pp 225–7, 234.   [6] *Correspondence*, I, p 219.

died in 1861.[1] His resignation was a disengagement from a (religious) institution, not a stage in the development of his thought.

The influences which provoked him to resignation were more mixed than such a summary would suggest, however. There was more to it than a lingering sense of dishonesty. A primary influence was the visit of Ralph Waldo Emerson, who had resigned from the congregational ministry on very similar grounds in 1832: in meeting him, Clough was made to feel how untenable his own position had become. But most of the influences on Clough's decision to resign were not so obvious, and were strikingly similar to the 'unconscious' influences which Susan Budd has described in her sample of working-class secularists.[2] Clough was relatively detached from close links with his family – he had been separated from them through most of his childhood and all his adolescence, and through the 1840s saw his mother only for fairly brief visits. He was relatively detached too from any links with local communities; he had few friends in Liverpool (except the Coneybeares and the unitarian Martineaus). At Oxford, because of his financial impoverishment following his father's second bankruptcy in 1841, he had always been something of an outsider, and in 1847–8 this feeling was intensified as he became one of a very small party pushing for rather extreme university reform.[3] He was also a radical in politics, as Miss Budd's secularists were, and like them extremely individualist. In 1848, he was in an aimless stage of his life, for his fellowship was due to lapse at the end of another year, and he would then in any case have to search for a livelihood outside Oxford: a college tutorship, he wrote, is 'a mere parenthetical occupation, uncontemplated in the past, and wholly alien to the future'.[4] He had left it rather longer than most non-clerical fellows before making the move that had to be made into another career – in his case, eventually, in the civil service. While all the discussion of Clough's resignation in his letters makes the question of the articles the central cause, these other, non-intellectual, factors – of aimlessness, friendlessness, social isolation, and so on – were also important in leading him to make his public gesture. They, rather than intellectual problems, may be the variables, which explain why he detached himself from religious

---

[1] A case is made for the continuity and coherence of Clough's thought by Michael Timko, *Innocent Victorian* (Ohio 1966) pp 19–60.

[2] Susan Budd, 'The Loss of Faith; Reasons for Unbelief among members of the Secular Movement in England, 1850–1950', *Past and Present*, xxxvi (Oxford 1967) pp 106–25.

[3] Clough published a pamphlet against Oxford extravagance in 1847: in *Prose*, pp 226–40.

[4] *Prose*, p 308.

institutions, while other Oxford dons holding very similar opinions – Jowett, for instance, or Mark Pattison – could stay within the Church. Stanley describes Clough as resigning 'with delight', hardly the conventional picture of the Victorian doubter, 'the higher glumness facing the Higher Criticism'.[1]

It was because in Clough's case the development of his ideas and his disengagement from the Church could be clearly distinguished, that late Victorian agnostics could identify with him so closely. His poetry of doubt, with its subtle self-irony, and sharp satire of traditional beliefs, expressed their own attitudes, far better than more theological works such as F. W. Newman's *The Soul*. 'What should I do without Clough?' wrote Henry Sidgwick in 1866; 'he is the wine of life to me.' 'There are several at Cambridge and Oxford', reported John Addington Symonds in the same year, 'who look on Mr Clough's poems as the expression of their deepest convictions, and seek in him a mirror of themselves, deriving strength and support from his example.'[2] James Russell Lowell, the American critic, went further: 'We have a foreboding that Clough...will be thought a hundred years hence to have been the truest expression in verse of the moral and intellectual tendencies, the doubt and struggle towards settled convictions, of the period in which he lived.'[3] After the publication of the very full two-volume *Poems and Prose Remains* there grew up round Clough a vast agnostic hagiography, and over thirty editions of his poems were called for before the First World War.

Oxford dons cannot be taken as typical of the average Victorian, but Clough's case suggests one explanation for the suddenness of the decline in religious practice in the early twentieth century. The loosening of social pressures which Clough, as an untypical Victorian, felt in the eighteen-forties, and which disengaged him from the Church whose formularies he already disbelieved, was not felt generally until some fifty or sixty years later, except in large towns. One would like now to be able to find out how much agnosticism there was in the pew before the decline in church attendance.[4]

---

[1] A. P. Stanley, *Daily News* (London 8 January 1862) p 2: Ian Fletcher, *New Statesman* (London 19 December 1969) p 899.

[2] D. G. James, *Henry Sidgwick* (Oxford 1970) p 50; *Letters of John Addington Symonds*, ed R. L. Peters and H. M. Schueller, I (Detroit 1967) p 670.

[3] J. R. Lowell, *My Study Windows* (Boston 1899) p 211: a full list of Victorian comment is given in R. M. Gollin, W. E. Houghton, and M. Timko, *Arthur Hugh Clough, A Descriptive Catalogue* (New York 1967) part III.

[4] Certainly some: see E. E. Kellett, *As I Remember* (London 1936) p 106, and Louis Grey, 'The Agnostic at Church', *Nineteenth Century*, XI (London 1882) pp 73–6.

AFRICAN SEPARATISTS:
HERESY, SCHISM OR PROTEST
MOVEMENT?

by PETER HINCHLIFF

AFRICA has never been an absolutely dark continent to those who live elsewhere. From the days of the Phoenician traders of Carthage to the Afro-Arab mercantile empires of the fifteenth century Africa was always a source of what more literate peoples wanted. Long before modern Europeans began to explore the continent others had been there and taken their literary skills with them. In 1857 Richard Burton – the real Richard Burton – went on a journey to find the 'reputed great Lake Tanganyika' for the Royal Geographical Society. One hundred and thirty-four days' journey into the interior he was the guest of an Arab dealer in slaves and ivory, of whom he said, 'He had read much, and, like an oriental, for improvement, not only for amusement: he had a wonderful memory, fine perceptions and passing power of language'.[1] Arabic and Islamic culture penetrated into, and made a lasting impression on, many parts of Africa. Reading and writing sometimes accompanied this penetration and there are fascinating traces of attempts to reduce African languages to writing in Arabic script.[2] Nevertheless, writing a history even of modern Africa requires a very different technique from that which is needed to write a history of Europe in the same period because it is far less concerned with documents.

Such written sources as there may be, moreover, will usually represent precisely that expansion-of-Europe attitude from which nowadays the historian of Africa must try to escape. The stately footnote referring to the archives of chancelleries or the letters of society hostesses is not a great deal of use. One finds oneself moving naked in what seems a far less certain and familiar world of linguistics, anthropology, oral tradition and form criticism. And one is having to take account of a somewhat patchy archaeology – patchy because it is relatively recent and

[1] Richard F. Burton, *Lake Regions of Central Africa*, 1 (London 1860) p 325.
[2] See for example [Basil] Davidson, [*Africa in History*] (London 1968) p 221.

tentative, because of the unhelpful climatic conditions of much of Africa, and because of the very nature of the civilisation one is hoping to uncover. For someone like myself, trained in a conventional school of theology, it all seems much less like what we did for the church history papers and much more like the 'history, language and literature of the Old Testament'. Genealogies come into their own again.[1] Myths about eponymous heroes are found to be, in fact, experiences through which the nation itself passed.[2] One is always wrestling with the slippery problem of finding a fixed point from which to calculate other dates.[3] One is compelled to weave together written sources and oral tradition, using, simultaneously, very different techniques to discount the distortions to which each is likely to be subject.[4]

All this is further complicated by the passionate presuppositions which one is likely to embrace. Nearly everyone who is sufficiently interested to attempt African history has such presuppositions and these affect not merely the attitudes he brings to the study or the conclusions to which he comes but the very techniques he employs. If one conceives of the history of Africa as part of the expansion of Europe one will be far less concerned with oral tradition than if one thinks of it as the history of African peoples in which white men are largely an intrusive and transient factor.

A study of the African separatists lands one very much in the midst of these difficulties because the whole thing turns upon the relationship between indigenous African Christians and the missionaries, and the missionaries are notoriously the centre of a dispute about their rôle in European imperial expansion.[5] Consciously or not, and even if they were opposed to that expansion, the white missionaries of the nineteenth century played their part in the spread of white rule. The most devoted and orthodox of modern African Christians will understandably exhibit an ambivalent attitude to those white Christians to

---

[1] In many cases genealogies are the only way in which an approximate chronology can be established, see [Monica] Wilson and [Leonard] Thompson, [*Oxford History of South Africa*], I (Oxford 1969) pp 74ff.

[2] For example Davidson, p 139.

[3]. See the attempt to date the movement of Nguni peoples in Wilson and Thompson, pp 74ff.

[4] See for example G. Shepperson and T. Price, *Independent African* (Edinburgh 1958).

[5] See for example H. Debrunner, *A Church Between Colonial Powers* (London 1965): R. Oliver, *The Missionary Factor in East Africa* (2nd ed London 1965): and n.b. R. T. Rotberg, *Christian Missionaries and the Creation of Northern Rhodesia* (Princeton 1965) and a critique of it by P. Bolink in *Nederduitse Gereformeerde Teologiese Tydskrif*, VII, 3 (Capetown 1966) pp 168ff.

whom he owes his faith but to whom also he owes denominationalism on the one hand and foreign imperial rule on the other.[1]

When, therefore, one asks the question whether African separatist movements are to be classed as heresy, schism or protest movement the answer one gives will, in part at least, be determined by one's view of the missionaries. If one regards the missionaries as those who brought the true faith to Africa one tends to think of the separatists as heretics or schismatics. If one regards the missionaries as tools of imperialist aggression, then the separatists are easily seen as constituting an entirely justifiable protest movement.

The difficulty of finding the right words reveals just how 'loaded' the whole subject has become. By what standards is one to determine heresy or schism? It used to be fashionable to call these African movements 'the sects'. Understandably such a prejudging term has come to be regarded as better avoided. But the usual substitute 'Independent Churches' is at least as misleading for those who are accustomed to thinking of 'independency' as having quite another meaning. I have chosen to talk of 'separatists',[2] recognising that any term will probably have pejorative overtones. But religious movements have been 'separating', with good and bad motives, since before Christianity. The Pharisees, the Donatists, the gathered Church of the seventeenth-century Puritans, were all separatist and I hope that I may be allowed so to describe these modern African Christians, who have deliberately created *African* Churches, without committing myself to the view that they were necessarily schismatic or sectarian in doing so.

The revolution brought about by the Africanising of African history has had an effect upon precisely this question of the way in which the separatists are regarded. Earlier in this century they were almost always treated as a manifestation of evil or as a rather comic curiosity.

The evils which they were thought to manifest were political as well as religious. In South Africa the special circumstances resulting from permanent white settlement, as opposed to colonial rule, meant that the separatists there were, in one sense, atypical of those in the rest of the continent yet, in another sense, only a more obvious expression of what existed elsewhere. Early in this century, before there was a Union

---

[1] See V. Rakotoarimanana, 'The Problems of Reunion Negotiations in Africa seen by a Malagasy Pastor', *Midstream*, IV, 2 (Indianapolis 1964) pp 35ff.

[2] I know that this terminology is not new and is open to certain objections – see [*Christianity in Tropical Africa*, ed C. G.] Baëta (London 1968) p 261 – but in this particular context I believe it is still the least misleading. Ancestor cult, used later in this paper, is also open to objection but again it is difficult to find a satisfactory substitute.

of South Africa, the four colonial governments in the sub-continent appointed a joint commission on 'Native Affairs'.[1] One of the duties of this commission was to investigate the separatists and try to determine how far they really represented a subversive political force. In fact the commission did not think this to be an important factor in the growth of separatism, but the fear was plainly there.

Ecclesiastics also regarded separatists with grave suspicion. While the joint colonial commission was at work, the South African General Missionary Conference met for the first time. This body was the earliest ecumenical organisation in southern Africa on which the Churches were even semi-officially represented and its membership included some very distinguished men of considerable academic ability. Yet a paper delivered to this gathering described the separatist movement as a serious evil cutting at the foundation of all missionary work.[2] Another argued that it was a carnal Christianity which sought privileges and shirked responsibility.[3] And the conference finally 'deplored' the lack of christian comity, the low morals and lax discipline and the mistrust of white men, exhibited by the 'Ethiopians' (as they were called), though it also recognised that Ethiopianism ought to be guided not repressed.[4]

If there were those who continued to regard the separatists as a manifestation of evil, there were many others who seem to have thought of it all as a joke, pathetic perhaps but undeniably funny. One eminent clergyman writing forty years ago about Anglicanism in South Africa saw the separatist movement as very largely caused by two things. Dissatisfied Africans, he thought, wished to qualify for a clergyman's fare concessions on the railways. Resentful misbehavers under church discipline wished to enhance their own importance.[5] He described separatists who, when invited to produce an official statement of their doctrine, found the whole of the XXXIX Articles too expensive to reprint. Forced by financial necessity to become selective they asserted that 'the foundation of their Christian belief' was a conviction that 'the Romish doctrine concerning Purgatory, Pardons, and adoration of Images as of Reliques, is a fond thing, vainly invented, and plainly repugnant to the Word of God'.[6] This High Church

---

[1] *Report of the South African Native Affairs Commission* (Cape Town 1905) and see especially p 63.
[2] Minutes of the South African General Missionary Conference; the reverend J. S. Morris, 14 July 1904.
[3] *Ibid* the reverend F. Bridgeman, 20 July 1904.   [4] *Ibid* Resolutions, 20 July 1904.
[5] O. Victor, *The Salient of South Africa* (London 1931) pp 106ff.   [6] *Ibid* p 107.

Anglican was, no doubt, amused by the idea of barely literate people taking out of context a fragment of the statement his own ancestors had used to justify their separation from sixteenth-century Rome. Others were even more amused by the fanciful conglomeration of nouns and adjectives that served as denominational labels for some of the bodies. The 'Castor Oil Dead Church' and the 'King George V Win the War Church' are, perhaps, the choicest examples.[1]

Three things have contributed to a growing feeling that these bodies are not just hilarious curiosities. Anthropologists and sociologists have done some very serious studies in the field. A good deal of this work has been done by Christians, some of them trained in theology as well as in the social sciences. The rapid growth of separatist bodies (so that there are now reckoned to be well over 3000 in South Africa alone, with a membership of over a million and a half) has been almost matched by the staggering size of the literature about them. The bibliography issued by a former anthropologist colleague of mine to his students in this field runs to five quarto pages and is not exhaustive. Perhaps the most impressive piece of evidence of all is that in 1967 the Oxford University Press published a two-volume work, running to about 600 pages and costing over £11, which dealt with one single West African Church.[2] This evidence of academic respectability, together with the rapid expansion of the movement and the very real sympathy which now exists for anything that could be described as an indigenous African Christianity has brought a completely different attitude. In 1969 one of these African Churches applied for membership of the World Council of Churches and not one single voice in the Central Committee of the World Council was openly raised in objection.

But, of course, the World Council of Churches is the one context in which the question whether a christian body is heresy, schism or protest movement, is a question not to be raised. One needs to look elsewhere for some basis of classification. Bishop Sundkler's *Bantu Prophets in South Africa*[3] has become something of a classic, as one of the first of the serious post-war studies of the separatists which is both sociological and theological. Sundkler originally attempted to classify the separatists as Ethiopian or Zionist.[4] By 'Ethiopian' he meant

---

[1] See [B. M.] Sundkler, [*Bantu Prophets in South Africa*], (2 ed. London 1961) appendix B, pp 354ff for a list of several thousand names of Churches.
[2] H. W. Turner, *African Independent Church*, 2 vols (Oxford 1967).
[3] 1 ed, London 1948.   [4] Sundkler (1 ed) pp 53ff.

those bodies who had broken away from some mission Church for political, disciplinary or personal reasons but had continued to hold the doctrinal beliefs of the parent body. By 'Zionists' he meant those separatists whose doctrines had changed, usually because of an attempt to combine christian beliefs with traditional African religion. At first sight this appears to be a classification which will fit very neatly with the classical distinction between schism and heresy. Ethiopians, who separated while continuing to hold a faith which was orthodox in terms of the Church from which they came, look like schismatics. Zionists, with changed and perhaps syncretistic beliefs, look like heretics (measured again by the standards of the Church from which they separated).

But the equation is not really as simple as this, for there is a sense in which both types of separatist Church could be defined as 'protest movement'. Sundkler himself seemed to show that one of the most important factors in the rise of Zionist bodies was a resurgence of traditional African beliefs and practices repressed by christian missionaries or white colonisers.[1] A considerable part of Sundkler's book, for instance, is devoted to an examination of the way in which many Zionist Churches are an embodiment of the Zulu concept of kingship translated into simple ecclesiological terms. This makes Zionism look like a protest movement, even if a partly unconscious one. And Ethiopian movements, again, have often contained a strong element of protest. At least in South Africa, overtones of political and racial resentment have been regularly present among reasons given for separation. The very first seceding body to take the name 'Ethiopian' was a Church set up in 1892 by the reverend Mangena Mokoni, who left the Methodist Church because he believed that Africans were not being given equal rights with white members of that Church.[2]

Sundkler has now added a third category to his types of movement – the Messianic.[3] Again, there has been some considerable literature on the subject[4] but it is not always easy to draw a precise distinction between strictly Messianic movements and the type of Zionist body which is focused upon a single visionary leader. Yet it is plain that in some cases at least, these movements offer a new black Messiah as an

[1] See, for example, the chart on pp 262ff of the first edition.
[2] E. Roux, *Time Longer than Rope* (London 1948) p 88.
[3] Sundkler, 2 ed, London 1961, pp 323ff.
[4] For example M. L. Martin, *The Biblical Concept of Messiahs and Messianism in Southern Africa* (Morija 1964); G. C. Oosthuizen, *The Theology of a South African Messiah* (Leiden 1967).

alternative to (or alongside) the white man's Christ. It is plainly felt that since the white Christian does not seem to love his black brother, the white man's Christ cannot be a very effective symbol of God's love for the black man, either. Ought there not to be some black and African person to focus that love?

I have attempted elsewhere to summarise the way this may be expressed in terms of the emergence of a Messianic group.

Isaiah Shembe's Nazareth Movement is a case in point. Isaiah Shembe died a few years ago and his son now leads the movement. Shembe himself has become a quasi-divine figure. He is spoken of in language which suggests that he is a kind of Melchizedek-cum-Christ type. His birth was not normal and human. His origins are unknown. He was born of the Spirit. He was Spirit. He was not of the world but of heaven. He was a servant sent by God and through him we know that God is not beyond the ocean but here, among us.[1]

One is almost bound to ask whether this is like the claim of some Montanists to represent a new manifestation of the divine, super-seding the Incarnation. And we know how much argument there has been about the nature of Montanism – whether it was simply a heresy or whether it was really a protest against institutionalism and the repression of prophecy.

It is possible to argue, of course, that every heresy is a protest against the neglect or repression of some legitimate element of the christian gospel. Very few heresies are the deliberate invention of creative minds indulging in pure malevolent speculation, with the possible exception of the patriarch Photius who invented a heresy to tease his rival Ignatius.[2] It may well be that 'heresy', 'schism' and 'protest move-ment' are not comparable terms – or, rather, that as we have tradition-ally defined 'heresy' and 'schism', 'protest movement' is not a third category that can be placed alongside them. All heresies and all schisms may be, in a sense, a protest against something and it certainly looks as though all three of Sundkler's classes of separatists could be described as protest movements in some degree or other.

Sundkler's attempted analysis is not the only one in the field. A World Council of Churches' report published in 1963 attempted a different kind of classification and proposed a terminology to clarify the complexity afflicting all discussion of the separatist movements.[3]

---

[1] P. Hinchliff, *The Church in South Africa* (London 1968) p 104.

[2] S. Runciman, *The Eastern Schism* (Oxford 1955) p 25.

[3] *African Independent Church Movements*, ed V. E. W. Hayward (London 1963).

Yet it is still possible to become quite drowned in a semantic sea in which terms like orthodox, millennial, initiatory, nativistic, imitative and prophetic can be used (singly or in an almost limitless series of combinations and permutations) with no guarantee that one writer means by any one of them what any other writer does. And the more one immerses oneself in one system of classification or another, the more certain one becomes that none of these systems is going to enable one to answer the question, 'heresy, schism or protest movement?'

To return to the idea that it is a kind of category mistake to put these three terms on the same level, it may well be that the separatist movements are all protests against something.[1] It may be possible to describe some of them as heresy and some as schism and, at the same time, to be compelled to recognise them all as protest movements. The real question is, perhaps, 'protest against what?' And this involves exploring some of the causes of separation.

In some individual cases, like one or two I have mentioned already, it is possible to say fairly simply that one particular matter has been the immediate cause of separation. In others any attempt to unravel the causes involves one in all the problems presented by African history, with the attendant uncertainties.

Part of the difficulty is to disentangle the actual story of how Christianity first made its impact upon the people concerned. In some cases it is almost impossible to get behind the overlay of christian ideas to the original beliefs of the people.[2] In others one discovers from the missionary records that the christian missionaries themselves had a most peculiar view of the religious ideas of the tribe amongst whom they worked.[3] Often they treated Africans as though their minds and lives were a complete blank, so far as religious things were concerned, a *tabula rasa* on which anything one liked could be engraved.[4] One is sometimes told, on the other hand, that the missionaries brought very little that was new and that African traditions contained myths very

---

[1] See R. T. Rotberg and A. A. Mazrui (eds) *Protest and Power in Black Africa* (New York 1970) pp 377ff for a consideration of religious protests seen in the broad context of protest as a sociological phenomenon. See also pp 1191ff for a tentative analysis of the causes of protest, identified as 'anger, fear and frustrated ambition'.

[2] See for example W. D. Hammond-Tooke, 'Some Bhaca Religious Categories', *African Studies*, XIX, 1 (Witwatersrand 1960) p 1.

[3] I am indebted on this point to a former pupil of mine, the reverend C. Garner, who has allowed me to see the results of his research in this field.

[4] *African Initiatives [in Religion*, ed D. B. Barrett] (Nairobi 1971) p viii.

like, for instance, the Christmas story. In my own experience the most vigorous attempt to make such a case was in a paper read at a consultation for staff of seminaries and theological colleges held at the university of Botswana, Lesotho and Swaziland in January 1966. The speaker maintained that almost every New Testament story had a parallel in traditional African legend.[1] When one cannot be sure what an African people believed, what the missionaries thought they believed or how the missionary message tied up with previous beliefs, it is almost impossible to tell why that message should be rejected.

As soon as one begins to enlarge the scope of the enquiry and to ask what causes in general are responsible for the existence of separatism as a widespread phenomenon, the answers are many and varied. The doyen of Dutch Reformed missionary historians in South Africa has this to say,

The main cause seems to be the awkward stage of adolescence through which every individual passes to manhood or womanhood. This is usually accompanied by growing pains and emotional outbursts. Feeling against whites is certainly not the whole, perhaps not even the principal, cause. The Church offers almost the only legitimate outlet for the urge of leadership, and consequently becomes the arena of competition to lead and rule. To satisfy this urge, the patterns of Bantu life and thought with their systems of rank and kingship tradition are eagerly copied.[2]

He believes there are three aggravating factors: the existence of a multiplicity of denominations, often dominated by whites; the failure to create autonomous and indigenous African Churches; and periods of war and unrest in Africa.

At the opposite end of the scale to this paternalistic and very subjective account is Dr David Barrett's sociological analysis of 6000 African religious movements.[3] Dr Barrett is not so much concerned with causes as with factors. He has constructed a scale of eighteen such factors and the number of factors present are, he argues, an indication of the degree of strain to which the tribal unit is subjected. When the strain reaches a certain intensity, measured by the number of factors present, separatism is almost certain to result. The factors are: if the tribe is of Bantu stock, over 115,000 in population, commonly

---

[1] See also the interesting parallels cited by C. K. Omari in *African Initiatives*, p 7.
[2] G. B. A. Gerdener, *Recent Developments in the South African Mission Field* (Cape Town 1958) p 190.
[3] D. Barrett, *Schism and Renewal in Africa* (Nairobi 1967) and 'Church Growth and Independency', in Baëta, pp 269ff.

practising polygamy; if the ancestor cult is important, if there is an earth-goddess cult; if colonial rule began over 100 years ago, if white settlers have occupied tribal land and if the national average income is over £25 a year; if missions arrived more than sixty years ago, if some or all of the Bible has been published in the tribal language, if this publication took place more than sixty years ago and if protestant missionaries number more than twenty-two per million of the population; if Muslims number less than fifty per cent, if Protestants or Catholics number more than twenty per cent and if there is separatism in any adjoining tribe. Barrett makes a good case for arguing that once thirteen or more of these factors are present separatism is frighteningly inevitable.

In trying to summarise Barrett's argument I have inevitably clothed it with caricature. Deprived of explanation, his factors may appear arbitrary and slightly comic. His full argument is, I believe, convincing to this extent, that it indicates that separatism is the result of many different forces in combination and is, in large part, a protest (conscious or unconscious) against much that Europe has introduced into Africa.

This is, admittedly, not an historical analysis in any normal sense. Barrett has used history to provide some of the information on which his analytical method has been constructed. Where there is clear evidence of the causes of separatism in some areas, this has enabled him to know what sort of factors to look for in others and it is always possible that some factors have been missed altogether. But Barrett would argue that it is essential to use every method one can lay hands on. European historians can afford to be scathing for they have documents in plenty, covering more than ten centuries. The historian of Africa lacks such resources and must 'employ a host of new techniques drawn from other disciplines as diverse as ethnography, haematology and astronomy'.[1]

What Barrett has really done is to construct a generalisation, more precise and more elaborate than the usual generalisation but serving the purpose of all generalisation in history. Without generalisation one becomes absorbed in the trees rather than the wood. Using generalisation sensibly is a way of achieving proper focus. Barrett provides a general picture of a society shattered by the impact of newcomers from another culture, whose religious ideas have been widely received, but whose practice has seemed to differ markedly from their preaching, who have not managed to harness African leader-

---

[1] *African Initiatives*, p 147 where Barrett explains and defends his method.

ship and African ideas, who have not understood African culture and have vigorously condemned some aspects of it. This general picture is based on areas for which there is evidence. It has then become a generalised hypothesis and is no more unjustified than the sort of hypothesis which an historian might construct from what little evidence there is about the shape of the ministry in the early Church. In areas where there is no evidence about the origin of the separatists, the general hypothesis will allow us to make a guess at the kind of situation that probably gave birth to them. One has to realise that, as with any other generalisation or any other hypothesis, it may not fit with what evidence there is in every given case. Indeed, in the same volume in which Barrett makes his defence, from which I quoted a moment ago, professor Terence Ranger shows how the hypothesis needs considerable modification before it could be made to fit with what has happened in large parts of Tanzania.[1]

Yet it is clear that the element of protest is strong within the separatist movement. Some of these protests are against the destruction of traditional culture as well as of traditional religion. Some are protests against colonial rule. Some are protests against the failure of christian missionaries to be true to christian principles, as in matters of racialism. But few, if any, of them can be neatly docketed as being against any one thing only. Social and religious factors are inextricably mixed together. Nevertheless it is possible to begin to see that separatism is *against* a variety of different things and what these things are may help to provide an answer to the question, 'heresy or schism?'. In other words, it may be possible to use the third term to answer the rest of the question.

Separatism may be a protest against the destruction of traditional culture. This is Sundkler's classic type, like the resurgence of Zulu kingship patterns. But it may take very simple and direct forms, and these may be of prime importance as Barrett's inclusion of polygamy among his eighteen factors indicates.[2] Bishop Colenso knew that to attack polygamous marriage was to undermine the whole structure of society by calling in question the status of husbands, wives and children alike.[3] Nor is polygamy a 'dead' issue. The question whether the Churches are right in insisting on monogamy is still being asked – and being asked more and more insistently. It is still one of those issues

---

[1] *African Initiatives*, pp 122ff.
[2] For the importance of polygamy in separatism see J. B. Webster in Baëta, p 224.
[3] P. Hinchliff, *John William Colenso* (London 1964) p 84.

which are particularly acute because they are concerned with the structure of society.

The frontier between religion and culture is almost impossible to draw in traditional African society. The ancestor-cult stands four-square on the frontier itself, being related on the one hand to the family and the tribe and the whole structure of society and, on the other, to the way in which one worships and how one is related to the divine and to the immortal. It is sometimes thought that one can 'baptise' the practice, as it were, and relate it to the communion of saints. But this is to ignore the fact that ancestors are by definition one's *own* ancestors. The question that is really being asked here is whether the missionaries were right in attacking the ancestor-cult with the enormous vigour which they undoubtedly employed.[1]

One is poised here on the brink of a whole series of questions in the area where theologians and anthropologists have both had a great deal to say.[2] Is it possible to detach religion from society and bring a pure essence of Christianity, as it were, out of the context of western culture and into an African culture in place of traditional religion? Can one preach Christianity to a people with another culture and hope that they will receive it without destroying their culture on the one hand or producing a syncretistic Christianity on the other? It is interesting to note how African christian thinkers themselves stress the importance of converting the family rather than the individual,[3] taking the line, followed by at least some sociologists and anthropologists,[4] that the revolution is less destructive if it is corporate. This contrasts sharply with the sort of attitude we tend to adopt when looking at the coming of Christianity to Europe in the Dark Ages, when we usually argue that mass tribal conversions are bad and that a more individual approach might have produced a less superficial and more stable religion.[5]

No one can doubt that there are real attempts among the separatists to seize what Christianity claims to offer and at the same time to make it more immediate than it often is for western Christians. There is a deep desire to make it African, sometimes even to blend it with the

[1] See D. Barrett in Baëta, p 279.
[2] For a fuller treatment of these questions see P. Hinchliff, 'Letter from South Africa', *Theology*, LXII, 463 (London 1959) pp 17ff.
[3] J. Mbiti, 'The Ways and Means of Communicating the Gospel', in Baëta, pp 337ff.
[4] See for example E. de Vries, *Man in Rapid Social Change* (London 1961) p 23 and compare p 41.
[5] For example L. G. D. Baker, 'The Shadow of the Christian Symbol', in *SCH*, VI (1970) pp 17ff.

raditional beliefs of Africa. Resentment of colonialism and racialism complicates the already complex mixture of syncretism and creative religious longings. This extract from an account of one of the 'messianic' bodies shows all these factors at work.

My senior informant quotes statements that were repeatedly made by members of the Mai Chaza Church at a meeting held near his home: 'I want to confess this before god, meaning before Vamatenga [the leader of the Church]'. 'The man whom you see here is Mwari [the high god of traditional religion] himself, our creator.' 'There is no other god but the one before you.' 'God is sitting in the hut.' 'Vamatenga is the god of Africa.'

Vamatenga's special place is within the holy stone enclosure where worship is held. Another informant told me that Vamatenga covers his face during services when sitting on a chair in his stone enclosure because 'man cannot see God and live'.

The informant then had the opportunity of attending a service in which Vamatenga was present. He sat next to him, but was strictly forbidden to address him. He reports: 'The leader is treated as the old Mwari of Matopos. A Shona king or chief was divine and no one was allowed to look at him. He was the embodiment of divinity and always remained in seclusion.' Vamatenga is also regarded as the Jesus of Africa.

Here then is the merging of various ideas: the sacral kingship of African tradition, the Old Testament notion of God's holiness, and the messianic concept of the New Testament.

It is nevertheless an amazing claim that Vamatenga makes. Among the Shona, Mwari is the god of heaven, the great king, the creator, the spirit of spirits, the holy one who is, but cannot be seen. By calling himself Vamatenga he makes the claim that the creator god, the holy one who used to speak in the caves, is now present in him. Mwari of Matopos and Yahweh of the Old Testament are, as it were, identified, and appear here and now in the powerful church-leader Vamatenga.

It is the desire for Immanuel, God with us, that is expressed in this tremendous claim; it is the desire for revelation here and now, here in Africa, through an African. Too often God and Jesus Christ are thought of, unconsciously no doubt, as being white and therefore irrelevant to the African community.[1]

How much of what results is a form of Christianity? Western Christians, if they think about these African Churches at all, tend to do so in terms which imply that it is the West which ought to decide how orthodox the Africans are. It is not for the historian to get himself involved in doctrinal pronouncements, but at least one African theologian (himself undoubtedly orthodox) has suggested

[1] M.-L. Martin in *African Initiatives*, pp 114ff.

that, where theology has to be expressed in such a very different form, as is required by African language and thought, Western Europeans may be quite incapable of judging its orthodoxy.

The time may have come, now, for western Christianity to be more humble in its approach to other religions and cultures, if it is to be effective here in Africa. Christianity has to approach this traditional background with an open mind, with a readiness to change it and be changed by it. In particular I would appeal to our brethren in and from Europe and America to allow us to make what in their judgement may be termed mistakes; allow us to make a mess of Christianity in our continent just as, if one may mildly put it, you have made a mess of it in Europe and America. When we speak or write on particular issues about Christianity or other academic matters, we should not be expected to use the vocabulary and approach used in Europe and America: please allow us to say certain things our own way, whether we are wrong or not. We sometimes reach a point of despair when what we say or do is so severely criticised and condemned by people in or from Europe and America – often because we have not said it to their satisfaction or according to their wishes. Are we not allowed to become what we wish to become? The Independent Churches, as a movement, may in fact be doing a great deal more to deepen Christianity in Africa than are the strictly historical churches which are too stiff to be shaped within the African situation. I have no doubt in my own mind that historical churches have a better theology, but the Independent Churches (speaking broadly) are more realistic and practical when it comes to taking the African situation seriously.[1]

It is not only some early missionaries who have given the impression that they knew little and cared less about African religious thought and feeling. Western scholars in general have sometimes given the impression that African religion was an interesting but barbarous or childish subject.[2] It is at least possible that the Separatist Churches are evidence of the existence of an African feeling for religion[3] which has more often than not been stifled or despised. These Churches may, in fact, have come into being as a genuine and justifiable attempt to take an initiative which has otherwise been denied to African Christians. This does not necessarily mean that they are not also 'heresy' or 'schism', in precisely the same way in which many of Europe's attempts to make Christianity its own have been given those labels.

[1] J. Mbiti, 'Christianity and Traditional Religions in Africa', *International Review of Missions*, LIX (Geneva 1970) pp 439ff.
[2] See Okot p'Bitek, *African Religions in Western Scholarship* (Nairobi 1971).
[3] *African Initiatives*, pp 274ff.